The **Rough Guide** to

Sri Lanka

written and researched by

Gavin Thomas

**ROUGH
GUIDES**

NEW YORK • LONDON • DELHI

www.roughguides.com

△ South coast beach between Galle and Matara

Introduction to
Sri Lanka

Sri Lanka has seduced travellers for centuries. Marco Polo described it as the finest island in the world, while successive waves of Indian, Arab and European traders and adventurers flocked to its palm-fringed shores, attracted by reports of rare spices, precious stones and magnificent elephants. Poised just above the equator amidst the balmy waters of the Indian Ocean, the island's legendary reputation for natural beauty and plenty has inspired an almost magical regard even in those who have never visited the place. Romantically inclined geographers, poring over maps of the island, have compared its outline to a teardrop falling from the tip of India or to the shape of a pearl (the less impressionable Dutch likened it to a leg of ham), whilst even the name given to the island by early Arab traders – Serendib – became (through the English word serendipity) a synonym for the making of happy accidents by chance.

Marco Polo's bold claim still rings true. Sri Lanka packs an extraordinary variety of natural and man-made attractions within its modest physical dimensions, and few islands of comparable size can boast a natural environment of such beauty and diversity. Lapped by the Indian Ocean, the **coast** is fringed with idyllic – and often refreshingly undeveloped – **beaches**, while the interior boasts a compelling variety of landscapes ranging from wildlife-rich lowland **jungles**, home to extensive populations of elephants, leopards and rare

iii

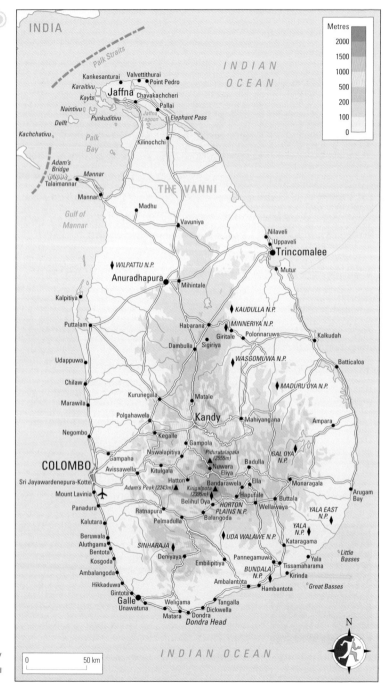

INDIA

Palk Straits

INDIAN
OCEAN

Kankesanturai
Valvettithurai
Point Pedro
Karaitivu
Kayts
Jaffna Chavakachcheri
Naintivu
Pallai
Delft
Punkuditivu
Jaffna
Lagoon
Elephant Pass
Kachchativu

Palk
Bay

Kilinochchi

Adam's
Bridge
Mannar
Talaimannar

THE VANNI

Mannar

Gulf of
Mannar

Madhu

Vavuniya

Nilaveli
Uppaveli
Trincomalee

WILPATTU N.P.
Anuradhapura

Mutur

Kalpitiya

Mihintale

KAUDULLA N.P.

Puttalam

Habarana

MINNERIYA N.P.

Giritale
Polonnaruwa
Kalkudah

Udappuwa

Dambulla
Sigiriya

WASGOMUWA N.P.

Batticaloa

Chilaw

Marawila

Kurunegala

Matale

MADURU OYA N.P.

Polgahawela

Kandy
Mahiyangana

Ampara

Negombo

Kegalle

Gampola

Nawalapitiya
*Pidurutalagala
(2555m)*

COLOMBO
Gampaha
Avissawella
Kitulgala
Nuwara
Eliya
Badulla

*GAL OYA
N.P.*

Sri Jayawardenepura-Kotte
Adam's Peak (2243m)
*Kirigalpota
(2395m)*
Bandarawela
Ella

Mount Lavinia
Hatton
Belihul Oya
Haputale
Wellawaya
Monaragala

Arugam
Bay

Panadura
Ratnapura
*HORTON
PLAINS N.P.*
Buttala

*YALA EAST
N.P.*

Kalutara
Pelmadulla
Balangoda

Beruwala
Aluthgama
UDA WALAWE N.P.

Bentota
SINHARAJA
Kataragama

*YALA
N.P.*

Kosgoda
Deniyaya
Embilipitiya
Pannegamuwa
*Little
Basses*

Ambalangoda
*BUNDALA
N.P.*
Tissamaharama

Hikkaduwa
Ambalantota
Kirinda

Gintota
Galle
Weligama
Tangalla
Hambantota
Great Basses

Unawatuna
Dickwella

Matara
Dondra

Dondra Head

INDIAN OCEAN

Metres
2000
1500
1000
500
200
100
0

N

0   50 km

△ Hill country tea factory

endemic bird species, to the misty heights of the **hill country**, swathed in immaculately manicured tea plantations. Nor does the island lack for man-made attractions. Sri Lanka boasts over two thousand years of recorded history, and the remarkable achievements of the island's early Sinhalese civilization can still be seen in the sequence of ruined cities and great religious monuments which litter the island's northern plains.

The glories of this early Buddhist civilization continue to provide a benchmark of national identity for the island's Sinhalese population, and Sri Lanka's historic role as the world's oldest stronghold of Theravada **Buddhism** lends it a unique cultural unity and character which permeate life at every level. There's more to Sri Lanka than just Buddhists, however. The island's geographical position at one of the most important staging posts of Indian Ocean trade laid it open to a uniquely wide range of influences, as generations of Arab, Malay, Portuguese, Dutch and British **settlers** subtly transformed its culture, architecture and cuisine, while the long-established Tamil population in the north have established a vibrant Hindu culture which owes more to India than to the Sinhalese south.

In fact, it is this very diversity which has threatened to tear the country apart. The last two decades of the twentieth century were marked by one of Asia's most pernicious **civil wars**, as Sri Lankan government forces and the LTTE, or Tamil Tigers, battled it out in the island's north and east. This debilitating conflict was finally halted in 2002, and Sri Lankans of all ethnic

v

Fact file

- Lying a few degrees north of the equator, Sri Lanka is slightly smaller than Ireland and a little larger than the US state of West Virginia.
- Sri Lanka achieved independence from Britain in 1948, and did away with its colonial name, Ceylon, in 1972. The country has had a functioning democracy since independence, and in 1960 elected the world's first ever female prime minister.
- Sri Lanka's population is a mosaic of different ethnic and religious groups, the two largest being the mainly Buddhist Sinhalese (74 percent), and the predominantly Hindu Tamils (18 percent); there are also considerable numbers of Christians and Muslims. Sinhala, Tamil and English are all officially recognized languages.
- Sri Lankans enjoy a healthy life expectancy of 72 years and a literacy rate of 92 percent, though they have also set some less enviable records in recent years, including achieving the world's highest suicide rate and its highest incidence of alcoholism – not to mention the highest death rate from snakebite.
- The country's main export is clothing, followed by tea; rubber, coconuts and precious gems are also important. Revenues from tourism are vital to the national economy, while remittances from the hundreds of thousands of Sri Lankans working overseas (mainly in the Gulf) are also significant.

origins are now looking forward with guarded optimism towards a new and peaceful future, whilst the ceasefire has opened up huge new areas of the north and east which were previously off limits to travellers.

Where to go

All visits to Sri Lanka begin at the international airport at **Colombo**, the island's capital and far and away its largest city – a sprawling and chaotic metropolis whose contrasting districts offer an absorbing introduction to Sri Lanka's myriad cultures. Many visitors head straight for one of the west-coast beaches, whose innumerable resort hotels still power the country's tourist industry. Destinations include the package-holiday

▽ Chillies, the Pettah, Colombo

The high, wet terrain of Sri Lanka's hill country is ideally suited to tea growing, and the country's premier tea-growing areas are internationally famous for the quality of their produce – the higher the plantation, the more delicate and highly prized the tea. The plant was introduced to Sri Lanka by the British during the nineteenth century following the catastrophic collapse of the island's coffee industry, and the success of the first plantations led to the rapid establishment of the massive tea gardens which still blanket the hill country today. The new industry also had an important cultural byproduct: the lack of sufficient local labour led to the British encouraging large numbers of Tamils to emigrate here to work on the plantations, radically changing the ethnic make-up of the central highlands – the sight of Tamil women tea pickers in brightly coloured saris is still one of the country's emblematic images. Although garment manufacture has long taken over as the country's leading export, tea is still crucial to the national economy and Sri Lanka remains one of the world's largest exporters, although relatively little finds its way to Britain, most instead now going to Russia, the Gulf and the Middle East.

resorts of **Negombo** and **Beruwala**, the more stylish **Bentota**, and the old hippy hangout of **Hikkaduwa**.

Beyond Hikkaduwa, the south coast presents a more laid-back and budget-oriented face. Gateway to the region is the marvellous old Dutch city of **Galle**, Sri Lanka's finest colonial townscape, while beyond here a string of outstanding beaches remain largely the preserve of independent travellers. The foremost of these is at the personable village of **Unawatuna**, currently the

Elephants

No animal is as closely identified with Sri Lanka as the elephant. The kings of Anuradhapura used them to pound down the foundations of their city's huge religious monuments, while the rulers of Kandy employed them to execute prisoners by trampling them to death. During the Dutch era they helped tow barges and move heavy artillery, and under the British they were set to clearing land for tea plantations – even today, trained elephants are used to move heavy objects in places inaccessible to machinery. Elephants also play an integral role in many of the island's religious festivals, and remain revered creatures – killing an elephant was formerly a capital offence, while the death of the great Maligawa Tusker Raja in 1998 prompted the government to declare a national day of mourning. And given Sri Lanka's world-famous Pinnewala Elephant Orphanage as well as its numerous national parks, few other countries offer such a wide range of opportunities to see them both in captivity and in the wild.

island's most popular backpacker hangout, whilst further along the coast are a string of quieter beaches including **Weligama**, **Mirissa** and **Tangalla**, as well as the lively provincial capital of **Matara**, boasting further Dutch remains. East of here, the amenable town of **Tissamaharama** serves as a convenient base for the outstanding **Yala** and **Bundala national parks**, and for the fascinating temple town of **Kataragama**, one of Sri Lanka's most important pilgrimage destinations.

Inland from Colombo rise the verdant highlands of the **hill country**, swathed in the tea plantations (first introduced by the British) which still play a vital role in the island's economy. The symbolic heart of the region is **Kandy**, Sri Lanka's second city and the cultural capital of the Sinhalese, its colourful

▽ Street sign, Galle

traditions embodied by the famous Temple of the Tooth and the magnificent Esala Perahera, Sri Lanka's most colourful **festival**. South of here, close to the highest point of the island, lies the old British town of **Nuwara Eliya**, centre of the country's tea industry and a convenient base for visits to the spectacular **Horton Plains National Park**. A string of characterful towns and villages – **Ella**, **Haputale** and **Bandarawela** – along the southern edge of the hill country offer an appealing mixture of magnificent views, wonderful hill walking and olde-worlde British colonial charm. Close to the hill country's southwestern edge, the soaring summit of **Adam's Peak** is another of the island's major pilgrimage sites, while the gem-mining centre of **Ratnapura** to the south offers a convenient base for visits to the elephant-rich **Uda Walawe National Park** and the rare tropical rainforest of **Sinharaja**.

△ Monks at postcard stall, Polonnaruwa

North of Kandy, the hill country tumbles down into the arid plains of the northern dry zone. This area, known as the **Cultural Triangle**, was the location of Sri Lanka's first great civilization, and its extraordinary scatter of ruined palaces, temples and dagobas still give a compelling sense of this glorious past. Foremost amongst these are the

ix

■

Dagobas

The pure white dome of the Buddhist stupa – or dagoba, as they are called in Sinhala – is one of the most emblematic features of the Sri Lankan landscape. Dagobas traditionally enshrine relics of the Buddha himself or of other holy personages, and offer a focal point for worship and contemplation. The form of the dagoba is laden with symbolism, ranging from the mundane to the cosmic – to some, the dagoba represents the Buddha's upturned begging bowl and walking stick; to others, it serves as an abstract symbol of the entire hemispherical cosmos, out

of which a spire points up towards nirvana. However you interpret it, the dagoba represents a classically simple symbol of Buddhism's essential message of renunciation and spiritual aspiration. Though Sri Lankan dagobas preserve their original hemispherical shape, there are myriad different nuances in their design; there are six basic shapes (from "heap of rice paddy" to "bubble"), and while some are severely plain, others are ornately decorated with stylized bo tree leaves and vines. Dagobas also come in many different sizes, from the miniature cluster at Kantharodai, just a few metres tall, to the three great dagobas of Anuradhapura, amongst the largest man-made structures of the ancient world – it's been estimated that the biggest of these, the Jetavana dagoba, uses almost a hundred million bricks.

fascinating ruined cities of **Anuradhapura** and **Polonnaruwa**, the marvellous cave temples of **Dambulla**, the hilltop shrines and dagobas of **Mihintale** and the extraordinary rock citadel of **Sigiriya**.

The regions north and east of the Cultural Triangle have only recently reopened to visitors after the civil war. Gateway to the **east** is the personable city of **Trincomalee**, virtually the only place of any size along the entire east coast. The huge swathe of pristine coastline itself remains almost completely undeveloped, save for the tourist enclaves of **Nilaveli** and **Uppaveli**, just north of Trincomalee, and the surfing centre of **Arugam Bay**, at the southern edge of the region. The **north**, meanwhile, bore the brunt of Sri Lanka's two decades of civil war and remains a destination for the adventurous only, although if you have the time it's well worth making the long journey to the fascinating city of **Jaffna**, the war-torn capital of Tamil Sri Lanka.

When to go

ri Lanka's **climate** is remarkably complicated for such a small country, due to the fact that opposite sides of the island are affected by two separate monsoons – though this also means that there is always good weather somewhere on the island, whatever the time of year. The **southwest monsoon** brings rain to the southwest quarter of the island (the so-called Wet Zone) from mid-May to October. The less severe **northeast monsoon** hits the east coast from December to March. There are two **inter-monsoonal periods** which can produce unsettled weather right across the island. The first, from March to mid-May, brings clear nights and mornings along with intermittent thunderstorms during late afternoons and evenings, especially in the southwest. The second inter-monsoonal period, from October to November, brings squally weather to many areas of the island. It's worth bearing in mind, however, that this basic pattern can vary from year to year, and that global warming has in recent times disrupted these already complicated weather patterns and caused severe periods of drought.

In practical terms, all of the above means that the **best time to visit** the **west coast** is from around mid-October to mid-April; from mid-May to October the southwest monsoon hits, bringing daily deluges and overcast skies. It's still feasible to visit during the monsoon months, since rain is usually confined to a couple of hours in the afternoon, although many guesthouses and restaurants shut up shop for the duration. The situation on the **east coast** is more or less the reverse of that on the west, with the best time to visit being from around April to October. The **hill country** sees

△ Budunuwagala

xi

significant rainfall all year and is particularly affected by the southwest monsoon – the southwestern corner of the hill country around Ratnapura and Sinharaja is particularly wet. As such, the best time to visit is during the early months of the year, from January to April/May. The **southeast** and **north** are the driest parts of the island and see little rain for most of the year, although the Cultural Triangle receives sporadic (and sometimes severe) inundations from October to December.

The island's position close to the equator means that **temperatures** remain virtually constant year-round. Coastal and lowland areas enjoy a high temperature of 27–29°C. Temperatures decrease with altitude, reducing to the temperate average of around 20°C in Kandy, and a pleasantly mild 16°C in Nuwara Eliya and the highest parts of the island – nights in the hills can be quite chilly, with temperatures sometimes falling close to freezing. **Humidity** is high everywhere, rising to a sweltering ninety percent at times in the southwest, and averaging sixty to eighty percent across the rest of the island.

Average monthly temperatures and rainfall

	Jan	Feb	Mar	Apr	May	Jun	Jul	Aug	Sep	Oct	Nov	Dec
Colombo												
Av. max. temp. (˚C)	30	31	31	31	31	29	29	29	29	29	29	29
Av. rainfall (mm)	89	69	147	231	371	224	135	109	160	348	315	147
Nuwara Eliya												
Av. max. temp. (˚C)	19	21	22	22	21	19	18	19	19	20	20	20
Av. rainfall (mm)	170	43	109	119	175	277	300	196	226	269	241	203
Trincomalee												
Av. max. temp. (˚C)	27	28	29	32	33	33	33	33	33	31	29	27
Av. rainfall (mm)	173	66	48	58	69	28	51	107	107	221	358	363

things not to miss

It's not possible to see everything that Sri Lanka has to offer in a single trip – and we don't suggest you try. What follows is a selective taste of the island's highlights: outstanding religious and cultural sites, memorable scenery and wildlife, spectacular festivals. They're arranged in five colour-coded categories with a page reference to take you straight into the guide, where you can find out more.

01 **Kandy** Page **208** • Beautifully situated amidst the central highlands, this historic city remains the island's most important repository of traditional Sinhalese culture, exemplified by the great Esala Perahera festival and the Temple of the Tooth.

02 **Adam's Peak** Page **274** • One of Sri Lanka's foremost pilgrimage sites, this soaring summit bears the revered impression of what is said to be the Buddha's own footprint, and offers the island's most magical – and enigmatic – views.

03 **Bentota** Page **133** • The pleasantly unspoilt southern end of Bentota beach is home to the island's finest selection of luxury beachside hotels.

04 **Ayurveda** Page **128** • Sri Lanka's ancient system of holistic health care uses herbal medicines and a range of traditional techniques, from gentle massages and steam baths to blood-letting and treatments with leeches and fire.

05 **Rice and curry** Page **41** •
Eat your way through this classic Sri Lankan feast, with its mouthwatering selection of contrasting dishes and flavours.

06 **Galle** Page **153** • Sri Lanka's most perfectly preserved colonial townscape, with sedate streets of personable Dutch villas enclosed by a chain of imposing ramparts.

07 **World's End** Page **259** • Marking the point at which the hill country's southern escarpment plunges sheer for almost a kilometre to the plains below, the dramatic cliffs here offer one of the finest of the hill country's many unforgettable views.

08 **Pinnewala Elephant Orphanage** Page **242** • One of the island's most popular attractions, Pinnewala is home to the world's largest troupe of captive elephants, from dignified elderly matriarchs to the cutest of babies.

09 **Kandyan dancing and drumming** Page **232** • Traditional Sinhalese culture at its most exuberant, with brilliantly costumed dancers performing limb-twisting feats of acrobatic dancing to an accompaniment of explosively energetic drumming.

10 **The Pettah** Page **88** • Colombo's colourful and chaotic bazaar district offers an exhilarating slice of Asian life, crammed with markets selling a bewildering assortment of merchandise from cheap saris to sackfuls of chillis.

12 **Yala National Park** Page **196** • Sri Lanka's most popular and rewarding national park, home to birds, monkeys, crocodiles and elephants, as well as the island's largest population of leopards.

11 **Polonnaruwa** Page **317** • Home to the island's finest collection of ancient Sinhalese art and architecture, from the giant Buddha statues of the Gal Vihara to the remarkable religious buildings of the Quadrangle.

13 **Bawa hotels** Pages **38 & 132** • With their memorable blend of modern chic and traditional design, the hotels of architect Geoffrey Bawa exemplify contemporary Sri Lankan style at its most seductive.

14 **Dambulla** Page **305** • These five magical cave temples are a little treasure box of Sri Lankan Buddhist art, sumptuously decorated with a fascinating array of statues, shrines and the country's finest of collection of murals.

15 Big Buddhas Page **437** • The Buddha's superhuman attributes are captured in a sequence of massive statues which dot the island, from the majestic ancient figures of the Gal Vihara, Aukana and Sasseruwa to the contemporary colossi at Dambulla and Wehurukannala.

16 Cricket Page **54** • Take part in a knock-around on the beach, or join the crowds of cricket-crazy spectators for a test match in Colombo, Kandy or Galle.

17 Anuradhapura Page **338** • From immense dagobas to mysterious forest monasteries, this vast ruined city bears witness to the great Sinhalese civilization which flourished here for almost two thousand years.

18 Kandy Esala Perahera Page 212 • One of Asia's most spectacular festivals, with huge processions of magnificently caparisoned elephants accompanied by ear-splitting troupes of Kandyan drummers, plus assorted dancers and acrobats.

19 Unawatuna Page 163 • Sri Lanka's most popular backpacker beach boasts a sheltered swathe of sand tucked into a picturesque bay, and a lively cluster of beachfront cafés and guest houses.

20 **Jaffna** Page **394** • Only recently reopened after the civil war, the vibrant town of Jaffna offers a fascinating microcosm of Sri Lanka's unique Tamil culture and heritage.

21 **Birds** Pages **56 & 446** • Sri Lanka is one of Asia's classic birdwatching destinations, with species ranging from delicate bee eaters and colourful kingfishers to majestic waterbirds and strutting peacocks.

xxiii

22 **Ella** Page **262** • Sri Lanka's most beautiful village, offering verdant walks amongst the surrounding tea plantations and a marvellous view through Ella Gap to the plains below.

23 Sigiriya Page **310** • Sri Lanka's most remarkable sight, this towering rock outcrop is home to the fascinating remains of one of the island's former capitals, complete with ancient graffiti, elaborate water gardens, a giant lion statue and perfectly preserved frescoes of voluptuous heavenly nymphs.

24 Kataragama Page **198** • Join the crowds thronging to the colourful nightly temple ceremonies at this remote pilgrimage town, held sacred by Buddhists, Hindus and Muslims alike.

Contents

Using this Rough Guide

We've tried to make this Rough Guide a good read and easy to use. The book is divided into six main sections, and you should be able to find whatever you want in one of them.

Colour section

The front colour section offers a quick tour of Sri Lanka. The **introduction** aims to give you a feel for the place, with suggestions on where to go. We also tell you what the weather is like and include a basic country fact file. Next, our author rounds up his favourite aspects of Sri Lanka in the **things not to miss** section – whether it's great food, amazing sights or a special hotel. Right after this comes a full **contents** list.

Basics

The **basics** section covers all the **pre-departure** nitty-gritty to help you plan your trip. This is where to find out which airlines fly to your destination, what paperwork you'll need, what to do about money and insurance, about internet access, food, security, public transport, car rental – in fact just about every piece of **general practical information** you might need.

Guide

This is the heart of the Rough Guide, divided into user-friendly chapters, each of which covers a specific region. Every chapter starts with a list of **highlights** and an **introduction** that helps you to decide where to go, depending on your time and budget. Likewise, introductions to the various towns and smaller regions within each chapter should help you plan your itinerary. We start most town accounts with information on arrival and accommodation, followed by a tour of the sights, and finally reviews of places to eat and drink, and details of nightlife and entertainment. Longer accounts also have a **directory** of practical listings and a box on **onward travel**. Each chapter concludes with **public transport** details for the region.

Contexts

Read **contexts** to get a deeper understanding of what makes Sri Lanka tick. We include a brief history, articles about Sri Lankan Buddhism, Buddhist art and architecture, and wildlife, and a detailed further reading section that reviews dozens of books relating to the country.

Language

The **language** section gives useful guidance for speaking Sinhala and Tamil and pulls together all the vocabulary you might need on your trip, including a menu reader. Here you'll also find a glossary of words and terms peculiar to Sri Lanka.

Small print and index

Apart from a **full index**, which includes maps as well as places, this section covers publishing information, credits and acknowledgements, and also has our contact details in case you want to send in updates and corrections to the book – or suggestions as to how we might improve it.

Chapter list and map

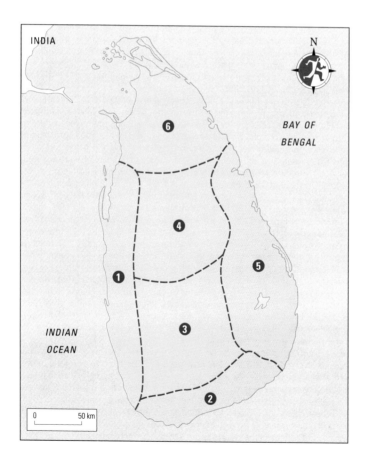

The Asian tsunami and its aftermath in Sri Lanka

Early on the morning of Boxing Day 2004 a huge sub-oceanic earthquake off the coast of Indonesia generated a massive **tsunami** which devastated the coastlines of countries around the Indian Ocean as far apart as Malaysia and Tanzania. Lying unprotected directly in the path of the tsunami, Sri Lanka was (after the Indonesian island of Sumatra) the place most badly affected: over forty thousand people were killed, and large sections of the coastline were devastated, with thousands of buildings destroyed, along with at least half the island's fishing boats and significant sections of road and railway line.

The scale of the devastation was astonishing, although perhaps even more extraordinary has been the national and international **response** to the event and the collective determination to get Sri Lanka back on its feet as soon as possible. The **tourist industry** was immediately targeted as a vital element in regenerating the island's economy, and foreigners have been urged to return to the island as soon as possible. The pictures of coastal devastation beamed around the world by the media unfortunately tended to mask the fact that the whole of the island's interior, four-fifths of its hotels and even certain beaches remained totally unaffected by the tsunami. Tourists wishing to travel to Sri Lanka should have absolutely no qualms about going: the island wants and needs visitors – now more than ever. And although it's difficult to make predictions, it seems likely that much of the island's tourist infrastructure will have been patched up by late 2005.

Around two-thirds of Sri Lanka's coast was inundated by the tsunami. Villages and towns all along the **south coast** – **Weligama**, **Mirissa**, **Tangalla** and **Hambantota**, to name only a few – were seriously damaged, while the **train line** from Colombo to Matara was largely destroyed south of Kalutara. **Galle** was particularly hard hit (although the old Fort area, protected by its huge Dutch ramparts, escaped serious damage and remains open for visitors); the nearby village of **Unawatuna** was almost completely flattened by the waves. The coastal areas of **Yala National Park** were also inundated (and the *Yala Safari Game Lodge* destroyed), although miraculously the resident wildlife survived unharmed and the park was reopened soon afterwards. The nearby town of **Tissamaharama**, lying a few miles inland, was completely unscathed.

The **west coast** as far north as Kalutara was also affected – mercifully, **Colombo** was largely untouched, as was the coast to the north. The resort of **Negombo** was almost entirely unaffected, and its hotels and guesthouses remain open for business as usual. **Hikkaduwa** and **Ambalangoda** were both severely damaged, however, while some hotels in **Kalutara**, **Bentota** and **Beruwala** were also affected (although many have since reopened). Lying directly in the path of the tsunami, damage on the **east coast** was predictably severe. Most of the nascent tourist infrastructure at the resorts of **Arugam Bay**, **Nilaveli** and **Uppaveli** was destroyed, while the towns of **Batticaloa** and **Trincomalee** were also badly hit.

In terms of this **guide**, inevitably much of the information on the coastal areas covered in chapters 1, 2 and 5 is now obsolete, though other regions remain unaffected. The usual pre-tsunami **precautions** still apply: make sure you have adequate insurance (see p.19); that your innoculations are up to date (see p.20); and take special care only to drink bottled water in coastal areas.

The best source of **online information** about the effects of the tsunami in Sri Lanka can be found at ⊛www.contactsrilanka.org. This site also has a comprehensive list of the status of the island's larger hotels, detailing which are closed. Further information can also be found at ⊛www.roughguides.com. Comprehensive links to aid organizations currently working in Sri Lanka (and to other sources of news and informations) can be found at ⊛www.aidsrilanka.com.

Contents

Colour section

Basics

Guide

Contexts
411–453

Language
455–464

Small print and index
469–480

Basics

Basics

Getting there

At present, the only way to get to Sri Lanka is to fly into the island's international airport at Katunayake, just north of Colombo. Sri Lanka is reasonably well served by international airlines, although you'll probably have to change planes somewhere en route. The island is also well connected to regional Asian air networks, with regular nonstop services to India, Thailand, Malaysia, Singapore, Indonesia, Hong Kong and Japan, as well as numerous points in the Gulf and Middle East. The long-awaited resumption of ferry services from India (see p.15) will offer an interesting alternative route into the country, if they ever materialize.

Air fares remain fairly constant year-round, assuming you book through a **discount flight agent** (see p.10, p.13 and p.15), or **purchase a ticket online** (see opposite) – in general, the further ahead you book your flight, the better chance you have a getting a good deal. Another possibility is to pick up a **package deal** from a high-street travel agent – even if you don't use the accommodation provided (or only use it for a few days), these deals can work out to be reasonable value thanks to the cheap flight.

If you want to visit Sri Lanka as part of a longer journey, you could consider buying a **Round the World** (RTW) ticket – though as Sri Lanka doesn't feature in any ready-made RTW itineraries, you'll have to either get a travel agent to put together an itinerary specially for you (usually more expensive than buying an "off-the-shelf" RTW ticket) or simply buy a return ticket from somewhere on a standard RTW itinerary, such as Delhi, Mumbai, Kuala Lumpur, Bangkok or Singapore.

Booking flights online

Many discount travel websites allow you to book tickets, hotels and holiday packages **online**, cutting out the costs of agents and middlemen. There are some bargains to be had on auction sites too. When searching for flights on the Internet, note that the airport code for Colombo is CMB.

Online booking agents and general travel sites

Ⓦ**www.cheapflights.co.uk** (UK & Ireland),
Ⓦ**www.cheapflights.com** (US),
Ⓦ**www.cheapflights.ca** (Canada),
Ⓦ**www.cheapflights.com.au** (Australia).
Comprehensive links to airlines and travel agents.
Ⓦ**www.cheaptickets.com** (US) Discount flight specialists. Also at ☎1-888/922-8849.
Ⓦ**www.ebookers.co.uk** (UK),
Ⓦ**www.ebookers.com** (Ireland) Efficient, easy-to-use flight finder, with competitive fares.
Ⓦ**www.etn.nl/discount** (US) Online airfare quotes, emailed to you within one hour by specialist discount agents.
Ⓦ**www.expedia.co.uk** (UK),
Ⓦ**www.expedia.com** (US), Ⓦ**www.expedia.ca** (Canada). Discount airfares, all-airline search engine and daily deals.
Ⓦ**www.flyaow.com** Online air travel info and reservations.
Ⓦ**www.geocities.com/thavery2000** (US) An extensive list of airline websites and US toll-free numbers.
Ⓦ**www.hotwire.com** (US) Last-minute savings of up to forty percent on regular published fares. Travellers must be at least 18 and there are no refunds, transfers or changes allowed. Log-in required.
Ⓦ**www.kelkoo.co.uk** (UK) Useful price-comparison site, checking several sources of low-cost flights.
Ⓦ**www.lastminute.com** (UK),
Ⓦ**www.lastminute.com.au** (Australia). Good last-minute holiday packages and flights.

Ⓦ **www.opodo.co.uk** (UK) Reliable source of low airfares, run in conjunction with nine major European airlines.

Ⓦ **www.orbitz.com** (US) Comprehensive web travel source, with the usual flight and hotel deals, plus great follow-up customer service.

Ⓦ **www.priceline.co.uk** (UK),

Ⓦ **www.priceline.com** (US). Name-your-own-price website that has deals at around forty percent off standard fares.

Ⓦ **www.skyauction.com** (US). Auctions tickets and travel packages to destinations worldwide.

Ⓦ **www.travelocity.co.uk** (UK),

Ⓦ **www.travelocity.com** (US),

Ⓦ **www.travelocity.ca** (Canada),

Ⓦ **www.zuji.com.au** (Australia). Discount fares and accommodation deals.

Ⓦ **www.travelshop.com.au** (Australia). Discounted flights, packages, insurance, and online bookings. Also on ☎ 1800/108108.

Flights from the UK and Ireland

The only nonstop scheduled flights **from the UK** to Sri Lanka are with SriLankan Airlines from London Heathrow; flying time to Colombo is around eleven hours. A number of operators – Gulf Air, Emirates, Qatar Airlines and Kuwait Airlines – offer one-stop flights from Heathrow via the Gulf. There are also more circuitous routeings via various points in Southeast Asia, including Singapore, Kuala Lumpur, Bangkok and Hong Kong. Travelling **from Ireland**, you can either make your way to Heathrow and pick up an onward connection there, or fly via one of the various European cities which have direct connections with Colombo – these include Paris, Frankfurt and Zurich (SriLankan Airlines) and Vienna (Austrian Airlines).

Average scheduled **fares** from London to Colombo are £450–500 return year-round. The cheapest tickets are usually offered by SriLankan Airlines, Emirates and Gulf Air, and you may also find good deals on Qatar Airways and Czech Airlines if you book far enough in advance. Fares for more circuitous routeings with Thai Air (via Bangkok), Malaysia Airlines (via Kuala Lumpur), Singapore Airlines (via Singapore) and Cathay Pacific (via Hong Kong), are generally significantly more expensive – in the area of £600–700.

Airlines

Austrian Airlines ☎ 0870/124 2625,
Ⓦ www.aua.com. One flight weekly from Dublin and London Heathrow to Colombo via Vienna.

Cathay Pacific UK ☎ 020/8834 8888,
Ⓦ www.cathaypacific.com/uk. Daily from London Heathrow to Colombo, via Hong Kong and Bangkok or Singapore.

CSA (Czech Airlines) UK ☎ 0870/444 3747, Republic of Ireland ☎ 01/814 4626, Ⓦ www.csa.cz. Twice weekly from London to Colombo via Prague (and sometimes Dubai).

Emirates UK ☎ 0870/243 2222,
Ⓦ www.emirates.com. Daily from London Heathrow to Colombo via Dubai.

Gulf Air UK ☎ 0870/777 1717,
Ⓦ www.gulfairco.com. Daily from London to Colombo via Abu Dhabi.

Kuwait Airways UK ☎ 020/7412 0006,
Ⓦ www.kuwait-airways.com. Five flights weekly from London Heathrow to Colombo via Kuwait City.

Malaysia Airlines UK ☎ 0870/607 9090, Republic of Ireland ☎ 01/676 2131,
Ⓦ www.malaysia-airlines.com. Five times weekly from London to Colombo via Kuala Lumpur.

Qatar Airlines (via Doha) UK ☎ 020/7896 3636, Ⓦ www.qatarairways.com. Twice daily from London to Colombo via Doha, and four times weekly from Manchester to Colombo via Doha.

Singapore Airlines UK ☎ 0870/608 8886, Republic of Ireland ☎ 01/671 0722,
Ⓦ www.singaporeair.com. Daily from London to Colombo via Singapore.

SriLankan Airlines UK ☎ 020/8538 2001,
Ⓦ www.srilankan.lk. Eight nonstop flights weekly from London Heathrow to Colombo, plus three flights weekly via Male in the Maldives.

Swiss International Airlines ☎ 0845/601 0956, Ⓦ www.swiss.com. Five flights weekly from London Heathrow to Colombo via Zurich.

Thai Air UK ☎ 0870/606 0911,
Ⓦ www.thaiair.com. Daily from Heathrow to Bangkok, then four times weekly from Bangkok to Colombo.

Travel agents and discount flight agents

Apex Travel Republic of Ireland ☎ 01/241 8000, Ⓦ www.apextravel.ie. Specialists in flights to Australia, East Asia & USA. Consolidators for BA, American and SAS Scandinavian.

Bridge the World UK ☎ 0870/443 2399,
Ⓦ www.bridgetheworld.com. Specialists in long-haul

travel, with good-value flight deals, Round the World tickets and tailor-made packages, all aimed at the backpacker market.

ebookers UK ☎0870/010 7000, ⓦwww.ebookers.com; Republic of Ireland ☎01/241 5689, ⓦwww.ebookers.ie. Low fares on an extensive selection of scheduled flights and package deals.

Flightcentre UK ☎0870/890 8099, ⓦwww.flightcentre.co.uk. Rock-bottom fares worldwide.

Flights4Less UK ☎0871/222 3423, ⓦwww.flights4less.co.uk. Good discount airfares. Part of Lastminute.com.

Go Holidays Republic of Ireland ☎01/874 4126, ⓦwww.goholidays.ie. City breaks and package tours.

Holidays4Less UK ☎0871/222 3423, ⓦwww.holidays4less.co.uk. Discounted package deals worldwide. Part of Lastminute.com.

Joe Walsh Tours Republic of Ireland ☎01/676 0991, ⓦwww.joewalshtours.ie. Long-established general budget fares and holidays agent.

Lee Travel Republic of Ireland ☎021/427 7111, ⓦwww.leetravel.ie. Flights and holidays worldwide.

Link Air Travels Ltd ☎020/8665 0206, ⓦwww.linkair.co.uk. India and Sri Lanka flight specialist.

McCarthys Travel Republic of Ireland ☎021/427 0127, ⓦwww.mccarthystravel.ie. Established travel agent offering cheap flights.

North South Travel UK ☎01245/608 291, ⓦwww.northsouthtravel.co.uk. Friendly, competitive travel agency, offering discounted fares worldwide. Profits are used to support projects in the developing world, especially the promotion of sustainable tourism.

Premier Travel UK ☎028/7126 3333, ⓦwww.premiertravel.uk.com. Discount flight specialists.

Red Dot Tours ☎01937/842846, ⓦwww.reddottours.com. Sri Lankan specialists, and a good source of cheap flights.

Rosetta Travel UK ☎028/9064 4996, ⓦwww.rosettatravel.com. Flight and holiday agent, specializing in deals direct from Belfast.

Skylord Travel ⓦwww.skylorduk.com. Cheap plane tickets worldwide.

STA Travel UK ☎0870/160 0599, ⓦwww.statravel.co.uk. Worldwide specialists in low-cost flights, overland and holiday deals. Good discounts for students and under-26s.

Taprobane Travel/Sri Lanka Tours ☎020/7434 3921, ⓦwww.srilankatours.co.uk. Sri Lanka specialist and one of the best sources of discount airfares.

Thomas Cook UK ☎0870/750 0512, ⓦwww.thomascook.co.uk. Flights and basic beach packages to Sri Lanka.

Top Deck UK ☎020/7244 8000, ⓦwww.topdecktravel.co.uk. Long-established agent offering discount flights and tours.

Trailfinders UK ☎020/7938 3939, ⓦwww.trailfinders.com, Republic of Ireland ☎01/677 7888, ⓦwww.trailfinders.ie. One of the best-informed and most efficient agents for independent travellers.

Travel Bag UK ☎0870/890 1456, ⓦwww.travelbag.co.uk. Discount deals worldwide.

USIT Northern Ireland ☎028/9032 7111, ⓦwww.usitnow.com, Republic of Ireland ☎0818/200 020, ⓦwww.usit.ie. Specialists in student, youth and independent travel – flights, trains, study tours, TEFL, visas and more.

World Travel Centre Republic of Ireland ☎01/416 7007, ⓦwww.worldtravel.ie. Excellent fares worldwide.

Specialist tour operators

Lots of companies based in the UK, North America and Australasia run tours to Sri Lanka. These can be a convenient way to get an introduction to the island, though many tend to be much of a muchness – if you want something a bit more unusual you might be better off contacting one of the Colombo-based operators listed on p.113. The tours usually feature a mix of wildlife and culture followed by a few days on the beach, although some are oriented more towards a particular interest, while others offer more adventurous possibilities such as trekking, cycling and whitewater rafting. Many of the operators below can also arrange honeymoon, wedding and cricketing packages, and virtually all of them will customize tours on request. Some tours are by private car, with your own personal chauffeur; others are in larger groups of up to sixteen people travelling by minibus.

Adventure Company ☎0870/794 1009, ⓦwww.adventurecompany.co.uk. Hands-on "adventure" tours (12–16 nights; from £539 plus flights) with the emphasis on nature and wildlife, including some cycling and walking and perhaps whitewater rafting. Tours are run to ensure profits reach local communities.

Ampersand Travel ☎020/7723 4336, ⓦwww.ampersandtravel.com. Luxury island tours

(8–17 nights; from £1230) focusing on nature or culture, with accommodation in top-end hotels or luxury villas. Also does wedding and honeymoon packages, and twin-centre holidays combining Sri Lanka with India or India and Dubai, are also available.

Carolanka ☎01822/810230,
Ⓦwww.carolanka.co.uk. Small Sri Lankan specialist offering two general island tours (15 nights; £600–1200), plus customized itineraries and special-interest trips – anything from birdwatching or meditation to golf.

Cox & Kings Travel ☎01235/824414,
Ⓦwww.coxandkings.co.uk. Two luxury group tours of Sri Lanka (12 and 8 nights; from £1045) visiting an interesting selection of cultural and natural attractions (but no beaches).

Holidays 2 Sri Lanka ☎0870/350 0045,
Ⓦholidays2srilanka.com. Cricketing specialists, offering supporters' tours combining sightseeing with visits to matches, as well as a very inexpensive general island tour (7 nights; from £220 plus flights).

Intrepid Travel UK ☎020/8960 6333,
Ⓦwww.intrepidtravel.com. Unoriginal but very cheap tours (6 or 13 nights; from £290 plus flights).

Kumuka Expeditions UK ☎0800/068 8855,
Ⓦwww.kumuka.co.uk. Tours (14 nights; from £820 plus flights) offer a mix of culture and wildlife, plus two days' whitewater rafting. Fourteen-day tours with a mix of culture and wildlife, plus two days' whitewater rafting.

Magic of the Orient UK ☎01293/537700,
Ⓦwww.magic-of-the-orient.com. Wide range of interestingly designed tours (4–7 nights; from £548 plus flights) with the emphasis on culture and wildlife (including one elephant-spotting tour), plus two-centre holidays with the Maldives or Dubai.

Red Dot Tours ☎01937/842846,
Ⓦwww.reddottours.com. Sri Lankan specialists offering a wide range of island tours (from around £1000 for 9 nights), including activity, wildlife and ayurveda holidays, plus beach holidays and cricket tours.

Somak Holidays ☎020/8423 3000,
Ⓦwww.somak.co.uk. General introductory island tour, or a nature-oriented jaunt around the hill country and Uda Walawe (7 or 8 nights; from £959).

Sri Lanka Insider Tours ☎01233/811771,
Ⓦsrilanka-insider-tours.com. Sri Lanka specialist offering small-group and customized tours from budget to luxury standards. Tours (3–14 nights; from £181/712 plus flights) are run in conjunction with Sri Lankan guides and organizations to create unusual itineraries, giving visitors a real first-hand taste of the island and offering stimulating encounters with locals.

Time Travel & Tours ☎020/8429 8333,
Ⓦwww.ucanfly.co.uk. Beach vacations, wedding and honeymoon packages, adventure and bird-watching tours, plus general tours (10 nights; around £900) and tailor-made holidays.

Trans Indus ☎020/8566 2729,
Ⓦwww.transindus.co.uk. Reputable India specialist offering a luxurious and extremely comprehensive cultural tour of Sri Lanka (15 nights; £1450–1700), including visits to some lesser-known sites as well as the big attractions.

Travelpack ☎0870/121 2050,
Ⓦwww.travelpack.co.uk. Three contrasting tours (6–13 nights; from £791), including "Kings of the Jungles", with a strong wildlife focus. Also arranges wedding packages.

Travel & Tours Anywhere ☎020/8589 7303,
Ⓦwww.exploresrilanka.biz. Sri Lanka specialists, offering several standard tours (8–15 nights; from £899) with varying mixtures of culture, nature and beach, plus interesting elephant-watching and cycling trips (15 nights; from £1549), and Sri Lanka's only turtle-watching tour (9 nights; from £1299).

Voyages Jules Verne ☎0845/166 7009,
Ⓦwww.vjv.com. Culturally oriented tours (8–11 nights; from £695), including tailor-made trips with a private vehicle.

Worldwide Holidays ☎01202/743907,
Ⓦwww.worldwideholidays.co.uk. Several tours (8–14 nights; £479–1099 plus flights) oriented variously towards culture, elephants, wildlife, golf and outdoor activities (cycling, trekking, camping and rafting).

Wildlife Encounters UK ☎01737/218802,
Ⓦwww.wildlife-encounters.co.uk. Interesting tours (16 nights; from £1795) of national parks and sanctuaries, run by well-established wildlife specialists.

Wildlife Worldwide UK ☎020/8667 9158,
Ⓦwww.wildlifeworldwide.com. Nature-oriented island tour (15 nights; from £1150) including visits to four national parks.

World Expeditions UK ☎020/8870 2600,
Ⓦwww.worldexpeditions.co.uk. Adventurous island tour (14 nights; from £790) focusing on outdoor activities and wildlife, including an ascent of Adam's Peak and whitewater rafting at Kitulgala, plus visits to cultural sites and Kandy.

Flights from the US and Canada

It's a long journey from North America to Sri Lanka, and chances are you'll want to break your flight somewhere or include the island as part of a longer visit to the region. The journey from North America to Sri Lanka takes at least 24 hours, and necessitates at least one change of plane, and probably more like two or three. From the **east coast**, there are various routeings via Europe. One possibility to is to fly to London and then pick up one of the onward connections covered on p.10. Alternatively, you could fly to Paris, Zurich, Frankfurt, Prague or Vienna, all of which have nonstop connections on to Colombo with various airlines. There are also various routeings via Europe and the Middle East with Gulf Air, Emirates, Qatar Airways and Kuwait Airlines. Travelling from the **west coast**, the most direct routes go via east and Southeast Asia, flying via Hong Kong, Kuala Lumpur, Singapore or Bangkok, all of which have nonstop connections on to Colombo.

From Canada, there are flights from Vancouver to Hong Kong, Singapore and Tokyo, from where there are direct connections to Colombo; and from Toronto and Montreal to Colombo via various European cities.

Year-round **fares** to Colombo are in the margin of US$1500–1700 from **New York**; from around US$2000 from **Los Angeles**; or about Can$3300 from **Vancouver**.

Airlines

Air Canada ☎1-888/247-2262, ⓦwww.aircanada.com. Flights from Vancouver to London, Hong Kong and Tokyo, and from Toronto to Delhi, London, Paris, Zurich and Frankfurt.
American Airlines ☎1-800/433-7300, ⓦwww.aa.com. Flights from many US cities to London, Frankfurt, Paris, Zurich and Tokyo
Austrian Airlines ☎1-800/843-0002, ⓦwww.aua.com. One flight weekly from Washington and New York to Colombo via Vienna.
Cathay Pacific ☎1-800/233-2742, ⓦwww.cathay-usa.com. Flights from 27 US cities, plus Vancouver and Toronto, to Hong Kong, from where there are daily services to Colombo via Bangkok or Singapore.
Continental Airlines ☎1-800/231-0856, ⓦwww.continental.com. Direct flights from New York to Hong Kong and from New York and Houston to Tokyo, with connections from numerous other cities in the US and Canada.
CSA (Czech Airlines) US ☎1-800/223-2365, Canada ☎416/363-3174, ⓦwww.csa.cz. New York, Toronto and Montreal to Colombo via Prague.

Delta ☎1-800/241-4141, ⓦwww.delta.com. Connections from numerous US and Canadian cities to London, Paris, Zurich, Frankfurt, Tokyo and Bombay.
Emirates ☎1-800/777-3999, ⓦwww.emirates .com. Daily flights from New York to Colombo via Dubai.
Gulf Air ☎1-888/FLY-GULF, ⓦwww.gulfairco .com. Nonstop flights from New York, Boston, Chicago, Miami and Los Angeles to London, from where there are connecting Gulf Air flights on to Colombo via Abu Dhabi.
Kuwait Airways US ☎1-800/458-9248, ⓦwww.kuwait-airways.com. Twice-weekly flights from New York and Chicago to Colombo via Kuwait City.
Singapore Airlines US ☎1-800/742-3333, Canada ☎1-800/387-8039 or 663-3046, ⓦwww.singaporeair.com. Flights to Colombo from New York, Los Angeles, San Francisco and Vancouver via Singapore.
SriLankan Airlines US ☎1-877/915-2652, Canada ☎1-800/667-2252, ⓦwww.srilankan .aero. No services to North America, but direct onward connections from London, Paris, Zurich, Frankfurt, Tokyo, Jakarta, Bangkok, Kuala Lumpur, Singapore and Delhi.
Swiss ☎1-877/FLY-SWISS, ⓦwww.swiss.com. Flights from New York, Boston, Chicago, Miami, Los Angeles and Montreal to Colombo via Zurich.
Thai Airways US ☎1-800/426-5204, Canada ☎1-800/668-8103, ⓦwww.thaiair.com. One- or two-stop flights from New York, San Francisco, Los Angeles, Toronto, Washington DC, Miami, Atlanta, Chicago, Dallas/Fort Worth and Denver to Bangkok, from where there are direct connections on to Colombo.
United Airlines ☎1-800/538-2929, ⓦwww.united.com. Connections from the US and Canada to London, Paris, Frankfurt, Tokyo, Hong Kong, Singapore and Bangkok.

Travel agents and discount flight agents

Air Brokers International ☎1-800/883-3273, ⓦwww.airbrokers.com. Consolidator and specialist in Round the World tickets.
Airtech ☎212/219-7000, ⓦwww.airtech.com. Standby seat broker and consolidator.
Airtreks ☎1-877/AIR-TREKS, ⓦwww.airtreks.com. Interactive online database on which to build and price your own Round the World itinerary.
Educational Travel Center ☎1-800/747-5551 or 608/256 5551, ⓦwww.edtrav.com. Low-cost

fares worldwide, plus student/youth discount offers.

Flightcentre US ☎1-866/WORLD-51, ⓦwww .flightcentre.us, Canada ☎1-888/WORLD-55, ⓦwww.flightcentre.ca. Rock-bottom fares.

STA Travel US ☎1-800/329 9537, Canada ☎1-888/427 5639, ⓦwww.statravel.com. Specialists in independent travel.

Student Flights ☎1-800/255-8000 or 480/951-1177, ⓦwww.isecard.com /studentflights. Student/youth fares.

TFI Tours ☎1-800/745-8000 or 212/736-1140, ⓦwww.lowestairprice.com. Well-established consolidator with a wide variety of global fares.

Travel Avenue ☎1-800/333-3335, ⓦwww.travelavenue.com. Discount travel agent.

Travel Cuts US ☎1-800/592-CUTS, Canada ☎1-888/246-9762, ⓦwww.travelcuts.com. Popular, long-established student travel organization, with worldwide offers.

Travelers Advantage ☎1-877/259-2691, ⓦwww.travelersadvantage.com. Discount travel club, with cash-back deals. Membership required ($1 for three months' trial).

Travelosophy US ☎1-800/332-2687, ⓦwww.itravelosophy.com. Good range of discounted and student fares worldwide.

Worldtek Travel ☎1-800/243-1723, ⓦwww.worldtek.com. Discount travel agency for worldwide travel.

Specialist tour operators

Absolute Asia ☎1-800/736-8187, ⓦwww.absoluteasia.com. Luxury tours (5–9 nights; from US$1700), six- to ten-day tours, mainly around the Cultural Triangle, plus a an eighteen-night combined tour with South India.

Adventures Abroad ☎1-800/665-3998, ⓦwww.adventures-abroad.com. Wide range of tours (7–40 nights; from US$985 plus flights) either of Sri Lanka alone or in conjunction with the Maldives or India/Nepal.

Cox & Kings ☎1-800/999-1758, ⓦwww.coxandkingsusa.com. Standard island tours (7 nights; from US$1725 plus flights) in luxury accommodation.

Goway Travel Experiences ☎1-800/387-8850 or 416/322-1034, ⓦwww.goway.com. Basic island tours (5 nights; around US$860 plus flights), with the option of an extra three days in Colombo at the end.

Journeys International ☎1-800/255-8735 or 734/665-4407, ⓦwww.journeys-intl.com. Three interesting tours, focused on Sri Lanka's ancient heritage (14 nights; US$2375); nature and wildlife

(12 nights; US$2275) and a comprehensive birdwatching tour (14 nights; US$2275).

Trek Holidays Canada ☎1-800/661-7265, ⓦwww.trekholidays.com. A range of island tours (11–14 nights; from Can$1255) comprise a well-planned mix of culture, nature and beach, and include several camping options. From Can$1255

Worldwide Adventures ☎1-800/387-1483, ⓦwww.worldwidequest.com. One islandwide tour (14 nights; US$1690) that includes walks in the hill country and Sinharaja, and a two-day canoe trip on the Kalu Ganga

Flights from Australia and New Zealand

Flying **from Australia** to Sri Lanka is straightforward, although you'll have to change planes at least once; the most direct routeings to Colombo are via Singapore, Kuala Lumpur, Bangkok or Jakarta. There are also a couple of one-stop options from **New Zealand**, via Singapore, Bangkok and Kuala Lumpur. **Fares** from Sydney to Colombo start at around Aus$1800, and from Auckland at around NZ$2500.

Airlines

Air New Zealand Australia ☎13 24 76, ⓦwww.airnz.com.au, New Zealand ☎0800/737 000, ⓦwww.airnz.co.nz. Regular nonstop flights from Auckland and Christchurch to Singapore, from where there are connections on to Colombo.

Garuda Indonesia Australia ☎1300/365 330 or 02/9334 9944, New Zealand ☎09/366 1862, ⓦwww.garuda-indonesia.com. Flights from Sydney, Melbourne, Brisbane, Darwin, Perth, Adelaide and Auckland to Jakarta. All except the Sydney service are via Denpasar (Bali), from where there are direct flights with SriLankan Airlines to Colombo.

Malaysia Airlines Australia ☎13 26 27, New Zealand ☎0800/777 747, ⓦwww.malaysia -airlines.com. Flights to Colombo via Kuala Lumpur from Sydney, Melbourne, Perth, Brisbane, Adelaide and Auckland.

Qantas Australia ☎13 13 13, New Zealand ☎0800/808 767 or 09/357 8900, ⓦwww.qantas.com. Flights from Melbourne, Brisbane and Adelaide to Singapore; from Perth to Singapore and Jakarta; and from Sydney to Jakarta, Singapore, Bangkok and Mumbai. SriLankan have connections to Colombo from all these cities.

Singapore Airlines Australia ☎13 10 11, New Zealand ☎0800/808 909,

ⓦwww.singaporeair.com. Flights from Sydney, Melbourne, Perth, Adelaide, Brisbane, Auckland and Christchurch to Colombo via Singapore.

SriLankan Airlines Australia ☎02/9244 2234, New Zealand ☎09/308 3353, ⓦwww.srilankan.lk. No flights to Australia or New Zealand, but regular connecting services from Bangkok, Jakarta, Singapore and Kuala Lumpur to Colombo.

Thai Airways Australia ☎1300/651 960, New Zealand ☎09/377 3886, ⓦwww.thaiair.com. Flights to Colombo via Bangkok from Sydney, Melbourne, Perth, Brisbane and Auckland.

Travel agents and discount flight agents

Flight Centre Australia ☎13 31 33, ⓦwww .flightcentre.com.au; New Zealand ☎0800 243 544, ⓦwww.flightcentre.co.nz. Rock-bottom fares worldwide.

Holiday Shoppe New Zealand ☎0800/808 480, ⓦwww.holidayshoppe.co.nz. Great deals on flights, hotels and holidays.

OTC Australia ☎1300/855 118, ⓦwww.otctravel .com.au. Deals on flights, hotels and holidays.

Plan It Holidays Australia ☎03/9245 0747, ⓦwww.planit.com.au. Discounted airfares and accommodation packages in Southeast Asia.

STA Travel Australia ☎1300/733 035; New Zealand ☎0508/782 872; ⓦwww.statravel.com. Worldwide specialists in low-cost flights, with good discounts for students and under-26s.

Student Uni Travel Australia ☎02/9232 8444, ⓦwww.sut.com.au; New Zealand ☎09/379 4224, ⓦwww.sut.co.nz. Good flight deals for students.

Trailfinders Australia ☎02/9247 7666, ⓦwww.trailfinders.com.au. One of the best-informed and most efficient agents for independent travellers.

travel.com.au and **travel.co.nz** Australia ☎1300/130 482 or 02/9249 5444, ⓦwww.travel.com.au; New Zealand ☎0800/468

332, ⓦwww.travel.co.nz. Comprehensive online travel company, with discounted fares.

Specialist tour operators

Abercrombie & Kent Australia ☎1300/851 800; New Zealand ☎0800/441 638; ⓦwww .abercrombiekent.com.au. Leisurely and luxurious island tour (9 nights; from Aus$1440), travelling from Polonnaruwa down to Nuwara Eliya.

Adventure World Australia ☎02/8913 0755, ⓦwww.adventureworld.com.au; New Zealand ☎09/524 5118, ⓦwww.adventureworld.co.nz. Standard island highlights tour (7 nights; from Aus$781 plus flights) with a mix of culture, nature and beach.

Intrepid Travel Australia ☎1300/360 667 or 03/9473 2626, ⓦwww.intrepidtravel.com. Two island tours (7 or 14 nights; from Aus$690 plus flights) – nothing very original, but cheap.

Kumuka Expeditions Australia ☎1800/804 277 or 02/9279 0491, ⓦwww.kumuka.com. Tours (13 nights; Aus$2100 plus flights) combine culture and wildlife, plus two days' whitewater rafting.

Passport Travel Australia ☎03/9867 3888, ⓦwww.travelcentre.com.au. A challenging and interesting cycling tour (15 nights; Aus$2499 plus flights), covering (16 days; Aus$2499 plus flights) of the island (covering up to 80km per day), with spot of canoeing and camping.

San Michele Travel Australia ☎1800/22 22 44 or 02/9299 1111, ⓦwww.asiatravel.com.au. Several Sri Lanka tours including beach packages and cultural tours (4–10 nights; from Aus$1399).

World Expeditions Australia ☎1300/720 000; New Zealand ☎0800/350 354; ⓦwww .worldexpeditions.com.au. Long-established and environmentally conscious operator offering stimulating adventure tours (14 nights; Aus$1990 plus flights) featuring hiking, canoeing, wildlife-spotting and cultural excursions, plus an ascent of Adam's Peak.

The ferry from India

The **ferry service** which formerly connected Rameswaram in India and Talaimannar in Sri Lanka was suspended in 1983 at the outbreak of civil war. Following the ceasefire in 2002, the reintroduction of ferry services was repeatedly promised but has so far failed to materialize. The entire subject has become something of a running joke, to the point where many now doubt that services will ever recommence. The latest proposed route for the ferry is from Colombo to Thiruvananthapuram (Trivandrum) in Kerala; it's unlikely that services will recommence from anywhere in the north of the island for the foreseeable future. Until ferries do resume, the closest equivalent to travelling by boat from India is to fly to Colombo from Tiruchirappali in Tamil Nadu with SriLankan Airlines.

Getting there from the rest of Asia

Sri Lanka isn't normally considered part of the overland Asian trail, although the island is well connected with other countries in **south and Southeast Asia**. There are regular nonstop flights with SriLankan Airlines to various places in India, including Delhi, Mumbai (Bombay), Chennai (Madras), Bangalore, Trivandrum and Tiruchirappali; to Bangkok with Sri Lankan Airlines and Thai Air; Kuala Lumpur with SriLankan and Malaysia Airline; Singapore with SriLankan and Singapore Airlines; Jakarta and Tokyo with SriLankan; and Hong Kong with Cathay Pacific. There are also direct connections to many places in the Gulf.

Red tape and visas

Nationals of the UK, Ireland, Australia, New Zealand, Canada and the US visiting Sri Lanka for tourist purposes are issued with a free one-month tourist visa on arrival (the same applies to nationals of most other European countries; if in doubt, check with your nearest embassy in advance).

This one-month visa can be easily extended to three months by visiting the **Department of Immigration** (☏011-259 7511), at Tower Building on Station Road in the southern Colombo suburb of Bambalapitiya; the office is just outside Bambalapitiya Station (see map on p.76–77), a short train ride from central Colombo. You can extend your visa as soon as you get to Sri Lanka; the month you're given on arrival is included in the three months. Visa extensions are dealt with on the first floor; the whole process takes about an hour and is surprisingly efficient, despite the initial impression of chaos (the way in which you're passed down the line of clerks during the procedure offers an interesting insight into the baroque machinations of Sri Lankan bureaucracy). You'll need to show a return or onward airline ticket out of the country, along with a credit card or other proof of funds, such as travellers' cheques. Fees for three-month visa extensions are

Sri Lankan embassies and consulates overseas

Australia 35 Empire Circuit, Forrest, Canberra ACT 2603 ☏02/6239 7041, ⓦwww.srilanka-highcommission.com.
Canada Suite 1204, 333 Laurier Ave West, Ottawa, Ontario KIP 1C1 ☏613/233 8449, ⓦwww.srilankahcottawa.org.
India 27 Kautilya Marg, Chanakyapuri, New Delhi 110021 ☏011/301 0201; 9d Nawab Habibullah Ave, Anderson Rd, Chennai ☏044/827 0831; Sri Lanka House, 34 Homi Modi St, Mumbai ☏022/204 8303.
New Zealand Contact Australian embassy.
Republic of Ireland Contact UK embassy.
UK 13 Hyde Park Gardens, London W2 2LU ☏020/7262 1841, ⓦwww.slhclondon.org.
US 2148 Wyoming Ave NW, Washington DC 20008 ☏202/483-4026, ⓦwww.slembassy.org.

Rs.4950 for UK nationals, Rs.1470 for citizens of the Republic of Ireland, Rs.2750 for Australians, Rs.3160 for New Zealanders, Rs.4580 for Canadians, and a hefty Rs.17,400 for US citizens. The three-month visa can be extended to six months upon payment of the same fee again, plus an additional Rs.10,000.

For a list of **foreign embassies and consulates** in Colombo, see p.110.

Customs

Entering Sri Lanka you are allowed to bring in 1.5 litres of spirits, two bottles of wine and 200 cigarettes. **Leaving Sri Lanka** you are permitted to export up to 3kg of tea duty-free. In theory, you're not allowed to take out more than Rs.250 in cash, though this is rarely checked. If you want to export antiques – defined as anything more than fifty years old – you will need authorization from both the Director of the National Archives (7 Reid Avenue, Colombo 7 ☎011-268 8757) and the Director General of the Archaeology Department (Sir Marcus Fernando Mawatha, Colombo 7 ☎011-269 5255). The export of any coral, shells or other protected marine products is prohibited; taking out flora, fauna or animal parts is also prohibited.

Information, websites and maps

Considering the importance of tourism to the national economy, there are surprisingly few sources of official tourist information in Sri Lanka, with just three offices of the Sri Lanka Tourist Board (still sometimes known as the Ceylon Tourist Board) in the entire country. The overseas branches of the tourist board (see below) are good sources of glossy leaflets about the island, and staff should be able to answer general questions.

For detailed information about specific areas, the best sources are the independent tour operators listed on pp.11–12 and p.14 & p.15, and staff at hotels and guest houses. For information about the country's national parks and other protected areas, you could (in theory) try contacting the **Department of Wildlife Conservation**, 18 Gregory's Road, Colombo 7 (☎011-269 4241, ⓦwww.dwlc .lk), although they are so poor at responding to enquiries, either by mail, email or in person, that it's usually not worth the effort.

Tourist-oriented **publications** are also fairly thin on the ground. The free monthly *Travel Lanka*, available from the tourist office in Colombo (see p.78), contains listings of

---

Sri Lanka Tourist Board offices overseas

Australia 29 Lonsdale St, Braddon, ACT 2612 ☎02/6230 6002, ⓕ6230 6066.

Ireland 59 Ranelagh Rd, Dublin 6 ☎01/496-9621, ⓔaelred@ireland.com.

New Zealand 157 Somerville Road, Howick, Auckland ☎09/534 0101, ⓔdhane@ihug.co.nz.

UK 26–27 Clareville House, Oxendon St, London SW1Y 4EL ☎020/7930 2627, ⓔsrilankatourism@aol.com

USA 111 Wood Avenue South, Iselin, NJ 08830 ☎0732/516-9800, ⓔctbUSA@anlusa.com.

accommodation, shops, services and transport in the capital and across the island; the tourist board also produce a free annual *Accommodation Guide*, although it's very hit-and-miss and far from complete. Also look out for the free glossy magazine, *Explore Sri Lanka*, which you can sometimes pick up from shops and hotels in Colombo; this has features on the island, news of upcoming events and some useful adverts.

Internet

Online information on Sri Lanka is patchy. There's a fair selection of general-interest sites, though the information they provide is a very mixed bag, but there's a good selection of news sites. For the latest information on **safety issues** in Sri Lanka, check out either the British Foreign & Commonwealth Office website (ⓦwww.fco.gov.uk) or the US State Department Travel Advisories (ⓦtravel.state .gov/travel_warnings.html).

Note that Sri Lankan websites tend to be quite temperamental; a site that's down one day may well be up again the next, so keep trying.

Maps

There are several good **country maps** of Sri Lanka. The best and most comprehensive is the *Rough Guide Sri Lanka Map* (1:500,000); it's also printed on indestructible waterproof synthetic paper. Another good country map is *Nelles Sri Lanka* (1:450,000), which also includes good town maps of Colombo, Kandy, Galle and Anuradhapura.

The entire island is covered by a series of 92 **1:50,000 maps** – detailed, but somewhat dated. These are only available from the Survey Dept on Kirulla Rd, Havelock Town, Colombo 5 (☎011-258 5111; Mon–Fri 10am–3.30pm); you'll need to show your passport to get in. Each sheet costs Rs.135, and they also sell a few other Sri

Sri Lanka online

General
Sri Lanka Tourist Board ⓦ www.srilankatourism.org
Official tourist board site, with general background and tourist information.
Ari Withanage's Sri Lanka pages ⓦ members.tripod.com/~withanage
Created by an expatriate Sri Lankan who now works for the London Fire Brigade, with lots of photos and text on Sri Lankan sites, culture and history.
Lanka Library ⓦ www.lankalibrary.com
Loads of background on sites, culture, history and cuisine; note that some links lead to sites for which a paid suscription is needed.
Lanka Net ⓦ www.lanka.net
Useful links to newspapers and radio stations, plus weather reports.
Travel Lanka ⓦ www.travelanka.com
Useful if slightly patchy general site with a hotel search, information on destinations, history and activities.
Travel Sri Lanka ⓦ www.travelsrilanka.com
Easily the best general site for visitors, with well-written background information, town guides and lots of practical tips.

Current affairs
Newspapers' websites are listed on p.48.
BBC News ⓦ www.bbc.co.uk/news
Huge searchable archive of news stories dating back to 1997.
The Academic ⓦ www.theacademic.org
Comprehensive links to Sri Lanka-related news stories across the web.
Peace in Sri Lanka ⓦ www.peaceinsrilanka.org
Official website of the Peace Process.
Tamil Net ⓦ www.tamilnet.com
The leading Sri Lankan Tamil website, with latest news stories from a Tamil perspective – an interesting correlative to Sinhalese sites.

Lankan maps, including town maps, historical maps and specialist geographical maps.

Map outlets

In the UK and Ireland

Stanfords 12–14 Long Acre, London WC2E 9LP
☎ 020/7836 1321, 🖥 www.stanfords.co.uk. Also at
39 Spring Gardens, Manchester ☎ 0161/831
0250; and 29 Corn St, Bristol ☎ 0117/929 9966.
Blackwell's Map Centre 50 Broad St, Oxford
OX1 3BQ ☎ 01865/793 550, 🖥 maps.blackwell.co
.uk. Other branches in Bristol, Cambridge, Cardiff,
Leeds, Liverpool, Newcastle, Reading and Sheffield.
National Map Centre 22–24 Caxton St, London
SW1H 0QU ☎ 020/7222 2466,
🖥 www.mapsnmc.co.uk.
National Map Centre Ireland 34 Aungier St,
Dublin ☎ 01/476 0471, 🖥 www.mapcentre.ie.
The Travel Bookshop 13–15 Blenheim Crescent,
London W11 2EE ☎ 020/7229 5260,
🖥 www.thetravelbookshop.co.uk.
Traveller 55 Grey St, Newcastle-upon-Tyne NE1
6EF ☎ 0191/261 5622, 🖥 www.newtraveller.com.

In the US and Canada

110 North Latitude ☎ 336/369-4171,
🖥 www.110nlatitude.com.

Book Passage 51 Tamal Vista Blvd, Corte
Madera, CA 94925; San Francisco Ferry Building
☎ 1-800/999-7909 or 415/927-0960;
🖥 www.bookpassage.com.
Longitude Books 115 W 30th St #1206, New
York, NY 10001 ☎ 1-800/342-2164,
🖥 www.longitudebooks.com.
Travel Bug Bookstore 3065 W Broadway,
Vancouver, BC V6K 2G9 ☎ 604/737-1122,
🖥 www.travelbugbooks.ca.
World of Maps 1235 Wellington St, Ottawa, ON
K1Y 3A3 ☎ 1-800/214-8524 or 613/724-6776,
🖥 www.worldofmaps.com.

In Australia and New Zealand

Mapland 372 Little Bourke St, Melbourne
VIC 3000 ☎ 03/9670 4383,
🖥 www.mapland.com.au.
Map Shop 6–10 Peel St, Adelaide SA 5000
☎ 08/8231 2033, 🖥 www.mapshop.net.au.
Map World 371 Pitt St, Sydney NSW 2000
☎ 02/9261 3601; also at 900 Hay St, Perth WA
6000 ☎ 08/9322 5733; Jolimont Centre, Canberra
☎ 02/6230 4097; and 1981 Logan Road, Brisbane
QLD 4122 ☎ 07/3349 6633;
🖥 www.mapworld.net.au. 173 Gloucester St,
Christchurch ☎ 0800/627 967,
🖥 www.mapworld.co.nz.

Insurance

It's essential to take out an insurance policy before travelling to cover against
theft, loss and illness or injury. Before paying for a new policy, however, it's worth
checking whether you are already covered: some all-risks home insurance policies may cover your possessions when overseas, and many private medical
schemes include cover when abroad. In Canada, provincial health plans usually
provide partial cover for medical mishaps overseas, while holders of official stu-
dent/teacher/youth cards in Canada and the US are entitled to (albeit meagre)
accident coverage and hospital inpatient benefits. Students will often find that
their student health coverage extends during the vacations and for one term
beyond the date of last enrolment.

After exhausting the possibilities above, you
might want to contact a specialist travel
insurance company, or consider the travel
insurance deal we offer (see the box on

p.20). A typical **travel insurance policy**
usually provides cover for the loss of
baggage, tickets and – up to a certain limit –
cash or cheques, as well as cancellation or

Rough Guides Travel Insurance

Rough Guides offers a low-cost travel insurance policy, especially customized for our (statistically low-risk) readers. There are five main Rough Guides insurance plans: **No Frills**, for the bare minimum for secure travel; **Essential**, which provides decent all-round cover; **Premier**, for comprehensive cover with a wide range of benefits; **Extended Stay**, for cover lasting four months to a year; and **Annual Multi-Trip**, a cost-effective way of getting Premier cover if you travel more than once a year. Premier, Annual Multi-Trip and Extended Stay policies can be supplemented by a "Hazardous Pursuits Extension" if you plan to indulge in sports considered dangerous, such as scuba diving or trekking. For a policy quote, call the Rough Guides Insurance Line: toll-free in the UK ☎0800/015 09 06 or +44 1392 314 665 from elsewhere. Alternatively, get an online quote at ⓦ www.roughguides.com/insurance.

early curtailment of your journey. Most of them exclude so-called dangerous sports unless an extra premium is paid: in Sri Lanka this can mean scuba diving, whitewater rafting, windsurfing and trekking, though probably not kayaking or jeep safaris. Many policies can be chopped and changed to exclude coverage you don't need – for example, sickness and accident benefits can often be excluded or included at will. If you do take medical coverage, ascertain whether benefits will be paid as treatment proceeds or only after return home, and whether there is a 24-hour medical emergency number. When securing baggage cover, make sure that the per-article limit – typically under £500 – will cover your most valuable possession. If you need to **make a claim**, you should keep receipts for medicines and medical treatment, and in the event you have anything stolen, you must obtain an official statement from the police.

Health

Sri Lanka is less challenging from a health point of view than any other country in south Asia: standards of hygiene are reasonable, medical care is of a decent standard and in significant parts of the island you don't even have to worry about malaria. Nevertheless, Sri Lanka does inevitably play host to the usual gamut of tropical diseases, and it's important to make sure you protect yourself against serious illness. You should start planning the health aspect of your trip well in advance of departure, especially if you're having vaccines for things like rabies or Japanese encephalitis, which need to be administered over the course of a month. Vaccinations and medical advice are available from your doctor or – more conveniently but expensively – a specialist travel clinic (see box on pp.21–22). It's also crucial to have adequate medical insurance (see p.19).

Before travelling you should ensure that you are up to date with the following standard **vaccinations**: diphtheria, tetanus, hepatitis A and polio. Other jabs you might consider are tuberculosis, meningitis and typhoid. Most importantly, you should have adequate protection against **malaria**, assuming you're visiting an affected area (see p.24). The

The diseases listed in this section are not the only health hazards in Sri Lanka. For information about **general security**, see p.60; information about **road traffic safety** appears on p.60.

excellent website ⓦ www.waypointclinic.com has comprehensive advice on travel health in Sri Lanka for both visitors and residents. For a detailed general guide, get hold of the *Rough Guide to Travel Health*.

The best way to avoid falling ill is to look after yourself. Eat properly, make sure you get enough sleep and don't try to cram too much strenuous activity into your holiday, especially in the first few days, before you've acclimatized to the sun, water and food and while you're probably still suffering jetlag. If you do get ill in Sri Lanka, standards of medical care are good. Many **doctors** speak English and a significant number have trained in Europe. All large towns have a **hospital**, and you'll also find private **medical clinics** in Colombo. If you pay for treatment, remember to get receipts so that you can claim it back on your insurance policy. All larger towns have well-appointed **pharmacies** (signed by a red cross on a white circle) and can usually produce an English-speaking pharmacist. If stuck, any reputable hotel or guest house should be able to put you in touch with a local English-speaking doctor.

For more on Sri Lanka's remarkable home-grown system of holistic medical care, **ayurveda**, see p.128.

Medical resources for travellers

ⓦ **www.fitfortravel.scot.nhs.uk** Scottish NHS website carrying information about travel-related diseases and how to avoid them.

ⓦ **www.istm.org** The website of the International Society for Travel Medicine, with a full list of clinics specializing in international travel health. Publishes outbreak warnings, suggested inoculations, precautions and other background information for travellers.

ⓦ **www.tmvc.com.au** Contains a list of all Travellers' Medical and Vaccination Centres throughout Australia, New Zealand and Southeast Asia, plus general information on travel health.

ⓦ **www.tripprep.com** A comprehensive database of necessary vaccinations for most countries, as well as destination and medical service provider information.

In the UK and Ireland

British Airways Travel Clinics 156 Regent St, London W1 (Mon–Fri 9.30am–6pm, Sat 10am–5pm, no appointment necessary; ☎ 0845/600 2236); 101 Cheapside, London EC2 (Mon–Fri 9am–4.45pm, appointment required; ☎ 0845/600 2236); ⓦ www.britishairways .com/travel/healthclinintro. Vaccinations, tailored advice from an online database and a complete range of travel health-care products.

Dun Laoghaire Medical Centre 5 Northumberland Ave, Dun Laoghaire, County Dublin ☎ 01/280 4996, ℱ 01/280 5603. Advice on medical matters abroad.

Hospital for Tropical Diseases Travel Clinic 2nd floor, Mortimer Market Centre, off Capper St, London WC1E 6AU (Mon–Fri 9am–5pm by appointment only; ☎ 020/7388 9600, ⓦ www.masta.org; a consultation costs £15, which is waived if you have your injections here). A recorded Health Line (☎ 0906/133 7733; 50p per

A traveller's first aid kit

Insect repellent
Antiseptic spray
Calamine lotion, tiger balm or aloe vera
Plasters (band-aids)
Sunscreen
Rehydration salts
A course of antibiotics, such as Flagyl
Water sterilization tablets or tincture of iodine
Immodium (lomotil) or loperamide for emergency suppression of diarrhoea
Multi-vitamins

min) gives hints on hygiene and illness prevention as well as listing appropriate immunizations.

Liverpool School of Tropical Medicine Pembroke Place, Liverpool L3 5QA ☎0151/708 9393, ⓦwww.liv.ac.uk/lstm/lstm. Walk-in clinic (Mon–Fri 1–4pm); appointment required for yellow fever, but not for other jabs.

MASTA (Medical Advisory Service for Travellers Abroad) ⓦwww.masta.org. 40 regional clinics (call ☎0870/6062782 for the nearest). Also operates a prerecorded 24-hour Travellers' Health Line (UK ☎0906/822 4100, 60p per min), giving written information tailored to your journey by return of post.

Nomad Pharmacy Surgeries at 40 Bernard St, London WC1N 1LE, and 3–4 Wellington Terrace, Turnpike Lane, London N8 0PX (Mon–Fri 9.30am–6pm; ☎020/7833 4114 to book a vaccination appointment). Advice is free if you visit in person; alternatively, the telephone helpline (☎0906/863 3414, 60p per minute) gives tailor-made information.

Travel Health Centre Department of International Health and Tropical Medicine, Royal College of Surgeons in Ireland, Mercers Medical Centre, Stephen's St Lower, Dublin 2 ☎01/402 2337. Expert pre-trip advice and inoculations.

Travel Medicine Services PO Box 254, 16 College St, Belfast BT1 6BT ☎028/9031 5220. Offers medical advice before a trip and help afterwards in the event of a tropical disease.

Tropical Medical Bureau Grafton Buildings, 34 Grafton St, Dublin 2 ☎1850/487 674, ⓦwww.tmb.ie.

In the US and Canada

Canadian Society for International Health 1 Nicholas St, Suite 1105, Ottawa, ON K1N 7B7 ☎613/241-5785, ⓦwww.csih.org. Distributes a free pamphlet, *Health Information for Canadian Travellers*, containing an extensive list of travel health centres in Canada.

Centers for Disease Control 1600 Clifton Rd NE, Atlanta, GA 30333 ☎1-800/311-3435 or 404/639-3534, ⓦwww.cdc.gov. The US government's official site for travel health. Publishes outbreak warnings, suggested inoculations, precautions and other background information for travellers. Useful website plus International Travelers Hotline on ☎1-877/FYI-TRIP.

International Association for Medical Assistance to Travellers (IAMAT) 417 Center St, Lewiston, NY 14092 ☎716/754-4883; and 1287 St Clair Avenue West, Suite #1, Toronto, Ontario M6E 1B8 ☎416/652-0137; ⓦwww.iamat.org. A nonprofit organization,

supported by donations, which can provide a list of English-speaking doctors in Sri Lanka, climate charts and leaflets on various diseases and inoculations.

International SOS Assistance Eight Neshaminy Interplex Suite 207, Trevose, PA 19053 ☎1-800/523-8930, ⓦwww.intsos.com. Members receive pre-trip medical referral info, as well as overseas emergency services designed to complement travel insurance coverage.

MEDJET Assistance ☎1-800/963-3538 or 205/595-6658, ⓦwww.medjetassistance.com. Annual membership programme for travellers (US$195 for individuals, US$295 for families) that, in the event of illness or injury, will fly members home or to the hospital of their choice in a medically equipped jet.

Travel Medicine ☎1-800/872-8633, ⓦwww.travmed.com. Sells first-aid kits, mosquito netting, water filters, reference books and other health-related travel products.

In Australia and New Zealand

Travellers' Medical and Vaccination Centres ⓦwww.tmvc.com.au 27–29 Gilbert Place, Adelaide, SA 5000 ☎08/8212 7522; 5/247 Adelaide St, Brisbane, Qld 4000 ☎07/3221 9066; 5/8–10 Hobart Place, Canberra, ACT 2600 ☎02/6257 7156; 270 Sandy Bay Rd, Sandy Bay Tas, Hobart 7005 ☎03/6223 7577; 2/393 Little Bourke St, Melbourne, Vic 3000 ☎03/9602 5788; Level 7, Dymocks Bldg, 428 George St, Sydney, NSW 2000 ☎02/9221 7133; 1/170 Queen St, Auckland ☎09/373 3531; Shop 15, Grand Arcade, 14–16 Willis St, Wellington ☎04/473 0991.

Water and food

Avoid drinking **tap water** in Sri Lanka. Although it's generally chlorinated and safe to drink, the unfamiliar micro-organisms it contains (compared with what you're used to at home) can easily precipitate a stomach upset. Also avoid **ice**, unless you're happy that it's been made with boiled or purified water. **Mineral water** is widely available (see p.44), although always check that the seal hasn't been broken – it's not unknown for bottles to be refilled with tap water. There are also various ways of making tap water safe. Most simply, it can be **boiled** for at least five minutes. You're unlikely to have the equipment to do this yourself, though some restaurants and hotels serve – or claim to serve – only boiled water. Alternatively, water can be **chemically sterilized** using chlorine or iodine **water purification tablets**, though these leave an unpleasant taste and do not remove all organisms. More effective is **tincture of iodine**, available in most camping shops, though this also leaves an unpleasant taste (you can buy crystals which remove some – though not all – the taste; alternatively, try a squeeze of lemon or lime). Avoid using iodine if you have a thyroid problem or are pregnant. The most effective treatment is to clean tap water using a **portable water purifier**, which both filters and chemically sterilizes the water, though these are expensive and relatively bulky. Despite all these precautions, you're still likely to come into contact with local water at various points – your eating utensils will be washed in it, and it will probably be used without your knowledge in things like fruit juices – so it's not worth getting paranoid about.

Though Sri Lankan standards of **food hygiene** are reasonable, and stomach troubles are much less common than in India, it still pays to be careful, and the old traveller's adage usually applies: if you can't cook, boil or peel something, don't eat it (although if you can't peel something, you can always wash it thoroughly in purified water). Another good rule of thumb is to stick to hot food which has been freshly prepared. Avoid salads and anything which looks like it has been sitting uncovered for a while; short eats (see p.42) are particularly likely to be old and to have been poked by everyone in the café. The busier the establishment, the better, since there's less probability that the food's been sitting around all day. Obviously you'll need to use your discretion: the buffet at a five-star hotel has more chance of being OK than a local café's tureen of curry which has been keeping the flies fat since dawn. Finally, remember that refrigerators stop working during power cuts, so unless you're eating at a place with its own generator, avoid any food (including meat and ice cream) which might have been unfrozen and then refrozen.

Diarrhoea, dysentery and giardia

Diarrhoea remains the most common complaint amongst tourists visiting Sri Lanka. It can have many causes, including serious diseases like typhoid or cholera, but in the vast majority of cases diarrhoea is a result of contaminated food or drink and will pass naturally in a few days. Such diarrhoea is also often accompanied by cramps, nausea and vomiting, and fever in more severe cases.

You should seek medical advice if diarrhoea continues for more than five days or if there is blood mixed up in the faeces, in which case you could be suffering from giardiasis or amoebic dysentery (see below).

Treatment

One of the biggest problems with diarrhoea, particularly in a hot climate such as Sri Lanka's, is **dehydration**; it's vital you keep topped up with fluids – aim for about four litres every 24 hours (the colour of your urine is the best guide). If you're having more than five bouts of diarrhoea a day or are unable to eat, take **oral rehydration salts** to replace lost salt and minerals. These can be bought ready-prepared in sachets from camping shops; alternatively, you can make you own by mixing eight teaspoons of sugar and half a teaspoon of salt in a litre of purified water. Coconut milk is a good alternative, especially if you add a pinch of salt; flat coca-cola or lemonade with a pinch of salt could also be used. **Children** with diarrhoea dehydrate much more quickly than adults, and it's even more vital to keep them hydrated. If you have to go on a long journey where you won't have access to a toilet, you can temporarily bung yourself up with a blocking drug like lomotil or loperamide, though these simply suppress symptoms and have no curative value. Whilst recovering, stick to bland foods (rice and yoghurt are traditionally recommended, and bananas help replace lost potassium) and get plenty of rest – this is not the moment to go rushing up Adam's Peak.

If you have persistent diarrhoea, you may be suffering from giardiasis or amoebic dysentery. With **giardiasis**, the onset of diarrhoea is slow and the diarrhoea less watery and severe (although associated with severe flatulence). You may also suffer stomach cramps, nausea and a bloated stomach. In

amoebic dysentery, diarrhoea is severe, with bloody stools and fever. If any of the above symptoms apply, the first thing to do is to get a **stool test** in order to establish what you're suffering from. Both giardiasis and amoebic dysentery respond to **antibiotics** – ciprofloxacin is the most commonly prescribed.

Malaria

Of the four strains of malaria, two exist in Sri Lanka. The **vivax** strain accounts for around eighty percent of cases in the island and, though it's extremely unpleasant, it is rarely dangerous and is fairly simple to diagnose and cure (although sufferers may suffer a relapse if the disease isn't properly treated to begin with). The second type, **falciparum**, makes up the other twenty percent of cases and is much more serious, and is occasionally fatal if treatment is delayed. One complication of falciparum infection, **cerebral malaria**, is particularly dangerous; symptoms include a reduced level of consciousness, leading to fits, coma and, if untreated, death; in ten percent of cases there may be lasting damage to the nervous system.

Malaria risk in Sri Lanka varies enormously depending on where in the country you are and when you visit. The west coast from Negombo right the way round to Tangalla is malaria-free, except for a low risk in Matara. Malaria is also absent from the hill country – roughly everywhere from Kandy and above; the mosquitoes responsible for transmitting malaria rarely venture above 1500m. There's a varying risk of contracting malaria everywhere else in the country; for a detailed area-by-area seasonal breakdown, see ⓦwww.waypointclinic.com/male/htm.

Avoiding bites

Even if you're on medication, it's important to avoid being bitten, since no antimalarial offers total protection, and mosquitoes in Sri Lanka also transmit other diseases such as dengue fever and Japanese encephalitis. Malarial mosquitoes come out at dusk and remain active throughout the night. Standard avoidance techniques are to wear light-coloured clothing with long sleeves; use a repellent containing DEET on exposed parts of your body; and (if your room's not air-conditioned) always sleep under a net. You might also want to spray your clothing with a permethrin spray, while burning a mosquito coil in your room or putting one under the table while you eat are also recommended. An alternative to coils is the Pyrethroid tablets which you place on a tray and put in a plug; the electricity heats the tray and vaporizes the Pyrethroid. Citronella oil (available from many chemists in Sri Lanka) is also thought to be good for repelling mosquitoes.

Antimalarial drugs

Ideas about appropriate **antimalarial medication** tend to vary from country to country, and prophylaxis remains a controversial subject; it's important that you get expert medical advice on which treatment is right for you. In addition, resistance to established antimalarial drugs is growing alarmingly – none of the following provide complete protection, so avoiding being bitten in the first place remains important.

The most established regime – widely prescribed in Europe, but not in North America – is a combination of **chloroquine** (trade names Nivaquin or Avloclor) taken weekly either on its own or in conjunction with a daily dose of **proguanil** (Paludrine). You need to start this regime a week before arriving in a malarial area and continue it for four weeks after leaving. **Mefloquine** (Lariam) is a newer and stronger treatment. As a prophylactic, you need take just one tablet weekly, starting two weeks before entering a risk area and continuing for four weeks after leaving. Mefloquine is a very powerful and effective antimalarial, though there have been widely reported concerns about its side effects, including psychological problems.

Doxycycline is often prescribed in Australasia. One tablet is taken daily, starting a day or two before entering a malarial zone and continuing for four weeks after leaving. It's not suitable for children under ten and it can cause thrush in women, while three percent of users develop a sensitivity to light, causing a rash, so it's not ideal for beach holidays. It also interferes with the effectiveness of the contraceptive pill.

Malarone (a combination of Atovaquone and Proguanil) is the most recent drug to come on the market. The bonus is that you only have to start taking it on the day you enter a malarial zone and continue for just a week after leaving, meaning that, although it's expensive, it can prove economical for short trips.

Finally, note that malaria has a typical incubation period of nine to sixteen days, sometimes longer – hence the importance of continuing with the medication once you get home. Initial **symptoms** are virtually indistinguishable from severe flu, coming in three waves: cold, hot and sweating. If you think you might have malaria, have a blood test done as soon as possible.

Sun

The potential health risks associated with the **sun** are easily underestimated – especially since being in it is presumably a major factor in why you decided to come to Sri Lanka in the first place. The tropical sun is probably far stronger than you're used to at home, and can cause various problems. The most obvious is **sunburn**. Remember that sunlight increases in strength when reflected off water and sand, meaning that you can burn badly even when sea or river breezes keep you feeling cool. You can also burn whilst swimming or snorkelling (wear a T-shirt in the water to avoid getting a burnt back), as well as through cloud cover (hence sunscreen should always be applied to exposed skin when outdoors). Young children are particularly vulnerable to burns and should be kept out of the sun at all times. Older kids should wear the highest factor sunblock and a hat, at the minimum. For all ages, eyes also need to be protected by proper sunglasses. In general, take time to acclimatize, don't go charging around for the first few days after arrival, and drink lots of water; the latter is particularly important if you do get sunburnt. Other measures to soothe burnt skin include warm (not cold) showers, or applying calamine lotion or aloe vera gel.

A common but minor irritant is **prickly heat**, usually afflicting newly arrived visitors. It's caused by excessive perspiration trapped under the skin, producing an itchy rash. Keep cool (air-conditioning is good), shower frequently, use talcum powder on the affected skin and wear loose (ideally cotton) clothing. At its worst, prolonged exposure to the sun and dehydration can lead to **heatstroke**, a serious and potentially life-threatening condition. Symptoms are a lack of sweat, high temperature, severe headaches, lack of coordination and confusion. If untreated, heatstroke can lead to potentially fatal convulsions and delirium. If you're suffering from heatstroke, get out of the sun, get into a tepid shower and drink plenty of water.

Marine hazards

Drowning is the second-most common cause of death amongst tourists in Sri Lanka (after road accidents). Currents can be strong and beaches may shelve into the sea with unexpected steepness – and there are no lifeguards to come and pull you out if you get into trouble. *Always* ask local advice before venturing in the water anywhere that is obviously not a recognized swimming spot. Conditions can vary radically even within a few hundred metres, so don't assume that because lots of people are swimming at one end of the beach, the other, deserted, end will be safe. The only warning signs of dangerous swimming conditions are the red flags are posted on the beaches outside major resort hotels. The unregulated use of **power boats** and **jet skis** presents another hazard to swimmers. Sensible precautions include always keeping within your depth and making sure that someone on the shore knows that you're in the water. *Never* swim under the influence of alcohol – newspaper stories of locals washed out to sea after too many bottles of arrack are an almost weekly occurrence.

Another potential hazard is **marine stings**. Jellyfish are common, and some can inflict painful stings; coral scratches and cuts can also be painful (although more of a problem for the coral itself, which dies on contact – be careful). Occasionally people develop quasi-allergic reactions to stings; if you start to wheeze or swell up around the face, go to hospital immediately.

The other thing you need to think about is how **clean** the water is: beaches in the vicinity of town centres are obviously prone to pollution. In addition, parts of some beaches are filthy. Look out for broken glass, fishing hooks, syringes and other rubbish; dog shit is also common. If you cut your foot, disinfect it immediately and seek medical advice, since you may need a tetanus booster and/or a hepatitis B vaccine.

Hepatitis

Hepatitis is an inflammation of the liver. The disease exists in various forms, though with a shared range of symptoms, typically jaundiced skin, yellowing of the whites of the eyes, dark urine, pale faeces and a general range of flu-like symptoms. **Hepatitis A** and **hepatitis E** are spread by contaminated food and water. If you become infected, there's little you can do except rest, drink lots of fluids and eat lightly – unfortunately, it can take upwards of a couple of weeks to shake off the effects. The much more serious **Hepatitis B** can result in long-term liver damage and liver cancer. Like the HIV virus, it's spread via infected blood or body fluids, most commonly through sex or needle sharing, but also by contaminated shaving, tattooing or ear- or body-piercing equipment. **Hepatitis C and D** are similar.

You can (and should) be **vaccinated** against hepatitis A. The hepatitis B vaccine is usually only recommended to those at especially high risk, such as health-care workers. There are no vaccines for other types of hepatitis.

Japanese encephalitis

Japanese encephalitis (JE) is a virus which attacks the brain and is transmitted by mosquitoes which bite at night. It's particularly associated with rural areas, as the virus lives in wading birds, pigs and flooded rice fields. The two main areas in Sri Lanka where JE is prevalent are the flat, rice-cultivating areas around the southwest coasts from Colombo to Hambantota, and the northern districts stretching from Kurunegala via Puttalam to Anuradhapura and Polonnaruwa. JE is most prevalent from October to January, with the onset of monsoonal rains.

JE is an extremely dangerous disease, with mortality rates of up to forty percent (though tourists are only very rarely affected). As with malaria, you won't contract JE if you don't get bitten (see p.24). Symptoms include drowsiness, sensitivity to light and confusion. An effective **vaccine** exists for JE (three shots administered over 28 days), though the standard advice is that it's only worth considering if you're travelling in high-risk areas during the monsoon for a period of over a month, especially if you'll be spending a lot of time in the country and/or camping out a lot. If you're just lounging around on the beach or making a quick visit to the Cultural Triangle, the vaccine's not necessary.

Dengue fever

Dengue fever is another mosquito-borne infection, though in contrast to Japanese encephalitis, dengue is an urban disease – Colombo is particularly affected, and it is also present in Galle, Kandy, Ratnapura and Matara. As mosquitoes lay their eggs in water, dengue outbreaks tend to peak during or after periods of rain. There are four **subtypes** of dengue fever, so unfortunately it's possible to catch it more than once. The disease is typically characterized by the sudden onset of high fever accompanied by chills, headache, a skin rash and muscle or joint pains (usually affecting the limbs and back, hence dengue fever's nickname "break-bone fever"). Dengue is also associated, in around a third of cases, with mild bleeding: typically nosebleeds, bleeding from the gums whilst brushing your teeth or heavier-than-usual menstrual flow. The fever usually lasts three to seven days, while post-viral weakness, lethargy and sometimes depression can persist for anything up to several weeks.

A rare but potentially fatal complication is **dengue haemorrhagic fever** (DHF), which is almost entirely confined to children aged under 15 who have previously been infected with dengue fever. Victims can become pale, clammy and faint, with a rapid pulse and breathing; abnormal bleeding may also be present. Urgent medical attention should be sought.

There is no vaccine for dengue fever. Unfortunately, the mosquitoes which transmit dengue bite during the day, making them harder to guard against than malarial mosquitoes. If you think you've contracted dengue fever, go to a doctor – it's easily confused with malaria in its early stages, so you'll need to have a blood test to determine what you've got. Take plenty of fluids, get lots of bed rest, keep any rashes cool and use an antihistamine.

Rabies

Rabies is an animal disease which is transmitted to humans by bites, scratches or even by licking; it's usually associated with dogs, but can also be transmitted by cats, monkeys, bats and even domestic livestock – in fact, any warm-blooded animal. Rabies, once symptoms have developed, is invariably fatal. There is, however, an effective vaccine, as well as other precautions you can take if you have been bitten or scratched. You are at risk if you suffer a bite which draws blood or breaks the skin, or if you are licked by an animal on an open wound. Bites to the face, neck and fingertips are particularly dangerous.

The good news is that a safe and effective **vaccine** exists (three shots over 28 days). Casual tourists on short holidays to the island may well feel that they are not sufficiently at risk to go through the hassle of a rabies vaccine, but if you're going for a long period or are likely to be in close contact with animals, you might decide it's worth the trouble. In general, Sri Lankan dogs are fairly well behaved, and it's rare that you'll encounter the sort of aggressive and unpredictable strays (or packs of strays) that you sometimes find in other parts of Asia.

Regardless of whether you've been vaccinated or not, if you're **bitten** or scratched (or licked on an open wound) by an infected animal, clean the wound thoroughly with disinfectant as soon as possible. Iodine is ideal, but alcohol or even soap and water are better than nothing. If you've already been vaccinated, you'll need two booster shots three days apart. If you haven't been vaccinated, you will need to be given five shots of the rabies vaccine over 28 days (the first must be administered as soon as possible after you've been bitten), along with a single injection of rabies antibody serum.

Other diseases

Typhoid is a gut infection, caused by contaminated water or food and leading to a high fever accompanied by headaches, abdominal pains and diarrhoea. If left untreated, serious complications may ensue, so seek medical help. Oral and injected vaccines are available and vaccination is recommended if you're visiting the north or the east of the island, especially if you'll be staying in budget accommodation. A vaccination against **meningitis** is also available. This cerebral virus, transmitted by airborne bacteria, can be fatal. Symptoms include a severe headache, fever, a stiff neck and a stomach rash. If you think you have it, seek medical attention immediately. Sri Lanka has experienced occasional outbreaks of **cholera**, although this typically occurs in epidemics in areas of poor sanitation, being transmitted by contaminated water, and almost never affects tourists.

The **tetanus** virus lives in soil and animal faeces; infection is via a cut or scratch on the skin. As befits tetanus's old name of "lockjaw", initial symptoms can be discomfort in swallowing and a stiffness in the jaw and neck, followed by convulsions – potentially fatal. The vaccination is a standard childhood jab in developed countries. **Typhus** is spread by the bites of ticks, lice and mites. Symptoms include fever, headache and muscle pains, followed after a few days by a rash, while the bite itself often develops into a painful sore. A shot of antibiotics will shift it.

Animals and insects

Leeches are common after rain in Sinharaja and Adam's Peak. They're difficult to avoid, attaching themselves to your shoes and climbing up your leg until they find flesh, and are quite capable of burrowing through a pair of socks. Once latched on, leeches will suck your blood until sated, after which they drop off of their own accord – perfectly painless, but not terribly pleasant. You can make leeches drop off harmlessly with the end of a lighted cigarette or the flame from a lighter, or by putting salt on them. Don't pull them off, however, or bits of leech might break off and become embedded in your flesh, increasing the risk of the bite becoming infected.

Sri Lanka has the dubious distinction of having the highest number of **snakebite** fatalities, per capita, of any country in the world, and any form of bite should be treated as quickly as possible. The island boasts five species of poisonous snake, all relatively common, especially in northern dry zones; they include the cobra and the extremely dangerous Russell's viper. Avoid wandering through heavy undergrowth in bare feet and flipflops; wear proper shoes or boots, socks and long trousers. If you're bitten, you should wrap up the limb, as for a sprained ankle, and immobilize it with a splint – this slows down the speed at which venom spreads through the rest of the body; keeping as still as possible also helps. Popular advice recommends catching and killing the snake so that the doctor knows what type of antivenin to administer, although it's unlikely you'll be able to do this, and you'll probably have to settle for a description of the creature. Unfortunately, reliable antivenins have not yet been developed for all types of snake – that for the Russell's viper, for instance, has been developed from the Indian Russell's viper, and is not always effective in treating bites administered by the Sri Lankan sub-species.

STDs, HIV and AIDS

Sexually transmitted diseases (STDs) are common in the chilled-out, uninhibited and scantily clad world of the average Sri Lankan tourist beach. The island has partly shaken off its reputation as a destination for sex tourists, but STDs remain common, and may rise as tourist numbers increase. Practise safe sex, or you might come home with an unwelcome souvenir of your visit.

Compared to other parts of Asia, Sri Lanka has relatively few reported **HIV** and **AIDS** cases – around 5000 as of 2002, or 0.07 percent of the population, although there is probably significant under-reporting given the stigma attached to the disease – awareness of AIDS and HIV is poor and the government has its head buried firmly in the sand. Again, there are obvious risks if you have unprotected sex. Contaminated **needles** are not considered a problem in Sri Lanka, so there's no need to carry your own – although don't be shy about asking to have the packet opened in your presence if you want to check this for yourself. Contaminated **blood** poses a potentially greater risk – blood transfusions should only be accepted in an absolute emergency.

Costs, money and banks

Despite a general rise in prices over the last few years, Sri Lanka is still excellent value for money – it's one of the least expensive tourist destinations in Asia. Accommodation, transport and food are all a bargain: those on a tight budget could survive quite happily on under US$10 a day, while if you've got cash to splash you can enjoy the best the island has to offer without breaking the bank.

Money

The Sri Lankan currency is the **rupee** (abbreviated variously as R., R/ or R/- and in this book as Rs.). Each rupee is divided into **100 cents**, though these are seldom encountered nowadays. **Coins** come in denominations of 25 and 50 cents, and Rs.1, 2, 5 and 10. **Notes** come in denominations of Rs.10, 20,

50, 100, 200, 500 and 1000. Try to avoid accepting particularly dirty, torn or disreputable looking notes, and break big notes and stock up on change whenever you can – don't expect to be able to pay for a Rs.10 cup of tea with a Rs.1000 note.

At the time of writing the **exchange rate** was around Rs.100 to the US dollar, and

Rs.150 to the pound; you can check current exchange rates at ⓦwww.xe.com. The Sri Lankan rupee continues to devalue steadily against hard currencies. To guard against the effects of this devaluation, top-end hotels always give their prices either in **US dollars** or (increasingly) in **euros**, though you'll be expected to pay in rupees, with the bill converted at the current bank exchange rate. Many other tourist services are also often priced in dollars or euros – anything from entrance tickets at archeological sites to tours, balloon trips or diving courses – though, again, payment will be expected in rupees.

Costs

Sri Lanka is still one of Asia's less expensive tourist destinations, and the cost of basic travel, food and accommodation is a bargain. You can travel from one end of the island to the other for US$10 or less, get a filling meal at local cafés for under a dollar, and find a decent double room for as little as US$5 per night. The major expense in visiting the island are the entrance charges to **national parks** and to the government-run archeological sites of the **Cultural Triangle**, most of which charge an admission fee of around US$15. **Tours** or **renting a vehicle** also bump things up – a car and driver normally goes for around US$25 to US$30 a day, whilst the better tour operators charge around US$50 per person per day. However even when these prices are taken into account, Sri Lanka still represents good value for money. Assuming you're travelling as a couple or in a family group, you can backpack around the island in relative comfort for US$15–20 per person per day, while for US$25–30 per day you can hire your own vehicle and enjoy good mid-range accommodation. For US$50 per day you're already edging into the luxury category, and for US$100 per day you can enjoy the best the island has to offer in terms of luxury hotels, personalized tours and top-notch cuisine.

Note that some hotels and restaurants levy a ten percent **service charge**. In addition, a ten percent **government service tax** (GST) is also sometimes added to the bill. The more upmarket the establishment,

the more likely it is that one or both of these charges will apply, and it's always worth checking beforehand – the extra twenty percent added at a top hotel can add a nasty twist to the bill if you're not expecting it.

Tourist prices and ethical bargaining

As a tourist, you're likely to pay slightly over the odds for a range of services, from tuktuk fares to items in shops and markets, but overcharging is generally less widespread and severe than in some other parts of Asia. Having said that, prices in Sri Lanka are often inherently fluid. Many hoteliers, for instance, chop and change their prices according to demand, while the price of anything from a tuktuk ride to an elephant carving may depend on time of day to the weather or the mood of the seller. Given this, it's always worth **bargaining** – even five-star hotels are sometimes responsive to requests for a "special price" or "small discount" (see the accommodation section on p.37 for more on bargaining in hotels and guest houses). Remember, though, that the key to effective bargaining is to retain a sense of humour and proportion. There is nothing more ridiculous – or more damaging for local perceptions of foreign visitors – than the sight of a Western tourist arguing bitterly over the final few rupees of a budget room or an item of shopping. The fact is that even the most cash-strapped Western backpacker is, in Sri Lankan terms, extremely rich, as their very presence in the country proves. And however tight one's budget, it's important to realize the difference that even a few rupees can make to a guest house owner who is struggling by on a couple of dollars a day.

On the other hand, it's also important not to be outrageously **overcharged**. Visitors who lack a sense of local prices and pay whatever they're asked contribute to local inflation, pushing up prices both for other tourists and (more importantly) for locals – the implications of just one tourist paying US$10 for a tuktuk ride that should cost US$1 can have serious implications for the local economy.

Government prices for foreigners

At all national parks and reserves, and at government-run archeological sites, the authorities operate a **two-tier price system** whereby foreigners pay a significantly higher entrance price than locals. In some places, foreigners pay almost a hundred times more than Sri Lankan nationals, as, for instance, at the country's national parks, where locals pay an entrance fee of around US$0.25, while overseas visitors can pay almost US$25 once various taxes and additional charges have been taken into account. A similar situation obtains at the sites of the Cultural Triangle – at Anuradhapura, for instance, foreigners pay US$15 per day, whilst locals pay nothing (the fact that many of these sites have been restored with funds donated by the international community is, for many visitors, merely another insult). Some visitors oppose this two-tier pricing system in principle; others object not to the basic idea, but to the scale of the difference between the prices. These charges have also damaged the businesses of innumerable Sri Lankan tour guides, who find themselves unable to offer trips to many cultural sites or national parks due to prohibitive entrance charges.

In practice, government prices can put a strain on many budgets, especially if you're a solo traveller, when it will generally cost you about US$50 for a half-day trip to pretty much any national park in the country once you've included transport. And if you want to stay overnight in one of the basic park bungalows, you're looking at well over US$100 – a sum which would get you into most of the country's luxury hotels.

Banks and foreign exchange

Sri Lanka is well supplied with **banks**. The six main chains (most larger towns will have a branch of at least three or four of these) are the Bank of Ceylon, Hatton National Bank, Sampath Bank, Commercial Bank, People's Bank and Seylan Bank. All are open Monday to Friday from 8am or 9am in the morning until 2pm or 3pm in the afternoon. All banks shut at weekends. **Exchange rates** for foreign currency,

whether travellers' cheques, cash or making withdrawals by credit or debit card, are fairly uniform across the various banks; you may get fractionally better rates if you shop around, but you won't make any dramatic savings.

If you need to change money outside banking hours, most top-end hotels change cash or travellers' cheques, though at rates which are up to ten percent poorer than bank rates. Failing this, you could try at local guest houses or shops – the more tourist-oriented the place you're in, the better your chances, though you'll probably have to accept poor rates.

There are a few licensed **moneychangers** in coastal resort towns such as Hikkaduwa and Aluthgama, which change money and travellers' cheques at slightly below bank rates, plus a useful bureau de change in Colombo (see p.110), but otherwise no dedicated cambios.

Credit and debit cards

Pretty much every major town in the country now has at least one bank with an **ATM** which accepts foreign-issued Visa and/or MasterCard **credit cards** (Visa ATMs are slightly more common), so you can rely on plastic as a standard way of accessing funds in the country. (Note that Sri Lankan ATMs can be slightly confusing: you'll have to enter 15,000.00 to get 15,000 rupees.) If you can't find an ATM which accepts foreign cards, all banks issue over-the-counter **cash advances** against Visa and MasterCard. You might like to take two credit cards, stored in separate places, in case one gets lost or stolen. If you do take two, keep them separate from one another, and make sure you also have a record (again, stored separately) of card details and the numbers you'll need to call if they're lost or stolen and you need to cancel them.

Remember that all cash advances are treated as loans, with interest accruing daily from the date of withdrawal; there may be a transaction fee on top of this. However, you can also use ATMs in Sri Lanka to make withdrawals from your home account using your **debit card**, which is not liable to interest payments, and the flat transaction fee is usually quite small – your bank will able to advise on this. Make sure you have a personal identification number (PIN) that's designed to work overseas.

Travellers' cheques and cash

Despite the usefulness of plastic, you might still feel it's worth taking at least a few **travellers' cheques**. It pays to get a selection of denominations. Make sure you keep the purchase agreement and a record of cheque serial numbers safe and separate from the cheques themselves, along with a record of the number you'll need to call to report them missing – if your cheques are lost or stolen, the issuing company will expect you to report the loss promptly. Most companies claim to replace lost or stolen cheques within 24 hours.

Travellers' cheques can be changed rapidly and painlessly at any bank in Sri Lanka – the entire process rarely takes more than fifteen minutes. You may pay a small amount in commission and government tax, though this won't add up to more than a couple of hundred rupees, and is often much less. In general, branches of the Commercial and Sampath banks tend to be the most efficient, though you shouldn't have any significant problems anywhere. Sterling-, euro- and dollar-denominated travellers' cheques are all universally accepted, but take a standard brand (Amex, Thomas Cook and Visa are the best known) to avoid problems.

You might also want to carry some **cash** with you for emergencies. US dollars, euros, pounds sterling and Australian dollars are all widely recognized and easily changed. New Zealand or Canadian dollars can occasionally cause problems, but are generally accepted in most banks.

Wiring money

Having money **wired from home** using one of the companies listed below is neither convenient nor cheap, and should be considered a last resort. It's also possible to have money wired directly from a bank in your home country to a bank in Sri Lanka, although this is somewhat less reliable because it involves two separate institutions. If you go this route, your home bank will need the address of the bank branch where you want to pick up the money and the address and telex number of the bank's Colombo head office, which will act as the clearing house; money wired this way normally takes two working days to arrive, and costs around £25/US$40 per transaction.

Money-wiring companies

Travelers Express/MoneyGram
ⓦ www.moneygram.com
US ℡ 1-800/444-3010; Canada ℡ 1-800/933-3278; UK, Ireland and New Zealand ℡ 00800/6663 9472; Australia ℡ 0011800/6663 9472.
Western Union ⓦ www.westernunion.com
US and Canada ℡ 1-800/CALL-CASH; Australia ℡ 1800/501 500; New Zealand ℡ 0800/005 253; UK ℡ 0800/833 833; Republic of Ireland ℡ 66/947 5603. Customers in the US and Canada can send money online.

Getting around

Given Sri Lanka's fairly modest size, getting around can be a frustratingly time-consuming process. The island's narrow roads, congested with pedestrians, cyclists and tuktuks, make bus travel laborious, while in many cases travel by rail is even slower. Even with your own vehicle you shouldn't expect to make rapid progress. Getting from Colombo to either Galle or Kandy, for instance (a distance of not much over 100km), takes around three hours by bus or train, while the bus trip across the island from Colombo to Arugam Bay takes at least ten hours by public transport for a distance of 320km.

Buses are the standard means of transport. Services reach even the remotest corners of the island, though they're usually a nerve-shredding and uncomfortable way of travelling. **Trains** offer a more characterful, if generally slower, means of getting about, and will get you to many parts of the country – eventually. If you don't want to put up with the vagaries of public transport, hiring a **car and driver** can prove a surprisingly cheap and extremely convenient way of seeing the island in relative comfort. For short journeys within towns and cities, and for shorter excursions, the island's innumerable **tuktuks** offer a standard means of getting around. Finally if you want to get off the beaten track and travel at a less frenetic pace, there's plenty of scope for **cycling** and, especially, **walking**.

Buses

Buses are the staple mode of transport in Sri Lanka. Any town of even the remotest consequence will be served by fairly regular connections, whilst buses screech past on the island's major highways every few seconds. That's the good news. The bad news is that bus travel in Sri Lanka is almost uniformly uncomfortable and often nerve-wracking as well, given that most drivers are willing to try anything to gain an extra yard. The average Sri Lankan bus journey is a stop–start affair: stomach-tightening bursts of speed alternate with periods of creeping slowness, all played out to an accompaniment of constantly parping horns, blaring Sinhala pop music and the awful noises of mechanical protest as the long-suffering bus careers around yet another corner with

every panel rattling – before the inevitable slamming-on of brakes sends everyone lurching forward in their seats. If you haven't got a seat, so much the worse. If you do, you'll probably find yourself serving as an impromptu armrest to one of the countless unfortunates standing packed in the aisle. The rear seats in large buses are the best place to sit, both because there's usually enough legroom to stow luggage comfortably under the seat in front, and because you won't have a very clear view of whatever craziness the driver is attempting.

Buses come in assorted forms. The basic distinction is between government, or CTB (Ceylon Transport Board), buses, and private services. Almost all **CTB buses** are rattling old TATA buses, painted yellow (though a few red buses survive in parts of the island). These tend to be the slowest and cheapest on the road, stopping wherever there is a passenger to be collected, no matter how full the vehicle already is.

Private buses come in various different forms. At their most basic, they're essentially the same as CTB buses, consisting of large, arthritic old vehicles (usually old Ashok Leyland rustbuckets) which stop everywhere; the only difference is that private buses will usually be painted white and emblazoned with the stickers of whichever company runs it. Some private companies operate slightly faster services, again in large buses known variously as "semi-express", "express", or "inter-city", which (in theory at least) make fewer stops en route.

At the top end of the scale, **private minibuses**, often described as "express" and/or "luxury" services (although the description should be taken with a large pinch of salt) offer the fastest way of getting around. These are smaller vehicles with air-conditioning and tinted, curtained windows, though the tiny seats and lack of luggage space (your rucksack will often end up on your lap or between your legs) can make them more uncomfortable than CTB services, especially if you're tall. (If the vehicle isn't packed to capacity you could try paying for an extra seat on which to put your luggage.) In theory, express minibuses only make limited stops at major bus stations en route – although in practice it's up to the whim of the driver and/or conductor as to where they stop and for how long, and how many people they're willing to cram in.

Most bus **fares** are so cheap as to be almost not worth noticing. For journeys on non-express buses, count on around Rs.10 per hour's travel, rising to around Rs.25–30 on express minibuses. Note that on the latter you'll usually have to pay the full fare for the entire route served by the bus, irrespective of where you get off. If you do want to get off before the end of the journey, let the driver/conductor know when you board. Seat **reservations** are almost unheard of except on services between Colombo and Jaffna, where they're obligatory.

Another problem with Sri Lankan buses is the difficulty of finding the relevant service. Many bus terminals are chaotic, at least to non-Sinhala speakers, and most timetables and signs are in Sinhala only, as are many of the destination boards displayed by buses – it's useful to get an idea of the characters you're looking for (see the list of place names on p.461). The larger terminals often have some kind of **information booth** – usually little wire-mesh enclosures in the middle of the station – whose staff will usually be able to point you in the right direction. If arriving at a larger terminal by tuktuk, it's a good idea to enlist the help of your driver in locating the right bus. Be careful, too, when walking around terminals, many of which can be gridlocked confusions of reversing and manoeuvring vehicles. Don't expect anyone to stop for you; the onus is on you to get out of the way.

Express services generally only halt at bus terminals or other recognized stops. Other types of services will usually stop wherever there's a passenger to be picked up – just stand by the roadside and stick an arm out. If you're flagging down a bus by the roadside, one final hazard is in **getting on**. Drivers often don't stop completely, instead slowing down just enough to allow you to jump aboard. Keep your wits about you, especially if you're weighed down with a heavy rucksack, and be prepared to move fast when the bus pulls in – or risk seeing it simply pull off again without you.

Trains

Sri Lanka's **train** network, constructed by the British during the nineteenth century and little changed since, offers a characterful way of getting around the island, and for many visitors a trip aboard one of these chuntering old relics (especially on the marvellously scenic hill country line) is a highlight of a trip to Sri Lanka. Travel by rail is, however, generally slower than by bus, and the charm of the experience is often leavened with a fair dose of frustration – delays are the norm and progress can be incredibly laborious, and can seem even more tedious if you end up standing up in an overcrowded carriage. Nonetheless, Sri Lankan trains are worth experiencing, if only once.

The network comprises three principal lines: the **coast line**, which runs along the west coast starting from Puttalam in the north and heading south via Negombo, Colombo, Kalutara, Bentota, Beruwala, Aluthgama, Ambalangoda, Hikkaduwa and Galle to Matara. The **hill country line** runs from Colombo to Kandy then on to Hatton (for Adam's Peak), Nanu Oya (for Nuwara Eliya), Haputale, Bandarawela, Ella and Badulla. The **northern line** runs from Colombo through Kurunegala to Anuradhapura and Vavuniya (the old service from here north to Jaffna may be resumed during the next few years). Two additional branches run off this line: the first to Polonnaruwa and Batticaloa, the second to Trincomalee.

Trains comprise three classes. Most consist exclusively of **second-** and **third-class** carriages. There's not actually a huge amount of difference between the two: second-class seats are slightly more padded and comfortable, and there are fans in the carriages, but the main bonus is that the carriages tend to be (very slightly) less over-crowded. **First class** covers three different types of seating, which are only available in selected trains. These are seats in the observation carriage on hill country trains; seats in the a/c carriage on trains to Anuradhapura and Vavuniya; and sleeping berths on overnight services.

Observation cars in the hill country trains have large windows and what passes on the Sri Lankan railways network for plush seating. You'll need to book ahead – and you'll be lucky to get seats anything less than a week in advance, especially on the popular Colombo to Kandy run. The observation car doesn't necessarily get you a much better view; the main advantage is a guaranteed seat. **Booking observation car seats** is slightly complicated. They are available from ten days in advance of the date of travel. There are 24 seats in the whole observation car; twenty of these are sold in Colombo and the other four in Kandy. You can buy tickets over the counter at Kandy or Colombo and it's possible to buy tickets in Colombo to travel from Kandy and vice versa. If you want to reserve an observation car seat from other stations along the line, they'll have to be ordered through either Kandy or Colombo, which obviously requires time and a degree of pre-planning. There's a Rs.50 booking fee for these seats. Sample fares in the observation car are: Kandy to Colombo Rs.170, Kandy to Badulla Rs.231, Kandy to Nanu Oya Rs.150, Kandy to Ella Rs.211. There are also a few **overnight trains**. These comprise first-class sleeping berths (booking fee Rs.75) and second- and third-class "sleeperettes" (fold-down seats), plus ordinary seats.

As with buses, **fares** are so cheap as to be virtually negligible. Train travel costs about Rs.1 per kilometre in first class, Rs.0.6 in second, and Rs.0.2 in third – the second class fare from Colombo to Kandy, for example, costs Rs.68, while that from Colombo to Galle costs Rs.133. **Advance bookings** are only available for first-class seats and sleeper berths, and for

sleeperettes and second-class seats on the four daily intercity express services between Colombo and Kandy. Reservations can be made up to ten days in advance at the Berths Booking Office (Mon–Sat 8.30am–3.30pm, Sun 8.30am–noon) at Fort Railway Station in Colombo. You can also make reservation at other stations, though they'll have to contact Colombo, so try to reserve as far ahead of the date of travel as possible. Tickets for all other types of seat can only be bought on the day of travel.

We've given current train **timetables** in the various "travel details" throughout the guide. Timetables are also available online at Ⓦ www.atsrilanka.com.

Planes

One dividend of the peace process has been the resumption of **domestic flights** within Sri Lanka. Three companies now operate regular services between Colombo (Ratmalana airport) and Jaffna, and one company also flies from Colombo to Trincomalee – see p.372 & p.397 for full details. Fares are very reasonable (from US$42 return from Colombo to Jaffna), and flights can be a real lifeline if you're in a hurry, getting you to Jaffna in just one hour, as opposed to at least ten hours by bus.

Another recent development is SriLankan Airlines' **air taxis**. These small amphibious Cessna caravan planes fly from Colombo to Kandy, Koggala, Bentota, Trincomalee, Dambulla, Anuradhapura and Hingurakgoda, near Polonnaruwa. Services aren't scheduled, but operate on demand; there's a flat fare of US$100 per person to all destinations. To reserve a seat, contact SriLankan Airlines (see p.10, p.13 & p.15).

Driving

As Sri Lankans say, in order to **drive** around the island you'll need three things: "good horn, good brakes, good luck". Although roads are generally in quite good condition, the myriad hazards they present – crowds of pedestrians, erratic cyclists, crazed bus drivers and suicidal dogs, to name just a few – plus the very idiosyncratic set of road rules followed by Sri Lankan drivers, means that you shouldn't contemplate driving yourself unless you are both familiar with local attitudes to road usage and an extremely confident driver.

If you're determined to get behind the wheel, it's best to come equipped with an **International Drivers' Licence**. If you only have your own national licence, you'll need to get a **Government Permit** (Rs.600; valid one month), which can take half a day to obtain (or longer if your licence isn't in English and needs to be translated). The two most reliable places to hire a car in Colombo are Quickshaws and Avis (see p.110), both of which can advise about the necessary licence regulations and paperwork.

Car and driver

Given the hassle of getting around by public transport, a large proportion of visitors opt to tour Sri Lanka by hiring a **car and driver**, which offers unlimited flexibility and is often surprisingly cheap. The main caveat is that drivers (and the travel companies they represent) work on commission, which they receive from some, but not all, hotels, plus assorted restaurants, shops, spice gardens and jewellers. This means that you and your driver's opinions might not always coincide as to where you want to stay and what you want to do – your driver will always want to head for wherever he gets the best kickbacks (and you'll also pay over the odds at these places, since the hotelier, restaurateur or shopkeepers have to recoup the commission they're paying to the driver). Unfortunately, despite the fact that you're paying, it's often not as easy to get your own way as you would imagine – stories of manipulative and dishonest drivers abound, and if you find you're spending more time stressing out about dealing with your driver than enjoying your holiday, find another one. It's not worth messing up your holiday for.

It's best, of course, to find a decent driver in the first place – it pays to go with a reputable company or a CTB-registered guide. Make sure your driver speaks at least some English and emphasize from the outset where you do and don't want to go. To avoid being led a merry dance around every spice garden and souvenir shop of your driver's choice, you could try to agree an additional payment to compensate them for lost commission (drivers will usually expect a tip of around ten percent in any case). Some drivers impose on their clients' good nature to the point of having meals with them and insisting on acting as guides and interpreters throughout the tour. If this is what you want, fine; if not, don't be afraid to make it clear that you expect to be left alone when not in the car. Finally, don't hire a driver at the airport. As ever, you get what you pay for, and although the operators here are extremely cheap, they have a poor reputation. You'll find more reliable drivers in Negombo and Colombo.

Prices depend more on quality than size of transport – a posh a/c car will cost more than a non-a/c minivan. Count on roughly US$30 per day for a non-a/c minivan, plus food and accommodation. Cars and drivers can be hired through any of the Colombo tour operators listed on p.113, or from many other tour operators and travel agents around the island – we've listed the most reliable outfits in the relevant places in the Guide. Alternatively, most hotels and guest houses can fix you up with a vehicle, or you could come to some arrangement with a taxi driver.

Tuktuks

The lines of motorized rickshaws which ply the streets of every city, town and village are one of Sri Lanka's most characteristic sights. Usually referred to, Thai-style, as **tuktuks**, but also variously called three-wheelers, trishaws or (rather more optimistically) "taxis", they are the staple means of travelling short distances in Sri Lanka, principally short hops within towns, although they can also be useful for excursions and can even, at a pinch, be useful for long journeys if you get stranded or can't be bothered to wait around for a bus. The vehicles themselves are mainly Indian-made Bajaj rickshaws, usually beige, sometimes green or red, and often decorated by their drivers with whimsical fluorescent stickers, statuettes, plastic flowers or other items both decorative or talismanic.

It's impossible to walk far in Sri Lanka without being solicited for custom by the owner of one of these vehicles, though drivers are far less persistent than in India –

a smile and a quick shake of the head will almost always suffice as a refusal, and you'll rarely find that they chase you down the street, as can happen in other parts of Asia. If you do need a ride, tuktuks are extremely convenient and can even be fun, in a slightly scary way, as they weave through the traffic, often at surprising speeds. In addition, the sheer number around (except in a couple of places, notably Jaffna and Batticaloa) means that you always have the upper hand in bargaining – if you can't agree a decent fare, there'll always be another driver keen to take your custom.

Tuktuks do have their drawbacks, however. They're not particularly comfortable for long journeys, and you can't see much. Also, be aware that they can capsize on steep gradients, making them potentially dangerous for out-of-town journeys in the hill country. In addition, tuktuks' diminutive size compared with the buses and lorries they share the road with (and the often gung-ho attitudes of their drivers) can put you at a certain risk, and you're likely to experience at least a couple of near misses with speeding traffic if you use them consistently for longer journeys.

Sri Lankan tuktuks are never metered; the **fare** will be whatever you can negotiate with the driver. *Never* set off without agreeing the fare beforehand, or you run the risk of laying yourself open to all sorts of trickery. The majority of tuktuk drivers in Sri Lanka are more or less honest, and you'll often be offered a decent fare without even having to bargain. A small minority of drivers, however, are complete crooks who will (at best) simply try to overcharge you or, at worst, set you up for some kind of scam. Given the wildly varying degrees of probity you'll encounter, it's often difficult to know exactly where you stand. As a general rule of thumb, locals would expect to pay around Rs.20 per kilometre, though as a tourist you might have to settle for Rs.30–40 – obviously this depends on how ruthlessly you're prepared to bargain. As a basic rule, the fewer tourists around, the more likely you are to be offered a reasonable fare. In

populous or heavily touristed places like Kandy, Colombo, Negombo and Beruwala/ Bentota you're likely to have to bargain much harder – aim to knock at least a third off the first quoted price to get a decent rate.

Finally, beware of tuktuk drivers who claim to have **no change** – this can even apply when trying to pay for a Rs.50 fare with a Rs.100 note, with the driver claiming (perhaps truthfully) to have only Rs.20 or Rs.30 change, and hoping that you'll settle for a few rupees less. If you don't have change, check that the driver does before you set off. If you make the position clear from the outset, you're guaranteed that your driver will go through the hassle of getting change for you rather than risk losing your fare.

Bicycle

For many Sri Lankans, the **bicycle** remains the standard means of locomotion – you'll be amazed at how many people can simultaneously get on a bicycle or what it's possible to carry on one. Bikes are available for **hire** in most tourist towns (alternatively, just ask at your guest house – they'll probably have or know someone who has a spare bike knocking around, or who will be prepared to surrender their own to you for a small price). Costs vary wildly, but will rarely be more than a few dollars a day, often much less. Cycling can make for an extremely enjoyable way of getting around and exploring the island's backroads, although as a cyclist you are extremely vulnerable – bus and truck drivers consider cyclists a waste of valuable tarmac, and as far as they're concerned you don't really have any right to be on the road at all. Be prepared not only to get out of the way quickly, but even to get off the road completely. You are at risk not only from traffic coming from behind, but also from oncoming vehicles overtaking another vehicle, who will think nothing of forcing you into the ditch, even though they're on what is technically your side of the road.

An increasing number of tour operators are offering specialist **cycle tours** of the island – see pp.11–12, p.14 & p.15 for details.

Accommodation

Sri Lanka has an excellent range of accommodation in all price brackets, from basic beachside palm shacks to elegant colonial mansions and sumptuous five-star resorts – indeed staying in one of the country's luxury establishments can be one of the principal pleasures of the visit to the island. Rates generally represent excellent value, and in many places you can sample the best that the island has to offer for a fraction of the price you would pay in many other countries.

Some good **internet resources** include Ⓦ www.srilankahotels.co.uk, Ⓦ www .srilankahotelstravel.com and Ⓦ www .reddottours .com, all of which feature most of the island's larger hotels, with latest rates and an online booking facility. Although not all hotels have their own websites, pretty much all the island's larger establishments feature on myriad websites run by overseas tour operators – typing the hotel name into a search engine will usually turn up a fair number of photos and reviews.

Types of accommodation

Travellers on a budget will spend most of their time in **guest houses**, usually family-run places either in or attached to the home of the owners. Some of the nicer guest houses can be real homes from home, with good cooking and sociable hosts, although if you're in the family house itself they can be noisy and lacking in privacy. Rates are generally a bargain, usually between US$5 and $10 per night. Note that there are no **youth hostels** in Sri Lanka.

Hotels come in all shapes and sizes, from functional concrete boxes to luxurious establishments which are virtual tourist attractions in their own right. Some of the finest hotels (particularly in the hill country) are located in old colonial buildings, offering a wonderful taste of the lifestyle and ambience of yesteryear, while the island also boasts a number of stunning modern hotels, including many designed by Sri Lanka's great twentieth-century architect Geoffrey Bawa (see p.132 and box overleaf). The coastal areas are also home to innumerable **resort hotels**, the majority of which – with a few honourable exceptions – are fairly bland places, populated largely by European package tourists on full-board programmes and offering a diet of horrible buffet food and plenty of organized fun.

Sri Lanka is gradually waking up to its massive **ecotourism** potential, and now boasts a few good eco-oriented hotels and lodges (see box overleaf). You can also stay in bungalows or camp within most of the island's national parks, although this is very expensive – see p.53 for details. The national parks are the only places in Sri Lanka with official **campsites**, and elsewhere camping is not a recognized activity. Pitching your tent unofficially in rural areas or on the beach is likely to lead to problems with local landowners and villagers – and given the cheapness of accommodation, is not worth the hassle.

Ten top Sri Lankan hotels

Galle Face Hotel, Colombo (p.81)
Helga's Folly, Kandy (p.216)
The Hill Club, Nuwara Eliya (p.252)
Kandalama, Dambulla (p.309)
The Lighthouse, Galle (p.156)
Mount Lavinia Hotel, Mount Lavinia (p.83)

St Andrew's, Nuwara Eliya (p.252)
The Tea Factory, Nuwara Eliya (p.252)
The Sun House and The Dutch House, Galle (p.157)
Club Villa, Bentota (p.136)
Bandarawela Hotel, Bandarawela (p.268)

Geoffrey Bawa hotels

Blue Waters, Kalutara (p.126)
Club Villa, Bentota (p.136)
Kandalama, Dambulla (p.309)
Kani, Kalutara (p.126)
The Lighthouse, Galle (p.156)

Neptune, Beruwala (p.129)
Royal Oceanic, Negombo (p.117)
Serendib, Bentota (p.136)
Triton, Ahungalla (p.138)
Villa Mohotti, (p.137)

Another recent trend is towards **villas** and **boutique hotels**, many set in old colonial villas and offering stylish and luxurious accommodation – ⓦ www.villasinsrilanka .com has a list of superb luxury boutique hotels and villas, mainly in the Galle area. Finally, for something a bit different, some tea companies have recently begun to let out **tea estate bungalows** (see p.247).

Hotels are **classified** using the usual one- to five-star system. In addition, some smaller hotels and guest houses are officially approved by the Sri Lanka Tourist Board, though it must be said that such approval means absolutely nothing – indeed, if anything, approved places often tend to be worst than their non-approved rivals.

Checking in

Sri Lanka has its fair share of accommodation **touts**, particularly active in Tissamaharama, Ella, Kandy and Galle (see p.60 and the individual town accounts in the guide for more details). One way of avoiding hassle is to ring ahead; most guest houses will pick you up for free from the local bus or train station if given advance warning.

What you'll need from your room depends on where you are in the island; basic necessities change as you move up into the hill country, and things become progressively colder as you gain altitude. Virtually all accommodation in Sri Lanka, even the cheapest, comes with **private bathroom** (we've mentioned any exceptions in the relevant listings). In low-

land areas, you'll virtually always get a **fan** (or, in smarter places, **air-conditioning**), while in the hill country, most places have **hot water** (again, we've mentioned any exceptions). As a general rule, you'll need a fan in all places up to and including Kandy, and hot water in Kandy and anywhere higher. In the highest parts of the island, particularly Nuwara Eliya, you'll usually need some form of heating and/or a good supply of blankets.

There are a few other things worth bearing in mind when choosing a room. In lowland areas, size and ceiling height are both important in determining how hot a room will be – those with low ceilings can become unbearably stuffy. In some areas (notably Tangalla and Arugam Bay) many places are built with their roofs raised slightly above the top of the walls, so that cool air can circulate freely through the gap (although, equally, it provides free access to insects). You should ensure that the fan works properly (both that it runs at a decent speed and doesn't make a horrible noise), and check how many lights there are and whether they work: Sri Lankan hoteliers have a penchant for twenty-watt bulbs, and rooms can be very dingy (some people even travel with their own light bulb). If you're staying in a family guest house, keep an eye out for noisy children, dogs or television sets in the vicinity of your room. And make sure you get a room away from any noisy nearby roads.

Seven top eco-lodges and hotels

Boulder Garden, Sinharaja (p.287)
Ella Adventure Park, Ella (p.264)
Galapita Eco-Lodge, Kataragama (p.381)
Hunas Falls, Kandy (p.217)

Tasks Safari Camp, Tamanalwila (p.284)
Tree Tops, Buttala (p.380)
Yala Safari Game Lodge, Yala National Park (p.197)

Other recurrent problems include **power cuts** (particularly common during periods of low rainfall, when the country's hydroelectric system runs dry). Many mid- and top-end places have their own generators; in budget places it pays to keep a torch handy. Finally, remember that most Sri Lankans go to bed very early. If you're staying at a small guest house and you go out for dinner and a few beers, it's not uncommon to find yourself locked out on your return – any time after 9pm. Let them know when to expect you back.

Room rates

Room rates in lower-end places reflect Sri Lanka's bargaining culture – exact rates are often only notional, as owners will vary prices to reflect the season, levels of demand and how rich they think you look. It's always worth bargaining (but also see the section on ethical bargaining on p.29), even in top-end places, especially if you're planning to stay a few nights, or if business is slow. If you're travelling on your own, you'll have to work harder to get a decent price since many establishments don't have **single rates** (where they exist, they're usually two-thirds to three-quarters of the price of a double). Try to establish what the price of a double would be, and bargain from there.

In many places, your hotel or guest house will also be the place you're most likely to eat (see p.41), and **half-** and **full-board** rates are common. These can often work out to be extremely good value, though the food can be bland; obviously, the attractiveness of these inclusive options depends on the presence or absence of other places to eat in the vicinity.

Prices are also subject to strong **seasonal variations**, although these vary confusingly across the island and from hotel to hotel. Rates often rise during the main tourist seasons (see the guide chapters for details), during holidays, over "long weekends" (where the Monday or Friday is a public holiday) or if there's a big procession or festival going on – as during the Esala Perahera at Kandy (see p.212) or during the New Year in Nuwara Eliya (p.249), when accommodation prices everywhere treble or quadruple. There's no real method to this, however. One hotel's rates might increase by fifty percent in season, while rates at the place next door stay exactly the same. The price codes given in the guide are all for high season.

Room rates at mid- and top-end places are often quoted in **dollars** for convenience, but are payable in rupees. Make sure you clarify whether any additional **taxes** will be added to the bill – the more upmarket the place you're staying in, the more likely this is. Many places levy a **service charge** of ten percent, while some also charge a **Government Service Tax** of ten percent – taken together, these can add a nasty twist to a bill, especially since they are also added to food and drink.

Finally, note that many top-end hotels operate a **dual-pricing system** whereby foreigners pay more (sometimes significantly more) than locals. There's nothing you can do about this unless you have a resident's visa, in which case you may be able to wangle local rates.

Accommodation price codes

All the accommodation in this book has been categorized according to the following **price codes**. These are for the price of a **double room in high season**, inclusive of any taxes (in some places these prices also include breakfast, and in all-inclusive resorts they also cover other meals and drinks for two people in a double room).

❶ Under US$6	❹ US$18–25	❼ US$65–100
❷ US$6–12	❺ US$25–40	❽ US$100–150
❸ US$12–18	❻ US$40–65	❾ Over US$150

Eating and drinking

In culinary terms, Sri Lanka is totally overshadowed by the world-renowned cuisine of neighbouring India, and the island's distinctive culinary style is little known abroad. The common perception is of Sri Lankan food as a local variant on the classic dishes of the subcontinent, but while the island's cooking has a certain amount in common with Indian (particularly South Indian) food, Sri Lanka's culinary heritage and traditions are actually quite distinct, the result of a unique fusion of local produce along with recipes and spices brought to the island over the centuries by Indians, Arabs, Malays, Portuguese, Dutch and English.

The staple Sri Lankan dish is **rice and curry**, at its finest a miniature banquet whose contrasting flavours – cinnamon, chillies, curry leaves, garlic, coconut milk, pandanus leaves and "Maldive fish" (an intensely flavoured pinch of sun-dried shrimps) – bear witness to Sri Lanka's status as one of the original spice islands. There are plenty of other unique island **specialities** to explore and enjoy – hoppers, string hoppers, kottu rotty, lamprais and pittu – as well as plentiful **seafood**.

Sri Lankan cuisine can be incredibly fiery – sometimes on a par with Thai, and far hotter than traditional Indian cuisine. Many of the island's less gifted chefs compensate for a lack of culinary subtlety with liberal use of chilli powder; conversely as a tourist you'll often be seen as a weak-kneed individual who is liable to faint at the merest hint of spice. You'll often be asked how **hot** you want your food; "medium" usually gets you something that's neither bland nor requires the use of a fire extinguisher. If you do overheat during a meal, remember that water only adds to the pain of a burnt palate; a mouthful of plain rice or a spoonful of yoghurt are much more effective.

Sri Lankans say that you can't properly enjoy the flavours and textures of food unless you **eat with your fingers**, although tourists will always be provided with cutlery on request. As elsewhere in Asia, you're meant to eat with your right hand, although this taboo isn't really strictly observed – if you'd really prefer to eat with your left hand, you're unlikely to turn heads.

Costs are uniformly low. You can get a filling meal of rice and curry for under a dollar at a local café, while main courses at most guest-house restaurants usually cost less than US$3, and even at the island's poshest restaurants it's difficult to find anything costing more than US$10. Note that many places add a ten percent service charge to the bill, while more upmarket restaurants usually add an additional government service tax of ten percent on top of that.

Be aware that the typical vagaries of Sri Lankan **spelling** mean that popular dishes can appear on menu in a bewildering number of forms: *idlis* can become *ittlys; vadais* turn into *wadais, kotthu rotty* transforms into *kotturoti* and *lampraise* changes to *lumprice*. You'll also be regaled with plenty of unintentionally humorous offerings such as "cattle fish", "nazi goreng" or "sweat and sour".

Where to eat

Although Sri Lankan cooking can be very good, few **restaurants** really do justice to the island's cuisine. There's no particular tradition of eating out and, except in Colombo, few independent restaurants of note. Locals either eat at home or patronize the island's innumerable scruffy little **cafés**, often confusingly signed as "hotels", which serve up filling meals for well under a dollar: rough-and-ready portions of rice and curry, plus maybe hoppers or kotthu rotty. However as the food is usually pretty ordinary, eating in local cafés is more of a social than a culinary experience.

Given the lack of independent tourist restaurants, most visitors end up taking the majority of their meals in their **hotel** or **guest house**. The sort of food and setting you'll encounter varies wildly, from the big bland restaurants at the coastal resorts to the cosy guest houses of Ella and Galle, where you can experience the marvellous home-cooking which rarely makes its way onto menus at larger hotels. In general, however, choice is limited, with most places offering a standard assortment of fried noodles or rice, a small range of seafood and meat dishes (usually including a couple of devilled options) and maybe a few kinds of curry.

Most of the island's independent **rest-aurants** can be found in Colombo and, to a lesser extent, Kandy and Negombo, where tourism has inspired the growth of a modest local eating scene. The most common restaurants are **Chinese** (see p.42), and you'll also find a few **South Indian** restaurants, especially in Colombo.

In terms of **opening hours**, the vast majority of restaurants and cafés open daily from early or mid-morning until reasonably late in the evening (around 9pm or 10pm), although some places (especially in Colombo) close from around 3pm to 6pm or 7pm. Unless otherwise stated, all the places listed in the guide are open daily for both lunch and dinner.

If you want to eat like the locals, you'll find **lunch packets** on sale on streets all over the country between around 11am and 2pm. These usually include a big portion of steamed rice along with a piece of curried chicken, fish or beef (vegetarians can get an egg), some vegetables and sambol. At Rs.50–100, they're the cheapest way to fill up in Sri Lanka, although they're probably best avoided until you're properly acclimatized to the local cooking.

What to eat

The island's staple is **rice and curry** (not "curry and rice" – it's the rice which is considered the principal ingredient). Basic rice and curry, as served up in cafés island-wide, consists of a plate of rice topped with a few dollops of veg curry, a hunk of chicken or fish and a spoonful of sambol. More sophisticated versions comprise the inevitable mound of rice accompanied by as many as fifteen side dishes. These generally include a serving of meat or fish curry plus accompaniments such as pineapple and potato curries, caramelized aubergine, sweet potatoes and dhal, although you might encounter more exotic offerings – anything from curried jackfruit to whole garlic cloves slow-cooked in fenugreek and ginger. If you're going to be eating a full-blown rice and curry, arrive with a huge appetite or you'll be full to bursting before you've even sampled half the dishes. Rice and curry is usually served with a helping of **sambol**, designed to be mixed into your food to give it a bit of extra kick. This comes in various forms, the most common being *pol sambol* (coconut sambol), an often eye-watering combination of chilli powder, chopped onions, Maldive fish, salt and grated coconut. Treat it with caution. Another common accompaniment is **mallung**: shredded green vegetables, lightly stir-fried with spices and grated coconut.

Funnily enough, however, what you won't get is a really good plate of **rice**. Although Sri Lanka produces many types of **rice**, what makes it to the nation's tables is usually fairly low-grade stuff, with a greyish colour and a tendency to clump. Don't expect to find the delicately spiced pilaus and birianis of north India, although what you get is usually sufficient for its purpose.

Other Sri Lankan specialities

The engagingly named **hopper** (*appa*), usually eaten either at breakfast or as an evening snack, is a small, bowl-shaped pancake traditionally made from a batter

---

Five good places for rice and curry

Ella-Gap Resthouse, Ella (p.266)
Mrs Khalid's, Galle (p.16)
Ravana Heights, Ella (p.267)

Refresh, Hikkaduwa (p.146) and
Tissamaharama (p.193)
Curry Leaf, Colombo (p.103)

containing coconut milk and palm toddy. Hoppers are cooked in a small wok-like dish, meaning that most of the mix sinks to the bottom, making hoppers soft and doughy at the base, and thin and crisp around the edges. Various ingredients can be poured into the hopper. An egg fried in the middle produces an egg hopper, whilst sweet ingredients like yoghurt or honey are also sometimes added. Alternatively, plain hoppers can be eaten as an accompaniment to curry. Not to be confused with the hopper are **string hoppers** (*indiappa*), tangled little balls of steamed noodles, often eaten with curry in place of rice for breakfast or lunch.

Another rice substitute is **pittu**, a mixture of flour and grated coconut, steamed in a cylindrical bamboo mould – it looks a bit like coarse couscous. Derived from the Dutch *lomprijst*, **lamprais** is another speciality: a serving of rice baked in a plantain leaf along with accompaniments such as a lump of chicken or a boiled egg, plus some veg and pickle.

Muslim restaurants are the place to go for **rotty** (or *roti*), a fine, doughy pancake – watching these being made is half the fun, as the chef teases small balls of dough into huge sheets of almost transparent thinness. A dollop of curried meat, veg or potato is then plonked in the middle and the rotty is folded up around it; the final shape depends on the whim of the chef – some prefer crepe-like squares, others opt for samosa-style triangles, some a spring roll. Rottys can also be chopped up and stir-fried with meat and vegetables, a dish known as **kotthu rotty**. You'll know when kotthu rotty is being made because of the noise – the ingredients are usually simultaneously fried and chopped on a hotplate using a large pair of meat cleavers, producing a noisy drumming sound – part musical performance; part advertisement.

Devilled dishes are also popular, and can be delicious. These are usually prepared with a thick, spicy sauce plus big chunks of onion and chilli, though the end-product often isn't as hot as you might fear. Devilled chicken, pork, fish and beef are all common – the last is generally considered the classic devilled dish and is traditionally eaten during drinking

binges. Another local staple is the **buriani**. This has little in common with the magnificent, saffron-scented North Indian biriani, being nothing more than a mound of rice with a hunk of chicken, a bowl of curry sauce and a boiled egg, but it makes a good lunchtime filler and is usually less fiery than a basic plate of rice and curry.

South Indian food

Colombo is home to numerous "pure vegetarian" **South Indian** restaurants (vegetarian here meaning no meat, fish, eggs or alcohol). These cheerfully no-nonsense places cater to a local clientele and serve up a delicious range of Tamil-style dishes at giveaway prices – well worth sapling if you're in the capital. The standard dish is the **dosa**, a crispy rice pacake served in various forms: either plain, with ghee (clarified butter), onion or, most commonly, as a **masala dosa**, folded up around a filling of curried potato. You'll also find **uttapam**, another (thicker) type of rice pancake that's usually eaten with some kind of curry, and **idlis**, steamed rice cakes served with curry sauces or chutneys. Another classic Tamil savoury which has entered the Sri Lanka mainstream is the **vadai** (or wadai), a spicy doughnut made of deep-fried lentils – no train journey is complete without the sound of hawkers marching up and down compartments shouting "Vadai-vadai-vadai!". Platefuls of vadais and rottys are often served up in cafés under the name of **short eats** – you help yourself and are charged for what you eat, though be aware that these plates are passed around and their contents indiscriminately prodded by all and sundry, so they're not particularly hygienic. Some South Indian places (again, particularly in Colombo) serve a fascinating array of **sweets**, luridly coloured and heavily spiced.

Other cuisines

There are plenty of **Chinese restaurants** around the island, though many are just glorified local drinking holes serving up plates of fried rice and noodles. Genuine places, as listed in the guide, are often good,

Vegetarian food in Sri Lanka

Surprisingly for such a Buddhist country, **vegetarian** food as a concept hasn't really caught on in Sri Lanka. Having said that, a large proportion of the nation's cooking is meat-free: vegetable and fruit curries, vegetable rottys, hoppers and string hoppers – not to mention the bewildering variety of fruit on offer. Colombo's numerous pure veg South Indian restaurants are a delight, while if you eat fish and seafood, you'll have no problems finding a meal, especially around the coast.

with predominantly Cantonese-style menus which are often spiced up for Sri Lankan tastes. As usual, Colombo has easily the best range of such places.

Indonesian dishes introduced by the Dutch are also sometimes served in tourist restaurants – most commonly nasi goreng (fried rice with meat or seafood, topped with a fried egg) and gado gado (salad and cold boiled eggs in a peanut sauce), although these rarely taste much like their Indonesian originals.

Other cuisines are restricted to Colombo. **Thai** food has made limited inroads, while **Japanese** cuisine is also popular, and the city's **Korean** population support a few restaurants. Colombo is also where you'll find Sri Lanka's surprisingly small number of decent **North Indian** restaurants, and there are also a few excellent **European** places. Smarter hotels all over the island also make some attempt to produce European cuisine, though with wildly varying results.

Seafood

Not surprisingly, **seafood** plays a major part in the Sri Lankan diet, with fish often taking the place of meat. Common fish include tuna, seer (a firm-bodied white fish), mullet and the delicious melt-in-the-mouth butterfish, as well as pomfret, bonito and shark. You'll also find lobster, plentiful crab, prawns and cuttlefish (calamari). The Negombo lagoon, just north of Colombo, is a particularly prized source of crab and prawns. Seafood is usually a good bet if you're trying to avoid highly spiced food. Fish is generally prepared in a fairly simple manner, usually fried (sometimes in breadcrumbs) or grilled and served with a twist of lemon or in a mild garlic sauce. You will, however, find some fiery fish curries, while chillied seafood

dishes are also fairly common – chilli crab is particularly popular.

Sri Lankan desserts and sweets

The classic Sri Lankan dessert is **curd** (yoghurt made from buffalo milk) served with honey or **kitul** (a sweet syrup from the kitul palm). When boiled and left to set hard, kitul becomes **jaggery**, an all-purpose Sri Lanka sweet or sweetener. Other characteristic desserts are **wattalappam**, an egg pudding from Malaysia which tastes faintly like crème caramel, but with a sweeter and less slippery texture. **Kiribath** is a dessert of rice cooked in milk and served with jaggery – it's also traditionally made for weddings, and is often the first solid food fed to babies. **Ice cream** is usually factory made, and safe to eat; the most widely available brand is the delicious Elephant House. You'll also find a wide selection of **cakes**, often in fluorescent colours and in a bizarre variety of curried flavours.

Fruits

Sri Lanka has a bewildering variety of **fruits**, from the familiar to the bizarre. The months given in brackets below refer to the periods when each is in season (where no months are specified, the fruit is available year-round). Familiar fruits include pineapple, mangoes (April–June & Nov–Dec), avocados (April–June) and coconuts, as well as a wide variety of bananas, from small sweet yellow specimens to enormous (but still tasty) red monsters. **Papaya** (pawpaw), a distinctively sweet and pulpy fruit, crops up regularly in fruit salads, but the king of Sri Lankan fruits is undoubtedly the **jackfruit** (*jak*; April–June & Sept–Oct), the world's largest fruit, a huge, elongated dark-green monster, rather like an

43

enormous marrow in shape, whose sweet and slightly chewy flesh can either be eaten raw or used as an ingredient in curries. **Durian** (May–July) is another outsized fruit: a large green beast with a spiky outer shell. It's very much an acquired taste: though the flesh smells rather like blocked drains, it's widely considered a great delicacy, and many also believe it to have aphrodisiacal qualities. Its distinctive aroma wafts across the island from July to September, when it's in season. The strangest-looking fruit, however, is the **rambutan** (July–Sept), a delicious, lychee-like fruit enclosed in a bright-red skin that's covered in tentacles. Again, it's in season from July to September. Another prized Sri Lankan delicacy is the **mangosteen** (July to Sept), which looks a little like a purple tomato, with a rather hard shell-like skin which softens as the fruit ripens. The delicate and delicious flesh tastes a bit like a grape with a slight citrus tang. Equally distinctive is the **wood apple**, an apple-shaped fruit covered in an indestructible greyish bark, inside which is a red pulpy flesh, rather bitter-tasting and full of seeds. It's sometimes served with honey poured over it. The tiny **gulsambilla** (Aug–Oct) is a strange little fruit – like a large, furry green seed enclosing a tiny, tartly flavoured kernel.

What to drink

It's best to avoid tap water in Sri Lanka (see p.22). **Bottled water** is available absolutely everywhere, sourced from various places in the hill country and retailed under a baffling range of names – every town seems to have its own brand. Bottles come in half-litre, litre and 1.5 litre sizes. A litre usually costs Rs.40–50, though prices vary wildly – anything between Rs.30 and Rs.90. Check that the seal hasn't been broken – note that they're all usually pretty grubby.

International brands of **soft drinks** – Pepsi, Coca-Cola, Sprite – are widely available, but it's much more fun (and better for the Sri Lankan economy) to explore the glorious range of outlandish soft drinks produced locally by Olé, Lion and Elephant. These include old-fashioned favourites like cream soda and ginger beer and unique local brands like Portello (which tastes a bit like Vimto) and the ultra-sweet, lollipop-

flavoured Necta. **Ginger beer** is particularly common, and very refreshing – the Elephant brand uses natural ginger, which is meant to be good for the stomach and digestion. Bottles cost from Rs.20 and up.

The slightly sour-tasting **coconut milk** (*thambili*) isn't to everyone's taste, although it's guaranteed safe, having been locked up in the heart of the coconut. It's also claimed to be an excellent hangover cure thanks to its mix of glucose and potassium, which also makes it good to drink if you're suffering from diarrhoea.

Tea and coffee

Despite the fame of Sri Lanka's **tea**, most of the best stuff is exported and you have little chance of getting a top-class cuppa unless you buy your own and make it yourself. Tea is usually made weak and milky here, and you won't find the marvellous masala teas of India. Normal tea is often called "milk tea"; "bed tea" is just ordinary tea brought to your room for breakfast. **Coffee** is often a better bet. This is generally either Nescafé or locally produced coffee – the latter is usually perfectly drinkable, although you're normally left with a big layer of silt at the bottom of the cup.

Alcoholic drinks

Sri Lanka has a strong drinking culture – beer was introduced by foreign captives during the Kandyan period, and the islanders have never looked back. The island's two staple forms of alcohol are lager and arrack. **Lager** is usually sold in large (625ml) bottles; draught lager is rare. There's not a great choice of brands; all clock in with an alcohol content of just under five percent. The staple national tipple, the slightly sweetish Lion Lager, divides opinion: locals either swear by it or at it. Other beers include Carlsberg (brewed under licence in Sri Lanka), and the less frequently encountered Three Coins and Goldbrew lagers, both dry and pale. Lion also produce a form of **stout**, while Guinness is also brewed locally. As you'd expect, lager is relatively expensive in Sri Lankan terms, ranging from around Rs.50 in a liquor shop or supermarket to Rs.100–150 in most bars and restaurants, and up to Rs.250 in a posh hotel. Imported beers, on the rare occasions you can find them, come with a hefty mark-up.

Two more distinctively local types of booze come from the versatile coconut. **Toddy**, tapped from the flower of the coconut, is non-alcoholic when fresh but ferments into a beverage faintly reminiscent of cider – it's sold informally in villages around the country, though unless you're travelling with a Sinhala-speaker it's difficult to track down. When fermented and refined, toddy produces **arrack** (33% proof), Sri Lanka's national beverage for the strong-livered – you won't go far before finding a group of voluble Sri Lankan men clustered around a bottle. Arrack is either drunk neat, mixed with coke or lemonade, or used in tourist-oriented bars and restaurants as a base for cocktails. It's available in various grades and is usually a darkish brown, though there are also clear brands like White Diamond and White Label; the smoother, double-distilled arrack tastes faintly like rum. Aficionados reckon that the DCSL Old Arrack is the best stuff. A 750ml bottle costs between Rs.260 and Rs.400. Some brands are also available in small (375ml) bottles. Imported **spirits** are widely available, but are predictably expensive. There are also locally produced versions of most spirits, including rather rough whisky, brandy, rum and vodka, as well as lots of brands of quite palatable lemon gin.

Most people drink in their hotel bar or guest house. There are a few decent **bars** and English-style pubs in Colombo, Kandy and a few tourist resorts, but most local bars are gloomy and rather seedy places, and very much a male preserve – potentially fun for blokes on a bender, although women will feel less comfortable. Alcohol is available from supermarkets in larger towns. In smaller places, there are usually a few rather disreputable-looking **liquor shops** – usually a small kiosk, piled high with bottles of beer and arrack and protected by stout security bars. You hand over the money and your bottle(s) are passed to you through the bars. You're technically not allowed to buy alcohol on full-moon (poya) days, although tourist hotels and bars will often discreetly serve visitors.

Post, phones and email

Sri Lanka is reasonably well connected with the outside world. There's an abundance of ways to make phone calls, while most tourist towns now have at least one place offering email facilities.

Phones

Phoning home from Sri Lanka is straightforward but expensive – if you're planning a long trip and are likely to be calling a lot, using your own mobile (see below) is the most cost-effective option. Without a mobile, the easiest way to make a call is to go to one of the island's innumerable **communications bureaux**, little offices offering phone, fax and photocopying services, and sometimes email as well (look out for signs advertising IDD calls); there will usually be at least a couple on the main street of even the smallest town. You make your call, either from a private cubicle or from a phone at the counter, and then pay the bill at the end. Some places have phones with built-in LCD timers so you can see exactly how long you've been on the line for; in other places they just use a stop watch (in which case it's worth keeping an eye open to make sure its not fiddled with while you're on the phone). Calls to the UK, Australasia and North America cost between Rs.120 and Rs.150 per minute (largely irrespective of when you make them, although a few places offer slight discounts on Sundays or late at night) – you could try bargaining, since rates aren't

Making calls

To **call home from Sri Lanka**, dial the international access code (☏00), then the country code (UK ☏44; US & Canada ☏1; Ireland ☏353; Australia ☏61; New Zealand ☏64), then the area code and subscriber number. Note that the initial zero is omitted from the area code when dialling the UK, Ireland, Australia and New Zealand from abroad.

To **call Sri Lanka from abroad**, dial your international access code (UK, Ireland & New Zealand ☏00; US & Canada ☏011; Australia ☏0011) then the country code for Sri Lanka (☏94), then the area code, minus the initial zero, then the subscriber number.

fixed. A few post offices also offer IDD phone facilities at similar rates to communications bureaux. Calls within Sri Lanka cost Rs.5–10 per minute from a communications bureau.

There are relatively few public payphones in Sri Lanka. **Cardphones** are operated by various companies, each of which issues its own, non-interchangeable, cards; these are available (in theory, at least) from shops near cardphones and from post offices. In practice, the small saving you might make by using these phones compared to a communications bureau is easily outweighed by hassle of buying the correct type of card and finding a phone that actually works – while the noise and lack of privacy is a further disincentive. There are also a few **coin-operated public phones**, though unless you want to spend the entire call shovelling in change these are only really useful for local numbers. One final possibility is to phone from your **hotel room**, though this will always cost significantly more than from a communications bureau, and can become positively astronomical in top-end hotels. Finally, a few Internet cafés (especially in Colombo) now offer **Webcalls** – international phone calls via the Internet. These are far cheaper than standard phone calls, usually costing around Rs.30 per minute; quality is quite reasonable, albeit not as good as using a proper phone line.

Most communications bureaux also have **fax** machines; count on around Rs.100 to send an A4 page to an overseas destination.

Mobile phones

If you want to use your **mobile phone** in Sri Lanka, ask your service provider whether your handset will work abroad and what the call costs are. Not surprisingly,

charges are generally steep – around US$3 per minute is common. Most mobiles in the UK, Australia and New Zealand use GSM, which works well in Sri Lanka. US mobiles (apart from tri-band phones) won't work in Sri Lanka. For further information about using your phone abroad, check out ⊕www.telecomsadvice.org.uk/features /using_your_mobile_abroad.htm.

If you're likely to be making a lot of inter-national phone calls, an alternative is to replace the **SIM card** in your phone with a new SIM from a Sri Lankan phone compa-ny. This will give you a Sri Lankan phone number and you will be charged domestic rates – typically an extremely modest Rs.25–30 for international calls, and around Rs.5–7 for local calls. SIM cards cost around US$25 and are available from the myriad phone shops which sprung up to cater to the Sri Lankan mobile boom; these places also sell chargers and adap-tors for Sri Lankan sockets and cards with which you can top up your airtime (or look for any shop displaying the relevant stick-er). The two biggest operators are Dialog (⊕www.dialog.lk) and Celltel (⊕www .celltel.lk). Both now cover pretty much every town of any consequence as far north as Jaffna, although you won't be able to get a signal in smaller villages such as Sigiriya and Unawatuna.

Telephone charge cards

One of the most convenient ways of phoning home from abroad is via a **tele-phone charge card** bought from your phone company back home. Using a PIN number, you can make calls from most

Changes to telephone numbers

During 2003, all Sri Lankan phone numbers were changed in order to convert the country's motley assortment of seven-, eight- and nine-digit phone numbers to a consistent **ten-digit format**, made up of a three-digit area code and seven-digit subscriber number. This involved two main changes. Firstly, the area codes of Colombo, Kandy and Galle changed from (respectively) 01, 08 and 09 to 011, 081 and 091 (other area codes remained unaffected). Secondly, additional 2s were added as needed to subscriber numbers to create ten-digit numbers. So, for example, the old Colombo number ☎01-345 678 changed to ☎011-234 5678, while the old Negombo number ☎031-12345 changed to ☎031-221 2345, and so on. Other changes (too complex to summarize here) affecting numbers prefixed 073, 074, 075 were also made. For full details visit ⊕www.trc.gov.lk.

In practice, telephone numbers are likely to carry on being advertised in their old formats for at least a couple of years, so you'll have to change the area codes and add 2s as necessary. At present, dialling the old numbers triggers a recorded message telling you the new numbers.

All the telephone numbers in this book have been given in the new format.

hotel, public and private phones which are then charged to your account back home (or, alternatively, a credit card). Since most major charge cards are free, it's worth getting one if only for emergencies; enquire first whether Sri Lanka is covered, and bear in mind that rates aren't necessarily cheaper than calling from a communications bureau.

In **the UK and Ireland**, charge cards are issued free to customers by British Telecom (☎0800/345144, ⊕www.payphones.bt.com/2001/phone_cards/menu.html); AT&T (dial ☎0800/890 011, then 888/641-6123 when you hear the AT&T prompt to be transferred to the Florida Call Centre; free 24 hours); and NTL (☎0500/100 505). In the **US and Canada**, AT&T, MCI, Sprint, Canada Direct and other North American long-distance companies all issue charge cards to their customers. In **Australia**, telephone charge cards include the Telstra Telecard (☎1800/038 000) and Optus Calling Card (☎1300/300 937), while in **New Zealand** Telecom NZ's Calling Card (☎04/801 9000) can be used to make calls abroad.

Post

A **postcard** or **aerogramme** to the UK, Australasia and North America costs Rs.18; an airmail letter under 10g costs Rs.28. Sending up to 2kg by registered airmail costs about US$20 to the UK, US$30 to the US. Airmail takes six to ten days to reach the UK and US. Surface mail is about half to one-

third the cost of airmail, but is so slow and offers so much potential for things to get lost or damaged in transit that it's really not worth bothering with. If you want **to send a parcel** home from Sri Lanka, you must take the contents unwrapped to the post office so that they can be inspected before wrapping (all larger post offices have counters selling glue, string and wrapping paper).

A useful alternative to standard airmail is the **EMS Speed Post**, a kind of high-speed airmail which takes two to three days to reach the UK, or five to seven days to reach the US and Australasia. Rates to the UK and Australasia run from a minimum Rs.1200 for under 250g up to Rs.2300 for up to 1.5kg. Rates to North America are slightly higher. Alternatively, a number of reputable **international couriers** have offices in Colombo – try Fedex at 300 Galle Rd, Kollupitiya.

Free **poste restante** services are available (at least in theory) at all post offices, though in practice staff may be unfamiliar with the concept – you're more likely to receive mail at the better organized post offices in larger towns. Poste restante mail should be addressed "Poste Restante (c/o The Postmaster)", with the recipient's surname clearly underlined. When picking up mail, check under both your first and last names.

Email and Internet

Large parts of Sri Lanka remain resolutely offline, and except in a very few places

(Negombo, Kandy and parts of Colombo) **email and Internet access** remains relatively scarce. Having said that, pretty much all places in the island which see significant numbers of tourists will have at least one place offering an Internet connection. The **cost** of access varies wildly – anything from Rs.2 per minute or less in Colombo and Kandy, rising to Rs.10 per minute or more in the island's backwaters; connections can be slow and erratic pretty much everywhere.

The media

Sri Lanka has an extensive English-language media, including numerous newspapers and radio stations, though journalistic standards are not especially high thanks, at least partly, to the state control exercised on large sections of the media.

Newspapers and magazines

Sri Lanka has a good spread of English-language **newspapers**, including three dailies – The Island (Ⓦwww.island.lk), the Daily News (Ⓦwww.dailynews.lk) and the Daily Mirror (Ⓦwww.dailymirror.lk) – and two Sunday papers, The Sunday Observer (Ⓦwww.sundayobserver.lk) and the Sunday Times (Ⓦwww.sundaytimes.lk). The best two are the Daily Mirror and the Sunday Times, which are independently owned. The others are all owned by the government, and therefore tend to reflect the opinions of whichever political party has control of the Information Ministry (a fact dramatically borne out in late 2003, when government-owned titles switched political allegiance virtually overnight following President Kumaratunga's seizure of power). Journalistic standards are not high in any of these publications, which tend to labour under a surfeit of political and administrative jargon which is difficult for outsiders to penetrate. All devote the majority of their coverage to domestic politics and cricket. Despite the number of titles, English-language newspapers can be a bit tricky to find – look out for people selling them by the roadside or at small stalls – and you'll usually only find one or two available in any one place; the Daily News is perhaps the most widely distributed. All these papers are also available online, though The Island, The Mirror and the Sunday Times sites require you to pay a subscription.

Lanka Monthly Digest **magazine** (Ⓦwww.lanka.net/LMD) is essentially a business publication, but usually has one or two articles of general interest about Sri Lanka every issue. There are also a number of tourist-oriented publications available in Colombo (see p.78) which are worth looking out for.

Radio

There are a surprising number of **English-language radio stations** in Sri Lanka, although reception can be hit and miss outside Colombo and most don't broadcast at night. The best is generally reckoned to be TNL Radio (101.7 FM; Ⓦwww.tnlradio.com), which has a good mix of music, news and chat. The most widely broadcast, however, is Sun FM (95.3 FM islandwide; 99.9 FM in Colombo and Kandy), which churns out a diet of mainstream Western pop presented by a roster of unforgettably naff DJs – their "Late-Night Love" show is unquestionably the funniest programme on Sri Lankan radio. Other stations include Yes FM (89.5 FM; Ⓦwww.yesfmonline.com), which broadcasts mainstream western pop 24 hours a day; Gold FM (93.0 FM) – "Old Time Hits All The Time" – which dishes up retro-pop and easy listening; and the similar

Classic Radio FM (92.6 FM). Two **Sinhala-language stations** which you'll also end up hearing a lot of (especially if you do much bus travel) are Sri FM (99.0/99.3 FM) and Shah FM (96.7 FM) – the former, in particular, is beloved of bus drivers all over the island and offers a toe-curling diet of Sinhala pop interspersed with terrible adverts. For a more interesting selection of local music, try Sirasa FM (88.8FM; www.sirasa.com)

Television

You're not likely to spend much time watching **television** in Sri Lanka. There are three state-run **channels** (Rupavahini, Channel Eye and ITN), which broadcast almost entirely in Sinhala and Tamil, plus various local satellite TV channels which offer a small selection of English-language programming, though this is a fairly deadly mixture of shopping programmes, children's shows, pop music and the occasional duff film. Some satellite channels carry international news programmes from the BBC, Sky and CNN.

Cinema

Sri Lankan **cinema** has a long history, although it continues to struggle to escape the huge shadow cast by the film industry in neighbouring India; the increasingly wide availability of television poses another challenge. The first film made in Sri Lanka and using the Sinhala language was *Kadawunu Poronduwa* (Broken Promise), premiered in 1947, although the first truly Sinhalese film is generally considered to be **Lester James Periris's** *Rekawa* (Line of Destiny), of 1956,

which broke with the Indian all-singing all-dancing model and attempted a realistic portrayal of Sri Lankan life. Peiris went on to to score further triumphs with films like *Gamperaliya* (Changing Village), based on a novel by Martin Wickramasinghe (see p.169), and served as a role model for a new generation of Sri Lankan directors. Modern Sri Lankan film-makers have tended to focus on themes connected with the country's civil war, most famously in Prasanna Vithanage's *Death on a Full Moon Day* (1997), which portrays a blind and naive father who refuses to accept the death of his soldier son. At present, about a hundred films are released each year in Sri Lankan cinemas, with offerings in English, Tamil, Sinhala and Hindi. Sri Lankan-made films are almost exclusively in Sinhala, apart from a few in Tamil.

There are only a very modest number of cinemas on the island, concentrated largely in Colombo. A couple show recent Hollywood blockbusters in English; others specialize in Tamil, Hindi and Sinhala releases, and are easily spotted by their huge advertising hoardings showing rakish, moustachioed heroes clutching nubile heroines. Tickets for all movies rarely cost more than a dollar. You might also catch screenings of more highbrow Sri Lankan movies at the various cultural centres in Colombo and Kandy.

Funnily enough, the most visible cinematic offerings in Sri Lanka are the soft-porn Western films – with titles like *Almost Pregnant* – which you'll see advertised on posters all over the island.

Festivals and public holidays

It's sometimes claimed that Sri Lanka has more festivals than any other country in the world, and with four major religions on the island and no less than 29 public holidays, things can seem to grind to a halt with (to a Westerner) disconcerting frequency.

Virtually all the festivals are religious in nature and follow the **lunar calendar**, with

every full moon signalling the start of a new month (an extra month is added every two

Festival calendar

January

Duruthu Poya Marks the first of the Buddha's three legendary visits to Sri Lanka, celebrated with a spectacular perahera at the Raja Maha Vihara in the Colombo suburb of Kelaniya (see p.102). The Duruthu poya also marks the beginning of the three-month pilgrimage season to Adam's Peak.

Thai Pongol (Jan 14/15) Hindu festival, honouring the sun god Surya, Indra (the bringer of rains), and the cow, in no particular order. It's marked by ceremonies at Hindu temples, after which the first grains of the new paddy harvest are ceremonially cooked in milk in a special pot – the direction in which the liquid spills is thought to indicate good or bad luck in the coming year.

February

Navam Poya Commemorates the Buddha's announcement, at the age of 80, of his own impending death, celebrated with a major perahera at the Gangaramaya temple in Colombo. Although this dates only from 1979, it has already become one of the island's biggest festivals, featuring a procession of some fifty elephants.

Independence Day Celebrates Sri Lanka's independence on February 4, 1948, with parades, dances and games.

March

Medin Poya Marks the Buddha's first visit to his father's palace following his enlightenment.

Maha Sivarathri (Feb/March) Hindu festival dedicated to Shiva, during which devotees perform a one-day fast and an all-night vigil.

April

Bak Poya Celebrates the Buddha's second visit to Sri Lanka.

New Year (April 13–14) Coinciding with the start of the southwest monsoon and the end of the harvest season, the Buddhist and Hindu new year is a family festival during which presents are exchanged and the traditional *kiribath* (rice cooked with milk and cut into diamond shapes) is prepared. Businesses close, rituals are performed, new clothes are worn and horoscopes are cast. April 13 is New Year's Eve; April 14 is New Year's Day.

Good Friday An Easter Passion play is performed on the island of Duwa, near Negombo.

May

Vesak Poya The most important of the Buddhist poya*s*, this is a three-fold celebration commemorating the Buddha's birth, enlightenment and death, all three of which are traditionally thought to have happened on the day of the Vesak poya. In addition, the last of the Buddha's three alleged visits to Sri Lanka is claimed to have been on a Vesak poya day. Lamps are lit in front of houses, and platforms decorated with scenes from the life of the Buddha (*pandals*) are erected throughout the country. Buses and cars are decorated with streamers, and free food (from rice and curry to Vesak sweetmeats) is distributed in roadside booths (*dansal*). Meanwhile, devout Buddhists visit temples, meditate and fast. The day after the Vesak poya is also a public holiday. Vesak also marks the end of the Adam's Peak pilgrimage season.

Labour day (1 May) The traditional May Day bank holiday.

National Heroes' Day (22 May) Honours soldiers who have died in the civil war.

June

Poson Poya Second only in importance to Vesak, Poson poya commemorates the introduction of Buddhism to Sri Lanka by Mahinda, marked by mass pilgrimages to Anuradhapura, while thousands of white-robed pilgrims climb to the summit of Mihintale.

July

Esala Poya Celebrates the Buddha's first sermon and the arrival of the Tooth Relic in Sri Lanka. The lunar month of Esala is the season of festivals, marked by elephant peraheras at Kataragama (see below), Dondra, Bellanwila (a southern Colombo suburb) and, most flamboyantly, the great Esala Perahera in Kandy (late July to early Aug; see p.212), Sri Lanka's most extravagant festival.

Kataragama (late July/early August) Festival at Kataragama (held at the same time as the Esala perahera) during which devotees fire-walk and indulge in various forms of ritual self-mutilation, piercing their skin with hooks and weights, and driving skewers through their cheeks and tongues.

August

Nikini Poya Marks the retreat of the Bhikkhus following the Buddha's death, commemorated by a period of fasting and of retreat for the monastic communities.

Vel (July/August) Colombo's most important Hindu festival, dedicated to Skanda/Kataragama (see p.198) and featuring two exuberant processions during which the god's chariot and *vel* (spear) are carried across the city from the Pettah to temples in Wellawatta and Bambalapitiya.

Nallur Festival Held at the Nallur Temple in Jaffna in honour of Skanda, this is the biggest and longest festival in Sri Lanka, a mammoth 26-day affair, ending on Nikini poya. See p.402.

September

Binara Poya Commemorates the Buddha's journey to heaven to preach to his mother and other deities.

Dussehra (Sept/Oct) Also known as Durga Puja, this Hindu festival honours Durga and also commemorates the day of Rama's victory over Ravana.

October

Vap Poya Marks the Buddha's return to earth and the end of the Buddhist period of fasting.

Deepavali (late Oct/early Nov) The Hindu Festival of Lights (equivalent to north India's Diwali), commemorating the return from exile of Rama, hero of the Ramayana, with the lighting of lamps in Tamil households, symbolic of the triumph of good over evil, and the wearing of new clothes.

November

Il Poya Commemorates the Buddha's ordination of sixty disciples.

December

Unduvap Poya Celebrates the arrival of the Bo tree sapling in Anuradhapura, brought by Ashoka's daughter, Sangamitta.

Christmas (25 December)

Christian New Year's Eve (31 December).

or three years to keep the solar and lunar calendars in alignment). **Buddhist festivals** revolve around the days of the full moon – or **poya days** – which are official public holidays as well as having special religious significance (the Buddha urged his disciples to undertake special spiritual practices on each poya day, and according to traditional belief he himself was born, attained enlightenment and died on the poya day in the lunar month of Vesak). On poya days, Sri Lankan Buddhists traditionally make offerings at their local temple and perform other religious observances, while the less pious section of the population mark the occasion with riotous behaviour and widespread drunkenness. The island's most important Buddhist festivals are traditionally celebrated with enormous **peraheras**, or parades, with scores of fabulously accoutred elephants accompanied by drummers and dancers. People often travel on poya days, so transport and accommodation tends to be busy; there's also (in theory) a ban on the sale of alcohol, although tourist hotels and guest houses will usually serve you.

Sri Lanka's main **Hindu festivals** rival or outdo the island's Buddhist celebrations in colour – in addition to the ones listed below, there are numerous other local temple festivals across the Jaffna peninsula. Sri Lanka's **Muslim festivals** are more modest affairs, generally only involving the Muslim community itself, with special prayers at the mosque. The three main celebrations are the **Milad un-Nabi** (May 3, 2004), celebrating the Prophet's birthday; **Id ul-Fitr** (Nov 14, 2004), marking the end of Ramadan; and **Id ul-Allah** (Feb 1, 2004), marking the beginning of pilgrimages to Mecca.

Most (but not all) Sri Lankan festivals follow the lunar calendar, meaning that **dates** vary considerably from year to year. Muslim festivals also follow a lunar calendar but without the corrective months which are inserted into the Buddhist lunar calendar, meaning that the dates of these festivals gradually move backwards at the rate of about eleven days per year, completing one annual cycle roughly every 32 years. You can find an exact list for forthcoming events at ⓦwww.srilankatourism .org/events_festivals.htm.

National parks and reserves

Nature conservation has a long and illustrious history in Sri Lanka – the island's first wildlife reserve is said to have been established by King Devanampiya Tissa in the third century BC, while many of the national parks and reserves that make up today's well-developed network date back to colonial times and earlier. Administered by the Department of Wildlife Conservation (ⓦwww.dwlc.com), these protected areas cover over thirteen percent of the island's land area and encompass a wide variety of terrains, from the high-altitude moorlands of Horton Plains National Park to the coastal wetlands of Bundala. Almost all harbour a rich selection of wildlife and birds, and several are also of outstanding scenic beauty. The only fly in the ointment are the absurdly discriminatory entrance fees imposed on foreign tourists.

Of Sri Lanka's fourteen **national parks**, the most touristed are Yala, Uda Walawe, Horton Plains, Bundala, Minneriya and the recently established Kaudulla. A number of

the parks lie in civil-war affected areas, and several were closed for long periods during the war, including Wilpattu, Maduru Oya, Gal Oya and Yala East (all now reopened), and

Somawathiya Chaitiya and Lahugala, which remain closed (although some people visit Lahugala unofficially). The Department of Wildlife Conservation's *A Guide to National Parks of Sri Lanka*, available from their office in Colombo (see p.111), has detailed information about all the national parks, apart from Kaudulla including a map of each one.

There are numerous other protected areas dotted across the island and run under government supervision. These are categorized variously as **nature reserves**, **strict nature reserves** (entry prohibited) and **sanctuaries**. In general these places possess important botanical significance but lack the wildlife found in the national parks, as at (to name just one example) the unique, World Heritage-listed Sinharaja Forest Reserve, Sri Lanka's last undisturbed pocket of tropical rainforest.

Visiting national parks

All national parks are open daily from 6.30am to 6.30pm. Other than in Horton Plains, where you're allowed to walk, you'll have to hire a **jeep** to take you around. There are usually jeeps (plus drivers) for hire at park entrances, though it's generally easier to hire one at the place you're staying to take you to and from the park, as well as driving you around it. Count on around US$15–20 for half a day's jeep (and driver) hire, or US$30 for a full day.

Except in Horton Plains, all visitors are allocated an obligatory **tracker**, who rides with you and acts as a guide. Some are very good, but standards do vary considerably and unfortunately many trackers speak only rudimentary English, which can seriously impair their effectiveness as a guide – it's entirely a matter of chance whether you get a good tracker or one who only speaks three words of English, has a bad hangover and wouldn't recognize an elephant at three paces. One way of insuring yourself against the chance of getting a dud tracker is to go with a good **driver** – the best are expert wildlife trackers and spotters in their own right, and also carry binoculars and wildlife identification books or cards.

Note that except at designated spots, you're supposed to stay in your vehicle at all times; in Yala, you're also obliged to keep the hood on your jeep down. It goes without saying that you should respect the park's wildlife and environment. Keep noise to a minimum; don't try to feed animals; don't chase or harass them; don't smoke; don't use flash photography; and don't litter.

The standard **entrance charge** to the majority of national parks is currently US$13.80 per person, converted into rupees (locals pay US$0.20, incidentally); Bundala and Kaudulla national parks cost half this. Children aged 6–12 pay half price; under 6s get in free; in addition, various other charges apply. There are minor variations from park to park, but in general you will also pay a **service charge** (around US$7 per vehicle), which covers the services of your tracker; a **vehicle charge** (US$1.50 per vehicle); plus **tax** on everything at a whopping twenty percent. The exact entrance cost per person thus becomes cheaper the more people you share a vehicle with – two people sharing a vehicle will pay a total of around US$22 per person.

Staying in a national park

It's possible to stay in many national parks, most of which are equipped with simple but adequate **bungalows** for visitors. These have to be booked in advance through the Department of Wildlife Conservation, 18 Gregory's Road, Colombo 7 (℡011-269 4241, ⓦwww.dwlc.com). Unfortunately, charges reflect the rip-off ethos that permeates the department's attitude to foreign tourists. You will have to pay US$24 per person to use the bungalow, plus two days' park entrance fees at US$13.80 per day, plus a service and linen charge of US$32 per group, plus tax at twenty percent. Thus, for a couple it will cost around US$150 per night to stay in a park bungalow. To put this into context, this is almost twice the price of a room in one of Colombo's cheaper five-star hotels – and this is before you've even begun to cover your transport costs to, from and around the park.

You can also **camp** in any of the national parks, though again at punitive pecuniary expense. You'll have to pay two days' entrance charges, plus a US$6 "occupation" fee, a US$2 "service charge", plus tax on everything at twenty percent – a grand total of around US$40 per person (locals pay about US$3). Again, you'll have to pre-book a camping space through the Department of Wildlife Conservation in Colombo, though some tour operators can arrange trips for you.

Sport and outdoor activities

Sri Lanka's vast potential for outdoor and activity holidays is only just starting to be tapped. Water-based activities like diving and surfing are reasonably well covered, but other outdoor pursuits such as mountain biking and trekking remain the preserve of a few pioneering operators. The island's eco-tourism potential is huge, but although its reputation amongst birdwatchers is well established, other wildlife attractions – from turtle-spotting to whale-watching – remain almost completely unexploited. Finally, if you fancy something a bit livelier and you're lucky enough to coincide with a match, a trip to watch Sri Lanka's cricket team in action – always an occasion of huge national excitement – is an absolute must.

Cricket

Of all the legacies of the British colonial period, the game of **cricket** is probably held dearest by the average Sri Lankan. As in India and Pakistan, cricket is undoubtedly king in the Sri Lankan sporting pantheon. Kids play it on any patch of spare ground, improvising balls, bats and wickets out of rolled-up bits of cloth and discarded sticks, whilst the country virtually grinds to a halt during international matches, with excitable crowds clustered around every available radio or television set.

Although the national team is a relative newcomer to international cricket – they were only accorded full test status in 1982 – they've more than held their own since then, with a famous demolition of England at Lord's in 1998 amongst their various triumphs. It's in the one-day game, however, that Sri Lanka have really taken the world by storm, capped by their triumph in the **1996 World Cup**, when their fearsomely talented batting line-up – led by elegant left-hander Aravinda da Silva and the explosive Sanath Jayasuriya – blasted their way to the title. The style of cricket played by the Sri Lankans during this tournament turned the old cricketing order on its head, establishing a new strategy for the one-day game based on all-out attack played at a breathtaking tempo which left opposition teams floundering in their wake – widely imitated since by other nations, though only rarely equalled.

Not surprisingly, the success of the Sri Lankan team has proved an important source of national pride and cohesion. Although Sinhalese players have traditionally dominated the squad, the Tamil population has provided present-day Sri Lanka's finest player, **Muttiah Muralitharan** (or "Murali", as he's known to linguistically challenged commentators the world over). Perhaps the world's most lethal spin bowler of recent years, Muralitharan became the leading wicket taker in the history of test cricket in May 2004.

If you get the chance, it's well worth taking in a cricket match – the vociferous crowds and carnival atmosphere are a world away from the rather staid ambience of most English cricket grounds. The island's three **test-match venues** are the Sinhalese Sports Club in Colombo (see p.98), the Asigiriya Stadium in Kandy (see p.230), and the cricket ground in Galle (see p.161). **One-day internationals** are held at the stadia in Galle and Kandy, at the Premadasa Stadium in Colombo and at the cricket ground in Dambulla. Tickets for matches are available from the relevant venues. Note also that many of the tour operators listed on pp.11–12 offer **cricketing tours** to Sri Lanka.

Diving and snorkelling

Sri Lanka isn't usually thought of as one of Asia's premier **diving** destinations, and although you probably wouldn't come here specifically to dive, there are enough underwater attractions to make a couple of days' diving a worthwhile part of a visit. Sri Lanka is also a good and cheap place to **learn to dive**, with schools in Colombo, Negombo, Bentota, Beruwala, Hikkaduwa, Unawatuna, Tangalla, Weligama, Nilaveli and Uppaveli – see the relevant guide accounts for details.

Unfortunately, however, Sri Lanka's marine environment, and a significant proportion of its coral, has been adversely affected by a host of factors: dynamite fishing; the collection of coral for souvenirs and limestone production; damage caused to reefs by boats; and the El Niño effect of 1998. The **west coast** has relatively little living coral but, in compensation, boasts plenty of marine life, including big fish such as barracuda, whale shark, tuna and seer plus various smaller pelagic species such as angel, lion, Koran, scorpion, parrot and butterfly fish (to name just a few). In addition, the diving here is three-dimensional and technically challenging, with deep dives, swim-through cave complexes, drop-offs and various **wreck dives**. Popular targets include the wreck of an old steam-driven oil tanker from 1860s known as the *Conch*, near Hikkaduwa, which is a favourite amongst less experienced divers. The most impressive wreck currently diveable in Sri Lanka lies 9km offshore from Colombo, and comprises the remains of a car ferry, sunk by the Japanese in World War II and lying at a depth of around 40m, with cars and trucks scattered all over the seabed around.

By contrast, Trincomalee on the **east coast** offers better coral but a relative paucity of marine life. Diving here is more two-dimensional, with shallow, flat coral beds. No wrecks have yet been opened up for divers along the east coast, although there are some excellent possibilities near Batticaloa,

including the wreck of the *Hermes*, a 270m-long aircraft carrier sunk during World War II and lying at a depth of 60m. Diving the Snake (see p.134) has plans to open up a centre there depending on the progress of the peace process, although at the time of writing there were no organized trips.

The **diving season** on the west coast runs roughly from October to April, and on the east coast from May to September; pretty much all the island's diving schools shut up out of season, although if you're really keen and don't mind diving in rough seas with poor visibility you might be able to find someone willing to take you out off-season. **Diving packages and courses** are extremely cheap. A three-day Open-Water PADI course goes for around US$350, a PADI Advanced Open-Water course for around US$225, and single dives for US$20–25. Introductory diving packages (including two dives) can also be had for around US$60.

There's not a lot of really good **snorkelling** around Sri Lanka: little coral survives close to the shore, although this lack is compensated by the abundant shoals of tropical fish which frequent the coast. The island's one outstanding snorkelling spot is around Coral Island at Nilaveli (see p.375); other decent places include the Coral Gardens at Hikkaduwa and the beach at Polhena.

Surfing

Many of the waves which crash against the Sri Lankan coast have travelled all the way from Antarctica, and not surprisingly there are several excellent **surfing** spots. The outstanding destination is **Arugam Bay** on the east coast, the one place in Sri Lanka with an international reputation amongst surfheads. The low-key south coast village of **Midigama** is another good spot, while **Hikkaduwa** is also popular. Boards are available to rent at all three places. Mambo Surf Tours at Hikkaduwa (see p.143), Blue Fin Tours in Unawatuna (see p.164) and various places in Arugam Bay arrange surfing trips around the coast, sometimes combined with visits to other attractions. The surfing **season** runs from April to October at Arugam Bay, and from November to April at Midigama and Hikkaduwa.

Whitewater rafting and other water sports

The island's premier spot for **whitewater rafting** is around **Kitulgala** (see p.278), where the Kelani Ganga river comes tumbling out of the hill country, creating boulder-strewn grade 3–4 rapids. You can either arrange trips locally or plan something in advance. The island's leading rafting specialists are Adventure Sports Lanka (see p.111); Jetwing Eco Holidays (see p.111) also arrange comprehensive fourteen-day whitewater rafting trips.

Sri Lanka's **water sports** capital is Bentota, whose lagoon provides the perfect venue for all sorts of water-based activities, including jet-skiing, windsurfing, speed-boating, waterskiing, inner-tubing and banana-boating.

Trekking

Sri Lanka's huge **trekking** potential remains almost totally unexploited, although the growing number of eco-lodges and eco-oriented tours is beginning to change matters. The hill country, in particular, offers the perfect hiking terrain – spectacular scenery, marvellous views and a pleasantly temperate climate – while trekking through the wildlife-rich lowland jungles is also a deeply rewarding experience. A few of the tour operators listed on pp.11–12 & p.113 offer walking tours; alternatively, contact Sumane Bandara Illangantilake (see p.233), who can arrange walking tours pretty much anywhere in the island.

Cycling

So long as you avoid the hazardous main highways (see p.36 for more on these), **cycling** around Sri Lanka can be a real pleasure, and a welcome change from sitting in a stuffy car or braving the anarchic bus system. For serious cyclists, the island's modest dimensions and scenic diversity offer the perfect ingredients for a varied tour on two wheels, while for the less committed renting a bike is the perfect way to explore the ancient cities of Anuradhapura and Polonnaruwa – or indeed any other corner of the island. Athough the main highways are busy, smelly and dangerous, Sri Lanka has myriad byways on which vehicles are relatively infrequent, and a National Cycling Path has recently been established along the coast from Kalutara to Galle. A number of the operators listed on pp.11–12 & p.113 offer cycling or mountain-biking tours, usually including a mixture of on- and off-roading and with a backup vehicle in support. Good options include Adventure Sports Lanka and Jetwing Eco Holidays, both of which run extended fifteen-day tours, plus shorter trips.

Eco-tourism

Sri Lanka's small but growing number of **eco-lodges** and **eco-hotels** (see p.38) make good bases for nature-activity holidays, and offer a more interactive experience than sitting in the back of a jeep and being driven around a national park. A few of these lodges – *Tree Tops*, *Galapita* and *Tasks Safari Camp* – are very remote and rustic and offer a real wilderness experience, if few five-star comforts.

Birdwatching is well established, and even if you've never previously looked at a feathered creature in your life, the island's outstanding range of colourful birdlife can prove surprisingly fascinating. A number of companies run specialist tours (see pp.11–12 & p.113), while bird-spotting usually forms a significant part of trips to the island's national parks – although you'll see birds pretty much everywhere you go, even in the middle of Colombo. See p.446 for more on the island's avifauna.

Elephants can be seen in virtually every national park in the country, at the famous Pinnewala Elephant Orphanage and in temples and at work on roads around the country. For **leopards**, the place to head for is Yala National Park (see p.196). Sri Lanka is an important nesting site for **sea turtles**; there are various hatcheries along the west coast (see p.135 & p.137), but the only turtle-watching site currently accessible is the ad hoc operation at Rekawa (see p.187). Similarly, the island's significant **whale-watching** potential remains untapped – recent studies have discovered seven whale species in the waters around Sri Lanka, including blue, sperm, humpback and the rare melon-headed whale. Unfortunately, no operators have yet succeeded in setting up trips, though this may change in future. The main centres are likely to be Kirinda and Trincomalee.

Yoga and meditation

Yoga isn't nearly as established in Sri Lanka as in India, although many of the island's numerous ayurvedic centres now offer classes as part of their treatment pans, and it's sometimes possible to enrol for them without taking an ayurveda course. Otherwise, your options are pretty limited. Serious students of yoga might consider signing up for a two-week stay at **Ulpotha** (Ⓦwww.ulpotha .com), a wonderful rural retreat in the Cultural Triangle attracting leading international yoga teachers – although at around US$1800 per person per fortnight, the experience doesn't come cheap.

Meditation courses are mainly concentrated around Kandy – see p.217 for further details.

Other activities

Ballooning has begun to take off in a big way in Sri Lanka, offering hot-air enthusiasts the chance to enjoy spectacular trips around Sigiriya, near Dambulla (from either the *Kandalama* or *Culture Club* hotels), and over Uda Walawe National Park – you can even get married during the flight. Several companies have recently begun arranging trips, and things are still a bit up in the air at the moment. The longest established operator is Adventure Centre Asia (Ⓣ077-758 8360, Ⓦwww.ac-asia.com); a standard one-hour flight costs US$230 per person. Adtech Lanka (Ⓦwww.balloons.lk) also offer trips.

Sri Lanka has three gorgeous **golf** courses, at Colombo, Kandy and Nuwara Eliya (see p.234 & p.253), and a number of the operators listed on pp.11–12 offer special golfing tours.

Mercifully, the island hasn't yet got a single **bungy jump**.

Shopping

Sri Lankan craftsmanship has a long and vibrant history. A visit to any museum will turn up objects testifying to the skill of the island's earlier artisans, who have for centuries been producing exquisitely manufactured objects in a wide variety of media, ranging from lacework and ola-leaf manuscripts to carvings in ivory and wood and elaborate metalwork and batiks.

Unfortunately, despite these fine traditions, modern Sri Lankan craftsmanship has largely degenerated into the mindless mass production of a few stereotypical items, and shopping is generally a disappointment compared to nearby countries such as India or Thailand. The decline in creativity is exemplified by the nationwide chain of government-run **Laksala** shops, the official state handicrafts emporium, whose outlets are stuffed to the gills with a predictable assortment of clumsily painted wooden elephants, kolam masks, ugly batiks and other tourist tat. It's not all bad news, however, and there are still a few worthwhile exceptions, especially in **Colombo**, which is also the best place to buy everything else Sri Lanka has to offer, from books to tea and discount clothing.

All larger shops have fixed, marked **prices**, although if you're making a major purchase or buying several items, a polite request for a "special price" or "small discount" might knock a few rupees off, especially for gems or jewellery. The smaller and more informal the outlet, the more scope for bargaining there's likely to be – if you're, say, buying a sarong from an itinerant hawker on the beach, you can haggle to your heart's content.

Finally, there are a couple of things you shouldn't buy. Remember that buying **coral or shells** (or any other marine product) contributes directly to the destruction of the island's fragile ocean environment; it's also illegal, and you're likely to end up paying a heavy fine if you try to take coral out of the country. Note that it's also illegal to export **antiques** (classified as anything over fifty years old) without a licence (see p.17).

Handicrafts

The most characteristic – and clichéd – Sri Lankan souvenirs are brightly painted **masks**, originally designed to be worn during kolam dances (see p.139) and now found for sale wherever there are tourists (though the sheer quantity churned out means that many are of indifferent quality and sloppily painted). Masks vary in size from the tiny to the huge; the vast majority depict either the pop-eyed Gara Yaka or the bird demon Gurulu Raksha, though if you hunt around you may find other designs – the excellent display at the National Museum in Colombo gives a good overview of the range of masks which have traditionally been made, even if you won't find as wide (or as well executed) a selection in any of the island's shops. Some masks are artificially but attractively aged to resemble antiques – a lot easier on the eye than the lurid colours in which most are painted. The centre of mask production is at Ambalangoda (see p.138), where there are a couple of large shops selling a big range of designs.

Second in popularity are **elephant carvings**. These range from small wooden creatures painted with bright polka-dot patterns, to the elegant stone carvings sold at the Gallery Cafe and Paradise Road in Colombo (see pp.108–109). **Batiks** (an art introduced by the Dutch from Indonesia) are also widespread. Designs are often stereotypical (the Sigiriya Damsels and naff beach scenes are ubiquitous), though a few places produce more unusual and interesting work. More entertaining are the **puzzle boxes** offered for sale around Sigiriya (and sometimes elsewhere in the Cultural Triangle) – delicately carved little wooden boxes which can only be opened by a series of Rubik-cube-like manoeuvres. Also fun are the beautifully made **wooden models** of tuktuks

and other vehicles – wonderful souvenirs or children's toys. They're most commonly found in Negombo, but are also increasingly available in Colombo and elsewhere on the island.

A number of other traditional crafts struggle on with a little help from the tourist trade. **Metalwork** has long been produced in the Kandy area, and intricately embossed metal objects such as dishes, trays, candlesticks and other objects can be found in all the island's handicraft emporia, though they're rather fussy for most foreign tastes. **Leatherwork** can also be good, and you'll find a range of hats, bags, boots and footrests (the shops at Pinnewala Elephant Orphanage have a particularly good selection). **Lacquerware** can also sometimes be found, along with Kandyan-style **drums** and, occasionally, **carrom boards** (see p.167).

Finally, if you've had a day in Colombo, it's well worth seeking out the **modern handicrafts** found at a few Colombo boutiques (see pp.108–109), such as Paradise Road, the Gallery Cafe or, especially, Barefoot, whose range of vibrantly coloured fabrics have become synonymous with modern Sri Lankan style.

Religious items

Wood or stone **Buddha carvings** of varying standards are common, while Kandyan Antiques (see p.108) in Colombo has a wide and interesting range of real and fake antiques of Buddhist and Hindu deities. For something a bit more unusual, the brightly coloured **posters** or strip-pictures of Buddhist and Hindu deities which adorn tuktuks and buses across the island are sold at pavement hawkers and stationers' shops across the island and make a cheap and characterful souvenir, while a visit to Kataragama or a trawl along St Anthony's Mawatha in Colombo (see p.92) will uncover an entertaining assortment of other **religious kitsch**, from bleeding Catholic saints to illuminated Ganesh clocks. If you really want to get into character, equip yourself with a begging bowl, fan and a set of saffron robes from one of the island's shops for Buddhist monks.

Tea and spices

Virtually all top-quality Ceylon **tea** is exported, although there's still plenty on sale which is likely to satisfy all but the most dedicated tea-fancier. A few factories around the hill country sell their tea directly to the public; alternatively, plenty of shops around the island stock a fairly wide range of Ceylon teas. The stuff on offer is pretty much the same wherever you go, and generally includes unblended high-grown teas (from around Rs.50) plus a wide range of flavoured teas (Rs.70–115) made with a huge range of ingredients, including standard offerings like lemon, orange, mint and vanilla, as well as the more outlandish banana, rum, kiwi fruit or pineapple. The main tea-shop chain is Mlesna, with branches in Colombo, Kandy and at the airport. You'll also find good selections in Cargills supermarkets islandwide.

Sri Lanka's spice gardens, mostly concentrated around Kandy and Matale, pull in loads of visitors on organized tours and sell packets of **spices**, often at outrageously inflated prices. You'll get much better deals in local shops and markets.

Gems and jewellery

Sri Lanka has been famous for its precious stones since antiquity, and gems and jewellery remain important to the national economy even today. This is nowhere more obvious than at the gem-mining centre of **Ratnapura** (see p.279), where locally excavated uncut gems are traded daily on the streets. All foreign visitors to the town will be offered stones to buy, but unless you're an expert gemologist there's a strong chance that you'll end up with an expensive piece of coloured glass. Another variant on this scam is that you will be persuaded to buy gems at a special "cheap" price with assurances that you will be able to resell them back home for several times the price you paid for them. Again, unless you're an expert, steer well clear of these deals.

Ratnapura apart, you'll find gem and jewellery shops all over the island – the major concentrations are in Negombo, Galle and Colombo. These include large chains, such as Zam Gems or Sifani, and smaller local outfits. There are no outstanding bargains to be had here, and if you are going to buy, it's worth doing some homework before you arrive so you can compare prices with those

back home. In Colombo, there's a big selection of gem shops at the Sri Lanka Gem and Jewellery Exchange, 310 Galle Rd, Kollupitiya. There's also a **gem-testing service** here (about US$2 per stone) if you want to get a purchase checked out. The obvious drawback is that it will be difficult to get something tested without buying it first, although you might be able to persuade Colombo jewellers to send a representative with you and the gem(s) before you part with your cash.

For silver and, especially, **gold** jewellery, try Sea Street in the Pettah district, which is lined with shops. These see few tourists, so prices are reasonable, although the flouncy designs on offer aren't to everyone's taste.

Clothes and books

Sri Lanka is a bit of a disappointment when it comes to **clothes**, and doesn't boast the gorgeous fabrics and nimble-fingered tailors of, say, India and Thailand. Having said that, the island is a major garment-manufacturing centre for overseas companies and there are lots good-quality Western-style clothes knocking around at bargain prices. In Colombo, two obvious places to try are the fancy Odel department store (see p.108), or the more downmarket House of Fashions (see p.108). Colourful but flimsy beachware is flogged by shops and hawkers at all the major west coast resorts – it's cheap and cheerful, but don't expect it to last much longer than your holiday. Most Sri Lankan women now dress Western style in rather boring skirts and blouses, but you can still find a few shops in Colombo and elsewhere selling beautiful saris and shalwar kameez (pyjama suits) – these shops are usually easily spotted via their enormous picture windows stuffed with colourfully costumed mannequins.

Books are relatively cheap: new paperbacks are about two-thirds of European and North American prices, and there are also lots of colourful coffee-table books and weird and wonderful works on Sri Lankan history, culture and religion that you won't find outside the island. The Vijitha Yapa bookshop has branches islandwide, and there are a number of other good bookstores in Colombo.

Crime, scams and personal safety

The good news is that Sri Lanka is a remarkably safe country to travel in and violent crime against foreigners is virtually unheard of – this is still a country where, despite twenty years of brutal civil war, the theft of two bicycles is considered a crime wave. The only bad news is that scams and aggressive touting are widespread in a few places.

Petty theft is less common than in many other parts of Asia (and rarer than in most European and American cities), though you should still take sensible care of your belongings. Pickpockets sometimes work in crowded areas, while thefts from hotel rooms are occasionally reported. Many hotels and guest houses ask guests to deposit valuables in their safe, and it's sensible to do so when you can. **Muggings** are very rare, though single travellers (especially women) should avoid dark beaches late at night – Negombo and Hikkaduwa have particularly bad reputations. In addition, make sure you keep a separate record of travellers' cheques and credit card numbers (along with the phone numbers needed in case of their loss) plus your passport details; it's worth taking a photocopy of the pages from your passport that contain your personal details.

If you do have anything stolen, you'll need to report it to the **police** – there's little chance that they will be able to recover it for you, but you'll need a report for your insurance claim. Given the fact that you might not find any English-speaking policemen on duty, you might try to get someone from your guest house to come along as an interpreter. The process of reporting a crime is usually a laborious affair, with much checking of papers and filling in of forms. Unfortunately, although **tourist police** offices have been set up in a few parts of the island, they're not much cop.

Dangers

Unless you've volunteered to clear minefields, the most dangerous thing you'll do in Sri Lanka is **cross the road**. The island has the dubious distinction of being in the world's top ten offenders when it comes to traffic-related fatalities, and as a pedestrian you're at the very bottom of the food chain in the dog-eats-dog world of Sri Lankan road use. Never rely on pedestrian crossings, avoid blind corners and oncoming buses like the plague, and always look for central reservations or, in Colombo, functioning traffic lights (which are rare). The incipiently suicidal might like to try imitating the local style of road crossing, which involves walking calmly out into the fray with an arm extended towards the oncoming traffic. A safer alternative is to wait until a group of locals begin to cross, and walk behind them.

In the north, the major safety hazard is **mines** – see the box on p.389 for more information.

Travel advisories

For current information on the security situation in Sri Lanka, visit one of the sites listed below.
Australian Department of Foreign Affairs ⓦ www.dfat.gov.au.
British Foreign & Commonwealth Office ⓦ www.fco.gov.uk.
New Zealand Ministry of Foreign Affairs ⓦ www.mft.govt.nz.
US State Department ⓦ www.travel.state.gov.

Scams and hassles

Sri Lanka has an unfortunate but well-deserved reputation for its **hustlers** and **con artists**, who range from simple gem shop and guest house touts to virtuoso scam merchants who run well-oiled schemes to entrap the unwary. At its simplest, you'll encounter low-level hassle from people who want you to visit their shop, stay in their guest house or be your guide (or, alternatively, who want to take you to a shop or guest house where they'll receive commission).

Common scams

Elephant festival in Colombo The capital's Galle Face Green is a well-known hangout for con artists – watch out for their classic chat-up line, "Sri Lanka very hot!". Having engaged you in conversation they will tell you how fortunate you are because there is a big elephant festival happening that very day (unless you've coincided with the Navam Perahera in February – see p.50 – they are lying). They will then whisk you off to see the "festival" (it's usually the temple elephant at the Gangaramaya temple; see see p.95) before setting you up for a ludicrously inflated tuktuk fare.

Taking you for a ride Many scams involve gaining your trust, then getting you into a tuktuk to visit some temple/"elephant festival"/handicraft shop or other attraction. Having driven you around for a while, you will be dumped in some remote and seedy part of town at which point the tuktuk driver will demand a wildly inflated fare for the ride. Alternatively, someone you meet on the train tells you there will be no tuktuks at your destination, and rings ahead for one, with the same end result. *Never* get into a tuktuk without agreeing a fare beforehand.

Free tea You are offered free tea by someone claiming to own or work on a plantation, on condition you pay a "small sum" to cover the export duty or postage. Needless to say, the tea never arrives.

Fake charity collectors Often elderly and respectable-looking gents with clipboards and official-looking letters; especially common around the lake in Kandy, but also in Colombo and on beaches everywhere. Real Sri Lankan charities do not collect on the streets.

Foreign coins You are approached by a respectable-looking gent who claims to be collecting foreign coins for his children or local school. You hand over some spare currency. Your coins are then passed on to a second person, who approaches you a few minutes later, claiming to have been given the coins some time previously as a tip or whatever, and asking you to change them back into rupees for them, since they are otherwise worthless.

Having a drink You fall into conversation with a friendly local who asks if you would like to have a drink with him. Having taken you to some obscure drinking den, he claims to have forgotten his wallet, leaving you to pay the (usually vastly inflated) bill. Once you've gone, he will return to collect his share of your money from the bar staff.

The card trick Someone asks you where you plan to stay. When you tell them, they produce a business card (purloined) from the relevant establishment and claim that they work there/are related to the owner. They then tell you that the said guest house or hotel is closed/full/undergoing renovations, then propose you come with them to their own guest house, or one where they earn commission.

War refugees Claims to be a war refugee followed by a request for money. Unless you're travelling in the north or east, these claims are likely to be false, and if you're in a touristy part of the island, you can be almost certain that you're dealing with an opportunist.

Gems Any transaction involving the purchase of gems is potentially risky except in the most reputable outlets. Also see Shopping, p.59.

Tuktuk drivers are the main source of this sort of pressure (never tell a tuktuk driver where you're staying or what your plans are, or they'll be camped out on your hotel doorstep waiting for you), although it can come from pretty much anyone with even a few words of English.

The island's con artists are a completely different kettle of fish – a breed of often plausible and cunning folk who live by their (often considerable) wits; they're mainly (but not exclusively) found in Colombo, Kandy and Galle. Convincing you of their trustworthiness is an important part of any scam, and con artists will often attempt to boost their own credentials by claiming to be a member of a professional elite (a SriLankan Airlines pilot; a former international cricketer). A standard ploy in Colombo is for con artists to claim to be visiting from the Maldives, thereby implying that they too are visitors and therefore to be trusted. Another common introductory ploy is for a con artist to claim to be a cook (or other backroom member of staff) at your hotel, hoping thereby to gain your confidence. Sometimes the lengths to

which con artists will go to wheedle themselves into your confidence are uncanny – in Kandy, for instance, visitors walking around the lake are sometimes approached by a respectable-looking gentleman who points out splashes in the lake, explaining that they are caused by water snakes (whereas, in fact, they are caused by a hidden accomplice chucking stones into the lake).

You shouldn't get too paranoid about these characters, but you should be aware that they exist and know how they operate. If you know the basic signs, they're fairly easily spotted; if you don't, you risk being taken for a (potentially expensive) ride. Do keep a sense of perspective, however; it's important not to stop talking to people because you're afraid they're going to rip you off. The vast majority of Sri Lankans that approach you will be perfectly honest, and simply keen to have a chat (or at least find out which country you are from – see p.64). Look out for the classic scams detailed in the box and, if you suspect that you are being set up, simply withdraw politely but firmly from the situation.

Voluntary work

There are all sorts of voluntary work projects in Sri Lanka – anything from teaching football to mucking out elephants – and a quick trawl through the Web will turn up dozens of possibilities. Note, however, that although volunteering is richly rewarding, it demands a real commitment of time and energy, and most placements cost at least as much as you'd expect to pay on an equivalent-length backpacking holiday on the island. The following organizations give a good idea of what's available.

i to i International Projects ☎ 0870/333 2332 (UK), ☎ 058/40050 (Ireland), ☎ 1-800/985-4864 or 303/765-5325 (US & Canada), ⓦ www.i-to-i.com. TEFL training provider operating voluntary teaching, conservation, business and medical schemes. Note that the website is only accessible on a PC (not a Mac).
Global Crossroad ☎ 0225/922-7854 (US), ⓦ www.globalcrossroad.com. Inexpensive two- to

twelve-week projects, including teaching English and working in orphanages and with rural women. From US$780 for two weeks to around US$1500 for twelve weeks.
Jetwing ⓦ jetwingeco.com. This leading ecotourism company (see p.113) runs several wildlife projects, including an ongoing bird-ringing project. They'll contribute towards expenses for volunteers with relevant experience.

Millennium Elephant Foundation This leading elephant sanctuary near Kandy (see p.243) offers three- and six-month placements (US$1450 and US$2100 respectively). Volunteers are expected to contribute with fundraising, website maintenance and public relations, as well as accompanying the foundation's mobile veterinary unit.

Teaching Abroad ☎01903/859911 (UK), ⊛www.teaching-abroad.co.uk. Recruits volunteers to teach English and other subjects, such as computer skills, and also offers medical/nursing

placements, journalistic and business work and conservation work, including placements at the Kosgoda Sea Turtle Project (see p.137). Three-month placements cost around £1400–1700.

Travellers Worldwide ☎01903/502595 (UK), ⊛www.travellersworldwide.com. Wide range of projects including English teaching, football coaching and placements at Colombo zoo and the famous Pinnewala Elephant Orphanage. Costs from around £1000 for one month or from £1400 for three months depending on the project.

Cultural values and etiquette

Sri Lanka is the most Westernized country in South Asia – superficially at least – and this, combined with the widespread use of English and the huge tourist industry, can often lure visitors into mistaking the island for something more familiar than it actually is. Scratch the surface, however, and examples of cultural difference can be found everywhere.

Behaving yourself

They are all very rich, and for a thing that costs one shilling they willingly give five. Also they are never quiet, going here and there very quickly, and doing nothing. Very many are afraid of them, for suddenly they grow very angry, their faces become red, and they strike any one who is near with the closed hand.

From *The Village in the Jungle,* by Leonard Woolf

Sri Lankans place great emphasis on **politeness** and **manners**, as exemplified by the fabulously courteous staff at top-end hotels, and raising your voice in a dispute is usually counterproductive and makes you look foolish and ill-bred.

Sri Lankans are very proud of their country – "Sri Lanka good?" is one of the questions most commonly asked of visitors – and they tend to take a simple and unquestioning pride in their island, its national achievements and (especially) their cricket team. Criticisms of Sri Lanka are not usually appreciated; remember that because something

about the country seems archaic, hopelessly bureaucratic or just plain stupid to you, it doesn't mean that Sri Lankans will agree – or appreciate hearing your views.

A few Western concepts have yet to make their way to the island. Nudity and toplessness are not permitted on any Sri Lankan beaches. Overt physical displays of affection in public are also frowned upon – Sri Lankan couples hide behind enormous umbrellas in the quiet corners of parks and botanical gardens. You should eat and shake hands with people using your right hand. For more on money and ethical bargaining, see p.29.

Temple etiquette

All visitors to Buddhist and Hindu temples should be appropriately dressed: this means taking off shoes and headgear and covering your shoulders and legs. Beachwear is not appropriate and can cause offence. In large temples the exact point at which you should take off shoes and hats is sometimes ambiguous; if in doubt, follow the locals. Never have yourself photographed with a Buddha image. Two traditional Buddhist observances are only loosely followed in Sri Lanka: the rule about not pointing your feet at a Buddha image is not as widely followed as in, say, Thailand, though you occasionally see people sitting in front of Buddhas with their legs neatly tucked under them. Equally, the traditional Buddhist rule that you should only walk around dagobas in a clockwise direction is not widely observed.

The same shoe and dress rules apply in Hindu temples (with a couple of twists). In some, non-Hindus aren't permitted to enter the inner shrine; in others, men are required to take off their shirt before entering, and women are sometimes barred entirely. In some temples you will be shown around by one of the resident monks and expected to make a donation. At other places, unofficial "guides" will sometimes materialize and insist on showing you round – for a consideration. Try not to feel pressured into accepting their services unless you want them.

Begging, bon-bons and schoolpens

Begging is far less widespread in Sri Lanka than in India. Whether or not you decide to give to beggars is of course a personal decision, though there's nothing wrong with handing out a few coins to the obviously old and infirm, who often congregate outside temples, churches and mosques. What is important, however, is that you do not contribute to a cycle of excessive dependence or create unrealistic expectations of foreign beneficence. For this reason, be sparing in the amounts you distribute (it's always better to give small amounts to lots of people rather than a big sum to a single unfortunate who catches your fancy) and never give handouts to children. In addition, avoid giving to beggars who specifically target tourists.

What is unfortunately widespread is a kind of pseudo-begging practised by perfectly well-to-do schoolchildren (and sometimes teenagers and even adults). This generally takes the form of requests for **bon-bons** (sweets), **schoolpens** or **money** (sometimes in the form of "one foreign coin?"). Sadly, this behaviour is the result of the misguided munificence of previous visitors, who have handed out all of the above in the mistaken belief that they are helping the local population, but who have instead created a culture of begging that both demeans Sri Lankans themselves and creates hassles for all the visitors who follow in their wake. If you really want to help local communities, make your donation to a local school or contribute to a recognized charitable agency working in the area.

"Where are you going?"

Western concepts of privacy and solitude are little understood or valued in Sri Lanka, whose culture is based on extended family groupings and closely knit village societies in which everyone knows everyone else's business. Natural curiosity usually expresses itself in the form of repeated **questions**, Most often "Where are you going?", closely followed by "What is your country?" and "What is your name?". These may drive you crazy if you're spending a long time in Sri Lanka, but it's important to stay polite and remember how potentially negative an impact any rudeness or impatience on your part will have on perceptions of foreigners, and on the treatment of those who follow in your wake. A smile (even through gritted teeth) and a short answer ("Just walking. England. John.") should suffice. If you really can't bear it any more, a little surreal humour usually helps relieve the tension ("To Australia. Mars. Lord Mountbatten.") without offending local sensibilities – Sri Lankans usually take great pleasure in being given first-hand proof of the generally recognized fact that all foreigners are completely mad.

Directory

DEPARTURE TAX A departure tax of Rs.1500 is levied when leaving the country.

ELECTRICITY 220–240V, 50 cycles A/C. Round, three-pin sockets are the norm.

GAY AND LESBIAN TRAVELLERS There is little understanding of gay issues in Sri Lanka – gays and lesbians are generally stigmatized and homosexuality is technically illegal (although no one has been arrested since 1950), so discretion is advised. There is a small and rather secretive scene, however. ⓦ www.geocities.com/srilankangay is a good first port of call for gays and lesbians, with info about contacts, events and meeting places.

GETTING MARRIED IN SRI LANKA Sri Lanka is one of the world's leading honeymoon destinations, and many couples go a step further and actually get married on the island – beach weddings are particularly popular. Arranging the ceremony independently and dealing with the attendant paperwork and bureaucracy can be difficult, however, and it's much easier to leave the details to a specialist operator. Most large hotels and a number of the tour operators listed on pp.11–12 & p.113 can arrange the whole wedding for you, including (if you fancy) extras like Kandyan drummers and dancers, plus optional elephants and a chorus of local girls. The tourist board publish a brochure, "Weddings and Honeymoons", which gives an idea of the sort of packages on offer.

OPENING HOURS Most businesses, including banks and government offices, work a standard five-day working week from Monday to Friday 9 or 9.30am to 5 or 5.30pm. Major post offices generally operate longer hours (typically 7am–9pm), and stay open on Saturdays as well. Many museums shut on Fridays, while Hindu temples stay shut until around 4–5pm, when they open for the evening puja.

Buddhist temples, by contrast, generally stay open all the time.

PHOTOGRAPHY Sri Lankans are very photo-friendly, and most people love having their picture taken – though obviously it's polite to ask. Some might expect to be paid, however, notably stilt fishermen and tea pickers in the highlands. You're not allowed to have your photo taken with a Buddha image; in addition, note that flash photography can potentially damage old murals; if you're asked not to take photos, don't. There are fairly well-equipped camera shops in most main towns, but if you're using slide or black and white film it's best to bring it from home. If you buy film in Sri Lanka, check the expiry date on the box and don't buy film which has been left lying around in the sun. Processing is widely available, though won't always match the standards you're used to back home.

TIME GMT plus six hours.

TIPPING Many hotels and restaurants add a ten percent service charge to the bill, which should be sufficient unless service has been especially good. If a service charge hasn't been added, a tip won't necessarily be expected, although it is of course always appreciated. If you tour the island by car, your driver will probably expect a tip of around ten percent, though you shouldn't feel obliged to give anything unless you're genuinely pleased with the service you've received. Unofficial "guides" will sometimes materialize to show you around temples and will expect a tip for their troubles (you might also be expected to make a donation to the temple itself).

TORCH Very useful during power cuts, to which Sri Lanka is extremely prone, especially during periods of low rainfall (much of the island's power is generated by hydroelectricity).

Guide

Guide

Colombo and the west coast

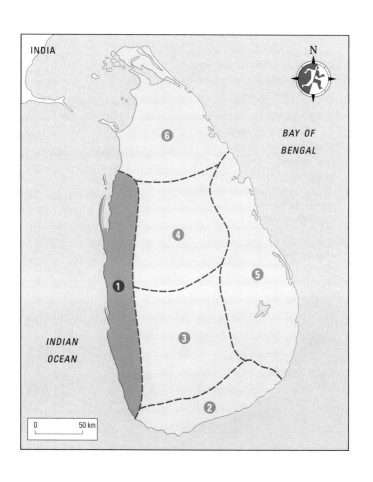

CHAPTER 1 # Highlights

* **Bawa hotels** Sample contemporary Sri Lankan style at its most seductive with a stay in one of the many west coast hotels designed by Geoffrey Bawa, the island's foremost twentieth-century architect. See p.38 & p.132

* **The Pettah** Colombo's absorbing bazaar district, stuffed full of every conceivable type of merchandise, from Japanese television sets to ayurvedic herbs. See p.86

* **Galle Face Green** A stroll along the oceanfront promenade here amongst the kite-flyers and food hawkers is the perfect way to end a day in Colombo; round off the evening with a sundowner at the historic *Galle Face Hotel*. See p.91

* **Gangaramaya and Seema Malaka** Step out of the urban melee of Colombo into the serene enclosures of these two contrasting Buddhist temples. See p.94

* **Colombo festivals** Mingle with the crowds of worshippers and elephants during Colombo's vibrant Vel festival or the spectacular Navam Perahera. See p.95

* **Eating in Colombo** The capital has Sri Lanka's best selection of places to eat by far, from cheap-and-cheerful local cafés to glitzy five-star palaces. See p.102

* **Bentota** With an idyllic swathe of sand and a string of elegant small-scale hotels, the southern end of Bentota beach offers an oasis of style and tranquillity amongst the brash west coast package resorts. See p.133

△ *Oruwa* boat, Negombo

Colombo and the west coast

S ri Lanka's **west coast** is the island's front door, and the point of arrival for all visitors to the country – indeed, until the long-awaited ferry service from India finally resumes, the international airport at Katunayake, just outside Colombo, provides the only link between Sri Lanka and the outside world. This is Sri Lanka at its most developed and populous – the busiest, brashest, noisiest and most westernized region in the country, home to the capital city and the principal coastal resorts, which have now all but fused into an unbroken ribbon of concrete and traffic which meanders along the seaboard for over a hundred kilometres. The west coast's **beaches** have long been at the heart of Sri Lanka's tourist industry, though relentless development has now overwhelmed much of the idyllic Indian Ocean scenery which brought the tourists here in the first place, and for most independent travellers, the region is largely a place to be negotiated en route to less spoilt parts of the island. A few oases survive amidst the development, however, and if you're after a touch of barefoot beachside luxury, the west coast has Sri Lanka's best selection of top-end places to stay, both large and small, many of which combine serenity with considerable style.

Situated about two-thirds of the way down the west coast, Sri Lanka's sprawling capital, **Colombo**, is usually low on visitors' list of priorities, but beneath the unprepossessing surface lies an intriguing and characterful city which offers a fascinating microcosm of contemporary Sri Lanka. North of Colombo is the lacklustre resort of **Negombo**, whose proximity to the airport makes it a popular first or last stop on many itineraries. The coast north of Negombo remains little visited and relatively undeveloped, punctuated by the workaday towns of **Chilaw** and **Puttalam** and bounded at its northern end by the vast natural wilderness of the **Wilpattu National Park**, only recently reopened after many years off limits due to its position near the frontline of the civil war.

South of the capital lie the island's main beach resorts. The principal areas – **Kalutara**, **Beruwala** and **Bentota** – are home to endless oversize hotels catering to vacationing Europeans on two-week packages. Pockets of serenity remain, even so, along with some characterful hotels and guest houses, while the lively little coastal town of **Aluthgama**, sandwiched between Beruwala and Bentota, offers a refreshing budget alternative to the big resorts at a fraction of the price. Further south lies shabby **Hikkaduwa**, Sri Lanka's original hippy hangout. Now all but choked on its own success, it does retain

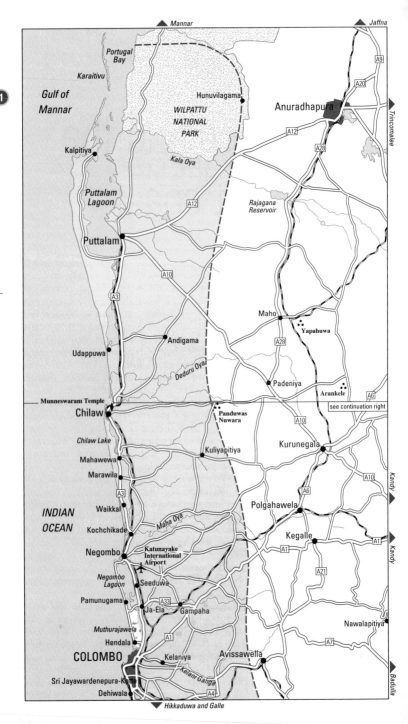

▲ *Mannar*
▲ *Jaffna*

A9

A20

Portugal Bay

Karaitivu

Gulf of Mannar

Hunuvilagama ●

Anuradhapura

WILPATTU NATIONAL PARK

A12

A28

Kalpitiya ●

Kala Oya

Puttalam Lagoon

A12

Rajagana Reservoir

● Puttalam

A10

A3

Maho ●

Yapahuwa

A28

● Andigama

A10

Udappuwa ●

Deduru Oya

Padeniya ●

Arankele

A6

Munneswaram Temple ●

see continuation right

Chilaw ●

Panduwas Nuwara

A10

Chilaw Lake

Kurunegala ●

Mahawewa ●

● Kuliyapitiya

Marawila ●

A6

A10

A3

Kandy ▶

Waikkal ●

Maha Oya

Polgahawela ●

INDIAN OCEAN

Kochchikade ●

Kegalle ●

A1

Negombo ●

Katunayake International Airport

A1

Kandy ▶

Negombo Lagoon

● Seeduwa

A21

Pamunugama ●

A33

Ja-Ela ● Gampaha

Nawalapitiya ●

Muthurajawela

Hendala ●

A1

COLOMBO

● Kelaniya

Avissawella ●

A7

Sri Jayawardenepura-Kotte ●

Kelani Ganga

Badulla ▶

Dehiwala ●

A4

▼ *Hikkaduwa and Galle*

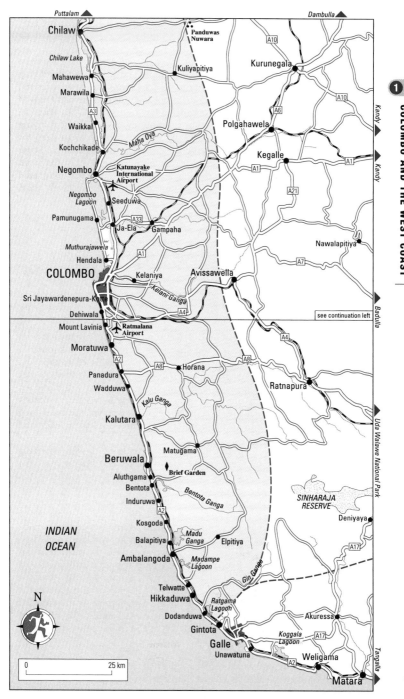

Puttalam

Chilaw

Chilaw Lake

Mahawewa

Marawila

A3

Waikkal

Kochchikade

Negombo

Negombo Lagoon

Pamunugama

Muthurajawela

Hendala

COLOMBO

Sri Jayawardenepura-Kotte

Dehiwala

Mount Lavinia

Moratuwa

A2

Panadura

Wadduwa

Kalutara

Beruwala

Aluthgama

Bentota

Induruwa

A2

Kosgoda

Balapitiya

Ambalangoda

INDIAN
OCEAN

N

0   25 km

A3

Panduwas Nuwara

Kuliyapitiya

Dambulla

A10

Kurunegala

A10

Polgahawela

A6

A1

Kegalle

A1

A21

Nawalapitiya

A7

Avissawella

A4

see continuation left

A4

Katunayake International Airport

Seeduwa

A33

Ja-Ela   Gampaha

A1

Kelaniya

Kelani Ganga

Ratmalana Airport

A8   Horana

A8

Ratnapura

Kalu Ganga

Matugama

◆ **Brief Garden**

Bentota Ganga

Elpitiya

Madu Ganga

Madampe Lagoon

Gin Ganga

SINHARAJA RESERVE

Deniyaya

A17

Telwatte

Hikkaduwa

Dodanduwa

Ratgama Lagoon

Gintota

Galle

Unawatuna

Akuressa

Koggala Lagoon

A17

Weligama

A2

Matara

Kandy

Kandy

Badulla

Uda Walawe National Park

Tangalla

Maha Oya

73

a certain down-at-heel charm and (by sleepy Sri Lankan standards at any rate) a refreshingly upbeat atmosphere, thanks to the backpackers who still flock here for cheap sun, sand and surf.

The **best time to visit** is from mid-October to mid-April, when the coast is blessed with perfect blue skies, rainfall is minimal, and swimming and diving conditions are good. During the rest of the year the monsoon downpours roll in. It's perfectly possible to visit during the monsoon months (the rain tends to come in short sharp bursts for no more than a few hours a day), but skies can be grey, many hotels and restaurants shut up shop, and swimming and diving become difficult – some places, such as Hikkaduwa, virtually go to sleep for the duration. **Getting around** the west coast is straightforward enough. There are regular train services along the coast, while endless buses ply the main coastal highway, the Galle Road – though the clogged traffic and antiquated trains mean that it can take a surprisingly long time to cover relatively short distances.

Colombo

Sri Lanka's frenetic capital, **COLOMBO**, seems totally out of proportion with the rest of the country. Congested and chaotic, it sprawls for sixty kilometres along the island's western seaboard in a bewildering straggle of suburbs and shantytowns which are home to over two million people. Colombo's vast extent and confusing layout make it difficult to get to grips with, however, while a lack of obvious charms means that it's unlikely to win many immediate friends, especially if (as is likely) your first taste is via the hour-long drive from the airport through the northern city's breeze-block suburbs and hooting files of weaving traffic.

There's plenty to enjoy beneath the unpromising exterior, though, especially if you're interested in getting behind the tourist clichés and finding out what makes contemporary Sri Lanka tick. Although specific sights are relatively thin on the ground, Colombo offers a heady admixture of Asian anarchy, colonial charm and modern chic. Shiny modern office blocks and air-conditioned boutiques rub shoulders with tumbledown local cafés and shops, while serene Buddhist shrines and colonial churches stand next to the garishly multi-coloured towers of Hindu temples. All of which offers a rewarding insight into the rich stew of races and religions which have gone into the making of this many-faceted city, and even if you're only on a short trip it's worth spending a day exploring the maze. Most of all, however, it's Colombo's energy which is likely to make the strongest impression, especially if you've spent time in the island's quieter backwaters – for sheer adrenaline, a walk through the crowded bazaars of the Pettah or a high-speed rickshaw ride amidst the kamikaze traffic of the Galle Road have no rival anywhere else in the country.

Some history

In the context of Sri Lanka's almost two and a half thousand years of recorded history, Colombo is a relative upstart. Situated on the delta of the island's fourth-longest river, the Kelani Ganga, the Colombo area only became important following the collapse of the great Sinhalese cities of Anuradhapura and Polonnaruwa in the north of the island, and the gradual southwards shift of power and population which followed from the thirteenth century onwards (see p.416). The first significant settlement in the area was 13km northeast of the modern city centre at **Kelaniya** (see p.102), site of a famous Buddhist shrine which had developed by the thirteenth century into a major town; the nearby settlement of **Kotte** (see p.102), 11km southeast of the modern city, served as the capital of the island's main Sinhalese lowland kingdom from the fourteenth to the sixteenth centuries.

Colombo itself began life as the minor fishing village of **Kalamba**, but despite the proximity of both Kelaniya and Kotte, its fortunes began to rise only after the arrival of the **Portuguese** in 1501. After being temporarily expelled by Muslims from Calicut in south India, the Portuguese returned in 1518, constructing the fort which subsequently formed the nucleus of modern Colombo. In 1597 they conquered and destroyed both Kotte and Kelaniya, swinging the pendulum of regional power decisively in Colombo's favour. Portuguese control of the city only survived until 1656, however, when the **Dutch** captured the fort after a seven-month siege. The Dutch remained for almost 150 years, rebuilding the fort, reclaiming land from the swampy delta using the system of canals which survive to this day, and creating new and spacious tree-lined suburbs.

In 1796, Colombo fell to the **British**, following Dutch capitulation to the French in the Napoleonic Wars. Colombo was made capital of Ceylon, transforming the city into a bustling mercantile centre, while an important new road link with Kandy further enhanced its prosperity. With the construction of a new harbour at the end of the nineteenth century, Colombo overtook Galle as the island's main port, becoming one of the great entrepôts of Asia and acquiring the sobriquet the "Charing Cross of the East" thanks to its location at the crossroads of Indian Ocean trade. The city retained its importance following **independence**, and has continued to grow at an exponential rate, attracting those displaced by poverty or ethnic strife from other parts of the island.

Arrival and information

Because getting in and out of Colombo is usually one big gridlocked drag – especially if you've just staggered off a long-haul flight – many visitors opt to spend their first night close to the airport in Negombo (see p.114) rather than venturing straight into the city. Entering or leaving the capital by train is smoother and generally faster than by road.

For full details of **moving on from Colombo** by bus or train, see p.111.

By air

Sri Lanka's only **international airport** is at Katunayake, 30km north of Colombo and 10km from Negombo. The modest arrivals terminal houses a **Sri Lanka Tourist Board** kiosk (open 24hr), where staff may be able to help you with general queries and hotel bookings, and various **bank** kiosks which change money at identical – and fairly competitive – rates. Several **tour operators** also have offices here, offering very cheap tours with car and driver – from as little as US$350 for two people for ten days, staying in cheap guest

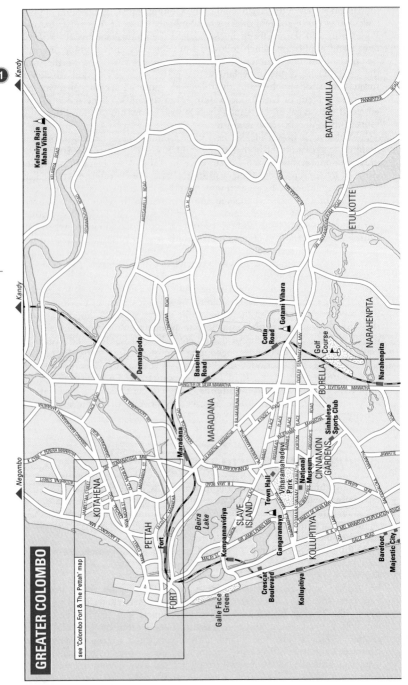

GREATER COLOMBO

see 'Colombo Fort & The Pettah' map

▲ Avissawella

MAHARAGAMA

Nawinna

Maharagama

Parliament
Building

Udahamulla

SRI JAYAWARDENEPURA

Sri Jayewardenepura
University

BORALESGAMUWA

NUGEGODA

Nugegoda

KOTTAWA ROAD

HIGH LEVEL ROAD

SUNETHRADEVI ROAD

PAMANKADA ROAD

ANDERSON ROAD

JAYANTHA WEERASEKARA MAWATHA

MAMADUWA ROAD

POLHENGODA ROAD

PEPILIYANA ROAD

HIGH LEVEL ROAD

DUTUGEMUNU STREET

KIRULAPONE AVENUE

BELLANTHARA ROAD

KOHUWALA ROAD

HOTANA ROAD

BORELLA ROAD

HAVELOCK
TOWN

BAMBALAPITIYA

HAVELOCK ROAD

DICKMANS ROAD

KIRULA ROAD

RAJA STREET

ASPATHANA MAWATHA

ELVITIGALA MAWATHA

THIMBIRIGASYAYA ROAD

POLHENGODA ROAD

WELLAWATTA

Wellawatta
Market

Chanuka
Guest House

Beach Wadiya

Wellawatta

SRI SARANANKARA ROAD

DUTUGEMUNU STREET

HILL STREET

Dehiwala
Zoo

Big John
Guest House

DEHIWALA

KANDAWALA ROAD

ANULA ROAD

SALAPORA ROAD

Dehiwala

MOUNT LAVINIA

HOTEL ROAD

HILL STREET

see 'Mount Lavinia' map

KANDAWALA ROAD

▼ Galle

▼ Galle

see 'Central Colombo' map

INDIAN
OCEAN

500 m

N

77

houses. However, they have a reputation for supplying pushy drivers (see p.35 for more on choosing a driver), and you're better off sorting out something in Negombo or Colombo, where there are plenty more reputable agents and guides.

Once you've passed through customs and immigration, you'll pounced on by one of the **airport taxi** drivers. You're unlikely to be ripped off but, equally, you're unlikely to be able to bargain down the quoted prices. Fares are roughly Rs.1200 for the tediously slow trip into Colombo (1hr); Rs.600 to Negombo (20min); and Rs.3000 to Kandy (3hr). There are no regular **buses** from the arrivals terminal. If you want a bus, you can either walk the 300m to the airport entrance and try to flag down a passing service on the main road (Negombo is left; Colombo is right); alternatively, take a tuktuk to **Katunayake bus station** (around Rs.50), from where there are regular buses to Colombo and Negombo.

In theory, you could catch a **train** from Katunayake to either Colombo or Negombo, though the station is a confusing 750m walk from the airport and services are very erratic (every 30min to 1hr 30min; 1hr to Colombo, 10min to Negombo). It's also possible to catch a **tuktuk** into Colombo, though it's not recommended, since you're likely to pass out from asphyxiation on the appallingly fumy main road long before you reach your destination.

By train and bus

Arriving by train, you'll come in at **Fort Railway Station** (though it's actually in the Pettah rather than Fort district). It's convenient for the cluster of top-end hotels in Fort and around Galle Face Green, though some way from the city's southern areas. Flocks of rickshaws wait for arriving passengers – a trip to anywhere in Fort shouldn't cost more than Rs.30–40, while the ride to hotels at the bottom of Galle Face Green (including the *Galle Face Hotel*, *Holiday Inn* and *Taj Samudra*) will cost about Rs.80. If you're staying further south in the city, you might prefer to pick up a suburban train (see p.80).

Arriving by bus, you'll come in at one of the city's three **bus stations** – Saunders Place, Bastian Mawatha or the Central Bus Stand – which lie side by side about 500m to the east of Fort station; lack of space in the terminals means that some services drop off passengers in the surrounding side streets. Wherever you're deposited, there are always plenty of tuktuks hanging around; fares are similar to those from Fort Railway Station.

Information

The city's **tourist office** (Mon–Fri 9am–4.45pm, Sat 9am–12.30pm; ℡011-243 7571, Ⓦwww.srilankatourism.org) is at 80 Galle Road, just south of the *Galle Face Hotel*. Staff can assist with general queries and may be able to help arrange accommodation and tours. They also dish out copies of the free monthly tourist guide, *Travel Lanka*, which contains listings of accommodation and services across the island, plus a free (but not very useful) accommodation guide and various glossy leaflets. Other free publications to look out for are *Leisure Times*, a free monthly listings magazine available from Barefoot (see p.109) with details of what's on in Colombo, and the excellent *Travel Sri Lanka*, available in bookshops and some other outlets (including Barefoot), which has excellent general articles and information about Sri Lanka.

Orientation

Colombo is a confusing city, and as there's no single focal point, it's more helpful to think of it as a collection of disparate neighbourhoods than a single, coherent urban space. At the heart of the old colonial city is the former administrative and financial centre of **Fort** district, while to the west lie the teeming markets of the **Pettah**, the city's main commercial district. South of Fort, **Galle Face Green** and **Slave Island** connect colonial Colombo with the city's modern districts, which are strung out along the sulphurous **Galle Road**, running south from chic **Kollupitiya** and **Cinnamon Gardens**, via **Bambalapitiya**, **Wellawatta** and **Dehiwela**, to the attractive beachside suburb of **Mount Lavinia**, 10km from the city centre.

Greater Colombo is divided into fifteen numbered suburbs, and districts are often identified by their **district code** rather than their name. The ones you're most likely to encounter are: Colombo 1 (Fort); Colombo 2 (Slave Island); Colombo 3 (Kollupitiya); Colombo 4 (Bambalapitiya); Colombo 6 (Wellawatta); Colombo 7 (Cinnamon Gardens); and Colombo 11 (Pettah).

A fruitful source of confusion is provided by recent changes to the city's **street names**. Dozens of streets have now lost their simple colonial originals and have been renamed in honour of various polysyllabic Sinhalese notables – four of the most important renamings are R.A. de Mel Mawatha (formerly Duplication Road); Ananda Coomaraswamy Mawatha (Green Path); de Soysa Circus (Lipton Circus); and Ernest de Silva Mawatha (Flower Road). We've used the new names throughout the guide, but have given the former name in brackets where helpful – many of these are still widely used. In addition, the vagaries of local **spelling** on street signs provide further pitfalls for the unwary. Thus, Campbell Road becomes "Camble", while Bagatelle Road becomes "Bagatalle Road" on one side of R.A. de Mel Mawatha (or Duplication Road) and "Bagathale Road" on the other, and so on.

City transport

Given how spread out Colombo is – not to mention the heat, humidity, traffic and crowds, which can make walking around the city a tiring experience – you'll need to make liberal use of **public transport** to explore the city. This is mainly likely to involve the frequent use of tuktuks, along with the occasional train or bus ride.

Tuktuks

Colombo has a superabundance of **tuktuks** – the recurrent calls of "Taxi?!" (as tuktuk drivers like to optimistically describe their vehicles) will quickly become one of the most familiar sounds of life in the city. **Fares** per kilometre are generally higher here than anywhere else in the country apart from Kandy – locals pay about Rs.20 per kilometre, though you'll have to bargain hard to get near this figure. You might well find it cheaper to order a metered taxi (see below).

Taxis

Taxis (often minivans rather than cars) can be ordered by phone or picked up outside the major hotels. There are plenty of firms operating metered **radio taxis**; these operate city-wide and charge around Rs.20 per kilometre in a minivan taxi, or about Rs.35 per kilometre in an a/c car – excellent value, and often cheaper than a tuktuk, unless you're a determined bargainer. Reputable companies for cars include 688 Cabs (℡011-268 8688) or Yellow Radio Cabs (℡011-294 2942); and Kangaroo (℡011-258 8588) or Excel (℡011-288 9889) for vans.

Buses

Endless lines of antiquated **buses** chunter along Colombo's major thorough-fares, though given the difficulty of working out routes and the cheapness of tuktuks, they're of little use to the casual visitor (and if you've got luggage, forget it). The only time you might want to catch a bus is to get up and down the Galle Road in the southern half of the city between Kollupitiya and Mount Lavinia. Buses tear up and down between Galle Face Green and the southern suburbs literally every few seconds; stops are marked by signs showing a picture of a bus set in a blue border.

Trains

Suburban **trains** are a useful way of getting around the southern part of the city, although they can get packed at rush hours (roughly Mon–Fri 7.30–9.30am & 4.30–6.30pm). Trains run roughly every half-hour (less frequently on Sundays) from Fort Railway Station, calling at Kollupitiya, Bambalapitiya, Wellawatta, Dehiwela and Mount Lavinia. The journey from Fort to Mount Lavinia takes around half an hour.

Accommodation

Colombo has plenty of top-end **hotels** aimed at business travellers, most of them located in Fort; the shortage of cheaper options reflects the small number of tourists visiting the city. It pays to **book in advance**, especially if you're planning on staying at one of the smaller guest houses, when you may need to reserve weeks ahead. Never turn up at a small family-run guest house unannounced; you're unlikely to find a vacancy and the owners won't appreciate having unexpected visitors on their doorsteps, especially if you arrive at some ungodly hour of the night or morning.

Given the fact that Colombo is so spread out, there's no obvious best area to stay in, and where you choose to base yourself largely depends on what you're planning to do in the city. Most of the top-end hotels, plus a couple of very basic cheapies, are located in **Fort** – convenient for exploring the northern areas, but very sleepy by 8pm and a long way from most of the best eating, drinking and shopping. The hotels at the southern end of **Galle Face Green** are generally a better option, conveniently equidistant between the northern and southern parts of the city, and offer the bonus of having the breezy Green right on your doorstep. There's a further selection of places – including some of the city's best budget options – scattered around the southern suburbs, mainly in the posh districts of **Cinnamon Gardens** and **Kollupitiya**.

On the southern edge of Colombo, the beachside suburb of **Mount Lavinia** is a popular city escape with locals and tourists alike and has heaps of accom-modation options, although many places are rather unsavoury. Having said that, you shouldn't go far wrong if you stick to the places listed here, and a stay at the *Mount Lavinia Hotel*, if you can afford it, is highly recommended.

Fort

The following places are marked on the map on p.89.

Ceylon Continental Janadhipathi Mw ☏ 011-242 1221, ⊛ www.colombocontinental.com. The smallest and most intimate of Colombo's five-stars, perched right on the oceanfront, with chintzy orangey-pink decor. Rooms are surprisingly cheap, if rather small (as are the double beds), though all have at least partial sea views. There's a big pool, gym, sauna and tennis courts, and the staff are frighteningly polite. ❼

Grand Oriental York St ☏ 011-232 0391, ⊛ www.grandorientalhotel.com. Famous old establishment, though little remains of its erstwhile colonial charm – service is poor and its setting at the end of a heavily policed and barricaded road is rather cheerless. Rooms are good value, however: characterless but spacious, with TV, fridge, a/c, hot water and town or harbour views. The restaurant and bar affords one of Colombo's best views. ❻

Hilton Sir Chittampalam A. Gardiner Mw ☏ 011-254 4644, ⊛ www.hilton.com. Colombo's classiest hotel, with stunning public areas and heaps of facilities including a swimming pool (a wallet-emptying Rs.880 for non-guests), tennis courts, six excellent restaurants and the city's best nightclub. Rooms are spread over nineteen floors and get more expensive the higher you go; for real pie-in-the-sky luxury, try the Executive Plus rooms on the top two floors. All have at least partial ocean views, though they're rather bland and not particularly big. ❾

YMCA Bristol St ☏ 011-232 5252. Dingy, labyrinthine institute offering a range of basic and erratically maintained doubles (couples accepted, but not single women) with or without private bathroom, and very cheap singles with clean communal bathrooms; there's also a men-only dormitory (Rs.125 per person). The Christian ambience is emphasized by the ban on alcohol, a 10pm curfew and a minatory picture of Jesus in the entrance. Fills up quickly with locals, so book ahead or arrive early. ❷

Galle Face Green

The following places are marked on the map on p.84.

Galle Face Hotel Galle Face Green ☏ 011-254 1010, ⊛ www.gallefacehotel.com. A famous Colombo landmark, this large colonial building is still the city's only real oceanfront hotel. The imposing entrance has bags of character, complete with antique lifts, liveried attendants and quasi-Kandyan architecture, and there's also a romantic seafront bar and restaurant. The rooms are rather musty and a bit shabby – avoid the extremely noisy ones overlooking the Galle Rd. ❼

Holiday Inn Sir M.M. Markar Mw ☏ 011-242 2001, ⊛ www.lanka.net/holiday. Tucked away in a quiet side street just off the bottom of Galle Face Green, this is reasonable value overall, and a decent alternative to the *Galle Face* if you're prepared to sacrifice atmosphere for comfort. The unusually spacious rooms come with safe, cable TV and phone. Facilities include a coffee shop, swimming pool (non-guests Rs.200), bar and a good Indian restaurant. ❽

Taj Samudra 25 Galle Face Centre Rd ☏ 011-244 6622, ⊛ www.tajhotels.com. Rivalling the *Hilton* as Colombo's smartest hotel, this immense five-star palace is set in huge, lush grounds straddling the southeastern side of Galle Face Green. Half of the three hundred rooms overlook the green and sea; they're comfortable if anonymous, and not particularly large. Facilities include a health club, squash and tennis courts, yoga classes, a business centre and swimming pool (guests only), plus several excellent restaurants. ❽

Kollupitiya

The following places are marked on the map on p.84.

Hotel Renuka & Renukah City 328 Galle Rd ☏ 011-257 3598, ⊛ www.lanka.net/renuka. Set in adjacent buildings (each with a different name), this smart, mid-range hotel is aimed at local business travellers, with modern a/c rooms, many with at least partial ocean views (though get one away from the noisy Galle Rd). There's a small swimming pool and a good basement restaurant. ❻

YWCA National Centre 7 Rotunda Gardens ☏ 011-232 8589, ✉ natywca@sltnet.lk. Soothingly tranquil place, with a rather convent-school atmosphere (lots of young girls live in dormitories here whilst studying in the capital) and clean, attractive private rooms with hot water set around a courtyard garden. Couples are admitted, but single men aren't. Good value, and a very convenient location. ❸

Slave Island

The following places are marked on the map on p.84.

Lake Lodge 20 Alvis Terrace ☎011-232 6443, ⓔlakelodge@eureka.lk. Pleasant guest house, with sixteen clean if rather faded rooms (some with a/c), tucked away at the end of a cul-de-sac in a quiet location near Beira Lake (it's right at the end of the road, and there's no sign – not even a street number). ❸

Nippon 123 Kumaran Ratnam Rd ☎011-243 1887, ⓕ233 2603. Situated in an interestingly down-at-heel part of town within the characterful, colonnaded Mannings Mansion of 1883. Rooms are spacious but variable: those with fans are a bit dog-eared (and some are downright shabby); those with a/c (US$5 extra) are smarter and good value – but avoid the noisy rooms overlooking the road at all costs. No single rates. ❸

Trans Asia 115 Sir Chittampalam A. Gardiner Mw ☎011-249 1000, ⓦwww.transasiahotel.com. Set in a slightly out-of-the-way location next to an arm of the sluggish Beira Lake between Fort and Slave Island, this big and rather ugly five-star is less appealing than its rivals, although the rooms are larger and it does boast a couple of excellent restaurants. ❼

YWCA International Guest House 393 Dr A. Colvin A. De Silva Mw (Union Place) ☎011-232 4181. Atmospheric old Dutch colonial mansion with antique furniture scattered around the veran-dah and a plant-filled garden, and with plenty of genuine, if rather ramshackle, olde-worlde charm. The twenty rooms are basic but clean, though a bit expensive for what you get. ❸

Cinnamon Gardens

The following places are marked on the map on p.84.

Parisare 97/1 Rosmead Place (no sign; the bell is to the right of the big iron gates) ☎011-269 4749, ⓔsunsep@visualnet.lk. Set in an unusually designed family house – there seem to be no walls – surrounded by lush gardens in a very quiet loca-tion in the heart of Cinnamon Gardens. The three rooms are simple but adequate, and there's solar-heated water, a nice roof terrace and delightful owners. Good single rates. Advance reservations essential. ❸

Mr Samarasinghe's 53/19 Torrington Ave ☎011-250 2403, ⓔranjitksam@hotmail.com.

Three very comfortable and homely a/c rooms (one with a shared bathroom) in a modern family house. Ring in advance; and note that it's not actu-ally on Torrington Ave, but on a side road just off it to the east. ❹

Wayfarers Inn 7 Rosmead Place (no sign) ☎011-269 3936, ⓔwayfarer@slt.lk. Set in a quiet residential area, this attractive colonial-style guest house has three comfortable doubles (two with a/c) with TV and hot water, plus one economy room and one studio apartment with kitchen. No single rates. Advance booking almost always necessary. ❸–❺

Bambalapitiya and Havelock Town

The following places are marked on the map on p.84.

Colombo House 26 Charles Place, Bambalapitiya ☎011-257 4900, ⓔcolombohse@eureka.lk. This attractive old mansion boasts a superb location amidst some of Colombo's smartest and leafiest streets – very quiet but very central. The four rooms (three doubles and one triple) are rather plain and old-fashioned, but perfectly comfortable. No single rates. ❹

Empress Hotel 383 R.A. de Mel Mw, Bambalapitiya ☎011-257 4930, ⓔhaesong@sltnet.lk. Slightly shabby lower mid-range hotel in a convenient downtown location. All rooms have phone, Star TV and hot water, and all but two have a/c. It's all a bit ramshackle, although ongoing renovations may mean that the establish-ment exudes a less obvious sense of falling to bits in future. ❹.

Havelock Place Bungalow 6 Havelock Place, Havelock Town ☎011-258 5191, ⓦwww .bungalow.lk. One of Colombo's most alluring places to stay, set in a pair of intimate and stylishly converted colonial villas which combine old-fashioned charm with all modern comforts. There's also a small pool, a beautiful garden and a peaceful café-restaurant. ❽

KSP Guest House 39 Shrubbery Gardens, Bambalapitiya ☎011-259 6461. Right by the sea at the end of a quiet side street, this is aimed squarely at locals, but the four sea-facing rooms (with optional a/c) are bright, cheery and good value, with fine views. ❷

Mrs Settupathy's 23/2 Shrubbery Gardens (on the left directly behind the Church of Christ), Bambalapitiya ☎011-258 7964. Cosy and good-value family guest house, with six spacious, clean rooms (three have hot water; one has a/c), and a nice upstairs communal seating area. ❷

Ottery Tourist Inn 29 Melbourne Ave, Bambalapitiya ⓣ011-258 3727. Comatose guest house close to the seafront. It looks like it hasn't had a guest for years, but despite the mild shabbiness and neglect, it's not without a sort of peaceful, grubby charm. The mothball-scented rooms are bright, reasonably spacious, and you can't complain at the price, which is about as cheap as it gets in Colombo. Good single rates. ❷

Wellawatta and Dehiwela

The following places are marked on the map on p.76.

Big John Guest House 47 Albert Place, Dehiwala ⓣ011-271 5027, ⓔselwyna@slt.lk. Pleasant modern guest house in a totally out-of-the-way location midway between Wellawatta and Mount Lavinia. Very good value, and a useful standby if you can't get in anywhere else. No single rates. ❷

Chanuka Guest House 29 Frances Rd, Wellawatta ⓣ011-258 5883. Close to the seafront and Wellawatta Station, with five large, simple but perfectly decent rooms; nothing special, but the cheapest in the city. ❶

Mount Lavinia

The following places are marked on the map on p.101.

Blue Seas 9/6 De Saram Rd ⓣ011-271 6298. Homely modern guest house in a quiet location, though the rooms are a bit musty, and not quite as nice as those at similarly priced *Ivory Inn*. Good single rates. ❷

Cottage Gardens 42–48 College Ave ⓣ011-271 9692. Five large cottages in a beautiful and very private walled garden. Each sleeps two, and has a kitchenette, high ceilings, elegant cane furniture and a wooden slatted verandah with bamboo blinds. ❹

Ivory Inn 21 De Saram Rd ⓣ011-271 5006. One of Mount Lavinia's best cheapies, with sixteen spotless, nicely furnished rooms with private balcony (but no hot water) in an attractive modern red-brick and timber building in a quiet location. Breakfast included. ❷

Mount Lavinia Hotel ⓣ011-271 5221, ⓦwww.mountlaviniahotel.com. Famous old hotel where the bellboys and commissionaires still put on their Kaiser Bill helmets or solar topees to welcome guests. Most rooms are in the modern Sea & Garden Wing or the slightly smarter, more expensive Bay Wing – all have sea views, a/c, TV, phone, minibar and private balcony. There are also a few much cheaper, rather musty non-a/c rooms in the gorgeously atmospheric original mansion, with its beautiful old wooden staircase and colonnaded corridors illuminated by old brass lamp fittings. There's also a biggish swimming pool and a huge swathe of idyllic private beach if you want to escape from the hoi polloi (non-guests can use both pool and private beach for Rs.300). ❻–❽

Rivi Ras Hotel 50 De Saram Rd ⓣ011-271 7786. Unusual but attractive-looking place, with its series of detached red-brick colonnaded buildings set in very spacious gardens. Rooms are large and minimally but stylishly furnished in quasi-colonial style; some have bathtubs, all have hot water. Poor service, though, and no single rates. ❸

Tropic Inn 6 College Ave ⓣ011-273 8653, ⓔabdeen@mail.lgo.lk. Pleasant, small hotel, with attractive wrought-iron and latticed-wood effects. Rooms are clean, modern and nicely furnished; all have hot water, and a/c is available for an extra US$4. Breakfast included. ❸

The City

Colombo musters few specific sights but offers plenty of atmosphere and sometimes quirky character, especially if you're prepared to spend some time unravelling the various contradictory strands which go into the making of this surprisingly cosmopolitan city – it's definitely a place which grows on you the longer you stay, and is worth a day out of even the shortest itinerary. At the heart of the city, the moribund and bomb-afflicted **Fort** district offers a stark reminder of the conflicts which have beset modern Sri Lanka, while to

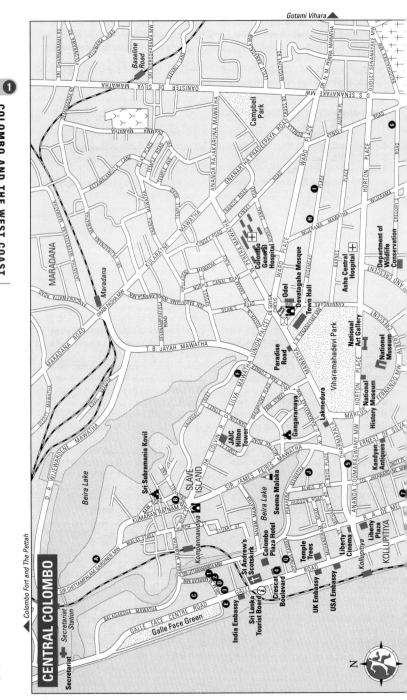

CENTRAL COLOMBO

Colombo Fort and The Pettah

Gotami Vihara

Secretariat
Secretariat Station

Galle Face Green

BALAMAKSHA MAWATHA

GALLE FACE CENTRE ROAD

India Embassy

Sri Lanka Tourist Board

Crescent Boulevard

St Andrew's Scotskirk

Colombo Plaza Hotel

Temple Trees

UK Embassy

USA Embassy

Liberty Cinema

Liberty Plaza

KOLLUPITIYA

Kollupitiya

Beira Lake

Seema Malaka

Gangaramaya

Lakmedura

Kandyan Antiques

National History Museum

National Museum

National Art Gallery

Viharamahadevi Park

Town Hall

Devatagaha Mosque

Odel

Colombo General Hospital

Asha Central Hospital

Department of Wildlife Conservation

Campbell Park

Baseline Road

Maradana

MARADANA

MARADANA ROAD

Beira Lake

SLAVE ISLAND

Sri Subramania Kovil

JAIC Hilton Tower

Paradise Road

Kompannavidiya

T B JAYAH MAWATHA

N

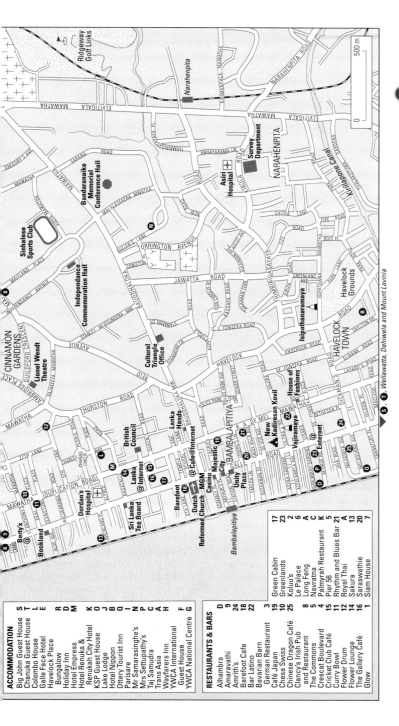

S, T, Wellawatta, Dehiwela and Mount Lavinia

ACCOMMODATION

Big John Guest House	S
Chanuka Guest House	T
Colombo House	L
Galle Face Hotel	E
Havelock Place	
Bungalow	R
Holiday Inn	D
Hotel Empress	M
Hotel Renuka &	
Renukah City Hotel	K
KSP Guest House	O
Lake Lodge	J
Hotel Nippon	B
Ottery Tourist Inn	Q
Parisare	I
Mr Samarasinghe's	
Mrs Settupathy's	N
Taj Samudra	P
Trans Asia	C
Wayfarers Inn	A
YWCA International	H
Guest House	F
YWCA National Centre	G

RESTAURANTS & BARS

Alhambra	D	Green Cabin	17
Amaravathi	9	Greenlands	23
Amrith's	24	Kolulu's	2
Barefoot Cafe	18	Le Palace	6
Bar Latino	22	Long Feng	A
Bavarian Barn		Navratna	C
German Restaurant	3	Palmyrah Restaurant	K
Café Japan	19	Pier 56	5
Chesa Swiss	10	Rhythm and Blues Bar	21
Chinese Dragon Café	25	Royal Thai	A
Clancy's Irish Pub		Sakura	13
and Restaurant	8	Saraswathie	20
The Commons	4	Siam House	1
Crescat Boulevard			
Cricket Club Café	11		
Curry Bowl			
Flower Drum	12		
Flower Lounge	14		
The Gallery Café	16		
Glow	7		

85

the east and south lie the bustling mercantile district of the **Pettah** and the engaging temples and old-fashioned street life of **Slave Island**. From here, it's a short walk or tuktuk ride to **Galle Face Green** – perfect, after a hard day's exploring, for an evening stroll along the seafront promenade and a sundowner at the historic *Galle Face Hotel*.

South of the green, **Galle Road** runs through the suburbs of **Kollupitiya** and **Bambalapitiya**, the heart of the modern city, and home to many of Colombo's best shopping and eating venues. Inland, the leafy streets of **Cinnamon Gardens** provide further places to stay, eat and drink, and are also home to the tropical oasis of the **Viharamahadevi Park** and the city's excellent **National Museum**.

Fort

Fort district lies at the heart of colonial Colombo, occupying (as its name suggests) the site of the now-vanished Portuguese defences. Under the British, Fort developed into the centrepiece of the colonial capital, adorned with handsome Neoclassical buildings and boasting all the necessities of expatriate life in the tropics, right down to the inevitable clocktower and statue of Queen Victoria. Following independence, Fort retained its position as Colombo's administrative and financial hub until the onset of the civil war, when repeated LTTE attacks – most notably the massive **bomb** that was detonated outside the Central Bank on Janadhipathi Mawatha in 1996 – all but killed off the life of the district. Despite these reverses, the area retains something of its former commercial importance, with myriad banks, airline offices, a clutch of five-star hotels and an optimistically modernist skyline (presided over by the two soaring towers of the unfortunately named World Trade Center), though these tokens of progress give little indication of the ravages of the war years. At street level, central Fort remains one of Sri Lanka's strangest urban spaces, its moribund and eerily deserted streets lined with the grandiose shells of semi-derelict nineteenth-century buildings, and carved up by security barriers and wire-mesh fences into a perplexing maze of blocked-off streets and security checkpoints – even in the wake of the ceasefire, almost half the district remains closed to visitors, and it's impossible to walk far before being waved back by gun-toting soldiers.

Around the Clocktower

Thanks to the presence of the President's Palace, almost the entire western side of Fort (effectively, everything between Janadhipathi Mawatha and the seafront Chaitiya Road) is currently closed to visitors. Aside from the places described here, the area's few sites of interest are now largely out of bounds. More or less at the centre of the district is the quaint **Clocktower-lighthouse**, ignominiously hemmed in on three sides by security fences and now a rather forlorn sight. The clocktower was originally constructed in 1857, apparently at the behest of the punctilious wife of governor Henry Ward as a result of her exasperation with Oriental standards of time-keeping. Ten years later, a lighthouse-style beacon was constructed on top of the clock, and it served simultaneously as time-keeper and as a signal for approaching shipping for a century until the surrounding buildings grew so high that they blocked out the lighthouse's beam (a new lighthouse now stands on the seafront just to the west). East of the clocktower, **Chatham** and **Hospital streets** are a hopeless mix of variously derelict buildings, dotted with the shops of jewellers, travel agents and insistent moneychangers, whose shouts of "Change dollar?" are usually the only sign of life hereabouts.

At the time of writing, the area north of the clocktower was closed to the general public, with the only exit from the clocktower east along Chatham Street to **York Street**, at the edge of the high-security zone. On the far side of the crash barriers, something approaching normal Sri Lankan street life resumes, with rushing traffic (banned from central Fort) and occasional hawkers flogging fake designer jeans, fluorescent underwear and Mickey Mouse watches under the graceful colonial arcades that flank the west side of the road. A block north of here, the corner at the junction with Mudalige Mawatha is dominated by the stolidly mercantile frontage of **Cargills** department store, whose expansive red-brick facade is one of Fort's most famous landmarks. Inside, the wood-panelled fittings and display cases look as though they haven't changed since the store's opening in 1906, though the disconcertingly bare shelves appear not to have been restocked since independence.

Immediately north of Cargills, turn left along Sir Baron Jayatilaka Mawatha. The end of the road is blocked off, though you can just make out the white, neoclassical **President's House** and the guards outside, who still wear the brilliant red tunics first sported by their colonial predecessors.

The port area

Continuing north from Cargills, York Street becomes increasingly down-at-heel before reaching Colombo's **port**, hidden behind high walls and strictly off limits. Until the early twentieth century, the island's main port was Galle, but Colombo's improved road and rail links with the rest of the country and Sri Lanka's strategic location on Indian Ocean sea routes between Europe, Asia and Australasia encouraged the British to invest in a major overhaul of the city's rather unsatisfactory harbour, during which they constructed three new breakwaters (the largest, built in 1885, is over a kilometre long). Opposite the main entrance to the port stands the famous old **Grand Oriental Hotel** – passengers arriving in Colombo would stagger straight off their liner into the palatial hotel foyer, to collapse over a revivifying cocktail. Little of the establishment's former colonial splendour remains, though its *Harbour Room* restaurant-bar (photography prohibited) affords marvellous port views. The area east of the hotel is currently out of bounds, meaning that you are unable to visit **St Peter's Church**, almost next door, whose cavernous nave was converted from part of the old Dutch governor's banqueting hall in 1804.

Southern Fort and Marine Drive

Heading straight back down York Street for 500m brings you to the southern end of Fort, where modern high-rises offer a sharp contrast to the district's otherwise colonial appearance. Southern Fort is dominated by a triumvirate of five-star **hotels** (see p.81) the slender, cylindrical **Bank of Ceylon Tower**, and the twin towers of the **World Trade Center**, whose glassy facades and expanses of bland concrete embody Sri Lanka at its most forward-looking and internationalist. These prestigious commercial symbols were repeatedly targeted by LTTE bombers during the civil war, and although most of the damage has now been patched up, the bombed-out remains of the buildings opposite the top end of Janadhipathi Mawatha provide a bleak reminder of the events of June 31, 1996, when a truck laden with 200kg of explosives was exploded outside the Central Bank, killing 91 people and injuring over 1500 – the most devastating of all the LTTE's various attacks against Colombo.

From the *Ceylon Continental* hotel, Chaitiya Road (Marine Drive) sweeps north along the ocean front, passing the modern lighthouse en route to the **Sambodhi Chaitiya**, a huge dagoba on stilts, built in 1956 to mark the

2500th anniversary of the Buddha's death – resembling an enormous lava lamp, this thoroughly peculiar structure is quite the oddest thing in Colombo. Just beyond here, the newly opened **Maritime Museum** (daily 3–7pm; free) has some rather tenuous exhibits featuring large (and largely conjectural) models of the ships on which various significant personages – Prince Vijaya, Fa-Hsien, Ibn Battuta – arrived in the island, plus later colonial vessels, miscellaneous bits of maritime bric-a-brac (including an enormous sling once used to load elephants onto ships) and some unintentionally scary life-size models of Sri Lankan fishermen.

You're now close to the main entrance to the port and the *Grand Oriental* hotel, though roadblocks just beyond the Maritime Museum bar your progress, meaning that (for the time being at least) you'll have to retrace your steps back to the *Ceylon Continental*.

The Pettah and Kotahena

East of Fort, the helter-skelter bazaar district of the **Pettah** is Colombo's most absorbing area, and feels quite unlike anywhere else in Sri Lanka. The crush and energy of the gridlocked streets, with merchandise piled high in tiny shops and on the pavements, holds an undeniable, chaotic fascination, although exploring can be a slow and rather exhausting process, made additionally perilous by the barrow boys and porters who charge through the crowds pulling or carrying enormous loads and threatening the heads and limbs of unwary tourists.

Shops in the Pettah are still arranged in the traditional **bazaar layout**, with each street devoted to a different trade: Front Street, for example, is full of bags, suitcases and shoes; 1st Cross Street is devoted to hardware and electrical goods; 3rd Cross Street and Keyzer Street are stuffed with colourful fabrics, and so on. The wares on display are fairly mundane – unless you're a big fan of spare car parts, Korean household appliances or fake Barbie dolls – although traces of older and more colourful trades survive in places, particularly on the quieter eastern side of the district, where you'll find the goldsmiths of Sea Street, the ayurveda merchants of Gabo's Lane and the spice merchants of 4th Cross Street.

Unlike the rest of Colombo, the district retains a strongly **Tamil** (the name Pettah derives from the Tamil word *pettai*, meaning village) and **Muslim** flavour, as evidenced by its many pure veg and Muslim restaurants, quaint mosques, Hindu temples and colonial churches (many Sri Lankan Tamils are Christian rather than Hindu). Even the people look different here, with Tamil women in gorgeous saris, Muslim children dressed entirely in white and older men in brocaded skull caps – a refreshing change from the boring skirts and shirts which pass muster in the rest of the city.

Fort Railway Station to the Jami ul-Aftar

On the south side of the Pettah stands Colombo's principal train terminus, **Fort Railway Station**, a rambling Victorian barn of a building, its footbridges emblazoned with garbled instructions on correct passenger etiquette ("FOOTBOARD TRAVELLING IS DANGEROUS BE IN THE COMPARTMENT AND MAKE OTHERS TOO COMFORTABLE"). In front of the station stands a statue of **Henry Steel Olcott** (1842–1907), the American Buddhist and co-founder (with Madame Blavatsky, the celebrated Russian clairvoyant and spiritualist), of the Theosophical Society, a quasi-religious movement which set about promoting Asian philosophy in the West

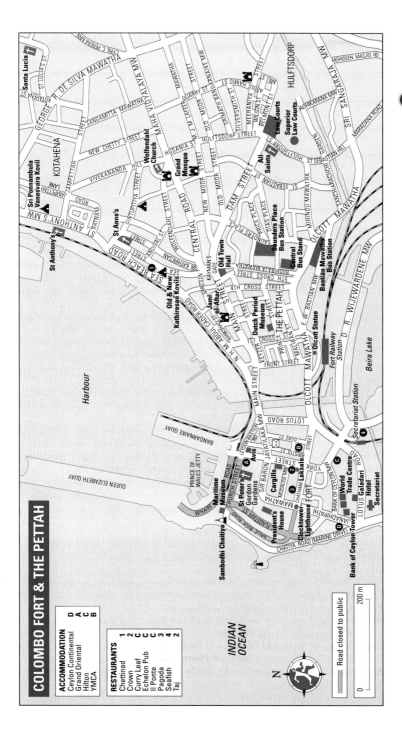

COLOMBO FORT & THE PETTAH

ACCOMMODATION
Ceylon Continental	D
Grand Oriental	A
Hilton	C
YMCA	B

RESTAURANTS
Chettinad	1
Crown	2
Curry Leaf	C
Echelon Pub	C
Il Ponte	C
Pagoda	3
Sealish	4
Taj	2

Road closed to public

0   200 m

INDIAN OCEAN

N

and reviving Oriental spiritual traditions in the East to protect them from the attacks of European missionary Christianity. The society's utopian (if rather vague) objectives comprised a mixture of the scientific, the social, the spiritual and the downright bizarre: the mystical Madame Blavatsky, fount of the society's more arcane tenets, believed that she had the ability to levitate, render herself invisible and communicate with the souls of the dead, as well as asserting that the Theosophical Society was run according to orders received from a group of "masters" – disembodied tutelary spirits who were believed to reside in Tibet. In 1880, Blavatsky and Olcott arrived in Ceylon, formerly embracing Buddhism and establishing the **Buddhist Theosophical Society**, which became one of the principal driving forces behind the remarkable worldwide spread of Buddhism during the twentieth century. Olcott spent many of his later years touring the island, organizing Buddhist schools and petitioning the British colonial authorities to respect Sri Lanka's religious traditions, though his most visible legacy is the multicoloured Buddhist flag (composed of the five colours of the Buddha's halo) which he helped design, and which now decorates temples across the island.

A couple of blocks north of the station on Prince Street, amongst some of the most densely packed of the Pettah's bazaars, the **Dutch Period Museum** (Mon–Thurs, Sat & Sun 9am–5pm; Rs.65, camera Rs.60) occupies the old Dutch town hall, a fine colonnaded building of 1780. The mildly interesting displays on the Dutch colonial era feature the usual old coins, Kandyan and Dutch artefacts, military junk and dusty European furniture, plus a couple of miserable-looking waxworks of colonists dressed in full velvet and lace despite the sweltering heat. Look out too for the picture of the devilishly good-looking Gerard Hulft, commander of the Dutch forces at the siege of Colombo in 1656, during which he was killed – his consolation was to have the nearby suburb of Hulftsdorf named after him. The main attraction, however, is the wonderfully atmospheric mansion itself, whose groaning wooden floors and staircases, great pitched roof and idyllic garden offer a beguiling glimpse into the lifestyle enjoyed by the eighteenth century's more upwardly mobile colonists.

Return to 2nd Cross Street and fight your way north for two blocks to **Main Street**, the district's principal thoroughfare, usually a solidly heaving bedlam of vehicles and pedestrians, with porters weaving through the throng pushing carts piled high with every conceivable type of merchandise. On the far side of the road is Colombo's most eye-catching mosque, the **Jami ul-Aftar**, a gloriously kitsch red-and-white construction of 1909 which rises gaudily above the cluttered shops of Main Street like a heavily iced cake.

The Old Town Hall to Sea Street

Continue east from the Jami ul-Aftar past a memorably malodorous fish market before reaching the intersection known as **Kayman's Gate** – the name probably refers to the crocodiles which were once kept in the canals surrounding Slave Island and in the fort moat to deter slaves from attempting to escape. Kayman's Gate is dominated by the fancifully Moorish-style **Old Town Hall** of 1873. Following an incarnation as a public market, the building was restored and reopened, in 1984, as a now-defunct municipal museum. The wrought-iron market building to one side still houses various marooned pieces of industrial and municipal hardware – including a steamroller, old street signs, and a former van of the Colombo Public Library – which you can peak at through the railings. You may be able to talk your way into the museum itself, up the Burma teak staircase to the old council chambers, whose austere wooden fittings and stalled fans exude a positively *Marie Celeste*-like charm.

△ Sea Street, The Pettah

The small room next door houses a petrified huddle of waxwork figurines sitting around a table re-enacting a council meeting of yesteryear – unquestionably one of Colombo's most surreal sights.

The fruit and veg sellers who line the western side of the town hall building make this one of the most photogenic sections of the Pettah, while just behind lies another half-submerged remnant of colonial times in the form of an elaborate wrought-iron **market building**, now occupied by a miscellany of shops. Just behind here, **4th Cross Street** is usually full of colourful lorries loading and unloading: great sacks of chillies clutter the pavements, while merchants sit behind huge ledgers and piles of spices inside the picturesque little office-warehouses that line the street.

North of the Town Hall, the crowds begin to thin. The south side of **Gabo's Lane** is home to a few easily missed shops selling ayurvedic ingredients: outlandish-looking sacks and pallets sit outside shops stuffed with bark, twigs and other strange pieces of vegetable matter. North of here, **Sea Street**'s eye-catching selection of fluorescent Sinhala signs advertise a long line of tiny jewellers shops, usually full of local women haggling over ornate gold rings, earrings and necklaces. Sea Street's middle section is dominated by the colourful **New Kathiresan** and **Old Kathiresan kovils**, dedicated to the war god Skanda and the starting point for the annual Vel Festival (see p.51). The temples' three gateways fill one side of the street with a great clumpy mass of Hindu statuary: the middle gateway is the most interesting, supported by six green dragons which look more like stunned frogs.

Kotahena

Continuing north along Sea Street and St Anthony's Mawatha, you enter the adjacent suburb of **Kotahena**, home to numerous colonial churches and small but brightly coloured Hindu temples. Walking north along St Anthony's Mawatha, you'll pass a string of colourful shops selling Hindu and Christian religious paraphernalia before reaching **St Anthony's Church**, where people of all faiths come to pay homage to a statue of St Anthony which is said to work miracles in solving family problems.

If you've still got some energy left, a further clutch of sights awaits. A fifteen-minute walk from St Anthony's, along Jampettah, Kotahena and St Lucia's streets, lies the cathedral of **Santa Lucia**, perhaps the most imposing church in Sri Lanka. Built between 1873 and 1910, and sporting a huge grey classical facade inspired by St Peter's in Rome, it seats some six thousand people, though not since the pope conducted a service here in 1994 has it been even half full. The tombs of three French bishops of Colombo are about as exciting as it gets inside. Two further Neoclassical buildings – a Benedictine monastery and a convent – sit by the cathedral, creating an unexpectedly impressive architectural ensemble in this slightly out-of-the-way corner of the city.

Back at St Anthony's, retrace your steps along Jampettah Street, then head south up Vivekananda Hill to reach the Dutch Reformed **Wolfendhal** (or Wolvendaal) **Church** of 1749, Colombo's oldest and one of Sri Lanka's most interesting Dutch relics. The rather severe neoclassical exterior conceals an attractive period-piece interior complete with old tiled floor, simple stained glass, wicker seating and wooden pews, organ and pulpit. There are lots of memorials on the walls, plus numerous finely carved eighteenth-century floor tablets in the south transept commemorating assorted Dutch officials, including various governors whose remains were moved here from Fort in 1813. The whole structure exudes a sense of beautiful quiet and longevity which seems to have survived in a curious bubble amidst the ramshackle surrounding streets.

The area just south of here is dotted with a number of small, fanciful-looking mosques – the largest (but plainest) is the **Grand Mosque** on New Moor Street, the most important in the city, which hides behind shyly latticed orange walls. The large and striking modern building with the hat-shaped roof you can see from here is the **Superior Law Courts** (the original Neoclassical courts stand stolidly next door, two dumpy little buildings with dour Doric facades). Next to it rises the soaring spire of the pale grey Gothic Revival church of **All Saints**.

Galle Face Green

Running along the sea front south of Fort, the grassy sweep of **Galle Face Green** is one of the city's few open public spaces, bounded to the north by the modern towers of Fort and to the south by the venerable facade of the *Galle Face Hotel*. The green was created by Sir Henry Ward, governor from 1855 to 1860 (an easily missed memorial plaque to him stands halfway along the prom-enade, in which the green is "recommended to his successors in the interest of the Ladies and Children of Colombo") and such is its place in the city's affec-tions that even the railway line south – which elsewhere runs straight down the coast – was rerouted inland to avoid it. The Fort end of the green is bounded by the ponderous Neoclassical **Secretariat**, now dwarfed by the *Galadari* hotel and the World Trade Center towers, which rise behind it. Statues of independent Sri Lanka's first four prime ministers stand in front; in the centre is a purposefully moustachioed D.S. Senanayake, the first post-independence PM, who died in 1952 from injuries sustained when he fell from his horse on the Green.

A turn along the Green's seafront promenade makes a pleasantly salty stroll, with the waves crashing a few feet below and breezy views along the coast and out to sea, where lines of gargantuan tankers and container ships line up wait-ing to enter the harbour. Late in the day is the best time to visit, when half the city seems to come here to gossip, fly kites and eat the curious-looking snacks served up by the line of hawkers stretched out along the sea front.

Unfortunately, the green is also plagued with **con artists** preying on tourists staying at the various nearby hotels – see p.61 for more details.

Slave Island

Immediately east of Galle Face Green is the area known as **Slave Island** – not actually an island, it's encircled on three sides by **Beira Lake**, an inland waterway built by the Dutch whose various sections are connected by stagnant, pea-green canals. This is a ramshackle but personable district, dotted with a number of intriguing religious structures and retaining colourful pockets of local life. The name dates back to its Dutch-era title, **Kaffir Veldt**, from the African slaves (Kaffirs) brought to Sri Lanka by the Portuguese in 1630, and who were used by the Dutch to build their fort – at one time there were as many as four thousand slaves in the city. After a failed insurrection in the seventeenth century, the Dutch insisted that all slaves were quarantined overnight in the Kaffir Veldt, and stocked the surrounding canals and lake with crocodiles in order to discourage escapes.

The heart of Slave Island, around the intersection of Dr A. Colvin A. De Silva Mawatha (still universally known as Union Place) and Kumaran Ratnam Road, preserves a ramshackle charm – flanked by halal cafés and neat piles of fruits and vegetables on market stalls, **Malay Street** is particularly appealing. The area is sprinkled with places of worship, including several fairly undistinguished mosques built during the British colonial era for soldiers from Malaya serving in the British army, who were garrisoned on the island.

Indian troops were also stationed here, and it was for them that **Sri Subramania Kovil**, one of central Colombo's most imposing Hindu temples, was built. The entrance, just off Kumaran Ratnam Road, is marked by a towering gopuram, a great mountain of kitsch masonry flanked with incongruously Victorian-looking miniature clock towers. The interior follows the standard pattern of Sri Lankan Hindu temples, with an inner shrine constructed from solid stone enclosed in a shed-like ambulatory. This outer **ambulatory** has a strangely improvised look, with corrugated-iron walls and roofing and various shrines seemingly constructed from a medley of leftover building materials (the largest shrine, holding five gorgeously garlanded statues in funny little silver hats, appears to have been fashioned out of a converted kitchen, whilst another has a smart marble floor and metal handrails that look as if they've been filched from the building site of a five-star hotel). The images in the temple are similarly mismatched, with conventional Hindu deities – including many blackened images of the maleficent Durga – alongside curious Buddha statues dressed as Hindu deities in robes and garlands. Just to the left of the entrance are the wooden animal chariots and palanquins used to carry images in temple processions, plus two caged peacocks, the symbol and chariot of the god Subramanian (or Kataragama, as he is known to the Sinhalese; see p.198), to whom the temple is dedicated. The **main shrine** is built from stone and has a more solid appearance, though again the marbled floor and illuminations give it a rather chintzy look. The main image sits right at the back, behind two golden makara torana arches. buried under garlands. Men are required to take their shirt off if they enter the main shrine.

The temple, like all in Colombo, is usually closed except during the morning and evening pujas (around 8–9am & 5–6pm), when you're free to wander around inside.

The Seema Malaka and Gangaramaya temples

Just south of the Sri Subramania Kovil the streets open up to reveal the southern arm of **Beira Lake** – not a place of any great beauty, though it's surrounded by fine old trees and provides welcoming breezes throughout the day, as well as attracting pelicans, egrets and cormorants. Two of the city's most interesting Buddhist temples lie close to one another on the southern lake's eastern side. The more modern, the **Seema Malaka**, is attractively situated at the end of a causeway jutting out into the middle of the lake – an unexpected and beautiful sight against the drab tower blocks behind, and particularly pretty when illuminated with fairy lights at night. Designed by Sri Lanka's foremost twentieth-century architect, Geoffrey Bawa (see pp.132–133), this unusual temple is used for inaugurations of monks from the nearby Gangaramaya temple – though it was actually paid for by a Colombo Muslim who, having fallen out with his co-religionists, decided to revenge himself by endowing a Buddhist shrine. Set on three linked platforms rising out of the lake, Seema Malaka's novel structure was apparently inspired by the design of Sri Lankan forest monasteries such as those at Anuradhapura and Ritigala, which feature similar raised platforms linked by bridge-like walkways. The buildings are roofed with lustrous blue tiles, with a small bo tree and delicately carved kiosk on the outer platforms standing either side of the larger central structure, an intricately latticed wooden pavilion lined inside and out by two rows of delicate Thai Buddhas in various mudras.

A couple of hundred metres east lies the older and more traditional **Gangaramaya** (entrance Rs.100; guide available), Colombo's most absorbing Buddhist temple and a peaceful retreat from the city. The buildings and images are of no particular antiquity, but the entire complex is lavishly decorated and worth a visit even if you've seen even the far more historic temples of the Kandy region and Cultural Triangle. Gangaramaya sits behind an unusually elaborate perimeter wall faced with polished brass panels decorated with dwarfs (symbols of prosperity) and topped with Buddhas, whose beady eyes protect the building against maleficent influences. To one side of the courtyard, a venerable old bo tree grows out of a raised platform draped in prayer flags; next to it sits a richly decorated Kandyan-style wooden pavilion. Across the courtyard lies the principal **image house**, its base supported by further dwarfs in quasi-yogic positions. Inside, the entire building is occupied by an eye-popping *tableau vivant*, centred on a gargantuan orange Buddha sitting majestically in the meditation posture, flanked by elephant tusks and surrounded by dozens of other larger-than-life Buddhas and devotees bearing garlands, fans, musical instruments and conch shells – thoroughly kitsch, but undeniably impressive. Just behind the main courtyard are a tier of stacked-up Buddha statues from Thailand – making these is regarded as a sure-fire way of earning spiritual merit, hence the enthusiasm with which they have been reproduced. Close by is the temple's most surprising feature: a fine selection of vintage **cars**, presented by well-wishers over the years.

Next to the entrance, the temple **museum** fills two big rooms with an astonishing treasure-trove of weird and wonderful objects: precious stones, coins, innumerable Buddha images and statues of other Buddhist and Hindu deities, oil lamps, votive dagobas, old clocks, porcelain, ivory carvings and gramophones. The overall effect is of an enormous antique warehouse, with objects of great delicacy and value alongside pieces of pure kitsch (such as a banana carved out of ivory).

The temple is also the focus of a major festival, the **Navam Perahera**, held on poya day every February, when up to fifty elephants descend. Although only established in 1979, this has quickly grown to be one of the most popular peraheras in Colombo.

Viharamahadevi Park and the museums

Just south of the Gangaramaya temple stretches the city's principal open space, **Viharamahadevi Park**, originally called Victoria Park but renamed with characteristic patriotic thoroughness in the 1950s, after the famous mother of King Duttugemunu (see p.192). The park makes a welcome spot to crash out in between forays to nearby museums and temples and boasts gorgeous tropical trees, plentiful bird life and the occasional visiting elephant; it's also a magnet to local courting couples, who sit discreetly snogging under umbrellas. At the northern end of the park lies lively **De Soysa Circus** – still widely known by its old name of Lipton Circus – one of central Colombo's major intersections and home to a couple of the city's best shops (see p.108), the huge Osu Sala state pharmacy and the eyecatching **Devatagaha Mosque**, a big white Moorish-looking structure that adds a quaint touch of architectural whimsy to the otherwise functional junction. Immediately south of here, facing the park, stands Colombo's **Town Hall**, built in 1927 – a severely functional white Neoclassical structure that's something like a cross between the US Capitol and a municipal waterworks. Opposite, a huge **gilded Buddha** stares fixedly down the park's principal avenue.

The National Museum

The southern section of the park is home to three state museums, most notably the extensive **National Museum** (Mon–Thurs, Sat & Sun; Rs.65, camera permit Rs.60), set in an elegant white Neoclassical building and opened in 1877. Exhibits are fairly well laid out, although only erratically labelled.

Ground floor: rooms 1, 3 and 4

The first three rooms have a largely religious slant. **Room 1** shows changing representations of the Buddha through the centuries, starting with early abstract representations – sacred footprints (*sri pada*), dagobas – followed by figurative carvings in wood, stone, bronze and coral from the third to the nineteenth centuries, exemplifying the transition in Buddhist art from the symbolic to the figurative (for more on which, see p.437). There are many images in the meditation (*dhyani mudra*) pose particularly popular amongst the island's sculptors, including the large limestone figure opposite the entrance, a classic image whose simplicity, serenity, lack of decoration and very human features embody all that is most characteristic of Sri Lankan art. The nearby figures of Surya, Durga and a voluptuous, black, wasp-waisted *tara* (a Mahayana Buddhist goddess) look hauntingly exotic and extremely Hindu in comparison.

More Indian-influenced sculpture can be found to the left of the entrance in **Room 4** (immediately left of the entrance), where an outstanding collection of twelfth-century bronzes, mainly from the Shiva Devale no. 1 at Polonnaruwa, show the strength of Hindu influence on this avowedly Buddhist city. Exhibits include fine bronzes of Shiva Nataraja, along with other Hindu deities and holy men related to this god, including a number of Parvatis and a cute Nandi (Shiva's bull). **Room 3** (immediately right of the entrance) is devoted to the island's architectural heritage and is dominated by a huge exhibit showing a fine moonstone and steps flanked by *nagarajas* – an architectural combination you'll see repeated all over the sites of the Cultural Triangle. Look out too for the model and cross-section of an ancient urinal pot from Anuradhapura, whose intricate workings show a concern for hygiene sadly not matched by many modern Sri Lankan conveniences.

Ground floor: rooms 5–10

On the far side of room 4, rooms 5–8 have a more secular theme. **Room 5** has an extensive collection of coins dating back to the third century BC from regions as far-flung as Rome, Byzantium, Greece, Scythia and Bactria – concrete evidence of the remarkably extensive international trading links forged by early Sri Lankan merchants. Nearer to home, there are Indian coins from the Pandyan and Pallava empires, while coins from the reigns of Parakramabahu I and Vijayabahu I (see p.318) show what the people of ancient Polonnaruwa would have used to go shopping with. Other exhibits include examples of later Portuguese, Dutch and British coins, plus a selection of *larins*, or "fish-hook" coins, consisting of a tin strip folded in half with Arabic inscriptions on either side – the standard currency of the Indian Ocean region throughout the sixteenth century.

Room 6 contains Sri Lankan artefacts from the seventeenth to nineteenth centuries, exemplifying the incredibly intricate craftsmanship, in a variety of materials, which was achieved by the Kandyan-era craftsmen – everything from minutely embossed brass plates and huge spoons chiselled from coconuts to delicately carved ivory figurines. **Room 7** is largely occupied by a worthy collection of Chinese porcelain, plus various ridiculous knick-knacks – everything from a commemorative gold coin struck for Ferdinand

and Imelda Marcos to a plate commemorating a visit of the under-19 Pakistani cricket team.

Much more interesting is **room 8**, where you'll find various bits of regalia and jewellery. Pride of place goes to the glittering regalia of the kings of Kandy – one of the museum's highlights – which was surrendered to the British during the handover of power in 1815 and kept in Windsor Castle until being returned by George V in 1934.

Rooms 9 and **10** contain a huge miscellany of eroded statuary and masonry – pillars, friezes, statues – salvaged from archeological sites across the island, and ranging in time from third-century Anuradhapura right through to a few colonial coats of arms and tombstones. The majority of pieces come from Anuradhapura and Polonnaruwa, including a forest of the pillar inscriptions which were commonly used to record administrative decrees and grants of land. It's difficult to make much sense of it all, although the sheer quantity of the exhibits is impressive, and they do testify to certain recurrent motifs – dwarfs, lions, *nagarajas* – which you'll see repeated island-wide. Room 10 also has some more very Indian-style figures from Polonnaruwa, principally of Shiva and related divinities.

The first floor

Heading up the stairs opposite the main entrance brings you to the large **room 13**, home to an outstanding selection of kolam masks (see p.139): a large and entertainingly gruesome collection showing myriad personages – policemen, government officials, ministers, Muslims, Tamils, Kaffirs, moneylenders and mythical demons and diseases – all variously deformed, with leering expressions, bizarre teeth and mad moustaches.

The remaining rooms are a bit of a hotch-potch. **Room 14** has a feeble display on the veddahs (see p.245), while **rooms 16** and **17** house life-size copies of frescoes from places such as Sigiriya and the Tivanka Pilimage in Polonnaruwa, plus some original Kandyan-era painted cloths. **Room 18** is devoted to watercolours by the Irish artist Andrew Nichol (1804–1886), who lived in Sri Lanka from 1846 to 1850. His mistily idealized landscapes offer a classic example of the way early colonial artists tended to wildly over-romanticize the landscapes of the empire's exotic new dominions: the peaks of the hill country end up looking like the Himalayas, whilst even the smallest temple is blown up to the scale of Westminster Abbey.

The museum peters out in the enormous **Room 19**, full of random pieces of dusty Dutch furniture; a extension of this room is devoted to the memory of independent Sri Lanka's first prime minister, D.S. Senanayake. From here, stairs lead back down to room 10 on the ground floor.

The Natural History Museum and National Art Gallery

Just behind the National Museum, the **Natural History Museum** (Mon–Thurs & Sat–Sun 9am–5pm; Rs.45) fills three gloomy and labyrinthine floors with exhibits ranging from stuffed leopards and pickled snakes to quaintly didactic presentations on the island's ecology and economy ("Easy Ways To Make Agricultural Chemical Safe for You And Everyone Else", and the like). It all looks like the sort of thing you'd expect to find in Bulgaria, although the vast quantity of stuffed animals posed in moth-eaten pomp is enough to turn a conservationist's hair grey.

Next door to the Natural History Museum, Sri Lanka's **National Art Gallery** (daily 9am–5pm; free) comprises a single large room full of twentieth-century Sri Lankan paintings. The majority treat Sri Lankan themes in a range of European styles from neo-Degas to faux-Picasso – all rather derivative, although the quality is actually quite good. Sadly there are no labels, and exhibits are roped off, so you can't get close enough to read the signatures or even look at the paintings in any detail, meaning that the whole experience is rather unedifying.

Cinnamon Gardens and Borella

South and east of Viharamahadevi Park stretches the smart suburb of **Cinnamon Gardens** (also known as **Colombo 7**), named for the cinnamon plantations which flourished here during the nineteenth century. The capital's most sought-after addresses, the leafy streets here preserve their aura of haughty Victorian privilege – along with their colonial street names – and are lined with elite colleges and enormous old colonial mansions (most now occupied by foreign embassies and government offices) concealed behind dauntingly high walls. There's not actually much to do or see here, though there are a couple of places to stay and eat. The heart of the district is formed by the rectangle of streets between Ward Place and Gregory's Road, the latter home to a whole string of embassies in spectacularly opulent colonial residences. South of here, Maitland Place runs down to the **Sinhalese Sports Club**, whose engagingly old-fashioned stadium, complete with antiquated, manually operated score-board, serves as Colombo's venue for test match cricket. Just south of here at the end of Independence Avenue lies the bombastic **Independence Commemoration Hall**, an overblown stone replica of the wooden Audience Hall at Kandy.

East of Cinnamon Gardens, in the adjacent suburb of Borella, the **Gotami Vihara** is home to a striking series of murals, by Sri Lanka's best-known twentieth-century artist **George Keyt** (1901–1993), depicting the life of the Buddha. Although a Christian Burgher, Keyt was deeply influenced by Buddhist and Hindu culture, as well as by Western artistic developments, creating an unusual and distinctive synthesis, sometimes rather reminiscent of Matisse in style, if not always in subject. The temple is rather out of the way – it's easiest to take a tuktuk or taxi. Go down Dr N.M. Perera Mawatha (the continuation of Ward Place) for about 500m, then take a left up Gotami Road.

Southern Colombo: Kollupitiya to Dehiwela

Immediately beyond Galle Face Green, **Galle Road** runs purposefully south, bisecting a string of coastal suburbs – **Kollupitiya**, **Bambalapitiya**, **Wellawatta** and **Dehiwela** – before reaching Mount Lavinia (see p.100). Much of the commercial activity driven out of Fort by repeated bombings has now established itself in this part of the city, moving Colombo's centre of gravity decisively southwards and transforming Galle Road – the area between Kollupitiya and Bambalapitiya especially – into the city's de facto high street.

It's a far from pleasant sight, however: choked with traffic for eighteen hours a day, enveloped in a constant film of smog and accompanied by a perpetual cacophony of screeching bus horns – the overall filthiness being made all the more obvious by the enticing sight of the Indian Ocean just a couple of hundred metres away down countless side roads. There's no way you could possibly consider Galle Road a tourist attraction, but it offers a good example of contemporary Sri Lanka at its most diverse: garish cinema hoardings stand next to serene Buddhist temples and colonial colleges, while shiny modern office blocks and air-conditioned shopping malls rub shoulders with ramshackle cafés and tiny lock-up shops, all boasting plenty of noisy character and in places even a strange, smelly sort of charm.

Running parallel to the Galle Road on its landward side, R.A. de Mel Mawatha – still often referred to by its former name of **Duplication Road** – is leafier and more salubrious, edged by smart shops and restaurants, though still busy with traffic during the day.

Kollupitiya and Bambalapitiya

Immediately south of Galle Face Green, Galle Road has a decidedly military atmosphere, with a trio of heavily fortified diplomatic compounds and **Temple Trees**, the prime minister's official residence, all but hidden behind sandbagged gun emplacements and high walls topped by army watchtowers. The only spot of architectural relief is supplied by the quaint Gothic **St Andrew's Scotskirk** of 1842, just north of Temple Trees. Continuing south, Colombo's ordinary commercial life resumes as Galle Road passes through central **Kollupitiya** (still occasionally signposted under its colonial name of Colpetty), with strings of cafes, banks and assorted shops. Many of the buildings here are functionally nondescript, with lots of the reflective, glassy facades favoured by modern Sri Lankan architects, though the occasional dog-eared little café, colourful sign or curious shop survives amongst the bland modern office blocks.

There are more flashes of character in the helter-skelter commercial suburb of **Bambalapitiya**. Following the decline in Fort's fortunes, the area around Bambalapitiya Junction has now to all intents and purposes become the centre of modern Colombo. It's a slightly anarchic mix of the old and new, ranging from the large and shiny Majestic Plaza shopping mall to little lopsided shops selling bits of rope or packets of spices, while a series of determinedly local cafés and South Indian restaurants brighten the fume-filled Galle Road with their fanciful signs. This is one of the busiest areas of Colombo: the pavements are clogged during daylight hours with office workers, beggars and tuktuk drivers touting for custom, while the handcarts of vadai-sellers and modest piles of merchandise laid out by street hawkers – anything from Buddha posters to recycled computer innards – add to the congestion.

Dehiwela Zoo

Some 10km south of Fort in the suburb of Dehiwela, the national **Zoo** (daily 8.30am–6pm; Rs.200) is home to a good range of Sri Lankan, Asian, African and South American wildlife housed in mostly tolerable conditions – ongoing renovations will hopefully soon put paid to the few distressingly small cages for some of the monkeys and big cats. Sri Lankan species here include cute sloth bears, sambhur and spotted deer, monkeys, lots of birds and a number of leopards, part of the zoo's good collection of **big cats**, which also includes jaguars, lions, tigers, cheetah and a rather miserable-looking ocelot. The zoo is also home to a number of Asian and a couple of African **elephants**; they can be seen performing during the zoo's elephant dance (daily at 5.15pm), if you're that way inclined.

The zoo's large assortment of **monkeys** includes examples of all the native primates, such as purple-faced leaf monkey, grey langur and toque macaque. There's also a wide array of other mammals, from African giraffes and spring-boks or South American guanacos and tapirs to Australian red-necked wallabies and giant red kangaroos. There's also an excellent collection of **birdlife**, including some fabulously large and fluffy owls, lots of cockatoos and macaws (including an astonishing – and very rare – hyacinth macaw) and toucans. There's also a huge walk-in aviary full of Sri Lankan species; a good place to practise your bird-spotting skills. In addition to the caged birdlife, a flooded quarry at one end of the zoo serves as a magnet to Colombo's aquatic birds, which are fed here daily. Egrets, herons and pelicans from all over the city flock here – a fine sight at feeding times, when hundreds swoop down onto the water. If you feel like eating yourself, there's a **restaurant** inside the zoo, as well as plenty of kiosks selling drinks and snacks.

About 500m from the zoo (follow the signs) is one of Colombo's more curious sights: a full-scale replica of two of the massive rock sculptures (the sleeping and standing Buddhas) from the **Gal Vihara** (see p.330) at Polonnaruwa – worth a quick look if you've never seen the originals. It's a peaceful spot and the replicas are meticulously done, though carved out of a coarse black stone.

Mount Lavinia

Ten kilometres south of Colombo Fort, the leafy beachside suburb of **Mount Lavinia** is bounded by the small headland (the so-called "Mount") that is one of the few punctuating features on the coastline near the capital. The area supposedly takes its name from a certain Lavinia, the lady friend of British governor Sir Thomas Maitland, who established a residence for himself here in 1806.

Maitland's residence was subsequently expanded by successive governors before being turned into the **Mount Lavinia Hotel**, now one of the most venerable colonial landmarks in Sri Lanka and the main reason most foreign visitors come here. Even if you can't afford to stay at the hotel, there are a few other pleasant small-scale guest houses nearby, and the suburb's proximity to the international airport makes it a handy first or last stop on a tour of the island – or just a convenient bolthole if you just want to escape the hectic streets of central Colombo for a day or two.

Mount Lavinia is also home to Colombo's closest half-decent **beach**, and on Sunday afternoons half the city seems to come here to splash around in the

---

Ayurveda in Mount Lavinia

There are a couple of good places for ayurveda in Mount Lavinia. The **Rankema Ayurveda Centre** at the *Mount Lavinia Hotel* (℡271 5221, ⓔrankema@sltnet.lk) is one of Sri Lanka's most attractive, with beautiful treatment rooms right on the beach and the divine smells of ayurvedic medicinal ingredients everywhere – all medicines are made here, and the main entrance is decorated with sackfuls of wild herbs, bits of bark and root, and other intriguingly unidentifiable vegetable matter. There's also a meditation room, and an ayurveda doctor in residence. Individual treatments cost from US$13; a one-week Panchakarma treatment is US$515.

For something rather more serious, try the **Mount Clinic of Oriental Medicine**, 6A Cross Rd (℡011-272 3464, ⓔmtclinic@sti.lk). This is run by a doctor qualified in both ayurveda and Chinese medicine, and the main emphasis here is on the serious treatment of chronic conditions, rather than on "soft" ayurveda massages and baths. A hundred different therapies are offered – perhaps the largest range of anywhere in Sri Lanka – including no fewer than 25 different types of ayurvedic massage and four Chinese, plus medieval-sounding treatments including blood-letting and cauterization with fire (so-called "moxibustion"), as well as the rare *ashtakarma* (eightfold treatment). Complete Panchakarma treatments go for US$450 per week; individual treatments from around US$8.

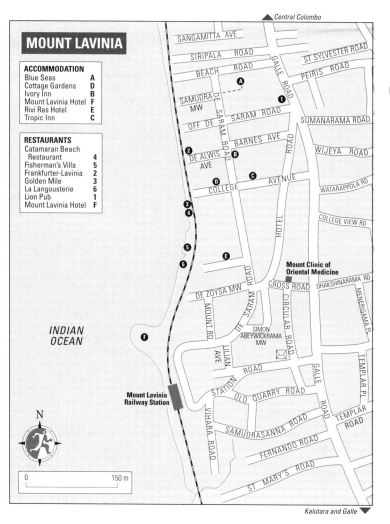

MOUNT LAVINIA

ACCOMMODATION
Blue Seas	A
Cottage Gardens	D
Ivory Inn	B
Mount Lavinia Hotel	F
Rivi Ras Hotel	E
Tropic Inn	C

RESTAURANTS
Catamaran Beach Restaurant	4
Fisherman's Villa	5
Frankfurter-Lavinia	2
Golden Mile	3
La Langousterie	6
Lion Pub	1
Mount Lavinia Hotel	F

SANGAMITTA AVE
SIRIPALA ROAD
BEACH ROAD
ST SYLVESTER ROAD
PEIRIS ROAD
GALLE ROAD
SAMUDRA MW
DE SARAM ROAD
SARAM ROAD
SUMANARAMA ROAD
OFF DE
BARNES AVE
WIJEYA ROAD
DE ALWIS AVE
AVENUE
COLLEGE
WATARAPPOLA RD
COLLEGE VIEW RD
HOTEL

Mount Clinic of Oriental Medicine

DE ZOYSA MW
CROSS ROAD
DHAKSHINARAMA RD
CIRCULAR ROAD
MENERIGAMA PL
MOUNT RD
DE SARAM ROAD
SIMON ABEYWICKRAMA MW
LILIAN AVE
ROAD
GALLE ROAD
TEMPLAR PL

INDIAN OCEAN

STATION
OLD QUARRY ROAD
TEMPLAR ROAD
VIHARA ROAD
SAMUDRASANNA ROAD
FERNANDO ROAD
ST MARY'S ROAD

Mount Lavinia Railway Station

N

0   150 m

water, play cricket and smooch under umbrellas. The proximity of the city means that the water is bordeline for swimming, while the beach itself is a bit messy, with piles of fishing tackle scattered here and there. It's not an idyllic tropical beach by any means, but does have a decent stretch of sand and a certain scruffy charm, especially at night, with the lights of the towers in central Colombo twinkling away to the north, and the more modest illuminations of the *Mount Lavinia Hotel* framing the beach to the south.

Mount Lavinia has a good spread of **places to eat**, some of them quite swish. Both the beach and the *Mount Lavinia Hotel* are attractive spots for an evening meal if you're staying in Colombo and fancy a break from the city, although it's a bit of a trek down the Galle Road unless you're staying in one of the southern suburbs. Plenty of taxi and tuktuk drivers hang out around the hotel until late at night, so you won't have any problems getting home.

Kelaniya and Kotte

Ten kilometres east of Fort lies Colombo's most important Buddhist shrine, the **Kelaniya Raja Maha Vihara** – the Buddha himself is said to have visited on the last of his three visits to the island. Various temples have stood on the present site – earlier structures were destroyed first by the Indians, then by the Portuguese – and the present one dates from the eighteenth and nineteenth centuries. A dagoba marks the exact spot where the Buddha is said to have preached. Next to it are a large bo tree and an elaborate **image house** (mainly dating from the twentieth century, though parts are older), home to a fine reclining Buddha plus images of various Hindu gods and the naga king, Maniakkhika, who invited the Buddha here to preach. There are also some striking modern murals by Soliyas Mendis showing the Buddha's three legendary visits to Sri Lanka and the destruction of the temple by the Portuguese. The temple is the focus of the extravagant two-day **Duruthu Perahera** celebrations every January. Bus 235 runs to Kelaniya from just outside Bastian Mawatha bus station.

Some 7km inland southeast from Fort lies the medieval regional capital of **Kotte** (see p.417). In 1984 President J.R. Jayawardene decided, rather bizarrely, to transfer the administrative capital of Sri Lanka from Colombo to here, and also to revive Kotte's old name of **Sri Jayawardenepura** (fortuitously similar to that of the president himself, it might be noted). Technically, Sri Jayawardenepura is therefore the official capital of Sri Lanka, even though it's really only a suburb of Colombo, and pretty much everyone continues to think of Colombo as the island's capital. The main physical sign of the suburb's status is the grandiose modern **Parliament Building**, designed by Geoffrey Bawa, which stands in the middle of an artificial lake, though unfortunately it's not open to the public, so you can only admire it from a distance.

Eating

Eating in Colombo is a wonderful contrast to the desultory restaurant scene of just about everywhere else on the island – the city boasts pretty much the full range of Asian and European cuisines, including French, Italian, Swiss, German, Middle Eastern, Korean, Japanese, Indonesian, Mongolian and Thai, as well as plenty of Sri Lankan and Indian cooking and a decent range of seafood. There are many ever-popular **Chinese** restaurants serving up quasi-Cantonese dishes sexed-up for Sri Lankan palates with lots of chilli and lemongrass, as well as plenty of excellent **South Indian vegetarian** restaurants – often lively and characterful places dishing up remarkably good (and good-value) food in cheerfully no-nonsense surroundings. If your stomach's acclimatized, there are innumerable lively little **local cafés** – clustered all over Slave Island, down Galle Road and the Pettah – which really come alive after dark.

For **fast food**, there are branches of *KFC* on Galle Road in Bambalapitiya and in the JAIC Hilton Tower, and a *McDonald's* on Galle Road, Kollupitiya. There are also branches of *Pizza Hut* past JAIC Hilton Tower and south of Bambalapitiya, and branches of *Délifrance* in Crescat Boulevard (see p.108) and Odel (see p.108). Prices at all are about a half to two-thirds cheaper than in Europe or the US. For **Sri Lankan fast food**, there are outlets of *Perera's Bakers* and *Caravan* all over town – good for short eats, snacks and confectionary. Finally, **lunch packets** are sold by pavement stalls and cafés all over the city.

Many of the restaurants listed below close from around 2.30 or 3pm until 6.30 or 7pm. We've given telephone numbers for the (few) places where it's advisable to book ahead.

Fort and Pettah

The places below are marked on the map on p.89.

Chettinad 293 Sea St, Pettah. A good lunch stop in the depths of the Pettah, dishing up delicious and dirt-cheap south Indian food – dosas, vadais, uttapam – in an authentically subcontinental atmosphere complete with banana leaf "plates", metal utensils and a colourful display of sweets in the entrance.

Crown York St, Fort. This shabby little basement café next door to Laksala (see p.108) offers an authentic slice of local life and reasonable South Indian vegetarian fare at suitably bargain-basement prices. The small menu features vadais and dosas, string hoppers and rice and curry, plus a few South Indian sweets. Open daytime only.

Curry Leaf *Hilton* hotel, Sir Chittampalam A. Gardiner Mw, Fort ☎ 011-249 1000. Tucked away in the *Hilton* grounds in a rather naff faux-jungle village construction. The nightly buffet (Rs.790) provides Colombo's best introduction to the full range of Sri Lankan cuisine – string hoppers, hoppers, kotthu rotty, wattalapan, plus all sorts of

rice and curries – all marvellously prepared. Open evenings only.

Il Ponte *Hilton* hotel, Sir Chittampalam A. Gardiner Mw, Fort ☎ 011-254 4644. Informal Italian restaurant in the far corner of the hotel grounds, with seating either in an indoor a/c section or outside by the pool. The small menu features pizzas, calzones, pastas and salads (mozzarella, salade niçoise) plus Australian steaks, burgers, Italian ice cream and tiramisu. It's all pretty low-key, but the food is delicious, and the thin-crust pizzas (from Rs.450) are the best in Sri Lanka.

Seafish Sir Chittampalam A. Gardiner Mw, Slave Island. Good fish and seafood (mains from around Rs.350) in a low-key little restaurant, just off the main road south of the *Hilton*, complete with a tankful of Colombo's ugliest fish.

Taj York St, Fort. A fun and lively place at lunchtimes, when local office workers pile in for the cheap and good burianis, rice and curry, and short eats (much prodded). It's also the only cheapie in Fort that stays open in the evenings.

Slave Island

The following are shown on the map on p.84.

Long Feng *Trans Asia* hotel, Slave Island ☎ 011-249 1000. Colombo's best Chinese restaurant, specializing in spicy Sichuan cuisine (plus a few Cantonese dishes), with meat, seafood and vegetarian offerings including tempting specialities like hot and sour soup with chilli oil, steamed pork belly with preserved vegetables, and braised ma po bean curd with chilli sauce. Mains from around Rs.350.

Royal Thai *Trans Asia* hotel, Slave Island ☎ 011-249 1000. The most beautiful place to eat in the city, this exquisite little jewel-box of a restaurant serves Columbo's best Thai food, including all the usual standards (*pad thai*, red and green curries, *tom yam*) as well as many more outré dishes, all vividly flavoured and fiery hot. Mains from around Rs.420.

Around Galle Face Green

The following are shown on the map on p.84.

Alhambra *Holiday Inn*, Sir M.M. Markar Mw. Long-running Indian restaurant (despite the Moorish name and decor), with a solid range of North Indian dishes (from around Rs.300), including Mughal-style birianis, tandooris and tikkas – plus a couple of South Indian-style fish curries, plenty of vegetarian options and a good selection of naans and rotis. Mains Rs.300–480.

Bavarian Barn German Restaurant Galle Rd. The rather gloomy interior full of chunky wooden

furniture provides a suitably Bavarian setting for Central European dishes like goulash, pickled beef, pepper steak, pork and Vienna schnitzels, bratwurst and chicken (most around Rs.400). There's also some seafood and vegetarian dishes.

Koluu's Sir M.M. Markar Mw. Tucked away behind the *Holiday Inn* – look for the fluorescent pink sign in the first-floor window, this is a lively and modern international restaurant whose vivid, camp pink decor doesn't detract (much) from its excellent European and Asian cuisine. Mains (Rs.350–500) include pasta, vegetarian choices plus tasty Southeast Asian dishes like ayam sakang, Malaysian fried rice and Singapore chilli crab; there's also a huge drinks list. Popular with expats, and can get riotous on Fridays.

Navratna *Taj Samudra* hotel, Galle Face Centre Rd. Colombo's swankiest Indian restaurant, with a range of standard subcontinental dishes plus more unusual regional specialities like saag bhutta (corn and spinach curry), shahi subz kofta (vegetable

dumpling curry) and avial (Keralan mixed vegetable curry). Mains from around Rs.400.

Seaspray *Galle Face* hotel. The food here won't win awards, but the oceanside setting is the most romantic in central Colombo, with seating either indoors or out on the sand close to the waves. The smallish selection of fish and seafood, plus a few meat dishes and a couple of vegetarian options, is OK if rather expensive (most mains around Rs.550). Portions are small and service is erratic, but given the setting, you probably won't care.

Kollupitiya and Cinnamon Gardens

The following are shown on the maps on p.84.

Amaravathi Mile Post Ave. Functional a/c restaurant serving up a huge range of cheap South Indian dishes. Popular with locals at lunchtimes, when there's an enormous selection of burianis plus gargantuan veg, fish and meat banana-leaf thalis – it's all fairly rustic, but makes a change from rice and curry.

Chesa Swiss Deal Place, corner of R.A. de Mel Mw (Duplication Rd) ☏ 011-257 3433. Very swish restaurant in a gorgeous colonial-style villa, with garden or indoor a/c seating. The mouthwatering Swiss and international dishes (mains Rs.430–1800) include the inevitable fondues, along with delicacies like deep-fried camembert, vegetable rösti with raclette cheese and deliciously creamy Swiss barley soup. Carnivores can tuck into Australian prime beef steaks, and there's also seafood and good vegetarian options. It gets busy with expats, so worth booking ahead.

The Commons Dharmapala Mw. Slightly arty little café with a pool table and a small garden terrace. The tasty light meals and snacks – sandwiches, melts, pasta, burgers – are all around Rs.300. The entrance is below the stairs up to *Pier 56* (see opposite column), and the door is often kept shut during opening hours. Daily 10am–6pm.

Crescat Boulevard Galle Rd, Kollupitiya. The food court in the basement of Colombo's smartest shopping mall teems with kiosks dishing up everything from *Pizza Hut* to Mongolian cuisine, as well as Sri Lankan, Indian, Chinese, Malaysian, pizza, pasta, wraps and ice cream. There's also a branch of *Délifrance* upstairs by the entrance.

Curry Bowl Deal Place. A good place to introduce yourself to the joys of Sri Lankan cuisine, this cheerful and very cheap little locals' café has piles of hoppers and trays of curry, plus string hoppers, kottu rotty, pittu and burianis, all for under Rs.150.

Flower Drum Thurston Rd. Old Colombo stalwart, with cheap Sri Lankan-style Chinese dishes, including the usual Cantonese standards plus various

spiced-up chillied and devilled dishes, all for under Rs.300. There are a few Indonesian and Singaporean dishes, too, though there's not much for veggies.

Le Palace Gregory's Rd. One of Colombo's poshest restaurants, set in a gorgeous colonial mansion on one of the city's most exclusive streets – seating is in four intimate dining rooms with plenty of fresh linen and cutlery polished to within an inch of its life, and there's a genuine French chef. The menu (which changes regularly) features gourmet French and international cuisine (mains from Rs.400), or you can stick to excellent (and surprisingly cheap) coffee and cake on the verandah outside.

Palmyrah Restaurant *Hotel Renuka*, Galle Rd. This plush basement restaurant is a good place to try Sri Lankan cuisine, with a range of dishes including string hopper pilau, kottu, curries, *meen sambol* (fried fish with chopped onions and green chillies) and cheap hoppers – all flavoured with unusual delicacy. Mains from around Rs.300.

Pier 56 Dharmapala Mw ☏ 011-257 6509. Classy, modern little restaurant upstairs from *The Commons* (see opposite), offering a big international-style menu of seafood, meat and lots of vegetarian options – prawns in spicy pineapple, aubergines stuffed with spicy potato and cheese and Arabic-bread pizza – as well as a huge selection of sushi. Reservations advisable. Open evenings only; mains from around Rs.400.

Sakura Rheinland Place. Cosy, low-key little Japanese restaurant with a big range of dishes (and a board full of pictures to help you choose) including sashimi, sushi, udon, tempura, ramen (from Rs.250), and set-menu lunches for Rs.400–500.

Siam House Abdul Kapoor Mw. Occupying a colonial-style villa on a quiet side street, this is Colombo's best option for budget Thai food, and is much cheaper than the rather smart appearance would suggest, with many dishes under Rs.200. All the usual favourites are on offer – red and green curries, fish curries, spicy Thai salads, pad thai and rice noodles.

Bambalapitiya

The following are shown on the map on p.84.

Amrith's Dickman's Rd. Peaceful a/c restaurant with a reasonable range of north and South Indian meat and veg standards (Rs.150–200) including thalis at lunchtime and dosas and idlis in the evenings.

Barefoot Café Galle Rd. Set in the beautiful courtyard at the back of Colombo's most personable shop (see p.108), with outdoor seating dotted around under the trees and a small but excellently prepared menu of moderately priced café-style fare: sandwiches, juices, milkshakes, cakes, coffees, pasta, plus excellent daily lunch specials and sinful desserts. Daytime only.

Café Japan 22 Lauries Place, R.A. de Mel Mw (Duplication Rd). Informal little café providing a homely, low-key setting for outstanding Japanese fare, with delicately flavoured sushi, sashimi, soba, somen, udon, tofu and tempura (from Rs.200) and set meals from around Rs.500. Wash it all down with sake. Slightly out of the way, but worth a special trip.

Chinese Dragon Café Milagiriya Ave, off Galle Rd. A Colombo institution, this friendly Chinese restaurant is tucked inconspicuously away down a side street off Galle Rd in a rambling old mansion. The extensive menu has loads of choices – chicken, beef, seafood, meat, veggie (mock duck, tofu) – all well prepared and reasonably priced, with most mains around Rs.275.

Cricket Club Café Queen's Rd, off Duplication Rd. This shrine to cricket is deservedly popular with expats, tourists and locals alike, with fascinating (if you're that way inclined) memorabilia ranged around the walls and nonstop live or recorded matches on TV. The food is top-notch, with a bistro-style menu of burgers, steaks, veggie dishes and imaginative daily specials (the Dickie Bird Burger; the Jayasuriya Triple Century, and so on).

The Gallery Café Alfred House Rd. Occupying the former offices of architect Geoffrey Bawa, Colombo's most stylish (and expensive) café is a real oasis, and definitely one of *the* places to be seen. The outer courtyard hosts temporary art and photographic exhibitions, plus a small shop (see p.108), while the inner courtyard is home to the café itself, with open-air seating. The food is as stylish as the building, with an extensive international menu featuring all sorts of tempting dishes, many with an Asian twist, plus good veggie options and a huge range of calorie-busting puddings; it's also good for a drink and some people-watching.

Green Cabin Galle Rd. Cheap and cheerful local place on Galle Rd serving up tastier-than-average rice and curry, lamprais and other Sri Lankan offerings.

Greenlands Shrubbery Gardens, off Galle Rd. A Colombo institution hidden away in an old colonial house, this sedate South Indian vegetarian restaurant offers a big range of excellent, dirt-cheap food including vadais (masala, ulundu, curd), dosas (paper, ghee, onion) and other goodies including idlis, pooris and bonda (a kind of bhaji). Lurid piles of Indian sweets are sold at the entrance.

Saraswathie Galle Rd. This long-established, no-nonsense South Indian vegetarian restaurant is ultra-cheap, interestingly hectic and offers a quintessential slice of Colombo life. Food includes various types of dosa (plain, masala, onion, ghee), string hoppers, veg buriani, potato curry, idlis and vadais, all at virtually giveaway prices – you can stuff yourself stupid for well under a dollar.

Wellawatta

The following is shown on the map on p.76.

Beach Wadiya 2 Station Ave ☎011-258 8568. Colombo's best seafood, cooked fresh out of the boat and served in a magical beachfront setting which combines informality with elegance: sand underfoot, fresh linen tablecloths and sparkling wine glasses. Best to sit outside, though if you get stuck indoors check out the candid shots of former guests plastered all over walls (including loads of famous drunk cricketers). Surprisingly cheap, given the quality (mains from Rs.250).

Mount Lavinia

The following are shown on the map on p.101.

Catamaran Beach Restaurant Low-key beach-shack with tables on the sand under a palm-thatched roof, serving good cheap snacks and seafood, plus the usual noodles, rice and devilled dishes.

Fisherman's Villa Attractive seafood restaurant in an open-air wooden pavilion by the beach. The extensive menu (mains Rs.265–425) has interesting Southeast Asian, Chinese and European touches (everything from minestrone to tom yam); try the grilled barracuda, cooked with chilli in banana leaf.

Frankfurter-Lavinia Rustic restaurant for dedicated carnivores, serving hardcore German and Central European meat dishes – pork knuckle in beer sauce or goulash soup – from Rs.420. Follow the signed track opposite *Ivory Inn*.

Golden Mile The ritziest place on the beach, in a slightly naff way, with floodlit palms, obsequious waiters and (at weekends) lots of pretty young things spending daddy's hard-earned cash. Seating is either on the beach or on the terrace above. Food is slightly pricey (mains from Rs.300) but good – mainly seafood, plus a few meat and veggie options.

La Langousterie Set in a large pavilion on the beach with vaguely Kandyan-style wooden decor, this seafood restaurant has a rather somnolent atmosphere, but dishes are well prepared and moderately priced, and service is good.

Lion Pub Entered via a gaping lion's mouth, this is a popular drinking hole amongst locals and tourists alike, with pleasant outdoor seating on a square of palm tree-studded beach, cheap beer and a holiday atmosphere.

Mount Lavinia Hotel The food at this landmark hotel is generally excellent, with a sumptuous Western buffet spread here and a popular Sri Lankan "curry corner", plus à la carte options. There's also an informal seafood restaurant on the private beach; choose what you want from catch of the day. Even if you don't eat here, it's worth coming for a drink on the beautiful terrace above the sea – gorgeous at sunset.

Drinking, nightlife and entertainment

There can be few other cities of three million people which have as little after-hours action as Colombo, where large parts of the metropolis go to sleep by about eight in the evening, turning swathes of downtown into a virtual ghost town. Colombo does have a bit of **nightlife**, though, mainly kept going by a small band of westernized locals and the expat community. The scene is small and secretive, and venues tend to come and go on an annual basis.

A lot of the city's nightlife is focused around the **bars** listed below – *Glow* and *Clancy's* are currently the liveliest spots; both stay open until the small hours (all the other places below are open every evening until around 11pm or midnight). There's also a smattering of **nightclubs**, though these only really get going at weekends, plus a selection of **casinos**, most of which stay open 24 hours and offer free food and drink if you play. If none of the above appeal, there are also a couple of cinemas screening Western **films**, and one small **theatre** with low-key performances most nights.

Bars and pubs

Bar Latino R.A. de Mel Mw (Duplication Rd), Bambalapitiya. Fashionable new bar-café with a laid-back ambience, reasonable Spanish food, a decent drinks list, an arty, mainly local crowd and – if you're really keen – dancing lessons.

Bavarian Barn German Restaurant Galle Rd. Principally a restaurant, though the bar sports a decent list of moderately priced beers (happy hour daily 6pm–7pm, plus a second happy hour Thurs 11pm–midnight) and there's live music every Thursday from 8pm, when things can get pretty noisy.

Clancy's Irish Pub Maitland Crescent, Cinnamon Gardens ⊛www.clancys.lk. Colombo's Irish pub – Guinness and Caffreys on tap, but otherwise about

as Celtic as chicken tikka masala. There's cheap drinks, live rock music (Tues & Thurs), dance music (Fri), a quiz and band (Wed), and a DJ (Sat & Mon), as well as five pool tables upstairs, and a café-style menu (from Rs.250). Rs.300 entrance.

Cricket Club Café 34 Queen's Rd, off R.A. de Mel Mw (Duplication Rd, Bambalapitiya. The cosy little pub-style bar at this popular café (see p.105) gets packed with expats and locals most nights.

Echelon Pub *Hilton*, Fort. Big English-style pub, popular with well-heeled tourists and local businessmen; often has live music in the evenings.

Ex-Serviceman's Club Bristol St, Fort. The noisy, down-at-heel bar here is usually full of voluble locals getting smashed on Johnnie Walker. About the cheapest beer in Colombo, and conveniently close to the teetotal YMCA, if you're staying there, so it's not too far to stagger back after a heavy night.

Galle Face Hotel Romantic, colonial-style bar overlooking the courtyard of this atmospheric old hotel, with the Indian Ocean breaking just beyond. Wildly popular amongst honeymooners.

Glow Sir M.M. Markar Mw. This minimalist bar on the third floor of the Millennium Building (the entrance is around the back) is currently Colombo's hottest venue, with cool decor, beautiful people, lots of cocktails with dirty names (including the inevitable "Glow Job"), imported beers (Guinness, Murphy's, Boddingtons) and plenty of spirits. When you leave, try saying the full name of the street – Sir Mohammed Macan Markar Mawatha – to find out how drunk you are.

Rhythm and Blues Bar Daisy Villa Ave, Bambalapitiya. Relaxed nightspot, with good live music most days of the week.

Nightclubs and casinos

Almost all Colombo's tiny handful of **nightclubs** are hidden away in top-end hotels. **Music** tends to be a mix of dance, house and Western pop spiced up with the occasional Indian track. Clubs are free to hotel guests, and usually charge a few hundred rupees entrance to non-guests – the younger, more beautiful and more female you are, the greater your chances of wangling your way in for free. The best place in town is the *Blue Elephant* at the *Hilton*, a stylish little underground venue with big video screens and cool lighting, which is usually packed with the glamorous young things of Colombo. The nearby *The Boom* at the *Galadari* is a dated black box which seems to have escaped intact from one of the more Gothic moments of the 1980s. The brash *Cascades* at the *Colombo Plaza Hotel*, on Galle Road just south of the tourist office, is usually the liveliest, if not the most stylish, place in town – it's probably Colombo's nearest equivalent to a pick-up joint. *The Library* at the *Trans Asia* is officially guests-only, though you may be able to blag your way in – though the atmosphere can be as sedate and hush-hush as the name suggests. The *Blue Leopard* at the *Grand Oriental* is only for those whose idea of a good time involves watching crowds of middle-class Sinhalese and their frumpy teenage daughters singing along to Boney M.

There are five glitzy but fairly small-scale casinos dotted around town: in Bambalapitiya, there's *MGM*, 772 Galle Rd; while Kollupitiya is home to *Bally's*, 14 Dharmapala Mw; *Bellagio's*, 430 R.A. de Mel Mw; *The Ritz Club*, 5 Galle Face Terrace; and S*tar Dust*, 15th Lane. These places cater to a mainly Chinese and Southeast Asian clientele, offering a basic range of games – blackjack, poker, baccarat and roulette – with minimum stakes of Rs.300–500 (Rs.50 for roulette).

Cinema, theatre and performing arts

Colombo's only modern **cinema** is the Majestic, on the third floor of Majestic City (see overleaf), which shows the latest Hollywood blockbusters on its one and only screen (4–5 screenings daily; Rs.150). The dog-eared Liberty Cinema, opposite Liberty Plaza, sometimes shows Hollywood blockbusters, while the British Council (see p.110) occasionally screens more highbrow Western and Sri Lankan films. Named after the famous Sri Lankan photographer and musician, the **Lionel Wendt Theatre and Art Gallery** on Guildford Crescent in Cinnamon Gardens stages a varied programme of dance, music and English- and Sinhala-language drama. Offerings include adaptations, original plays and even ballet, plus school performances, with something different pretty much every night; tickets generally go for under Rs.500. The complex also has two galleries showing mainly photographic exhibitions – again, these change regularly.

Shopping

Colombo has an excellent range of shops, and a day trawling through the city's handicraft emporia and chic boutiques can be an enjoyable way to end a visit and offload surplus rupees. You'll find the best of Sri Lanka's modest traditional **handicraft** production on sale in the city, although it's more interesting to hunt out the characterful modern shops, such as Barefoot and Paradise Road, which offer chic contemporary takes on traditional designs – everything from stationery and stuffed toys to fabrics and kitchenware – and all at bargain-basement prices. Colombo also boasts an excellent selection of **bookshops**, a plethora of **jewellers** and, of course, plenty of **tea** shops.

Department stores and shopping malls

Cargills York St, Fort. The grand old lady of Colombo department stores, though its beautiful colonial-era shelves and display cases are chronically understocked save for a few postcards and a handful of English-language books. There's a good little supermarket at the back, though, which has a wonderful array of arrack.

Crescat Boulevard Galle Rd, Kollupitiya, next to the *Colombo Plaza Hotel*. Sri Lanka's ritziest mall – if you've spent some time out in the sticks, you might appreciate the crisp a/c and bland con-sumerism of it all. Home to branches of *Délifrance*, Vijitha Yapa Bookshop and Mlesna Tea Centre, as well as a Keells supermarket in the basement, and a food court.

House of Fashions R. A. de Mel Mw, Wellawatta, on corner of Visaka Rd. Huge and incredibly popular store that acts as a clearing house for the surplus production of Sri Lanka's massive garment industry. Three floors are stuffed with all sorts of clothing and sportswear at giveaway prices, including Western labels at under a tenth of their retail price back home. It's a bit hit and miss, though, depending on which orders have been over-fulfilled recently.

Majestic City Galle Rd, Bambalapitiya. Formerly the city's flagship mall and still a popular hangout with wannabe-Western local teenagers. Lots of shoe and clothes shops, a couple of good photo places (see p.111), a Cargills supermarket and a Mlesna Tea Centre.

Odel De Soysa Circus (Lipton Circus). The poshest department store in Sri Lanka, divided up into lots of little boutique sections. There's a good range of clothes, including both international and local labels, as well as a Dilmah Tea Shop and a bookshop well stocked with Sri Lanka-related titles. There are also branches of *Délifrance*, the *Nihonbashi Sushi Bar* and *Il Gelati* (Italian ice cream).

Handicrafts

Barefoot Galle Rd, Bambalapitiya ⓦ www .barefootceylon.com. Colombo's most interesting and original shop, and a serene retreat from the pollution and noise of Galle Road (the sense of escape enhanced by the deliberate lack of street-facing windows). It's perhaps best known for its vibrantly coloured woven fabrics, which are sold on their own or made into all sorts of objects including clothes, tablecloths, fabric-covered stationery, marvellous stuffed toys (grown-ups will love them too), and much more besides. There's also an excellent little bookshop (see opposite); temporary exhibitions are often held here as well, while a local weaver can often be seen at work in the courtyard at the back.

Gallery Café Alfred House Rd. The small shop at this wonderful café (see p.105) has a stylish assortment of assorted knick-knacks, including cute minimalist elephant sculptures, fabrics, photo frames and leatherbound books, plus some beautiful coffee-table books.

Kandyan Antiques Ernest de Silva Mw (Flower Rd), Kollupitiya. Specializing in objects from Kandy and around, and stocking a good selection of genuine antiques (from around US$35) alongside cheaper but extremely convincing forgeries. Offerings include Buddhist and Hindu religious items, and everyday artefacts like lime boxes and betel pounders.

Laksala York St, Fort. Worth visiting just to get an idea of the tat that often passes for Sri Lankan craftsmanship: the ground floor is a cavern of kitsch, including leather poufs, shiny orange Buddhas and various other monstrosities. Upstairs has a predictable selection of third-rate kolam masks, several herds of gruesomely coloured wooden elephants and some truly bizarre little Sri Lankan people with wobbling heads. Other offer-ings include mediocre fabrics, wood carvings and some memorably awful batiks; there's jewellery and tea downstairs.

Lakmedura Dharmapala Mw, Cinnamon Gardens. Basic selection of masks, tea, the usual lurid

elephants, tiny wooden rickshaws and lots of ultra-kitsch metalwork and embossed plates.
Lanka Hands Bauddhaloka Mw, Bambalapitiya. An upmarket alternative to the ubiquitous Laksala, selling similarly touristy stuff, but of a somewhat higher quality. Wares include decent wood and stone carvings, brasswork, fun toys, lacquered bowls, a mixed bag of batiks, and better-than-average kolam masks. Also has a reasonable selection of Western and Sri Lankan CDs.

Paradise Road De Soysa Circus (Lipton Circus). Set in a lovely, chintzy colonial villa, this is one of the top names in Colombo chic, stocking a mix of superior household items (glassware, china, cutlery, fabrics and tablecloths) alongside decorative stuff like scented candles, random *objets d'art* (including cute elephant carvings) and posh stationery. There's a second branch around the corner from the Gallery Café (see p.105), called *Paradise Road Studio*.

Tea

There are **tea** shops all over Colombo, although they tend to stock an almost identical range (see p.58). The main chain is the Mlesna Tea Centre, which has branches at Majestic City (see opposite), Crescat Boulevard, Liberty Plaza in Kollupitiya, and the *Hilton* (see p.81). Other tea shops include Dilmah, at Odel bookshop (see opposite); the Sri Lanka Tea Board, 574 Galle Rd, Kollupitiya; and the Tea Shop, on Sir M.M. Markar Mawatha between the *Holiday Inn* and *Galle Face Hotel*. The city's various Cargills and Keells supermarkets (see p.111) also have extensive selections.

Bookshops

New English-language **books** are sold in Sri Lanka for about two-thirds of the retail price in Europe and North America, though the stock is often rather dog-eared. All the city's bookshops also offer huge selections of Sri Lanka-related titles ranging from gorgeous coffee-table volumes to arcane tomes on a baffling range of historical, cultural and religious topics. The best selection can be found on Galle Road between Kollupitiya and Bambalapitiya; in Fort, Cargills (opposite) or the tiny bookshops at *Hilton*, *Galadari* or (best) *Taj Samudra* hotels are your only options.

Barefoot Galle Rd, Bambalapitiya ⓦwww .barefootceylon.com. The bookshop here manages to cram an excellent range of titles into a relatively small space, including the city's best selection of English-language fiction, plus lots of gorgeous coffee-table books and loads of volumes on Sri Lankan art, culture and history.
Bookland 430–432 Galle Rd. Rambling, musty bookstore with fair selection of English-language titles.
Odel De Soysa Circus (Lipton Circus). Excellent outlet in the city's flashest department store – particularly good for glossy coffee-table tomes,

and has a decent selection of local and foreign magazines.
Vijitha Yapa The island's main bookstore chain has branches in the basement of Unity Plaza (next door to Majestic City; see opposite), and Crescat Boulevard (see opposite), plus a smaller branch at the British Council (p.110). The first two branches have a good range of books on Sri Lanka, plus a big selection of English-language novels – mainly bodice-rippers, but with a few more worthwhile titles. A good selection of guidebooks, a few magazines and some stationery are also stocked; the Crescat Boulevard branch sells English newspapers and a few magazines.

Listings

Airlines, domestic Expo Aviation, 466 Galle Rd, Kollupitiya ☎011-451 2666; Lion Air, 14 Trelawney Place, Bambalapitiya ☎011-451 5615, ⓔlionairsales@sierra.lk; Serendib Express, 500

Galle Rd, Col 6 ☎011-250 5632, ⓦwww .serendibexpress.com.
Airlines, international Air Canada, East Tower, World Trade Center, Echelon Square, Fort

⏲011-254 2875; Air France, Shopping Village, *Galle Face Hotel*, Kollupitiya ⏲011-232 7605; Air India, 108 YMBA Building, Sir Baron Jayatilaka Mw, Fort ⏲011-232 5832; Austrian Airlines, c/o Browns Tours, 21 Janadhipathi Mw, Fort ⏲011-242 4973; British Airways, *Trans Asia Hotel*, 115 Sir Chittampalam A. Gardiner Mw, Slave Island ⏲011-234 8495; Cathay Pacific, 186 Vauxhall St, Slave Island ⏲011-233 4145; Emirates, Hemas House, 75 Braybrooke Place, Slave Island ⏲011-471 6565; Gulf Air, 11 York St, Fort ⏲011-244 0880; Indian Airlines, Bristol Complex, 4 Bristol St, Fort ⏲011-232 6844; Lufthansa, c/o Lewis Brown's Air Services, 2nd Floor, EML Building, 61 W.A.D. Ramanayake Mw, Slave Island ⏲011-230 2823; Malaysia Airlines, Hemas Building, 81 York St, Fort ⏲011-234 2291; Qatar Airlines, 201 Sir James Peiris Mw, Col 2 ⏲011-452 5700; Royal Jordanian Airlines, 40a Kumaratunge Mw, Kollupitiya ⏲011-230 1621; Singapore Airlines, 315 Vauxhall St, Slave Island ⏲011-230 0757; SriLankan Airlines, East Tower, World Trade Center, Fort ⏲011-242 1161 (reservations), ⏲01973-35500 (reconfirmations), ⏲01973-32677 (flight information); Thai Airways, JAIC Hilton, Union Place, Slave Island ⏲011-230 7100; United Airlines, East Tower, World Trade Center, Fort ⏲011-234 6026.

Airline tickets George Travel (see p.113) is a good source of discounted international airline tickets.

Airport ⏲011-225 5555.

Ayurveda Colombo's only ayurveda centres are in Mount Lavinia (see p.100).

Banks and exchange All banks in Colombo change cash and travellers' cheques, and many also have ATMs, which accept foreign cards; these are often open 24hr and most accept both Visa and MasterCard (a few only accept Visa); all the banks marked on our maps of Colombo have ATMs which accept foreign cards. As well as banks marked on the maps, there are useful ATMs in Fort at the *Galadari Hotel* and on the third floor of the World Trade Center; and in Kollupitiya in the corridor between Crescat Boulevard shopping mall and the *Colombo Plaza Hotel*. The Bank of Ceylon Bureau de Change, York St (Mon–Fri 8.30am–6pm, Sat & Sun 8.30am–4pm; open 365 days a year) changes money and travellers' cheques at fractionally lower than bank rates but is useful since it's open at weekends.

British Council 49 Alfred House Gardens, Kollupitiya (Tues–Sat 9am–6pm; ⊛www .britishcouncil.lk). Has an extensive library, including a good selection of Sri Lanka-related titles, plus online British newspapers, a small cafeteria and a branch of the Vijitha Yapa bookshop chain;

also stages occasional talks, readings, concerts and exhibitions.

Bus information Central Transport Board ⏲011-258 1120.

Car rental Most people opt to hire a car with driver, most easily done through your hotel or via one of the tour operators listed on p.113. For self-drive, the most reliable options are Quickshaws (see p.113), and Avis, 4 Leyden Bastian Mw, Fort (⏲011-232 9887, ⊛www.avis.com). Rates at both start from around US$20 per day including 100km free mileage and insurance.

Couriers Fedex, 300 Galle Rd, Kollupitiya.

Cricket Test matches are played at the Sinhalese Sports Club (SSC), centrally located on Maitland Place in Cinnamon Gardens. The BCCSL shop (Board of Cricket Control of Sri Lanka; ⏲011-471 4599) here sells tickets for forthcoming internationals. One-day internationals are played at the Premadasa Stadium, Maligawatha, Dematagoda. Tickets are available direct from the stadia.

Cultural associations Alliance Française, 11 Barnes Place, Cinnamon Gardens ⏲011-269 4162; British Council (see above); Goethe Institute, Gregory's Rd, Cinnamon Gardens ⏲011-269 4562; Indian Cultural Centre, 133 Bauddhaloka Mw, Kollupitiya ⏲011-250 0014.

Cultural Triangle tickets Central Cultural Fund office at 212/1 Bauddhaloka Mw, Cinnamon Gardens ⏲011-258 1944 (Mon–Fri 9am–4.30pm).

Customs ⏲011-242 1141.

Diving Underwater Safaris, 25c Barnes Place, Cinnamon Gardens (⏲011-269 4012, ⊛underwatersafaris.org) are the oldest diving school in Sri Lanka, offering PADI courses and reef and wreck dives to local sites.

Embassies and consulates Australia, 3 Cambridge Place, Cinnamon Gardens ⏲011-269 8767; Bangladesh, 47 Flower Rd, Cinnamon Gardens ⏲011-268 1310; Canada, 6 Gregory's Rd, Cinnamon Gardens ⏲011-269 5841; India, 36–38 Galle Rd, Kollupitiya ⏲011-242 1605; Indonesia, 400/50 Sarana Rd, off Bauddhaloka Mw, Cinnamon Gardens ⏲011-267 4337; Malaysia, 92 Kynsey Rd, Cinnamon Gardens ⏲011-268 6090; Maldives, 23 Kaviratne Place, Colombo 6 ⏲011-258 6762; Pakistan, 221 De Saram Place, Colombo 10 ⏲011-269 6301; Thailand, 43 Dr C.W.W. Kannangara Mw, Cinnamon Gardens ⏲011-268 9037; UK, 190 Galle Rd, Kollupitiya ⏲011-243 7336; US, 210 Galle Rd, Kollupitiya ⏲011-244 8007.

Emergencies Fire and ambulance ⏲011-242 2222.

Hospitals and health clinics If you need an English-speaking doctor, first ask at your hotel or guest house (or at the nearest large hotel). For minor medical problems, contact one of the following private medical clinics: Medicheks, 383 Galle Rd, Kollupitiya ☎011-257 5273; Healthcare Laboratories, 108 Horton Place, Cinnamon Gardens ☎011-269 6984; or Glass House, Edinburgh Crescent, Cinnamon Gardens ☎011-269 1322. Reputable private hospitals include Asiri, 181 Kirula Rd, Havelock Town ☎011-250 0608; Nawaloka, 23 Sri Saugathodaya Mw, Slave Island ☎011-254 6258; Asha Central, Horton Place, Cinnamon Gardens ☎011-269 6412; or Durdans, Kollupitiya ☎011-257 5205.

Golf The beautifully manicured Royal Colombo Golf Club (☎011-269 5431) is in the suburb of Borella, a couple of kilometres east of Fort. Nonmembers can play on Saturdays and Sundays with advance reservation (green fees Rs.2400; club hire Rs.1000; caddy Rs.250).

Internet access Berty's, Galle Rd, Kollupitiya (daily 8am–10pm; Rs100 per hour); The Café@inter.net and Surf Play, 491 Galle Rd, Bambalapitiya (daily 9am–7pm; Rs.70–140 per hour); Lanka Internet, 443 Galle Rd, Kollupitiya (daily 8.30am–7pm; Rs.65 per hour); Enternet Box, corner of Galle Rd and De Fonseka Place, Bambalapitiya (daily 9am–10pm; Rs.50 per hour). Another possibility is the *Empress Hotel* (see p.82) in Bambalapitiya, which has a 24hr cyber-café (Rs.150 per hour).

Laundry There are no public laundries in Colombo, although your hotel or guest house should be able to do your laundry for you. Alternatively, visit the Taj Laundrette, around the back of the *Taj Samudra* hotel (Mon–Sat 9am–12.30pm & 1.30–6pm; shirt Rs.80, trousers Rs.95, dress Rs.120).

Left luggage There's a left-luggage office at Fort Railway Station in the cloakroom outside the station to the left of the entrance.

Maps Survey Department, Kirula Rd, Havelock Town (see p.18). There's also a Survey Department Map Sales Centre on Chatham St in Fort, though this is only irregularly open and doesn't have much stock.

Pharmacies Osu Sala, the huge state-owned pharmacy, is at de Soysa Circus (Lipton Circus), Cinnamon Gardens (☎011-269 4716). There are well-stocked pharmacies in Cargills on York St, Fort, and in the basement of Majestic City, Kollupitiya. Other useful pharmacies include I. C. Drug Stores, Bambalapitiya Junction, Galle Rd, Bambalapitiya ☎011-581 770; The City Dispensary, Union Place, Slave Island ☎011-259 5897; and Union Chemists, Union Place, Slave Island ☎011-269 2532.

Police Tourist police, Fort Police Station, Bank of Ceylon Mw, Fort ☎011-243 3333.

Post office The main post office on Bristol St in Fort (Mon–Sat 7am–6pm) offers free poste restante service (post is held for only 14 days), and there are agency post offices all over the city, especially along Galle Rd. Note that there are vague plans to move the main post office back into the old General Post Office building near the clock tower in the middle of Fort (see p.84) in the next year or two, depending on the security situation.

Phones There are clusters of communications bureaux all over the city; try Bristol St in Fort, and the southern end of Galle Rd. Most of the Internet places listed opposite do webcalls (around Rs.20–30 per minute to the UK, US and Australia).

Photos The reliable Millers Colour Lab (Kodak Express) has branches in the basement of Majestic City (see p.108) and in Cargills (see p.108), and there's a large Fuji Film bureau next to the Majestic City branch. As well as all the usual products and services, these places sell slide and black-and-white film.

Supermarkets The main chains are Cargills, which has branches at York St, Fort (see p.108) and in the basement of Majestic City (see p.108); and Keells, in the basement of Crescat Boulevard (see p.108).

Train information ☎011-243 5838.

Wildlife Conservation Department 18 Gregory's Rd, Cinnamon Gardens ☎011-269 4241, ⓦ www.dwlc.lk.

Moving on from Colombo

As you would expect, Colombo has the island's best **transport connections**; however as the density of traffic means it takes a good hour to get out of the city by bus, the train is an attractive option for short hops down the coast. For longer journeys, though, the bus is almost always quicker.

For more detailed journey times and frequencies, see p.147.

By train

Colombo is the hub of the Sri Lankan **railway** system, with direct services to many places in the country – see p.147 for detailed timetable information. The principal terminus, **Fort Railway Station** can be somewhat anarchic, especially during rush hours. Different ticket windows sell tickets to different destinations – if in doubt, check with the helpful enquiries window; it's left along the platform from the entrance. The **Railway Tourist Information Service**, outside next to the main entrance (Mon–Fri 9am–5pm, Sat 9am–1.30pm; ☎011-244 0048) is a useful source of general information and arranges tours; you may also be able to buy a railway timetable.

If you're taking the **train to Kandy**, be sure to sit on the south side of the train (i.e. on the right as you face the front of the train) – you'll get much better views.

By bus

All **long-distance buses** out of Colombo leave from one of the Pettah's three bus terminals (see p.78). **Bastian Mawatha** handles private buses to Kandy and Nuwara Eliya, as well as all destinations along the south coast as far as Kataragama, including Hikkaduwa, Galle, Matara, Tangalla and Tissamaharama. Although cramped, the station is relatively orderly, with plenty of information kiosks.

Saunders Place Bus Station handles all other long-distance private buses: services to Negombo, Chilaw, Puttalam, Ampara, Haputale, Badulla, Trincomalee, Mannar, Kurunegala, Vavuniya, Ratnapura, Anuradhapura, Dambulla, Sigiriya and Polonnaruwa. Note, though, that signage is minimal here, and that there are far too many vehicles jockeying for position in far too small a space. Watch your back.

The **Central Bus Depot** handles CTB bus departures to destinations all over the island. It's well laid out and spacious, although you're unlikely to use it, since it's generally easier and quicker to pick up a private bus.

Useful **bus numbers** include: Kandy #1, Galle #2, Negombo #240, International Airport #187, Matara #32, Kataragama #32, Kurunegala #5 and #6, Anuradhapura #4, #14 and #57, Nuwara Eliya #79, Badulla #99 and Trincomalee #79. Private and CTB buses to the same destination share the same number.

By car

The easiest way to leave Colombo is to hire a **car**, which can be done through any of the major hotels or through one of the city's travel agents (see opposite). All the bigger hotels have travel desks where you can arrange a car and driver for any length of time to anywhere in the island – as ever, it pays to shop around. Three of the best set-up places are the branch of Hemtours at the *Holiday Inn*, the travel desk at the *Galle Face Hotel* and the travel desk at the *Grand Oriental* – the last is usually the cheapest. Count on US$14 and up for a trip to the airport, and US$50–60 for transfers or day tours to Galle and Kandy.

By air

The easiest but most expensive way to reach the **international airport** is to hire a taxi (see p.79). Alternatively, there's an **airport bus** from Bastion Mawatha station (every 15 min; 1hr 15min) – note, though, that buses don't actually go into the terminal, but dump you outside the airport gates, from where it's a 200-metre walk. Avaricious tuktuk drivers prey on disoriented tourists at the gates and charge rip-off rates to take you the short distance down the airport approach road.

Sri Lanka's **domestic airport** is at **Ratmalana**, south of Mount Lavinia; the easiest way to get there is by taxi or tuktuk, though if you're counting the pennies you could catch a train or bus to Mount Lavinia first, and pick up a taxi or tuktuk there. There are daily flights to Jaffna operated by the three domestic airline companies listed on p.109. Serendib Air also operate flights five times weekly to Trincomalee.

Tour operators in Colombo

Setting up a **tour** with a Colombo-based operator is a very viable alternative to arranging one at home, and local knowledge gives several of the following companies a distinct edge over foreign rivals – Jetwing Eco-Tours and Adventure Sports Lanka are particularly well regarded, whilst Jetwing and Aitken Spence between them own many of the island's finest hotels.

Adventure Sports Lanka 366/3 Rendapola Horagahakanda Lane, Talangama, Koswatta ⓣ011-279 1584, ⓦwww.actionlanka.com. Offerings from Sri Lanka's leading outdoor adventure specialists include kayaking and whitewater rafting (at Kitulgala and near Kandy), mountain biking (from half-day fun rides to two-week tours), river and lagoon canoeing trips, and trekking trips, including hikes in the Knuckles range and around Adam's Peak.

Aitken Spence Travels 315 Vauxhall St, Slave Island ⓣ011-230 8408, ⓦwww.aitkenspencetravels.com. Well-organized travel wing of one of Sri Lanka's top hotel chains, offering six- and eight-day general island tours, plus an interesting selection of wildlife and nature tours through their ecotourism arm, Nature Voyagers (ⓦwww.naturevoyagers.com).

Connaissance de Ceylan 58 Dudley Senanayake Mw, Borella ⓣ011-268 5601, ⓦwww.connaissanceceylon.com. Big operator which owns several top-end hotels and arranges a wide variety of tours, including mountain-biking, whitewater rafting, surfing, camping, trekking, diving and safari and cultural tours.

George Travel Bristol St, Fort ⓣ011-242 2345, ⓕ242 3099. Tucked away in a sign-posted building about halfway up Bristol Street, this small but long-established travel agent offers very cheap car-and-driver transfers and tours island-wide. Also a good source for cheap air fares.

Jetwing Travels Jetwing House, 46/26 Navam Mw, Slave Island ⓣ011-234 5700, ⓦwww.jetwingtravels.com. Travel division of Sri Lanka's largest hotel group, with a small selection of island-wide tours (7 or 8 days). Their subsidiary company, Jetwing Eco-Holidays (ⓦwww.jetwingeco.com) is Sri Lanka's leading eco-tourism operator, offering an excellent range of wildlife and adventure activities including birdwatching, leopard-spotting, trekking, cycling, whitewater rafting, whale-watching and more. Nature activities are led by an expert team of guides.

Quickshaws Tours 3 Kalinga Place, Wellawatta ⓣ011-258 3133, ⓦwww .quickshaws.com. With a wide range of vehicles for hire (with or without driver), this is one of the best options if you want to drive yourself (from around US$25 per day; minimum age 25; US$150 deposit). Customized tours also available.

Walkers Tours 130 Glennie St, Slave Island ⓣ011-242 1101, ⓦwww.walkerstours .com. Large operator, offering general tours island-wide along with twelve-day mountain-biking, rafting, trekking and birdwatching trips, and golf, watersports and diving packages. They also arrange fancy weddings – if you want to ride into your marriage service on an elephant whilst dressed as an eighteenth-century Kandyan princeling, these are the people to talk to.

North of Colombo

The coast **north of Colombo** is much less developed than that to the south. The principal destination is the resort of **Negombo**, close to the international airport, beyond which a few further hotels and guest houses dot the largely unspoilt coast through **Waikkal** and **Marawila**. Few visitors make it beyond here to the unremarkable fishing town of **Chilaw**, notable only for the important Munnesvaram Hindu temple nearby, or the equally unexciting fishing settlement of **Puttalam**, which you might pass through if you're travelling from Negombo to Anuradhapura. The area north of Puttalam was affected by its proximity to the front line of the civil war, though the area's major attraction, the extensive **Wilpattu National Park**, has now reopened after many years of war-enforced closure.

Negombo and around

The sprawling town of **NEGOMBO** is of interest mainly thanks to its proximity to the international airport, just 10km down the road – many visitors stagger off long-haul flights straight into one of the beach hotels here, or use the town as a last stop before flying home; it's also a good place to arrange

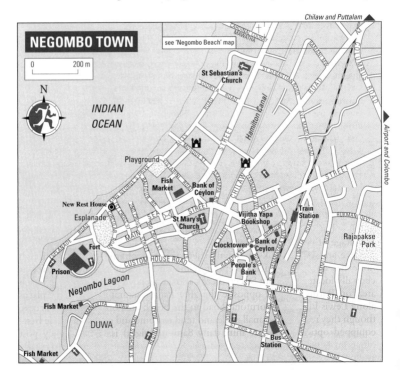

Chilaw and Puttalam

NEGOMBO TOWN

see 'Negombo Beach' map

0   200 m

N

INDIAN OCEAN

St Sebastian's Church

Hamilton Canal

Playground

Fish Market

Bank of Ceylon

New Rest House

Esplanade

St Mary's Church

Vijitha Yapa Bookshop

Train Station

Fort

Clocktower   Bank of Ceylon

Rajapakse Park

Prison

Negombo Lagoon

People's Bank

Fish Market

DUWA

Bus Station

Fish Market

Airport and Colombo

onward tours and transport, and is convenient for boat trips to the wildlife-rich wetlands of **Muthurajawela**, just south of town. Negombo's beach is very wide in places, but can feel rather shabby if you've visited any of the more pristine resorts further south (although if you've just arrived from Europe or North America, you'll appreciate even Negombo's rather down-at-heel tropical charms).

Negombo is also the heartland of **Christian Sri Lanka**, as borne out by the enormous churches and florid wayside Catholic shrines scattered about the town and its environs. The people of Negombo are **Karavas**, Tamil fishermen who converted en masse to Catholicism during the mid-sixteenth century under the influence of Portuguese missionaries, taking Portuguese surnames and becoming the first of Sri Lanka's innumerable de Silvas, de Soysas, Mendises and Pereras. The **Dutch** made the town an important commercial centre, building a canal (and a fort to guard it) on which spices – particularly cinnamon, which grew profusely in the surrounding areas – were transported from the interior to the coast prior to being shipped abroad.

Thanks to its position between the rich ocean waters and the Negombo Lagoon inland, Negombo has also developed into one of the most important **fishing ports** on the island. Fishing still dominates the local economy, with the sea providing plentiful supplies of tuna, shark and seer, while the lagoon is the source of some of the island's finest prawns, crabs and lobster. The Karavas are also famous for their unusual fishing boats, known as **oruwas**, distinctive catamarans (the word itself is derived from the Tamil *ketti-maran*) fashioned from a hollowed-out trunk attached to an enormous sail. Hundreds of these small vessels remain in use even today, and are an unforgettable sight when the fleet returns to shore.

Arrival and accommodation

Negombo's position near the airport guarantees a steady year-round trade, although things become fairly sleepy – and some shops and restaurants close down – during the monsoon (mid-April to mid-Oct). The resort area sprawls for a considerable distance along the coast, dividing broadly into two areas: the **town** itself, and **Negombo beach**. The latter straggles north for several kilometres and is backed by the long main drag, **Lewis Place** (which later turns into **Porutota Road**): a ramshackle thoroughfare dotted with endless shops, cafés, guest houses and heaps of refuse, each home to a few goats and huge flocks of crows.

The **bus** and **railway** stations are close to one another in the town centre, some way from most of Negombo's accommodation. A tuktuk from either station to the Lewis Place guest houses shouldn't cost more than Rs.60; or about Rs.100 to the north end of the beach (for instance the *Royal Oceanic* hotel) – but you might have to bargain hard; drivers here are used to taking advantage of newly arrived tourists.

There are several banks in town where you can **change money** (though none has an ATM which accepts foreign cards), while the **post office** is centrally located on Main Street; there's also an agency post office in the beach area, on Porutota Road opposite the *Alta Italia* restaurant. Dozens of places along Lewis Place and Porutota Road in the beach area offer **Internet** access, though they're all pretty small-scale and tend to come and go quickly. The best-equipped option (Rs.4 per min; daily 8am–midnight) is at the agency post office on Lewis Place opposite the *Golden Star Beach Hotel*. **Webcalls** (usually around Rs.30 per min) are also available at a number of these places. The (nameless) handicrafts shop just north of the *Alta Italia* restaurant and opposite the *Oasis Beach Hotel* has a range of **motorbikes** and trail bikes for Rs.600–1500 per day.

There's a modest branch of the Vijitha Yapa **bookshop** close to the train station. If you need to do some last-minute souvenir shopping, there are lots of **handicraft** shops all along the main road (itinerant hawkers also sell along the beach). Quality and choice here is as high as anywhere in Sri Lanka – the beautifully made wooden cars and tuktuks are something of a local speciality. **Ayurveda** treatments are available at the beautiful (though expensive) *Ayurveda Pavilions* (see opposite).

Accommodation

There's heaps of **accommodation** in Negombo, though the easy custom generated by proximity to the airport means that standards are generally indifferent. The resort as a whole caters to a mainly German clientele – as do most places down the west coast – and the larger **hotels** here service an endless supply of all-inclusive package tourists who appear to demand nothing more of Sri Lanka than cheap beer, execrable quasi-European cuisine and ping-pong tournaments. The good news for budget travellers is that some of Negombo's nicest places to stay are also its cheapest. Most of the **budget** places are clustered along Lewis Place; more **upmarket** options are concentrated to the north along Porutota Road.

Other than the New Rest House (see Negombo Town map, p.114), all accommodation below appears on the Negombo Beach map (p.118).

Budget

Dephani (also signposted as *Deepani*) 189/15 Lewis Place ☎031-223 8225, ✉dephanie@slt.lk. One of Negombo's best budget guest houses – sleepy and homely, with a beautiful garden running down to the beach. The twelve large, clean and spacious rooms come with big frame nets and attractive old furniture; the nicer upstairs ones have ocean views through the palms. Very cheap airport transfers and tours, plus bicycle hire. ❷

Jeero Guest House 239 Lewis Place ☎031-223 4210. Small, good-value family place in a neat modern house – the four rooms (two sea-facing) are spacious, nicely furnished and come with hot water. Laundry service and bike rental. The helpful owner is a CTB-registered guide (see p.119). ❷

New Rest House 14 Circular Rd, Negombo Town ☎031-222 2299. If you want to stay in town, this is your best (indeed almost your only) option. Set in an attractive old colonial building, the old wing has eight huge, atmospheric suites with bags of character, albeit of a rather gloomy type; the more modern rooms in the new wing are decent value and fairly clean, though a bit musty. No single rates. ❷

Ocean View 104 Lewis Place ☎031-223 8689, ✉oceanview@wow.lk. Run by a charming family, one of whom is a CTB-registered guide (see p.119). The downstairs rooms are simple and clean, if a bit musty and dark; those upstairs are smarter, more modern and about twice the price.

The owners' nearby *Peace Villa* has another six cheap, simple rooms. ❶

Silver Sands 229 Lewis Place ☎031-222 2880, ⓦwww.silversands.go2lk.com One of Negombo's best budget options, set in attractive white arcaded buildings running down to the beach. The rooms (a few with a/c) are a mite old and musty, but are scrupulously clean and very good value – most overlook the courtyard garden and come with private balconies and unusual but effective hooped mosquito nets. There's also a good little restaurant, bikes and motorbikes for hire, and very cheap airport transfers. ❷

Starbeach 83/3 Lewis Place ☎031-222 2606. Very similar to the adjacent *Dephani*, this extremely low-key guest house is set in attractive gardens on the beach, with simple but comfortable rooms (three with sea-facing balconies; upstairs rooms are breezier and have slight views), plus a nice beachfront garden and restaurant. Downstairs ❶, upstairs ❷

Sunflower Beach Hotel 289 Lewis Place ☎031-222 4308, ✉sunflo@eureka.lk. Surprisingly good-value hotel set in an unusual semicircular building – ignore the grotty entrance, which looks like the rear end of a public convenience. Rooms are spacious, with parquet floors, wooden furniture and balconies overlooking one of the biggest pools in town (non-guests Rs.150). A/c supplement Rs.300. ❸

Topaz Beach Hotel 21 Porutota Rd ☎ 031-227 9265, @ topaz@sltnet.lk. Very basic resort-style hotel on the beach. The sea-facing, balconied rooms are pretty basic – and a bit musty and old-fashioned – but are OK at the price. ❸

Moderate and expensive

Ayurveda Pavilions Porutota Rd ☎ 031-227 6718, ⊛ www.jetwinghotels.com. Easily the classiest and priciest place in town, with a pretty little ochre huddle of twelve gorgeous "bungalows", each hidden behind high walls in its own private garden. All come with bags of mod-cons and gorgeous open-air bathrooms, while there's an army of staff to cater to your every whim, including four ayurveda doctors, fifteen therapists and a sitar-playing music therapist. Courses include "soft" (1–3 days), preventative (14–21 days) and curative (according to need), and rates are inclusive of treatments, accommodation and meals. Treatments are also available to guests for US$120 per day; individual treatments start at US$18, and one-week programmes are US$540 (treatment only). ❾

Blue Oceanic Beach Hotel Porutota Rd ☎ 031-227 9000, ⊛ jetwinghotels.com. Big beachside hotel with some of the nicest rooms in Negombo: all are large, sea-facing with a/c and right on the beach, with nice big French windows and private verandahs. The public areas are less appealing, although there's a decent-sized pool (non-guests Rs.250) and an expensive ayurveda centre. No single rates. ❼

Brown's Beach Hotel Lewis Place ☎ 031-222 2031, ⊛ www.aitkenspenceholidays.com. Contender for the title of Negombo's best resort hotel, with spacious and attractive public areas backing onto the beach. Standard rooms in the main building are pleasant and decent value; superior rooms and the rather unappealing bunga-lows on the beach are comparatively overpriced. There's also a huge pool (non-guests Rs.200), two restaurants, an ayurveda centre, children's play-ground, coffee shop, karaoke bar and even an *oruwa* boat for ocean trips (Rs.1000/1–2hr). Standard ❻ , superior and bungalows ❼

Golden Star Beach Hotel Lewis Place ☎ 031-223 3564, @ goldenst@cga.slt.lk. Attractive medium-scale beachfront hotel with a nice pool (non-guests Rs.125). Rooms are pleasant (and some are very spacious), with slightly old-fashioned furniture and feel; most have sea views, and all come with a/c and hot water. ❹

The Icebear 103 Lewis Place ☎ 031-223 3862, ⊛ www.icebearhotel.com. Unusual Swiss-owned place, with five rooms of various sizes and prices scattered around a gorgeous rambling garden and furnished with a bizarre assortment of kitsch – everything from dancing Shivas to grandfather clocks. It's weird and full of character, if rather expensive for what are essentially quite basic rooms. Watch out for the chained monkey in the garden, which will make a grab for the unwary. ❷–❹

Sea Garden Hotel Porutota Rd ☎ 031-227 9000, ⊛ www.jetwinghotels.com. Small, unpretentious hotel: rooms (some overlooking the beach) are a bit past their best, but are cheerily furnished in bright colours, and are good value. There's an attractive restaurant, guests have free use of the pools at the nearby *Blue Oceanic* and *Royal Oceanic* hotels, and also get ten percent off food and drink there. No single rates. ❸

Hotel Sunset Beach 5 Senaviratna Mw, Lewis Place ☎ 031-223-8758. This relatively small-scale, friendly and pleasantly understated hotel is one of Negombo's best mid-range options, and is good value, particularly in high season. All rooms are sea-facing and come with hot water (though no a/c); they're quite simple but bright, with tiled floors and nice French windows opening onto private balconies. Medium-size pool (non-guests Rs.200). ❹

Royal Oceanic Porutota Rd ☎ 031-227 9000, ⊛ www.jetwinghotels.com. Negombo's most stylish resort, set in nicely landscaped grounds and with an attractive pool (non-guests Rs200) running partly underneath the main building. Rooms are very spacious (if slightly musty), and come with private balcony, a/c, TV, phone, minibar and writing desk. No single rates. ❼

The town and beach

Negombo's **old town** preserves a clutch of colonial remnants and some lively splashes of local life that can fill an interesting couple of hours. The heart of the old town is situated on the tip of a peninsula enclosing the top of the Negombo lagoon. Close to the western end of the peninsula lie the modest remains of the old Dutch **fort**, mostly demolished by the British to make way for the prison that still stands behind the gateway. There's little to see beyond a semi–derelict

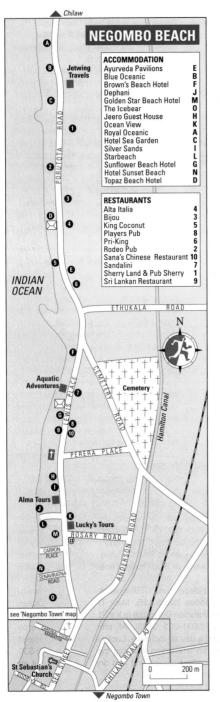

Chilaw

NEGOMBO BEACH

ACCOMMODATION	
Ayurveda Pavilions	E
Blue Oceanic	B
Brown's Beach Hotel	F
Dephani	J
Golden Star Beach Hotel	M
The Icebear	O
Jeero Guest House	H
Ocean View	K
Royal Oceanic	A
Hotel Sea Garden	C
Silver Sands	I
Starbeach	L
Sunflower Beach Hotel	G
Hotel Sunset Beach	N
Topaz Beach Hotel	D

RESTAURANTS	
Alta Italia	4
Bijou	3
King Coconut	5
Players Pub	8
Pri-King	6
Rodeo Pub	2
Sana's Chinese Restaurant	10
Sandalini	7
Sherry Land & Pub Sherry	1
Sri Lankan Restaurant	9

Jetwing Travels

PORUTOTA ROAD

INDIAN OCEAN

ETHUKALA ROAD

N

Aquatic Adventures

CEMETERY ROAD

Cemetery

Hamilton Canal

LEWIS PLACE

PERERA PLACE

Alma Tours

Lucky's Tours

ROSARY ROAD

CARRON PLACE

SENAVIRATNA ROAD

ANDERSON ROAD

see 'Negombo Town' map

CORONAL ROSARY MAWATHA

St Sebastian's Church

SEA STREET

CHILAW ROAD

A3

0   200 m

Negombo Town

archway emblazoned with the date 1678, and a very short section of ramparts topped with a miniature clocktower.

Continuing east, Custom House Road takes you past the northernmost arm of the Negombo lagoon, with myriad multicoloured fibreglass boats tied up under huge tropical trees. A couple of hundred metres down the road, a bridge crosses to the diminutive island of **Duwa**, home to the town's second fish market and venue for a locally famous Passion play, staged here every Easter. There are fine views of the lagoon from here.

A further 150m along Custom House Road, head north to reach one of Negombo's finest churches, **St Mary's**, a grandiose pink Neoclassical edifice, constructed over fifty years from 1874 onwards, which rises aristocratically out of the low-rise streets. The plain pink interior is largely bare apart from a few simple statues of saints and Stations of the Cross, plus a kitsch altarpiece in a kind of Sri Lankan rococo style and an image of Our Lady of Madhu (see p.392) on the pulpit, which devout locals touch in supplication. Old colonial buildings flank the west side of the church, one of which is home to various Christ images – an interesting place to see how local Buddhist, Hindu and Muslim traditions have seeped into Sri Lankan Christian customs: worshippers remove their shoes before entering and keep their feet pointed away from images, as in a Buddhist temple, while some prostrate themselves, Muslim fashion, before the images. North of here, the **Dutch canal** (known here as Hamilton Canal) arrows due north, continuing all the way to Puttalam. Once the major conduit for Dutch trade in the area, it now looks rather forlorn – you can walk along the towpath for a couple of hundred metres, but no further. Alternatively, head just north of St Mary's to reach Negombo's principal **fish market**, occupying a crumbling concrete pavilion surrounded by ramshackle clapboard shacks and piles of fishing nets.

A couple of kilometres north of the old town lies Negombo's **beach** area: a long strip of hotels and guest houses strung out along the sand or the main thoroughfare of **Lewis Place** (**Porutota Road** at its northern end). The beach scene here is rather desultory. The whole resort is too spread out to really have any central focus or atmosphere, and most of the package tourists (who make up the bulk of Negombo's visitors) tend to stay in their hotel slumped out around the pool – not altogether suprising, since the exposed nature of the coast here means that the sea is often rough and not great for swimming. The stretches of sand outside the main resorts are raked and cleaned daily, but the sections in between are still very much the province of the local Karavas, with crowds of fishermen mending their nets and kids playing cricket, accompanied by the occasional pig rooting around in the rubbish that litters the tar-stained sands.

If you want to get out onto the water, locals offer a variety of interesting **boat trips**. The simplest trip is a short turn up and down the beach in an oruwa boat, or a trip out in a motorboat to see the oruwa fleet at it comes into shore. Longer trips include visits (either on their own or in various combinations) to stretches of reef for snorkelling; trips around the Negombo lagoon; and up the Maha Oya river and the Dutch canal, which offers the chance to see lots of bird life and water monitors – you might also be taken to visit a coir factory and arrack distillery, and watch toddy tappers at work. You can also arrange **deep-sea fishing** and **night-fishing** trips. A few operators (try Alma Tours, see below) also organize trips to the Muthurajawela lagoon (see p.121).

Tour operators and guides in Negombo

Negombo is a good starting point from which to arrange onward **tours** and **transport**. All the larger hotels and various tour operators along the main road can arrange day-tours or transfers to Kandy, Colombo, Pinnewala Elephant Orphanage or pretty much anywhere else you fancy (count on around US$30 to Kandy, half that to Colombo) or longer tours island-wide. One of the more reliable general operators is **Alma Tours**, in Negombo Beach at 217 Lewis Place (T031-223 7532), which can arrange island-wide trips (including camping and trekking trips to places like Horton's Plains or Bundala) and all sorts of vehicle hire, including self-driving cars (Rs.2000 per day), vans (Rs.3000 per day), car or van with driver (around Rs.3300 per day all-inclusive), motorbikes (Rs.900–1100 per day) and good-quality Japanese bicycles, including ladies' bikes (Rs.250 per day). Negombo is also the centre of operations for Jetwing (see p.113), who own no less than five of the town's hotels – for tours, ask either at the *Royal Oceanic* or *Blue Oceanic* hotels, or at the Jetwing office just opposite the latter.

There are also several excellent independent CTB-registered **guides** in town, including Terry at the *Jeero* guest house (see p.116), Mark Thamel at the *Ocean View* guest house (see p.116), and Lakshman Bolonghe (a.k.a. "Lucky") at 146 Lewis Place, just south of Alma Tours (T031-223 3733). All offer island-wide trips customized to suit for around US$50 a day all-inclusive. Lucky also leads specialist birdwatching excursions, including an interesting half-day trip to Chilaw (US$30 per group), whose position on the border between wet and dry zones makes it an excellent place for birdlife – expect to see around fifty species.

There are various ways of arranging trips. There are usually a number of boatmen and their vessels pulled up on the beach, touting for custom; they often hang out by the *Royal Oceanic* and *Brown's Beach Hotel*. Alternatively, many guest houses and hotels can arrange something (try the *Dephani* or *Silver Sands*), while travel agents in town can also usually arrange trips. These usually last two to three hours and combine several attractions (for instance the lagoon, reef and a wreck, or the Maha Oya and canal); expect to pay between Rs.1200 and Rs.2000 for a three-hour trip (a bit extra if there are more people).

For **diving** in Negombo, contact the Anglo-Dutch-run Aquatic Adventures, 321 Lewis Place, opposite the *Sandalini* restaurant (☎077-764 8459), offering all the usual PADI courses and dives at around forty different sites, including remote and unspoilt reefs around 9km offshore at depths of 16–20m, plus wreck dives and deep dives with abundant marine life.

Eating and drinking

The town's location between the sea and the Negombo lagoon, source of some of the island's finest prawns and crabs, makes it a good place for **seafood**, while the number of tourists passing through means it also has one of Sri Lanka's better selections of **places to eat** – although disappointingly most are strung out along the main road, rather than on the beach itself. If you do end up in one of the resort hotels, note that buffet food at these places is almost uniformly dreadful; you'll get much better food by going à la carte, which is often no more expensive (and sometimes cheaper) than opting for half- or full-board rates.

As for **drinking**, *Players Pub* and *Rodeo* are usually fairly lively (the former is only open in high season), while *Pub Sherry* has a big list of cocktails, plus imported and local spirits and beers including rum, tequila, Corona beer, Red Bull and – yes – sherry.

All the places below appear on the Negombo Beach map (p.118).

Restaurants

Alta Italia (aka *The Italian Restaurant*) 36 Porutota Rd. Pleasant Italian-managed place which makes a decent stab at producing authentic Italian cuisine in the tropics. Offerings include gnocchi, polenta, risotto, lasagne, ravioli and heaps of other pasta dishes (Rs.250–400), plus pannacotta, tiramisu and Italian coffee.

Bijou 44 Porutota Rd. The best restaurant in Negombo, this homely Swiss-managed place has a tempting menu of excellent Swiss-Italian dishes including fondues (from Rs.1760; order in advance), pastas such as home-made spinach ravioli, and Malfatti cheese with fried potatoes; there's also a range of perfectly prepared seafood. Mains from around Rs.400.

King Coconut 11 Porutota Rd. A giant metal crab with flaying claws welcomes you to one of Negombo's few independent beachfront restaurants (although it's on a rather shabby bit of sand). The pizzas (Rs.230–300) are a bit weird but OK, and there's also pasta and seafood, including cheap grilled prawns.

Pri-King 10 Porutota Rd. One of the cheapest places in town (though in a rather unatmospheric roadside setting), with plenty of seafood, Chinese, Sri Lankan and tourist favourites like the inevitable Wiener schnitzel from around Rs.250.

Sana's Chinese Restaurant 212 Lewis Place. Cavernous, attractive restaurant whose Chinese chef concocts a huge range of unusually authentic and good-value Chinese dishes (from Rs.200). The emphasis is on seafood – lobster, crab, prawns, pomfret, grouper – but there are plenty of other choices, with big portions and cheap beer to wash it down with.

Sandalini 270 Lewis Place. Cheerfully eye-catching baby-blue establishment offering a small but good, authentic and cheap selection of Italian dishes using imported ingredients – this is one of the few places in Sri Lanka where you'll get real parmesan, capers and olives in your pasta – as well as seafood, noodles and devilled dishes. Wash it all down with imported wines (including Italian) at just Rs.500 a bottle.

Sherry Land 74 Porutota Rd. Set in a pleasant garden towards the north end of town, this restaurant does a bit of everything – rice and

Moving on from Negombo

All Negombo's guest houses should be able to arrange **taxis**; the international airport should cost Rs.500–600. The **bus station** is relatively orderly. CTB buses leave from the northern half of the terminal; private buses from the southern part; each has its own information kiosk. A few services leave from the road outside the terminal, including some to Colombo. Express minibuses (#240) leave every 10–15 minutes to **Colombo** (1hr) and the **airport** (20min). There are fairly regular departures to **Kandy** (3hr 30min) in the early morning, plus a few services in the afternoon. Alternatively, change at Kurunegala or Kegalle – the route via Kegalle is more direct. There's one early morning departure to **Anuradhapura** (5hr), otherwise, change at Kurunegala; this is also where you'll need to change for buses to **Dambulla**.

The **train** service between Negombo and Colombo is frustratingly slow, taking between 1hr and 1hr 30min to cover the forty kilometres to the capital, and there are only twelve services daily; it's easier and just as quick (or quicker) to catch the bus. Heading north, there are a similar number of departures to **Chilaw** (1hr 15min) and **Puttalam** (2hr 45min).

If you're **driving** from Negombo to Colombo, it's well worth travelling via the **coastal road** through Pamunugama and Hendala, which runs along the narrow spit of land which divides Negombo Lagoon from the ocean, passing innumerable churches en route – it's surprisingly unspoilt, and infinitely preferable to the dreary suburban sprawl of the main road.

curry, Chinese food, salads, steaks – though the main emphasis is on seafood. Prices are cheap and the cooking's good.

Sri Lankan Restaurant Lewis Place. Cosy and popular little restaurant offering the usual range of tourist dishes at the usual prices – portions are big and quality is high, but don't come if you're ravenously hungry, as service can be agonizingly slow. Look out for the signs saying "Sea Food"; the restaurant's proper name isn't clearly marked.

Around Negombo: Muthurajawela

Around 15km south of Negombo (and 20km north of Colombo), at the southern end of the Negombo lagoon and close to the northern edge of the airport, **Muthurajawela** comprises a considerable area of saltwater wetland which attracts an outstanding range of water-loving birds, including various species of colourful kingfisher, plus assorted herons, egrets, moorhen, duck, painted stork and many others. You might also spot crocodiles and macaque monkeys, and the marshes are also home to rarely seen otters, painted bats, slender loris, fishing cats and mouse deer.

The entrance to the wetland in on the mainland coastal road through Pamunugama. The small **visitor centre** (☎011-483 0150) here is the starting point for two-hour boat trips through the wetlands (Rs.600 per person including guide) – although not strictly necessary, you might want to ring in advance to make sure there's a boat available. The return trip from Negombo by taxi should cost around Rs.1000; alternatively, catch a train to Ja-Ela, on the main Colombo to Negombo line, and take a tuktuk from there for the one-kilometre trip to the entrance.

North of Negombo

North of Negombo the coastline becomes increasingly rocky and wild, with narrow beaches and crashing waves that make swimming impossible for most of the year. Not surprisingly, the area remains largely undeveloped, although there are a pair of good hotels at **Waikkal** and, further north, the bustling fishing town of **Chilaw** and the interesting **Munnesvaram Temple**, one of the island's most important Hindu temples. North of Chilaw is the fishing town of **Puttalam**, beyond which lies the extensive, and only recently reopened, **Wilpattu National Park**.

Waikkal to Mahawewa

Twelve kilometres north of Negombo, the small village of **WAIKKAL** is a major **tile-making** centre, thanks to the good clay found hereabouts, and the area is dotted with quaint tile factories sporting tall chimneys attached to barn-like buildings with sloping sides and huge roofs, with great mounds of freshly baked tiles stacked up beneath them. The village is also home to a couple of good **places to stay**. The best is the beautiful *Ranweli Holiday Village* (☎031-227 7359, ⓦecoclub.com/ranweli; ❻), an idyllic eco-friendly resort squeezed in between the ocean and the canal, with rustic but stylish rooms set in low red-brick buildings connected by covered walkways. Activities include yoga, boat trips on the canal and birdwatching trips with the hotel's excellent guide. The other place here is the *Club Hotel Dolphin* (☎031-227 7788, ⓦwww.serendibleisure.com; ❻), a huge resort which straggles along the coast for the best part of a kilometre, though it manages to feel surprisingly intimate even so, and retains a certain elegance despite its size. Activities include boat trips and canoeing on the nearby Dutch canal, and there are also floodlit tennis courts, squash courts and two pools: the smaller one has underwater music; the impressive larger one is allegedly the longest in South Asia.

Twenty kilometres north of Negombo, the strongly Catholic village of **MARAWILA** has several large churches and produces good batiks – a trade introduced by the Dutch from Indonesia. There's another small strip of rather wild and rocky beach here, and a cluster of uninspiring hotels, including the large and charmless *Club Palm Bay* resort (☎032-225 4954; ❽ all inclusive with drinks) and a couple of cheaper options, though it's far preferable to press on to Waikkal or Negombo.

Beyond Marawila, organized tourism ceases, as the beautiful coastal road runs north through an endless succession of fishing villages, past toppling palms, Christian shrines and cemeteries, palm shacks and prawn hatcheries. A few kilometres north of Marawila is **MAHAWEWA**, also renowned for its batiks. There are various tiny "factories" dotted around the village if you want to buy, or just watch how it's made.

Chilaw

Some 32 kilometres north of Negombo lies the predominantly Catholic fishing town of **CHILAW** (pronounced, Portuguese-style, "chilao"). Small but lively, it's home to a big fish market and is dominated by the eye-catching, orange-pink **St Mary's Cathedral**. Pretty much the only place **to stay** in Chilaw is the *Rest House* (☎032-222 2299; Rs.950, ❸). **Buses** run from Negombo to Chilaw every half-hour or so; there are frequent onward connections from Chilaw northwards to Puttalam. Alternatively, there are fairly regular **trains** north from Negombo to Puttalam throughout the day.

The only real reason for visiting Chilaw, however, is the **Munnesvaram Temple**, 4km to the east of town, one of the four most important Shiva temples on the island and an important pilgrimage centre. Its origins are popularly claimed to date back to the mythical era of the *Ramayana*, and legend states that

Vishnu himself worshipped here. The original temple was destroyed by the Portuguese, and the present building dates from the British era. The best time to visit is for the evening **puja**, held around 5pm, when the whole place comes alive with pilgrims, drumming and temple ceremonies. A lively local **festival** is celebrated here each year in either August or September, with fire walking.

Munnesvaram follows the usual plan of Sri Lankan Hindu temples, with a solidly built inner shrine of stone enclosed within a larger, barn-like wooden structure, its stout outer walls painted in the traditional alternating red and white stripes. The darkly impressive **inner shrine** (*cella*) is very Indian in style; a huge Shiva pillar stands in front of the entrance door. Inside the shrine is the temple's main Shiva lingam and a gold figure of Parvati, festooned in garlands. The **outer building** is a fine old wooden structure, despite the bits of modern bathroom tiling which are creeping into this – as into so many other – Sri Lankan Hindu temples. To the left of the entrance are various chariots (including a beautiful wooden horse) used to carry images and other paraphernalia during temple festivities. Past here, the rear end of the inner shrine is flanked by statues of Ganesh and Skanda, both framed by delicate makara torana arches. In the far corner stands an enormous eleven-headed composite figure, each head belonging to a different god; the stone next to it is used for the characteristic Sri Lanka ritual of coconut smashing (see p.200). More festival chariots can be found beyond here, including a peacock (for Skanda), a Garuda (Vishnu) and a lion (Parvati). On the other side of the inner shrine are images of various gods – Vishnu flanked by Garuda and Hanuman; Sarasvati playing a sitar; Kali killing a buffalo; and Lakshmi. Outside, the surrounding **courtyard** is full of stalls selling puja offerings – fruit, flowers – and other religious paraphernalia. The huge chariot used in the festival is usually parked outside too.

North to Puttalam and Wilpattu National Park

North of Chilaw, you enter the dry zone, the luxuriant palm trees giving way to more arid scrubland and dry forest. **PUTTALAM** (pronounced "Pootalam") sits 50km from Chilaw near the southern end of the enormous Puttalam Lagoon, and is of interest mainly as a transit point on the little travelled (at least by tourists) road between Negombo and Anuradhapura, or possibly as a base for visiting the recently reopened Wilpattu National Park. There are a couple of places **to stay** in town: the basic *Rest House*, on Beach Road (℡032-226 5299; ❷, ❸ with a/c); or the more appealing *Senatilake Guest Inn* at 81a Kurunegala Rd (℡032-226 5403; ❷).

Wilpattu National Park

Some 25km north of Puttalam, **Wilpattu National Park** is the largest in Sri Lanka, and was one of the most popular until its position close to the front line of the civil war led to its closure in 1985. It was finally reopened in 2003, though at the time of writing only about 50km of track was passable to visitors; the remainder of the park remains closed pending rehabilitation work. Wilpattu was formerly one of best places in Sri Lanka to spot leopards, not to mention deer, sloth bears and many types of bird. Poaching during the civil war has taken a significant toll on the wildlife, although you may see elephants, deer, crocodiles and giant squirrels.

An unusual feature of the park's topography are the numerous **villus**: these look like lakes, though they're actually just depressions filled with rainwater which expand and contract with the seasons, attracting a range of water-birds and wildlife. There are also fine stretches of monsoon forest around the entrance, while the coastal stretches along Portugal Bay and Dutch Bay (currently inaccessible) are thought to support rare populations of dugong.

The **park entrance** is at **Hunuvilagama**, about 40km west of Anuradhapura and 50km northeast of Puttalam. You may be able to arrange a tour in Anuradhapura through one of the guest houses or hotels. The usual **entry fees** apply (see p.53) and the park is open from 6am to 6pm daily. If you want **to stay** near the park, your only option is the *Preshamel Safari Hotel* (☎025-225 7699, or ☎011-252 1866 in Colombo and ask for Prasanna; ❷), near the turn-off to the park from the main Puttalam–Anuradhapura road. This has four simple but adequate rooms (one with a/c), and you can also arrange trips into the park here. Alternatively, contact Lionel Sirimalwatte of Wilpattu Safaris (☎077-724 9888) to arrange a jeep.

South of Colombo

Heading south out of Colombo, the fulminating Galle Road passes through a seemingly endless succession of ragtag suburbs before finally shaking itself clear of the capital, though even then a more or less continuous ribbon of development straggles all the way down the coast – according to Michael Ondjaate in *Running in the Family*, it was said that a chicken could walk along the roofs of the houses between Galle and Colombo without once touching the ground. The endless seaside buildings mean that although the road and railway line run close to the coast for most of the way, you don't see that much of the sea, beaches or actual resorts from either.

Beyond Colombo, the towns of **Moratuwa** and **Panadura** have both now been pretty much absorbed by the capital; the former is a major carpentry and furniture-making centre, and you might see the odd sight of lines of chairs and other furniture set out alongside the road for sale.

Kalutara

Just over forty kilometres from Colombo, bustling **KALUTARA** is the first town you reach travelling south which retains a recognizably separate identity from the capital. It's one of the west coast's largest settlements, but the long stretch of beach north of town remains reasonably unspoilt, dotted with a string of top-end hotels which make a decent first or last stop on a tour of the island, given the town's relative proximity to the international airport

> The best season for diving and swimming on the west coast is roughly November to mid-April; at other times, heavy breakers and dangerous undertows mean that it can be risky to go in beyond chest height. For more about swimming and other marine hazards, see p.25.

(although it's still a tedious two-hour drive by the time you've negotiated Colombo).

Sitting next to the broad estuary of the Kalu Ganga, or "Black River", from which it takes its name, Kalutara was formerly an important spice-trading centre, controlled at various times by the Portuguese, Dutch and British. Nowadays it's more famous as the source of the island's finest **mangosteens** (in season June to September). Kalutara announces its presence via the immense white dagoba of the **Gangatilaka Vihara**, immediately south of the long bridge across the Kalu Ganga. The dagoba was built during the 1960s on the site of the former Portuguese fort, and has the unusual distinction of being the only one in the world which is entirely hollow – you can go inside the cavernously echoing interior, largely covered in a sequence of 74 murals depicting various scenes from the Buddha's life. Outside, a sequence of dona-tion boxes line the roadside, popular with local motorists, who frequently stop here to say a prayer and offer a few coins in the hope of a safe journey – if you're travelling south, you'll soon understand why.

The remainder of the temple buildings are situated in a compound on the other side of the road, featuring the usual bo tree enclosures and Buddha shrines. It's a lively complex, and a good place to watch the daily rituals of Sri Lankan Buddhism: the Buddha images here are "fed" three times a day (rather like the package tourists at the nearby resorts); devotees place food in boxes in front of the images, as well as offering flowers (sometimes arranged in pretty stupa designs), lighting coconut-oil lamps, tying prayers written on scraps of cloth to one of the bo trees (sometimes with coins wrapped up inside them), or pouring water into the conduits which run down to water the bo trees' roots. The temple's size and position on the main road mean that there are lots of pushy guides hanging around, though you're under no obligation to go around with one if you don't want to.

Kalutara's fine stretch of **beach** extends north of the bridge all the way to the village of **WADDUWA**, some 8km away; it's surprisingly unspoilt and quiet, given the proximity of Colombo, and boasts some good top-end hotels (though there's not much for budget travellers). The end of the beach nearest the bridge is covered in fishing boats and is rather dirty; it gets cleaner the further north you go, although (as along much of the west coast) the sea can be rough, and most people swim in their hotel pools.

Practicalities

Buses drop passengers right in the middle of town on Main Street. Services head north and south along the Galle Road every ten minutes or so; the run to Colombo takes around an hour. The **train station**, Kalutara South, is on the seaward side of the town centre, south of the river; see p.147 for timetable details. There are several **banks** along Main Street; the **ATMs** at the Commercial and Sampath (Visa and MasterCard) and Seylan (Visa only) banks all accept foreign cards.

Aside from the guest houses and resorts, there's very little choice when it comes to **eating** in Kalutara, though there are a few informal beachside restau-rants along the southern section of the beach.

Accommodation

Most **accommodation** in Kalutara straggles up the beach north of the lagoon, spreading from Kalutara itself to **Wadduwa**. Distances are given from the bridge across the Kalu Ganga at the north end of Kalutara.

Kalutara

Dugong 750m north of the bridge ☎034-222 4330. Acceptable cheapie, set just back from southern end of the beach in a deeply somnolent part of town, with eight clean and comfortable (though rather dark) rooms arranged around a small courtyard. Free bikes for guests. ❷

Golden Sun 3km north of the bridge ☎034-222 8484, ⓦaitkenspenceholidays.com. Big resort hotel in an attractively isolated position at the northern end of Kalutara beach. Rooms have a/c, private balconies, minibar, hairdryer, safe, TV and phone, and there's also a shopping arcade, two restaurants, a gym, sauna, health centre and floodlit tennis court. ❼

Kani 1.5km south of the bridge ☎034-226 5377, ⓦwww.kanilanka.com. Stylish, Geoffrey Bawa-designed resort hotel in an excellent location on a narrow spit of land between the ocean and the Kalutara lagoon, with grand views over the town to one side and the ocean to the other. Rooms are elegantly furnished in a kind of minimalist-colonial style and diversions include a spa, tennis courts and dinner cruises, and you can also arrange watersports (waterskiing, sailing, canoeing) on the adjacent lagoon. ❼

Royal Palms 1.5km north of the bridge ☎034-222 8118, ⓦwww.tangerinetours .com/hotels.htm. Fancifully designed resort hotel virtually surrounded by an enormous serpentine pool (non-guests Rs.200). Rooms are comfortably bland, with a/c, satellite TV and minibar, and facilities include a gym, tennis court and the Pancha Karma ayurveda centre (actually in the *Tangerine Beach Hotel* next door). It's all very pleasant, though a bit lacking in style, given the hefty price tag. ❽

Tangerine Beach Hotel 1.5km north of the bridge ☎034-222 6640,

ⓦwww.tangerinehotels.com. One of Kalutara's oldest resorts, this attractively rustic four-star establishment is a bit cheaper than its nearby rivals, with cheery blue a/c rooms and nicely designed public areas with linked ponds and miniature fountains, and an ayurveda centre. ❼

Wadduwa

The Blue Water ☎038-223 5067, ⓦwww .jetwinghotels.com. Serene, Geoffrey Bawa-designed hotel set around a superb pool and beautifully screened by a grove of coconut palms. The attractive rooms have a/c, minibar, satellite TV, safe and sea-facing balconies; other facilities include a beauty salon, tennis and squash courts, three bars and a nightclub. ❽

Siddhaleepa Ayurveda Health Resort ☎038-229 6967, ⓦwww.ayurvedaresort.com. One of the island's best-known and oldest ayurveda resorts, offering intensive residential treatments plus hydrotherapy, yoga and meditation classes. Accommodation is in an unusual medley of themed rooms styled after various types of island architecture. All-inclusive one-week ayurveda packages cost US$775–1050 per person in a double room.

Around Kalutara

Glenross Neboda village, 21km inland from Kalutara ☎011-234 5719, ⓦwww.jetwinghotels .com. This beautiful hideaway in a stylishly refur-bished colonial planter's villa offers a very quiet rural retreat, with just four rooms and no phones or TV to intrude. There's a small pool, and a resident chef who can conjure up gourmet meals on demand. The bungalow is only let out to one group at a time, so you're guaranteed total privacy even if you only book one room. ❾

Beruwala, Aluthgama and Bentota

Some 15km south of Kalutara, the beaches at **Beruwala** and **Bentota** are home to Sri Lanka's biggest concentration of resort hotels, catering to a predominantly German clientele (the adaptable local touts and tuktuk drivers are as likely to hassle you in German as in English). This is the best-established package-holiday destination on the island, and some parts have largely sold out to the tourist dollar – if you're looking for unspoilt beaches and a taste of local life, this isn't the place to find them. Although some areas of the coast here – the main section of Beruwala beach in particular – are now eminently missable, there are still exceptions, including a cluster of excellent (though relatively expensive) hotels at the quiet southern end of Bentota, and a handful of attractive (and much cheaper) guest houses on the beautiful lagoon which backs the busy little town of **Aluthgama**, sandwiched between Bentota and Beruwala. Many of the hotels here are the work of local architect

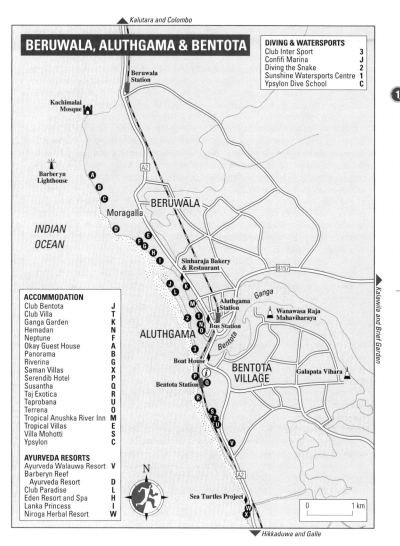

BERUWALA, ALUTHGAMA & BENTOTA

DIVING & WATERSPORTS

Club Inter Sport	3
Confifi Marina	J
Diving the Snake	2
Sunshine Watersports Centre	1
Ypsylon Dive School	C

Kalutara and Colombo

Beruwala Station

Kachimalai Mosque

Barberyn Lighthouse

INDIAN OCEAN

A2

BERUWALA

Moragalla

Sinharaja Bakery & Restaurant

B157

Ganga

Aluthgama Station

Wanawasa Raja Mahaviharaya

Bus Station

ALUTHGAMA

Bentota

Boat House

BENTOTA VILLAGE

Galapata Vihara

Bentota Station

Kalawila and Brief Garden

ACCOMMODATION

Club Bentota	J
Club Villa	T
Ganga Garden	K
Hemadan	N
Neptune	F
Okay Guest House	A
Panorama	B
Riverina	G
Saman Villas	X
Serendib Hotel	P
Susantha	Q
Taj Exotica	R
Taprobana	U
Terrena	O
Tropical Anushka River Inn	M
Tropical Villas	E
Villa Mohotti	S
Ypsylon	C

AYURVEDA RESORTS

Ayurveda Walauwa Resort	V
Barberyn Reef Ayurveda Resort	D
Club Paradise	L
Eden Resort and Spa	H
Lanka Princess	I
Niroga Herbal Resort	W

N

A2

Sea Turtles Project

0   1 km

Hikkaduwa and Galle

Geoffrey Bawa (see pp.132–133) – it's well worth splashing out to stay in one of his classic creations, whose artful combination of nature and architecture offers an experience both luxurious and aesthetic.

Needless to say, most people come here to loaf around on the beach, but there are plenty of distractions, including a wide range of **diving** and **watersports** (see box on p.134) as well as **boat trips** on the Bentota Ganga and the beautiful estate at **Brief Garden**. In addition, the area is a major centre for **ayurvedic treatments** (again, aimed at an overwhelmingly German clientele); most of the larger hotels offer massages and herbal or steam baths, and there are also a number of specialist resorts (see box on p.130).

Ayurveda – from the Sanskrit, meaning "the science of life" – is an ancient system of health care which is widely practised in India and Sri Lanka. Its roots reach back deep into Indian history: the basic principles are supposed to have been handed down personally from Brahma, the supreme Hindu deity, to Dhanvantari, the god of medicine, and descriptions of a basic kind of ayurvedic medical theory are found as far back as the second millennium BC, in the sacred proto-Hindu texts known as the Vedas.

Unlike allopathic Western medicines, which aim to determine what's making you ill, then destroy it, ayurveda is a holistic system which regards illness as the result of a derangement in a person's basic make-up. The ayurvedic system holds that all bodies are composed of varied combinations of five basic **elements** – ether, air, fire, water and earth – and that each body is governed by three **doshas**, or life forces: **pitta** (fire and water); **kapha** (water and earth); and **vata** (air and ether). Illness is seen as an imbalance in the proportions of three influences, and specific diseases are considered symptoms of more fundamental problems. Ayurvedic treatments aim to rectify such imbalances, and ayurveda doctors will typically examine the whole of a patient's lifestyle, habits, diets and emotional proclivities in order to find the roots of a disease – treatment often consists of encouraging a more balanced lifestyle as much as administering specific therapies.

With the developed world's increasing suspicion of Western medicine and pharmaceuticals, ayurveda is gaining an increasing following amongst non-Sri Lankans – it's particularly popular with Germans, thousands of whom visit the island every year specifically to take ayurvedic cures, so fuelling a massive explosion in the island's industry. Genuine courses of ayurveda treatment need to last at least a week or two to have any effect, and resorts and clinics which offer them will have resident ayurveda doctors who, after an initial consultation, will prescribe a programme of treatment based on each patient's individual constitution and state of health. These programmes usually consist of a range of herbal treatments and various types of baths and massages in combination with cleansing and revitalization techniques including yoga, meditation, special diets (usually vegetarian) and abstention from alcohol. Some of the more serious ayurveda resorts and clinics offer the **panchakarma**, or "five-fold treatment", comprising the five basic therapies of traditional ayurveda: therapeutic vomiting; purging; enema; blood-letting; and the nasal administration of medicines – a rather stomach-turning catalogue which offers the serious ayurveda devotee the physical equivalent of a thorough spring cleaning. A few places offer other yet more weird and wonderful traditional therapies such as treatments with leeches and fire ("moxibustion").

Although a sizeable number of people visit Sri Lankan ayurvedic centres for the serious treatment of chronic diseases, the majority of treatments offered here are essentially cosmetic, so-called "soft" ayurveda – **herbal** and **steam baths**, and various forms of **massage** are the overwhelming staples, promoted by virtually every larger resort hotel along the west coast. These are glorified beauty and de-stress treatments rather than genuine medicinal therapies, and whether there's anything truly ayurvedic about many of them is a moot point, but they're enjoyable enough, if you take them for what they are and don't confuse them with genuine ayurveda.

The principles of ayurveda spill over into many other Sri Lankan products. "Ayurveda tea" is ubiquitous, while local toiletries, beauty products and food may often contain ayurvedic ingredients – even basic spices such as salt, pepper, nutmeg, coriander and turmeric are claimed to have ayurvedic benefits, if used correctly. In addition, you'll occasionally see **ayurveda pharmacies**, intriguing places with long shelves closely packed with jars full of herbs, roots and other vegetable matter. Such medicines generally remain cheaper than imported Western medicines, and the treatment of choice for many Sri Lankans, although the fact that many ingredients only grow wild, and in small quantities, has created a national shortage of some remedies.

Heading south from Bentota, things become progressively more low-key through the villages of **Induruwa** and **Kosgoda**, where you'll find the coast's leading turtle hatchery, along with further hotels and guest houses.

Beruwala

BERUWALA is Sri Lanka's resort destination par excellence, perfect if you're looking for a naff tropical holiday with heaving beaches, bland food and characterless accommodation. Big resort hotels stand shoulder to shoulder along the broad and still attractive **beach**, separated by stout fences and armed guards from any possible contact with the ordinary life of Sri Lanka outside, while the locals poke their noses through the fences and ogle the fantasyland of foreign luxury within, deriving endless fascination from the strange sight of innumerable comatose Europeans laid out in pink heaps around the various hotel grounds and swimming pools. Things are, however, a lot better at the quieter northern end of the beach, which preserves a fine swathe of relatively unspoilt sand and offers a couple of reasonable budget options. There are lifeguards all along the main stretch of Beruwala beach; flags outside the resort hotels indicate whether it's safe to swim or not.

North of the resorts, scruffy **Beruwala town** is where Sri Lanka's first recorded Muslim settlement was established, during the eighth century. On a headland at the northern end of town, the **Kachimalai Mosque** is believed to be the oldest on the island, and to mark the site of this first Arab landing; it contains the shrine of a 10th century Muslim saint and is an important pilgrimage site at the end of Ramadan.

Practicalities

Beruwala's **train and bus stations** are in the town proper, two to four kilometres north of the various resorts and guest houses (the train station is served only by irregular, slow services). It's easiest to go to Aluthgama (see p.130) and get a tuktuk from there. The larger hotels all **change money** or travellers' cheques at lousy rates; if you want a bank (or a post office), you'll have to go down the road to Aluthgama. The **tourist police** office is on the east side of the Galle Road, almost opposite *Tropical Villas*.

Accommodation and eating

Some of Beruwala's hotels only take guests on an all-inclusive basis; this usually includes unlimited quantities of local booze. The buffet food dished up in the resort hotels is usually execrable; you'll generally get much better grub by ordering à la carte. There are also a few cheap and cheerful cafés along the beach if you fancy a drink or a snack.

For **ayurveda resorts** in Beruwala, see the box opposite.

Neptune ☎ 011-230 8408, ⓦ aitkenspenceholidays.com. The most attractive of the Beruwala resort hotels, with elegant, rather Andalucian-looking white buildings enclosing neat gardens, a big T-shaped swimming pool, attractive public areas and lots of facilities, including an ayurveda centre, beauty salon, mini-shopping arcade and four bars. Rooms (all with a/c and hot water) are slightly more characterful than elsewhere. ❽ all-inclusive

Okay Guest House ☎ 034-227 6248. Named with admirable accuracy: it's okay, though nothing more, with large and clean (if characterless) rooms at what by Beruwala standards is a reasonable price. ❷

Panorama ☎ 034-227 7091. The cheapest accommodation in the town, with eight breezy and good-value rooms set in a family home above the beach – all are clean and comfortable and have hot water, while four have sea views. Simple meals available on request. ❷

Riverina ☎ 034-227 6044, ⓦ www.confifigroup .com. Not quite as attractive as the *Neptune*, but better than all the other beachfront resorts, with

Ayurveda and health resorts in Beruwala and Bentota

Ayurveda Walauwa Resort Bentota ☏034-227 5372, ⓦwww.sribudhasa.com. In a high-walled compound on the land side of the Galle Road (just under 1km south of *Club Villa*), this looks a bit like a prison from the outside, though the tree-filled interior is leafy, shady and peaceful, with soothingly old-fashioned rooms. Ayurveda courses cost US$840 per week including accommodation (based on two people sharing), ayurveda meals and all treatments.

Barberyn Reef Ayurveda Resort Beruwala ☏034-227 6036, ⓦwww.barberyn.com. The oldest of the area's ayurveda resorts, and still one of the best. Seekers of physical and mental well-being will appreciate the low-key ambience, with a variety of accommodation (rooms, cottages, beach cottages) set in tranquil shaded grounds laden with frangipani. Courses go for a very moderate US$420 per week on top of accommodation. Rates include vegetarian ayurvedic meals and free yoga and meditation classes. ⑥

Club Paradise Bentota ☏034-227 5354, ⓔherbal@slt.net. Sister hotel to the *Ayurveda Walauwa* in a nicer location on Paradise Island; slightly more expensive, though the actual hotel is rather unprepossessing. Complete treatment courses go for a pricey $950 per person per week including accommodation (based on two people sharing) and meals.

Eden Resort and Spa Beruwala ☏034-227 6075, ⓦwww.confifigroup.com. This luxurious five-star establishment is a combination of plush holiday resort and spa/health club, the latter offering hydrotherapy, herbal baths, reflexology, pedicures, beauty treatments and free yoga lessons. Facilities include a gym, squash court, billiards room, outdoor jacuzzi, children's play area and even a glitzy nightclub. ⑧

Lanka Princess Beruwala ☏034-227 6711, ⓦwww.lankaprincess.com. Very smart German-owned place offering cosmetic rather than medicinal treatments in a big, luxurious resort setting; some more hard core treatments are also available. A six-day "wellness cure" goes for $370 per person. ⑧ all-inclusive of meals (treatments extra).

Niroga Herbal Resort Bentota ☏034-227 0312, ⓦwww.niroga.com. Next door to *Saman Villas*, this pleasant ten-room ayurveda resort is one of the cheapest around, with good-value twelve-day all-inclusive courses for around US$600 per person (including accommodation and ayurvedic meals). The emphasis here is on the treatment of chronic medical conditions – anything from high blood pressure to alcohol addiction – rather than on "soft" ayurveda, with treatment plans personally customized after an initial doctor's consultation.

curving white buildings set around extensive, palm-studded gardens. Rooms come with satellite TV, minibar and a/c, and there's an ayurveda centre, disco, coffee shop, myriad bars and an attractive glassed-in restaurant. ⑦

Tropical Villas ☏034-227 6157, ⓦwww .jetwinghotels.com. Unusual and extremely stylish hotel, five minutes' walk from the beach, with buildings forming an intimate quadrangle enclosing a beautiful garden with lots of trees and birdlife. The split-level rooms are little works of art, and

there's also a good restaurant serving Sri Lankan and Western fare. The only minus point is the proximity of the noisy Galle Rd – get a room as far away from it as possible. ⑦

Ypsylon ☏034-227 6132, ⓔypsylon@slt.net. Nice, laid-back guest house at the northern end of Beruwala beach. The 25 rooms (one with a/c) are all sea-facing and have hot water, though they're a tad musty and gloomy, and relatively pricey for what you get. There's a swimming pool and reasonable restaurant. ③

Aluthgama and around

Dividing Beruwala from Bentota, the lively little town of **ALUTHGAMA** offers a welcome dose of everyday life amidst the big resorts, and remains refreshingly unaffected by the local package tourist trade. The main street is a colourful succession of trades: a fish market straggles up its west side, with all sorts of seafood lined up on benches supervised by machete-wielding fishmongers, while at the south end of the road, local ladies flog great piles of lurid, factory-made cloth. A photogenic vegetable market is held just south of here, past the Nebula supermarket – Mondays are particularly lively.

Aluthgama's other attraction is its good and relatively cheap selection of **guest houses**; these places aren't actually on the beach, but just behind it at the edge of the beautiful lagoon at the mouth of the Bentota River – in many ways just as attractive a location as the oceanfront, especially at night, when the lights of the northern Bentota resorts twinkle prettily in the darkness across the waters. A couple of guest houses have their own boats to shuttle you quickly across the lagoon to the beach opposite, depositing you on the spit of land known as Paradise Island (see p.133); otherwise it's a ten-minute walk, or a quick tuktuk ride, to the nearest section of beach at Bentota.

Practicalities

Aluthgama is the area's major transport hub, with **train and bus stations** close to one another in the middle of town. Count on Rs.20–30 for the tuktuk ride to any of the Aluthgama guest houses, Rs.50–75 to places in Bentota and the main section of Beruwala beach, or Rs.100 to the northern end of Beruwala beach – as ever, the more upmarket the hotel you're heading to, the more you'll have to haggle to get a decent fare. **Leaving Aluthgama**, buses head north and south along the Galle Road every ten to fifteen minutes; for details of train services, see p.147. There are two **banks** – a Bank of Ceylon immediately north of the bus station, and a Commercial Bank further north along the main road – the latter has an ATM (Visa and MasterCard). Various places offer erratic **Internet** access – try Happy New Year (daily 9am–11pm; Rs.5 per minute) or the Rameesha Agency Post Office, although its promised "cybercafé" is just one erratically functioning machine (daily 8am–7pm; Rs.6 per min). There's also a well-stocked Cargills **supermarket** next to the Commercial Bank.

Accommodation and eating

All the guest houses listed below do decent **food** – that at the *Tropical Anushka River Inn* is especially good, with a fabulous rice and curry for a measly Rs.250. The cheap and cheerful *Sinharaja Bakery and Restaurant* on the main road at the north end of town has short eats and snacks downstairs, and simple noodle and rice lunches and dinners upstairs – a refreshing and package tourist-free pocket of local life.

Guest houses

Ganga Garden Off the Galle Rd, behind the *Sinharaja Bakery* ☎034-428 9444, @ ggarden@sol.lk. UK-owned and managed lagoon-side guest house. Rooms (with hot water) are dazzlingly clean and equipped with handsome, locally made mahogany furniture, while the communal verandah and the surrounding gardens are exquisite. ❹
Hemadan 25 River Ave ☎034-227 5320, @ hemadan@stmail.lk. The most attractive guest house in Aluthgama, with a definite, understated and slightly old-fashioned charm, a gorgeous garden running right down to the lagoon and pleasantly

spacious, attractively furnished rooms with high ceilings (a couple have a/c for around Rs.400 extra). Free boat shuttle to beach opposite. ❹
Terrena River Ave ☎ & @034-428 9015. Austrian-owned place in a fine location overlooking the lagoon, with five serviceable rooms (including one triple) with hot water. ❷
Tropical Anushka River Inn 97 River Ave ☎ & @034-227 5377. Four clean, modern rooms (one a/c) with hot water in an extremely friendly guest house right on the edge of the lagoon – the restaurant leans right out over the water, there's a nice roof terrace and a free boat to the beach, as well as top-notch food. ❸

Around Aluthgama: Brief Gardens

About 10km inland from Aluthgama, the idyllic **Brief Gardens** (daily 8am–5pm; Rs.125 including guided tour) comprise the former house and surrounding estate of the writer and artist **Bevis Bawa**, elder brother of the architect Geoffrey Bawa – the name alludes to Bawa's father, who purchased the land with the money raised from a successful legal brief. Bevis Bawa began landscaping the five-acre gardens in 1929 and continued to work on them almost up until his death in 1992, creating a series of terraces which tumble luxuriantly down the hillside below the house. The gardens are nice for a stroll, but the main attraction is the **house**, a low-slung orange building stuffed with quirky artworks, some by Bawa himself; several pieces (including two entertaining aluminium sculptures and a big mural of Sri Lankan scenes) are by the Australian artist Donald Friend, who came to Brief for a week's visit and ended

---

Geoffrey Bawa (1919–2003)

We have a marvellous tradition of building in this country that has got lost. It got lost because people followed outside influences over their own good instincts. They never built right "through" the landscape . . . You must "run" with the site; after all, you don't want to push nature out with the building.

Geoffrey Bawa

One of the twentieth century's foremost Asian architects, **Geoffrey Bawa** was born in 1919 to a wealthy family of Colombo Burghers (see p.158), the small but colourful community of English-speaking Sri Lankans of European descent. Bawa's own family boasted English, Dutch, German, Sinhalese and Scottish ancestors, a heady cocktail of cultures which mirrors the eclectic mix of European and local influences so apparent in his later architectural work.

Bawa spent a large proportion of his first forty years abroad, mainly in Europe – indeed he seems to have considered himself more Western than Sri Lankan for much of his early life. Having studied English at Cambridge and law in London, Bawa finally dragged himself back to Sri Lanka and followed his father and grandfather into the legal profession, though without much enthusiasm – his only positive experience of the law seems to have been driving around Colombo in his Rolls-Royce whilst wearing his lawyer's robes and wig. After scarcely a year he threw in his legal career and went to Italy, where he planned to buy a villa and settle down.

Fortunately for Sri Lanka, the villa didn't work out, and Bawa returned to Sri Lanka and stayed with his brother Bevis at his estate at Brief Garden (see above), which Bevis had been busily landscaping and improving. Inspired by his brother's house and garden, Bawa decided to do something similar himself, and soon purchased a nearby estate which he christened **Lunuganga**. This was the turning point in Bawa's life, and the pleasure he found in working on Lunuganga convinced him to swap careers. Another trip to England to train as a professional architect ensued, and having finally qualified (at the advanced age of 38), Bawa returned to Colombo and flung himself into his work.

Bawa's early leanings were modernist, encouraged by his training in London and by his close working relationship with the Danish architect Ulrik Plesner, a keen student of functional Scandinavian design. The style of his early buildings is often described as "Tropical Modernism", but local conditions gradually changed Bawa's architectural philosophy. The pure white surfaces favoured by European modernists weathered badly in the tropics, while their flat rooflines were unsuitable in monsoonal climates – and in any case, shortages of imported materials like steel and glass encouraged Bawa to look for traditional local materials.

up staying five and a half years. Other exhibits include old colonial furniture and a fascinating collection of photographs of the imposing Bawa himself (he was six foot seven inches tall), both as a young man serving as a major in the British Army and as one of Sri Lanka's leading social luminaries, posing with house guests such as Laurence Olivier and Vivien Leigh. The return journey from Aluthgama by tuktuk, including an hour's waiting time, should cost Rs.400–500. Avoid visiting at weekends, when the place gets overrun.

Bentota

South of Aluthgama, **BENTOTA** offers a further clutch of package resorts plus an outstanding selection of more upmarket places. The **beach** divides into two areas. At the **north** end, facing Aluthgama, lies "Paradise Island" (as it's popularly known), a narrow spit of land beautifully sandwiched between

The result was a style in which the strong and simple forms of modernism were beautifully softened and enriched by local influences and landscapes. Bawa revived the huge overhanging tiled roofs traditionally used by colonial architects in the tropics, whose broad eaves and spacious verandahs offered protection against both sun and rain, while buildings were designed with open interconnecting spaces to obviate the need for air-conditioning. The use of local materials, meanwhile, allowed his buildings to blend seamlessly with their setting and to age gracefully. His former offices in Colombo, now the *Gallery Cafe* (see p.105), are a good example of this, with airy interior courtyards, a largely open-plan layout and the use of rustic local materials and objects throughout.

Bawa also worked hard to ensure that his buildings sat harmoniously within the landscape (he often designed to fit around existing trees, for example, rather than cutting them down), and attempted to blur the distinction between interior and exterior spaces so that architecture and landscape became joined – perhaps most spectacularly at the **Kandalama Hotel**, which appears to grow out of the jungle-covered ridge on which it's set. Bawa's architecture also provided a showcase for other local artists. Sculptures and murals by the outstanding Laki Senanayake are a prominent feature of many Bawa buildings (such as the extraordinary staircase at the Lighthouse Hotel), while the batik artist Ena de Silva and designer Barbara Sansoni, the founder of the famous Colombo shop Barefoot (see p.108), were also frequent contributors.

The arrival of package tourism in the 1960s brought with it the need for modern hotels, a genre with which Bawa became inextricably associated (a list of his principal hotels appears on p.38). His first major effort, the **Bentota Beach Hotel**, set the style for hotels all over the island. The main wooden pavilion, topped by a hipped roof, used natural local materials throughout and paid distant homage to traditional Kandyan architecture in its overall shape and conception; at its centre lay a beautifully rustic courtyard and pond set within a cluster of frangipani trees, giving the sense of nature not only being around, but also inside the building (sadly, subsequent alterations have changed many of these telling details, although the broad plan of the hotel survives intact).

Around a dozen other hotels followed – most notably the **Kandalama** and **The Lighthouse** – as well as the mammoth new **Sri Lankan Parliament** building in Kotte and **Ruhunu University** at Matara. Not surprisingly, Bawa's architectural practice became the largest on the island during the 1970s, and most of Sri Lanka's finest young architects started their careers working for him. Many took his influence with them when they left, and buildings (hotels especially) all over the island show the influence of the Bawa style, executed with varying degrees of competence and imagination.

Diving and watersports

The calm waters of the Bentota lagoon provide a year-round venue for all sorts of **watersports** (approximate prices are given in brackets) including waterskiing ($10 per 15min), jetskiing ($15 for 15min), speed boating ($15 for 15min), windsurfing ($5 per hr), canoeing ($3 per hr), lagoon boat trips (see below), deep-sea fishing ($100 for 4 people) and banana-boating ($5 per person; minimum of about five people); note that all the above prices are in US dollars. The places listed below are the main operators, but almost every hotel and guest house in the area seems to now have some kind of watersports centre attached, offering all sorts of deals. Bentota also has good **diving**, and one of the best selections of dive schools in the country.

Club Inter Sport *Bentota Beach Hotel* (about 200m northeast of Bentota railway station) ⌖034-227 5178. This all-purpose house of fun offers a bit of everything: waterskiing, jetskiing, windsurfing (tuition and board rental), speedboating, deep-sea fishing and banana-boating, and has PADI-registered dive instructors in season.

Confifi Marina Next to *Club Bentota* ⌖034-558 1416, ⓦwww.LSR-srilanka.com. Dive centre offering a full range of dives and courses, plus snorkelling trips, water-skiing, jetskiing, windsurfing, boat trips, banana-boating, tube-riding and canoeing.

Diving the Snake Paradise Island, Bentota ⌖034-558 8818, ⓦwww.divingthesnake .com. Recently established dive centre under expert Swiss management, offering a full range of PADI and CMAS courses, plus a wide range of one-off dives at various sites along the west coast.

Sunshine Water Sports Center Aluthgama, just north of the *Hemadam* guest house ⌖034-227 0401. Full range of watersports, and particularly good for windsurfing and waterskiing, with tuition available from two former Sri Lankan champions. Other offerings include jetskiing, body-board hire, snorkelling trips, deep-sea fishing and Bentota river cruises.

Ypsylon Dive School ⌖034-227 6132, ⓔypsylon@slt.net. One of the area's biggest and longest-established dive schools, offering the usual range of single dives, PADI courses, night dives, introductory "discovery" dives, and wreck dives.

---

the choppy breakers of the Indian Ocean and the calm waters of the Bentota lagoon; however the "island" is heavily developed and covered in a sequence of big and rather pedestrian hotels. Backing Paradise Island, the tranquil **Bentota lagoon** provides the setting for the island's biggest range of watersports (see above), along with interesting boat trips up the Bentota river. The attractive **southern end of Bentota beach** (south of the station) comprises a wide and tranquil swathe of sand that's home to one of the island's finest clusters of top-end hotels, set at discrete intervals from one another down the coast. Inland from here lies **Bentota village**, a traditional coastal settlement which is home to a couple of temples and a few other minor attractions which the entrepreneurial locals will be happy to show you – for a consideration.

Despite the number of visitors, Bentota beach remains surprisingly quiet, particularly south of the station. Unlike Hikkaduwa or Unawatuna, there's virtually no beachlife here, and the oceanfront lacks even the modest smattering of impromptu cafes, handicraft shops and hawkers you'll find at Beruwala – it's this somnolent atmosphere which either appeals or repels, depending on which way your boat's pointing. If you're staying at Aluthgama or Beruwala and fancy a day on the beach here, you can eat and drink at all the guest houses and hotels listed on p.136; most also allow non-guests to use their pools for a modest fee.

Bentota village

Sprawling under an endless canopy of palm trees between the lagoon and the land-side of the busy coastal highway, sleepy **Bentota village** has a smattering of low-key sights, although the place is full of opportunistic locals hanging around waiting to pounce on tourists – harmless but tiresome. You might be offered a village tour, which could include seeing a local toddy tapper in action or a visit to one of the village's many small coir factories, where coconut husks are turned into rope (you'll see huge piles of coconut husks piled up around the village, waiting for processing). In general, though, the self-appointed village "guides" are a pain and largely uninformative – the only real reason for having one is to stop other would-be guides pestering you. Prices for tours are whatever you can bargain, and beware of people who refuse to agree a price, saying "whatever you like". Name a sum you are willing to pay at the outset to avoid recrimination later.

There are also two village temples. At the eastern end of the village, next to the lagoon, is the **Wanawasa Raja Mahaviharaya**, a large and unusually ugly building full of kitsch pictures, dayglo statues and a memorable model of Adam's Peak equipped with a kind of flushing mechanism which sends water streaming down the mountainsides at the tug of a lever. The remains of an older section of underground temple can be seen by looking down the well behind the modern image-house. Further south, also on the lagoon-side, is the much more attractive **Galapata Vihara**, a venerable temple which dates back to the twelfth century and sports interesting wall paintings, peeling orange Buddhas and a large boulder outside carved with a long extract from the *Mahavamsa*, written in Pali.

Bentota River safaris

The Bentota lagoon is the last section of the broad **Bentota River** (Bentota Ganga), a popular spot for boat safaris which ply the river as it meanders inland for a few kilometres from the Bentota bridge before losing itself in another mazy lagoon dotted with tiny islands and fringed with tangled mangrove swamps. These trips aren't the greatest natural adventure you're likely to have: the boats themselves are usually noisy and smelly, and the standard of guiding pretty hopeless. Even so, you should see a fair selection of aquatic birds – herons, cormorants and colourful kingfishers – as well as water monitors and crocodiles, while your boatman might also ferry you right in amongst the mangroves themselves, a mysterious and beautiful sight as you drift though still, shaded waters beneath huge roots. Obviously, the longer the trip and the further upriver you travel, the more unspoilt the scenery becomes – you're unlikely to see much of interest on a one-hour trip. Longer excursions usually include extras such as trips to coconut factories or handicrafts shops – you'll probably also be chased by various hawkers in boats flogging handicrafts or waving baby water monitors in your face in the hope that you'll give them money. You may also be taken to visit the Galapata Vihara (see above).

Trips can be arranged through most Bentota or Aluthgama guest houses and hotels, or through the area's many watersports centres (see the box opposite). The standard trip lasts three hours and costs around Rs.400 per person in a group of at least four.

Sea Turtles Project

About 3km south of the Bentota bridge, on Bentota beach just north of *Saman Villas*, the **Sea Turtles Project** (daily 8am–6pm; Rs.100) is one of several turtle hatcheries along this part of the coast which have been set up by locals in response to the rapidly declining numbers of marine turtles visiting Sri Lanka. Turtle eggs, which would otherwise be eaten, are bought for a few rupees each from local fisherman and re-buried along the beach. Once hatched, the baby turtles are kept in holding tanks for a few days before being released into the sea by night – the very few female turtles which survive to maturity will return ten years later to lay their own eggs here. There's not actually an awful lot to see, apart from lots of tiny hatchlings in concrete tubs and a few adult turtles which cannot be returned to the wild (including a rare albino), but the staff are informative and enthusiastic about all matters turtle-related, and it's an eminently worthwhile cause.

Practicalities

Bentota has its own **train station**. Some (but not all) express services stop here; alternatively, get off at Aluthgama and catch a tuktuk. If arriving by **bus** it's also easier to get off at the terminal in Aluthgama, unless you know exactly where you want to be set down. As usual, most people **eat** in their guest houses or hotels – and there's not much reason to venture out unless you fancy a meal in the beautiful surroundings of *Club Villa* or *Villa Mohotti*; both have very reasonably priced menus, though the food is competent rather than outstanding. There's a useless Ceylon Tourist Board **information centre** (Mon–Sat 8.30am–4.45pm) in the shopping complex just behind the *Serendib Hotel*.

For **ayurveda resorts** in Bentota, see the box on p.130.

Club Bentota ☎034-227 5167, ⓦwww .clubbentota.com. Large but attractively under-stated resort, with low-rise, red-tiled wooden build-ings in an unrivalled location near the tip of the Bentota peninsula between the ocean and lagoon. Facilities include an ayurveda centre and a wide range of watersports, and there's also a decent pool (non-guests Rs250). All-inclusive rates only. ❾

Club Villa ☎034-227 5312. One of Sri Lanka's most personable small hotels, this intimate and serene Geoffrey Bawa-designed establishment is set just back from the beach at the southern end of Bentota in a wonderfully tranquil location. The fifteen rooms (five with a/c; US$10 supplement) are discretely scattered around several modern colonial-style buildings, while trees and artworks are dotted strategically about the grounds. There's also a small swimming pool and an attractive restaurant. ❼

Serendib Hotel ☎034-227 5248, ⓦwww .serendibleisure.com. Serene and very low-key Geoffrey Bawa-designed resort, occupying a clas-sically simple white building in a tranquil setting on Bentota beach. The brightly furnished rooms (all a/c with private balcony and hot water) are good value compared to the competition; there are no facilities beyond a couple of bars, a restaurant and a pool – though for many visitors this is part of the charm of the place. ❼

Saman Villas ☎034-227 5435, ⓦwww .samanvilla.com. Much-hyped hotel beautifully

perched on a isolated headland 3km south of Bentota bridge. The swimming pool – seemingly suspended in mid-air above the sea – is extraordi-nary, but despite being stuffed full of every modcon conceivable, the hotel itself lacks the quiet distinction of the nearby Bawa-designed establishments. Prices vary wildly according to season; you may even be able to bargain during periods of low demand. Decent value in low season, but rather expensive at other times. ❾

Susantha ☎034-227 5324, ⓔsusanthas @sltnet.lk. Set immediately behind the railway station, this pleasant guest house is Bentota's cheapest option – although still relatively expensive. The eighteen clean, quite smart rooms are set around a shady courtyard garden and come with nice furniture, large mosquito nets and tiled bathrooms; the deluxe ones upstairs have nice balconies. ❸

Taj Exotica ☎034-227 5650, ⓦwww .tajexoticasrilanka.com. Set in magnificent isolation on a beautiful headland at the southern end of Bentota beach, this huge but stylish hotel sports lots of Kandyan-style wooden eaves and roof lines, imaginatively interlocking balconies and plenty of tropical greenery. Rooms are luxurious in a rather bland way. Non-guests can use the pool if they take buffet lunch (Rs.950). No single rates. ❽

Taprobana ☎034-227 5618, ⓦwww.taruvillas .com. Beautiful villa in shades of orange and pink with nine rooms – stylishly if rather minimally furnished in a kind of modern colonial idiom – around a small swimming pool. It's all very nice, but not quite as special as the hefty price tag would suggest, and even then you have to pay an extra US$10 to get a/c. Breakfast included. ❽

Villa Mohotti (aka *The Villa*) ☎ 034-221 3818. Gorgeous 1880s colonial mansion, with sensitive extensions designed by Geoffrey Bawa in the 1970s. Rooms are widely spread out, so there's plenty of privacy, and are very elegantly – if rather minimally – furnished, with lots of pure white surfaces and antique wooden furniture. The beautiful garden runs down to the beach, and there's a small swimming pool and a tranquil restaurant. ❼

Induruwa, Kosgoda and Balapitiya

South of Bentota, the straggling villages of **INDURUWA** and **KOSGODA** are backed by a stretch of sleepy and as yet relatively undeveloped beach, dotted with a few hotels and guest houses which are becoming increasingly popular with visitors looking to avoid the major west coast resorts. The atmosphere hereabouts is deeply somnolent, although if you get bored there are a couple of nearby attractions.

Kosgoda is home to the west coast's biggest and longest established **turtle hatchery** (daily 8am–6pm; Rs.100). As at the Bentota Sea Turtles Project (see p.135), this was originally established as an independent local venture, though the project has now been taken over by the Department of Wildlife Conservation. Turtle eggs are bought from local fishermen and reburied in safe locations; once hatched, the babies are kept here for a few days before being released into the sea – the short time they spend growing stronger in captivity gives them significantly higher chances of surviving when returned to the ocean. As at the Bentota hatchery, there are usually plenty of baby turtles swimming around in holding tanks – all five species of turtle which visit Sri Lanka lay eggs here, and depending on when you visit, you might see newly hatched examples of them all.

Some 20km south of Bentota, and about 5km north of Ambalangoda, the village of **BALAPITIYA** is the starting point for interesting boat safaris along the **Madu Ganga**, a good place to spot water monitors and a wide array of birdlife, including myriad colourful kingfishers. There are also no less than 66 islands along this stretch of river, one of which is home to a large Buddhist temple adorned with lurid modern paintings and sculptures. Boats cost around Rs.1000 for one person, slightly more for additional passengers. Operators in Unawatuna (such as G.G. Happy Tour; see p.164) offer trips for around Rs.2500 for transport to Balapitiya and boat.

Practicalities

Frequent **buses** run up and down the Galle Road past the various hotels and guest houses; if arriving by bus try to get the conductor to put you off in the right place – the hotels are spread out and quite difficult to spot from the road. There are no **banks** at Induruwa or Kosgoda, although you might be able to change money or travellers' cheques at the larger hotels. There's a similar shortage of places **to eat** apart from the hotels and guest houses – if you fancy a night out in style, head for the *Triton Hotel*.

Emerald Bay Hotel Induruwa ☎ 034-227 5363. Simple but comfortable rooms with hot water (but no a/c) on a nice stretch of quiet beach. ❹

Induruwa Beach Resort Induruwa ☎ 034-227 5445, ✉ inbeachr@sltnet.lk. Big four-storey resort with ninety a/c rooms, all with sea view, and lots of amenities including a health club, sauna, ayurveda centre, games room and billiards table. Good value, though not particularly inspiring. ❻

Janu's Paradise Rest Induruwa ☎ 034-229 0021. Welcoming place right on the beach with big airy rooms, sea views and friendly owners. ❸

Kosgoda Beach Resort Kosgoda ☎ 091-226 4017, ✉ kosgodab@eureka.lk. Fifty a/c rooms in an attractive three-star resort set between sea and lagoon, with all the usual facilities including an attractive pool and garden plus tennis court, games room and catamaran trips. ❼

Triton Hotel Ahungalla, 6km south of Kosgoda (and 9km north of Ambalangoda). ☎ 091-226 4041, ⓦ aitkenspenceholidays.com. Vast five-star resort which sprawls along a considerable section of unspoilt beach. It's luxurious but surprisingly intimate and low-key, with attractive landscaping, cheerfully designed rooms and an enormous main pool. Popular with wedding parties. ❼

Ambalangoda

Some 25km south of Bentota, the workaday coastal town of **AMBALANGODA** is the island's major production centre for the demonic wooden **masks** which leer at you from doorways and handicrafts shops across the island. These were originally designed to be worn by performers in kolam and other southern Sri Lankan dances (see box opposite), and although the dances themselves are now rarely performed, the masks have acquired a new lease of life as souvenirs, while many locals hang a Gurulu Raksha mask outside their houses to ward away demons (the Gurulu is a fearsome mythical bird which is believed to prey on snakes and related demonic beings). The main outlets are the two mask museums-cum-shops which face one another across the main coastal highway at the northern end of the town centre. These are run by two sons of the late mask-carver Ariyapala Wijesurya, who was largely responsible for establishing Ambalangoda as a centre of mask-carving. The larger of the two is the **Ariyapala and Sons Mask Museum** (daily 8.30am–5.30pm; donation), comprising two interesting and well-laid-out sections downstairs focusing on kolam dances and Sunni Yakuma healing dances respectively, with masks and photos of performances. The shop upstairs sells the island's biggest selection of masks, featuring all the characters you'll have encountered in the museum. All are made out of the light and easily carved Sri Lankan balsa wood, *kaduru* (*nux vomica*), and come in all sorts of different sizes, costing anything from Rs.250 to Rs.15,000 – larger masks can take up to six weeks to carve and paint. The quality isn't actually all that great: masks are churned out in the workshop next door (which you can also visit) in industrial quantities for the endless tour groups that stop here, and you might find better specimens in the smaller workshops around town, in Hikkaduwa, or even in Kandy or Colombo. Some masks are artificially aged to resemble antiques, their colours skilfully faded to a lustrous, mellow patina which makes a more aesthetic alternative to the lurid, day-glo colours of the standard items.

Just across the road, the second shop-museum, **Ariyapala Traditional Masks** (daily 8.30am–5.30pm; donation), is less interesting, but still worth a quick visit. The small downstairs display features enormous puppets of the tyrannical last king of Kandy, Sri Wickrama Rajasinha (see p.220) and his queen, plus gruesome tableaux showing the execution of Sri Wickrama's prime minister and his children. The items for sale upstairs are of a similarly humdrum standard to those over the road.

There are occasional performances of masked dances at the **Bandu Wijesurya School of Dance** opposite the two museums. Even if nothing formal is scheduled, you can often visit the school to see students practising from around 3pm onwards. You may even be able to enrol in dance classes yourself, if you're particularly interested.

Masks and dancing aside, Ambalangoda also boasts a fine swathe of largely untouristed **beach** – a low-key alternative to the much busier sands at Hikkaduwa.

Low-country dancing: devil dancing and kolam

The masks you'll see at Ambalangoda (and elsewhere around the island) were originally produced to be worn by performers in low-country (southern) dances, either in devil dances or kolam. Many Sri Lankans still believe that diseases and illness can be caused by demons, and the purpose of the **devil dance** – more strictly known as an exorcism ceremony (*bali*) or healing dance (*sunni yakuma*) – is to summon up the demons who are causing a person sickness, make offerings to them and then politely request that they leave their victim in peace. There are various groups of demons – five *yakka* demons, twelve *pali* demons and eighteen *sanni* demons; each is believed to be responsible for certain diseases, and each is represented by its own mask, which is worn by a dancer during the exorcism ceremony (all 35 individual masks are sometimes combined into a single enormous medicine mask). Devil dances are still occasionally performed in rural villages, although you'd have to be very lucky to see one.

The origins of the **kolam** dance-drama are popularly claimed to date back to the mythical Queen Menikpala, who whilst pregnant developed a craving to witness a theatrical performance. Vishvakarma, the god of craftsmen and artists, is said to have given the king the first kolam masks and the plot of the entire entertainment. The traditional kolam performance features a sequence of dances held together by a rather tenuous plot based around the visit of the pregnant Queen Menikpala and her husband, King Maha Sammatha, to a village. The performance traditionally comprises a medley of satirical and royal dances, featuring characters such as the king's drunken drummer, a lecherous village clerk, assorted village simpletons, a couple of propitious demons, a lion and, of course, the royal couple themselves. Unfortunately, complete kolam performances are no longer staged, so it's impossible to experience this unique Sri Lankan medley of folk tale, demonic superstition and history (laced with a touch of Buddhism) – though you can at least still enjoy the masks.

Practicalities

Buses run up and down the coast along the Galle Road every fifteen minutes or more. The **bus station** has neatly labelled bays inside, though many buses simply stop on the road outside. If you need to **change money**, there are branches of the People's Bank and Hatton National Bank just north of the bus station.

If you fancy overnighting here, you'll find there are a few reasonable **places to stay**. For **food**, the *Nirodh Tourist Restaurant*, on Main Street opposite (and signposted from) the bus station is a pleasant spot, with standard tourist grub – rather overpriced, though the portions are big.

Accommodation

Piya Nivasa Galle Rd, Akurella, 3km south of Ambalangoda ☎091-225 8146. In a quiet spot outside town, this charming little place has simple but comfortable rooms in a beautiful colonial villa opposite the beach. A tuktuk from Ambalangoda should cost around Rs.100. ❶

Rest House Just off (and signposted from) Galle Rd, 200m south of the bus station ☎091-225 8299. This old and atmospheric Dutch warehouse, boasting a beautiful verandah scattered with antique furniture, has thirteen immense but very basic and gloomy rooms in the old building;

those in the grotty new wing are also basic but just about acceptable, and have the bonus of nice ocean-facing balconies. No single rates. ❶

Shangrela 38 Sea Beach Rd ☎091-225 8342. Trim resort-style hotel; the new wing has bright and airy rooms (including triples) with hot water, which get more expensive the higher you go in the building; there are also cheaper but perfectly acceptable rooms in an older building – though the fastidious manager might try to persuade you that these aren't suitable for foreign tourists. ❷

Sumuda Guest House 418 Main St ☎ 091-225 8832. Just down the side road behind the main mask museum, this is Ambalangoda's nicest guest house, with six simple but pleasantly spacious rooms (including one triple) in a characterful old colonial villa. Rates include a very good breakfast and Sri Lankan dinner. ❷

Hikkaduwa and around

Back in the 1970s, **HIKKADUWA** was Sri Lanka's original hippy hangout, a budget travellers' alternative to the fancier resort hotels at Beruwala and Bentota. Three decades later, it embodies the worst aspects of the unconstrained development that has ravaged the coastline all the way from Negombo to Unawatuna. Years of unplanned building have reduced the beach to a narrow ribbon of sand; the once-beautiful Coral Sanctuary has become a circus of boats chasing traumatized fishes through a labyrinth of dead coral; while Hikkaduwa town's original hotels stand around in various stages of dereliction, monuments to a failed avarice which is steadily destroying the source of its own livelihood. And just a few yards inland, running the length of the town, the noxious Galle Road is the province of psychotic bus drivers who scream along at insane speeds, filling the ocean-fresh air with clouds of smog and making the simple act of stepping outside your guest house a potentially life-threatening experience. Meanwhile, the growing popularity of the far more attractive Unawatuna, just thirty minutes down the road, has delivered a potentially knock-out blow to the town's fading fortunes.

Trashy as it may be, however, Hikkaduwa preserves a kind of ramshackle, down-at-heel charm which still appeals to some. Compared to somnolent Bentota or Beruwala – not to mention the sleepier resorts further south – it still has a bit of atmosphere, with plenty of restaurants and shops to tempt you out of your guest house, and a crowd of predominantly young and independent travellers who give the place a liveliness that's lacking in most of the island's other beach towns. And if you do get fed up with the place, a smattering of interesting temples in the relatively unspoilt countryside inland make for rewarding escapes.

Arrival and accommodation

The **bus** and **train** stations are at the northern end of Hikkaduwa town. A tuktuk from here to Wewala will cost around Rs.40; to Narigama around Rs.60, to Thiranagama around Rs.80. When **moving on from Hikkaduwa**, note that many buses heading north don't leave from the bus station itself, but from the ocean side of the main road, about 50m south of the station.

Virtually every building in Hikkaduwa seems to offer accommodation of some kind, although despite the massive competition, the hotels and guest houses here are generally uninspiring, and relatively expensive to boot. Accommodation options here straggle for several kilometres down the coast. Noisy and shabby **Hikkaduwa town** itself, at the northern end of the beach, was formerly the centre of the area's tourist industry, and still boasts a fair number of hotels and guest houses, ranging from the merely run-down to the utterly derelict. Basically, it's not worth staying anywhere north of the huge *Coral Gardens* hotel (hence we haven't listed any of these places).

South of *Coral Gardens* stretches the far more appealing area of **Wewala**, effectively the heart of tourist Hikkaduwa, with the biggest concentration of rooms, food and other amenities. If you want something quieter (especially in

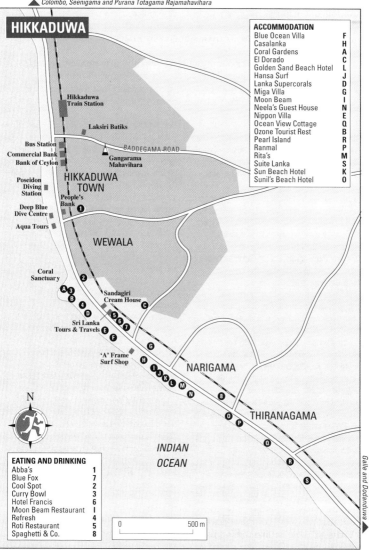

HIKKADUWA

ACCOMMODATION

Blue Ocean Villa	F
Casalanka	H
Coral Gardens	A
El Dorado	C
Golden Sand Beach Hotel	L
Hansa Surf	J
Lanka Supercorals	D
Miga Villa	G
Moon Beam	I
Neela's Guest House	N
Nippon Villa	E
Ocean View Cottage	Q
Ozone Tourist Rest	B
Pearl Island	R
Ranmal	P
Rita's	M
Suite Lanka	S
Sun Beach Hotel	K
Sunil's Beach Hotel	O

Hikkaduwa Train Station

Laksiri Batiks

BADDEGAMA ROAD

Bus Station
Commercial Bank
Bank of Ceylon

Gangarama Mahavihara

Poseidon Diving Station

HIKKADUWA TOWN

People's Bank

Deep Blue Dive Centre

Aqua Tours

WEWALA

Coral Sanctuary

Sandagiri Cream House

Sri Lanka Tours & Travels

'A' Frame Surf Shop

NARIGAMA

N

THIRANAGAMA

INDIAN OCEAN

EATING AND DRINKING

Abba's	1
Blue Fox	7
Cool Spot	2
Curry Bowl	3
Hotel Francis	6
Moon Beam Restaurant	I
Refresh	4
Roti Restaurant	5
Spaghetti & Co.	8

0   500 m

Galle and Dodanduwa ▶

season, when Wewala can get pretty busy), the areas of **Narigama** and **Thiranagama** offer increasing isolation and quiet the further south you go. (Indeed, as the northern end of town effectively dies as a tourist destination, so new places open further and further south, almost as if the whole town is gradually sliding down the coast.)

Most of Hikkaduwa's accommodation is squeezed into the narrow strip of land between the beach and the Galle Road, meaning that many places suffer from traffic noise – the further you can get from the road, the better. In addition, the majority of places are built end-on to the beach to maximize the use of the available space, so in most places you don't get any sea views. Pretty much everywhere can provide **meals**, and many places have cute, if small-scale, oceanside restaurants.

Out of season, rooms rates can fall by as much as fifty percent, though this is of largely academic interest, since Hikkaduwa during the monsoon is best avoided: from mid-April to mid-October many places close for repairs, and the entire town has all the charm and atmosphere of a building site.

Wewala

Blue Ocean Villa ⊤ & ⑤ 091-227 7566. Pleasant modern place, with spacious tiled rooms with high ceilings; best value are the two breezy sea-facing rooms upstairs (and make sure you get a room away from the road). ❸

Casalanka ⊤ 091-438 3002. This friendly and popular cheapie is becoming a touch ramshackle, but it's decent value nonetheless. Rooms upstairs are comfortable and reasonably furnished (although the front two are rather too close to the Galle Rd); those downstairs are darker and more basic. Upstairs ❸; downstairs ❷

Coral Gardens ⊤ 091-227 7023, ⓦ johnkeellshotels.com. The smartest hotel in town (though that's not saying much), looking like a cross between a Chinese pagoda and a multi-storey car park. Rooms are spacious, with a/c and at least a partial sea view – perfectly comfortable, albeit perfectly anonymous. There's also a pool (non-guests Rs.100), coffee shop, two restaurants and an ayurveda centre. No single rates. ❼

El Dorado ⊤ 091-227 7091. Haven of peace set in lush tropical gardens just a couple of minutes inland from the Galle Rd. The five rooms (one with a/c, ❷) are simple but perfectly respectable, and very good value. ❶

Lanka Supercorals ⊤ 091-227 7387, ⓔ supercor@banlanka.net. In face of stiff competition, this memorable eyesore carries off the prize of Hikkaduwa's ugliest building (as well as the largest swimming pool; non-guests Rs.200). Rooms are a bit gloomy, but decently furnished and with bathtubs. Deluxe and superior have a/c and sea views (deluxe also have TVs). Standard and superior ❻, deluxe ❼

Miga Villa ⊤ & ⑤ 091-545 1559. Characterful place set on landward side of Galle Rd in a quaint, century-old colonial house. Rooms are basic, but bright and clean, and good value at the price. No single rates, but you could try bargaining. ❶

Moon Beam ⊤ 077-790 3803, ⑤ 091-227 7567. Nice-looking place with a garden adjoining the beach and a good restaurant (see p.146). Rooms are smart and modern (though some are a bit small) and the bathrooms immaculate. The cheaper ones downstairs have cold water only;

smarter upstairs rooms come with sea view, hot water and private balcony. ❸

Nippon Villa ⊤ 091-438 3095. Brisk modern hotel done up in cheerily naff strains of blue and orange, with bright, spacious and nicely furnished rooms (a few with sea views) set around a pleasant two-storey courtyard. ❷

Ozone Tourist Rest ⊤ 091-438 3008. Set in a long, narrow green-and-brown concrete block running down to the beach, with simple but clean and cheap rooms. ❶

Narigama

Golden Sand Beach Hotel ⊤ 091-227 7060, ⓦ www.goldensandbeach.com. Twenty-odd acceptable rooms divided by a long, gloomy corridor – those on the right are a bit bigger and brighter than those on the left. Breakfast included. No single rates. ❸

Hansa Surf ⊤ 091-438 3088. One of the cheapest places in town – the rooms are basically just concrete boxes with a bed, but are habitable. There are some more expensive rooms upstairs, though they're nothing special. Downstairs ❶, upstairs ❷

Neela's Guest House ⊤ 091-438 3166. Long-established and popular, with very friendly owners and good food – although like most places in Hikkaduwa it's beginning to show its age. ❷

Rita's ⊤ & ⑤ 091-227 7496. Appealing little guest house with a neat red-and-white exterior. The rooms are OK value, although getting a bit shabby. ❷

Sun Beach Hotel ⊤ 091-438 3163, ⓦ www .sunbeachsurf.com. Friendly management and four-teen variable rooms, some with a/c: the five large, clean, modern tiled ones above the beach are the nicest; the others are a bit gloomy. Alternatively, try the unusual treehouse in the garden. ❷–❺

Thiranagama

Ocean View Cottage ⊤ 091-227 7237, ⓦ www.oceanviewcottage.net. One of Thiranagama's nicest places. Although rather close to the Galle Rd, the four older rooms are huge and quite smart, with fetching bathrooms in lurid shades of blue. The five smart and spacious new

rooms are further away from the road, with sea views, a/c, hot water and minibar. There's also a nice roof terrace and garden restaurant. ❸
Oriental Rest ☎ & ℱ 091-227 6331. Pleasant colonial-style house at the very southern end of town. Rooms are nicely done up with period furniture and attractive batiks, though the downstairs ones are disappointingly small and gloomy; those upstairs are much nicer, and share an attractive sea-facing balcony overlooking a scrubby garden. Breakfast included. ❸
Pearl Island ☎ 091-227 6392. Good-value two-storey white-balconied structure at the quiet end of the beach, with clean, modern rooms and some cheaper but shabbier ones in an older wing next door. There's also a pleasant restaurant in a thatched pavilion on the beach. Breakfast included. ❷
Ranmal ☎ 091-227 7114, ⓦ www.ranmal-rest

.com. Twelve rooms of varying price and standard. The smartest have hot water, nice furnishings and big French windows opening onto a peaceful courtyard. The cheaper rooms are simpler but good value. ❷–❹
Suite Lanka ☎ 091-227 7136, ⓔ suitelan @panlanka.net. Refreshing oasis of olde-worlde charm, with bijou rooms kitted out with colonial-style furniture (including unusual high beds). Standard rooms are a bit dark and stuffy, given the price, but superior ones upstairs are brighter and more spacious, and also have a/c and hot water. There's also a small pool. Standard ❺, superior ❻
Sunil's Beach Hotel ☎ 091-227 7186, ℱ 227 7187. One of the best mid-range options in town, this big resort-style establishment has attractive and spacious rooms, plus pool, bar and restaurant. A few rooms have a/c and hot water (US$8 extra). ❹

The town and beaches

You're unlikely to want to spend any longer than you have to in chaotic **Hikkaduwa town**, a run-down and depressing place whose numerous

---

Diving and surfing at Hikkaduwa

Hikkaduwa has the largest selection of **diving schools** in Sri Lanka – the four listed below are the best established, although other operations come and go. As usual, the dive season runs from November to April. There's a good range of dives close by, including **reef dives** down to 25m at the labyrinthine Hikkaduwa Gala complex, a well-known spot with swim-through caves, plus several **wrecks** including a much-dived old steam-driven oil tanker from the 1860s known as the *Conch*. You could also use Hikkaduwa as a base from which to visit nearby sites at Gintota, Galle and Unawatuna. **Prices** tend to be fairly similar, although you might find slightly cheaper deals by shopping around – as always, the most important thing is that you feel comfortable and confident with the set-up, something that's well worth paying a few dollars extra for. All the following also hire out snorkelling equipment, and may be able to arrange specialist snorkelling trips.

Aqua Tours *Coral Reef Hotel*, Hikkaduwa Town ☎ 091-227 7197.

Blue Deep Dive Centre Hikkaduwa Town, next to the *Hotel Blue Corals* ☎ 091-438 3190, ⓦ www.sri-lanka-reisen.de/english/hf_en_tauchen.htm.

Poseidon Diving Station Hikkaduwa Town, immediately south of the *Hikkaduwa Beach Hotel* ☎ 091-227 7294, ⓦ divingsrilanka.com.

Scuba Safari *Coral Gardens* hotel (see p.142) ☎ 091-227 7188, ⓦ www .underwatersafaris.org.

Surfing

Hikkaduwa has some of the best **surfing** in Sri Lanka, after Arugam Bay and Midigama. Mambo Surf Tours and "A" Frame Surf Shop in Narigama (☎ 091-545 8132, ⓦ www.mambo.nu) is the main place for surfing info and equipment in town, and does one-day surfing tours along the south coast, two-day surf and safari trips to Yala, plus longer trips to Arugam Bay – count on US$25–50 per person per day, depending on how much driving is involved. They also rent out surfboards (Rs.400 per day) and body boards (Rs.350 per day), and do quick board repairs.

abandoned and semi-derelict hotels offer a vivid example of the environmental perils of chasing the tourist dollar, epitomized by the shattered Coral Gardens (see below), which lie at the southern end of town. The area's tourist industry has largely fled south of here, to the villages of **Wewala** and **Narigama**, where a long string of hotels and guest houses line up along the oceanfront. Unplanned development has taken its toll here too, eating away at the beach and producing some memorable eyesores, such as the *Lanka Supercorals* hotel, probably the ugliest building in Sri Lanka. Vestiges of the beach's original charm remain, however, in the palm-shack restaurants and other improvised buildings, built up by cash-strapped local entrepreneurs out of a motley assortment of left-over materials, which possess a sort of ragamuffin charm – after dark, at least. Further south, the village of **Thiranagama** is quieter still, with a pleasantly broad stretch of sand and a few stilt fishing posts.

The Coral Sanctuary

Hikkaduwa's **Coral Sanctuary**, situated at the north end of town, was established in 1988 to protect the small, shallow area of reef, never more than a few metres deep, which stretches from the beach a couple of hundred metres out to sea, and is now enclosed and protected by a string of rocky outcrops. Sadly, the once-beautiful coral here is now almost completely dead, bleached a skeletal white thanks to the depredations of the local boatmen, who after decades of polluting and abusing the gardens have succeeded in transforming this natural wonder into an ecological disaster area. You'll see a few specks of colour here and there on reviving clumps of coral, but the gardens are now interesting principally for their rich populations of tropical **fish** – indeed the death of the coral has increased levels of algae in the water, and thus the number of feeding fish, including myriad colourful species such as parrotfish, unicornfish, trunkfish, angelfish, grunts, fusillerfish and balloonfish. Around full moon time you may also be fortunate enough to see **turtles**, a majestic sight, though as soon as one is spotted, every boatman in the vicinity is likely to go chasing after the poor creature.

The most popular way of seeing the sanctuary is to take a trip in one of the innumerable **glass-bottomed boats**. It's easiest to rent a boat from one of the touts on the beach – the going rate is about Rs.500 per boat for thirty minutes. Boats usually hold up to six people; it helps if you can get a boatman who speaks a few words of English, otherwise you won't get much idea of what you're looking at. It's not a great experience: visibility through the glass is generally poor, whilst the flotilla of boats chasing round the waters in search of big fish and turtles lends all the charm of a marine motorway. **Snorkelling** is much more eco-friendly, and you'll see more, although the number of boats tearing around can make it a bit unnerving. You can rent snorkelling equipment from one of the dive centres listed on p.143; count on around Rs.300 per day and check carefully for leaks before you hand over any money. Alternatively, various shops along the main road also hire out gear.

Temples around Hikkaduwa

There are several interesting Buddhist temples **around Hikkaduwa**, all easily reachable by tuktuk or bicycle (though be *very* careful cycling along the treacherous Galle Road). The closest to town, just 500m inland from the bus station along Baddegama Road, is the **Gangarama Mahavihara**, an attractive modern Buddhist temple perched atop a large terrace, whose pretty ensemble of neat white buildings is often busy with devout locals, including many old ladies in white saris making offerings at the bo tree and various shrines – a far cry from the bedlam of Hikkaduwa Town just down the road.

About 2km north of town lies the diminutive **Seenigama** temple, an eye-catching little white building squeezed onto a tiny island just offshore. Unusually, the temple is dedicated to Dewol, a malevolent deity who is approached by those seeking revenge.

Continue north for another kilometre then turn inland (there's a rather faded sign, and usually a few rickshaws parked up at the turning) for a few hundred metres to reach the **Purana Totagama Raja Mahavihara**, or Telwatta Monastery. This was a celebrated centre of learning as far back as the fifteenth century – the great teacher and poet Sri Rahula Maha Thera, celebrated both for his verse and for his powers of exorcism, lived here; he's commemorated with a bright modern copper statue. The original temple was destroyed by the Portuguese; the present buildings date from 1805, an atmospheric complex with well-preserved murals, peeling reclining Buddhas and fine makara toranas.

Around 4km south of Hikkaduwa, the traffic-plagued town of **DODAN-DUWA** is home to the **Kumarakanda Vihara**, looking for all the world like a Baroque Portuguese church rather than a Buddhist temple; you'll find it on the inland side of the Galle Road just past where it crosses the railway line, and is reached by a spectacular flight of steps. These lead up to the principal shrine, which contains a reclining Buddha and various murals, including depictions of the sacred footprint, lions and processions. Tour groups sometimes stop here, so there are usually a few "guides" (often bored local kids) hanging around to hassle you, although you're better off visiting on your own.

Inland from here (take the first left south of the temple and ask for directions) a sylvan country lane runs to **Ratgama lagoon**, one of the many which dot the southwestern coast. The Blue Lagoon Boat House down by the waterside offers **lagoon trips** (Rs.300 for about 2hr) in primitive wooden catamarans – late afternoon is the best time to see birds and other wildlife, including monkeys. They'll also take you to the two retreats on the lake, one for men, one for women. You may be offered similar trips but at much higher prices by touts at Dodanduwa.

Eating and nightlife

There are loads of **places to eat** in Hikkaduwa, though as with the town's accommodation, standards are very average, with one outstanding exception. The town has a certain amount of tourist-inspired **nightlife** during the season; all the venues are fairly impromptu and mainly revolve around drinking, although there might be live music some nights. *Top Secret*, just north of *Rita's* guest house (see p.142), the *Chill Space Surf Café*, next to the A Frame Surf Shop (see p.143), or the lively *King's Pub*, at *Abba's* restaurant, are popular at the moment, though different places come and go on a yearly basis, and there are several other places down in Narigama – just follow the music.

Restaurants

Abba's Waulagoda Rd, Hikkaduwa Town. Attractive-looking restaurant on a raised wooden terrace set a merciful distance away from the sup-purating Galle Rd, and offering a decent range of the usual tourist standards. It's also home to the lively *King's Pub*.

Blue Fox Narigama, Reasonable selection of basic tourist grub, including excellent cheap breakfasts (Rs.130), though the proximity of the Galle Rd doesn't make for restful eating.

Cool Spot Wewala. Cute little place that's been dishing up dirt-cheap grub to locals and tourists alike for over thirty years, from snacks and milk-shakes to basic rice and noodle dishes.

Curry Bowl Wewala. Unpretentious place, walled off from the main road, with a reasonable selection of cheapish curries and burianis for around Rs.200.

Hotel Francis Narigama. Large open-air restaurant specializing in seafood, with a big but not particularly exciting menu of tourist standards, with most mains around Rs.200. The quality is quite reasonable, though service can be moribund. **Moon Beam Restaurant** *Moon Beam Hotel* (not to be confused with the Moon Beam Restaurant opposite *Lanka Supercorals*), Narigama. One of the nicest beach restaurants (and about the only one that's likely to be open out of season), in a big wooden pavilion with a rustic bar in the centre. Standard menu of touristy dishes, but moderately priced, well prepared and with big portions.

Refresh Wewala. The best restaurant in town – indeed one of the best on the island – with a menu the size of a telephone directory stuffed full of Sri Lankan and international goodies: everything from gazpacho to falafel and gado-gado to nachos. There's also one of the best rice and curries you'll ever taste, and a stash of Sri Lankan breakfasts (hoppers, string hoppers or kiribath). The setting is beautiful, too, with a lantern-dotted terrace running down to the sea. Prices are a bit more expensive than elsewhere (mains from around Rs.300), but worth every rupee.

Roti Restaurant (House of Roti) Local café with touristic pretensions, dishing up a big choice of reasonable rotis for around Rs.40, plus a few curries.

Spaghetti & Co Thiranagama. This Italian-owned and managed place is, along with *Refresh*, one of the nicest places to eat in town, set in a colonial-style villa and garden on the land-side of the Galle Rd, and offering a good range of deliciously cooked, moderately priced pizza and pasta.

Listings

Banks and exchange There are branches of the Commercial Bank, the Bank of Ceylon and the People's Bank dotted along the main road south of Hikkaduwa's bus station; the former has a 24-hour ATM (Visa and MasterCard). If you're staying in Wewala and want to avoid traipsing up to Hikkaduwa, Sri Lanka Tours and Travels (see opposite column) changes cash and travellers' cheques at bank rates.

Bicycle rental A couple of places have selections of knackered old bikes for rent: try the place on the main road opposite the turn-off to *Miga Villa*; or International Travels (see Car rental, below). Both charge around Rs.10–20 per hour, or Rs.100 per day.

Car and motorbike rental Sri Lanka Tours and Travels (see opposite column) hires out cars or jeeps for US$36 per day self-drive, or US$42 per day with driver. They also have motorbikes for Rs.600–1200 per day; you don't need a licence, but you'll have to leave your passport or plane ticket as a deposit. International Travels (despite the grandiose name, basically a bloke with a sign by the roadside), just north of *Supercorals* hotel has mopeds for hire (Rs.300 per day for a 50cc machine).

Handicrafts A load of places along the Galle Rd offer all sorts of collectables, including plenty of kolam masks (the quality is actually often higher here than in Ambalangoda) and more unusual wooden pieces. Laksiri Batiks, 400m down Baddegama Rd by the bus station (just before the Gangarama Mahavihara), has a batik factory and a decent range of pieces from around US$5, as well as clothes and sarongs.

Internet Various places along the Galle Rd offer Internet access. Sri Lanka Tours and Travels (see below) is the best set up and most reliable (daily 9am–7.30pm; Rs.90 per hour).

Supermarkets Rangith Snacks, just north of and opposite *Nippon Villa*, and Sandagiri Cream House, just north of and opposite the *Reefcomber* hotel, are the best of the various general stores along Galle Rd.

Taxis Taxis (minivans) line up outside the *Coral Gardens* hotel. Transport to the airport can be arranged through many guest houses or through Sri Lanka Tours and Travels or New Berlin Tours (see below) for Rs.2500–3000.

Travel agents Sri Lanka Tours and Travels (℡091-227 7354), in Wewala opposite the *Reefcomber* hotel, offers island-wide guided tours for around US$50 per day, including transport and half-board accommodation. New Berlin, just north of and opposite *Coral Gardens* hotel, also does island-wide packages and customized tours including short trips to Galle and Unawatuna for around Rs.2000 for up to four people.

Travel details

Train

Aluthgama to: Ambalangoda (9 daily; 30min); Galle (9 daily; 1hr 20min); Colombo (9 daily; 1hr 30min); Hikkaduwa (9 daily; 45min); Kalutara (9 daily; 25min).

Ambalangoda to: Aluthgama (9 daily; 30min); Galle (9 daily; 50min); Colombo (9 daily; 1hr 55min); Hikkaduwa (9 daily; 15min); Kalutara (9 daily; 55min).

Colombo to: Aluthgama (9 daily; 1hr 30min); Ambalangoda (9 daily; 1hr 55min); Anuradhapura (4 daily; 4hr–5hr 30min); Badulla (4 daily; 10hr 20min); Bandarawela (4 daily; 9hr); Chilaw (7–9 daily; 2hr 40min–3hr); Ella (4 daily; 9hr 30min); Haputale (4 daily; 8hr 30min); Hatton (4 daily; 5hr 30min); Kalutara (9 daily; 1hr); Kandy (8 daily; 2hr 30min–3hr 30min); Kurunegala (8 daily; 2hr–2hr 45min); Galle (9 daily; 2hr 45min); Hikkaduwa (9 daily; 2hr 10min); Matara (5–6 daily; 3hr 45min–4hr 40min); Nanu Oya (4 daily; 7hr); Negombo (12 daily; 1hr–1hr 30min); Polonnaruwa (1 daily; 7hr 40min); Puttalam (3 daily; 3hr 30min–4hr 30min); Trincomalee (1 daily; 8hr).

Hikkaduwa to: Aluthgama (9 daily; 45min); Ambalangoda (9 daily; 15min); Colombo (9 daily; 2hr 10min); Galle (9 daily; 35min); Kalutara (9 daily; 1hr 10min).

Kalutara to: Aluthgama (9 daily; 25min); Ambalangoda (9 daily; 55min); Colombo (9 daily; 1hr); Galle (9 daily; 1hr 45min); Hikkaduwa (9 daily; 1hr 10min).

Negombo to: Chilaw (12 daily; 1hr 15min); Colombo (12 daily; 1hr–1hr 30min); Puttalam (12 daily; 2hr 45min).

Bus

The timings given overleaf are for the fastest express services, where they exist. Local buses are usually significantly slower, increasing journey times by anything up to fifty percent.

Principal train departures from Colombo Fort

In addition to the services listed below, other useful departures include: to **Badulla** and the hill country at 5.55am, 9.45am, 7.40pm and 10pm (see p.288 for full timetable); to **Trincomalee** and **Polonnaruwa** at 6.15am and 8pm; and to **Anuradhapura** at 5.45am, 10.40am, 2pm, 3.55pm (express) and 9.30pm.

Colombo to Galle and Matara (express and semi-express services only)

Train no.	50	40	86	56/54	58	94	760	766	775
Colombo	07.10	09.00	10.30	14.05	16.00	17.00	17.15	17.45	19.30
Kalutara South	08.20	09.59	11.29	15.02	16.50	–	18.25	19.06	20.42
Aluthgama	08.48	10.24	11.54	15.28	17.15	18.14	18.50	19.36	21.28
Bentota	08.52	10.27	–	15.32	–	–	18.55	–	21.34
Ambalangoda	09.18	10.52	12.25	16.12	17.45	18.39	19.40	20.06	22.30
Hikkaduwa	09.33	11.07	12.41	16.27	18.00	18.53	20.00	20.21	22.47
Galle	10.15	11.45	13.25	16.50	18.35	19.15	20.35	20.55	23.14
Ahangama	10.43	12.11	13.53	18.00	18.58	–	21.31	–	
Weligama	10.57	12.25	14.07	18.15	19.11	–	–	21.47	–
Matara	11.15	12.45	14.25	18.40	19.30	–	–	22.10	–

Colombo to Kandy
(for onward connections from Kandy, see p.288)

Train no.	5	9+	19	23	29+	35	39	45
Colombo	05.55	07.00	10.30	12.40	15.35	16.55	17.50	19.40
Kandy	08.42	09.35	13.51	16.10	18.05	20.00	21.00	22.54

+= express service

Aluthgama to: Ambalangoda (every 15min; 30min); Colombo (every 15min; 1hr 30min); Galle (every 15min; 1hr 30min); Hikkaduwa (every 15min; 45min); Kalutara (every 15min; 30min).

Ambalangoda to: Aluthgama (every 15min; 30min); Colombo (every 15min; 2hr); Hikkaduwa (every 15min; 20min); Kalutara (every 15min; 1hr).

Colombo to: Airport (every 15min; 50min); Aluthgama (every 15min; 1hr 30min); Ambalangoda (every 15min; 2hr); Anuradhapura (every 30min; 5hr); Badulla (hourly; 8hr); Bandarawela (every 20min; 6hr 30min); Batticaloa (2 daily; 8hr); Dambulla (every 20min; 4hr); Galle (every 15min; 2hr 30min); Hambantota (every 15min; 6hr); Haputale (every 30min; 6hr); Hikkaduwa (every 15min; 2hr 15min); Jaffna (2–3 daily; 10hr): Kalutara (every 15min; 1hr); Kandy (every 10–15min; 3hr); Kurunegala (every 20min; 2hr); Mannar (4 daily; 7hr); Matara (every 15min; 4hr); Negombo (every 10min; 1hr); Nuwara Eliya (every 30min; 4hr 30min); Polonnaruwa (every 30min; 6hr); Ratnapura (every 15min; 3hr); Tangalla (every 15min; 5hr); Tissamaharama (every 15min; 7hr); Trincomalee (hourly; 7hr); Vavuniya (every 30min; 7hr); Weligama (every 15min; 3hr 40min).

Hikkaduwa to: Aluthgama (every 15min; 45min); Ambalangoda (every 15min; 20min); Colombo (every 15min; 2hr 15min); Galle (every 15min; 30min); Kalutara (every 15min; 1hr 15min).

Kalutara to: Aluthgama (every 15min; 30min); Ambalangoda (every 15min; 1hr); Colombo (every 15min; 1hr); Hikkaduwa (every 15min; 1hr 15min).

Negombo to: Airport (every 10–15min; 20min); Anuradhapura (1 daily; 5hr); Chilaw (every 15min; 1hr 15min); Colombo (every 10min; 1hr); Kandy (12 daily; 3hr 30min); Kegalle (every 30min; 2hr 30min); Kurunegala (every 30min; 2hr 15min); Puttalam (via Chilaw; every 15min; 3hr).

Plane

Colombo (Ratmalana Airport) to: Jaffna (3–7 daily; 1hr); Trincomalee (5 weekly; 1hr).

2

The south

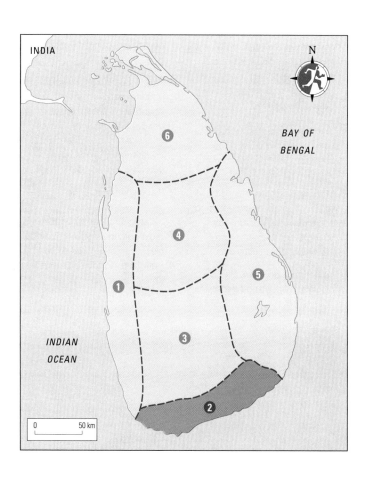

CHAPTER 2

Highlights

✷ **Galle** Spend a day in Sri Lanka's most perfectly preserved colonial town, its somnolent streets lined with historic Dutch villas and hidden behind enormous ramparts. See p.153

✷ **The Sun House** One of the island's most romantic hotels – and with some of its most memorable cuisine – set in a gorgeous nineteenth-century tea planter's villa high above Galle. See p.157

✷ **Unawatuna** Crash out on Sri Lanka's most popular beach at the personable little village of Unawatuna. See p.163

✷ **Mirissa** Tiny, intimate and idyllic beach, hidden away behind a thick swathe of palm trees near the southernmost point of the island. See p.174

✷ **Mulkirigala** Southern Sri Lanka's outstanding historical attraction, with a sequence of beautifully decorated rock temples carved into the flanks of a spectacular outcrop. See p.186

✷ **Bundala** Bundala's interlinked wetlands and lagoons support an huge range of birdlife and other fauna, including magnificent flocks of vivid pink flamingoes. See p.190

✷ **Yala** Sri Lanka's foremost national park, occupying a beautiful stretch of coastal dry-zone forest with marvellous scenery and abundant wildlife, from peacocks to leopards. See p.196

✷ **Kataragama** Join the crowds for the evening puja at Kataragama, one of Sri Lanka's most colourful religious spectacles, at a shrine held sacred by Buddhists, Hindus and Muslims alike. See p.198

△ Tangalla

The south

I n many ways, **the south** encapsulates all that is most traditional about Sri Lanka. Stretched out along a great arc of sun-baked coastline from Galle in the west to Tissamaharama in the east, the area remains essentially rural; a land of a thousand sleepy villages, sheltered under innumerable palms, where the laid-back pace of life still revolves around coconut farming, rice cultivation and fishing (the last still practised in places by the distinctively Sri Lankan method of stilt-fishing – one of the island's emblematic images). Culturally, too, the south remains relatively conservative and inward-looking, a bastion of Sinhalese traditions exemplified by the string of temples and giant Buddha statues which dot the coast, and by the colourful peraheras and festivals celebrated throughout the region, which culminate in the exuberant religious ceremonies which are enacted nightly at the ancient shrine of Kataragama.

The south's physical distance from the rest of the island, and from the waves of Indian invaders who periodically overran the north, meant that the ancient kingdom of **Ruhunu** (or Rohana) – a name still often used to describe the region – acted as a bastion of traditional Sinhalese values, exemplified by the legendary King Dutugemunu (see p.348), who launched his reconquest of the island and expulsion of the Indian invaders from his base in the southern city of Mahagama (modern Tissamaharama). In later centuries, despite the brief importance of the southern ports of Galle and Matara in the colonial Indian Ocean trade, Ruhunu preserved this separation, and with the rise of Colombo and the commercial decline of Galle and Matara in the late nineteenth century, the south became a relative backwater – as it remains, despite the more recent incursions of tourism.

The region's varied attractions make it one of Sri Lanka's most rewarding areas to visit. Gateway to the south – and one of its highlights – is the atmospheric old port of **Galle**, Sri Lanka's best-preserved colonial town and a wonderful place to idle away a couple of somnolent days. Beyond Galle stretch a string of picture-perfect beaches – **Unawatuna**, **Weligama**, **Mirissa** and **Tangalla** – whose relative inaccessibility has protected them from the swarms of package tourists who inundate the west coast. There's plenty to do besides lounging on beaches, though. The little-visited town of **Matara**, with its quaint Dutch fort and rambling streets of old British villas, offers a further taste of Sri Lanka's colonial past, while ancient **Tissamaharama** makes a good base from which to visit two of the country's finest national parks: the placid lagoons and wetlands of **Bundala**, home to crocodiles, monkeys and myriad species of birdlife, and **Yala**, famous for its elephants and elusive leopards. Beyond Tissamaharama (and also easily visited from it) lies the fascinating religious centre of **Kataragama**, whose various shrines are held sacred by Buddhists, Hindus and Muslims alike, and whose nightly temple ceremonies offer one of Sri Lanka's most colourful religious spectacles.

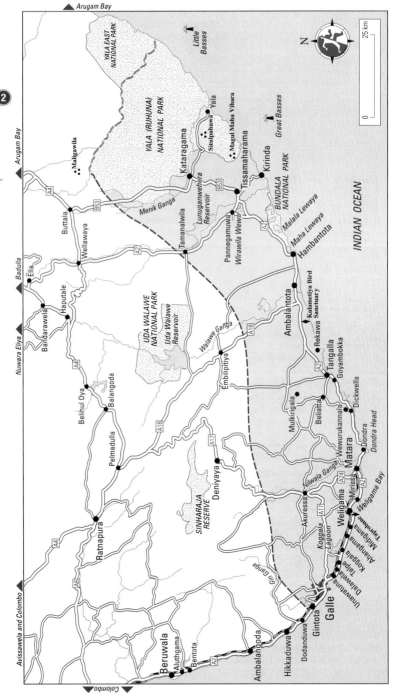

Arugam Bay

Little Basses

YALA EAST
NATIONAL PARK

Maligawila

YALA (RUHUNA)
NATIONAL PARK

Great Basses

Yala

A4

B53

Buttala

Menik Ganga

Situlpahuwa

Magul Maha Vihara

Kataragama

Lunuganwehera
Reservoir

Tissamaharama

Kirinda

Wellawaya

Tamanalwila

B53

A2

Pannegamuwa
Wirawila Wewa

BUNDALA
NATIONAL PARK

Malala Lewaya

INDIAN OCEAN

Badulla

Ella

Haputale

A2

Maha Lewaya

Hambantota

Bandarawela

UDA WALAWE
NATIONAL PARK

Uda Walawe
Reservoir

A4

Belihul Oya

Balangoda

A18

Walawe Ganga

Ambalantota

Kalametiya Bird
Sanctuary

Nuwara Eliya

Pelmadulla

Embilipitiya

A18

Rekawa Lagoon

A2

Tangalla

Goyambokka

Dickwella

Ratnapura

A17

Deniyaya

SINHARAJA
RESERVE

Mulkirigala

Beliatta

Wewurukannala

Dondra

Dondra Head

Matara

A4

A8

Akuressa

Nilwala Ganga

A24

Mirissa

Weligama

Avissawela and Colombo

Gin Ganga

Koggala
Lagoon

Weligama Bay

Midigama

Ahangama

Koggala

Talpe

Dalawella

Unawatuna

Galle

Gintota

Dodanduwa

Hikkaduwa

Ambalangoda

A2

Aluthgama

Bentota

Beruwala

Colombo

0   25 km

N

Getting around the south is straightforward: most of the places covered in this chapter are strung out along the main coastal highway, whose principal towns are served by innumerable buses; in addition, the southern coastal railway connects Galle, Weligama and Matara with Colombo. Most of the south, from Galle to just east of Tangalla, lies in the wet zone and shares broadly the same climate as the west coast south of Colombo, meaning that the **best time to visit** is from mid-October to mid-April, outside the monsoon season. Tissamaharama, Kataragama and Yala and Bundala national parks lie in the dry zone and experience relatively little rainfall year-round.

Galle

Perched on the coast close to the island's southernmost point, the venerable port of **GALLE** (pronounced "Gaul") has grown from ancient origins into Sri Lanka's fourth largest city. At the heart of modern Galle – but strangely detached from it – lies the old Dutch quarter, known as the **Fort**. Sri Lanka's best-preserved colonial townscape, it's enclosed within huge walls and bastions which now protect the area from modernization as effectively as they once protected Dutch trading interests from marauding adventurers. Declared a World Heritage Site in 1988, the Fort has an understated, quietly decaying charm, its low-rise streets lined with old churches and Dutch colonial villas, many of which retain their original street-facing verandahs, their white plaster now stripped by sea breezes and weathered to a peeling grey. There's not actually much to see (a few bizarre museums excepted): the main pleasure here is just ambling round the atmospheric old streets and around the walls, enjoying the easy pace of life and refreshing absence of traffic – you won't find a quieter town anywhere else in the island.

Some history

Galle is thought to have been the Biblical **Tarshish**, from whence King Solomon obtained gold, spices, ivory, apes and peacocks, and the combination of its fine natural harbour and strategic position on the sea routes between Arabia, India and Southeast Asia made the town an important trading emporium long before the arrival of the Europeans – the celebrated Moroccan traveller Ibn Battuta visited in the fourteenth century and described an already flourishing settlement. In 1505 a Portuguese fleet heading for the Maldives ran into a storm and were forced to take refuge in the harbour. The fanciful story goes that, upon hearing the town's cocks (in Portuguese, *galo*) crowing in the dusk, they christened the town **Punto de Gale**, a name later corrupted by the British into Point de Gale, though it's far more likely that the name is derived from the Sinhala *gala*, meaning rock, which is a common component of place names across the island and a thing of which Galle has plenty. Either way, the cockerel has become the town's de facto emblem, however suspect the etymology behind it.

It wasn't until 1588–89 that the Portuguese renewed their interest in Galle, building a small fort named Santa Cruz, which they later extended with a series of bastions and walls. The **Dutch** captured Galle in 1640 after a four-day siege, and in 1663 expanded the original Portuguese fortifications to enclose the whole of Galle's sea-facing promontory, establishing the street plan and system of bastions which survive to this day, as well as introducing marvels of

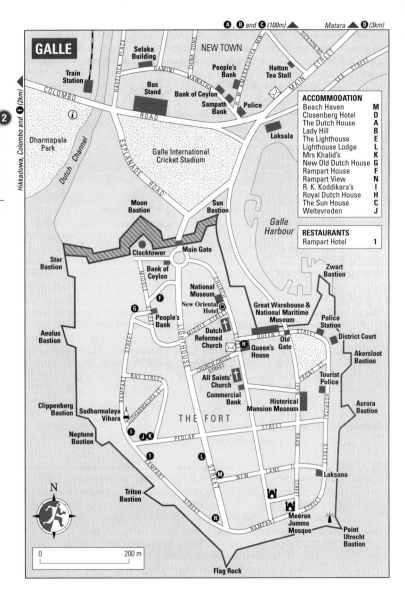

GALLE

NEW TOWN

Ⓐ, Ⓑ and Ⓒ (100m) ▲   Matara ▲ Ⓓ (3km)

Selaka Building

People's Bank

Hatton Tea Stall

Train Station

Bus Stand

Bank of Ceylon

Sampath Bank

Police

Laksala

Dharmapala Park

Galle International Cricket Stadium

ACCOMMODATION	
Beach Haven	M
Closenberg Hotel	D
The Dutch House	A
Lady Hill	B
The Lighthouse	E
Lighthouse Lodge	L
Mrs Khalid's	K
New Old Dutch House	G
Rampart House	F
Rampart View	N
R. K. Koddikara's	I
Royal Dutch House	H
The Sun House	C
Weltevreden	J

Moon Bastion

Sun Bastion

Galle Harbour

RESTAURANTS	
Rampart Hotel	1

Star Bastion

Clocktower

Main Gate

Bank of Ceylon

National Museum

New Oriental Hotel

Zwart Bastion

Great Warehouse & National Maritime Museum

Police Station

Aeolus Bastion

People's Bank

Dutch Reformed Church

Queen's House

Old Gate

District Court

Akersloot Bastion

Clippenberg Bastion

Sudharmalaya Vihara

All Saints' Church

Commercial Bank

Historical Mansion Museum

Tourist Police

Aurora Bastion

THE FORT

Neptune Bastion

Triton Bastion

Laksana

Meeran Jumma Mosque

Point Utrecht Bastion

N

0   200 m

Flag Rock

European engineering such as an intricate subterranean sewer system which was flushed out daily by the tide.

The **British** took Galle in 1796 during the largely peaceable islandwide transfer of power following Dutch capitulation in the Napoleonic Wars (see p.421) – ironically, after all the ingenuity and labour they had invested in the town's defences, Galle was finally surrendered with hardly a shot being fired. The city continued to serve as Ceylon's principal harbour for much of the eighteenth century, but Colombo's growing commercial importance and improvements to its harbour gradually eroded Galle's trade. By the early twentieth century, Galle had become an economic backwater, lapsing into a tranquil decline which happily, if fortuitously, allowed the old colonial townscape of the Fort to survive almost completely intact.

In the years since independence, Galle has recovered some of its lost dynamism. The bustling modern city is now one of Sri Lanka's largest, while despite playing second fiddle to Colombo, Galle's port still receives significant quantities of shipping; there are usually a few enormous container ships waiting to dock. More recently, the Fort has become Sri Lanka's most newly fashionable area: an influx of foreign cash has seen many of the colonial villas bought up and renovated by foreign investors, while the dilapidated *New Oriental Hotel* has been transformed into Sri Lanka's most luxurious (and expensive) place to stay.

Arrival, information and accommodation

There are two parts to Galle: the old town or **Fort**, within the ramparts of the old Dutch fort, and the **new town** to the north, home to the bus and train stations and virtually all the town's commercial activity. A tuktuk from either the train or bus station (both right in the middle of the new town) to any of the Fort guest houses shouldn't cost most than Rs.50.

There's a hopeless **Tourist Information Centre** (Mon–Fri 9am–4.45pm; ☏091-224 7676) in the park opposite the train station. The sign promises tourist information in three different European languages, although in practice you'll be lucky to get anything more than a few words of English.

Accommodation

Galle Fort has one of the best selections of inexpensive, family-run **guest houses** in Sri Lanka, offering sociable lodgings and good home-cooking. There are a couple of outstanding top-end options scattered around the fringes of the new town, though there's not much choice of mid-range accommodation. In addition to the places listed below, at the time of writing the historic but seriously dilapidated New Oriental Hotel in the Fort had been bought by Aman Resorts (Ⓦwww.amanresorts.com), who are currently transforming it into the most luxurious and – at a reported US$500 per night – most expensive hotel on the island. According to latest estimates, it's due to reopen early 2005 – check the website for an update.

Many colonial-era villas in Galle Fort and the surrounding countryside have been converted into spectacular **holiday homes**, offering luxurious lodgings in historic surroundings. Visit Ⓦwww.villasinsrilanka.com for a full listing.

Touts and scams in Galle

Galle has more than its fair share of **touts** and **con artists** – all the usual cautions (see p.61) apply. None of the Fort's guest houses are clearly signed, so if you take a tuktuk to reach one, check the address to make sure you're actually being taken to the right place; some guest-house owners will pick you up from the bus station if you ring in advance. Apart from trying to get you into a guest house of their choice, the town's touts are also keen to wheedle their way into visitors' confidence in order to get them into one of the town's many **gem shops** – a favourite trick is to offer to take you to see "crocodiles" (actually water monitors) in the canal alongside Havelock Place. These caveats aside, if you keep your wits about you and treat any unnaturally friendly approaches with due caution, you shouldn't have any problems.

Budget and moderate

Beach Haven (Mrs N.D. Wijenayakae's) 65 Lighthouse St ☏091-223 4663, Ⓔthalidh@sri.lanka.net. Very friendly guest house in a meandering family house right in the middle of the Fort, offering a varied range of good-value rooms. There's also a pleasant upstairs sitting area and communal verandah overlooking the street – good for idle people-watching – and tasty home-cooked meals. ❶–❷

Lighthouse Lodge 62b Lighthouse St ☏091-545 0514, Ⓔumayanga@eureka.lk. The cheapest accommodation in town, with small, dark rooms in a rather claustrophobic family house – basic, but OK at the price. ❶

Mrs Khalid's 102 Pedlar St ☏091-223 4907, Ⓔkhalid@dialogsl.net. A Galle institution, recently moved to a beautiful colonial house. Two smart upstairs rooms have a balcony, partial sea view and hot water, while three cheaper rooms downstairs have cold water only. There's also a small library, cheap email for guests (Rs.75 per hr) and excellent home-cooking (see p.162) from the owner. ❶–❸

New Old Dutch House 21 Middle St ☏091-438 5032, Ⓕ438 4920. Characterless, oxymoronically named establishment whose sign promises "sweet" rooms: they're actually not suites at all, just average-size doubles with twin beds. All are sparklingly modern, with TV, fridge, phone and carpet, though most share an (albeit immaculate) bathroom. ❸

Rampart House 3 Rampart St ☏091-438 0566. Three large and pleasant double rooms (which can sleep three) in a modern and very peaceful family house near the entrance to the Fort. Breakfast and dinner available. ❶

Rampart View 37 Rampart St ☏091-438 0566. Modern house right by the ramparts with five spacious, clean rooms – four are upstairs with sea views and a nice little breezy verandah. Great location and reasonable value, though less sociable than some of the other guest houses in town. ❷

R.K. Koddikara's (Beatrice House) 29 Rampart St ☏091-222 2351, Ⓔkodi.galle@ccom.lk. One of Galle's best and oldest guest houses, set in an attractive sea-facing house beautifully situated next to the ramparts. The breezy upstairs rooms (with hot water) are simple but spacious and clean, and have ramparts views, and there are cheaper options downstairs; all boast specially made extra-long beds, a rare pleasure for oversize foreigners. Downstairs ❶, upstairs ❷

Royal Dutch House Queen's House, corner of Church and Queen's streets ☏091-224 7160, Ⓔkengngsa@sltnet.lk. Set in this historic 1683 building, the rooms here are huge and have bags of colonial character, with creaking wooden floors, quaint swivel doors and immensely high ceilings (although there's not much in the way of furniture). It's all intensely atmospheric, though not wildly comfortable and a bit under-used and forlorn. There's a reasonable if pricey restaurant downstairs. ❸

Weltevreden 104 Pedlar St ☏091-222 2650, Ⓔpiyasen2@sltnet.lk. Peaceful family-run guest house set in a 250-year-old Dutch house arranged around a beautiful, flower-filled courtyard garden. Rooms are smaller and shabbier – but also cheaper – than some of the town's other guest houses. Good home-cooked food and Internet access available. ❷

Expensive

Closenberg Hotel 11 Closenberg Rd, Megalle ☏091-222 4313, Ⓕ223 2241. Tucked into a little bay 3km east from Galle, this nineteenth-century British villa has five pleasantly old-fashioned rooms complete with chunky teak furniture, plus fifteen more in a modern wing with sea-facing balconies. A tuktuk from Galle shouldn't cost more than Rs.100. A/c supplement US$5. ❺

The Dutch House (aka Doornberg) Upper Dickson Rd ☏091-438 0275, Ⓦwww.thesunhouse.com. Next door to *The Sun House* and under the same management, this meticulously restored Dutch villa of 1712 has four huge suites complete with reproduction antique furniture and all the amenities you'd expect at around $350 a night. Outside there's an immaculately manicured garden with croquet hoops, and a gorgeous L-shaped pool. ❾

Lady Hill 29 Upper Dickson Rd ☏091-224 4322, Ⓦwww.ladyhillsl.com. Modern five-storey hotel atop the highest hill in Galle. Rooms are small and a bit shabby, but all come with a/c, hot water, phone, TV and private balconies from where (on higher floors especially) there are superlative views over the town, coast and hills inland. There's also a small swimming pool. ❻

The Lighthouse Dadella ☏091-222 3744, Ⓦwww.jetwinghotels.com. On the main road 2km west of town, this enormously stylish – albeit enormously expensive (around $240 per double per night) – Geoffrey Bawa-designed hotel is one of Sri Lanka's finest, perched on a rather wild stretch of coast in an elegantly understated, slightly Tuscan-looking ochre building. The sixty rooms are masterpieces of interior design, complete with all modcons, and there are plenty of facilities, including two pools, a gym, spa, squash court, beauty salon and an attractive ayurveda centre. Good food, too (see p.162). ❾

The Sun House 18 Upper Dickson Rd ☎091-438 0275, ⓦwww.thesunhouse.com. One of Sri Lanka's most magical small hotels, set in a restored 1860s planter's villa perched on a hillside and offering memorable views across a sea of palm trees. The four standard rooms are on the small side, but lovingly furnished and brimful of character; there's also the magical Cinnamon Suite, occupying the whole first floor of the main house. Marvellous food (see p.162) and a small pool set in an enchanting, frangipani-studded garden. ❾

The Fort

The principal entrance to the Fort is through the **Main Gate**, one of the newest parts of the fortifications, having been added by the British in 1873 to allow easier vehicular access to the fort. The section of ramparts facing the new town is the most heavily fortified, since it protected the Fort's vulnerable land side. The Dutch substantially enlarged the original Portuguese fortifications here, naming the new defences the **Sun**, **Moon** and **Star bastions**. The sheer scale of the town-facing bastions here is brutally impressive, if not particularly aesthetic – a fitting memorial to Dutch Governor Petrus Vuyst (1726–29), who was largely responsible for their construction and whose cruelty and abuse of power was such that he was eventually recalled to Jakarta and executed by the Dutch authorities. The ugly clocktower on top of the bastions was erected by the punctilious British in 1883.

The National Museum to All Saints' Church

From the Main Gate, go left at the roundabout to reach one of the Fort's two main north–south thoroughfares, the atmospheric **Church Street** (originally Kerkstraat), named after a long-demolished Dutch church. An attractive old colonial building near the top of the street holds the **National Museum** (Tues–Sat 9am–5pm; Rs.45), a wildly over-optimistic name for three dusty rooms of rather sorry-looking exhibits, which give only the faintest sense of the exotic and luxurious items which would formerly have passed through Galle's harbour. The large and rather stately white building next door to the museum was originally built for the Dutch governor in 1684; it was converted into the venerable **New Oriental Hotel** in 1863.

Almost next door, the atmospheric **Dutch Reformed Church** (or Groote Kerk) is Galle's most absorbing colonial building. Built on the site of an earlier Portuguese Capuchin convent, the present structure was completed around 1755 – the traditional explanation states that it was an offering from the Dutch commander Casparus de Jong and his wife, erected in gratitude after the birth of their first child. The graceful and slightly Italianate lines of the facade belie the severity of the **interior**, in which the only decorative concessions are the enormous canopy over the pulpit (presumably for acoustic effect) and the attractive organ loft, reached by an elegant flight of balustraded stairs. The floor is covered in ornately carved **memorials** to the city's Dutch settlers, the earlier examples in Dutch (moved here from two earlier Dutch cemeteries which were dismantled by the British in 1853), later ones in English, many of them bearing witness to the lamentably brief life expectancy of Ceylon's early European colonists, such as the unfortunate Harriet Hynes, "Who departed this life after a short illness from fever on the 11th Decr 1867, aged 17 years, one month & four days", the painfully exact enumeration of each month and day adding its own poignant subtext. Most striking, however, is the memorial to **E.A.H. Abraham**, Commander of Galle, complete with skull, hourglass, a medieval-looking armoured helmet and the remains (for reasons not obvious) of his shirt.

Dutch Burghers

Many of the tombstones which cover the floor and fill the churchyard of the Dutch Reformed Church bear Dutch names – Jansz, De Kretser, Van Langenberg, and the like – dating from the colonial period right up to modern times. These commemorate the families of Sri Lanka's smallest, and oddest, minority: the **Dutch Burghers** (or Dutch-Portuguese Burghers, as they are sometimes called). These are Sri Lankans of Dutch or Portuguese descent.

At the time of Independence the community numbered around fifty thousand, based mainly in Colombo, and exerted a strong influence on the country, having held major government posts under the British as well as running many of the island's trading companies. However, their numbers declined significantly in the 1950s, when as many as half the country's Burgher families, disillusioned by Sinhalese nationalist laws based on language and religion, left for Australia, Canada or Britain.

Despite their Dutch (or Portuguese) ancestry, the Burghers have for centuries spoken English as their first language. Burgher culture preserves strong Dutch elements, however, and they would be horrified to be confused with the British, despite a certain amount of intermarriage over the years (not only with the British, but also with the Sinhalese and Tamils). Not that there is really such a thing as a single Burgher culture or community. Many of the wealthier Burghers arrived in Ceylon as employees of the Dutch East India Company, while working-class Burghers, more often from Portugal, came to help build the railways and settled largely on the coast between Colombo and Negombo. And to make things a little more confused, there are thousands of Sri Lankans with Dutch or Portuguese names, adopted during the years of occupation, yet who have no connection at all with Europe.

In recent years, the Burghers have made their mark in Sri Lanka, and beyond, in the arts. **Geoffrey Bawa** (see p.132), arguably Asia's greatest twentieth-century architect, belonged to the community (though his family, in typical Burgher style, also claimed Malay descent). **George Keyt** (1901–93), Sri Lanka's foremost modern painter, was also a Burgher, as are two of the leading contemporary Sri Lankan artists, **Barbara Sansoni**, founder of the Barefoot company in Colombo (see p.108), and **Ena de Silva**, the batik designer. Overseas, the best-known Burgher is Canada-based novelist **Michael Ondaatje**, author of the Booker Prize-winning *The English Patient*, whose memoir of island life, *Running in the Family*, gives a wonderful picture of Burgher life in the years before independence. Other Burgher novels include **Michelle de Kretser's** evocative *The Hamilton Case*, set in 1930s Ceylon, and **Carl Muller's** picaresque trilogy, *The Jam Fruit Tree*, about the "railway Burghers". There's also an interesting chapter on Sri Lanka's present-day Burgher community in **Riccardo Orizio's** *Lost White Tribes*.

A few steps further down the road is the dilapidated but still functioning **post office**, whose Dickensian-looking interior is worth a peek. Diagonally opposite stands **Queen's House**. Originally the offices of the Dutch city governor (it's still sometimes called the Old Dutch Government House), it's now an atmospheric hotel and restaurant (see p.156), hence the painting which currently disfigures the Church Street facade; the original entrance on Queen's Street, emblazoned with the date "Anno 1683" and a picture of a cock, remains unadulterated. Immediately south of here is the Fort's principal Anglican place of worship, **All Saints' Church**, a memorably ugly Romanesque basilica-style structure whose stumpy steeple is one of the area's most distinctive landmarks. The church was begun in 1868 on the site of a previous courthouse – the town's gallows might (as a sign outside gruesomely points out) have stood on the site of the current high altar; otherwise, the bare, mildewed interior gives disappointingly little insight into the history of the British in Galle.

The Great Warehouse to the Lighthouse

From All Saint's, retrace your steps for a few metres then turn right down Queen's Street to reach the **Great Warehouse**, one of the Fort's most striking buildings, completed around 1676 – a long, barn-like ochre structure punctuated by barred windows behind black shutters. Ships' provisions and valuable commodities such as cowries, sappan wood, salt, pepper and cinnamon were kept safe here, and the warehouse also served as a place of worship for the Dutch prior to construction of the Reformed Church – it's now largely occupied by the National Maritime Museum (see below). Built into the far end of the warehouse stands the **Old Gate**. Until the construction of the Main Gate in 1873, this was the only entrance to the Fort, strategically positioned between the Zwart and Sun bastions, both of which could fire on potential attackers heading for the gate. The arch on the Fort side of the gate is inscribed with the coat of arms of the VOC (Vereenigde Oost Indische Compagnie, or Dutch East Indies Company), showing two lions holding a crest topped by the inevitable cockerel), while the moss-covered arch on the exterior, port-facing side is decorated with the British crest, "Dieu et mon droit", and the date 1668.

A side-door inside the Old Gate leads through into the interior of the Great Warehouse and the second of Galle's quirky national museums, the **National Maritime Museum** (Mon–Thurs & Sun 9am–5pm; Rs.65), filled with murkily illuminated displays on marine life ranging from the merely tedious (corals, seaweed, seashells, models of fish and whales) to the thoroughly desperate (a tin of pilchards and a jar of fish paste).

The northeastern corner of the Fort is marked by a spacious green dotted with handsome old trees, one of which is being dramatically engulfed by an enormous banyan. Immediately south of here, the top of **Leyn Baan Street** (Rope Walk Street) is home to dozens of lawyers' offices, covered in an exuberant medley of signs. A couple of minutes' walk down the road, the entertaining **Historical Mansion Museum** (daily 9am–6pm; donation) is the result of the efforts of a certain Mr Gaffar, who over the past 35 years has accumulated an enormous collection of antiques, curiosities, bric-a-brac and outright junk, presumably in the belief that if you horde enough stuff for long enough, some of it might eventually turn out to be worth something. The fruits of his labours are stuffed into several chaotic rooms, items of general interest muddled up with all sorts of detritus: smashed plates, glassware, alarm clocks, accordions, knuckledusters, stethoscopes, cigarette lighters – in fact, pretty much any type of object which has been manufactured in Sri Lanka over the past century. The overall effect of this Aladdin's Cave of rubbish is strangely compelling, even when it becomes obvious that the principal object of the entire museum is to get you into Mr Gaffar's gem shop.

Return to the green and walk south down **Hospital Street**. The ramparts here are hidden behind buildings until the junction with Pedlar Street, though you can see parts of the **Zwart Bastion** (Black Fort), which is thought to incorporate the remains of the original Portuguese fortress of Santa Cruz, making it the town's oldest surviving section of fortification, although there's nothing to really distinguish it from the rest of the wall. Its neighbour to the south, the **Ackersloot Bastion** (1789) is named after the birthplace of Admiral Wilhelm Coster, the Dutch captain who captured Galle from the Portuguese in 1640. Capping Hospital Street is **Point Utrecht Bastion**, topped by a slender white **lighthouse** of 1938; the ruined structure standing below it was a British powder magazine. Overlooking it to the west is the large, early twentieth-century **Meeran Jumma Mosque**, which looks every inch a Portuguese Baroque church (it's actually built on the site of the former Portuguese cathedral), with only a couple of tiny minarets and a token

△ Meeran Jumma Mosque, Galle

scribble of Arabic betraying its true function. The mosque stands at the heart of Galle's **Muslim quarter**, whose white-robed and skull-capped inhabitants form a distinctive part of life in the old town's streets.

The ramparts

From the lighthouse, it's possible to walk clockwise along the top of the **ramparts** all the way to the main town-facing bastions – a beautiful stroll and an excellent way to get an overview of the town and orientate yourself (though between the lighthouse and Flag Rock, you'll probably be mainly concerned with avoiding the persistent attentions of hawkers and the local snake charmers, whose pythons are mercilessly goaded out of their baskets at the merest whiff of a tourist). At the southwestern corner of the Fort, **Flag Rock** is the most imposing of Galle's bastions – the name derives from the Dutch practice of signalling approaching ships to warn them of offshore hazards hereabouts (the warning signals would have been backed up by musket shots, fired from the huge Pigeon Rock, which you can see just offshore).

The well-preserved section of ramparts beyond here gives a clear idea of how the original Dutch fortifications would have appeared. Look closely at the stones and you'll see that many are actually formed from coral, which would have been hewed and carted into place by slaves. The next bastion along, the **Triton**, comes alive around dusk, as the townsfolk turn out en masse to promenade along the walls and take in the extraordinary red-and-purple sunsets enjoyed by this part of the coast, amidst the inevitable impromptu cricket matches and the ice cream hawkers (whose mechanical jingles will lodge in your head for weeks afterwards) – aim to be on the west-facing ramparts when the sun goes down.

Continuing north, the **Neptune** and **Clippenberg bastions** give increasingly fine views over the Fort, with the stumpy spire of All Saint's prominent amongst the picturesque huddle of red rooftops. Closer to hand stands the neat white dagoba of the 1889 **Sudharmalaya Vihara**, looking bizarrely out of place amidst its colonial surroundings. The **Aeolus Bastion** is still in military use, meaning that you'll have to descend briefly from the walls and detour around it. Just beyond here, the modest **tomb** of a Muslim saint lies in solitary splendour beneath the ramparts, said to mark the spot where the saint's body washed ashore. From here you can continue up to the Star Bastion and back across to the Main Gate.

The new town

Exiting the Fort by the Main Gate, you'll have a fine view of Galle's compact **Galle International Cricket Ground**, one of the country's three major test venues; the pitch occupies the site of the former British racecourse, built on reclaimed ground in the nineteenth century (match tickets are available directly from the stadium, or ask at your guest house or hotel). To the east, the **harbourside** is normally busy with fishing boats, their owners noisily bartering over piles of tuna, seer and crab. Beyond here the **new town** straggles northwards in an indeterminate confusion of hooting buses and zigzagging rickshaws. The most interesting place for a wander is the relatively traffic-free section of **Main Street** past the junction with Sea Street, where lines of small shops and local pavement traders cut a colourful dash.

Eating

For the fourth-largest city in Sri Lanka, Galle has a surprising paucity of decent **places to eat**: options comprise a dingy collection of local cafés and down-at-heel Chinese restaurants. The good news is that most of the Fort guest houses do good home-cooking, so you can usually get a reasonable meal where you're staying, while in *The Sun House*, *Mrs Khalid's* and *The Lighthouse*, the city boasts three of southern Sri Lanka's finest gastronomic experiences. In addition, it's easy enough to head out to Unawatuna (see opposite) for an evening's lounging on the beach; a tuktuk should cost Rs.120 each way, and there are plenty hanging around for the return trip until quite late at night. It's also worth the climb up to the fifth floor of the *Lady Hill* (see p.156) for a (pricey) **drink** at the rooftop bar, from where's there a marvellous view on one side out over the red-tiled roofs of the Fort and, on the other, across miles of palm trees stretching away inland to the Hill Country.

The Lighthouse Dadella, 2km west of Galle. This beautiful hotel (see p.156) provides the five-star setting for some excellent but surprisingly cheap Sri Lankan and international cuisine, either in the stylish Cinnamon Room (count on around $15 for a two-course meal with drinks) or the less formal Cardamom Café (open 24hr).

Mrs Khalid's 102 Pedlar St. The charming owner claims to be able to rustle up any dish you fancy, Western or Sri Lankan, and also serves one of the most memorable rice and curry spreads in the island: a delicately flavoured feast accompanied by cardamom-scented pilau for a bargain Rs.250. Order a few hours in advance. No alcohol.

Rampart Hotel 31 Rampart St. Pleasant, breezy location overlooking the ramparts (at least by day – you won't see much at night). Food from the standard, tourist-oriented menu is rather pricey, with most main courses over Rs.300, but is better than average – the devilled cashew nuts (Rs.360) are a treat.

The Sun House 18 Upper Dickson Rd ☎091-438 0275. The candlelit garden verandah of this magical colonial villa (see p.157) provides an incomparably romantic setting for daily-changing three-course set meals (Rs1800–2000), featuring fabulous Sri Lankan cuisine with Indian, Malay, Dutch and Portuguese influences – anything from chilli-roasted mahi-mahi fillet in lemongrass sauce to Cajun shark with mango salsa. Book by 1pm for dinner.

Listings

Banks There are branches of Sampath Bank, Hatton National Bank and the Bank of Ceylon clustered together around the junction of Gamini Mw and H.W. Amarasuriya Mw in the new town – Sampath is usually the most efficient. In the Fort, there are branches of the Bank of

Moving on from Galle

Galle's **bus station** is more than averagely chaotic – if arriving here by tuktuk it pays to ask your driver to help find your bus. Services in both directions along the main **coastal road** leave roughly every fifteen minutes; express a/c minibuses leave every fifteen minutes for **Colombo** via **Hikkaduwa**, **Aluthgama** and **Kalutara**. Long-distance services heading east usually originate in Colombo rather than Galle, meaning that you can't count on getting a seat. If you're heading to **Tangalla** or **Tissamaharama**, you may find it quicker to catch a bus to Matara and change there, rather than waiting for a through bus (on which you're also unlikely to find a seat). There are also a few direct buses to **Kataragama** (5 daily); otherwise, change at Matara and/or Tissa.

The easiest way to get to **Kandy** from Galle is to return to Colombo. To reach **Sinharaja**, you'll need to take a bus to **Akuressa** then change for **Deniyaya** (every 30min; there are also a few direct buses to Deniyaya). Reaching the southern **hill country** from Galle is a laborious process; there's currently a once-daily service departing in the morning to **Badulla** via **Haputale** and **Bandarawela**, and at least one service daily to **Nuwara Eliya**. Alternatively, catch the bus to Tissa, then another to **Wellawaya**, from where there are frequent services to Ella, Haputale and Badulla – this is a long day's journey, however.

Note that if you're heading along the coast, it's generally more comfortable to go by **train**; see p.202 for full details.

Ceylon and People's Bank on Middle St, and a Commercial Bank on Church St (Mon–Fri 9am–3pm), which has the only ATM in Galle which accepts foreign cards (Visa and MasterCard).

Bookshop Vijitha Yapa, on the second floor of the Selaka Building near the bus station, has a reasonable selection of English-language books.

Handicrafts Laksala, opposite the main post office, has the usual range of trashy masks, carved elephants and statues of ladies with wobbly heads. Laksana, at 30 Hospital St in the Fort, has a classier selection of antique items, including lots of silver jewellery.

Hospital General Hospital ☎ 091-222 2261

Internet Infolink Computer Systems (daily 9am–5pm; Rs.5 per min), on the second floor of the Selaka Building near the bus station, has cheap rates and a reasonable number of machines.

Pharmacies Silvas Drugs Store or Medimate Pharmacy, both on Havelock Place in the new town; or Steurt Remedica, just round the corner on the ground floor of the Selaka Building. Not much English is spoken at any of them.

Photography Selaka Colour Lab, on the first floor of the Selaka Building, is the town's main Kodak agent.

Police The tourist police have an office on Hospital St in the Fort (open 24hr).

Post and phones The main post office (Mon–Sat 7am–9pm), in the new town on Main St, has a well-organized poste restante section, plus an EMS mail service and stationers. There's also a dilapidated sub-post office in the Fort on Church St just south of the Dutch Reformed Church. For phone calls, Havelock Place in the new town holds the main concentration of communication bureaux.

Tea The Hatton Tea Stall (actually mainly a supermarket) has a very good selection; it's just off Main Street in the new town.

Unawatuna

Five kilometres southeast of Galle, the ever-expanding village of **UNAWATUNA** is now firmly established as Sri Lanka's most popular resort for independent travellers – and with good reason. Set snugly in a pretty semicircular bay, picturesquely terminated by a dagoba on the rocky headland to the northwest, the beach remains idyllic, while the sheltered bay gives safe year-round swimming, and a group of rocks 150m offshore further breaks up waves (though it can still get a bit rough during the monsoon).

It's far from unspoilt, of course. Virtually every home in the village offers rooms for rent, new guest houses continue to spring up, and much of the beach has now disappeared under a string of informal waterfront restaurants. But despite its growing popularity, Unawatuna retains a low-key, slightly ramshackle charm – for the time being, at least. Unlike Hikkaduwa or Negombo, it also manages to be lively without being trashy, and although it's not exactly a party village, you can at least stay up eating and drinking on the beach until fairly late at night, a rare pleasure in early-to-bed Sri Lanka. It also remains lively all year round, making it a good place to visit if you're on the west coast during the monsoon.

Arrival

Unawatuna is hidden away off the coastal Matara Road some 5km east of Galle. Take any bus heading east from Galle and ask to be dropped at the turn-off for the village, **Yaddehimulla Road** (formerly known as The Strand), which runs from the Matara Road for 500m down to the beach past a string of guest houses (no buses actually go into the village itself). Yaddehimulla Road isn't clearly signposted and is very easy to miss – look out for signs to the guest houses and make sure the conductor knows where you're getting off (if you're coming from Galle and you reach the Sri Udaya Musical Centre, you've just passed the turning). A **tuktuk** to or from Galle costs Rs.120.

Travel agents

Unawatuna has loads of **travel agents** and is a good place to arrange local **day-trips** or longer **tours** of the island. All the companies below should be able to fix you up with a car and driver (around US$30 per day), as well as organizing all-inclusive tours with accommodation of whatever standard you want, from cheap guest houses to hotels (US$40–60 per person per day). Transport is usually in minivans seating up to five or six people, so tours work out cheaper the larger the group. Closer to Unawatuna, most agents can arrange trips to Kosgoda lagoon and river safaris on the Madu Oya at Balapitiya.

Blue Fin Tours ☏091-438 0346. Surfing specialists, offering either day-trips or longer excursions, with cheap tours to Midigama and Arugam Bay. They can also arrange standard tours with car and guest house accommodation, plus more adventurous walking tours and camping trips. They also have motorbikes for hire (Rs.450 per day for a 250cc Honda).

G.G. Happy Tour ☏091-438 1441, ✉gghappy@wow.lk. Perhaps the best general tour operator in town, with a good reputation for interesting tours and informative guiding at quite reasonable rates. Day-trips to Sinharaja and Uda Walawe are also available.

Vista Travel Agency ☏091-224 7219, ✉vista3@slt.lk (signed as "Reisebüro Travel Office"). Reliable operator offering the usual all-inclusive islandwide tours plus a wide range of day-trips to Galle, Tangalla, Ratnapura and other destinations.

If you want a **bank**, you'll have to go to Galle, though you may be able to **change cash** (at poorish rates) at one of the travel agents or smarter hotels in town (try the *Unawatuna Beach Resort*). There are lots of places with **Internet** access. Right in the middle of the village, *InternetCafe@e-world* has plenty of good machines with ISDN connections (daily 9am–midnight; Rs.5 per min) and free coffee. You can make IDD international **phone calls** at lots of places in the village. The local **post office** is about a kilometre down the Matara Road towards Galle.

There's a smattering of handicrafts shops along Yaddehimulla Road and elsewhere in the village. The little-visited and rather forlorn **Handicrafts Shopping Complex** on the main road has a big range of handicrafts, some of it of reasonable quality. **Udaya Antiques** nearby is an Aladdin's cave of bric-a-brac, with genuine antiques mixed up with lots of junk. It's worth a rummage, but there are no marked prices, so you'll have to bargain.

Accommodation

There are heaps of **places to stay** in Unawatuna. Guest houses abound – it can seem as if every house in the village offers a couple of rooms for rent – but there are relatively few (and relatively poorer-value) mid-range options, and just one top-end hotel. You'll pay over the odds though to stay on the beach; the best-value accommodation is away from the water at either end of Yaddehimulla Road.

Seasonal variations and fluctuations in demand keep prices very fluid. High season runs roughly from mid-October to mid-April; outside this period rates fall by up to thirty percent in many places. In addition, the sheer number of places offering rooms keeps competition keen and means guest house owners are usually receptive to bargaining. Few places have fixed single rates; again there's plenty of room to bargain. Most guest houses also do food, though given the number of restaurants in town, it's usually more fun to eat out.

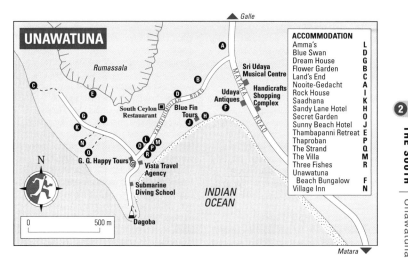

ACCOMMODATION

Amma's	L
Blue Swan	D
Dream House	G
Flower Garden	B
Land's End	C
Nooite-Gedacht	A
Rock House	I
Saadhana	K
Sandy Lane Hotel	H
Secret Garden	O
Sunny Beach Hotel	J
Thambapanni Retreat	E
Thaproban	P
The Strand	Q
The Villa	M
Three Fishes	R
Unawatuna Beach Bungalow	F
Village Inn	N

Budget

Amma's ☎091-222 5332. One of the oldest guest houses in Unawatuna, and still a decent – if slightly overpriced – choice, with clean, simple rooms in the heart of the village. ❷

Blue Swan ☎ & ℻091-222 4691. Set in a rather imposing-looking house at the quieter northern end of Yaddehimulla Rd, this British-owned and managed place has four large, well-furnished and good-value rooms (one with a/c; two with shared bath). It's a bit smarter than your average budget guest house, helped by the lovely rugs everywhere. ❷–❹

Flower Garden ☎091-222 5286, ℮flowerga@wow.lk. A secluded garden setting at the top end of Yaddehimulla Rd, the eighteen rooms here in neat little bungalows have hot water and optional a/c, lots of colonial-style furniture and private verandahs. There's also a small ayurvedic centre and a decent-size pool. Breakfast included. ❸

Land's End ☎091-438 0099, ⓦwww.lanka.net/landsend. Scenically located on a wild and rocky headland west of the village, with great views of the sea and sunsets over Galle, and clean, spacious and well-maintained rooms in an attractive Swiss chalet-style building with a nice verandah where meals can be served. Good value. ❷

Rock House ☎091-222 4948. Thirteen rooms of varying size and standard (the brighter upstairs ones are more expensive) set in two cheerful orange buildings. All are clean, bright and modern, with private balconies, big frame-nets and big fridges full of fatally cheap beer; some also have hot water. Functional, but very good value. ❶–❷

Saffron (no phone) Three doubles in a cosy yellow bungalow – on the small side, but clean, comfortable and amongst the cheapest in the village. ❶

Sandy Lane Hotel ☎077-755 3898, ℮sandylane@sltnet.lk. The clean and simple rooms here are some of the cheapest on the beach, especially out of season. Breakfast included. ❷

The Strand ☎091-222 4358, ℮strand_u@sltnet. Set in a gorgeous old 1920s colonial-style house and its surrounding modern buildings, all scattered around a lush garden. Rooms (of various sizes) are disappointingly ordinary compared to the beautiful house, but reasonable value even so. Advance bookings are only accepted on a weekly basis, though if you turn up on spec you may be able to get rooms on a per-night basis. ❶–❸

Sunny Beach Hotel ☎091-438 1456. Set right above the beach in a modern two-storey building; the six rooms (doubles and triples) are quite spacious, fairly clean and reasonable value. There's also a nice verandah overlooking the sea, and a breezy seafront terrace restaurant. ❷

Three Fishes ☎091-224 1857. Exquisite, compact colonial villa hidden behind palm trees right on the beach. The five rooms (including two cheap singles) have some period-style furniture and lots of charm, though they score higher on atmosphere than on creature comforts. Big discounts in low season. ❺

Unawatuna Beach Bungalow One of the nicer small guest houses in Unawatuna, set just behind the beach (and the drab *Unawatuna Beach Resort*). The comfortable modern rooms have pristine bathrooms and hot water. ❸

Village Inn T & F 091-222 5375. Rooms here are a bit gloomy and grubby, though set in a nicely secluded and peaceful location, and all have private verandahs overlooking an attractive garden. **①**

Mid-range and expensive

②

Dream House T 091-438 1541, F 438 1212. Italian-owned establishment set in a very attractive old colonial villa, with four characterful (if rather small) rooms with wooden floors, period furniture and hot water – very pleasant, but overpriced, and you'll have to battle with the treacherous iron spiral staircase every time you come in or out. There's reasonable food here, too. **⑥**

Nooite-Gedacht T 091-222 2349, E nooitged@sltnet.lk. Set in a delectable colonial mansion of 1735 this has bags of character and a very mixed assortment of rooms – most are stately but rather gloomy period pieces; a few are bright and modern and come with a/c. It's a wonderful hideaway, though rather a long way from the beach. The ayurveda centre here is one of the best on the south coast, offering the usual baths and massages, plus more extended courses of treatment, although the obligatory Rs.1000 doctor's consultation is a rip-off. **④**

Secret Garden T 091-222 4313. Exactly as the name suggests, with a tiny, easily missed door leading into a wonderful concealed walled garden full of trees, birds and the odd monkey. Accommodation is either in the old colonial villa,

which has four rooms of varying size and sophistication, or in four rooms in the less characterful modern bungalow. **④–⑥**

Thambapanni Retreat T & F 091-438 1722. Unawatuna's only top-end option, with fourteen classy, colonial-style rooms tucked away amidst the dense jungle which lines the slopes of Rumassala (see p.168) – it looks like a kind of rainforest retreat, even though you're just a couple of minutes from the beach. Rooms come with a/c, satellite TV, minibar, and there's a small swimming pool, spa, sauna and meditation facilities. **⑦**

Thaproban T & F 091-438 1722. One of Unawatuna's smartest options, housed in a bizarre-looking tower – painted a vivid orange for extra visibility and bang up against the equally odd-looking villa. The nine rooms (two with a/c) are on the small side, but neat, modern and with cheery blue-and-orange bathrooms; the room right over the beach is particularly inviting. There's also Internet access (Rs.5 per min) and a small library. Fills up quickly, so book ahead. **⑤**

The Villa T 091-438 0019, E thevilla@slt.net. Right on the beach in Unawatuna's most shamelessly kitsch building – you may feel like you're staying in an enormous cuckoo clock. The six rooms are quite small but nicely equipped with big frame-nets, colonial-style furniture and colourful blue bathrooms, as well as a/c, hot water, minibar, phone and satellite TV; all have sea views. Good value in low season, when rates fall significantly. Also has a quite smart restaurant. Reserve in advance. **⑥**

The village and beach

Unawatuna **beach** is small and intimate: a graceful semicircular curve of sand not much more than a kilometre from start to finish, enclosed by headlands at either end. Despite the increasing development, the beachside establishments retain an improvised, slightly ramshackle quality which is the essence of Unawatuna's charm for many visitors. It's easy to spend days here, idling purposelessly between the beach cafés and the ocean, playing endless games of carrom (see opposite page) – many of the cafés have boards, and the locals are usually only too pleased to initiate visitors into the game's mysteries – and enjoying the easy pace of life, which seems to strike just the right balance between liveliness and somnolence.

For the energetic, there are various **watersports** on offer (see box opposite), while **Siri Goonasekera** (c/o the *South Ceylon Restaurant*, on the main road through the village; T 091-224 5863, E goonas@sltnet.lk) can organize either individual or group **yoga** tuition for all standards (individual sessions Rs.400 per hour). He also has a meditation room (classes available) and can arrange ayurvedic herbal massages by a qualified doctor (Rs.1000). Other masseurs hang around the beach (though some look thoroughly disreputable, and assaults have been reported), along with wandering ladies flogging sarongs and beachwear. At the northern end of the beach, a footpath leads up to a small

Carrom

A kind of hybrid of pool, marbles and draughts (checkers), **carrom** is played throughout Sri Lanka, but particularly in the south, where the clatter of wooden pieces is a familiar sound in cafés along the coast. The game's origins are obscure: some say that it was invented by the maharajahs of India, although many Indians claim that it was actually introduced by the British, while Burma, Egypt and Ethiopia are also touted as possible sources.

Whatever its origins, carrom achieved increasing popularity in south India and Sri Lanka during the early twentieth century – the first serious carrom **tournament** was held in Sri Lanka in 1935. By 1958, India and Sri Lanka had established official carrom associations, whilst the 1960s saw the start of international competitions between the two countries; over the next two decades carrom tournaments were held in Pakistan, Afghanistan, Malaysia and the Maldives, and later in Germany, Holland and Switzerland. There are now carrom federations and board manufacturers not only in Asia, but also in a number of European countries, the US and even Australia.

The game is **played** using a square wooden board with a pocket at each corner; the aim is to flick all your pieces (which are very similar to draughtsmen) into one of the pockets, using the heavier "striker" piece, equivalent to the white ball in pool. Carrom can be played by either four or (more usually) two people, and various rules govern the set-up of the pieces, flicking methods and scoring. If you get hooked, a **carrom board** makes an unusual, if bulky, souvenir – there are usually a few for sale at *Laksala* in Colombo (see p.108). Alternatively, you could buy one from an overseas manufacturer or importer – visit ⊛ www.carrom.org for lists of these and for further details of the game's background, rules and national federations.

dagoba perched on the rocks above the bay, offering fine views over Unawatuna and north to Galle.

Behind the beach, **Unawatuna village** is, in places at least, a surprisingly attractive place. Its recreational possibilities have long been recognized, having originally developed as a country retreat for Dutch merchants and administrators living in Galle – the flouncy colonial villas built by them and their British successors still give parts of Yadehimulla Road a surprisingly

Diving, snorkelling and surfing at Unawatuna

Unawatuna has a modest range of watersports on offer, though dedicated divers and surfers are better served at nearby Hikkaduwa. The **Submarine Diving School** (☏091-438 0358), at the western end of the beach, offers the usual range of PADI courses, plus single and introductory dives and wreck and deep dives: there are no less than eight wrecks in the vicinity, including an old wooden English ship, the *Rangoon*, lying at a depth of 30m.

You can **snorkel** off the beach at Unawatuna, though there's not much to see apart from a few colourful fish. The best snorkelling is about 1km offshore, hence you'll need to hire the Submarine Dive School's **glass-bottomed boat** (Rs.1200 for 30–40min). Submarine also rent out snorkelling equipment (Rs.150 per hour or Rs.450 per day), as do a couple of cheaper shacks on the beach nearby. Check all equipment carefully; there are plenty of dud masks and snorkels in circulation.

A lot of locals **surf** at Unawatuna, though the waves aren't nearly as good as at nearby Hikkaduwa or Midigama. Boards can be rented on the beach (Rs.200 per hour or Rs.400 per day) near the diving school. You can also rent **inner tubes** on the beach, if you fancy a less strenuous way of getting wet.

Moving on from Unawatuna

If you're **heading west** from Unawatuna, it's easiest to take a tuktuk to Galle and pick up a bus or train there (see p.162 for details). **Heading east**, you should be able to flag down a bus to Weligama, Mirissa or Matara along the main Matara Road, though the local tuktuk drivers will tell you a pack of lies about buses not stopping at Unawatuna in an attempt to get you into their vehicle. If you wave at anything that passes, something will probably stop for you sooner or later – you'd be unlucky to wait more than fifteen minutes. If you do succumb to the tuktuk drivers, the ride to Weligama shouldn't cost more than Rs.400.

chintzy look. Unawatuna's most striking natural feature is **Rumassala**, an incongruously grand outcrop of rock whose sides rise up sheer behind the village; it's popularly claimed to be a fragment of the chunk of mountain carried from the Himalayas by the monkey god **Hanuman**. As recounted in the *Ramayana*, Hanuman was sent by Rama to collect a special herb from the Himalayas which was needed to save the life of Rama's wounded brother, Lakshmana. Arriving in the Himalayas, the absent-minded Hanuman realized he had forgotten the name of the required plant, so ripped up an entire chunk of mountainside in the hope that the necessary plant would be found somewhere on it. He then carried this fragment of mountain back to Sri Lanka, dropping a bit in Ritigala, in the north of the island, and another piece at Unawatuna. The rock still sports a large collection of medicinal herbs as well as entertaining troupes of boisterous macaque monkeys, Hanuman's latter-day relatives, who periodically descend from the rock to raid the villagers' papaya trees.

Eating

Unawatuna is chock full of **places to eat**, with a long line of low-key cafés along the beachfront offering tasty touristy standards at rock-bottom prices: lots of fish, the usual rice, noodle and curry dishes, devilled this and that, and what passes in Sri Lanka for pizza – though if you've been in the island's rural backwaters for a while, you'll appreciate even that. For wholesome food, cheap beer, good music and a romantic setting you can't beat the confusingly named *Hard Rock*, *Hot Rock* and *Rock View* cafés, side by side at the centre of the beach; along with the adjacent *Coral Light*, these are usually the liveliest places after dark, when candlelit tables are set out along the sand – a beautiful sight. The *Hard Rock* is normally the liveliest and loudest of the four. The beachfront restaurant at *The Villa* hotel is also pleasant, and does Sri Lankan breakfasts (order the day before), though the "Nescafe" is execrable. Perhaps the nicest place in town, however, is the lively and attractive restaurant at the *Thaproban* hotel (see p.166) – one of the few places in Unawatuna with any pretensions, though it's still surprisingly cheap, with most mains under Rs.200.

Dalawela to Midigama

Beyond Unawatuna, the straggle of small villages that dot the coastline hold a smattering of crashed-out guest houses and hotels, popular with Robinson Crusoe types. This section of coast is also home to one of Sri Lanka's most emblematic sights, **stilt fishermen**. The stilts consist of a single pole and crossbar planted out in the sea on which fishermen perch whilst casting their lines into the sea when the currents are flowing in the right direction. So abundant is the supply of fish along this part of the coast, even close to the shore, that positions are highly lucrative and are handed down from father to son.

Some 2km beyond Unawatuna, the village of **DALAWELA** has particularly striking clusters of fishing stilts, along with a few attractive **places to stay** on the beach which offer escape from the modest hustle and bustle of Unawatuna – guest houses aside, there's very little to the village. The best two places to stay stand next door to one another on the beach, right next to the main cluster of stilt fishing posts. The *Shanthi* (T091-438 0031; ❷) has six rooms and six cabanas, all sea facing. Rooms are pleasant, modern and tiled, with big frame-nets; the cabanas are more rickety and basic, but closer to beach. There's also a sea-water swimming pool and expensive Internet access (Rs.9 per min). Next door is the equally pleasant though significantly more expensive *Sri Gemunu* (T091-228 3202; ❷–❸; during Dec rooms are only available on half-board basis ❺), a pleasant, medium-size modern hotel on the beach. All rooms come with hot water and private balcony; there are good views from the top floors. There's also a sea-water swimming pool.

About 500m further along the coastal road, *Point de Galle* (T091-228 3206, F091-223 4360; ❹) is a family-oriented beachside resort, with thirteen decent-value sea-facing rooms, most of them extremely spacious and pleasantly old-fashioned. There's also a sea-water swimming pool in a natural rock enclo-sure, two restaurants and a big garden with a children's play area. Another 500m along is the immaculate new *Star Light Hotel* (T091-228 2216, Estarlight@sltnet.lk; ❺; no single rates), with fifteen big and very smartly fur-nished rooms (some with a/c), plus a smallish pool – good value, though some rooms are very close to the road, and views of the sea are obstructed by an adjacent building.

Koggala and around

Around 12km beyond Unawatuna lies the small and unprepossessing town of **KOGGALA**, dominated by a military airbase which was hurriedly con-structed here during World War II against the threat of Japanese attack. The town is home to one of the island's more rewarding museums, erected in honour of the famous Sinhalese writer **Martin Wickramasinghe**, as well as the fascinating **Kataluwa Purvarama Mahavihara** temple, while **Koggala Lagoon** is just a couple of kilometres away; dotted with islands and fringed with mangroves, it's good for birds and boat trips, although factories associated with the nearby Free Trade Zone have sullied the waters somewhat. G.G. Happy Tour in Unawatuna (see p.164) arrange boat and catamaran trips here, or you might be able to arrange something locally (ask at the hotels below).

Koggala is also the unlikely home to a pair of big **resort hotels**. The best is the *Koggala Beach*, just past the airbase and right on the beach (T091-228 3243, Ekogbeach@sltnet.lk; ❺; no single rates), a nice-looking, oldish resort with sea-facing, a/c rooms with hot water, private verandah or balcony, TV, phone, fridge – perfectly pleasant, though you're pretty much in the middle of nowhere.

Martin Wickramasinghe Museum

Directly opposite the large *Club Horizon* hotel (just east of the *Koggala Beach Hotel*), the excellent **Martin Wickramasinghe Museum** (daily 9am–5pm; Rs.15) is inspired by – and partly devoted to – the life, works and ideas of

Martin Wickramasinghe, one of the most important Sinhalese cultural figures of the twentieth century. A prolific writer, Wickramasinghe penned fourteen Sinhala-language novels and eight collections of short stories, plus some forty nonfiction books on subjects ranging from Buddhism to cultural anthropology. Much of his fiction explores the impact of the modern world on traditional Sri Lankan village life, while his nonfiction champions traditional Sinhalese customs and culture, and played an important role in asserting its value and importance at a time when the island was in danger of being swamped by European influences; Wickramasinghe's use of Sinhala in his novels and stories also played a crucial role in establishing the language as a viable literary alternative to English. A museum showcasing Sri Lanka's traditional culture was a long-cherished idea of Wickramasinghe's, though it wasn't realized until after his death. Wickramasinghe was deeply attached to Koggala and remained very much a local boy at heart – his birthplace and grave (both now part of the museum) lie just a few metres apart – although the traditional rural village which he grew up in (and idealized in his work) has now largely vanished.

The museum comprises several different sections, ranged around grounds full of carefully labelled tropical trees. The excellent **Folk Museum** houses an absorbing and well-labelled selection of exhibits pertaining to the daily practical or spiritual life of the Sinhalese – everything from catching a fish to chasing off malevolent spirits. Religious artefacts fill the **first room**, ranging from Buddha statuettes to more atavistic devotional objects such as rough clay figurines and cobra figures used as offerings to the gods. Most interesting are the "sand boards", trays of sand which were used to practise writing – the Sri Lankan equivalent of a blackboard, and one of the museum's many examples of simple but elegant local solutions to preindustrial problems. The **second room** contains agricultural and household utensils including cute wooden and metal cow bells, cunning fish traps, and the wooden rattles and bows and arrows used to scare birds from paddy fields. There's also an excellent collection of masks, some up to a century old and depicting a range of characters, including an unusual pair of pink-faced British officers, as well as exhibits relating to traditional industries, including rubber collection, toddy tapping and cinnamon gathering.

At the rear of the grounds stands the **house** in which Wickramasinghe was born and grew up with his nine sisters. The only dwelling in the area to survive World War II (the village's other houses were demolished to make way for the nearby airbase), it was used by local army officers as their own quarters. The **Hall of Life**, attached to the house, is devoted to Wickramasinghe's life, though it gives disappointingly little information on the man himself. Exhibits are limited to a selection of his books, plus various photos showing him hobnobbing with the great and the good at various international literary and political functions. Wickramasinghe's simple **grave** stands immediately in front of the house.

Kataluwa Purvarama Mahavihara

Around 5km beyond Koggala lies one of the south's most absorbing temples, the **Kataluwa Purvarama Mahavihara**. The temple is interesting principally for the remarkable Kandyan-style **wall paintings** in the main shrine, dating from the late nineteenth century – a resident monk will probably materialize to explain some of the most notable panels. The four walls were painted by different artists in competition (no one seems to know who won) and illustrate various *jatakas* and other cautionary Buddhist tales, peopled with detailed crowds of meticulously executed figures including various colonial bigwigs and – strangely enough – a rather lopsided, characteristically dour Queen Victoria, apparently placed here to commemorate her support for native Buddhism in the face of British missionary Christianity. Panels showing the punishments meted out to sinners run along the base, while images of the 24 previous Buddhas (see p.434) are painted on the outer wall of the inner shrine. The inner shrine (mind your head: the doors are built purposefully low to force you to bow as you enter the presence of the Buddha) contains further Buddha figures, as well as a black Vishnu and a blue Kataragama.

The turn-off to the temple is around 2km along the coastal road east of the Martin Wickramasinghe Museum – ignore the stone sign saying "Unique nine dagobas ancient temple" and take the turning about 100m further along. The temple lies about 3km inland from here (the road layout is slightly confusing, so you'll have to ask directions if making your own way); it's 150m down an unsignposted road on the right-hand side at a kind of T-junction. The return trip from Koggala by tuktuk should cost around Rs.200.

Ahangama and Midigama

The section of coastline from Koggala to Weligama is relatively undeveloped. The road runs close to the ocean for much of the way, in many places squeezing the beach into a narrow ribbon of sand between the tarmac and the waves. A few kilometres beyond Koggala, the town of **AHANGAMA** is famous for having the greatest concentration of **stilt fishermen** along the entire coast. There are also a few drab hotels and a little sliver of beach here, but once you've had a look at the stilt fishermen, it's best to push on.

A couple of kilometres further on, the scattered village of **MIDIGAMA** is popular amongst both local and foreign surfers. The waves here are some of the best in the island, though surfing apart, the rather narrow exposed beach hasn't much to recommend it and the village is very small and sleepy – unless you're here to catch waves, there's not a lot to do. West of tiny Midigama village, a clutch of low-key guest houses straggle along the beach and road (which are very close together here); the quaint little clocktower at the village's centre makes a useful landmark when you're trying to work out where to get off the bus. A few guest houses rent out **surfboards** (around Rs.500 per day): try *Subodinee* or *Surfer's Dream*; the latter also has bikes to rent (Rs.150 per day).

Accommodation

Note that of the following (all of which are in Midigama), only the *Villa Gaetano* functions all year round. Other places tend to close during the low season, or are turned upside down with repairs. Other than the *Subodinee*, all are on the main coastal road, meaning that traffic noise can be a problem. The following are listed in the order you reach them travelling from west to east, starting from the small river which separates Ahangama from Midigama.

Villa Gaetano 750m beyond the 137km post, just beyond the river ☎091-228 3968, ⓦwww .internet-window.de/gamini. Extremely pleasant and professionally run hotel. The clean, smart modern rooms have hot water and minibar, there's a pleasant garden-cum-restaurant looking out to Lace Rock, Internet access (guests only; Rs.350 per hour) and excellent seafood. ❸

Surfer's Dream 500m past Villa Gaetano, on the inland side of the main road ☎091-228 3968. A lot nicer (and only a little more expensive) than the other surfers' dives in town. Rooms are smallish but clean, modern and comfortable, and there's a nice outdoor restaurant. ❶

Hot Tuna 200m past Surfer's Dream, and 200m before the Midigama clocktower ☎091-228 3411. Aimed squarely at surfers, with six very cheap, basic rooms (some with shared bathroom). ❶

Subodinee Down the side road from the clock-tower, opposite the train station ☎091-228 3383, ⓔsubodinee@hotmail.com. Another cheap and cheerful surfers' place with colourful and slightly wacky decor, a big selection of basic rooms and a surprisingly good choice of Western and Sri Lankan food. ❶

Ram's Surfing Beach At the 139km post, 500m east of the clocktower ☎041-225 2639. Ultra-cheap surfer's place: the rooms are pretty basic – essentially just small concrete boxes – but OK at the bargain-basement price. ❶

Villa Samsara At the 140km post, 1.5km east of the clocktower ☎041-225 1144, ⓦwww

.members.aon.at/samsara. Wonderfully atmospheric verandahed house hidden away in an immaculate, palm-studded garden. The beautiful rooms are full of colonial charm (though they would be even more beautiful if the toilets had doors), as is the wonderful dining-cum-sitting room. Rooms are let on a half-board basis only, and usually by the week, although with prior reservation you might be able to arrange a shorter stay. ❼ half-board

Weligama

Twenty-three kilometres east of Unawatuna, the sleepy fishing town of **WELIGAMA** ("Sandy Village") meanders around a broad and beautiful bay, dotted with rocky outcrops and fringed with fine golden sand. It's an attractive spot, though it's never really caught on as a destination for foreign tourists, and despite a decent choice of accommodation, things are pretty somnolent and there's not much to do other than stare at the sea – which may be exactly what you're after.

Weligama itself is surprisingly attractive, as Sri Lankan towns go: quiet and relatively traffic-free, with a clutter of shops at the centre trailing off into lush streets of pretty gingerbread villas decorated with ornate *mal lali* wooden fretwork, peeking out from dense, green tropical gardens. At the western end of town, near the railway line, stands a large megalith carved (probably sometime during the eighth or ninth centuries) with a three-metre figure known as **Kusta Raja**, the "Leper King", usually thought to show an unknown Sinhalese monarch who was miraculously cured of leprosy by drinking nothing but coconut milk for three months. An alternative theory claims it as a depiction of a Mahayana Boddhisatva, possibly Avalokitesvara or Samantabhadra – a claim lent credence by the carvings of meditating Buddhas in the figure's tiara.

The waters of **Weligama Bay** are relatively exposed, and suffer from pollution close to the town – ask at your guest house about where's safe to swim. The bay's most prominent feature is the minuscule island of **Taprobane**, just offshore, virtually invisible under a thick covering of luxuriant trees. The island was owned during the 1930s by the exiled French Count de Maunay, who built the exquisite white villa that still stands, its red tiled roof poking up through the trees; the whole lot is available for rent (see p.174). The prettiest end of the bay is around Taprobane, where dozens of colourful outrigger **catamarans** pull up on the beach between fishing expeditions; you may be able to negotiate a trip round the bay with one of the local fishermen – count on around Rs.500 per hour.

If you want to get out into the water, you can arrange **diving** through Bavarian Divers at the *Bay Beach* hotel (see opposite; ☎041-225 0201, ⓦwww.cbg.de/bavariandivers), a German-run diving school offering the standard range of PADI courses plus dives to local sites including coral reefs, the underwater rocks of the Yala Rock complex and the wreck of the *SSS Rangoon*, which sank just outside Galle Harbour in 1863.

For something completely different, try the **Snake Farm**, about 14km from Weligama on the Akuressa Road, which has around fifteen different kinds of snake, including some enormous pythons, as well as some nasty-looking spiders. You can handle the snakes, if you think you're hard enough. The

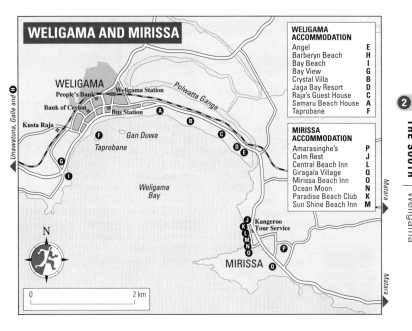

WELIGAMA AND MIRISSA

WELIGAMA
People's Bank
Bank of Ceylon
Kusta Raja
Weligama Station
Polwatta Ganga
Bus Station Ⓐ
Ⓑ
Ⓒ
Ⓓ Ⓔ
Ⓕ Gan Duwa
Taprobane
Ⓖ
Ⓘ
Weligama Bay
N
0   2 km

Ⓙ Kangeroo
Ⓚ Tour Service
Ⓛ
Ⓜ Ⓝ
Ⓞ
Ⓟ
MIRISSA Ⓠ

Unawatuna, Galle and Ⓗ
Matara
Matara

❷

admission price is negotiable: the owner has been known to ask anything up to Rs.1000, though Rs.200–300 should suffice.

Practicalities

Buses stop in the centre of Weligama, a block inland from the bay. Few services originate here (most are in transit between Galle, Matara and Colombo), so you'll have to take your chances with what's passing through. There should be at least one bus in each direction every fifteen minutes. Weligama is also a major stop on the Matara to Colombo railway; the **train station** is in the town centre a block inland from the bus station – see the timetable on p.202 for details. There are branches of the Bank of Ceylon and People's Bank in the town centre where you can **change money**, but no ATMs which accept foreign cards. The small **post office** is directly opposite the train station. There's currently no Internet access in Weligama.

Weligama has some quite good **accommodation** spread out along the beach, though nowhere particularly good **to eat** – you'll almost certainly end up having meals where you're staying.

The places below are marked on the map above.

Guest houses and hotels

Angel ☎ & 🖷 041-225 0475. A good, slightly upmarket alternative to the town's budget guest houses, with attractive and spacious modern rooms (some with hot water) in an airy modern house. Breakfast included. No single rates. ❷

Barberyn Beach 2km west of Weligama ☎034-227 6036, 🖳www.barberyn.com. Newly opened

offshoot of the long-established original in Beruwala (see p.130), this beautiful ayurveda resort has sixty rooms in extensive beachfront grounds and a huge range of expert courses and treatments for around US$400 per week. Full board only. ❽

Bay Beach ☎041-225 0201, 📧hashani@sltnet.lk. Weligama town's smartest

173

hotel, this pleasant but rather anonymous place has respectable modern rooms with a/c, fridge and gorgeous ocean views. There's also a coffee shop, pool and a restaurant with a stunning view of the bay – the food's average, but cheap. Breakfast included. Good value. **❺**

Bay View ☎041-225 1054. Friendly little family guest house, and one of the cheapest in town, offering three very basic rooms on land side of the main road, overlooking a slightly wild patch of garden. **❶**

Crystal Villa ☎041-225 0635, ☏011-273 5031. Friendly and good-value mid-range option, with a mix of pleasant standard rooms along with more smartly furnished "superior" rooms and attractive bungalows; all have hot water, private verandahs and overlook the pleasant pool (non-guests Rs.100) and sea; some also have a/c. **❺**

Jaga Bay Resort ☎041-225 0033. One of best places in town, set in spacious beachside grounds. The seventeen modern rooms and three spotless cabanas all have hot water and sea-facing private verandahs, and the restaurant is one of the best places to eat in town. **❷**

Raja's Guest House ☎077-796 0656. Cheapest in town (along with Bay View), with three shabby and basic rooms, though you can't complain at the price, and it's bang on the beach. **❶**

Samaru Beach House ☎041-225 1417. Along with Jaga Bay, the top budget option in town, right on the beach with spotlessly modern rooms outside the main building or darker and simpler rooms inside – all are excellent value. **❶**

Taprobane Contact the Sun House in Galle (see p.157) for bookings, ⊛ www.taprobaneisland.com. For one of Sri Lanka's ultimate romantic fantasies, try renting the island of Taprobane (see p.172). The solitary building, a beautiful colonial villa, sleeps ten people in five double rooms, and the resident staff of six will cook for you and minister to all your needs. US$1000 per night.

Mirissa

Tucked into the far eastern end of Weligama Bay, the picture-perfect swathe of sand at the village of **MIRISSA** was formerly the island's most famously "undiscovered" beach. The days when you could expect to have the place almost to yourself are long gone, but although the village now attracts a steady stream of visitors, its beach remains one of the prettiest in the island, with a narrow strip of sand backed by dense palm trees which manage to camouflage all signs of human presence. The fact that all the guest houses are concentrated in a much smaller area than Weligama means that Mirissa's a bit livelier, though it's still pretty comatose. There's reasonable **swimming**, though conditions vary considerably along different parts of the beach, so it's worth asking at your guest house about where's safe to swim before venturing into the water. You can also **snorkel** here, though you won't see much apart from the occasional pretty fish.

Practicalities

Mirissa village is strung out along the Matara Road, which runs just behind, and parallel to, the beach (though is largely hidden from it by a dense screen of palm trees). **Buses** whizz up and down the main road every few minutes; when arriving, make sure the conductor knows to let you off, since Mirissa is easily missed. When leaving, you'll have to flag something down along the main road. Mirissa has its own **train** station, though as only slow services stop here and it's a bit of a way from the village, it's easier to catch the bus. The useful Kangaroo Tour Service (☎041-225 2402) on the Matara Road has slightly pricey **Internet** access (Rs.8 per min), IDD **phone** facilities, motorbikes for hire (Rs.500 per day) and can arrange a car and driver (Rs.3000 per day), as well as tours.

There are no culinary treats in Mirissa, but if you want to eat away from your guest house the village boasts a few simple but acceptable **beach cafés**, all offering the usual seafood dishes, noodles, and rice and curry.

Accommodation in Mirissa is cheap and cheerful, while competition keeps guest house owners honest and makes the village good value for money. The following places are shown on the map of Weligama on p.173.

Guest houses and hotels

Amarasinghe's 200m inland from the coastal highway, signposted from almost opposite the Ocean Moon ☏ 041-225 1204. Some distance from the beach, but the idyllic and peaceful rural location, surrounded by lush gardens full of birds and the occasional monkey. Accommodation is in six adequate rooms of varying sizes and prices. ❶

Calm Rest ☏ & ℱ 041-225 2546. Middlingly pleasant place, slightly away from the beach, with a mixture of simple, clean and reasonable-value rooms, plus some fairly rustic and makeshift (but much more expensive) cabanas, all set in a pleasant garden. Rooms ❶, cabanas ❷

Central Beach Inn ☏ 041-225 1699. Six very cheap rooms in functional concrete blocks, plus two cabanas – all simple but nicely kept, and set in attractive flowering gardens. ❶

Giragala Village ☏ 041-225 0496, ☼ www .geocities.com/giragala. A nice, breezy location on a headland at the south end of the beach, with fifteen fairly basic and musty rooms in functional accommodation blocks dotted around pleasant,

spacious grounds – prices vary according to size and proximity to the beach. They also rent out snorkelling gear. ❶–❷

Ocean Moon ☏ 041-225 2328. Very friendly place, and slightly more upmarket than its neighbours, with six nice modern concrete cabanas and three rooms. The restaurant has a good and very cheap menu, including a selection of Sri Lankan breakfasts. Cabanas ❷, rooms ❶

Paradise Beach Club ☏ 041-225 1206, ✉ mirissa@sltnet.lk. Mirissa's only large-scale or remotely upmarket establishment, with accommodation in little chalets (with optional a/c) scattered around attractive gardens by the beach; all are perfectly pleasant and very good value, though quite simple. This is also where you'll find Mirissa's only pool (non-guests Rs.100). Half- or full-board only. Half-board ❹, full-board ❺

Sun Shine Beach Inn ☏ 041-225 2282. Nine basic but perfectly acceptable rooms in a functional concrete block. The restaurant has one of Mirissa's longer and more interesting menus, assuming it's all available. ❶

Matara and around

Standing close to the southernmost point of the island, the bustling town of **MATARA** (pronounced "*maat*-rah" the middle syllable is elided) provides a taste of everyday Sri Lanka that may (or may not) be welcome if you've spent time in the coastal resorts. Standing at the terminus of the country's southern railway line, the town is an important transport hub and a major centre of commerce – a lively place given a youthful touch by the presence of students from **Ruhunu University**, 3km east of town. Matara preserves a few Dutch colonial buildings and an atmospheric old fort area which has much of the charm but none of the tourists of Galle – well worth a couple of hours if you're in the vicinity. A few kilometres away, the attractively low-key beachside suburb of **Polhena**, with its small cluster of guest houses, quiet strip of beach and good snorkelling, offers a convenient escape from the hustle and bustle of the town itself. The area **around Matara** boasts a couple of mildy interesting and little-visited sights, including the giant Buddha and unusual underground temple at **Weherehena** and the town of **Dondra**, whose slender lighthouse marks the island's southernmost point.

Matara itself (from Mahatara, or "Great Harbour") is an ancient settlement, though no traces of anything older than the colonial era survive. The Portuguese used the town intermittently, but it was the Dutch, attracted by the deep and sheltered estuary of the Nilwala Ganga, who established a lasting presence here, fortifying the town and making it an important centre for cinnamon and elephant trading.

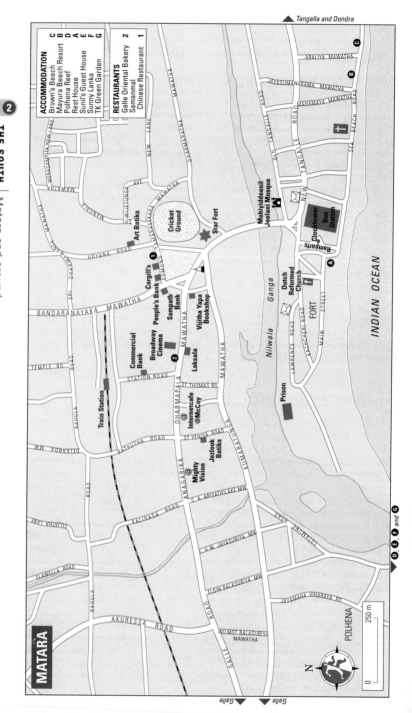

MATARA

ACCOMMODATION
Brown's Beach C
Mayura Beach Resort B
Polhena Reef D
Rest House A
Sunil's Guest House E
Sunny Lanka F
TK Green Garden G

RESTAURANTS
Galle Oriental Bakery 2
Samanmal
Chinese Restaurant 1

Tangalla and Dondra

ARALIYA MAWATHA

JAYASUMANARAMA MAWATHA

MAHAMAYA MAWATHA

SEA BEACH ROAD

OLD TANGALLE ROAD

NEW TANGALLE ROAD

Muhiyiddeenil
Jeelani Mosque

Clocktower
Bus Station

Ramparts

Dutch
Reformed
Church

FORT

LACCHERI ROAD

LAWRENCE ROAD

MAIN STREET

Nilwala Ganga

INDIAN OCEAN

Prison

ST THOMAS RD

Internetcafe
@McCoy

ST VEHVA ROAD

Jezlook
Batiks

Mighty
Vision

C. A. ARIYATHILAKE MW

KALIDASA ROAD

H.W. JAYASURIYA MW

LAXAPANA ROAD

ELGIN BALASURIYA MW

JAYAMAHA VIHARAYA RD

WILMOT BALASURIYA
MAWATHA

AKURESSA ROAD

POLHENA

GALLE ROAD

BAHULA

ELAWELLA ROAD

SULAHA LANE

BAHULA MW

DELKANDA MW

TEMPLE RD

Train Station

ROAD

BANDARANAYAKA MAWATHA

BAHULTHA ROAD

ANAGARIKA DHARMAPALA MAWATHA

KUMARATUNGA MAWATHA

Commercial
Bank

Broadway
Cinema

Laksala

Sampath
Bank

Vijitha Yapa
Bookshop

People's Bank

Cargill's

UDYANA ROAD

Art Batiks

Cricket
Ground

Star Fort

ABHASAGALA MAWATHA

NEW LANE

DHARMAPALA MAWATHA

EDMAND MAWATHA

WELITUNGA AVE

WEBAGAMPITIYA NEW LANE

MANGALA THISSA MW

MAWATHA

Galle

Galle

Galle

D, **E**, **F** and **G**

N

0   250 m

1

2

The Town

As at Galle, Matara divides into two areas: the **modern town** and the old Dutch colonial district, known as the **Fort**; the two are separated by the **Nilwala Ganga**, a fine swathe of water, edged by thick stands of palm trees, which appears remarkably unspoilt given that it runs straight through the middle of the bustling town centre. The Fort area lies on the narrow spit of land south of the Nilwala Ganga, its eastern side bounded by a long line of stumpy **ramparts**, built by the Dutch in the eighteenth century and topped by the inevitable ugly white British clocktower of 1883. Immediately behind the ramparts stands Matara's most impressive colonial building, the **Dutch Reformed Church**, a large and rather austere gabled structure almost invisible beneath its huge pitched roof. This is one of the earliest Dutch churches on the island – the memorial tablets inside go back to 1686 (the date of 1769 carved over the doorway apparently refers to a later remodelling of the facade). Unfortunately the church is usually locked.

To the west of the ramparts stands Matara's **old town**, entered via a dilapidated **gateway** (dated 1780) at the north end of the ramparts. It's a captivating district of lush, tree-filled streets dotted with fine old colonial houses in various stages of picturesque disrepair – some are surprisingly palatial, with big colonnaded facades and sweeping verandahs. At the far west end of the fort, the peninsula tapers off to a narrow spit of land at the confluence of the Nilwala Ganga and the sea, where dozens of colourful fishing boats are usually lined up on the sand.

Retrace your steps and head for the bridge which connects the new and old towns; the striking white building at its southern end is the **Muhiyiddeenil Jeelani** mosque, though it looks far more like a Portuguese Baroque church than a place of Islamic worship. Cross the bridge to the far side of the river to reach Matara's other stronghold, the diminutive **Star Fort**, a quaint little hexagonal structure built by the Dutch to protect the river crossing to the main Fort area. The entrance gate is emblazoned "Redoubte Van Eck 1763", commemorating the Dutch governor under whose administration it was constructed, and the whole structure is surrounded by a stagnant green moat in which the Dutch once kept crocodiles. The caretaker will show you around the interior for a tip, although there's not much to see apart from a couple of empty rooms, a central well and rainwater drain edged with coral paving stones, and two tiny prison cells to either side of the gate, each of which was allegedly used to hold up to 25 prisoners.

North of here, the **new town** sprawls away in all directions. Turn left beyond the prominent Buddhist temple to head down **Anagarika Dharmapala Mawatha**, the area's principal thoroughfare, usually a heaving, gridlocked confusion of vehicles and pedestrians. About 500m west along here, an unprepossessing house in a small side street hides **Jezlook Batiks** (☏041-222 2142), one of the best batik workshops in the south, with a list of customers which includes the British queen. The batiks are made to original designs by the owner, Jezima Mohamed, and they can also make up your own designs, if you fancy. Average-size batiks go for Rs.1000–3000; larger tablecloth-sized pieces for Rs.10,000. They also make gorgeous silk batiks, as well as clothes. If you're interested in batik, you might also want to visit **Art Batiks** (☏041 -222 4488), just north of the cricket ground on Udyana Road, which sells pieces designed by owner Shirley Dissanayake (a man, incidentally), many with Sri Lankan themes. It's a bit cheaper than Jezlook, though the designs aren't as original.

Practicalities

Matara's large and unusually well-organized **bus station** is next to the old ramparts, south of the river, and convenient for the *Rest House*, *Mayura* and *Brown's*. The **train station** is just north of the town centre. A tuktuk from either terminal to Polhena should cost around Rs.120. For information on moving on from Matara, see box opposite.

There are branches of Sampath and the People's **banks** north of the Star Fort, just past the cricket ground, and a Commercial Bank near the train station on Station Road; the last has an ATM which accepts foreign cards (Visa and Mastercard). The smart modern **post office** is opposite the north end of the bus station; you can make international **phone calls** here. The best place for **Internet** access is Internetcafe@McCoy (daily 8.30am–10.30pm; Rs.6 per min), 500m west of the centre along Anagarika Dharmpala Mawatha. Failing this, try Mighty Vision, slightly further along the same road (daily 9am–6pm; Rs.7 per min). There's a decent Vijitha Yapa **bookshop** near the cricket ground, also on Dharmapala Mawatha, and a Cargill's Food City **supermarket** just to the northeast.

There's not much choice when it comes to **eating** in Matara. The most characterful place in town is the *Galle Oriental Bakery*, on Anagarika Dharmapala Mawatha, a pleasantly old-fashioned local establishment with charmingly antiquated, white-smocked waiters. The very cheap food includes rice and curry, plus short eats, though with enough chilli in them to reduce you to tears. For something more formal, the restaurant at the *Rest House* (see below) is about as good as it gets, with seating inside and out within earshot of the sea and a standard selection of seafood, curries and meat dishes from around Rs.300. Alternatively, try the *Samanmal Chinese Restaurant*, immediately north of the cricket ground. This serves primarily as a local drinking hole, although the Sri Lankan-style Chinese food is cheap and surprisingly good – even though it's so gloomy inside you can hardly see what you're eating.

Accommodation

There's a definite lack of accommodation in Matara proper; most foreign visitors stay in the suburb of Polhena (see below). If you do want to stay in Matara itself, the following three places are as good as it gets.

Brown's Beach ☎041-222 6298. The best place in Matara, and cheap too (although service is erratic), with a couple of pleasant modern rooms overlooking the seafront (though there's a bit of road noise). There are another five quieter but gloomier rooms (some with a/c) away from the road and seafront, plus a small restaurant. ❷

Mayura Beach Resort ☎041-222 3274. Mainly used for parties and weddings, foreign tourists are rare here, but the rooms are surprisingly clean, modern and quiet (unless there's a function on, in which case forget it). A decent alternative to Brown's, though pretty unatmospheric. ❷

Rest House ☎041-222 2299. First appearances are promising, set right on the seafront behind an attractive garden, but the rooms, though large, are terribly gloomy, shabby and pretty much falling to bits. Official foreigners' rates are a total rip-off; try for the local price, though even then it's no bargain. ❸

Polhena

A couple of kilometres west of Matara city centre, the rambling beachside suburb of **Polhena** makes a pleasant alternative to Matara proper, and has a small selection of reasonable budget accommodation (though given the proximity of Mirissa, Weligama, Tangalla and Unawatuna, there's no compelling reason to visit if you're after a beach holiday). Polhena can be unnervingly quiet during the week, although things liven up with local visitors at weekends.

There's good **snorkelling** here straight off the beach, with lots of colourful fish and a small section of live coral. The knowledgeable local snorkelling guides Titus and Nisantha can be hired through *Sunil's*, *TK Green Garden* or *Sunny Lanka* guest houses (see below); they charge around Rs.300 (including equipment) for two- to three-hour trips, and can also arrange night-snorkelling. Snorkelling is best outside the monsoon period, though there are sometimes periods of good visibility at other times. Other activities here include three-hour afternoon **boat trips** along the Nilwala Ganga arranged by *Sunil's* guest house, which are good for bird- and croc-spotting, though at Rs.3000 per boat they're prohibitively expensive unless you can get a group together. *Sunil's* can also arrange tours (a day-trip to Uda Walawe, for example, costs Rs.4000); cars with driver (Rs.3500 per day for up to 150km); and a taxi to the airport (a hefty Rs.4500). They also rent out **motorbikes** (Rs.500 per day).

Practicalities

Polhena suffers from a few touts and dodgy tuktuk drivers; as ever, exercise discretion. Though not actually on the beach, *Sunny Lanka*, *Sunil's* and *TK Green Garden* are the most geared toward foreign budget travellers. There are lots of other **accommodation** options (including a number of shabby beachside places, not listed below) mainly catering to a local clientele – these can get noisy at weekends. Almost all the guest houses do some sort of **food**; your only other option at present is the attractive *Blue Corals* seafood restaurant on the beachfront.

Polhena Reef ☎041-222 2478. Right on the seafront, this is Polhena's poshest option, though it can get noisy with local parties at weekends. The spacious and pleasant rooms (including triples and family rooms) are good value and come with TV, phone, fridge, hot water and private balconies; a/c is available for an extra US$6. The restaurant has an extensive but slightly pricey menu. ❸
Sunil's Guest House ☎041-222 1983. Polhena's liveliest and best-organized guest house, with a range of accommodation including basic and very cheap but quite respectable rooms in the main building and fancier doubles in adjacent buildings

– one comes with mad furniture and a mechanical budgie door-chime. Food is available for guests only. Free bikes for guests. ❶
Sunny Lanka ☎041-222 3504. One of Polhena's budget stalwarts. Rooms (including one triple) are large, clean, bare and perfectly acceptable, and very good value at the price. Food is available if ordered in advance. ❶
TK Green Garden ☎041-222 2603. Set about 50m back from the beach, this pleasant two-storey structure with wooden touches is a bit grander than your average guest house. Rooms are a bit bare and tired, but very cheap. ❶

Moving on from Matara

Matara is the south's major transport hub. The **bus station** is unusually orderly, with clearly marked bays and a helpful information office (although it's not signposted) in the outside corridor in the corner nearest the bridge. Eastbound services leave from the eastern side of the terminal; westbound services from the west. There are 24-hour services to **Colombo**, with inter-city expresses leaving every fifteen minutes. Heading west, there are services to **Tissamaharama** via **Tangalla** and **Hambantota** every fifteen minutes (though few direct buses to **Kataragama**; easiest to change at Tissa). Matara is also a good place from which to head up to the hill country. There's at least one early morning departure to **Nuwara Eliya**, plus services to **Bandarawela** and **Ratnapura** (4 daily). If you're heading to **Sinharaja**, there are frequent buses to **Akuressa** (every 30min), where you'll need to change for Deniyaya (there are also a few direct buses to Deniyaya). As ever, it pays to check the latest schedules in the information office in advance.

Matara stands at the end of the southern **railway** line from Colombo; see p.202 for details of services.

Around Matara

A few kilometres east of Matara, the tiny village of **WEHEREHENA** is home to one of the island's most colossal Buddha statues, the focal point of a large, modern temple complex. The present temple and Buddha were begun in the early twentieth century on the site of a hidden underground temple, constructed in the seventeenth century to escape the evangelical attentions of the Portuguese. Thirty-nine metres tall and enclosed in a rather ugly shelter built in the 1990s, the giant Buddha figure itself, shown in the seated *samadhi* position, is a thing of impressive size, if no particular beauty. Most of the temple is actually buried underground, with endless corridors decorated with around twenty thousand inanely painted, cartoon-style depictions of various *jatakas*, plus unwittingly spooky black-and-white photos of past temple donors. Right underneath the giant Buddha, a monk will take your donation (Rs.100 is "suggested") and point out a mirror below in which you can see reflected a cache of precious gold and stone Buddhas buried in an underfloor vault. From here steps lead up to the giant Buddha itself. You can climb all the way up to the head, although there's not much to see. A big **perahera** is held here on the Unduvap poya day in early December.

The temple is a fifteen-minute bus ride from Matara. Take **bus #349** from the central aisle (east side) of the bus station; departures are every thirty minutes. Alternatively, a tuktuk will cost around Rs.250 return, including waiting time.

Dondra

Another large roadside Buddha (actually a copy of the Aukana Buddha – see p.337) announces the small town of **DONDRA**, 5km southeast of Matara. Dondra's sleepy present-day character belies its former significance. Also known as **Devi Nuwara**, or "City of the Gods", the town was formerly home to a great temple dedicated to Vishnu, one of the most magnificent on the island until it was destroyed by the Portuguese in 1588. However one ancient shrine, the **Galge**, survived. It's a small, plain structure thought to date back to the seventh century AD, making it the oldest stone building in Sri Lanka, and it has now been incorporated into the town's principal temple, an unusual blue pagoda-style construction dating from the early twentieth century. One of the south's major festivals, the **Devi Nuwara Perahera**, is held at the temple every year on the Esala poya day (early August) at the same time as the great Kandy Esala Perahera (see p.212).

Just over a kilometre south of town, a lighthouse marks the **southernmost point** in Sri Lanka. Built in 1889, the lighthouse stands 50m high and is sometimes open to visitors; you may be allowed inside to climb up the winding staircase to the top, from where there are sweeping views up and down the coast. South of here, there's nothing but sea between you and Antarctica, over ten thousand miles distant.

To reach Dondra, take any **bus** heading eastwards out of Matara; you'll have to either walk or catch a tuktuk (around Rs.75) to the lighthouse itself.

Tangalla and around

Strung out along one of the south's most beautiful stretches of coastline, **TANGALLA** (or **Tangalle**) is amongst the region's more developed beach destinations, although despite the burgeoning number of guest houses, tourism here hasn't yet taken off as much as the entrepreneurial locals would like, and

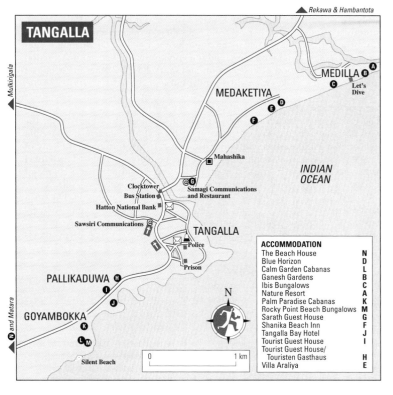

TANGALLA

Mulkirigala

MEDILLA Ⓐ
Ⓒ Let's
    Dive
MEDAKETIYA Ⓓ
Ⓔ
Ⓕ

INDIAN
OCEAN

Mahashika

Clocktower
Bus Station
Samagi Communications
and Restaurant

Hatton National Bank

Sawsiri Communications

TANGALLA

Police

PALLIKADUWA Ⓗ
Ⓘ
Ⓙ
GOYAMBOKKA
Ⓚ
Ⓛ
Ⓜ

Prison

N and Matara

Silent Beach

0   1 km

N

ACCOMMODATION	
The Beach House	N
Blue Horizon	D
Calm Garden Cabanas	L
Ganesh Gardens	B
Ibis Bungalows	C
Nature Resort	A
Palm Paradise Cabanas	K
Rocky Point Beach Bungalows	M
Sarath Guest House	G
Shanika Beach Inn	F
Tangalla Bay Hotel	J
Tourist Guest House	I
Tourist Guest House/ Touristen Gasthaus	H
Villa Araliya	E

the whole place remains resolutely low-key even compared to Unawatuna, let alone the big west coast resorts. If you want watersports, shops, restaurants and nightlife, this isn't the place to come; but if you just want great expanses of beautiful sandy beach to crash out on, Tangalla is worth a shout.

The area around Tangalla is also home to a number of rewarding attractions, including the **Hoo-maniya blowhole**, the giant Buddha and gaudy temple of **Wewurukanala** and the magnificent rock temples of **Mulkirigala**, all of which can be combined into a rewarding half-day excursion. In addition, the nearby beach at **Rekawa** is Sri Lanka's premier site for turtle-watching, offering the nightly opportunity to see these majestic creatures drag themselves ashore to lay their eggs in the sand. Dedicated ornithologists might also fancy a trip to the little-visited **Kalametiya Bird Sanctuary**, home to a rich selection of marine birdlife.

Arrival and accommodation

Buses stop right in the middle of town by the clock tower; a tuktuk from here to any of Tangalla's guest houses shouldn't cost more than Rs.50 (or Rs.80 to Goyambokka). There's a **Hatton Bank** right in the middle of town, and an agency **post office** just opposite; the main post office is slightly south of the centre. For **Internet** access, try either Sawsiri Communications, on the southern side of the town centre (Mon–Sat 8am–6pm, Sun 8am–2pm; Rs.6–8 per min), or Samagi Communications, at the southern end of Medaketiya Beach (daily 8am–10pm; Rs.7 per min). Samagi also rent out **bikes** (Rs.150 per day), motorbikes (Rs.600–700 per day) and have their own a/c vehicle (seats up to 10) for rent (Rs.3000 per day including driver and guide). The helpful owner can also arrange islandwide tours, and is a good source of general information on bus times and good places to swim and snorkel. Many other guest houses around town have bikes for rent at similar rates.

Accommodation

The beaches here stretch out for a couple of kilometres to either side of the workaday town of Tangalla itself: north of the town at **Medaketiya** and **Medilla** and south at **Pallikaduwa** and **Goyambokka**. All are furnished with plenty of budget guest houses, although they're generally poorer value than at Unawatuna or Mirissa. There's little in the way of upscale accommodation, bar a couple of average mid-range places and one outstanding (and very expensive) villa.

Many of Tangalla's cheaper places are built with slightly raised roofs. The small gap between the top of the walls and the roof tiles allows air to circulate freely and keeps things cool, but also means that you're at the mercy of mosquitoes; places right on the beach should be OK, since the sea breeze keeps insects away.

Medaketiya and Medilla

The best selection of accommodation in Tangalla is north of the town, in **Medaketiya** and **Medilla**. Note that to reach the two northernmost places (*Nature Resort* and *Ganesh Gardens*) by road you'll have to go inland along the Hambantota Rd.

Blue Horizon ☏ & ℱ 047-224 0721. One of the best-value places in Tangalla, with three rooms (and two more planned), including two family rooms, in an engaging, three-storey chalet-like structure above the beach. No single rates. ❶

Ganesh Gardens ☏ 077-761 2181. Seven pleasant little bungalows with verandahs at the quiet northern end of the beach; simple but perfectly adequate, though rather expensive for what you get. There's also a pleasant thatched pavilion restaurant with relatively cheap food. No single rates. ❷

Ibis Bungalows ☏ 077-790 5408, ℱ 047-224 0401. Three large clean but rather bare bungalows; good value for Tangalla, especially out of season. They also run the adjacent *Happy Bungalows* – simple rustic wooden structures with raised roofs, but cheap (❶). The friendly young owner is a good source of information, and there's also tasty cheap food; the fish is very fresh, and there's a live lobster trap from which to select your own victim; you can even catch and barbecue your own fish. Very cheap snorkelling gear (Rs.100/day). ❷

Nature Resort ☏ 047-224 0844, ⓦ srilanka -holiday.com. Situated at the remote northern end

of the beach, with lagoon and mangroves on one side and ocean on the other, this is the most upmarket place hereabouts, though still pretty low-key. Accommodation is in bijou two-storey green bungalows set amidst sandy gardens; they're adequate rather than special, and a bit overpriced, especially considering the lack of a/c or even hot water. There's a decent-size pool (non-guests Rs.150) and restaurant with a small and rather pricey menu. ❺

Sarath Guest House ☏ 077-740 3972. Appealing, good-value tiled rooms in an attractive house full of quasi-colonial furniture. Reasonably priced menu (including the famous "Aspaghethi A. Bolognees") is available. ❷

Shanika Beach Inn ☏ 047-224 2079. The cheapest place in Tangalla and very good value it is too, with bare but clean and reasonably sized rooms, and a very inexpensive menu. ❶

Villa Araliya ☏ & ℱ 047-224 2163. One of the most attractive places in Tangalla, with two nice bungalows (one large, one small; both with raised roofs) set in abundant gardens and furnished in quasi-colonial style. Pricey, but worth it. ❸

Pallikaduwa

There are lots of thoroughly unappealing budget guest houses south of the town in Pallikaduwa. The following are the only ones worth considering.

The Beach House c/o The Sun House in Galle (see p.157), ⓦ www.thesunhouse.com/villas.html. Nominated by *Condé Naste Traveller* as one of the world's top twenty villas, this exquisite Dutch colonial residence occupies its own stretch of deserted beach and is exquisitely designed and furnished throughout, with a magnificent ocean-facing terrace and a sizeable pool. The villa sleeps nine people in four bedrooms and comes complete with resident staff and chef. From US$750 per day.

Tangalla Bay Hotel ☎ 047-224 0346, ⒺIntence@sltnet.lk. The smartest place in Tangalla, this memorably ugly hotel sits on top of one of the town's loveliest promontories like an enormous concrete wart. The interior is modelled on a ship, and is kind of fun, in a rather mad and gloomy way. Rooms (or "cabins") are functional and past their best, but the setting above the

ocean is gorgeous. There's hot water and a small pool too. Also home to one of Tangalla's less awful (though totally moribund) restaurants. A/c supplement US$5. ❺

Tourist Guest House ☎ 047-224 0389. Not a great setting, right on the main road, but the rooms in a pleasant modern building are comfortable and spacious; a/c is available for an extra $5 and there's quite reasonable food. Prices are very flexible: get your bargaining hat on. ❷

Tourist Guest House/Touristen Gästhaus ☎ 047-224 0370, ⒺPacko@sltnet.lk. Seven rooms, including one with a/c and hot water (Rs.1000), and one with a self-contained kitchen – all are clean, modern, quiet and very good value. The owner likes to take his sign down for no apparent reason; it's immediately behind *Bay View* guest house on the corner (it's worth ringing in advance). ❷

Goyambokka

Accommodation in Goyambokka is expensive, though given the setting you might be prepared to cough up the extra rupees.

Calm Garden Cabanas ☎ 047-224 0523. Three functional concrete bungalows perched at the top of a scrubby plot of land – totally unatmospheric, and set away from the sea, but the cheapest in the village. ❷

Palm Paradise Cabanas ☎ 047-224 0842, ⓦ www.palmparadisecabanas.com. Very popular place, set in beautiful beachside gardens, with 22 rooms in rustic, rather basic individual bungalows. There's safe swimming nearby, a decent but costly range of food, plus expensive Internet access, ayurvedic oil massages, and bike and cheap motorbike rental. ❹

Rocky Point Beach Bungalows ☎ 047-224 0834, ⓦ hsrilankarockypoint.com. The nicest place in Goyambokka, wonderfully situated on a hillside overlooking a tiny beach and rocky headland, with pleasant bungalows and more basic rooms (including one family room). It's seriously overpriced, but given the location you might decide it's worth it. A good breakfast is included in the room rate, but otherwise the food is indifferent. Out of season rates allegedly fall by around 25 percent, but you may have to bargain for them. Rooms ❹, bungalows ❺

Around Tangalla

Claughton 11km west of Tangalla, signposted 400m off the main road ☎ 071-725 470. This rather exclusive, Bawa-designed establishment has just three rooms (one double and two twins) set in

a beautiful villa enclosed within spacious landscaped grounds running down to the sea. You can either rent an individual room (❻) or the entire villa for a measly US$345 per day full-board.

The town and beaches

Tangalla's beaches stretch for a couple of kilometres either side of **Tangalla town**, a busy but unremarkable provincial centre with a dusty selection of shops and cafés plus the obligatory clocktower and anarchic bus station. The most developed section of coast is to the north of town, along **Medaketiya** and **Medilla beaches**, a long, straight swathe of golden sand lined with an endless string of guest houses opened by optimistic local entrepreneurs in anticipation of a flood of tourists who have yet to arrive. What visitors there are tend to stick to their guest houses, and the mood is very somnolent.

Though just as sleepy, the coast immediately south of town, known as **Pallikaduwa**, is quite different in character, made up of a sequence of beautiful

Swimming, snorkelling and diving at Tangalla

Swimming in Tangalla can be hazardous: Medaketiya and Medilla beaches shelve steeply into the sea and there are dangerous currents in places, although the coves south of town at Pallikaduwa and Goyambokka are pleasantly sheltered. Always check at your hotel before venturing into the water: conditions vary considerably even within a few hundred metres – and the fact that the various beaches are often idyllically deserted means that there might not be anyone around to help if you get into trouble.

Tangalla's beaches offer some promising **snorkelling** – the best area is by the navy base in the middle of Tangalla Town, which still boasts a few bits of live coral; again seek local advice. **Diving** can be arranged through Let's Dive (℡077-790 2073), at the northern end of Medaketiya beach, which offers the usual range of PADI courses at average prices.

rocky coves – much more scenic than Medaketiya and Medilla, but with little sand. The rocky shoreline here has prevented building directly on the beach, so most of Pallikaduwa's accommodation is set back behind the main road – you'll be listening to passing traffic rather than crashing waves. The most scenic and unspoilt section of Tangalla coastline can be found a couple of kilometres further south at the village of **Goyambokka**, which sits atop the area's loveliest stretch of coast, with a superb rocky promontory flanked by two gorgeous beaches – that to the west of the headland, popularly known as **Silent Beach**, is an absolute picture, and totally untouched (for the time being at any rate).

Eating

Eating in Tangalla is a real disappointment, and you're probably best off having meals at your guest house (though in most instances the cooking's unlikely to consist of much more than boringly prepared fish or stodgy rice and curry). In terms of fully fledged restaurants, in **Tangalla town** itself, *Villa Ocean Waves* has a dirt-cheap menu with cheap fish plus rice and veg curry for a bargain Rs.60 – it's a pleasant place, and popular with locals. At **Medaketiya Beach**, the very basic but very friendly *Maheshika Restaurant* is set right on the sand, with gorgeous views and quite reasonably priced food from a simple menu of tourist standards. The *Samagi Restaurant*, attached to Samagi Communications (see p.181), also has a reasonably priced menu of standard dishes, plus a good range of cheap Sri Lankan breakfasts (order the evening before).

Things are even less promising at **Pallikaduwa**. There are several plausible-looking places along the seafront here, but the food's generally indifferent and can be wildly overpriced (the prominent *Sea-Beach*, in particular, is definitely one to avoid); a couple of these places also sell coral, so you might not want to patronize them for ecological reasons. You'd probably do better to stick to your guest house, or perhaps try the murky restaurant at the *Tangalla Bay Hotel*, which has the usual range of tourist favourites, acceptably prepared – about as good as it gets on this side of town.

Around Tangalla

A rewarding half-day trip from Tangalla combines the **Hoo-maniya blowhole**, the **Wewurukannala** temple with its enormous Buddha statue, and the absorbing rock temples of **Mulkirigala**. All local guest houses should be able to arrange a combined round-trip by tuktuk to these three places; the current going rate is around Rs.900. Another evening can be spent watching the turtles coming ashore at **Rekawa**, while halfway between Tangalla and Hambantota lie the little-visited wetlands of the **Kalametiya Bird Sanctuary**.

Hoo-maniya blowhole

Around 7km west of Tangalla, the village of Kudawala is home to the **Hoo-maniya blowhole** – the fanciful name derives from the low, booming "Hoo" sound which it produces prior to spouting water. The blowhole is formed from a deep, narrow cleft in the cliff, around twenty metres deep and a metre wide, which funnels plumes of water up into the air in great jets by some mysterious action of water pressure – it's most impressive during the monsoon (May to mid-Nov; June is reckoned to be best), when the jets can be fifteen metres high. At other times it can be slightly underwhelming. The blowhole is a popular spot with Sri Lankans, and gets busy at weekends, when the sight of great crowds of sari-clad ladies screaming and hopping around the rocks as they try to avoid getting drenched is at least as entertaining as the blowhole itself.

Wewurukannala

A few kilometres beyond Hoo-maniya, just inland from the village of Dickwella, the temple at **Wewurukannala** (Rs.50, plus tip for the informative resident guide if you want him to show you round) is home to the largest **Buddha statue** on the island, a 50m concrete colossus constructed in the late 1960s. The rather supercilious-looking Buddha is shown in the seated posture, draped in orange robes (unusually, both shoulders are covered) with his head crowned by a gaudy, polychromatic *sirsapata* (the Buddhist equivalent of the halo) – supposedly representing the flame of wisdom, though on this occasion it looks more like an enormous dollop of ice cream. Immediately to the rear of the statue is a seven-storey building, which the Enlightened One appears to be using as a kind of backrest. You can walk up the steps inside the building, past a big collection of boring, cartoon-style *jataka* paintings, and peer into the Buddha's head.

The main **image house** dates from the late nineteenth century and contains an impressive ensemble of huge Buddhas in various poses; like so many of the island's mosques and temples, the architect seems to have taken his inspiration from Portuguese Baroque architecture. The outer corridor has a wonderfully kitsch collection of statues plus the usual makara toranas; the side aisles are lined with representations of the 24 previous Buddhas, one shown as a lion. Outside and to the left of the main shrine is the oldest part of the temple, a small shrine some 250 years old, decorated with faded murals and housing a seated clay Buddha. Next door, another image house houses a kind of Buddhist **chamber of horrors** showing the punishments awaiting wrongdoers in the afterlife (Buddhist cosmology describes over twenty hells, including both hot and cold ones, in which sinners are incarcerated for unimaginably lengthy – albeit not infinite – periods). The gruesome collection of life-size statues here depict unfortunates being sawn in half, boiled in oil and impaled on stakes by rather jolly-looking devils. The corridor past the statues shows a long series of paintings (many unfinished): the upper panels depict various sins – everything from slapping your mother to urinating in front of a temple – the corresponding panel underneath shows the relevant punishment. You have been warned.

To reach the temple by public transport, catch the bus to Matara via **Beliatta**, which passes directly by.

Mulkirigala

Sixteen kilometres north of Tangalla lies the remarkable temple-monastery of **Mulkirigala** (daily 6am–6pm; Rs.100), the only monument in the south to rival the great ancient Buddhist sites of the Cultural Triangle. Mulkirigala (sometimes spelt Mulgirigala) consists of a series of **rock temples** carved out of the face of a huge rock outcrop which rises sheer and seemingly impregnable for over two hundred metres out of the surrounding palm forests; the temples date back to the third century BC, but were completely restored during the eighteenth century under the patronage of the kings of Kandy. Arranged on four terraces, each temple contains a reclining Buddha and is richly decorated with wall paintings and other statues. The overall effect is rather like a cross between the far better-known Dambulla and Sigiriya, though even if you've visited those sites, Mulkirigala doesn't disappoint. It's a bit of a climb to the top – over seven hundred steps – but unquestionably worth it both for the temples themselves and for the magnificent panoramas out over the surrounding countryside. Remember to remove your shoes and headgear when entering the temples; the site is still considered to be of religious significance, and a school for young monks stands at the base of the rock.

Immediately beyond the ticket office lies **terrace one**, home to two rock temples and a small dagoba; the unusual structures standing on elephant feet outside are oil lamps dating from the turn of the twentieth century. The temple nearest the entrance contains a reclining Buddha, plus paintings (along the side wall nearest the entrance) of Vishnu, Kataragama (by the door) and Vibhishana (he's the demonic blue figure with fangs), while the wall between the two doors into the first temple is decorated with pictures of *arhats* (enlightened Buddhist monks). The second cave here is one of the finest, with beautifully executed Kandyan-style paintings dating back to the eighteenth-century restoration – the wall between the two doors, decorated with *jataka* stories, is particularly striking. If you look at the outside of the doorway, you can see a watercourse cut into the rock to prevent drips falling into the cave. Retrace your steps past the ticket office to reach the steep flight of steps which lead up to **terrace two** – relatively uninteresting, with a single rock temple housing a reclining Buddha flanked by two disciples.

Further steps lead up to **terrace three**, the most interesting section of the complex. There are four temples here, ranged side by side, with a small rock pool at the left-hand end. Immediately behind the pool is the smallest of the four temples (you have to go through the adjacent temple to reach it), the so-called **Naga** or **Cobra temple**, named after the fearsome snake painted on the door at the rear – probably an allusion to the snake's status as a revered animal in Buddhist mythology, though literal-minded locals will claim that a genuine cobra still lives behind the door. The next temple along sports a gaudy reclining Buddha in its inner shrine; the frieze at the entrance shows the gods of the four cardinal points with colourful makara toranas between, while the terrace-facing wall shows pictures of various Buddhist shrines in Sri Lanka.

The third temple along, known as the **Raja Mahavihara**, is Mulkirigala's finest. The vestibule, paved with old Dutch floor tiles and supported by Kandyan-style wooden pillars, contains an antique chest which was once used to hold ola-leaf manuscripts of religious and other texts. It was in this chest, in 1826, that the British official and antiquarian **George Turnour** discovered a clutch of ancient manuscripts which enabled him to translate the *Mahavamsa* (see p.413), the first time Sri Lanka's famous historical chronicle had been deciphered in the modern era. Enter the inner shrine via the left-hand door, which is dated 1849 and carved with pineapples and cavorting squirrels. The shrine itself holds yet another sleeping Buddha, its feet intricately decorated with some of the 32 distinguishing marks with which local artists traditionally adorn their master's soles and toes. The small and delicate alabaster Buddha at the feet of the main reclining Buddha is from Burma – compare its decidedly Oriental-looking features which the far more Aryan faces of the Sri Lankan-made versions. The fantastically kitsch final temple is home to Mulkirigala's only *parinirvana* Buddha – that is to say a dead, rather than a merely sleeping, Buddha (for more on this, see p.438), surrounded by a lurid tableaux of grieving figures.

Next to the Raja Mahavihara, steps lead up again, past a set of treacherously narrow and steep rock-cut steps to **terrace four**, at the very summit of the site. There's not much to see here, apart from two young bo saplings, both grown from cuttings taken from the famous tree at Anuradhapura, and a derelict image house; the main attraction is the wonderful views south to Tangalla – scramble down the path behind the topmost dagoba for a wonderful unobstructed panorama northwards into the hills. On the far side of the summit, a "secret gate" – a kind of natural rock arch – leads to a concealed path down to the base of the rock.

You're free to explore the site by yourself, though if you want a tour, the informative resident **guide** will show you around for a tip. To reach Mulkirigala by public transport, take a **bus** from Tangalla to Beliatta (every 15min; 30min), then take one of the hourly buses to Walasmulle, which pass right by the temple.

Rekawa

The beach at **REKAWA** village, 10km east of Tangalla, is home to one of the most important **sea turtle nesting sites** in Sri Lanka, visited by five different species which lay their eggs in the sand here every night throughout the year (for more on Sri Lanka's turtles, see p.448). The nesting sites along the beach were formerly protected by the **Turtle Conservation Project** (TCP), which conducted research into visiting turtles and paid local villagers to protect eggs from predators. Despite the uniquely valuable nature of Rekawa, and the precarious state of worldwide sea turtle populations, funding for this project has now been removed. The villagers have continued the project as best they can in the absence of official support, and now make a basic living from entertaining visiting tourists.

The project, such as it is, now has a decidedly ad hoc character. The villagers don't speak a great deal of English, so it's difficult to get much idea of what's going on, and given the general lack of visitors (particularly out of season), the hours you'll probably have to spend waiting on the pitch-black beach for a turtle to arrive, and the general lack of evidence that you're even in the right place, it's easy to feel a bit disoriented by the whole experience, or even to believe (as many visitors do) that you're the object of some enormous scam. Despite appearances, however, the turtles do eventually appear. Watchers up and down the beach scout for their arrival – when one arrives (the vast majority are green turtles), it first crawls across the beach, away from the sea, leaving behind a remarkable trail which looks as if a one-wheeled tractor has driven straight up out of the sea. This takes the turtle an exhausting thirty minutes, since they are very badly adapted for travel on land, and can only move with agonizing slowness. Having reached the top of the beach, the turtles then spend about another 45 minutes digging an enormous hole; you'll hear periodic thrashings and the sound of great clouds of sand being scuffed up. As the turtle begins to lay its eggs, you're allowed in close to watch, although all you actually see is the turtle's backside with eggs – looking just like ping-pong balls – periodically popping out in twos and threes. The eggs are then taken to be re-buried in a secure location. The turtle then rests, fills in the hole and eventually crawls back down to the sea. It's an epic effort, the sight of which makes the whole evening-long experience (just about) worthwhile.

The **best time** to see turtles is between January and April; periods when there's a full or fullish moon are also good throughout the year, because there are both more turtles and more light to see them by. Rekawa's record is apparently 23 turtles in one night, and there's allegedly always been at least one turtle every night, though you might have to wait until around midnight to see one. The villagers levy a Rs.300 fee, while a tuktuk from Tangalla will cost Rs.600. For security reasons (it's a dark and lonely ride), it's best to book a reliable tuktuk through your guest house; note also that turtle-watching can make for a long and boring evening: take a sarong to sit on, as well as any food and drink you might fancy. Locals will suggest you arrive at the beach just after nightfall, though given that most turtles don't turn up till much later (often around midnight) you might want to delay your arrival until about 8.30 or 9pm. Finally, don't expect either the villagers or your tuktuk driver to have change – potentially a bit of a problem at 1am in the middle of nowhere: take the right money.

Kalametiya Bird Sanctuary

Twenty kilometres beyond Tangalla, the little-visited **Kalametiya Bird Sanctuary** comprises an area of coastal lagoons and mangroves which is rich in marine and other birdlife, similar to that found in Bundala and best seen from November to March. Access to the sanctuary is from the village of **Hungama**. There are no facilities at the sanctuary and no guides; entrance is free.

Hambantota

The area between Tangalla and Hambantota marks the transition between Sri Lanka's wet and dry zones, where the lush palm forests of the southwest give way to the arid and scrub-covered savannah that characterizes much of the island. Some 45 kilometres beyond Tangalla, the dusty and dispiriting little town of **HAMBANTOTA** is sometimes used as a base for visits to Bundala National Park by those who can afford to stay at one of the three pleasant mid-range hotels. If you're on a budget, press on to Tissamaharama (see p.191).

Hambantota was originally settled by Malay seafarers (the name is a corruption of "Sampan-tota", or "Sampan Port", alluding to the type of boat in which they arrived) and the town still has the largest concentration of Malay-descended people on the island, with a correspondingly high proportion of Muslims and mosques – you really notice the call to prayer here. A few inhabitants still speak Malay, and although you probably won't notice this, you're likely to be struck by the occasional local face with pure Southeast Asian features. Hambantota's other claim to fame is as the **salt** capital of Sri Lanka. Salt is produced by letting seawater into the **lewayas**, the sometimes dazzlingly white saltpans which surround the town, and allowing it to evaporate, after which the residue is scraped up and sold.

The Town and around

Hambantota's modest attractions are easily covered in an hour's walk. Starting right in the centre, the sadly neglected **Catholic Cemetery** is home to a few rapidly collapsing colonial memorials, including one poignant monument to the luckless George McKerrow Clark, Irrigation Engineer, aged 33, and

Edward Russell Ayrton, Archaeological Commissioner, aged 32, who drowned on May 18, 1914, in Tissa Tank "under circumstances tending to shew that each gave his life in an attempt to save the other" – a touching memento which stands virtually forgotten in the dusty centre of modern Hambantota.

Head north from here past the ramshackle bus station and clocktower, then follow the road as it winds around the headland, giving views over the pretty little **harbour**, Hambantota's best feature, and beyond along the denuded coast to the grand, saw-tooth hills around Kataragama away in the distance – a beautiful sight. The **beach** itself is scrubby and unappealing, and strong currents make swimming dangerous.

Beyond here, the road meanders around the headland to the attractive old *Rest House*. Just north of here sits an old British **martello tower** and a black-and-white-striped **lighthouse** surrounded by a few disconsolate maritime sculptures. The clutch of government buildings nearby were formerly home to Hambantota's British government agents, amongst them **Leonard Woolf**, who spent several years here in the pay of the Ceylon Civil Service before returning to England, where he married novelist Virginia Stephen, giving her the surname by which she is now remembered. Whilst here, Leonard penned the Sri Lankan classic *The Village in the Jungle*, an extraordinarily depressing tale of life in the backlands.

Practicalities

Buses stop at the terminal right in the middle of town. There are branches of Hatton National Bank and the Bank of Ceylon where you can change money, but none have ATMs which accept foreign cards. The main post office is directly opposite the Bank of Ceylon; there's also an agency branch on Main Street, roughly opposite the *Fine Curd Food Cabin*. For **Internet** access, try Singhe Communication and Print Shop, immediately north of the bus terminal on Main Street. **Leaving Hambantota**, note that through buses to Tissa don't stop at the bus station, but instead pick up passengers on the corner of Main Street and Jail Street, next to the Sathosa supermarket.

Accommodation and eating

There are a number of budget **guest houses** in Hambantota, but they're all uniformly awful and we haven't included them – if you can't afford one of the

Tours from Hambantota

All the town's hotels and guest houses can organize transport to Bundala and other parks, plus nearby birdwatching spots such as Wirawila Wewa, Malala Lewaya, Bundala Lewaya and Kalametiya. For **Bundala National Park**, count on Rs.1600–2600 for a half-day trip. A day-trip to **Yala National Park** costs around Rs.2500–3800, though you'd be much better off visiting the park from Tissa, which is a lot closer. You could also visit **Uda Walawe** as a long day-trip from Hambantota, though it's a bit of a slog, with a 130-kilometre round-trip to get to the park and back – count on around Rs.3800.

All these prices are for transport only, usually in some kind of jeep holding up to six or seven people; obviously the more people, the cheaper it becomes per person. Prices can vary quite significantly, so its worth shopping around; the town's budget guest houses offer cheaper deals than the big hotels. Alternatively, try the knowledgeable Samsiri (Flamingo Safaris), who can often be found hanging around in a green jeep outside the *Peacock*.

hotels below, go to Tissa. The hotels are also the only places you'd really want **to eat** in town. The best bet is the restaurant at the *Peacock* hotel, attractively situated overlooking the sea, with reasonably priced standards (from around Rs.300), both Eastern and Western, presented under various touching headings including "Gets on your mark" (starters) and the immortal "Crispies of Green Fields" (salads). The restaurant at the *Rest House* has plenty of character and wonderful harbour views, although the food's very average, and the curry should come with a fire extinguisher. The only other place you might want to try is the *Jade Garden* (not a Chinese restaurant, despite the name), opposite the entrance to the *Peacock*. This looks deceptively pleasant, but has poor and rather expensive food, enlivened only by hilariously bad service. The lunchtime buffet is probably the best option; their à la carte selection of tourist standards (from Rs.250) is very hit and miss. Given the lack of alternatives, however, you might give it a go.

If you want a **drink**, try the *Peacock* hotel's breezy rooftop *Lihiniya Bar*, the nicest spot in town, with a terrific view over the beach and houses (from this distance, even Hambantota looks almost attractive).

Hotels

Oasis Sisilasagama, about 7km west of Hambantota ☏047-222 0650, ⓦwww.lanka.net/oasis. Average but inoffensive modern resort-style hotel, with ten chalets scattered around the pleasant grounds and 38 standard rooms with phone, TV, hot water and bathtubs. ❻

Peacock ☏047-222 0159, ⓔpeacock@sltnet.lk. Attractive resort-style hotel on the beach, backed by luxuriant gardens and with plush, sea-facing a/c rooms, plus a few slightly more worn older rooms (same price). There's a swimming pool (non-guests Rs.100) and tennis courts. No single rates. ❻

Rest House ☏ & ⓕ047-222 0299. Beautifully located on a headland overlooking the harbour, with views of the parched coastline and distant hills. Rooms in the atmospheric old wing are huge and stuffed full of lovely old furniture; cheaper ones in the "new" wing are much less characterful, but still pleasant and comfy and with great views. Overall it's relatively expensive for what you get, but very appealing. Old wing ❺, new wing ❹

Bundala National Park

Around fifteen kilometres east of Hambantota (and a similar distance west of Tissa), **Bundala National Park** is one of Sri Lanka's foremost destinations for **birdwatchers**, protecting an important area of coastal wetland famous for its abundant aquatic (and other) birdlife, as well as being home to significant populations of elephants, crocodiles, turtles and other fauna, including the occasional leopard. Although it doesn't have quite the range of wildlife or scenery of nearby Yala National Park, Bundala is much quieter, and makes a good alternative if you want to avoid Yala's crowds.

The park stretches along the coast for around twenty kilometres, enclosing five shallow and brackish **lagoons**, or *lewayas* (they sometimes dry up completely during long periods of drought) separated by thick low scrubby forest running down to coastal dunes. A total of 197 bird species have been recorded here, made up of 139 resident species and 58 seasonal visitors, the latter arriving during the northern winter (Sept–March). The lagoons attract an amazing variety of **aquatic birds**, including ibis, pelicans, painted storks, egrets and spoonbills, though the most famous visitors are the huge flocks of **greater flamingos**. The Bundala area is the flamingos' last refuge in southern Sri Lanka, and you can see them here in variable numbers throughout the year; their exact breeding habits remain a mystery, though it's thought they migrate from the Rann of Kutch in northern India. Other non-aquatic birds commonly seen here include delicate green bee eaters, one of the south's prettiest residents (you may also see blue-tailed bee eaters, regular migrants from the Himalayas), along with spotted doves, common babblers, kingfishers, parakeets and bulbuls – all fascinating stuff, if you've got even a trace of ornithological enthusiasm in your system. Perhaps the park's most visible avian resident, however, is the **peacock** (or Indian peafowl, as it's correctly known): a memorable sight in the wild at any time, especially when seen perched sententiously amidst the upper branches of the park's innumerable skeletal palu trees.

Bundala is also home to 32 species of **mammals**, including leopards (very rare), sloth bears, civets, mongooses and giant squirrels, as well as rabbits (rare in Sri Lanka, and an incongruous sight as they bounce fluffily around amidst the arid tropical landscape), though the most commonly seen mammals are the excitable troupes of grey langur **monkeys**. There are also a few **elephants**, including around ten permanent residents and some twenty semi-resident; larger seasonal migratory herds of up to sixty, comprising animals that roam the Yala, Uda Walawe and Bundala area, also visit the park. Four species of **turtle** (olive ridley, green, leatherback and hawksbill) lay their eggs on the park's beaches, although there are currently no turtle watches. You'll probably also come across large **land monitors** and lots of enormous **crocodiles**, which can be seen sunning themselves along the sides of the park's lagoons and watercourses. Depending on how wet it is, your tracker might let you get within a couple of metres of their log-like forms, or even take you to have a peek inside their burrows: a memorable experience, though not one for the faint-hearted.

Practicalities

Bundala is about thirty minutes' drive from either Hambantota or Tissa (the main coastal road runs along the northern edge of the park) – drivers charge Rs.1500–2000 for a jeep trip from either town (see p.188 and below). The **entrance fee** is currently US$6.90, half the entrance price at Sri Lanka's other national parks; the usual additional charges and taxes also apply (see p.53). The **best time to visit** is between September and March, when the migratory birds arrive; as with all wildlife areas in Sri Lanka, early morning and late after-noon are the best times of day to visit. Take binoculars, if you have them. Your driver will ferry you around the park, which is criss-crossed by rough tracks; you can stop and get out of your vehicle anywhere you fancy (unlike Yala). Drivers will probably assume that you're most interested in seeing elephants; if you have other interests, tell them.

Tissamaharama and around

Beyond Bundala National Park the main highway turns away from the coast towards the town of **TISSAMAHARAMA** (usually abbreviated to **Tissa**), one of the most pleasant towns in the south. Tissa's main attraction is as a base for trips to the nearby national parks of Yala and Bundala or the temple town of Kataragama, but it's an agreeable place in its own right, with a handful of monuments testifying to the town's important place in early Sri Lankan history when, under the name of **Mahagama**, it was one of the principal settlements of the southern province of Ruhunu. Mahagama is said to originally

Queen Viharamahadevi

Early Sinhalese history has many heroes but very few heroines – with the notable exception of the legendary **Queen Vihara Maha Devi**. According to tradition, Vihara Maha Devi's father – a certain King Kelani Tissa – unjustly put to death a Buddhist monk, whereupon the waters of the ocean rose up and threatened to submerge his kingdom until he sacrificed his pious and beautiful young daughter to the sea, placing her in a fragile boat and casting her off into the waves. The brave young princess, who had patiently submitted to this ordeal for the sake of her father's kingdom, was carried away around the coast and finally washed ashore in Kirinda, on the coast near Tissamaharama. The local king, the powerful **Kavan Tissa**, came upon the delectable princess as she lay asleep in her boat, fell in love with her, and promptly married her. Their first son, **Dutugemunu** (see p.348), became one of the great heroes of early Sinhalese history.

Quite what the story of Vihara Maha Devi's sea journey means is anyone's guess – perhaps the folk memory of some catastrophic flooding, a forgotten dynastic alliance, or even some prehistoric fertility cult. Whatever the legend's basis, it provided the Sinhalese's greatest warrior-king with a suitably auspicious parentage, and created Sri Lanka's first great matriarch in the process.

have been founded in the third century BC by a brother of the great Devanampiya Tissa of Anuradhapura, and later rose to prominence under **Kavan Tissa**, father of the legendary Dutugemunu (see p.348). A cluster of dagobas and a beautiful tank dating from this era lend parts of Tissa a certain distinction and a sense of history which makes a pleasant change from the run-of-the-mill towns which dot much of the southern coast.

Arrival and accommodation

Buses stop in the middle of the town; a tuktuk to the guest houses around Tissa Wewa will cost Rs.30–40. There are branches of the Bank of Ceylon, Hatton National Bank and Sampath Bank along Main Street where you can **change money** – the last has an **ATM** which accepts foreign MasterCard and Visa. You can make international **phone calls** from loads of places along Main Street in town and at the **agency post office** on the same road. There's not much in the way of **Internet** access: try Dhammika Printers (Rs.7 per min) on Main Street opposite Sampath Bank, or the nameless place (it says "email" on the glass door) slightly further west along the same road (Rs.8 per min).

Accommodation

Accommodation in Tissa is split into three quite separate areas. A kilometre north of the town proper, the area around the placid waters of the **Tissa Wewa** is easily the nicest base, and has the widest selection of guest houses (although none really take advantage of their proximity to the lake). There are also a couple of recommendable alternatives away from the lake in **Tissa town** itself, and in the village of **Deberawewa**, about 2km west. There are also a few options out in the unspoilt countryside near the entrance to Yala National Park – see p.197 for details.

Tissa Wewa

All the places listed opposite are north of the lake, on (or just off) the Kataragama Road.

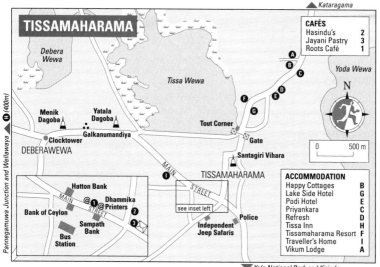

TISSAMAHARAMA

▲ Kataragama

CAFÉS
Hasindu's 2
Jayani Pastry 3
Roots Café 1

Debera Wewa

Tissa Wewa

Yoda Wewa

N

Menik Dagoba **Yatala Dagoba**

Clocktower Galkanumandiya

DEBERAWEWA

Tout Corner

Gate

Santagiri Vihara

TISSAMAHARAMA

0   500 m

ACCOMMODATION
Happy Cottages   B
Lake Side Hotel   G
Podi Hotel   E
Priyankara   C
Refresh   D
Tissa Inn   H
Tissamaharama Resort F
Traveller's Home   I
Vikum Lodge   A

Hatton Bank

@ Dhammika
@ Printers

Bank of Ceylon

Sampath Bank

Bus Station

see inset left

Independent Jeep Safaris

Police

MAIN STREET

▼ Yala National Park and Kirinda

Happy Cottages ☎047-223 7085. A handful of cheap older rooms – quiet, bright and reasonable value (❶–❷) – plus four smart new a/c rooms (❹ including breakfast) in a new annexe.

Lake Side Hotel ☎047-223 7216. Pleasant-looking hotel with attractive downstairs lounge and public verandahs. Rooms are slightly threadbare but quite pleasant, clean and tiled; some have hot water, and a few have a/c or (restricted) lake views; the cheaper rooms are not such good value. There's reasonable food in the pleasant restaurant, though service can be slow. No single rates. ❷

Podi Hotel ☎047-223 7698, ⓦwww.podihotel.com. Scottish-owned and-managed hotel with five clean and spacious rooms (two with a/c); those upstairs are a bit brighter and quieter. There's also an attractive restaurant downstairs. A/c supplement Rs.500. ❷

Priyankara ☎047-223 7206, ⓔprihotel@itmin.com. The poshest spot in town, but very reasonably priced. The a/c rooms are surprisingly smart; non-a/c ones are a bit shabbier, but perfectly OK and equally good value. All have nice verandahs with views over paddy fields, and there's good, moderately priced food. It's also one of the few places in town that doesn't arrange tours (most of the guests here are already on one), so you're guaranteed a hassle-free stay. A/c supplement US$5. ❺

Refresh ☎047-223 7357. Four rooms attached to Tissa's best restaurant (see p.195) – they're good value, spacious, spotless and surprisingly stylish, and would be the best in town if it weren't

for the noise from the attached restaurant, kitchen and communal TV (the situation isn't helped by the baffling lack of glass in the windows). A reasonable choice nonetheless. ❷

Tissamaharama Resort (formerly the Rest House) ☎047-223 7299, ⓦwww.ceylonhotels.lk. Large hotel nicely located next to Tissa Wewa – one wing faces directly onto the lake. The rustic wooden foyer conceals the full architectural horror of the place: a sludge-brown concrete box with peeling paint and prison-like corridors and stairwells. Rooms are OK but a bit worn and overpriced. The hotel also boasts Tissa's only swimming pool (non-guests Rs.125), and boat safaris on Tissa Wewa can be arranged (Rs.1000). Food is indifferent and wildly overpriced. A/c supplement US$7. ❺

Vikum Lodge ☎047-223 7585. Run by a charming elderly couple, this is Tissa's most personable guest house, slightly out of the way, but well worth the walk. Rooms (all with hot water) are unusually bright and lovingly maintained, and are arranged around a pretty garden and an attractive courtyard with a little vine-covered restaurant in the centre. Good single rates. ❷

Tissa town and Deberawewa

Tissa Inn Deberawewa, 1.5 km west of the clocktower ☎047-2237233, ⓔtissainn@cga.lk. Long-established place, still popular and good value, with twelve clean rooms plus a reasonable restaurant. ❷

Traveller's Home ☎047-223 7958, ℮supuncj@sltnet.lk. Popular guest house with two cheap rooms with bath and two even cheaper ones without. They're pretty basic, but good value at the price, and the family who run the place are almost pathologically friendly. They also arrange cheap tours (see below). ➊

The Town

➋ Modern Tissa is a bustling but unremarkable local commercial centre – essentially a single thoroughfare, **Main Street**, lined with banks, shops and

Tours from Tissa

A horde of local operators offer a wide range of trips from Tissa. Easily the most popular are the half- and full-day trips to **Yala** and **Bundala national parks** (see the relevant accounts to get an idea of how long you fancy spending in either park). It's suggested that you begin half-day trips at either 5.30am or 2.30pm, to be in the park for dawn or dusk. Some operators also offer **night safaris** to Yala and Bundala; these usually leave at 3.30pm and return at 10.30am the next morning and include two park drives, plus tent, dinner, breakfast and tea. Staying the night in the parks gives you the chance to see nocturnal animals, including snakes, crocs, owls, wild pigs, porcupines (rare) and nocturnal birds. During Yala's annual closure (Sept 1–Oct 15) you can arrange trips around the edge of the park, just outside the boundaries; the terrain is similar, and you might see some wildlife, but by and large this is a watered-down experience compared to visiting the park itself, and costs about the same.

Another increasingly popular option is the half-day excursion to the rock temple at **Situlpahuwa** (see p.197) followed by a visit to **Kataragama** (see p.198) for the evening puja. The journey to Situlpahuwa passes through the fringes of Yala (though you don't have to pay the entrance fee), so you might spot some wildlife en route, but this is much less interesting than a proper trip to the main portion of the park. Some drivers also offer a combined tour of five different local **tanks**, including Tissa Wewa, Deberawewa and Wirawila Wewa, all rich in birdlife (assuming they haven't dried up, as happens frequently in periods of low rainfall). It's also possible – in theory – to visit **Uda Walawe** from Tissa in a day, though this would be a long slog, and isn't recommended.

Tour operators and prices

Almost all the town's guest houses and hotels can fix up tours – the cheapest place is *Traveller's Home*. Alternatively, try the reputable **Independent Jeep Safaris**, in town just east of the bus station (☎047-223 7831, ℮supuncj@sltnet.lk). The other option is to take your chances with the rabble of jeep drivers at **tout corner**, by the archway at the southeastern corner of Tissa Wewa. Despite the initial impression many of these young men give of having just escaped from a stag party, the crowd here does contain a few fairly switched-on individuals – try Jayantha (☎047-223 7603), who has twenty years' experience and has good knowledge of the local flora and fauna. For more about choosing a driver, see p.35.

Prices don't vary an enormous amount between the different operators, but it's worth shopping around a little to get an idea of current rates; there's (very limited) room for bargaining if you can convince whoever you're talking to that you've found a cheaper deal elsewhere. The following prices are for a jeep seating up to six or seven people. A standard half-day trip to Yala or Bundala costs around Rs.1800, or Rs.3000 for a full day. Half-day trips – such as to Situlpahuwa combined with Kataragama, or around five different local lakes – cost Rs.1800; the long day-trip to Uda Walawe usually goes for around Rs.3500. Night safaris to Bundala and to Yala can also be arranged.

little cafés. Refreshingly compact, the town is bounded on its northern side by a beautiful expanse of paddy fields, in the middle of which stands the most impressive of Tissa's various dagobas, the **Santagiri** (or Sandagiri) **dagoba**, allegedly built by Kavan Tissa in the second century BC and now restored to its original glory. About a kilometre north of the modern town lies the beautiful **Tissa Wewa**, an expansive artificial lake thought to have been constructed in the second or third century BC – the shore nearest the town is often busy with crowds of people bathing (including the occasional tourist) and flocks of aquatic birds including bitterns, herons and egrets skimming across the waters. A beautiful walk leads along the massive **bund** (embankment) which encloses the lake's southern shore, shaded by a procession of majestic old trees. At the far end a track leads to the smaller adjacent lake of **Deberawewa**, another haven for birdlife, its surface prettily covered in water lilies.

Return to the southwest corner of the Tissa Wewa, from where a short walk along the road back towards the town centre brings you to two large dagobas dating back to the second century BC – each once probably formed part of a large monastery, though little now survives above ground. The first of these, the **Yatala dagoba**, is surrounded by a wall faced with sculpted elephant heads and may once have housed the Tooth Relic (see p.219). There's a small and only erratically open **museum** here, containing a very modest selection of carvings and masonry rescued from local archeological sites. Continue down the road for a couple of hundred metres to reach the **Menik dagoba**. The small cluster of pillars you pass en route is all that remains of the **Galkanumandiya**, thought to be some kind of monastic building.

Eating

Tissa is home to one of the best **restaurants** in the south, *Refresh* (see p.193), an offshoot of the excellent establishment in Hikkaduwa; the menu here is much smaller than at the original branch, but still excellent, with attractive open-air seating, well-prepared fish, rice and noodle dishes, plus a rice and curry (Rs.350) spread to dream of. There are also a couple of other moribund pseudo-Chinese places further up the road, though they serve mainly as local drinking holes. In addition, all the guest houses and hotels listed on p.193 do **food** – the *Priyankara* and *Lake Side Hotel* are two of the better places, offering a predictable but well-prepared range of touristy dishes.

In town, the sociable *Roots Café*, just off Main Street, doesn't look like much but has good cheap food (mainly Chinese and Sri Lankan) from a surprisingly

---

Moving on from Tissa

Tissa is a major terminus for buses travelling east along the coastal road, which stop here before heading back west (hence you should be able to get a seat). Services depart regularly for **Matara** and **Colombo**, though most are old CTB rustbuckets; if you're heading back to Colombo, you might find it easier to change onto an express bus in Matara. Tissa is also a convenient place to head up into the hills, though to get there you may have to change buses at **Pannegamuwa**, a small town located on a major road intersection 5km west of Tissa, and again at **Wellawaya**, from where there are plenty of buses to **Ella** or **Haputale**.

If you're staying around Tissa Wewa and going to **Kataragama**, there's no need to go into the bus station in town; just stand on the main road here, which is also the road to Kataragama, and flag down anything that passes. You're unlikely to have to wait more than a few minutes.

long menu. *Hasindu's Café*, just off Main Street, dishes up cheap rice and curry, burianis and devilled dishes, while *Jayani Pastry* (immediately west of the agency post office) does equally inexpensive short eats and rice and curry, and has Elephant House ice cream.

② Yala National Park

Around 20km southeast of Tissamaharama lies the entrance to **Yala National Park** (properly known as Yala West or Ruhunu National Park), Sri Lanka's most visited wildlife reserve. Yala covers an area of 1260 square kilometres, although four-fifths of this is designated a Strict Natural Reserve and closed to visitors. On the far side of the Strict Natural Reserve is Yala East National Park (see p.384), which is currently only accessible via Arugam Bay. There's no public transport to Yala West, and you're only allowed into the park in a vehicle, so you'll have to hire a jeep.

To avoid disappointment, it's important to understand what Yala is, and what it isn't – if you expect vast herds of elephants and other large mammals, with leopards dangling from every tree, you'll inevitably be disappointed. In addition, there's no limit to the number of vehicles allowed inside the park, and it can sometimes seem impossibly busy, with posses of belching jeeps careering around in frantic pursuit of elusive elephants or leopards. Despite this, Yala can be a richly rewarding place to visit. The park's dry-zone **landscape** is strikingly beautiful, especially when viewed from the vantage points offered by the curious rock outcrops which dot the park. From these you can look out over a seemingly endless expanse of low scrub and trees dotted with brackish lakes next to the dune-covered coastline; particularly magical from Situlpahuwa, at Yala's northern end. In addition, the park's wildlife has its own distinctive charm, with huddles of colourful painted storks perched on the edge of lagoons between the supine shapes of dozing crocodiles; fan-tailed peacocks kicking up clouds of dust while monkeys chatter in the treetops; or the incongruously conjoined sight of elephants marching sedately through the bush while rabbits scamper through the undergrowth.

The park's most famous residents are its elusive **leopards**, but you'll be very lucky to see one (at least unless you stay at the *Yala Safari Game Lodge* and avail yourself of that establishment's excellent resident naturalists; see opposite). Much more visible are the resident **elephants**, best seen during the dry season from around January to May, when they come to drink at the park's various lagoons. Other resident **mammals** include sambar and spotted deer, wild boar, wild buffaloes, macaque and langur monkeys, sloth bears, jackals, mongooses, pangolins, porcupines, wild boar, rabbits and (rare) wild cats. There are also plentiful **crocodiles**, though the fact that you're confined to your vehicle prevents the white-knuckle close encounters you'll get at Bundala – something which you might not entirely regret. Yala is also rich in **birdlife**. Around 130 species have been recorded here, including many migrants escaping the northern winter. Common aquatic birds include various storks (among them the rare black-necked stork), sandpipers, pelicans, egrets, herons, ibises, kingfishers and the magnificent Indian darter, along with birds of prey such as the hawk eagle and colourful smaller species including green and blue bee eaters, hoopoes, parakeets and bulbuls. Peacocks are ubiquitous throughout the park, while you should also spot at least a couple of jungle fowl, a singularly inelegant, waddling creature, like a feral hen, which has been adopted as the national bird of Sri Lanka.

Yala also has a certain historic interest. The remains of extensive settlements that once dotted the area during the Ruhunu period can still be seen, most notably the monastery at **Situlpahuwa**, which may once have housed over ten thousand people and remains an important site of pilgrimage en route to nearby Kataragama (see p.198). The temple comprises two rock-top dagobas separated by a small lake; there's a faded Pali inscription at the base of the first rock. The main draw, though, is the temple's lost-in-the-jungle setting and the marvellous views it affords of pretty much the entire park, with scarcely a single sign of human presence interrupting the majestic swathe of scrub and forest receding into the saw-tooth hills further away up the east cost. South of Situlpahuwa are the very modest remains of the first-century BC **Magul Maha Vihara**, built (according to legend) on the spot where Kavan Tissa and Vihara Maha Devi (see p.192) were married – *magul* means "wedding". Although these two temples lie within the national park, you can visit them without paying the entrance fee; combined with Kataragama, they make a good half-day excursion from Tissa.

Practicalities

For details of arranging a **jeep from Tissa** to Yala, see p.194. The usual national park fees apply (see p.53). Yala is **closed annually** from September 1 to October 15.

All vehicles entering the park are assigned an obligatory tracker; as ever, the standards of both tracking and English vary wildly. You're meant to stay inside your vehicle (except on the beach), keep your jeep's hood up, stick to roads and avoid all noise, although you are allowed to drive freely around the park, following whichever track takes your fancy – this obviously favours the more clued-up drivers and trackers, who are likely to have up-to-date information about recent leopard and elephant sightings, although it also means that the less expert trackers simply chase one another around the park at the merest hint of a sighting. October to December is the **best time** for bird-spotting, as migrant species arrive to escape the northern winter; the key time to see elephants is during the January to May dry season, when they congregate around the park's lagoons.

If you've got the money, it's worth staying at **Yala Safari Game Lodge** (☏047-223 8015, ⓦwww.jetwinghotels.com; ❼), set in a patch of jungle on the coast close to the park entrance. An extremely comfortable and pleasant place in its own right, its main attraction is the game drives led by three expert resident naturalists, whose inside knowledge allows them to turn up leopards with a frequency which other park drivers and trackers can only dream of. If you're desperate to see a leopard and are willing to devote a couple of days to exploring the park with these guys, you've got a roughly ninety percent chance of spotting one – or even several – of these majestic creatures. You can go on tours with the hotel's naturalists even if you're not staying there; contact the hotel for further information.

There are a couple of other **accommodation** options if you want to get a feel for the dry-zone landscape by staying out in the countryside around the park entrance. These are the simpler but still comfortable *Brown's Beach Motel* (☏060-247 3216, ⓕ011-276 4377; ❹–❺), by the sea on the edge of the park; and the luxurious new *Yala Village* (☏047-223 9450; ❼), a couple of kilometres from the park entrance, with sixty plush a/c bungalows scattered around ten acres of jungle between the sea and lagoon. To reach either, you'll need to hire a jeep from Tissa unless you have your own vehicle.

Kataragama and around

Nineteen kilometres inland from Tissa lies the small and remote town of **KATARAGAMA**, one of the three most venerated religious sites in Sri Lanka (along with Adam's Peak and the Temple of the Tooth at Kandy), held sacred by Buddhists, Hindus and Muslims alike – even Christians sometimes visit in search of divine assistance. The most important of the town's various shrines is dedicated to the god **Kataragama**, a Buddhist-cum-Hindu deity (see box below for more on his confused lineage) who is believed to reside here. The origins of this shrine are obscure. One theory has it that King Dutugemunu built a shrine to Kataragama here in the second century BC, while the adjacent Buddhist dagoba allegedly dates back to the first century BC.

Kataragama is easily visited as a day-trip from Tissa, but staying the night means you can enjoy the evening puja in a leisurely manner and imbibe some of the town's backwater charm and laid-back rural pace. The town is at its busiest during the **Kataragama festival**, held around the Esala poya day in late July or early August (at the same time as the great Esala Perahera in Kandy). The festival is famous for the varying forms of physical mortification with which some pilgrims express their devotion to Kataragama, ranging from crawling from the river to the Maha Devale to gruesome acts of self-mutilation: some penitents pierce their cheeks or tongue with skewers; others walk across burning coals – all believe that the god will protect them from pain. At

Kataragama

Perhaps no other deity in Sri Lanka embodies the bewilderingly syncretic nature of the island's Buddhist and Hindu traditions as clearly as the many-faceted **Kataragama**. The god has two very different origins. To the Buddhist Sinhalese, Kataragama is one of the four great protectors of the island. Although he began life as a rather unimportant local god, named after the town in which his shrine was located, he gained pan-Sinhalese significance during the early struggles against the South Indian Tamils, and is believed to have helped Dutugemunu (see p.348) in his long war against Elara. To the Hindu Tamils, Kataragama is equivalent to the major deity **Skanda** (also known as Murugan or Subramanian), a son of Shiva and Parvati and brother of Ganesh. Both Buddhists and Hindus have legends which tell how Kataragama came to Sri Lanka to battle against the *asuras*, or enemies of the gods. Whilst fighting, he became enamoured of Valli Amma, the result of the union between a pious hermit and a doe, who became his second wife. His cult waned amongst the Sinhalese following the accession of Tamils to the throne of Kandy, but was subsequently revived amongst the island's plantation Tamils, who considered Kataragama a manifestation of the god Skanda. Despite Kataragama's confused lineage, modern-day visitors to the shrine generally pay scant attention to the god's theological roots, simply regarding him a powerful deity capable of assisting in a wide range of practical enterprises.

Kataragama is often shown carrying a **vel**, or trident, which is also one of Shiva's principal symbols. His colour is red (devotees offer crimson garlands when they visit his shrines) and he is frequently identified with the peacock, a bird which was sacrificed to him. Thanks to his exploits, both military and amorous, he is worshipped both as a fearsome warrior and as a lover, inspiring an ecstatic devotion in his followers exemplified by the *kavadi*, or peacock dance (see p.200) and the ritual self-mutilations practised by pilgrims during the annual Kataragama festival (see above) – a world away from the chaste forms of worship typical of the island's Buddhist rituals.

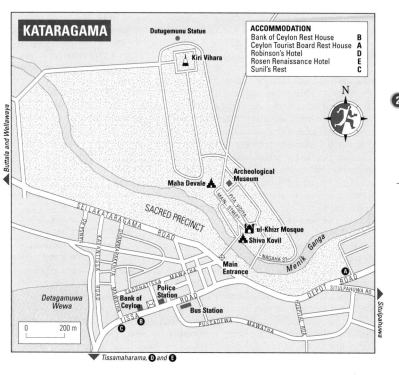

the end of the festival, the waters of the Menik Ganga are "cut" with a sword, symbolizing (according to different interpretations) either the division of the pure and impure, or the washing of the god's clothes, or the invocation of rain for the harvest. During the festival devotees flock to the town from all over Sri Lanka, some walking along the various pilgrimage routes which converge on Kataragama from distant parts of the island – the most famous route, the **Pada Yatra**, leads all the way down the east coast from Jaffna, through the jungles of Yala, and is still tackled by those seeking especial religious merit. Most of today's visitors, however, come on the bus.

The Town and Sacred Precinct

Kataragama town spreads out over a small grid of tranquil, leafy streets – outside poya days and puja times, the whole place is incredibly sleepy and peaceful, and its quiet streets offer a welcome alternative to the dusty mayhem that usually passes for urban life in Sri Lanka. During evening pujas, Kataragama is transformed, with throngs of pilgrims and streets of brightly illuminated stalls stuffed full of garlands, fruit platters and other colourful religious paraphernalia.

The town is separated by the Menik Ganga ("Gem River") from the so-called **Sacred Precinct** to the north, an area of beautiful parkland overrun by inquisitive grey langurs and dotted with myriad shrines; pilgrims take a ritual bath in the river before entering the precinct itself. The first buildings you'll encounter are the **ul-Khizr mosque** and the adjacent **Shiva Kovil** – the former houses the tombs of saints from Kyrgyzstan and India and is the main focus of Muslim devotions in Kataragama, although there's not much to see.

Continue up the main avenue, past a string of gaudy minor shrines, to reach the principal complex, the **Maha Devale**. This exhibits a quintessentially Sri Lankan intermingling of Hindu and Buddhist, with deities and iconography from each religion – trying to work out where one religion begins and the other ends is virtually impossible, and certainly not something which troubles the pilgrims who flock here every night. The main courtyard is surrounded by an impressive wall decorated with elephant heads, and is entered through an ornate metal gate – both wall and gate are decorated with peacocks, a symbol of the god Kataragama. Inside are three main shrines. Directly opposite the entrance gate is the **principal shrine**, that of Kataragama himself, its walls decorated with pink lotuses, green bo leaves and elephants, and its entrance secured with ornate silver doors bearing a massive padlock – despite the lavish detail, however, it's a surprisingly small affair. Kataragama **himself** is represented inside not by an image, but simply by his principal symbol of a *vel*, or trident. The two rather plain adjacent shrines are devoted to **Ganesh**, often invoked as an intermediary with the fearsome Shiva, and the **Buddha**.

Outside the door into the Kataragama shrine are two **stones** surrounded by railings, one marked by a trident, the other with a spear – supplicants bring coconuts here as offerings to Kataragama, setting fire to the coconut first, then holding it aloft while saying a prayer, before smashing it to pieces on one of the stones. It's considered extremely inauspicious if your coconut fails to break when you throw it on the stone, which explains the concentration and determination with which visitors perform the ritual. To the side of the three shrines stand two fine Bo trees, the larger surrounded by golden rails and an elephant wall, while to the north of the main enclosure stands a secondary complex of subsidiary shrines, including ones to Vishnu and Kataragama's wife, Valli Amma.

Next to the Maha Devale, the modest **Archeological Museum** (no set hours; donation; remove footwear) features huge fibreglass replicas of religious sculptures from various places in the island, along with other bits of religious

The evening puja

Kataragama's Sacred Precinct springs to life at **puja** times. Flocks of pilgrims appear bearing the fruit platters as offerings to Kataragama, and many smash coconuts in front of his shrine. According to tradition, if the coconut breaks cleanly down the middle, a wish will be granted; misfortune attends those whose coconut fails to break. As puja time approaches, a long queue of pilgrims line up to present their offerings, while a priest makes a drawn-out sequence of obeisances in front of the curtained shrine and a huge ringing of bells fills the temple. Meanwhile, musicians playing oboe-like instruments, trumpets and drums perambulate around the complex, followed by groups of pilgrims performing the **kavadi**, or peacock dance, spinning around like dervishes whilst carrying *kavadi*s, the semicircular hoops studded with peacock feathers after which the dance is named – the music is strangely jazzy, and the dancers spin with such fervour that it's not unusual to see one or two of the more enthusiastic collapsing in a dead faint on the ground. Eventually the main Kataragama shrine is opened to the waiting pilgrims, who enter to deposit their offerings and pay homage to the god, while others pray at the adjacent Buddha shrine or bo trees.

The evening puja starts at around 7.30pm, though it's worth arriving by not later than 7pm if you want to watch the whole build-up. There's another early-morning puja at around 5am (except on Saturdays), and a mid-morning one at around 10.30am, though these are pretty low-key compared to the evening ceremonies.

statuary and paraphernalia – conch shells, stone figurines; it's all mildly interesting, although in anticipation of a tip the resident staff will insist on trying to "explain" everything for you using their three words of English.

From the rear of the Maha Devale, a road leads 500m past further lines of stalls selling lotus flowers to the **Kiri Vihara**, an alternative focus for Buddhist devotions at Kataragama – it's basically just a big dagoba, its only unusual feature being the two sets of square walls which enclose it – but it's a peaceful place, surrounded by parkland and usually far less busy than the Maha Devale. A modern statue of King Dutugemunu stands just behind.

Practicalities

Kataragama is a thirty- or forty-minute bus journey north of Tissa. The **bus station** is right in the centre of town on the Tissa Road, a five-minute walk south of the temples. There's a Bank of Ceylon just west of the bus station where you can **change money** (but no ATM for foreign cards); the **post office** is next door.

Interesting **eating** options in Kataragama are totally nonexistent. The town's religious bent is reflected by the unusually high number of exclusively vegetarian places – but don't get too excited, this basically just means the usual rice and curry minus any form of fish or meat.

Accommodation

It's best to book ahead during the Kataragama festival, although at other times you shouldn't have problems finding a bed. If you do get stuck, there are numerous rather scruffy little flophouses, aimed at local pilgrims, dotted around town.

Bank of Ceylon Rest House Tissa Rd ☎047-223 5229. Rooms here are very good-value: clean, quiet and spacious, with nice private balconies and hill views. Technically you have to book in advance in Colombo on ☎011-254 4315, though if there are vacancies you'll be allowed in without a prior reservation. It's usually full at weekends and holidays, but there should be space at other times. ❶

Ceylon Tourist Board Rest House Depot Rd ☎047-223 5227. Large but peaceful place with very spacious, if rather bare and gloomy rooms (a few with a/c) – a reasonable fallback if you can't get into the Bank of Ceylon Rest House. No single rates. ❷

Robinson's Hotel Detagamuwa, 1km out of town on the road to Tissa ☎047-223 5175. Pleasant,

functional hotel in attractive garden setting, though some way out of town. ❷

Rosen Renaissance Hotel Detagamuwa, on the Tissa road 2km out of town ☎047-223 6030, ℮rosenr@sltnet.lk. A surprisingly smart and stylish hotel for sleepy Kataragama, and not at all the stuff of self-abnegating pilgrimage. The fifty a/c rooms come with all modcons including satellite TV, minibar and safe; there's also a gym, coffee shop, games room and three swimming pools (complete with underwater music). ❼

Sunil's Rest Tissa Rd ☎047-223 5300. Three very clean rooms (though one is rather small) in an attractive and friendly family guest house. No single rates. ❷

Travel details

Trains

The following timings are for express services. For timetables of services south from Colombo to Galle, and from Galle to Matara, see p.147.
Ahangama to: Aluthgama (5 daily; 2hr); Ambalangoda (5 daily; 1hr 30min); Colombo (5 daily; 3hr 15min); Galle (10 daily; 30min); Hikkaduwa (5 daily; 1hr 15min); Kalutara (5 daily; 2hr 30min); Matara (10 daily; 35min); Weligama (10 daily; 15min).
Galle to: Ahangama (10 daily; 30min); Aluthgama (11 daily; 1hr 30min); Ambalangoda (11 daily; 1hr); Colombo (11 daily; 3hr); Hikkaduwa (11 daily;

Express trains from Matara to Colombo

For services from Colombo to Matara, see p.147.

Matara	05.40	–	07.25 [+]	09.10	–	13.15	16.50
Weligama	05.57	–	07.49	09.30	–	13.35	17.10
Galle	06.45	07.40	09.05	10.40	14.10 [++]	14.45	18.05
Hikkaduwa	07.08	08.07	09.35	11.10	14.33	15.09	18.35
Ambalangoda	07.22	08.22	09.51	11.26	14.50	15.24	18.58
Aluthgama	07.55	08.46	10.25	11.55	15.30	15.55	19.38
Kalutara South	08.19	–	10.49	12.24	15.56	16.20	20.13
Colombo Fort	09.15	10.05	11.46	13.22	16.55	17.30	21.10

[+] = Mon–Fri only
[++] = Sun only

35–45min); Kalutara (11 daily; 2hr); Matara (10 daily; 1hr); Weligama (10 daily; 45min).
Matara to: Ahangama (10 daily; 35min); Aluthgama (5 daily; 2hr 30min); Ambalangoda (5 daily; 2hr); Colombo (5 daily; 4hr); Galle (10 daily; 1hr); Hikkaduwa (5 daily; 1hr 45min); Kalutara (5 daily; 3hr); Weligama (10 daily; 20min).
Weligama to: Ahangama (10 daily; 15min); Aluthgama (5 daily; 2hr 15min); Ambalangoda (5 daily; 1hr 45min); Colombo (5 daily; 3hr 45min); Galle (10 daily; 45min); Hikkaduwa (5 daily; 1hr 30min); Kalutara (5 daily; 2hr 45min); Matara (10 daily; 20min).

Buses

The timings given below are for the fastest express services, where they exist. Local buses are usually significantly slower, increasing journey times by anything up to fifty percent.
Galle to: Akuressa (every 30min; 45min); Aluthgama (15min; 1hr 30min); Badulla (1 daily; 8hr); Bandarawela (1 daily; 7hr); Colombo (every 15min; 2hr 30min); Hambantota (every 15min; 3hr); Haputale (1 daily; 6hr 30min); Hikkaduwa (every 15min; 30min); Matara (every 15min; 1hr); Nuwara Eliya (1–2 daily; 8hr); Tangalla (every 15min; 2hr); Tissamaharama (every 15min; 4hr); Weligama (every 15min; 40min).
Hambantota to: Colombo (every 15min; 6hr); Embilipitiya (every 15min; 1hr 30min); Galle (every

15min; 3hr); Matara (every 15min; 2hr 15min); Tangalla (every 15min; 1hr 15min); Tissamaharama (every 15min; 45min); Weligama (every 15min; 3hr).
Matara to: Akuressa (every 20min; 30min); Badulla (1 daily; 7hr); Bandarawela (3 daily; 6hr); Colombo (every 15min; 4hr); Deniyaya (4 daily; 2hr 30min); Embilipitiya (every 20min; 2hr 30min); Galle (every 15min; 1hr); Hambantota (every 15min; 2hr 15min); Monaragala (5 daily; 4hr); Nuwara Eliya (2 daily; 8hr); Ratnapura (4 daily; 5hr); Tangalla (every 15min; 1hr); Tissamaharama (every 15min; 3hr); Weligama (every 15min; 20min).
Tangalla to: Colombo (every 15min; 5hr); Embilipitiya (every 20min; 1hr 30min); Galle (every 15min; 2hr); Hambantota (every 15min; 1hr 15min); Matara (every 15min; 1hr); Tissamaharama (every 15min; 2hr); Weligama (every 15min; 1hr 20min).
Tissamaharama to: Colombo (every 15min; 7hr); Galle (every 15min; 4hr–4hr 30min); Hambantota (every 15min; 45min); Kataragama (every 10min; 40min); Matara (every 15min; 3hr); Monaragala (5 daily; 2hr); Tangalla (every 15min; 2hr); Weligama (every 15min; 3hr 20min); Wellawaya (hourly; 2hr).
Weligama to: Colombo (every 15min; 3hr 40min); Galle (every 15min; 40min); Hambantota (every 15min; 3hr); Matara (every 15min; 20min); Tangalla (every 15min; 1hr 20min); Tissamaharama (every 15min; 3hr 20min).

3

Kandy and the hill country

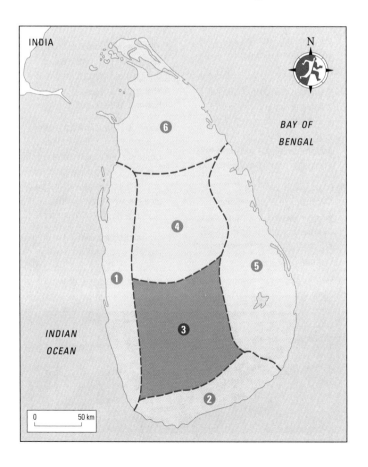

CHAPTER 3 # Highlights

✽ **Kandy** Hidden away amidst beautiful central highlands, historic Kandy remains the crucible of Sri Lanka's Sinhalese cultural traditions. **See p.208**

✽ **Esala Perahera, Kandy** Sri Lanka's most spectacular festival, honouring the Buddha's Tooth Relic with immense processions of drummers, dancers and richly caparisoned elephants. **See p.212**

✽ **Kandyan dancing** Watch a pulse-quickening display of Kandyan dancing, with fabulously costumed dancers accompanied by explosively energetic drumming. **See p.232**

✽ **Pinnewala Elephant Orphanage** Home to the world's largest troupe of captive pachyderms, from majestic old tuskers to the cutest of babies. **See p.242**

✽ **The Tea Factory** Stunning hotel set in a converted tea factory perched in a spectacular setting high amongst tea plantations near Nuwara Eliya. **See p.252**

✽ **Horton's Plains and World's End** Hike across the rain-swept moorlands of Horton's Plains to the vertiginous cliffs of World's End, which plunge sheer for almost a kilometre to the plains below. **See p.259**

✽ **Ella** The island's most beautiful village, with country walks through tea plantations and a string of excellent guest houses. **See p.262**

✽ **Adam's Peak** The ascent of Adam's Peak is the classic Sri Lankan pilgrimage, offering the island's most spectacular view and a peek at a footprint said to have been left by the Buddha himself. **See p.274**

✽ **Sinharaja** Comprising a unique tract of undisturbed tropical rainforest, Sinharaja is a botanical treasure-trove of international significance. **See p.285**

△ Train passing the Kotmale River, near Nuwara Eliya

Kandy and the hill country

O ccupying the island's southern heartlands, the sublime green heights of the **hill country** are a world away from the sweltering coastal lowlands – indeed nothing encapsulates the scenic diversity of Sri Lanka as much as the short journey by road or rail from the humid urban melee of Colombo to the cool altitudes of Kandy or Nuwara Eliya. The **landscape** here is a beguiling mixture of nature and nurture. In places the mountainous green hills rise to surprisingly rugged and dramatic peaks, whose craggy grandeur belies the island's modest dimensions; in others, the slopes are covered in carefully manicured tea gardens whose neatly trimmed lines of bushes add a toy-like quality, while the mist and clouds which frequently blanket the hills add a further layer of mystery.

The hill country has been shaped by two very different historical forces. The northern portion, around the historic city of **Kandy**, was home to Sri Lanka's last independent kingdom, which survived two centuries of colonial incursions before finally falling to the British at the beginning of the nineteenth century. The cultural legacy of this independent Sinhalese tradition lives on today in the city's distinctive music, dance and architecture, encapsulated by the **Temple of the Tooth**, home to the island's most revered Buddhist relic, and the exuberant **Kandy Esala Perahera**, one of Asia's most spectacular festivals. To the south lies **Adam's Peak**, whose rugged summit, bearing the imprint of what is claimed to be the Buddha's footprint, remains an object of pilgrimage for devotees of all four of the island's principal religions.

In contrast, the character of the southern hill country is largely a product of the British colonial era, when tea was introduced to the island, an industry which continues to shape the economy and scenery of the entire region. At the heart of the tea-growing uplands lies the town of **Nuwara Eliya**, which preserves a few quaint traces of its British colonial heritage and provides the best base for visiting the misty uplands of **Horton Plains** and **World's End**. To the south, in **Uva Province**, a string of small towns – **Ella**, **Bandarawela** and **Haputale** – offer marvellous views and walks through the hills and tea plantations. At the southwestern corner of the hill country lies the town of **Ratnapura**, the island's gem-mining centre and a possible base for visits to the national parks of **Sinharaja**, a rare and remarkable pocket of surviving tropical rainforest, and **Uda Walawe**, home to one of the island's largest elephant populations.

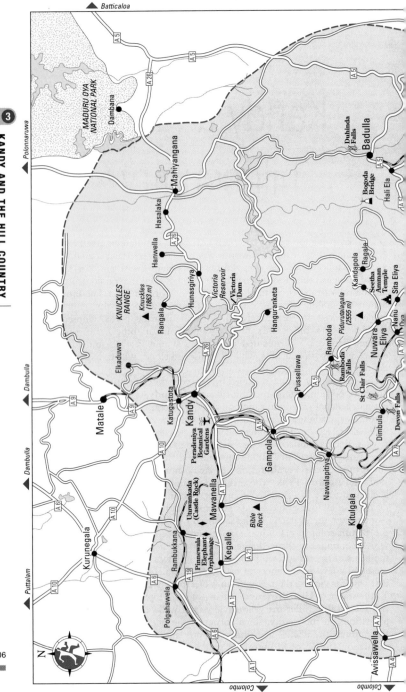

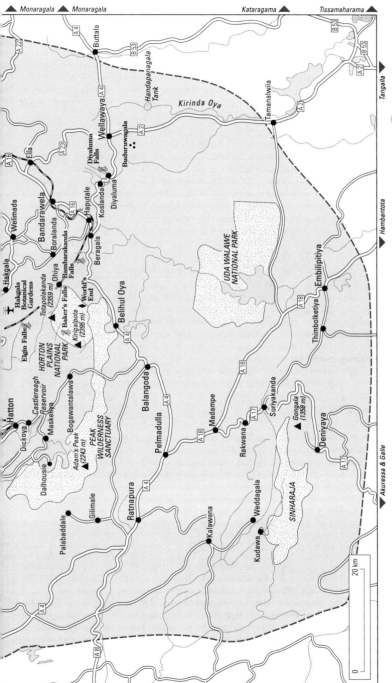

Tangalla ▶

Hambantota ▶

Akuressa & Galle ▶

A 22

A 4

Buttala

B 53

B 53

A 4

Handapanagala
Tank

Kirinda Oya

A 2

B 53

A 2

Wellawaya

A 4

Tamanalwila

Ella

A 16

A 23

Diyaluma
Falls

Badurwagala

Welimada

Bandarawela

A 16

Haputale

Koslanda

Diyaluma

Boralanda

Boralanda

Beragala

UDA WALAWE
NATIONAL PARK

Hakgala

Hakgala
Botanical
Gardens

Bambarakanda
Falls

Embilipitiya

Elgin Falls

Ohiya

Totapolakanda
(2359 m)

Baker's Falls

World's
End

Belihul Oya

A 4

Thimbolketiya

A 18

HORTON
PLAINS
NATIONAL
PARK

Kirigalpota
(2395 m)

Hatton

Castlereagh
Reservoir

Dickoya

Maskeliya

Bogawantalawa

Balangoda

A 4

Madampe

A 17

Suriyakanda

Gongala
(1358 m)

Deniyaya

A 18

A 17

PEAK
WILDERNESS
SANCTUARY

Adam's Peak
(2243 m)

Pelmadulla

A 18

Rakwana

Dalhouse

Palabaddale

Gilimale

Ratnapura

A 4

Kalawana

Weddagala

SINHARAJA

A 8

A 4

Kudawa

20 km

0

Kandy and around

Situated amidst precipitous green hills at the heart of the island, **KANDY** is the proud bastion of an independent Sinhalese tradition which preserved its freedom through two and a half centuries of attacks by the Portuguese and Dutch. Kandy's unique cultural heritage is everywhere apparent – in its music, dance and architecture – while the city is also home to the country's most important religious shrine, the **Temple of the Tooth**, as well as its most exuberant festival, the **Esala Perahera**. Kandy maintains a somewhat aristocratic air, enhanced by its scenic highland setting and its pleasantly temperate climate. And though the modern city, Sri Lanka's second largest, has begun to sprawl considerably, the twisted topography of the surrounding hills and the lake at its centre ensure that Kandy hasn't yet overwhelmed its scenic setting, and retains at its heart a modest grid of narrow, low-rise streets which, despite the crowds of people and traffic, retains a surprisingly small-town atmosphere.

The beautiful countryside **around Kandy** is home to a wealth of varied attractions. Most visitors head straight for the world-famous **Pinnewala Elephant Sanctuary** and the beautiful **Peradeniya Botanical Gardens**, while the region's cultural legacy can be traced in the various beautiful **temples**, dating from the heyday of the Kandyan kingdom, which dot the countryside. If you really want to get away from it all, the rugged **Knuckles Range**, just east of Kandy, is the hill country's last great wilderness area and a wonderful location for trekking, cycling and bird-spotting.

Some history

Kandy owes its existence to its remote and easily defensible location amidst the steep, jungle-swathed hills at the centre of the island. The origins of the city date back to the early thirteenth century, during the period following the collapse of Polonnaruwa, when the Sinhalese people drifted gradually southwards across the island (see p.416). During this migration, a short-lived capital was established at **Gampola**, just south of Kandy, before the ruling dynasty soon moved on to Kotte, near present-day Colombo. A few nobles left behind in Gampola soon revolted, and some time during the fifteenth century moved their base to the still more remote and easily defended town of **Senkadagala**. Senkadagala subsequently became known by the sweet-sounding name of **Kandy**, after Kanda Uda Pasrata, the Sinhalese name for the mountainous district in which it lay (although from the eighteenth century, the Sinhalese often referred to the city as **Maha Nuwara**, the "Great City", a name by which it's still sometimes known today).

By the time the Portuguese arrived in Sri Lanka in 1591, Kandy had established itself as the capital of the island's three main kingdoms (along with Kotte and Jaffna). The Portuguese swiftly turned their attentions to Kandy, though their first expedition against the city ended in failure when the puppet ruler they placed on the throne was ousted by the formidable **Vimala Dharma Surya**, the first of many Kandyan rulers who tenaciously resisted the European invaders. As the remainder of the island fell to the Portuguese (and subsequently the Dutch), the Kandyan kingdom clung stubbornly to its independence, remaining a secretive and inward-looking place, protected by its own inaccessibility – Kandyan kings repeatedly issued orders prohibiting the construction of bridges or the widening of footpaths into the city, fearing that they would become conduits for foreign attack. The city was repeatedly besieged and captured by the Portuguese (in 1594, 1611, 1629 and 1638) and the Dutch (in 1765), but each time the Kandyans foiled their attackers by burning the city to the ground and retreating into the surrounding forests, from where they continued to harry the invaders until they were forced to withdraw to the coast.

Despite its isolation, the kingdom's prestige as the final bastion of Sinhalese independence was further enhanced during the seventeenth and eighteenth centuries by the presence of the **Tooth Relic** (see p.219), the traditional symbol of Sinhalese sovereignty, while an imposing temple, the **Temple of the Tooth**, was constructed to house the relic. It had long been their tradition to take South Indian brides descended from the great Vijayanagaran dynasty, and when the last Sinhalese king of Kandy, Narendrasinha, died in in 1739 without an heir, the crown passed to his Indian wife's brother, Sri Vijyaya Rajasinha (1739–47), so ending the Kandyan dynasty established by Vimala Dharma Suriya and ushering in a new Indian **Nayakkar** dynasty.

The Nakayyars embraced Buddhism and cleverly played on the rivalries of the local Sinhalese nobles who, despite their dislike of the foreign rulers, failed to unite behind a single local leader. In a characteristically Kandyan paradox, it was under the foreign Nayyakars that the city enjoyed its great Buddhist revival. **Kirti Sri Rajasinha** came to the throne in 1747 and began to devote himself – whether for political or spiritual reasons – to his adopted religion, reviving religious education, restoring and building temples and overseeing the reinvention of the **Esala Perahera** (see pp.212–213) as a Buddhist rather than a Hindu festival. These years saw the development of a distinctively Kandyan style of architecture and dance, a unique synthesis of local Sinhalese traditions and southern Indian styles.

Having gained control of the island in 1798, **the British** quickly attempted to rid themselves of this final remnant of Sinhalese independence, although their first expedition against the kingdom, in 1803, resulted in a humiliating defeat. Despite this initial reverse, the kingdom survived little more than a decade, though it eventually fell not through military conquest but thanks to internal opposition to the excesses and cruelties of the last king of Kandy, **Sri Wickrama Rajasinha** (ruled 1798–1815; see box on p.220). As internal opposition to Sri Wickrama grew, the remarkable **Sir John D'Oyly**, a British government servant with a talent for languages and intrigue, succeeded in uniting the various factions opposed to the king. In 1815, the British were able to despatch another army which, thanks to D'Oyly's machinations, was able to march on Kandy unopposed. Sri Wickrama fled, and when the British arrived, the king's long-suffering subjects simply stood to one side and let them in. On **March 2, 1815**, a convention of Kandyan chiefs signed a document handing over sovereignty of the kingdom to the British, who in return promised to preserve its laws, customs and institutions.

Within two years, however, the Kandyans had decided they had had enough of their new rulers and **rebelled**, an uprising which soon spread across the entire hill country. The British were obliged to call for troops from India and exert their full military might in order to put down the uprising. Fears of resurgent Kandyan nationalism continued to haunt the British during the following decades – it was partly the desire to be able to move troops quickly to Kandy which prompted the construction of the first road to the city in the 1820s, one of the marvels of Victorian engineering in Sri Lanka. Despite the uncertain political climate, Kandy soon developed into an important centre of British rule and trade, with the usual hotels, courthouses and churches

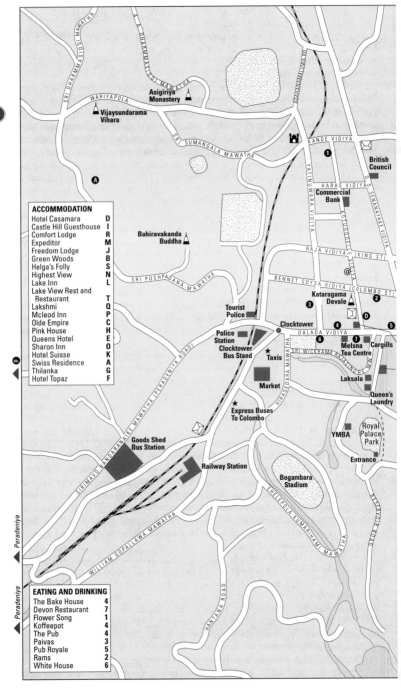

ACCOMMODATION

Hotel Casamara	D
Castle Hill Guesthouse	I
Comfort Lodge	R
Expeditor	M
Freedom Lodge	J
Green Woods	B
Helga's Folly	S
Highest View	N
Lake Inn	L
Lake View Rest and Restaurant	T
Lakshmi	Q
Mcleod Inn	P
Olde Empire	C
Pink House	H
Queens Hotel	E
Sharon Inn	O
Hotel Suisse	K
Swiss Residence	A
Thilanka	G
Hotel Topaz	F

EATING AND DRINKING

The Bake House	4
Devon Restaurant	7
Flower Song	1
Koffeepot	4
The Pub	4
Paivas	3
Pub Royale	5
Rams	2
White House	6

Asigiriya Monastery

Vijaysundarama Vihara

Wariyapola

Sri Dharmasidoi Mawatha

A.A. Dharmawijaya Mawatha

Kande Vidiya

British Council

Sri Sumangala Mawatha

Yatinuwara Vidiya

Das Senanayake Vidiya

Haras Vidiya

Commercial Bank

A

1

Bahiravakanda Buddha

Sri Pushpadana Mawatha

Raja Vidiya (King St)

Bennet Soysa Vidiya (Colombo St)

@

Kataragama Devale

2

3

Tourist Police

D

Police Station

Clocktower Bus Stand

Clocktower

Dalada Vidiya

4

5

6

7

Melsna Tea Centre

Cargills

Sri Wickrama Rajasinch...

Hiragedara Mawatha

Taxis

Market

Laksala

Queen's Laundry

Express Buses To Colombo

Sirimavo Bandaranaike Mawatha (Peradeniya Road)

Goods Shed Bus Station

Railway Station

YMBA

Royal Palace Park

Entrance

Bogambara Stadium

Ehelepola Kumarihami Mawatha

Keshevrina Hill

William Gopallawa Mawatha

Hantana Road

Peradeniya

Peradeniya

Peradeniya

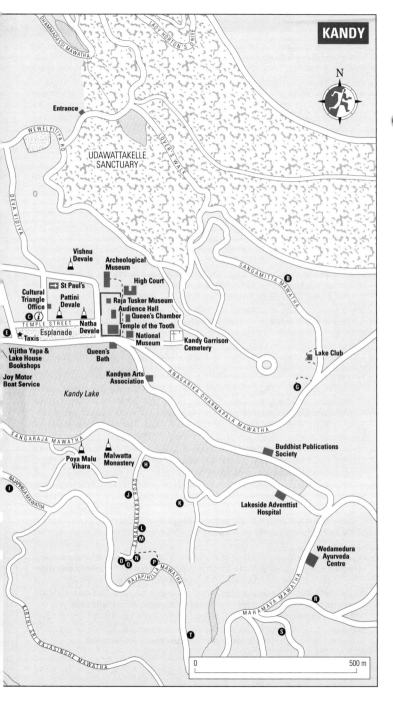

KANDY

N

Entrance

DHAMMADASSI MAWATHA

LADY HORTON'S DRIVE

WEWELPITIYA RD

UDAWATTAKELLE
SANCTUARY

DEVA VIDIYA

LOVER'S WALK

SANGAMITTA MAWATHA

B

**Vishnu
Devale**

**Archeological
Museum**

High Court

**Cultural
Triangle
Office**

St Paul's

**Pattini
Devale**

C (i)

TEMPLE STREET

**Natha
Devale**

E ★ **Taxis**

Esplanade

Raja Tusker Museum

Audience Hall

Queen's Chamber

Temple of the Tooth

**National
Museum**

**Kandy Garrison
Cemetery**

Lake Club

**Vijitha Yapa &
Lake House
Bookshops**

**Joy Motor
Boat Service**

**Queen's
Bath**

**Kandyan Arts
Association**

G

ANAGARIKA DHARMAPALA MAWATHA

Kandy Lake

SANGARAJA MAWATHA

**Buddhist Publications
Society**

**Poya Malu
Vihara**

**Malwatta
Monastery**

H

RAJAPIHILLA MAWATHA

I

J

K

L

M

O **N**

P

RAJAPIHILLA MAWATHA

**Lakeside Adventtist
Hospital**

**Wedamedura
Ayurveda
Centre**

S RAVANKARI ROAD

KIRTHI SRI RAJASINGHE MAWATHA

MAHAMAYA MAWATHA

R

T

S

0   500 m

3

211

The Esala Perahera

Held over the ten days leading up to the full moon during the lunar month of Esala (July to August), Kandy's **Esala Perahera** is the most spectacular of Sri Lanka's festivals, and one of the most colourful religious pageants in Asia. Its origins date back to the arrival of the **Tooth Relic** (see p.219) in Sri Lanka in the fourth century AD, during the reign of Kirti Siri Meghawanna, who decreed that the relic be carried in procession through the city once a year. This quickly developed into a major religious event – the famous Chinese Buddhist Fa Hsien, visiting Anuradhapura in 399 AD, described what had become a splendid festival, with processions of jewel-encrusted elephants.

Occasional literary and artistic references suggest that these celebrations continued in some form throughout the thousand years of upheaval which followed the collapse of Anuradhapura and the Tooth Relic's peripatetic journey around the island (see p.219). Esala processions continued into the Kandyan era in the seventeenth century, though the Tooth Relic lost its place in the procession, which evolved into a series of lavish parades in honour of the city's four principal deities: Vishnu, Kataragama, Natha and Pattini, each of whom had (and still has) a temple in the city.

The modern festival took shape in 1775, during the reign of **Kirti Sri Rajasinha**, when a group of visiting Thai clerics expressed their displeasure at the lack of reverence accorded to the Buddha himself during the festival. To propitiate them, the king ordered the Tooth Relic to be carried through the city at the head of the four temple processions, establishing the pattern which endures to this day. Sri Rajasinha's own enthusiastic participation in the celebrations, and that of his successors, also added a political dimension to the festival – the Nayyakar kings of Kandy (who were from South India) probably encouraged the festival in the belief that by associating themselves with one of Buddhism's most sacred relics they would reinforce their dynasty's shaky legitimacy in the eyes of their Sinhalese subjects. The Tooth Relic itself was last carried in procession in 1848, since when it's been considered unpropitious for the relic to leave the temple sanctuary – its place is now taken by an empty casket.

The festival

The ten days of the festival begin with the **Kap Tree Planting Ceremony**, during which cuttings from a tree – traditionally an Esala tree, though nowadays a Jak or Rukkattana are more usually employed – are planted in the four devales (see p.226), representing a vow (*kap*) that the festival will be held. The procession (*perahera*) through the streets of Kandy is held nightly throughout the festival: the first five nights are relatively low key; during the final five nights, the **Randoli Perahera**, things become progressively more spectacular, building up to the last night, featuring a massive cast of participants including fifty or sixty brilliantly caparisoned elephants and thousands of drummers, dancers and acrobats walking on stilts, cracking whips, swinging fire pots and carrying banners, while the replica casket of the Tooth Relic itself is carried on the back of the **Maligawa Tusker** elephant (see p.224).

Following the last perahera, the **water-cutting ceremony** is held before the dawn of the next day at a venue near Kandy, during which a priest wades out into the Mahaweli Ganga and "cuts" the waters with a sword. This ceremony symbolically releases a supply of water for the coming year (the Tooth Relic is traditionally believed to protect against drought) and divides the pure from the impure – it might also relate to the exploits of the early Sri Lankan king, **Gajabahu** (reigned 174–196 AD), who is credited with the Moses-like feat of dividing the waters between Sri Lanka and India in order to march his army across during his campaign against the Cholas.

After the water-cutting ceremony, at 3pm on the same day, there's a final **"day" perahera**, a slightly scaled-down version of the full perahera. It's not as spectacular as the real thing, though it does offer excellent photo opportunities.

The procession

The perahera is a carefully orchestrated, quasi-theatrical event – there is no spectator participation here, although the astonishing number of performers during later nights give the impression that most of Kandy's citizens are involved. The perahera actually comprises five separate processions, which follow one another around the city streets: one from the Temple of the Tooth, and one from each of the four devales. The exact route changes from day to day, although the procession from the Temple of the Tooth always leads the way, followed (in unchanging order) by the processions from the Natha, Vishnu, Kataragama and Pattini devales (Natha, as a Buddha-to-be, takes precedence over the other divinities). Each procession has as its centrepiece an elephant carrying the insignia of the relevant temple – or, in the case of the Temple of the Tooth, the replica Tooth Relic. Each is accompanied by other elephants, various dignatories dressed in traditional Kandyan costume, and myriad dancers and drummers, who fill the city streets with an extraordinary barrage of noise. Each procession follows a broadly similar pattern, although there are slight differences. The Kataragama procession – as befits that rather unruly god (see p.198) – tends to be the wildest and most freeform, with jazzy trumpet playing and dozens of whirling dancers carrying *kavadis*, the hooped wooden contrivances, studded with peacock feathers, which are one of that god's symbols. The Pattini procession, the only one devoted to a female deity, attracts mainly female dancers. The beginning and end of each perahera is signalled by a deafening cannon shot.

Perahera practicalities

The exact **dates** of the festival vary from year to year, but usually fall sometime in early August. You can check at Ⓦwww.sridaladamaligawa.lk, which also has lots of background information on the festival. **Accommodation** during the Esala Perahera gets booked up months in advance, and prices triple or quadruple – reserve a room as far ahead as you can. If you don't have a reservation, don't despair. Many locals rent out rooms in their homes during the festival – the tourist office (see p.214) should be able to help you out, but try to arrive as early in the day as possible; if you turn up late afternoon you might end up sleeping on a pavement somewhere. Note that the entire city more or less shuts down during the latter stages of the perahera. From mid-afternoon the centre fills with spectators, the streets are cordoned off and all businesses shut up shop.

The perahera itself begins between 8pm and 9pm. You can either claim a space on the pavement or pay to use one of the myriad seats which are set out along the route – virtually every house and shop in town crams its windows and balconies with seats, sometimes in unnervingly precarious positions. During the early days of the perahera it's fairly easy to find a space on the pavement; during the last few nights, however, you'll have to arrive four or five hours in advance. Unless you're prepared to spend this amount of time sitting immobile on a tiny square of tarmac with the locals, it's easier to pay for a seat, although you'll still have to be in it a couple of hours before the perahera begins or you risk not being able to get through the crowds which throng the pavements. **Seats can be reserved** through your hotel or guest house, the tourist office or, most easily, through touts on the street – even on the busiest nights, you should be able to find a seat by just turning up a couple of hours before the procession begins. On the later nights seats start at around US$10 and go up to US$60 or so for the very best street-level spots. There's reasonable scope for bargaining. Always check exactly which seat you're being offered before handing over any cash.

One other last thing worth doing during the festival is to wander around the **devales** in the couple of hours before the procession begins. This offers a fascinating back-stage view of the perahera preparations, with crowds of elephants chained up around the temples, each stationed in front of a great mound of leaves, whilst crowds of drummers don their costumes and tune their instruments, and other participants busy themselves preparing the myriad items used in the festival.

servicing a burgeoning community of planters and traders. In 1867, the **railway** from Colombo was completed, finally transforming the once perilous trek from the coast into a comfortable four-hour journey, and so linking Kandy once and for all with the outside world.

Post-colonial Kandy has continued to expand, preserving its status as the island's second city despite remaining a modest little place compared to Colombo. It has also managed to largely avoid the Civil War conflicts which traumatized the capital, suffering only one major LTTE attack, in 1998, when a **truck bomb** was detonated outside the front of the Temple of the Tooth, killing over twenty people and reducing the front of the building to rubble.

Arrival and information

Kandy's **train** and **bus stations** sit next to one another on the southwest edge of the city centre – if coming from Colombo by train, be sure to sit on the south side of the train (the right side as you face the engine) to get the best views. A **tuktuk** from the bus or train station to all but the most far-flung of the town's guest houses shouldn't cost more than Rs.75, though you might have to bargain hard as drivers here are amongst the most rapacious in the island. There are also plenty of **taxis** in town (see p.233), though you'll really only need these for longer journeys – the city centre is extremely compact.

The **tourist office** on Temple Street (Mon–Fri 9am–4.45pm; ☏081-222 2661) is a useful source of information about the city and surrounding area, as well as latest bus timetables. The **Cultural Triangle Office** (daily 9am–4pm; head office in Colombo ☏011-250 0733) is housed in a Greek-style orange colonnaded building, signed "Central Cultural Fund", diagonally opposite the tourist office. You can buy Cultural Triangle tickets here (see p.296 for more details), and they also have a few books for sale on Kandy and Cultural Triangle sites.

Accommodation

There's a huge selection of **accommodation** in all price ranges in an around Kandy, ranging from the clusters of budget guest houses around the lake to the string of top-end hotels which dot the surrounding countryside – many of the smarter places listed below are featured on ⓦ www.kandyhotels.com. The **temperature** in Kandy is markedly cooler than along the coast – you probably won't need air conditioning, but you probably will want hot water (all the following places have this unless specifically stated otherwise). In general, the better the view, the further from town – and the more taxing the walk.

Meals are available at all the places listed below, and most can also arrange tours (see p.233 for more details).

Budget

Most of the town's budget accommodation is clustered on just two roads. The first, **Saranankara Road** (known as "Kandy Hikkaduwa" thanks to its dense concentration of inexpensive guest houses), climbs steeply up from the southern side of the lake, about ten minutes' walk from the town centre. There are some wonderful views from places towards the top of this road, but even finer vistas over the city and lake can be had from the various places scattered along **Rajapihilla Mawatha**, which winds erratically around the hillside above – there's a useful shortcut up to Rajapihilla Mawatha via the steps from the lakeside to Royal Palace Park (see p.230), and another tiny footpath between the top of Saranankara Rd and Rajapihilla Mawatha.

Expeditor 41 Saranankara Rd ☏081-223 8316, ✉expeditorkandy@hotmail.com. Brand new guest house, owned and managed by Kandy's leading tour guide (see p.233) and with a range of cosy rooms of varying standards and prices. Good home cooking. ❶–❸

Freedom Lodge 30 Saranankara Rd ☏081-222 3506, ✉freedom@sltnet.lk. Good-value family guest house, with four comfy, nicely furnished rooms; two are right inside the family house, however, so have all the privacy of a goldfish bowl. ❷

Green Woods 34a Sangamitta Mw ☏081-223 2970. A real rural retreat, run by a charming owner and set in an attractive modern building in a beautifully secluded setting overlooking Udawattakele Sanctuary, whose birdlife can be ogled for free from the verandah. Rooms are fairly simple but perfectly comfortable, although only two have hot water. ❷

Highest View 129/3 Saranankara Rd ☏081-223 3778, ☏081-223 3778. At the top of Saranankara Rd, with wonderful views down to the lake and Temple of the Tooth. Rooms, all with private balconies, are very modern, smart, and sparklingly clean, though on the small side. There are also a few good-value budget rooms without views. No single rates. ❷–❸

Lake Inn 43 Saranankara Rd ☏081-222 2208, ✉matsui@slt.lk. Long-established guest house towards the top of Saranankara Rd, with a fine view of lake and town from the communal balcony. Rooms are clean and fairly modern, although there's a slightly institutional feel. ❸

Lake View Rest and Restaurant 71a Rajapihilla Mw ☏081-223 9420, ⊕www.lakeviewrest.info. Biggish guest house in a sublime position high above Kandy, with jaw-dropping views to lake and city below. Rooms (twins or doubles) are

comfortable and reasonable value, if unexceptional, and all have some sort of view. ❷

Lakshmi 57 Saranankara Rd ☏081-222 2154. One of the cheapest in town, with ten simple but large, clean and quite bright rooms. It's all a bit bare and there's no hot water, but it's OK at the price. Not much English spoken. ❶

Mcleod Inn 65a Rajapihilla Mw ☏081-222 2832. Kandy's best bargain, perched in a peerless location high above town. The six rooms are clean, modern, spacious, and excellent value; two of them have views to dream of through enormous French windows, as does the dining room. ❷

Olde Empire 21 Temple St ☏081-222 4284. Set behind a balconied colonial entrance, this venerable establishment is the only cheapie in the city centre, with a charmingly antiquated wood-panelled interior and six basic white rooms, reasonably clean and very good value. All share an OK bathroom. Also home to a characterful little bar-restaurant (see p.232). ❶

Pink House 15 Saranankara Rd ☏077-764 7468. Long-established, popular and sociable ultra-cheapie in a quaint if rather battered old house. The eight very basic and rather run-down rooms share two communal bathrooms; there's also one en-suite room. It's all pretty down at heel, but OK at the price, which is one of the cheapest in town. ❶

Sharon Inn 59 Saranankara Rd ☏081-222 2416, ✉sharon@sltnet.lk. The smartest and best set up of the Saranankara Rd guest houses, slightly more expensive but well worth the extra rupees. It's set right at the top of the road, with ten modern, nicely furnished rooms in a bright, white and scrupulously clean guest house; all rooms have marvellous bird's eye views over the town from private balconies. There's also Internet access, communal satellite TV and excellent rice and curry. ❸

Moderate and expensive

There's a further selection of mid- and top-end options in the countryside around Kandy; see overleaf.

Hotel Casamara 12 Kotugodelle Vidiya ☏081-222 4688, ✉casamara@sri.lanka.net. Bang in the city centre, this recently refurbished hotel doesn't look like much from the outside, but offers smart modern rooms with a/c, satellite TV and minibar – at an excellent price. The rooftop bar has a good view down into the hive of city streets below. ❹

Castle Hill Guest house 22 Rajapihilla Mw ☏081-222 4376, ✉ayoni@sltnet.lk. Colonial villa

perched in solitary splendour directly above the lake and town, offering one of the best of Kandy's many memorable views. Set in gorgeous gardens, the house itself has bags of character, although the four rooms are rather bare – and big enough to swing a sackful of cats in. ❹

Comfort Lodge 197 Rajapihilla Mw ☏081-447 3707, ✉comfort@sri.lanka.net. Pleasant if totally anonymous mid-range place with six functional and comfortable modern rooms, with nice balconies overlooking an attractive garden (but no real views), plus satellite TV, phone and cheap Internet access. ❹

Helga's Folly Off Mahamaya Mw ☏ 081-223 4571, ⓦ www.helgasfolly.com. Utterly maverick and magical place, set high above Kandy in the palatial former home of Sri Lanka Independence hero George E. de Silva – former house guests have included Gandhi, Nehru and Laurence Olivier. The extraordinary interior is a riot of colourful invention, with each room decorated in a different theme and colour, from the eye-popping yellow lounge, with petrified dripping candles, deer heads, Indonesian puppets, and colonial photos, to the individual bedrooms, each with a unique design featuring any combination of wacky murals, colonial furniture and unusual objets d'art. The overall effect is entirely quirky and captivating, although the charm doesn't come cheap. There's also a shallow swimming pool (non-guests Rs.150). No single rates. Standard rooms ❼, budget rooms ❻

Queens Hotel ☏ 081-222 2813, ⓦ www.ccom.lk/suisse. Dating back to the 1860s, this venerable hotel is one of central Kandy's most famous landmarks, and still has plenty of style, with smart staff, grand, high-ceilinged corridors and a gorgeous antique lift. The spacious rooms (most with a/c, TV and minibar) have plenty of colonial character, but almost all overlook busy roads and suffer from noise. Decent value nonetheless, and there's a pool (non-guests Rs.100). Breakfast included. ❺

Swiss Residence ☏ 081-447 9055, ⓦ www.jetwinghotels.com. Smart modern hilltop hotel at the summit of Sri Lanka's steepest driveway, with great views fore and aft over town and country. The forty rooms (with or without a/c) are bright, modern and comfortable; the slightly larger deluxe ones come with bathtub and TV. There's good food, plus the added attraction of Kandy's only nightclub, the *Blackout* (Fri & Sat) and a pool (non-guests Rs.75). No single rates. ❼

Hotel Suisse ☏ 081-223 3024, ⓦ www.ccom.lk/suisse. Famous old hotel – it served as Mountabatten's Southeast Asian headquarters during World War II – and still one of the nicest in Kandy. Rooms (some lake facing; all with a/c, minibar and satellite TV) are spacious and comfortable, with shiny parquet floors and vaguely colonial decor. The attractive public areas include a cosy bar, a restaurant set in the cavernous and atmospheric old ballroom, a billiards room and a pool (non-guests Rs.100). ❻

Thilanka 3 Sangamitta Mw ☏ 081-223 2429, ⓦ www.thilanka.com. Set high above the lake, with outstanding views and a large neon sign which disfigures the Kandyan skyline on a nightly basis. The good-value standard rooms are attractively old fashioned; deluxe a/c ones are smarter but more anonymous. The emphasis is on traditional Sri Lankan pleasures (yoga classes and a serene and reasonably priced ayurveda centre), plus there's the most spectacularly situated swimming pool in town (non-guests Rs.100). Standard rooms ❺, deluxe ❻

Hotel Topaz Anniewatte, about 1.5km from centre ☏ 081-222 4150, ⓔ topaz@eureka.lk. Set atop one of the biggest hills in town and with a vertiginous, top-of-the-world feeling and immense vistas into the surrounding hills. The hotel itself is rather sterile, and much favoured by package groups; rooms are plush, comfortable and cheerfully bland; all come with a/c, TV and private balconies. There's a free shuttle bus to town, plus a big swimming pool (non-guests Rs.125). ❼

Around Kandy

The marvellous countryside around Kandy is home to a string of smart resort hotels. All are attractively located and offer top-notch comforts, though they're all much of a muchness, with the exception of the eco-oriented *Hunas Falls* and the intimate *Stone House Lodge*.

The following hotels are marked on the map on p.236.

The Citadel 5km west of Kandy ☏ 081-223 4365, ⓦ www.johnkeellshotels.com. Occupying an attractive perch above the Mahaweli Ganga – this large complex is the cheapest of the big hotels around Kandy, and popular with tour parties. The deluxe rooms are attractively kitted out with Kandyan fabrics, and there's a large pool. ❼

Earl's Regency 4km east of Kandy ☏ 081-242 2122, ⓦ www.aitkenspenceholidays.com. In a stunning position overlooking the Mahaweli Ganga, this large and well-run establishment is one of only two five-star hotels in the hill country. The main building houses stylish executive rooms, with marvellous hill or river views; the second block has slightly cheaper and less memorable deluxe rooms; all have TV, minibar, safe and phone, and there's also a good-sized swimming pool, an ayurveda centre, gym and health centre. ❽

Kandy is the best place in Sri Lanka to study **meditation**. The following are the main centres.

Nilambe Meditation Centre Office ☎081-222 5471; centre ☎077-780 4555 (best to ring centre between 6pm and 8pm). Sri Lanka's most famous meditation centre, and the place most used to dealing with – and most popular among – foreign visitors. It's set in a beautifully tranquil spot in the hills near Galaha (around 22km from Kandy), and there's little to disturb you, since there's no electricity and just a single mobile phone. You can just turn up (though you might prefer to ring in advance just to be sure there's space) and there's no minimum length of stay, though obviously you'll have to spend at least a couple of nights to get anything out of the experience. The cost is Rs.400 per day, including basic food and lodging. All levels are welcome, from novices to experienced meditators, and there's a qualified teacher on hand, plus a library and meditation tapes. Days begin at 4.45am and comprise a mixture of solo and group meditation sessions and some practical manual labour around the centre. To reach the centre, take the Galaha bus from Kandy and ask the conductor to put you off at the junction with the road up to the centre, from where it's a 45-minute walk. Bring a torch and comfortable loose clothing.

Sri Jemieson International Meditation Centre ☎081-222 5057. Set in a temple 4km outside Kandy, and catering to all standards; women aren't allowed to stay overnight, but are welcome to attend during the day until 4.30pm. You can just turn up, but you'll be expected to do at least three days. It's free (but you can – and should – make a donation) and you're given local food. To reach the centre take the Ampitiya or Talatu Oya bus or a tuktuk (around Rs.100); it's past the seminary near the third kilometre post.

Hunas Falls Elkaduwa, 27km north of Kandy ☎081-247 0041, ⓦwww.jetwinghotels.com. This comfortable modern hotel is the most appealing of the big establishments hereabouts, set in a wonderfully rural location up against the flanks of the Knuckles Ranges, with a strong ecotourism focus and walks led by an expert resident guide. Rooms are functional but bland. ❽

Le Kandyan 7km southwest from Kandy ☎081-223 3521, ⓦwww.connaissanceceylon .com. The highest hotel in the immediate vicinity of Kandy, this large pink hotel seems to float in the clouds, with superlative views out over the hills. The themed Kandyan decor is reasonably stylish (although the restaurant is naff), and the rooms pleasantly anonymous. There's a large pool (though it's quite cool up here) and a gorgeous-smelling ayurveda centre. ❻

Mahaweli Reach 4km north of the city ☎081-447 2727, ⓦwww.mahaweli.com. One of the hill country's two five-star places (alongside *Earl's Regency*), this big, glizty white palace offers all the creature comforts you'd expect, in a fine setting by the Mahaweli Ganga. ❽

Stone House Lodge 42 Nittawella Rd, 2.5km north of town ☎081-223 2769, ⓔstonehse@sltnet.lk. Small upmarket guest house in a laid-back semi-rural setting, with an intimate and welcoming atmosphere and wonderful views of the hills from the immaculate garden. The four rooms are beautifully furnished in colonial style – and the master bedroom is a real work of art. ❻–❼

The City

Kandy's centrepiece is its large artificial **lake**, created in 1807 by Sri Wickrama Rajasinha in an area of the town previously used for paddy fields. Although nowadays considered one of Kandy's defining landmarks, the lake was regarded by the city's put-upon inhabitants as a huge white elephant at the time of its creation, and proof of their king's unbridled delusions of grandeur – a number of his subjects who objected to labouring on this apparently useless project were impaled on stakes on the bed of the lake. Rajasinha named the lake the

Kiri Muhuda, or Milk Sea, and established a royal pleasure house, or "harem", on the island in the centre, while the more practically minded British converted the island into an ammunition store, but also added the attractive walkway and parapet which encircles the lake. Despite the traffic which blights the southern shore (especially during Kandy's anarchic rush hour), the walk round the perimeter offers memorable views of the city, with the long white lakeside parapet framing perfect reflections of the Temple of the Tooth and old colonial buildings around the *Queen's Hotel*. If you want to get out onto the water, the **Joy Motor Boat Service** (daily 9am until 6pm or 8pm), at the western end of the lake, offers twenty-minute spins around the lake, or transfers to the *Hotel Suisse*, for Rs.150 per person.

On the south side of the lake, the **Malwatta Monastery** is one of the most important in Sri Lanka – the head of the monastery is one of the three religious dignitaries entrusted with a key to the casket in which the Tooth Relic is stored. Malwatta is reached from the lakeside through an impressive stone arch decorated with creatures both real (lions, geese, birds) and imaginary (toranas, centaurs). The drive leads to an octagonal tower, built in imitation of the Pittirippuva at the Temple of the Tooth, which faces it across the lake. Behind this lies the main **chapterhouse** (*poyage*), a solid-looking colonnaded building raised on a stone base and topped by a neat hipped roof; inside there's a stone pillared hall with a vividly painted ceiling and a seated Buddha. The chapterhouse is enclosed by further white monastic buildings. As an observer remarked in 1810, it's a pleasant spot, though the monastery isn't geared up to receiving tourists, and unless you arrive during puja time at around 6.45pm, everything will be shut. A tiny circular monks' bathing house stands right by the lakeside pavement.

A hundred metres along the lakeside road back towards town (go up the broad steps to the building signed Sri Sangharaja Maha Pirivena) are another cluster of monastic buildings belonging to the **Poya Malu Vihara**, including an interesting square colonnaded **image house**, with a colourfully painted upper storey and a finely carved stone doorway very similar to one at the Temple of the Tooth's main shrine.

The Temple of the Tooth

Posed artistically against the steep wooded hills of the Udawatakelle Sanctuary, Sri Lanka's most important Buddhist shrine, the **Temple of the Tooth**, or Dalada Maligawa (daily 6am–8pm; Rs.200, camera permit Rs.100; ⓦ www.sridaladamaligawa.lk), sits on the lakeshore just east of the city centre. The temple houses the legendary **Buddha's Tooth**, which arrived here in the sixteenth century after various peregrinations around India and Sri Lanka. Nothing remains of the original temple, built around 1600. The main shrine of the current temple was originally constructed during the reign of Vimala Dharma Suriya II (1687–1739) and was rebuilt and modified at various times afterwards, principally during the reign of Kirti Sri Rajasinha (1747–1781). It was further embellished during the reign of Sri Wickrama Rajasinha, who added the moat, gateway and Pittiripuwa; the eye-catching golden roof over the relic chamber was donated by President Premadasa in 1987.

The temple was badly damaged in 1998 when the LTTE detonated a massive **truck bomb** outside the entrance, killing over twenty people and reducing the facade to rubble – the Pittiripuwa was particularly badly damaged. Restoration work has been swift and thorough, and there's little visible evidence left of the attack, although crash barriers now prevent vehicular access to the temple, and all visitors have to pass through stringent security checks.

Guides of varying standards hang around at the entrance; count on around Rs.200 for a thirty-minute tour; some are very informative, but check how good their English is first. **Pujas** are held at 6am, 10am and 7pm (note that the temple operates its own archaic time zone, half an hour ahead of standard Sri Lankan time, according to which these times will be shown as 6.30am, 10.30am and 7.30pm). Tourists now tend to outnumber locals at the evening puja – you might prefer to go to one of the morning pujas. The main attraction of the puja is the noisy drumming which precedes and accompanies the ceremony, most of which is performed behind closed doors although at the end of the puja the upstairs room housing the Tooth Relic is opened to the public gaze. You're not actually allowed into the Tooth Relic chamber, but you are permitted to file past the entrance and look inside for a cursory glance at the big gold casket which holds the relic.

Note that buying a ticket for the temple also allows you access to the **Raja Tusker Museum** and **Audience Hall** (see p.224).

The Pittirippuva and outer buildings

The approach to the temple leads through two security checks and past flower stalls; there's often a temple elephant on duty here, too, posing for photographs.

The Buddha's Tooth

Legend has it when the Buddha was cremated in 543 BC at Kushinagar in north India, various parts of his remains were rescued from the fire, including one of his **teeth**. In the fourth century AD, as Buddhism was declining in India in the face of a Hindu revival, the Tooth was smuggled into Sri Lanka, hidden (according to legend) in the hair of an Orissan princess. It was first taken to Anuradhapura, then to Polonnaruwa, Dambedeniya and Yapahuwa. In 1284 an invading Pandyan army from South India captured the Tooth and took it briefly back to India, until it was reclaimed by Parakramabahu III some four years later.

During these turbulent years the Tooth came to assume increasing political importance, being regarded not only as a unique religious relic but also as a symbol of Sri Lankan sovereignty – it was always housed by the Sinhalese kings in their capital of the moment, which explains its rather peripatetic existence. After being reclaimed by Parakramabahu III, it subsequently travelled to Kurunegala, Gampola and Kotte. In the early sixteenth century, the Portuguese captured what they claimed was the Tooth, taking it back to Goa, where it was pounded to dust, then burnt and cast into the sea (Buddhists claim either that this destroyed Tooth was simply a replica, or that the ashes of the Tooth magically reassembled themselves and flew back to Sri Lanka). The Tooth finally arrived in Kandy in 1592 and was installed in a specially constructed temple next to the palace, later becoming the focus for the mammoth Esala Perahera (see pp.212–213).

The exact nature and authenticity of the Tooth remains unclear. Bella Sidney Woolf, writing in 1914 when the Tooth was still regularly shown to the public, described it as "a tooth of discoloured ivory at least three inches long – unlike any human tooth ever known," unconsciously echoing the sentiments of the Portuguese visitor, a certain de Quezroy, who in 1597 claimed that it actually belonged to a buffalo. Whatever the truth, the Tooth remains an object of supreme devotion for many Sri Lankans. Security concerns mean that it is no longer taken out on parade during the Esala Perahera, though it is put on display in the Temple of the Tooth for a couple of weeks once or twice every decade.

The last king of Kandy: Sri Wickrama Rajasinha

Few figures in Sri Lankan history are as famous – or as reviled – as the last king of Kandy, **Sri Wickrama Rajasinha** (1798–1815). His despotic excesses and cruelties have become the stuff of legend, though as the last king of an independent Sinhalese kingdom, Sri Wickrama is also seen as the final figurehead of a golden age – a complex and contradictory figure rather in the manner of England's Henry VIII (whom Sri Wickrama was even supposed to physically resemble).

The true nature of Sri Wickrama's rule, however, is more ambiguous than tradition would suggest. His hold on the Kandyan throne was, to begin with at least, extremely weak. The king came from the Aravidu royal dynasty of southern India, and arrived in Sri Lanka in 1785 at the invitation of the queen of King Rajadhi Sri Rajasinha. Kandyan kings were chosen through election by the kingdom's principal Sinhalese nobles rather than by direct dynastic succession, and three years after his arrival, upon the Rajadhi's death, Sri Wickrama was elevated to the throne by the ambitious Sinhalese courtier and *maha adikaram* (chief minister) **Pilimatalawe**, who saw in the young and inexperienced Sri Wickrama – who otherwise had "nothing to recommend him but a good figure" – a convenient and easily manipulated puppet ruler.

Sri Wickrama, however, showed more obstinacy than Pilimatalawe had bargained for. The new king quickly made himself unpopular, surrounding himself with South Indian cronies and attempting to introduce Hindu customs into Kandyan royal and religious life. The Buddhist clergy of Kandy twice sent representatives to the court of the king of Burma, asking for a Burmese Buddhist prince to be sent to replace Sri Wickrama – missions which may have been encouraged, and even arranged, by the British in Colombo, who schemed during these years to undermine Kandyan unity, largely through the efforts of the brilliant colonial official **Sir John D'Oyly** (see p.225). The British also ensured that a regular supply of liquor reached Sri Wickrama, encouraging a taste for alcohol which left him increasingly befuddled and unfit for the exercise of power.

Surrounded by the machinations of British officials and intriguing Sinhalese courtiers and clergy, Sri Wickrama's burgeoning despotism is not so surprising – as a contemporary British official observed: "his situation as king was attended with insuperable difficulties. Like a man blindfolded and in fetters, he could neither see nor move but as the *adikar* [chief minister] directed him . . . Not having a minister in whom he could place any confidence, he lived under the constant fear of conspiracies . . . He trusted none of his courtiers; and it is doubtful if any one of the chiefs deserved his confidence." In 1811, the scheming Pilimatalawe was executed,

You'll also pass a diminutive statue of the child-hero Madduwa Bandara (see box). The temple's exterior is classically plain: a rather austere collection of plain white buildings whose hipped roofs rise in tiers against the luxuriant green backcloth of the Udawatakelle Sanctuary. The most eye-catching exterior feature is the octagonal tower, the **Pittirippuva**, projecting into the moat which surrounds the temple; strictly speaking, it's not part of the temple at all. Sri Wickrama Rajasinha used the upper part as a platform from which to address his people, and it's now where all new Sri Lankan heads of state give their first speech to the nation. The **moat** itself is bounded by two walls adorned with rather Japanese-sounding names: the outer, with pointed tops, is the Diyareli Bemma (Wave-Swept Wall); the inner, with rounded tops, is the Walakula Bemma (Cloud-Drift Wall); the recesses in each are for oil lamps.

The entrance to the temple proper is through the **Maha Vahalkada** (Great Gate), which was formerly the main entrance to the royal palace as well as the temple. A sumptuous carving of Lakshmi stands by the entrance – a curious touch of Hinduism in such an important Buddhist shrine. Once through the

his place as *maha adikaram* taken by his son-in-law, **Ehelepola Maha Nilame**. This did little to crush dissent, however, which was further stimulated by the king's plans to comprehensively remodel Kandy along the lines of the Indian city of Madurai, including moving six of the city's principal Buddhist temples out of the city to Peradeniya and the creation Kandy's central lake.

Encouraged by John D'Oyly, Ehelepola declared war on the king in 1814 from the safety of the remote Uva province. The sequel to Ehelepola's revolt was swift and brutal. Sri Wickrama first executed seventy Kandyan chiefs whom he suspected of treachery, then seized Ehelepola's family, who had remained in Kandy, and sentenced them to death. Ehelepola's children, wife and brother were led before the executioner. The eldest child, aged 11, clung to his mother in terror. Seeing his brother, Ehelepola's second son, **Madduma Banda**, aged just 9, stepped forward, and declaring proudly that he would show his brother how to die, offered his neck to the executioner. As onlookers watched in horror, the executioner beheaded Madduma, then the remainder of Ehelepola's children, including a baby who had been suckling at his mother's breast, so that it was said that when the head was severed, the milk it had just drunk ran out and mingled with its blood. Following this carnage, it's claimed that the queen was forced to pound the decapitated heads of her children in a mortar, before being taken to a lake outside Kandy and drowned.

These horrific events shocked the entire island. Kandy, it is said, "was as one house of mourning and lamentation; and so deep was the grief, that not a fire was kindled, no food was dressed, and a general fast was held." The British in Colombo were no less affected, seeing in Sri Wickrama's actions the work of a tyrant, which conveniently unfitted him for rule and established the moral pretext required for launching an invasion of the kingdom. What is not generally remembered is that punishment meted out to Ehelepola's family, however merciless, was exactly that laid down under Kandyan law for the punishment of treasonable offences, the very same law which Sri Wickrama had sworn to uphold on coming to the throne; the detail of the queen being forced to pound the decapitated heads in a mortar is probably a fictional embellishment.

Events rapidly overtook Sri Wickrama. In 1815 the British, in collusion with dissident Kandyan nobles, invaded the kingdom under the leadership of John D'Oyly. The friendless king fled, but was soon captured and exiled to Vellore in southern India, where he lived in considerable style at British expense until finally expiring in 1832.

gateway, turn right and walk up further steps carved with dwarf figures and covered by a canopy painted with lotuses and pictures of the perahera. The **ticket office** is at the top of the steps by the entrance to the temple proper, via a gorgeously carved stone door adorned with a moonstone, guardstones and topped by a makara torana. Continue through a painted corridor, over another moonstone into the interior of the temple.

The shrine

The interior of the temple is relatively modest in size, and something of an architectural hotchpotch. In front of you lies the **Drummers' Courtyard** (Hewisi Mandapaya), into which is squeezed the two-storey **main shrine** itself (the Tooth Relic is kept upstairs). The shrine is a rather curious construction: some portions have been lavishly embellished (the three doors, for instance), but many of the painted roundels on the walls have been left unfinished, and the stone pillars which support the upper storey are utterly plain, giving the whole thing the effect of a job only half done – although the overall effect is still undeniably impressive.

The most intricate carving is on the two stone side-doors (that to the left is also equipped with splendid gold locks), while the main doors are fashioned of gorgeously decorated silver, though they're usually hidden behind a curtain except during pujas. The whole shrine is surrounded by gold railings and fronted by a moonstone and four elephant tusks sheltering two stone lions with gaping red mouths. The walls are decorated with a colourful and intricate confusion of entwined geese (a symbol of union or marriage), lotuses, vines and lions, and dotted with painted medallions (some unfinished) of the **sun and moon**, a symbol of the kings of Kandy which can be found all over the city – the image of the twinned heavenly orbs was designed to represent both the light-giving and the eternal nature of their rule. A more quirky touch is supplied by numerous paintings of **rabbits** curled up in the moon: where the West believes there is a man in the moon, the Sri Lankans – no less inexplicably – see a rabbit. What's perhaps strangest about all this decoration, however, is its largely royal and secular content: Buddha images, in this holiest of Sri Lankan temples, are notable largely by their absence.

From the drummers' courtyard, a set of stairs to the left (as you face the main shrine) lead to the upper level; halfway up you'll pass the casket in which a replica of the Tooth Relic is paraded during the Esala Perahera, along with golden "flags" and ceremonial fans which are also used during the procession, and a small dagoba. At the top of the steps is the **Pirit Mandapa** (Recitation Hall), a rather plain space whose unusual latticed wooden walls lend a faintly Japanese air (though the lino-clad floor is hideous). This leads to the entrance to the **Tooth Relic chamber** itself, on the upper level of the main shrine. You can't actually go into the relic chamber, and the entrance is railed off (except during the temple pujas; see below), although you can make out some of the details of the fantastically ornate brass doorway into the shrine, framed in silver and decorated in a riot of embossed ornament, with auspicious symbols including dwarfs, some holding urns of plenty, more entwined geese, peacocks, sun and moons and dagobas. Paintings to either side of the door show guardstone figures bearing bowls of lotuses, surmounted by makara toranas.

The **interior** of the Tooth Relic chamber is divided by golden arches into three sections, though the chamber is kept shut except during pujas, and even then you'll only be able to get a brief glimpse as you're hurried past the door. The Tooth Relic is kept in the furthest section, the **Vedahitina Maligawa** (Shrine of Abode), concealed from the public gaze in a dagoba-shaped gold casket which is said to contain a series of six further caskets, the smallest of which contains the Tooth itself. There are three different keys to the six caskets, one held by the temple's administrator, the others by the heads of the Malwatta and Asigiriya monasteries (see p.218 and p.230); the casket can only be opened when all three are in attendance.

On the far side of the Pirit Mandapa, another flight of stairs lead back down to the courtyard, passing a striking gilded Buddha from Burma and further objects used in the perahera.

The Alut Maligawa

From the rear of the Drummers' Courtyard, steps lead up to the **Alut Maligawa** (New Shrine Room), a large and undistinguished building completed in 1956 to celebrate the 2500th anniversary of the Buddha's death. The interior, as if to compensate for the lack of Buddhist imagery in the main section of the temple, is filled with a glut of Buddha statues, many donated by foreign countries, which offer an interesting opportunity to compare Asian variations of traditional Buddhist iconography. From left to right the images are from China (white marble); Sri Lanka (a classically simple orange ceramic figure, typical of Sri Lankan craftsmanship); Japan (a golden figure with black hair and a large golden halo); Japan again (sandalwood, backed by elaborate flames of enlightenment); Thailand (the main central image; a gilded seated figure surrounded by the stylized flames of enlightenment); Korea (black hair); Taiwan (a small white stone figure); India (white marble with a large backrest); and finally Sri Lanka again (a large golden standing figure). Beneath the central Thai image is a holographic Buddha face from France, set in a minute dagoba, which turns its head to follow you as you move around the room.

A sequence of 21 **paintings** hung around the chamber's upper walls depict the story of the Tooth Relic from the Buddha's death to the present day. The Buddhas below were a gift from Thailand to commemorate the fiftieth anniversary of Sri Lanka's independence.

The Sri Dalada Museum

Exit the back door of the Alut Maligawa and follow the signs up to the **Sri Dalada Museum** (Tooth Relic Museum; Rs.100), situated on the first and second floors of the building and devoted to anything and everything concerned with the Tooth Relic itself. **The first floor** shows pictures of all the various cities and shrines in which the Tooth Relic is supposed to have rested during its travels around Sri Lanka, along with photos of the damage caused by the 1998 bombing, bringing home the remarkable scale and skill of the restoration carried out since then. Other exhibits include fragments of murals destroyed in the blast, a selection of (mainly colonial) documents relating to the Tooth Relic and Kandy, and a few old fabrics, including a selection of the enormous handkerchiefs designed for the royal noses of the kings of Kandy.

The more interesting **second floor** is largely occupied by the bewildering assortment of objects offered to the Tooth Relic at various times. These include all sorts of bowls and vases, fans, fancy jewellery, incense burners, foreign coins, votive offerings (including a touching collection of little tin figures) and votive plaques, including several given by former presidents. The highlight is the gorgeous silk Buddha footprint which is said to have been offered to the temple in the reign of Kirti Sri Rajasinha.

The Royal Palace and around

The Temple of the Tooth originally lay at the heart of the sprawling **Royal Palace**, a self-contained complex of buildings immediately surrounding the temple and housing various royal residences, audience chambers and associated structures. Significant sections of the original palace complex survive, although it's difficult to get a very clear sense of how it would originally have looked, thanks to the many additions and alterations made to the area since 1815. Several of the buildings are now used as museums, and although none are of outstanding individual interest, taken together they provide a tantalizing glimpse of what the former royal precinct would have looked like, and of the sumptuous lifestyle enjoyed by the Kandyan nobility – the best overview of the complex is from the Vishnu Devale (see p.227).

The layout of the surviving palace buildings is rather confusing. Two of its buildings – the **Audience Hall** and **Raja Tusker Museum** – can only be reached by going through (and buying a ticket for) the Temple of the Tooth. The others, including the **National** and **Archeological museums**, are reached by walking around the outside of the temple along the lakeside (the Archeological Museum can also be reached via the Vishnu Devale, see p.227).

The Audience Hall and Raja Tusker Museum

Immediately north of the temple (and reached via a side exit from it) lies the imposing **Audience Hall**, an impressively complete Kandyan pavilion set on a raised stone plinth, open on all sides and sporting characteristic wooden pillars, corbels and roof, all intricately carved. The hall originally dates from 1784, though it was set on fire during the British attack of 1803 – the conservation-minded British invaders obligingly put out the fire and subsequently restored the building. It was here that the Kandyan chiefs signed the treaty that handed over power to the British on March 2, 1815.

Just north of the Audience Hall, in another handsome old palace building adorned with hipped roof, guardstones and moonstone, stands the **Raja Tusker Museum**, devoted to the memory of Sri Lanka's most famous elephant, **Raja**. The main attraction is Raja himself, the world's only stuffed elephant, now standing proudly in state in a glass cabinet. Raja died in 1988 after fifty years' loyal service as Kandy's **Maligawa Tusker** – the elephant which carries the Tooth Relic casket during the Esala Perahera. Such was the veneration in which he was held that Raja's death prompted the government to order a day of national mourning, while the animal's remains are now an object of devotion to many Sinhalese, who come to pray at Raja's glass case. The museum also has photos of Raja in various peraheras, plus sad snaps of him surrounded by anxious vets during his last illness in 1988.

No single elephant has yet proved itself able to fill Raja's considerable boots, and at present the role of Maligawa Tusker is shared between various different elephants. All Maligawa Tuskers must fulfil certain physical require-ments. Only male elephants are permitted to carry the relic and, most importantly, they must be **Sathdantha** elephants, meaning that all seven parts of their body – the four legs, trunk, penis and tail – must touch the ground when they stand upright. In addition, the elephant's tusks must be formed in the curved shape of a traditional winnow, and it must have a flat back and reach a height of around twelve feet. It is proving increasingly difficult to find such "high-caste" elephants locally, although the temple already owns several suitable elephants, including ones donated by notables including various prime ministers of Sri Lanka and India, as well as the king of Thailand.

The National Museum and around

The other surviving buildings of the royal palace lie outside the Temple of the Tooth enclosure. Exiting the Temple and turning left along the lakeside brings you to the two-storey **Queen's Bath** (Ulpenge), a grand but now rather dilap-idated structure built over the lake, rather like a boathouse; the upper storey was added by the British.

Beyond the Queen's Bath (and immediately behind the Temple of the Tooth, though not accessible from it) lies the **National Museum, Kandy** (Mon–Thurs & Sun 9am–5pm; Rs.65), set in a low white building which was formerly the Queen's Palace (or "King's Harem", as it's sometimes described by over-excitable historians). The museum contains a treasure trove of mementoes of Kandyan life before the coming of the Europeans, with many exhibits attesting to the high levels of skill achieved by local craftsmen, with a plethora of minutely detailed ivory objects (look for the cute figurines of various Kandyan bigwigs) along with lots of jewellery, fabrics, bracelets and ear ornaments. Look out too for the intriguing selection of **water clocks**: small copper bowls with a tiny pinhole in the bottom: floated on water, they sink after precisely 24 minutes, the equivalent to one Sinhalese hour, or *paya* (in a neat but coincidental reversal of Western time-keeping, the Sinhalese divided each day into sixty hours of 24 minutes). There's also an interesting collection of ola-leaf manuscripts, including treatises on charms, medicine and astrology, plus a few beautifully painted book covers showing the same kind of floral decoration found all over the Temple of the Tooth.

Next door to the National Museum sits the relatively modest **Queen's Chamber**, a discreet low white structure with tiny balustraded windows and stone pool inside – it's now used as a craft workshop by local girls. Just past here lie the large Neoclassical **High Courts** built by the British – the courtroom is open on two sides so you can watch proceedings within (though you're not allowed to take photographs or write notes). Just beyond here is the **District Court**, housed in an old-style Kandyan pavilion and again open on two sides.

Past the District Court lies the **Archeological Museum** (Mon & Wed–Sun 8am–5pm), also reachable from the Vishnu Devale (see p.227), which lies just to the other side of it. The museum is situated in the long, low white building which was formerly the **King's Palace**, built by Vimala Dharma Surya (1591–1604). The palace's ornate main doors are decorated with the Kandy kings' sun and moon symbol, while the interior of the gateway is adorned with lions and geese (the latter symbolizing purity). Inside, the museum holds a mildly interesting collection of assorted pots, bits of masonry, fragments of carved stones and old wooden pillars.

Note that the museum doesn't issue its own entrance tickets, being covered by the Cultural Triangle combined ticket. If you don't have one of these, you'll have to tip whoever lets you in and shows you around.

The Kandy Garrison Cemetery

Back on the lakeside just beyond the National Museum, a signposted turning points up to the evocative **Kandy Garrison Cemetery** (daily 10am–noon & 1–6pm; donation), established in 1817, shortly after the British seized control of Kandy, to provide a final resting place for expired British colonists. Having fallen into complete dereliction, the cemetery has recently been painstakingly restored and now offers a moving memorial to Ceylon's former colonial master. Shockingly few of the people buried here made it to the age of 30, and even those who avoided the usual hazards of tropical diseases and hostile natives found unusual ways to meet their maker, such as John Spottiswood Robertson (died 1856), trampled to death by a wild elephant; David Findlay (died 1861), killed when his house collapsed on top of him; or William Watson Mackwood (died 1867), who somehow managed to impale himself on a stake whilst dismounting his horse.

The most notable internee, however, is **Sir John D'Oyly**, the remarkable colonial official who brokered the surrender of the city to the British in 1815. D'Oyly was one of the most fascinating figures in the history of colonial Ceylon – at once a supreme diplomat who manipulated the Kandyan nobility with almost Machiavellian genius, and also a kind of proto-hippy who became a strict vegetarian, avoided European society and devoted himself to the study of Sinhala and Buddhism. As an observer remarked in 1810: "He lives on plantain, invites nobody to his house, and does not dine abroad above once a year. When I saw him . . . I was struck with the change of a Cambridge boy into a Cingalese hermit." Despite his brilliant orchestration of the bloodless coup at Kandy, D'Oyly's subsequent attempts to protect the Kandyans from British interference and Christian missionaries were little appreciated, and by the time of his death from cholera in 1824, he had become a lonely and marginalized figure.

The devales

Kandy traditionally lies under the protection of four gods, each of whom is honoured with a temple in the city. Three of these temples – the **Pattini**, **Natha** and **Vishnu** devales – sit adjacent to one another in a large compound next to the Temple of the Tooth, a magical quarter of the city whose myriad shrines, dagobas and bo trees offer a wonderful treasure-house of Kandyan arts and religious traditions, as well as providing marvellous views of the adjacent Temple of the Tooth and the buildings of the Royal Palace complex. The fourth devale, dedicated to **Kataragama**, lies a couple of blocks west in the city itself (see p.228). Besides their obvious artistic merits, the devales offer a fascinating lesson in the way in which Hindu and Buddhist beliefs shaded into one another in Kandy, as throughout Sri Lankan history – two of the four devales are dedicated to adopted Hindu gods, whilst the principal shrine of the Natha devale is housed in a building which wouldn't look out of place in South India.

The four devales are technically covered by the Cultural Triangle Ticket (see p.296), though it's extremely unlikely that you'll be asked to produce one. You might, however be asked for a **donation**, especially if you venture into the principal shrines at the Pattini and Natha devales (although if you steer clear of these shrines, you're unlikely to be asked for money). The devales are most easily visited from the city centre, entering from Deva Vidiya, although they can also be reached from the Archeological Museum, in which case you'll visit them in reverse order to that described below.

Pattini Devale

The **Pattini Devale** is the simplest of the four temples. The cult of the goddess **Pattini** (see box below) was introduced from South India in the second century AD by King Gajabahu (reigned 174–196 AD); she remains a popular deity amongst poorer Sri Lankans, thanks to her lowly origins. Her golden ankle bracelet, brought back from India by Gajabahu, is said to be kept here (though you can't see it). Entering from Deva Vidiya, you're confronted by the **Wel–Bodhiya**, a huge bo tree, perched on an enormous, three-tiered platform;

Pattini

Pattini (originally named Kannaki) was a humble Indian girl from the city of Madurai who married a certain **Kovalan**, an errant spouse with a weakness for dancing girls. Despite Pattini's considerable charms, the feckless Kovalan abandoned his wife and bankrupted himself in pursuit of one particular amour until, ashamed and penniless, he returned to Pattini to beg forgiveness. The pliable Pattini welcomed him back without even a word of reproach and handed over her last possession, a golden ankle bracelet, for him to sell. The unfortunate Kovalan did so, but was promptly accused of stealing the bracelet by the king's goldsmith and executed. The distraught Pattini, legend states, descended upon the royal palace, tore off one of her breasts, caused the king to drop dead and then reduced his palace to ashes before being taken up into the heavens as a goddess.

Pattini's cult was originally introduced to Sri Lanka by King Gajabahu in the second century BC, but enjoyed its heyday during the Kandyan era, when the kingdom's Hindu rulers revived her cult and built her Kandy temple. Pattini is now revered as the ideal of the chaste and devoted wife: pregnant women come her to pray for a safe delivery (rather inexplicably, since Pattini was childless), while she is also thought to protect against infectious diseases such as chicken pox, smallpox and measles.

it's believed to have been planted by **Narendrasingha**, the last Sinhalese king of Kandy in the early eighteenth century. The actual shrine to Pattini is off to the right, set in a modest little enclosure entered through gorgeous embossed brass doors decorated with the usual sun and moon symbols, makara toranas and guardstone figures. The shrine itself is set in a small but beautiful Kandyan wooden pavilion, and is usually the most popular of all the devales amongst visiting worshippers. To either side stand subsidiary shrines to the Hindu deities Kali and Mariamman – the latter, like Pattini, is a female deity of humble South Indian origins who is believed to protect against disease. You'll probably be approached by a temple flunkey at this point asking for a donation; he'll most likely show you a book in which previous donations are listed, many of which appear to have been wildly inflated by the addition of surplus zeros.

Natha Devale

From the Pattini Devale, a gate leads directly through to the **Natha Devale**. **Natha** is the most purely Buddhist of the gods of the four devales, and thus the most important in the city, being considered a form of the Mahayana Bodhisattva **Avalokitesvara**, who is still widely worshipped in Nepal, Tibet, China and Japan. Natha was thought to have influence over political events in the kingdom – new kings of Kandy were obliged to present themselves at the shrine on attaining the throne – although the god's exulted status means that his shrine is far less popular with the hoi polloi than that of humble Pattini next door.

Away to your right at the end of the enclosure is the **Natha Shrine** itself, built by Vikramabahu III in the fourteenth century, and thus the oldest building in Kandy. This low stone gedige, topped with a small *shikhara* dome at its end, is very reminiscent in style of similar temples at Polonnaruwa and shows strong Indian influence (the fact that the city's most Buddhist deity sits in its most Hindu-style temple is entirely characteristic of the syncretic nature of Kandyan culture). The shrine is fronted by a much later pavilion sporting beautifully carved wooden pillars. In the middle of the enclosure stands a **Buddha shrine**, its front steps decorated with no less than three moonstones, with two bo tree enclosures to the rear. Exit the temple through the archway to the north, its exterior wall richly carved and painted with makara torana and guardstone figures.

Vishnu Devale

Directly ahead of here stands a wooden pavilion, through which ornate stone steps, decorated with vines, lead up into the third and most interesting of the devales, the **Vishnu Devale** (also known as the Maha Devale, or "Great Temple"). The steps lead into the first of the temple's two courtyards, in the middle of which stands the wooden **digge** pavilion, in which drummers and dancers would formerly have performed in honour of the deity – you can still sometimes see trainee dancers being put through their paces here. Past the *digge*, a further set of sumptuously carved stone steps leads up to the main **Vishnu shrine**, fronted by a characteristically ornate gilded doorway; the Vishnu image worshipped here is thought to come from Dondra on the south coast. The main image inside is, as usual, hidden behind a curtain, though you can see elaborate ceremonial objects used in Esala Perahera, including the palanquin, ranged along the sides of the shrine. Behind and to the left of the Vishnu shrine stands a subsidiary shrine to **Dedimunda** (a local god of obscure origins), fronted with a beautifully carved stone door-frame and gorgeously embossed gilded doors featuring the ubiquitous sun and moon motif.

The rest of the city

Facing the entrance to the Pattini Devale, the **tourist office** is fronted by a replica Kandyan wooden pavilion constructed by the British. Opposite here sits an ornate metal **fountain**, adorned with eight rusty cherubs – Italian Renaissance in overall style, it's relieved with local touches such as the four central cupids, who wrestle with tiny crocodiles, and the egrets which top the whole structure. The fountain was erected by the coffee planters of Ceylon in 1875 to commemorate a visit by the Prince of Wales – one of the last fruits of the island's colonial coffee trade before it was wiped out by the insidious *hemileia vastratrix* leaf fungus.

Just north of the tourist office lies **St Paul's Church**, a quaint, ochre-coloured neo-Gothic structure, built in 1843, which offers a homesick and thoroughly incongruous memento of rustic English nostalgia amidst the myriad Buddhist monuments which cover this part of town – indeed the irreverent insertion of such a large Christian building into such a sacred Buddhist precinct says much about British religious sympathies (or lack of). The **interior** is a piece of pure English Victoriana, with beautiful wooden pews, floor tiles decorated with floral and fleur de lys patterns, wooden rood screen and choir stalls, naff stained glass, brass eagle lectern and a grand piano, all tenderly preserved. The various monuments date back to the 1840s, recording deaths in parts of the empire as far flung as Bombay, Port Said, Wei-Hai-Wei and South Africa. Opposite here, the walls of the buildings are all but buried underneath a much photographed surfeit of **signs** in English and Sinhala advertising the services of local lawyers, whose offices stand along the street, occupying a former Victorian-era army stables and barracks.

West of here lies the **city centre** proper, where you'll find the fourth of the city's principal devales, the **Kataragama Devale**, entered through a lurid blue gateway on Kotugodelle Vidiya (it's surprisingly easy to miss amidst the packed shops and crowds of pedestrians). This is the most Hindu-influenced of Kandy's temples, right down to the pair of resident Brahmins who serve here. The central Kataragama shrine is enclosed by an attractive balustraded terrace, topped by a wooden roof and protected by two intricately gilded doors, outside of which stands a splendid metal peacock, one of the god's most important symbols. Various Buddhas stand behind and to the left of the principal shrine, whilst on the opposite side is a temple housing a black Durga idol in an elaborate gold recess. A pillared walkway leads from here to two further tiny shrines, each fronted by an ornate gold door with tiny bells which devotees ring to attract the gods' attention.

The centre of the modern city spreads out around the Kataragama Devale. The hilliness of the terrain has confined it to a compact and crowded grid of streets lined with small shops and honeycombed in places with tiny alleyways. The most interesting area is along the eastern end of Bennet Soysa Vidiya (generally known by its old name of Colombo Street), running at right angles to Kotugodelle Vidiya, where fruit and veg sellers sell their wares from the pavements – although the crush is usually such that there's nowhere to stand still and take in the scene. At the far end of Dalada Vidiya stands Kandy's unusually ornate **clocktower**, with golden elephant friezes and a cute, hat-like top.

The Bahiravakanda Buddha and Asigiriya

West of the town centre, the immense white **Bahiravakanda Buddha** stares benevolently over the city centre from its hilltop perch – a fine sight when illuminated by night. The statue offers good views of the **Knuckles Range**

Robert Knox and seventeenth-century Kandy

In 1660, a party of English sailors who had gone ashore near the mouth of the Mahaweli Ganga were taken prisoner by soldiers of the king of Kandy, Rajasinha II. Among them was a nineteen-year-old Londoner named **Robert Knox**. Knox's subsequent account of his nineteen years as a hostage of the king was eventually published as *An Historical Relation of Ceylon*, a unique historical record which offers a fascinating snapshot of everyday life in the seventeenth-century Kingdom of Kandy. The book later served as one of the major sources of Daniel Defoe's *Robinson Crusoe*, and something of Knox's own industrious (if rather dour) character may have crept into Defoe's self-sufficient hero.

Upon arriving in Kandy, Knox was surprised to discover that he and his shipmates were not the only European "guests" being detained at Rajasinha's pleasure – also in Kandy were prisoners of war, shipwrecked sailors, army deserters and assorted diplomats. Knox seems to have admired many of the qualities of his hosts, though he did object (as have so many subsequent Western travellers to Asia) that "They make no account nor conscience of lying, neither is it any shame or disgrace to them, if they be catched in telling lies; it is so customary." He also recorded (with puritan disapproval) the kingdom's liberal attitude to sex: "Both women and men do commonly wed four or five times before they can settle themselves". Married women appeared free to have affairs with whoever took their fancy, so long as they were of an equal social rank, sometimes even leaving their husbands at home to look after the children. When important visitors called, husbands would offer them the services of their wives and daughters "to bear them company in their chamber". Men were allowed to have affairs with lower-caste women, but not to sit or eat with them. Polyandry, in which a wife was shared between two or more brothers, or in which one man married two or more sisters, was also accepted, while incest was reputedly common amongst beggars. If nothing else, the kingdom's sex drive was impressive. As Knox observed of the Kandyan women: "when their Husbands are dead, all their care is where to get others, which they cannot long be without".

In terms of material possessions, the life which Knox recorded was simple. Most Kandyans contented themselves with the bare necessities of life, encouraged in a life of indolence by the fact that the moment they acquired anything it was taken away by the king's mob of tax collectors. Justice was meted out by a court of local chiefs, but appeared to favour whoever was able to present the largest bribe – those convicted of capital offences were trampled to death by an elephant.

Despite being a prisoner, Knox and his fellow "guests" were free to live a normal life and, as time passed, to wander around the kingdom at will – although all escape routes were cut off by the dense jungle which surrounded the kingdom, while the only paths through and out were heavily guarded. Europeans enjoyed favoured status under Rajasinha II, even though many of them showed a loutish disregard for local customs and spent most of their time drunk – indeed the Europeans' major contribution to the development of Kandyan society was to help break down the taboos against beef and alcohol – although Knox himself kept a puritanical distance from such goings-on. Most eventually took Sinhalese wives and settled down to raise families, injecting a substantial splash of European blood into the Kandyan gene pool, although Knox steadfastly resisted all native female charms – he appears to have been a rather dour character, and perhaps something of a misogynist. He supported himself by a mixture of small-scale farming, knitting caps and peddling; in the latter guise Knox wandered all over the kingdom, acquiring the intimate knowledge of its geography that finally allowed him and a companion to escape to the Dutch-controlled north – the only Europeans to succeed in finding their way out of the maze of the Kandyan kingdom.

(see p.244), named for its uncanny resemblance to the knuckles of a clenched fist, which is particularly obvious from this vantage point, although the view over town and in other directions is largely blocked by trees. To reach the statue from the clocktower, walk along Bandaranaike Mawatha then up Sri Pushpadana Mawatha for five minutes, then follow the sign to the circuit bungalow opposite a flag-festooned bo tree. From here, it's a stiff ten-minute climb to the top. Foreigners pay Rs.100 to get into the enclosure in which the statue stands. Save your money: the views are just as good from outside.

On the north side of the Bahiravakanda hill lies the **Asigiriya monastery**, along with the Malwatta Monastery the most important in the city. The monastery was founded in the fourteenth century, and is thus the oldest religious foundation in the city. There's a small, though picturesque, quadrangle of rustic buildings here, with the chapterhouse in the middle. If you arrive during the evening puja (around 4.30pm), or succeed in button-holing a passing monk, you may be able to get inside to see the monastery's large reclining Buddha and collection of ola leaf manuscripts.

Immediately northeast of here lies the **Asigiriya Stadium**, one of Sri Lanka's three venues for test-match cricket, shoe-horned into a small hollow beneath towering hills – often and rightly described as one of the most beautiful cricket grounds in the world.

Royal Palace Park

Retrace your steps from the clocktower back down Dalada Vidiya and then head south along the road which bounds the west side of the lake. From the junction with Sangaraja Mawatha, steps ascend to the entrance to Rajapihilla Mawatha and the entrance to the modest **Royal Palace Park**, also known as Wace Park (daily 8.30am–4.30pm; Rs.25), another of Sri Wickramam Rajasinha's creations. The small ornamental gardens at the top of the park provide an unlikely setting for a Japanese howitzer, captured in Burma during World War II and presented to the city by Lord Mountbatten (who had his wartime headquarters here in the *Hôtel Suisse*) – a thoroughly useless and unattractive gift. Beyond the ornamental gardens, a series of terraced footpaths wind down a bluff above the lake, offering some fine views of the lake and Temple of the Tooth – though as the gardens are usually chock-full of snogging couples hiding in every available corner, you might feel a mite self-conscious. There are better views over the lake and into the green ridges of hills beyond from **Rajapihilla Mawatha**, the road above the park – the classic viewpoint is from the junction of Rajapahilla Mawatha and Rosmeath Road, though it's well worth walking all the way along the road for the peerless views it offers over the lake and into the hills beyond.

Udawattakelle Sanctuary

On the opposite (north) side of the lake, providing a dense green backdrop to the Temple of the Tooth, **Udawattakelle Sanctuary** (daily 7am–5pm; Rs.575) sprawls over two kilometres of densely forested hillside, with imposing trees, plenty of birdlife and a few monkeys – as well as lots of leeches if it's been raining. The sanctuary was formerly a royal reserve, and was subsequently preserved and protected by the British – foreign tourists are now charged a preposterous entrance fee, probably the most flagrant of Sri Lanka's many officially sponsored attempts to fleece overseas visitors. As if this wasn't enough, assaults on unaccompanied women have also been reported here, so single women should either stay away or at least stick to the main two paths, Lady Horton's Drive and Lady Gordon's Road, both named after the wives of British governors. If you still want to visit, the entrance to the park is a steep hike from town: go up past the post office along Kandy Vidiya and then Wewelpitiya Road.

Tea Museum

Some 4km south of Kandy on the Hantanta Road is the recently opened **Tea Museum** (Tues–Sun 9am–4pm; Rs.250). Housed in a disused tea factory, the museum hosts various imposing old pieces of Victorian-era machinery collected from defunct factories around the hill country, along with exhibits documenting the careers of James Taylor, Sri Lanka's pioneer tea planter, and the famous Thomas Lipton, whose name still adorns tea bags across the world, and other memorabilia from the early days of the Sri Lankan tea industry. The smart restaurant on the top floor offers panoramic views of the surrounding hills.

Eating, drinking and entertainment

Kandy has a reasonable selection of **places to eat**, though the range of food on offer is pretty limited, and there's certainly nothing to rival Colombo's cosmopolitan spread of cuisines. For **rice and curry**, it's best to try the guest houses – the *Sharon Inn* (see p.215) is a good bet, offering an interesting spread of fifteen or so dishes, often including unusual Sri Lankan vegetables. True to its name, Kandy has a pronounced sweet tooth, exemplified by the countless **bakeries** which dot the city centre, serving all sorts of strangely coloured and flavoured cakes.

Kandy also has a decent little selection of **bars and pubs** – a refreshing change from the usual smoky, men-only whisky and arrack dens.

Restaurants and cafés

The Bake House Dalada Vidiya. Cheap, cheerful and very lively local eatery, with cakes, short eats and cheap snacks or meals, including good-value set lunches, cellophaned examples of which are laid out in the entrance so you can see exactly what you're getting. Open until 8pm.

Devon Restaurant Dalada Vidiya. Shiny and modern, with lots of chrome and Formica and naff landscapes on the walls, but the food is no-nonsense and cheap, with a good selection of staples, including good hoppers at breakfast, plus burianis, lamprais, basmati fried rice, noodles and devilled dishes, almost all for under Rs.125. There's also a big cake shop in the entrance, as well as a self-service food court upstairs (reached by separate entrance from the street).

Flower Song Kotugodelle Vidiya. Pleasant restaurant dishing up Kandy's best Chinese cooking, with a long list of well-prepared standards plus a few Vietnamese and Thai dishes, including a modest selection of veg options; most mains are around Rs.250. There's also a few naff wines – if you've been hankering for Mateus Rosé or Blue Nun, now's your chance (from Rs.640).

Koffeepot Dalada Vidiya. Tiny café that's deservedly popular with tourists for its good cakes and excellent coffee.

The Pub Dalada Vidiya. Gloomy, chic and very tourist-oriented place, with loud Western pop, MTV videos and occasional English football highlights on the TV. The menu sounds good, with a refreshingly wide choice of soups, salads, pasta, fish and meat dishes (mainly chicken), though in practice it's distinctly hit and miss – and it's relatively expensive too. Still, it makes a change from your average Sri Lankan restaurant, and is a good spot for a drink (see overleaf).

Paivas Yatinuwara Vidiya. This scruffy-looking place won't win any design awards, but offers a decent selection of cheap and tasty north Indian standards including birianis, chicken tikkas and mutter paneer – the vegetarian dishes are particularly good value at under Rs.100.

Rams 87 Bennet Soysa Vidiya (Colombo St). The fetchingly psychedelic interior – complete with wooden parrots, paintings of sari-clad lovelies and a ceiling decorated in multicoloured lotus flowers – provides a memorable setting for Kandy's finest South Indian fare, including all sorts of (mainly vegetarian) dosas, vadais and thalis at bargain prices. Also has a good selection of juices and lassis. No alcohol.

White House Dalada Vidiya. Pleasant and bustling local restaurant with a big range of all the old favourites – noodles, curries, burianis, fried rice – plus sandwiches and snacks, all of them tasty and cheap, with pretty much everything under Rs.150. There's also a special Chinese section (the *Golden Wok*), while the bakery in the entrance offers an enticing selection of fancy cakes.

Pubs and bars

Hotel Casamara 12 Kotugodelle Vidiya. The rooftop bar in this pleasant hotel is one of Kandy's better-kept secrets, with fine views down to the city streets and ant-sized pedestrians below.
Olde Empire Temple St. Set within a charming old

colonial-era hotel, this gorgeously shabby bar-restaurant offers cheap beer served by superannu-ated waiters. A good place for a drink, though you'll have to be very drunk to enjoy the food.
Pub Royale Dalada Vidiya. Kandy's best stab at a traditional English pub. The atmosphere is usually pretty quiet, but the beer's cheap and it's a fun place to observe the chaos of the city traffic, especially during the evening rush hour.
The Pub Dalada Vidiya. The outdoor terrace over-looking Dalada Vidiya is *the* place in town for a drink or meal (see p.231), and is normally packed with tourists people-watching from the balcony over the busy street. Draught, local and imported beers and liqueurs, though all are relatively pricey.

Cultural shows

Three places in town put on nightly shows of Kandyan **dancing and drum-ming**. All are touristy but fun, with a fairly standard range of dances, generally including snippets of both southern as well as Kandyan dances and usually

Kandyan dancing and drumming

Sri Lanka's classic performance art, **Kandyan dancing and drumming** is a spectacular display of carefully choreographed acrobatics accompanied by a pulsat-ing, ear-shattering barrage of massed drumming. It originated as part of an all-night ceremony in honour of the god Kohomba, an elaborate ritual featuring some fifty dancers and ten drummers. This ceremony flourished under the patronage of the kings of Kandy and reached such heights of sophistication that it was eventually adopted into local religious ceremonies, becoming a key element in the great Esala Perahera festival. Some temples in the Kandyan area even have a special columned pavillion, or **digge**, designed for performances and rehearsals by resident dancers and drummers – becoming a key element in the great Esala Perahera festival.

There are various **types of Kandyan dance** (*ves*, *pantheru* and *udekki*), with subtle differences in costume and choreography, although in all forms the dancers (always male) are flamboyantly attired in ornate costumes, with a white sarong and a kind of breastplate made out of small rosettes, plus enormous belts and various other neck, arm and leg ornaments which jangle as they move about. The **ves** dance – for which performers also wear a kind of extravagantly decorated metal headdress – is at once highly mannered and hugely athletic, combining carefully stylized hand, head and body gestures with acrobatic manoeuvres including spectacular backflips, huge high-kicking leaps and dervish-like whirling pirouettes. In the **pantheru** dance, per-formers also play small tambourines, whilst during the **udekki** dance they beat small hourglass-shaped drums.

All forms are accompanied by **drumming**, which can reach extraordinary heights of virtuosity. The archetypal Sri Lankan drum is the **geta bera**, a double-headed instru-ment carried on a strap around the drummer's neck and played with the hands. Other types of drum are also used, some of them single-headed, and some played with sticks. Dance performances are usually accompanied by troupes of between four and eight drummers – the rhythmic coordination and ensemble achieved by these troupes (in the absence of any conductor) is remarkable, producing rhythmic effects of a dazzling complexity. Even if the finer points pass you by, the headlong onslaught of a Kandyan drum ensemble in full flight leaves few people unmoved, providing a fitting musical accompaniment to the gymnastic fireworks of the dancing itself.

culminating in a spot of firewalking. The biggest, gliztiest and most popular show is at the **Kandyan Arts Association** (daily at 6pm; Rs.300), on the north side of the lake just east of the Temple of the Tooth – a big, very touristy place whose flashy but good-fun shows draw coach parties galore. The **YMBA** (daily at 5.45pm; Rs.300), at the west end of Rajapihilla Mawatha, offers a similar programme but in a much less commercial and more intimate atmosphere, and with generally lower-key dancing and drumming (partly a result of the much smaller stage, which limits the range of acrobatics possible). The show at the **Lake Club** (daily at 5.45pm; Rs.250), east of the town centre on Sangamitta Mawatha, is midway in scale between the YMBA and Kandyan Arts Association, but not as good as either.

Listings

Ayurveda A number of hotels in and around Kandy offer ayurveda treatments, including the *Earl's Regency, Golden View, Le Kandyan*, and *Thilanka* (see listings on p.216). Alternatively, the well set-up Wedamedura Ayurveda Centre at 7 Mahamaya Mawatha (℡081-447 9484, ⓦwww.ayurvedawedamedura.com) offers the usual steam and herbal baths, as well massages, reflexology, pedicures and aromatherapy. A resident ayurveda doctor offers consultations and treatment plans, and you can arrange complete courses including accommodation and meals.

Banks and exchange There are heaps of banks in the city centre, the majority on Dalada Vidya The following banks have ATMs which accept foreign cards (all Visa and Mastercard, except the Bank of Ceylon): Bank of Ceylon (Visa only), Dalada

Vidiya; Commercial Bank, Kotugodelle Vidiya; Hatton Bank, Dalada Vidiya; HSBC, Kotugodelle Vidiya.

Bookshops Vijitha Yapa Bookshop, right in the city centre on Kotugodelle Vidiya, has a reasonable selection of English-language books, including lots of tomes about Sri Lanka. The Lake House Bookshop next door has a very small selection of English-language books. The Buddhist Publications Society, near the eastern end of the lake, has an enormous selection of Buddhist titles and books on Sri Lankan history.

British Council 178 D.S. Senanayake Veediya ℡081-222 2410 (Tues–Sat 9.30am–5pm). Kandy's rather unexciting branch of the British Council has old copies of *The Times*, a few British magazines and a library of English classics.

Hospital Lakeside Adventist Hospital (℡081-222

Tours from Kandy

Almost all the city's guest houses can arrange **tours**, and there are also plenty of taxis hanging around for custom. As usual, count on around US$25–30 per day for the hire of a car and driver. The main **taxi stand** (minivans and cars) is around the entrance to the Temple of the Tooth; there's another opposite the Clock Tower Bus Stand. Some approximate prices (for transport only, exclusive of any admission or accommodation charges) are: Pinnewala Rs.1500; Peradeniya Rs.800; three-temples circuit Rs.1500; three-temples circuit plus Peradeniya Rs.2000. All these prices are for a basic, non-a/c minivan; expect to pay twenty percent more for an a/c car.

The vastly experienced **Sumane Bandara Illangantilake**, c/o the *Expeditor Inn* (see p.215), offers islandwide tours, plus trips around Kandy including a two-hour Mahaweli Ganga sunset cruise in an inflatable dinghy (Rs.1000 per person), and an unusual off-road version of the three temples walk (see p.237; US$35 for two people). Sumane is the island's leading guide to the Knuckles Range (see p.244), an authority on the Veddahs (see p.245) and can arrange visits to pretty much anywhere you might fancy going. For tours, count on around US$50 per person per day half-board, not including entrance fees. He also arranges an "Eco-Challenge" (annually in Oct or Nov), featuring a five-day race (or "Chase") through the wilds of the hill country as part of a twelve-day holiday.

3466), on the lakeshore 100m beyond the *Hôtel Suisse*; there's also a dental clinic here.

Golf The magnificent eighteen-hole, par-73 course at the Victoria Golf Club (☎071-274 3003) is around 20km east of Kandy at Rajawella, tucked into a scenic spot between the Knuckles Range and the Victoria Reservoir. Green fees are Rs.2000 on weekdays, Rs.2500 at weekends.

Handicrafts A huge new shopping centre is currently under construction by the west end of the lake which will doubtless furnish all sorts of new shopping possibilities when open (planned for 2005). For the moment, the two biggest places are Laksala, on the road at the west end of the lake, and the Kandyan Arts and Crafts Association, towards the eastern end of the lake. Both are government-sponsored and turn out a very similar range of unimaginative tat. There's much better stuff at a couple of places on Rajapahilla Mawatha: Kandy Souvenirs, 61 Rajapahilla Mw, has a fairly wide range of wood carvings as well as metalwork, leatherwork, kolam masks and jewellery – all of quite good quality. Gunatilake Batiks, nearby at 173A Rajapahilla Mw, has a big stock of batiks from around US$12 and up, including some attractive, rather Indonesian-looking birds, peacocks and fish. There are also a couple of big crafts shops (and many jewellers) along the Peradeniya Rd en route to the Botanical Gardens.

Laundry Queen's Laundry (Mon–Fri 8am–6pm, Sat 8am–5pm, Sun 8am–12.30pm), on the road along the western edge of the lake next to Laksala, offers an 8hr service (shirt Rs.60, trousers Rs.80).

Internet access The cafe@inter.net (daily 8.30am–10.30pm; Rs.2 per min) on Kotugodelle Vidiya is the smartest cyber-café in Sri Lanka, and dead cheap to boot. Alternatively, the *Koffeepot* café on Dalada Vidiya (daily 8am–8pm; Rs.2 per min), has lots of machines in a rather poky room at the back.

Newspapers Local English-language newspapers are sold at pavement stalls by the Bank of Ceylon on the corner of Dalada Vidiya and Kotugodelle Vidiya.

Pharmacy Sri Lanka Pharmacy, 39 D.S. Senanayake Vidiya (Mon–Sat 8.30am–7.30pm).

Post office The main post office is opposite the train station (Mon–Sat 7am–9pm). There's a free poste restante service (ask at the enquiries desk; mail is held for up to three months), and EMS is also available. In the city centre, try the Seetha Agency Post Office (daily 7am–10pm), 29 Kotugodelle Vidiya, a couple of doors south of the Kataragama Devale, or the Senkadagala Sub-Post Office, just behind the Tourist Office.

Supermarket Cargills, Dalada Vidiya (daily 8am–9pm).

Tea Mlesna Tea Centre, opposite *The Pub* on Dalada Vidiya, has a reasonable selection, as does Cargills.

Tourist Police The tiny tourist police office is just west of the clocktower at the western end of town on Peradeniya Rd (no phone). It's allegedly open 24hr, though it's pot luck whether you'll actually find a policeman in attendance. Alternatively, try the main police station, just south of here on Bandaranaike Mawatha.

Around Kandy

The countryside around Kandy is full of attractions, comprising an interesting blend of the cultural and the natural – elephants, historic temples, hill walking and more – and you could easily spend a week exploring the area. Top of most visitors' list is a trip to the famous **Pinnewala Elephant Orphanage**, one of the highlights of a visit to the island for many people. More elephants can be seen at the **Millennium Elephant Foundation**, close to Pinnewala, and at the **Riverside Elephant Park**, just outside Kandy. Closer to hand, the idyllic **Peradeniya Botanical Gardens** offer a pleasant escape from the city and the chance to lose yourself amongst four thousand species of tree, while there's also a fascinating collection of Kandyan-era **temples** scattered around the countryside which make rewarding destinations if you want to get off the beaten track. Finally, the dramatic but still little-visited **Knuckles Range** boasts some of the island's finest wilderness trekking.

Peradeniya Botanical Gardens

Set 6km southwest of Kandy in a loop in the Mahaweli Ganga lie the expansive **Peradeniya Botanical Gardens** (daily 8am–5pm; Rs.300), the largest

Thanks to its position roughly in the centre of the island, Kandy is within fairly easy striking distance of pretty much everywhere in the country, although if you're heading directly to the south coast, it's probably easiest to go back to Colombo and start from there. Heading south into the **hill country**, the train connects Kandy with most places you're likely to want to go, while to the north, all the sites of the **Cultural Triangle** are no more than two to three hours away by road. For details of tours and taxis from Kandy, see p.233.

Regular trains connect Kandy with Colombo in one direction, and with the southern hill country in the other. The ride through the hills up to Nanu Oya (for Nuwara Eliya), Haputale, Ella and Badulla is unforgettable, and if possible it's well worth booking a seat in the **observation car** (see p.34). Travelling to Colombo, sit on the south side of the train (the left-hand side of the train, as you face the front) for the best views. Full details of train **timetables** from Kandy are given on p.288.

Most long-distance **bus** services (see p.287 for full details) depart from Kandy's main bus station, the memorably chaotic **Goods Shed Bus Terminal** opposite the train station. It's very difficult to make sense of the terminal: if you can't find the bus you're looking for, ask at one of the two wire-mesh information kiosks in the middle of the terminal. Heading north, there are regular CTB and private services to **Anuradhapura**, **Polonnaruwa** and **Dambulla**, plus one bus direct to **Sigiriya** daily at 8am (otherwise change at Dambulla, from where you can catch another bus either to Sigiriya or to Inamaluwa Junction; see p.316). There are also regular services south to **Nuwara Eliya**. Services to **Negombo** leave from the main road opposite the Goods Shed terminal. **Express services to Colombo** leave from the roadside on Station Road about halfway between the Goods Shed terminal and the clocktower. There's also an early-morning departure for the **airport** at 5am.

The **Clocktower Bus Stand**, south of the Clocktower at the west end of the city centre, is for local departures only.

---

and finest gardens in Sri Lanka, covering almost 150 acres and stuffed with a bewildering variety of local and foreign tree and plant species. The history of the site dates right back to the fourteenth century, when Wickramabahu III established a royal residence here. The park itself was originally created during the eighteenth century by King Kirti Sri Rajasinha to serve as a pleasure garden for the Kandyan nobility. It was transformed into a botanical garden by the British in 1821 during the enterprising governorship of Edward Barnes, who had Sri Lanka's first tea trees planted here in 1824, though their full commercial potential wasn't to be realized for another half-century.

There are around ten thousand trees in the gardens. Lots of the trees are labelled, though unfortunately many of these have weathered away to illegibility, while others show only the tree's Latin name – not much help unless you're an expert botanist. You can buy a leaflet with a map (Rs.20) at the entrance. The area around the entrance is largely given over to small-scale flora, including an **orchid house**, a **spice garden** and a tiny and rather unimpressive **Japanese garden** – the most interesting sight here is the bizarre-looking snake creeper, whose tangled aerial roots look just like a writhing knot of vipers.

Running from the entrance, the gardens' principal thoroughfare, stately **Royal Palm Avenue**, bisects the gardens, heading in an arrow-straight line from the entrance to the Mahaweli Ganga at the far northern end, via the **Great Circle** at the gardens' centre. To the west of the avenue stretches the **Great Lawn**, home to Peradeniya's most majestic sight: a huge Javan fig whose sprawling roots and branches create a remarkable natural pavilion. (There's also

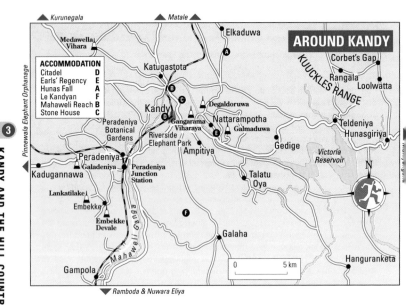

an overpriced **restaurant** near here, and cheaper drinks in the kiosk next door.) Running along the southern side of the Great Lawn, **Double Coconut Palm Avenue** is flanked with coco de mer trees, rather stumpy and unimpressive-looking things, though their massively swollen coconuts – which can weigh up to 20kg – are the world's largest and heaviest fruit. There are also a few stunning kauri pines here from Queensland (they're actually broadleaved trees, not pines). To the east side of the lawn runs a long line of strangely shaped Cook's pines.

The northern half of the gardens have an altogether wilder quality, and the trees here are home to enormous populations of **fruit bats**, which hang in ominous clusters from the branches overhead. At its northern end, Royal Palm Avenue curves around to the right, following the bank of the Mahaweli Ganga; you'll often see troupes of **macaque monkeys** here. A pleasant circuit leads right round, following the river through some of the gardens' most peaceful and shady areas to reach **Cabbage Palm Avenue**, lined with West Indian cabbage palms – very tall, slender trees, with a tiny fan of leaves at the top. **Palmyra Palm Avenue** leads off to the left, lined with spiky-crowned Palmyra palms, a familiar sight to anyone who has visited the Jaffna peninsula, where they are the dominant species – they're rarely found elsewhere in the island. South of here is a marvellous group of **Java almonds**, whose huge buttressed roots line the side of the path. Returning to Cabbage Palm Avenue and continuing south brings you to **Cannon Ball Avenue**, lined with beautiful cannon ball trees, wreathed in creepers from which hang the characteristically large, round fruits, after which the militaristic British named the tree. The Sinhalese (who call them *sal* trees) hold their beautiful flowers sacred, since they appear to comprise a tiny dagoba, shaded by a cobra's hood and surrounded by tiny florettes which are thought to represent a crowd of worshippers. Beyond here, the avenue curves around away from the river, before returning you to the Orchid House and entrance.

South of the Great Lawn lies a small but picturesque **lake**, covered in waterlilies and overlooked by a classical rotunda and an enormous clump of giant bamboo. Continuing south brings you to a didactic but dull little area of carefully laid out medicinal and aquatic plants, plus various types of grass. Next to these is a line of far more striking **talipot palms** (see box below), identifiable by the unusual criss-cross bark pattern at the foot of the trunk (the remains of old leaves) and by their enormous leaves – the trees as a whole look rather like enormous toilet brushes. Beyond here, at the southernmost edge of the gardens, is the pretty little **Students' Garden**, surrounding by weird cycads and ferns.

A tuktuk to the gardens will cost around Rs.400 return from Kandy, including waiting time. Alternatively, frequent buses leave the Clocktower Bus Stand for Peradeniya.

Close to the entrance lies **Peradeniya University**, one of the island's most illustrious places of higher education.

The three-temples loop

The countryside around Kandy is dotted with dozens of Kandyan-era **temples** which together make up a treasure-trove of Sinhalese Buddhist art and architecture. Few see any foreign visitors, and setting off into the local backwaters in search of these legacies of the Kandyan kingdom makes a wonderful alternative to joining the hoards flocking to Pinnewala or Peradeniya. The most interesting of these temples are the **Embekke Devale**, **Lankatilake** and **Galadeniya**, which lie some 10km west of Kandy and make a rewarding day-trip – they are often combined into a round-trip by vehicle or foot, known as the **three-temples loop** (a further trio of temples are described on p.240). All three temples were constructed during the fourteenth century, in the early days of the nascent Kandyan kingdom when the

---

| **The versatile talipot** | | |

A marvellous Mercy which Almighty God hath bestowed upon this poor and naked People in this Rainy Country

Robert Knox

The **talipot palm** is one of Sri Lanka's botanical celebrities, an arboreal oddity which flowers just once in its life, after about forty years, producing what is claimed by some to be the largest cluster of flowers in the world, sometimes reaching almost ten metres in height. From a practical point of view, however, it's the enormous leaves of the mature talipot which are of unusual interest. In Kandyan times they were often employed to construct shelters (three or four leaves sewn together produce a passable tent) or to serve as umbrellas – "one single Leaf being so broad and large, that it will cover some fifteen or twenty men, and keep them dry when it rains," according to Robert Knox.

Talipot leaves are best known, however, as the source of **ola leaf**, the local alternative to paper, which was manufactured in Sri Lanka and India from as early as 500 BC. Ola is produced using young talipot leaves, which are boiled, dried in the sun, then exposed to dew and smoothed and stretched. The treated leaf can then written on – or, more precisely, engraved – using a steel stylus to scratch out the characters. The engraved leaf is then smeared with a form of ink (a resin mixed with charcoal, although cow dung was used in South India) to pick out the characters. The efficacy of ola is proved by the fact that some books have survived over five hundred years, and have proved far more durable in the tropical climate than paper.

region was ruled from Gampola and Tamil influence was strong. They can all be visited (albeit with some difficulty) by bus or, far more conveniently, by taxi (count on around Rs.1500 for the round trip). The best way to visit, however, is to walk at least part of the way between the three, starting at the Embekke Devale and finishing at the Galadeniya (or vice versa). There's a Rs.100 entry change at each temple. You'll often see guides hanging around at the Embekke Devale and the Galadeniya.

Embekke Devale

To reach the **Embekke Devale**, and the start of the walk, take bus 643 from the Goods Shed Bus Terminal (every 20min; 1hr); alternatively, a taxi to the temple will cost around Rs.500. The bus drops you in **Embekke village**. It's a 1km walk from here to the temple: turn right onto the tiny road opposite the red postbox, then follow it straight ahead as it switchbacks up over a steep hill.

Dating from the fourteenth century, the rustic little Embekke Devale, dedicated to Kataragama, is famous principally for the fine pavilion (the *digge*) fronting the main **shrine**, with its intricately decorated wooden pillars – apparently brought here from another temple at Gampola. Each of the myriad pillars bears a different design, a marvellously carved assortment of peacocks, entwined swans, wrestlers, dragons, dancers, horsemen, soldiers and Bodhisattvas (shown as composite figures: part man, part fish, part bird). One of the most famous panels depicts an elephant and lion fighting; another shows what looks curiously like a Habsburg double-headed eagle. Two quaint lions flank the entrance to the main Kataragama shrine behind, which is topped by a delicate pagoda-tower. To the left of the main building stands an unusual **granary**, raised on stones above the ground to protect its contents from wild animals; to the right, a subsidiary shrine with sumptuously carved wooden doors houses a Buddha and a fine (but difficult to see) wooden statue of a peacock, a bird traditionally associated with Kataragama.

Lankatilake

From Embekke Devale, retrace your steps back up the road towards Embekke Village. At the top of the hill, about 200m from the temple, the road forks. Go left here, climbing a steep hill and continuing for 500m through the edge of the village, a pleasant spot, though you're likely to be hounded relentlessly by small children asking for sweets and schoolpens along the way. At the end of the village you reach a gorgeous bo tree and paddy fields, with a huge rock outcrop to your right. Continue straight along the road for a further 500m until the road forks. Keep right here and continue over the brow of a hill, from where you'll catch your first, magical sight of the **Lankatilake temple** rising out of the tea plantations ahead. Continue ahead, ignoring another road to the left, through further paddy fields. You can take a shortcut immediately below the temple by walking along the wall across the paddy fields by an electricity pylon (follow the locals); alternatively, continue along the road till you reach the temple's access road, which leads off on the left. Both wall and road lead to the base of the temple.

From here, a magnificent flight of rock-cut steps leads precipitously up to the temple itself, giving glorious views of the surrounding hills. Lankatilake is perhaps the finest temple in the district: an imposingly solid-looking structure built on a huge rock outcrop and painted a faint blue rather than the usual white. It was founded in 1344, and its architecture is reminiscent of the solid, gedige-style stone temples of Polonnaruwa rather than the later and more decorative Kandyan-style wooden temples. The building was

△ Lankatilake

formerly four storeys tall, though the uppermost storeys collapsed in the nineteenth century and were replaced by the present, rather ill-fitting wooden roof. The gloomy central **shrine**, with eighteenth-century Kandyan paintings, is magically atmospheric: narrow but tall, and filled with a great seated Buddha under a huge makara torana, above which rise tiers of decidedly Hindu-looking gods. The massive exterior walls contain a sequence of small shrines containing statues of Saman, Kataragama, Vishnu and Vibhishana, punctuated by majestic low-relief carvings of elephants. To the left of the temple, a large rock inscription in Pali records the details of the temple's construction.

If you want to reach Lankatilake by **bus** directly from Kandy, take service #666 from the Goods Shed bus station (every 30min; 1hr).

Galadeniya

Returning to the road by the pylon, continue along to the left. The road hairpins quickly up to reach a larger road and another village. Turn left along the main road and continue for about 3km, keeping right whenever the road forks, to reach the **Galadeniya temple**. This part of the walk is less special – the road is bigger and there's more traffic, although there are plenty of tuktuks around if you get bored (count on Rs.70 between Lankatilake and Galadeniya). The area is a major centre of metalworking, and you'll pass dozens of shops selling traditional oil lamps – they look something like a cross between a miniature spire and an overblown cake stand.

Galadeniya dates from the same year – 1344 – as the Lankatilake. The principal **shrine**, built on a rock outcrop at the top end of the site, has a pronounced South Indian appearance (it was designed by a Tamil architect, one Ganesvarachari), and the style of the corbelled roof and carvings of dancers, drummers and the two quaint elephants which flank the entrance is strongly reminiscent of the temples at the great Hindu capital of Vijayanagar in Karnataka. The interior houses a fine gold Buddha (with oddly close-set eyes) under a marvellous makara torana, plus a subsidiary Vishnu shrine. The whimsical subsidiary shrine, in the middle of the compound, consists of a cruciform building, each wing housing a tiny Buddha shrine and topped by a minuscule dagoba, with the entire structure being surmounted by a larger dagoba – a unique local take on the traditional Indian-style *shikhara* dome, which is a common feature of Hindu temples in the subcontinent.

To **return to Kandy**, carry on down the road for a further ten minutes to reach the main Gampola–Kandy highway. Buses back to Kandy pass every minute or so – just flag one down. To reach Galadeniya directly from Kandy, take any of the numerous non-express buses heading west along the road to Kegalle or Colombo and ask to be set down at the Galadeniya turn-off (it's a couple of kilometres beyond Kiribathgoda, and before you reach Kadugannawa).

Temples east of Kandy

There's a further trio of interesting temples just east of the city dating from the Buddhist renaissance which the Kandyan kingdom experienced under Kirti Sri Rajasinha (see p.209), who built all three temples. A round trip by tuktuk should cost around Rs.600–700.

Gangarama Viharaya

About two kilometres east of Kandy (head east along the Mahiyangana road, then turn north towards Madawela) on the banks of the Mahaweli Ganga, lies the

Gangarama Viharaya. This small monastery is notable mainly for its fine two-storey **image house**, decorated with Kandyan-era paintings and home to an eight-metre-tall standing Buddha statue, carved out of the natural rock outcrop around which the shrine is built. (You can see the rock outcrop poking out of the back of the image house, carved with an extensive rock inscription in Sinhala recording details of the temple's construction). The walls inside are decorated with the usual hundreds of tessellated sitting Buddhas, while the lower sections of the wall show Jataka stories and scenes from the Buddha's life, delicately painted in characteristic Kandyan style in narrow panels using a predominantly bright-red palette. A small **digge** stands opposite the entrance to the image house.

Degaldoruwa

A couple of kilometres further along the road to Gangarama lies **Degaldoruwa**, the most interesting of this group of temples. The temple is built into a large rock outcrop and consists of three small connected chambers: the first two – the *digge* and antechamber – are built outside the rock and topped by crumbling old wooden roofs, while the third, the main shrine, is hollowed out of the rock itself, and invisible from the outside. The **digge** has a few old wooden pillars and a couple of drums hanging from the rafters; it's unusual in that it's directly attached to the rest of the temple, rather than occupying a separate pavilion as is usually the case. Old wooden doors under a makara torana arch lead into the **antechamber**, which preserves a fine moonstone and a sequence of paintings showing scenes from the Jataka stories, painted in five vivid red panels.

The doors leading from here into the **main shrine** have metal fittings which were formerly studded with jewels. The principal image is a large reclining Buddha; the pillow on which the Buddha's head rests is inlaid with a glass copy of a huge amethyst – according to tradition, the painters who decorated the shrine worked by the light generated by this enormous jewel. The murals here are some of Sri Lanka's finest, though they're rather dark and difficult to make out, having until recently been covered in a thick layer of soot from fires lit in the temple – a tiny square of black wall has been left just next to one of the doors to show what the shrine looked like before restoration. The wall opposite the reclining Buddha is painted with Jataka scenes and pictures of dagobas at Sri Lanka's principal pilgrimage sites, but the finest painting is on the ceiling, a magnificent depiction of the **Buddha's battle with Mara**, dating from the 1770s and 1780s, and rivalling the far better known example at Dambulla.

Outside stands a belfry, apparently built in imitation of a Christian church tower. Steps to the left of the temple lead up to a large platform, where a stupa and bo tree stand facing one another above the temple.

Galmaduwa Gedige

Return to the main Mahiyangana road and continue east for about five kilometres to reach the village of **Kalapura**, home to the extremely unusual **Galmaduwa Gedige**. The bizarre shrine here is enclosed in a cloister-like stone structure (the gedige) and topped by a stone pyramid – an odd but endearing Kandyan version of a traditional South Indian temple. Apparently, the gedige was left unfinished, and its exact purpose remains unclear (the image house at the back was only added during a restoration of 1967). Old ola-leaf manuscripts suggest that the innermost section was originally built as a jail to contain a single prisoner of noble birth who had offended the king, and that the surrounding ambulatory was added later.

Riverside Elephant Park

If you don't have time to visit the Pinnewala Elephant Orphanage, or simply can't get enough of elephants, the **Riverside Elephant Park** (daily 7.30am–4.30pm; Rs.400), 4km southwest of Kandy, offers further opportunities to interact with these magnificent beasts. The park is set on a broad and picturesque section of the Mahaweli Ganga and is home to six elephants (five adults and one baby rescued from the jungle). The rather steep admission price includes an elephant ride, and you can also help wash them, or even sit on one whilst it's given a shower. Unlike at Pinnewala, there are no set times for any activities. Short **elephant safaris** to Kandy and back can be arranged for Rs.2000. You can also take a boat over to the pleasant **restaurant** on the island in the middle of the river.

The Pinnewala Elephant Orphanage and around

Situated just outside the town of Kegalle, some forty kilometres west of Kandy, the **Pinnewala Elephant Orphanage** (daily 8.30am–6pm; Rs.200, video cameras Rs.500 extra) is one of Sri Lanka's most popular tourist attractions. It was set up in 1975 to look after seven orphaned baby elephants, though the orphanage's population has now mushroomed to around 65, making it the world's largest collection of captive elephants. The elephants here range in age from newborns to elderly matriarchs, and include orphaned and abandoned elephants, as well as those injured in the wild (often in conflicts with farmers), amongst them famous residents such as the three-legged elephant, Sama, who stood on a land mine, and a blind elephant, Raja. In addition, the orphanage's population is constantly augmented by new arrivals born in captivity: about one elephant is born here every year (as of 2003, 22 elephants had been born in the orphanage), and the baby elephants here are without doubt the tiniest and cutest you're ever likely to see. The adult elephants work in the orphanage itself, earning their keep by helping with various chores, such as collecting food.

Practicalities

It's best to time your visit to coincide with one of the three daily **feeding sessions** (9.15am, 1.15pm & 5pm); an entertaining sight as the older elephants stuff their faces with trunkloads of palm leaves, whilst the youngsters guzzle enormous quantities of milk out of oversized baby bottles. Twice a day (10.30am & 2pm), the elephants are driven across the road to the Ma Oya river for a leisurely bath – you can observe their antics from the riverbank or, in greater comfort and for the price of an expensive drink, from the terraces of the *Pinnalanda* or *Hotel Elephant Park* restaurants above the river.

Pinnewala is on a side road a few kilometres north of the road between Colombo and Kandy, just to the east of Kegalle, near the 82km post. By far the easiest way to reach it is **by taxi** from Kandy (see p.233); count on Rs.1500. Some people visit by **tuktuk** from Kandy (around Rs.1200), though it's a smelly and (if there are two of you) uncomfortable ride, and not worth the small saving. The orphanage is also reachable by public transport from Kandy. By **bus**, take a service from the Goods Shed terminal towards Kegalle (every 15min; 1hr) and get off at Udamulla, a few kilometres short of Kegalle. From here you can catch another bus to Rambukkana and get off at Pinnewala (every 20min; 10min). By **train**, catch a service to Rambukkana (6.45am, 10.30am, 2.15pm 3.40pm and 6.40pm; 1hr 40min), 3km from the orphanage, from where you can either hop on a bus or take a tuktuk. The orphanage could also be visited from **Colombo**: take one of the regular buses from the Bastian Mawatha terminal to Kegalle, or a train from Fort Railway Station to Rambukkana (13 daily from Colombo; 2hr 30min). The orphanage is also easily visited from **Negombo** as a day-trip by taxi; expect to pay Rs.2500–3000.

There are a couple of **places to stay** at Pinnewala. The quiet *Greenland Guest House* (℡035-226 6316, ✉nandani@sltnet.lk; ❸), on the side road to the elephant bathing spot, is attractively located in a pleasantly shady garden, though the large and rather bare rooms are a bit overpriced. On the main road, the larger *Randaliya Hotel* (℡035-226 5321, ✉ralidid@sltnet.lk; ❸) is slightly more expensive and more anonymous, though the rooms are better value. There are lots of **handicraft shops** around the village (especially along the road leading from the orphanage to the river) with a wide range of stock, including leather goods and elephant paper (which is also sold at the orphanage) – see box below. There are also heaps of **spice gardens** en route to Pinnewala.

The Millennium Elephant Foundation

A few kilometres down the road from Pinnewala, the **Millennium Elephant Foundation** (daily 8am–5pm; Rs.300; ⊛www.eureka.lk /elefound) has a rather more didactic aim than Pinnewala – indeed the two places complement one another rather neatly. With the exception of the young Pooja, who was born at the foundation in 1986 (the only birth here to date), the eight elephants here are all retired working beasts. Guides will tell you everything you need to know about elephants and demonstrate how they are used as working elephants; you can also help clean them and interact with them, and it's possible to do voluntary work with the foundation's mobile veterinary unit – see the website for details. The foundation was also instrumental in introducing pachyderm paper (see below) to the Sri Lankan market.

The small **museum** here is full of elephant skulls and (remarkably heavy) bones, along with a few poster displays.

Shit happens: pachyderm paper

One of the most novel wildlife initiatives in Sri Lanka in recent years has been the invention of **pachyderm paper**: paper made from elephant dung. As well as their many remarkable abilities, elephants are also a kind of paper factory on legs. During feeding, they ingest a huge amount of fibre which is then pulped in the stomach and delivered in fresh dollops of dung, ready-prepared for the manufacture of paper. The dung is dried in the sun and boiled, and the resultant pulp used to make high-quality stationery with an artistically textured finish. The texture and colour varies according to the elephants' diet, while other ingredients including tea, paddy husks and onion peel are also added according to the required finish. More than just a novelty stationery item, pachyderm paper could prove an important source of income to locals – and thus a significant help in conservation measures. Customers to date have included the Colombo Hilton, SriLankan Airlines and the Bank of Ceylon. Pachyderm paper products can be bought online at ⊛www.paperhigh.com.

East and south of Kandy

The hill country **east of Kandy** remains largely off the tourist map. The main highway, the A26, twists and turns east through the hills, skirting the southern edge of the rugged **Knuckles Range**, the hill country's last great unspoilt wilderness, though its tourist potential remains largely untapped. East of here, the hills fall precipitously to the dry-zone plains of eastern Sri Lanka. At the foot of the hills, a turn-off heads north to the remote **Wasgomuwa National Park** (see p.334), while the main road continues to the town of **Mahiyangana**, important both in Buddhist legend and as the heartland of Sri Lanka's diminishing population of **Veddahs**.

The Knuckles Range

From Kandy, the A26 wriggles past the **Victoria Reservoir and Dam**, opened in 1989 as part of the huge Mahaweli Ganga Project and one of the island's major sources of electricity. North of the reservoir, the rugged peaks of the **Knuckles Range** – named by the British for their resemblance to the knuckles of a clenched fist – cover a rugged and still largely untouched area of great natural beauty and biodiversity. The steeply shelving mountain terrain, reaching 1863m at its highest point, includes stands of rare dwarf cloudforest, and is home to leopard, various species of deer (sambhur, barking and mouse), monkeys (purple-faced langur and macaque) and giant squirrels. The range is also an exceptionally good place to spot endemic bird species. The most straightforward approach to the Knuckles is from the main Kandy to Mahiyangana road. Some 27km east of Kandy, at **Hunasgiriya**, a left turn leads via **Rangala** into the range, hairpinning up via Loolwatta (1065m) to **Corbet's Gap**, from where there are magnificent views of the main Knuckles directly ahead.

The areas of the range above 1000m metres have recently been declared a World Heritage Conservation Area, and an **entrance fee** of Rs.575 is now charged; tickets can be bought at Udawattakelle in Kandy (see p.230) or, more conveniently, at Hunasgiriya en route to the range itself, where tickets are checked. There are all sorts of intriguing but still largely unexplored trekking possibilities in the Knuckles, although you'll really need to go with a guide if you plan on doing any extended walks; contact local expert Sumane Bandara Illangantilake (see p.233). Alternatively, you could explore the range whilst staying at the nearby *Hunas Falls Hotel* (see p.217) In addition, a few tour operators, such as Adventure Sports Lanka (see p.113), are beginning to offer visits to the area.

East to Mahiyangana

Beyond Hunasgiriya, on the far side of the village of Madugoda, the hills fall abruptly away to the dry-zone plains, giving marvellous views. The highway descends through precipitous hairpins – this stretch of the A26 is popularly known as Sri Lanka's most dangerous road, and although it's fairly small beer compared to Himalayan or Andean highways, the local bus drivers do their best to keep the adrenalin flowing. At the bottom of the hills, the village of **Hasalaka** is the starting point for the 45-kilometre road north to the remote Wasgomuwa National Park (see p.334).

Around 7km further east from Hasalaka, the small town of **MAHIYANGANA** is famous in Buddhist legend as the first of the three places in Sri Lanka which the Buddha himself is traditionally said to have visited (the others are Kelaniya and Adam's Peak). The large **Rajamaha Dagoba**, a kilometre or so south of town, is held to mark the exact spot at which the Buddha preached, and is believed to enshrine a lock of his hair. The dagoba's origins are lost in antiquity; it's said to have been rebuilt by King Duttugemunu, and has been restored many times since.

Mahiyangana is something of a crossroads town on the bus routes between Polonnaruwa, Kandy, Badulla, Monaragala and Ampara. If you do end up having to spend the night here, there are a couple of bearable options, both basic but acceptable. Try the *Venjinn Guest House* on Rest House Road (℡055-225 7151; ❶–❷), or the *New Rest House* (℡055-225 7304; ❷), by the river.

Northeast of Mahiyangana lies the huge **Maduru Oya National Park**, covered on p.378.

The Veddahs

The **Wanniyala-aetto** ("People of the forest"), more usually known by the name of **Veddahs** (meaning "hunter"), were the original inhabitants of Sri Lanka, and are ethnically related to the aborigines of India, Sumatra and Australia. The Veddahs may have arrived in the island as far back as 16,000 BC, and developed a sophisticated matrilineal hunter-gatherer culture based on ancestor worship and an intimate knowledge of their forest surroundings, the latter allowing them to coexist in perfect harmony with their environment until the arrival of the Sinhalese in the fourth century BC. Veddahs feature extensively in early Sinhalese legend, where they are described as *yakkas*, or demons, and this common perception of Veddahs as demonic savages has persisted through the centuries. One memorably smug Victorian colonial official described them as a:

strange and primitive race [whose] members are but a degree removed from wild beasts. They know nothing of history, religion or any art whatever. They cannot count, know of no amusement save dancing, and are popularly supposed not to laugh. During the Prince of Wales's visit, however, one of those brought before him managed to grin when presented with a threepenny piece. The Veddahs have, however, of late years shown some signs of becoming civilised under British influence.

Faced by successive waves of colonizers, the Veddahs were forced either to assimilate with the majority Sinhalese or Tamils, or retreat ever further into their dwindling forests. Despite the best attempts of successive British and Sri Lankan governments to "civilize" them, however, an ever-diminishing population of Veddahs still cling obstinately to their traditions. Most now live around Bintenne and Mahiyangana, and a small number have attempted to continue their traditional hunter-gatherer existence (even if they now use guns rather than bows and arrows). The creation of national parks, alongside government development and resettlement schemes and agricultural projects, have further encroached on traditional Veddah lands – in recent years they have campaigned vigorously for recognition and for the right to continue hunting on land now protected by the Maduru Oya National Park. Some "reserved" areas have now been set aside for their use, though their struggle for proper recognition continues.

Some tour operators arrange visits to Veddah villages, though many tourists find these experiences degrading for both visitors and Veddahs alike. If you have a genuine interest in the Veddahs, Sumane Bandara Illangantilake in Kandy (see p.233) has good connections with them and can arrange visits on a more equitable footing, including trips to the chief Veddah village of Kotabakina, near Mahiyangana ("King's Village"). For more on the Veddahs, see Ⓦwww.vedda.org.

South from Kandy: Ramboda, Dimbulla and around

The journey south from Kandy to Nuwara Eliya is spectacular both by train and by bus. The **bus** is far more direct and significantly quicker, cutting up through the hills and swinging round endless hairpins, passing the magnificent waterfalls at the village of **RAMBODA** en route, which plunge over the cliffs in two 100m cataracts.

The **train** is significantly slower, but makes for a quintessentially Sri Lankan experience, as the carriages bump and grind their way painfully up the interminable gradients towards Nuwara Eliya (and occasionally lose traction and slither a yard or so back downhill again). The track climbs slowly through pine and eucalyptus forest into a stylized landscape of immaculately manicured tea plantations which periodically open up to reveal heart-stopping views through the hills, nowhere more so than above the village of **DIMBULLA**, at the centre of a famous tea-growing area, where the line passes high above a grand, canyon-like valley between enormous cliffs.

This is one of the most scenically spectacular parts of the island, though its tourist potential remains almost totally unexploited. The easiest way to get a taste of the area is to go on one of the "waterfall tours" offered by various operators in Nuwara Eliya (see p.255), which usually include the Ramboda falls along with two picturesque cascades in the Dimbulla area – the **St Clair** and **Devon** falls. If you want to explore the region in more depth, you can **stay** in the area. The best option is the *Ramboda Falls Hotel* (☎052-225 9582; ❹), close to – and offering a spectacular view of – the Ramboda Falls. There's also the *Rest House* (☎081-247 8397; ❸) at **Pussellawa**, 45km south of Kandy on the Nuwara Eliya road – it's only got three rooms, though, so best to book ahead.

The southern hill country

The **southern hill country** is the highest, wildest and – for many visitors – the most beautiful part of Sri Lanka. Although the area was an integral part of the Kandyan Kingdom, little physical or cultural evidence survives from that period, and most of what you now see is the creation of the British colonial period, when the introduction of **tea** here changed the economic face of Sri Lanka for ever. The region's attractions are self-explanatory: a whimsical mixture of ruggedly beautiful scenery and olde-worlde colonial style, with sheer green mountainsides, plunging waterfalls and mist-shrouded tea plantations enlivened by quaint British memorabilia – clunking railways, half-timbered guest houses, Gothic churches and English vegetables – while a further, unexpected twist is added by the colourful Hindu temples and saris of the so-called "Plantation Tamils", who have been working the tea estates since colonial times.

The southern hill country's principal settlement, the faded resort of **Nuwara Eliya**, is the most British of all Sri Lankan towns, and sits at the heart of the tea industry; it's also the best jumping off point for the rugged **Horton Plains National Park**. To the southeast, in Uva Province, the villages of **Haputale**

Tea estate bungalows

For a true taste of the Sri Lankan colonial lifestyle, you can't beat a stay in one of the sumptuous **tea estate bungalows** which dot the southern highlands. Originally built for British estate managers in the nineteenth and early twentieth centuries, many offer beautiful and atmospheric lodgings, often in spectacular locations. **Information** about estate bungalows is hard to come by – details traditionally circulate by word of mouth, and few places advertise. Watawala Plantations (☎011 -237 2790, ℮sunshine@zesta.lk) run four beautiful bungalows in the Hatton area, near Adam's Peak (the *Craig Appen*, *Dickoya*, *Lindula* and *Strathdon*). Another beautiful option is the *Kirchhayn Bungalow* (☎011-250 8754, ℮henk@eureka.lk) on the Aislaby Tea Estate at Bandarawela. Rooms at all these places cost from US$15 to US$40 per night. In addition to the above, Dilmah Tea have plans to open up four luxury bungalows in the Adam's Peak area from late 2004, along with a spa featuring treatments using tea-derived products. For the latest information contact Forbes & Walker in Colombo (☎011-242 3281, ℮teatrails@forbestea.com).

and **Ella** and the modest town of **Bandarawela** lie strung out along the southern edge of the hills, offering marvellous scenery, panoramic views and wonderful hill walking. On the western edge of the region lies the spectacular mountain of **Adam's Peak**, whose summit – marked with what is claimed to be an impression of the Buddha's footprint – is one of the country's most important places of Buddhist pilgrimage. Just south of Adam's Peak, in the rolling foothills at the edge of the hill country, lies the gem-mining town of **Ratnapura**, which can also be used as a base for trips to the World Heritage rainforest of **Sinharaja** and the elephant-rich **Uda Walawe National Park**.

Nuwara Eliya and around

Sri Lanka's highest town, **NUWARA ELIYA** lies at the heart of the southern hill country, set amidst a bowl of green mountains beneath the protective gaze of Sri Lanka's tallest peak, Pidurutalagala (2555m). Nuwara Eliya (pronounced "Nyur-*rail*eeya") was established by the British in the nineteenth century, and the town and surrounding area continue to be touted as Sri Lanka's "Little England" – a remnant of the old country stuck in the heart of the tropics. The reality, however, is that Nuwara Eliya is far less of a period piece than the publicity would have you believe, although the town still boasts a triumvirate of fine old colonial hotels, along with scattered atmospheric villas and fusty guest houses whose misplaced architecture – a mixture of jaunty seaside kitsch and solemn faux-Tudor – lend some parts an oddly English (or perhaps Scottish) air, like a crazily transplanted fragment of Brighton or Balmoral, an illusion heightened by the luxuriant green spaces of the golf course, racecourse and Victoria Park. The memory of England lives on, too, in the small-scale market-gardening which is still one of the mainstays of the modern town's economy – the odd spectacle of dark-skinned Tamil men dressed up like English farm labourers in padded jackets and woolly hats, whilst carting around great bundles of turnips, swedes, marrows, radishes, and cabbages, is one of Nuwara Eliya's characteristic sights, adding a pleasantly surreal touch to the town's out-of-focus English nostalgia.

And yet, despite the faint traces of colonial magic which still cling to parts of the town, Nuwara Eliya is a frustratingly contradictory – and, for many visitors, disappointing – place. Much of it is now a functional and unappealing expanse of concrete shopping arcades and traffic intersections. The stress of altitude causes vehicles here to belch out great noxious clouds of fumes, so making a mockery of Nuwara Eliya's claim to be Sri Lanka's "Garden City", while the unpredictable weather can dampen even the brightest spirits. That said, if you take it with a pinch of salt, Nuwara Eliya still has a certain charm,

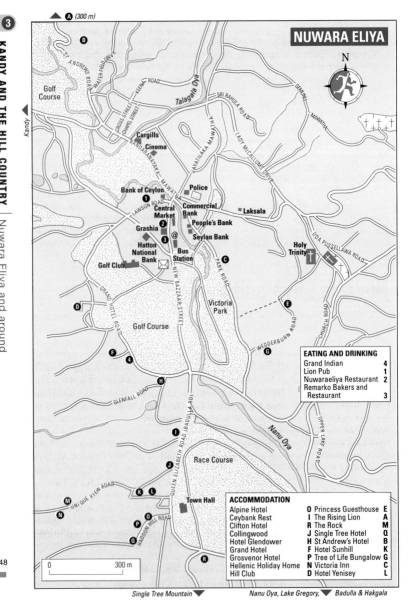

NUWARA ELIYA

N

EATING AND DRINKING

Grand Indian	4
Lion Pub	1
Nuwaraeliya Restaurant	2
Remarko Bakers and Restaurant	3

ACCOMMODATION

Alpine Hotel	O	Princess Guesthouse	E
Ceybank Rest	I	The Rising Lion	A
Clifton Hotel	R	The Rock	M
Collingwood	J	Single Tree Hotel	Q
Hotel Glendower	H	St Andrew's Hotel	B
Grand Hotel	F	Hotel Sunhill	K
Grosvenor Hotel	P	Tree of Life Bungalow	G
Hellenic Holiday Home	N	Victoria Inn	C
Hill Club	D	Hotel Yenisey	L

Single Tree Mountain ▼   Nanu Oya, Lake Gregory, ▼ Badulla & Hakgala

Spring in Nuwara Eliya

A popular resort amongst Sri Lankans, Nuwara Eliya is at its busiest during the Sinhalese–Tamil **new year** in April, when spring comes to the hill country, the flowers bloom and the Colombo smart set descend. For ten days the town gets overrun and accommodation prices go through the roof, while visitors are entertained by a succession of events, including horse racing, golf tournaments, motor-cross (motorcycles), clay-pigeon shooting and a mini-carnival.

especially if you can afford to stay in one of the town's nicer hotels, and also makes an excellent base for **excursions** into the spectacular surrounding countryside and tea estates.

Some history

Although there's evidence of Kandyan involvement in the region, Nuwara Eliya is essentially a British creation. The Nuwara Eliya region was "discovered" by the colonial administrator John Davy in 1819, while a decade later Governor **Edward Barnes** recognized its potential, founding a sanatorium and overseeing the creation of a road from Kandy, which he hoped would encourage settlement of the area. Barnes' plans slowly bore fruit, and during the 1830s the town gradually developed into a commercial and coffee-planting centre, with a largely British population. In 1847, **Samuel Baker** (who later distinguished himself by discovering Lake Albert and helping to identify the sources of the Nile) had the idea of introducing English-style agriculture to the area, laying the foundations for the town's important market-gardening industry: vegetables grown here are still exported all over the island, whilst many of the area's local Tamil tea plantation workers supplement their incomes by growing vegetables in their own allotments.

With the gradual failure of the coffee crop during the 1870s, local planters turned their attention to the beverage which would radically change the physical and social face of the region: **tea**. The first experimental plantation was established in 1867 by Sir James Taylor at the Loolecondera Estate, between Kandy and Nuwara Eliya, and the success of his experiment led to Nuwara Eliya becoming the centre of Sri Lanka's tea-growing industry. British influence went beyond quaint architecture and golf, however. Whereas the coffee industry had required only seasonal labour, tea required year-round workers, and this led to the arrival of massive numbers of Tamil migrant workers from South India – the so-called **Plantation Tamils** – who settled permanently in the area and decisively changed the region's demographic make-up; about sixty percent of the population here is now Tamil.

Nuwara Eliya continued to grow throughout the 1870s; Governor Sir William Gregory converted a patch of marshland just south of the town into Gregory's Lake, whilst the island's first large-scale brewery was opened in 1881 just outside town near Lover's Leap. In 1885 the railway line to nearby Nanu Oya was completed, and visitors began to flock to the town. Trout were introduced into the lake and local streams, the golf course was constructed and the first horse races held. Nuwara Eliya continued as a major centre of tea-planting as well as of British (and later Sinhalese) society until Independence and after. The town was briefly convulsed by riots in 1983, but the Plantation Tamils largely kept out of the Sinhalese–Tamil conflicts of the 1980s and 1990s. The modern town continues to serve as a focus of the tea industry, as an agricultural centre and tourist town – though local Sinhalese visitors now tend to outnumber foreign tourists.

Arrival and accommodation

Nuwara Eliya doesn't have it's own **train station**; the nearest stop is at **Nanu Oya**, about 5km down the road. Buses to Nuwara Eliya meet all arriving trains (despite what touts might tell you). Alternatively, a minivan-taxi into town will cost around Rs.100. Arriving **by bus**, you'll end up at the new bus station in the middle of town. A tuktuk from here to pretty much any of the guest houses shouldn't cost more than Rs.50.

Accommodation

More than anywhere else in Sri Lanka, your choice of **accommodation** in Nuwara Eliya is likely to have a decisive influence on how much you enjoy your visit. This really is a place where it's worth prising open your wallet and indulging in a bit of colonial nostalgia by staying in one of the patrician old colonial hotels – the *Grand Hotel*, *St Andrew's* and the *Hill Club*. Even if you can't afford one of the top-end places, there are plenty of attractive mid-range alternatives.

If you're counting the pennies, it also pays to choose with care; there are plenty of very indifferent places, a reflection of the fact that Nuwara Eliya is geared up as much for Sri Lankan visitors as for foreigners – come the weekend or holiday periods, many places get overrun by parties of hormonal schoolboys or pissed-up locals. Remember too that, given the vagaries of the local climate, you might spend much longer in your room than in other parts of the island, and a basic budget place that would be fine in sunny coastal climes can be depressing in rainy Nuwara Eliya. Wherever you stay, make sure you've got reliable hot water and plenty of blankets, and check to see how many lights there are in your room (and whether they work; Nuwara Eliya's hoteliers appear to have a constitutional aversion to buying new light bulbs – if you get stuck, buy your own from one of the town's supermarkets). The better places either include heaters in their room rates or offer them for hire for Rs.150–250 per day.

Prices can fluctuate to reflect local holidays. Many places hike rates at weekends, especially over "long" weekends, when the Friday or Monday is a poya day. Rates also rise during December and Christmas, and over the "mini-season" during the school vacations in August, whilst rates in most places double or triple during the April **new year** (see previous page). The price codes given below are for basic weekday room rates outside these peak times.

Incidentally, despite Nuwara Eliya's name (it means "City of Light"), it's well worth bringing or acquiring a **torch** if you plan to leave your guest house at night. The municipal budget hasn't yet extended to laying on any decent street lighting, and there's every chance that you'll end up knee deep in mud or, even less appetisingly, in one of the town's many open drains if you can't see where you're going.

Food is available in all the following places.

Budget

Clifton Hotel 154 Badulla Rd ☎052-222 2471. Pleasantly cosy and characterful old guest house kitted out with a mishmash of old-fashioned furniture and carpets – it's all a bit like going to stay with an elderly relative, right down to the pervasive smell of mothballs, but it's good value, and offers excellent single rates. ②

Grosvenor Hotel 6 Haddon Hill Rd ☎052-222 2307. One of the town's smarter budget places,

with attractive public areas and a slightly English B&B feel. The ten rooms are nicely furnished, though a tad gloomy, and there's a pleasant restaurant. ②

Hellenic Holiday Home 49/1 Unique View Rd ☎ & ☎052-223 4437. A stiff ten-minute walk up from the main road, though with correspondingly fine views, and the ten carpeted rooms are very comfy and nicely appointed. The restaurant has only a limited choice, however, so you'll have to

trudge back down to town if you want some culinary excitement – a long, dark walk at night. ❸
Princess Guest House 12 Wedderburn Rd ☎052-222 2462. Set in an atmospheric old villa, this place seems to have survived in a time-warp, complete with dotty but charming valetudinarian staff. Rooms are big and bizarrely furnished, with eccentric double beds, crazy bedclothes, fireplaces and even the odd roll-top bath – bags of maverick, if slightly frayed, character. ❸
The Rising Lion 3 Sri Piyatissapura Mw ☎052-222 2083, ⓕ223 4042. Located on a hill above the north end of town at an altitude of around 2600m, this place claims to be the highest hotel in Sri Lanka, offering memorable views from the restaurant and two front-facing rooms, as well as friendly management, wackily furnished public areas (featuring copious stag's antlers) and clean, bright good-value rooms. Heaters on request Rs.150. Free pick-up from bus stand; or from Nanu Oya railway station for Rs.150. No single rates. Without view ❷, with view ❸
Single Tree Hotel 1/8 Haddon Hill Rd ☎052-222 3009. Recently renovated guest house with ten smart, warm, wood-panelled rooms – it's all a bit like being in an enormous sauna. Excellent value, if not particularly atmospheric. Also a good place to arrange tours (see p.255). ❷
Hotel Sunhill 18 Unique View Rd ☎052-222 2878, ⓕ222 3770. One of Nuwara Eliya's largest and most popular budget places. Standard rooms are bright and reasonable value, though a bit shabby and rather small; the smart, modern deluxe ones are better value, with TV, nicely furnished and with good views. There's also a dark and very cosy pub-style bar, and good food in the main downstairs restaurant. Standard ❷, deluxe ❸
Victoria Inn 15 Park Rd ☎052-222 2321. Set in a tranquil and convenient location overlooking Victoria Park, with nine cheap and reasonably comfy rooms. Good value, if a bit basic. Staff can arrange all sorts of tours (see p.255). ❷
Hotel Yenisey 16b Unique View Rd ☎052-223 4000. Medium-sized guest house offering a mix of cosy and nicely furnished "luxury" rooms (mad bedspreads, carpets and nice bathrooms) and acceptable if rather gloomy standard rooms. Good single rates. Standard ❷, luxury ❸

Moderate

Alpine Hotel 4 Haddon Hill Rd ☎052-222 3500. Modern mid-range hotel with 25 sparkling rooms, all comfy and pleasantly furnished, with swish bathrooms (all with bathtubs) and a few period touches and facilities including phone, satellite TV

and heaters. Very comfortable and good value, but pretty unatmospheric. ❹
Ceybank Rest Badulla Rd ☎ & ⓕ052-222 3053. Set in an aristocratic old country house – a former British governor's residence – and boasting plenty of colonial ambience, with immaculately maintained wooden fittings and period furnishings. Popular with locals and tour groups, though, so it's not always the most tranquil of places. ❹
Collingwood 112 Badulla Rd ☎052-222 3550, ⓕ223 4500. Attractively old-fashioned place with a real English country hotel ambience, complete with shiny wooden fittings and nicely decorated rooms, plus lots of old-fashioned wooden furniture – all very pleasant and cosy, although could be cheaper. ❹
Hotel Glendower 5 Grand Hotel Rd ☎052-222 2501, ⓔhotel_glendower@hotmail.com. Perhaps the best mid-range option in town, this welcoming low half-timbered establishment makes an excellent halfway alternative to the town's posh hotels, with plenty of period character, including a cosy pub-style bar, a pleasant lounge and billiards table. The six rooms and three suites are comfortable and charming, with pleasant wooden floors and furniture and lots of lights; all but one have bathtubs. Also has the added bonus of the town's best restaurant (see p.253). Standard ❸ three suites ❹
The Rock 60 Unique View Rd ☎052-222 3096. A steep ten-minute walk up the hill from town, though compensated for with fine views. Rooms (all with one double and one single bed) are very good value – spacious and absolutely pristine, with pretty floral decor. There's also a nice bar and pleasant restaurant – just as well, since the alternative is a long walk into town. ❸
Tree of Life Bungalow 2 Wedderburn Rd ☎052-222 3685, ⓕ011-282 4350. Gorgeously atmospheric colonial villa with a beautiful garden to the front, ideal for quiet afternoons with a teapot and sandwiches. The six rooms are spacious and pleasantly furnished, though a bit pricey for what you get. ❺

Expensive

Grand Hotel Grand Hotel Rd ☎052-222 2881, ⓦwww.tangerinetours.com/hotels.htm. Doughty half-timbered pile, over a century old, which appears to have been lifted wholesale from a golf course in Surrey. The gorgeous public areas are painfully redolent of Blighty, with a marvellous wooden staircase and the heady aroma of wood polish everywhere. Sadly, the rooms themselves are fairly ordinary, albeit relatively cheap. Those in the deluxe Golf Wing are comfortable if not terribly atmospheric; standard rooms are shabbier. Facilities include two good restaurants (see p.253), a health centre, gym, sauna and massage centre. **6**

Hill Club Off Grand Hotel Rd ☎052-222 2653, ✉hillclub@eureka.lk. Founded in 1876, this baronial-looking stone and half-timbered structure is Sri Lanka's most famous exercise in nostalgia, right down to the comfy lounge, musty billiards room, and reading room with battered leather furniture, stuffed stags' heads and dog-eared books, lit up with a fire every evening. Misogynists can retire to the cosy, pub-style men-only bar (there's also a mixed bar). Rooms are characterful and homely, with creaky wooden floors and dark wood furniture. Even if you're not staying you shouldn't miss coming for dinner or a drink (see p.253). **7**

St Andrew's Hotel 10 St Andrew's Drive ☎052-222 2445, ⊛www.jetwinghotels.com. Set in a late Victorian former country club overlooking a swathe of immaculate lawn and the golf course, this serene colonial-style hotel is the smartest place in town, its oak-panelled bar and dining room and gorgeous lounge retaining a delightful Edwardian ambience. Rooms in the old wing (all twins) are characterful and pleasantly old-fashioned; those in the new wing are brighter and more modern, though less atmospheric. There's also an excellent restaurant (see p.254), while guests have free use of the resident naturalist (see p.255) – a real bonus. No single rates. **7**

Around Nuwara Eliya

Humbugs Badulla Rd, Hakgala ☎052-222 2709. Homely and pleasant rooms plus gorgeous views down the escarpment into the massed hills of Uva Province. The pleasant little café does a big line in strawberries – fresh strawberries and cream in season (Rs.70), plus strawberry milkshakes and strawberry preserves – plus a few other simple snacks and meals. **2**

The Tea Factory Kandapola, 14km east of Nuwara Eliya ☎052-222 9526, ⊛www .aitkenspenceholidays.com. Set on a hilltop at an altitude of over 2000m, this spectacular five-star hotel was created out of the old Hethersett Estate Tea Factory, which closed in the 1970s and reopened as a hotel in 1996. The tea factory's original exterior has been completely preserved, with corrugated-iron walls and green windows, and it's not until you step inside the stunning interior atrium that you realize the place isn't a working factory at all, although there's still plenty of old machinery lying around, giving the place a look which is at once industrial and futuristic. Rooms are stylish and extremely comfortable, with stunning views to all sides, and there are loads of facilities including a nine-hole putting green, sauna, massage centre and gym. The beautiful surrounding tea estates are good for walking, and there's also a resident naturalist for birdwatching walks in nearby the cloudforest and trips to Horton Plains and other nearby attractions. **8**

The Town

Though Nuwara Eliya's attractions are relatively modest – the real highlight here is the surrounding countryside – the town is worth a quick look. It's dominated by the thickly forested mountain of **Pidurutalagala** (whose tongue-twisting name was transformed by the linguistically challenged English into the cod-Spanish Mount Pedro). Sadly, the mountain's summit has been taken over by the government – it now houses the island's major air-traffic control centre – and is out of bounds. The dense cloudforest which covers the lower slopes of Pidurutalagala is a treasure-trove of flora and fauna, with myriad bird species (including several endemics) and even the occasional leopard, though to see it you'll have to arrange a walk with the resident naturalist at *St Andrew's Hotel* (see p.255), since the hotel owns much of the land (and in any case if you go on your own you run the risk of getting dangerously lost).

The centre of town, strung out along **New Bazaar Street**, is now a featureless procession of concrete shops, though it's worth sticking your nose into the determinedly local **Central Market**, a picturesque little covered alley-way of fruit and veg stalls alongside some smelly fish retailers. Opposite here on the other side of New Bazaar Street, a side alley is packed with clothes stalls – a good place to pick up cheap quilted jackets if you're feeling the cold.

South of here lies **Victoria Park** (daily 8am–5pm; Rs.20); the entrance is at its north end, by the roundabout opposite the post office. Though it provides a merciful respite from the fume-choked streets, it's nothing special, with a few neatly maintained trees and shrubs, and some of the tallest eucalypti you'll ever see. The park also has an unusual ornithological distinction: despite its proximity to the smelly town centre, it's something of an ornithological hotspot, being visited by a number of rare Himalayan migrant **birds**, including the Kashmir flycatcher, Indian blue robin and the pied thrush, as well as Sri Lankan endemics such as the Sri Lanka white-eye, yellow-eared bulbul and the dull-blue flycatcher.

Opposite the park, Nuwara Eliya's sylvan **golf course** (see p.254) adds a further welcome splash of green, while to the south lies the town's scrubby **racecourse**, the scene of Sri Lanka's only horse-racing meetings, held here in April, August and December; each meeting lasts for a day, with ten to fifteen races. Beyond the racecourse, shabby Lake Gregory marks the town's southern end; you can follow footpaths around the banks, but it's not a particularly pleasant walk.

If you want to get a bird's-eye view out over the surrounding hills, there's a pleasant short walk, starting near the racecourse, to **Single Tree Mountain**. Go straight up the road immediately before the *Clifton Inn*, and walk up through tea plantations to the electricity station at the top, from where (in clear weather) there are marvellous views out to Hakgala and beyond.

Eating and drinking

Virtually every guest house in Nuwara Eliya offers food, but if you want to venture out, there are several decent **restaurants** in the larger hotels offering heaps of colonial charm and wholesome, English-influenced menus where you're as likely to end up eating pork chops as rice and curry.

There are several places to **drink** in town, either in the cosy pub-style bars at the top-end hotels – those at the *Hill Club* and *St Andrew's Hotel* are both nice – or in the string of local dives around New Bazaar Street – try the determinedly down-at-heel upstairs bar in the *Nuwaraeliya Restaurant* if you're feeling brave, or the equally raucous *Lion Pub*. The gloomy pub-bar in the *Hotel Sunhill* (see p.251) is a decent alternative if you're staying at the south end of town.

Collingwood Hotel 112 Badulla Rd. Big and rather plush restaurant with mainly Chinese-inspired food plus curries, fish, devilled dishes and spaghetti, all quite moderately priced (Rs.150–300).

Hill Club Off Grand Hotel Drive. Dining at this famous old hotel is an experience not to be missed, and a taste of the colonial lifestyle of yesteryear. Dinner is served promptly at 8pm: you'll need to pay the temporary club membership fee (Rs.60) and wear a jacket and tie – if you don't have your own you can borrow the requisite clobber from the club wardrobe's tasteless selection of 1970s leftovers. Food is either a three-course set dinner (US$14.50) or a modest selection of à la carte dishes (US$4.50–7), including fish, rice and curry, or grilled pork or lamb chops – the food is average, but the setting is deeply romantic, complete with discretely shuffling white-gloved waiters. Retreat to the lounge afterwards for the coffee and brandy. There's also a set lunch (US$12).

Grand Hotel Grand Hotel Drive. This stately old hotel supplies all sorts of culinary experiences. The huge plush pink main restaurant (with live band nightly) provides a suitably grandiose setting for the set menus (breakfast US$10, lunch US$11, dinner US$14), while the cosy supper club has award-winning à la carte offerings (though you'll have to put up with the live saxophonist). There's also a pleasant pub-style bar.

Grand Indian *Grand Hotel*, Grand Hotel Drive. Set at the foot of the hotel's driveway, this small café dishes up cheapish, fast-food-style north Indian staples – channa masala, veg korma or jalfrezi (Rs.150–170) – plus tastier South Indian dosas, vadais and uttampams (Rs.70–85). The food is variable, though tends to blandness. Lunch 11am–3pm, dinner 6–11pm, snacks at other times. The attached pastry shop is a decent place for a cup of tea and a cake.

King Prawn *Hotel Glendower*, 5 Grand Hotel Rd. One of the island's best Chinese restaurants, with a menu full of unusual delights, all beautifully cooked and crisply spiced – choose from dishes like shark fin with shredded chicken deep-fried Thai-chilli style or kang kung fried in hot garlic sauce. Relatively expensive, with mains from Rs.300 to Rs.700, but worth every rupee.

Nuwaraeliya New Bazaar St. The best of the down-at-heel little local restaurants along the main drag, with decent and inexpensive Chinese food downstairs and what's possibly Sri Lanka's cheapest beer (Rs.56) in the chummy little bar upstairs – though be prepared to field dozens of "Where are you from?" enquiries from curious fellow drinkers.

Remarko Bakers and Restaurant New Bazaar St. Good, cheap fast food, with evening and lunchtime buffets (lamprais, rice and curry, veg fried rice plus occasional hoppers in the evening), short eats and rolls, plus a small à la carte selection (you'll have to ask for the menu) of Chinese, Sri Lankan and pasta dishes and a decent selection of cakes.

St Andrew's Hotel 10 St Andrew's Drive. Set in the oak-panelled dining room of Nuwara Eliya's poshest hotel, the *St Andrew's* restaurant is one of the best places in town for a (modest) splurge. The emphasis is on wholesome and warming meat dishes like rack of lamb or oaty pork medallions, plus a couple of fish and veg options (mains from around Rs.400). You can watch your dinner being prepared in the open-plan kitchen and choose wine from Sri Lanka's only walk-in wine cellar, which has vintages from fifteen countries (from Rs.900 per bottle), plus Sri Lankan wines (from Rs.400).

Hotel Sunhill 18 Unique View Rd. The restaurant here is often one of the liveliest places in town, churning out reasonable Chinese and Sri Lankan staples at budget prices – but make sure they charge you the prices printed on the menu, and not ones they've just made up in the kitchen.

Listings

Banks and exchange The People's Bank on Park Rd currently has the only ATM in town which accepts foreign cards (Visa and MasterCard). There are also branches of the Hatton National Bank on Badulla Rd and Bank of Ceylon on Lawson Rd.

Bookshop Cargills supermarket (see below) has a tiny selection of English-language titles, as does the bookshop in the *Grand Hotel* (see p.251).

Golf The gorgeous Nuwaraeliya Golf Club course (☎052-222 2835, ℱ052-223 4648) winds through the town centre, beautifully landscaped with magnificent old cypresses, pines and eucalyptus. Green fees (with clubs, caddy and balls) are Rs.2500 on weekdays, Rs.2800 at weekends (Rs.1600/Rs.1900 if you bring your own equipment and caddy).

Internet The only place in town is Aishhwarya Communication on New Bazaar St, which has one dodgy but wildly expensive machine (daily 8am–8pm; Rs.10 per min). Slightly

cheaper Internet access is planned at the *Alpine Hotel*.

Pharmacy There's a (nameless) pharmacy next door to *Remarkos* bakery on New Bazaar St. The City Clinic, opposite the Hatton Bank, has a pharmacy, dispensary and medical laboratory.

Phones There are several places along New Bazaar St offering IDD calls.

Police The police station (☎052-222 2222 or 222 2223) is next door to the *Windsor Hotel*, though you'll struggle to find an English-speaker.

Post The post office (Mon–Sat 7am–9pm) occupies a bowel-tighteningly ugly pink and half-timbered monstrosity on New Bazaar St, just south of the town centre. There's a free poste restante service.

Supermarkets Cargills on Bandaranayaka Mw (daily 8am–9pm) has a decent selection of food and drink, plus a tiny bookshop and a Mlesna Tea Centre; the Grashia supermarket on New Bazaar St is also good.

Moving on from Nuwara Eliya

Full details of trains and buses are given on pp.287–289. There are frequent private and CTB **buses** to Colombo, Kandy and the train station at Nanu Oya, plus regular direct buses (CTB only) to Badulla and Hatton. If you've got an iron-clad backside and want to make the long journey down to the south coast in a single sitting, there's at least one service daily to Matara and Galle, usually leaving around 8am. For **Ella**, **Bandarawela** and **Haputale** it's far easier to take the train; by bus, you'll have to head to **Welimada** (every 30min) and change there (and for Ella and Haputale you may have to change again in Bandarawela).

Around Nuwara Eliya

The main reason for visiting Nuwara Eliya is to get out into the surrounding countryside, which boasts some of the island's highest and most dramatic scenery. The most popular and rewarding trip is to Horton Plains and World's End (see p.259), though there are plenty of more accessible options closer to town, including a couple of **tea estates**, the fine botanical gardens at **Hakgala**, and some wonderful **walks** through the surrounding hills. You might also consider a trip to the stunning and spectacularly located **Tea Factory** hotel (see p.252), virtually a sight in its own right, and a good spot for some lunch followed by a walk in the beautiful surrounding estates. A taxi there and back with a couple of hours waiting should cost around Rs.700.

Tours from Nuwara Eliya

There are lots of interesting destinations within easy striking distance of Nuwara Eliya. The most popular is **Horton Plains National Park** (see p.259), though there are plenty of other places, including tea factories, walks and waterfalls. You could also, at a push, use Nuwara Eliya as a base for visiting **Adam's Peak** (see p.274) – you'll need to leave at 10pm to arrive at Delhouse at around 12.30am, then start climbing at 2am in order to reach the summit for dawn. Many guest houses in town offer tours. All the operators listed below (except St Andrew's) are run by the same family, and so can pool resources. As a very rough rule of thumb, count on around Rs.1500 per group for a half-day tour, or Rs.3000 for a full day, including guiding and a vehicle seating up to six people, although there are all sorts of different permutations (and some scope for bargaining) depending on what you're doing and how big a group you're in. The return trip to Horton Plains usually costs around Rs.1800 per vehicle.

Alpine Adventure Tours *Alpine Hotel*, 4 Haddon Hill Rd ☏052-222 3500. Staff here can arrange pretty much anything you can imagine, including islandwide trekking, camping and guest house tours with CTB-licensed guides; they can also provide a CTB guide to take you around Horton Plains, as well as arranging guided walks elsewhere. Other trips include tea factory tours, a day-trip combining over twenty local waterfalls, and guided mountain-bike tours; alternatively, you can rent a 21-speed mountain bike (Rs.550 per day) and head off on your own. More unusual offerings include rafting trips to Kitulgala and Gampola; rock-climbing and mountain-walking; horse-riding around Nuwara Eliya and Horton Plains); plus canoeing and fishing. They can also set you up with a car and driver (around Rs.2000 per day for up to 100km).

Single Tree Hotel Tours *Single Tree Hotel*, 1/8 Haddon Hill Rd ☏052-222 3009. The hotel's knowledgeable resident guide Krisantha has his own vehicle and does trips to Horton Plains, tea factory visits to Labookelie and Mount Pedro, waterfall tours (including St Clair Falls, Devon Falls and Lover's Leap), plus islandwide tours to Ella, Yala, the Cultural Triangle and so on.

St Andrew's 10 St Andrew's Drive ☏052-222 2445. The resident naturalist here (see p.252) leads walks up into the unspoilt cloudforest which blankets the slopes of Pidurutalagala behind the hotel, offering a fascinating insight into the botanical treasure-trove contained therein, with its marvellous array of medicinal plants and endemic bird species (such as the yellow-eared bulbul, dusky-blue flycatcher and Ceylon hill white-eye), plus other wildlife, including dusky and giant squirrels. These tours are free to guests at *St Andrew's*, and may also be available to non-guests – contact the hotel.

Victoria Inn 15 Park Rd ☏052-222 2321. Staff here can arrange tours to Horton Plains, Labookelie tea factory, tours of five local waterfalls and Adam's Peak. The guest house's resident guide, Ari, also leads a marvellous walk out to Shantipura (see p.258).

Incidentally, it can be risky to travel outside town by **tuktuk** because of the steep and twisting roads – tuktuks do occasionally capsize on steep gradients. **Taxis** line up along New Bazaar Street.

The Pedro Tea and Labookelie tea estates

If you're interested in finding out more about the local tea industry, the **Pedro Tea Estate** (daily 6.30am–5pm; Rs.50), set beneath a flank of Mount Pedro about 3km east of Nuwara Eliya, offers a convenient introduction. The factory building and tea fields are less picturesque than others in the highlands (there's rather too much suburban clutter, and pylons straggle impertinently across the views), but the estate's easy accessibility and informative resident guide make it a worthwhile short excursion. Established in 1885, it remained under British ownership until being nationalized in 1975 (it was re-privatized in 1985) – its factory is still home to a few impressive pieces of old British machinery, some still in operation. The company now employs around a thousand workers and its plantations sprawl for miles over the surrounding hillsides. The resident guide will take you on an interesting **tour** of the factory (included in entry

---

Ceylon tea

The first use of the leaves of the **tea** plant as a beverage is generally credited to the Chinese emperor Sheng-Nung, who – in truly serendipitous manner – discovered the plant's potable qualities around 2700 BC when a few leaves fell by chance off a wild tea bush into a pot of boiling water. Tea developed into a staple drink of the Chinese, and later the Japanese, though it wasn't until the nineteenth century that it began to find a market outside Asia. The British began commercial production in India in the 1830s, establishing tea plantations in Assam and, later, Darjeeling, where it continues to flourish today. Sri Lanka's first commercial tea plantation was established in 1867 at Looolecondera state, southeast of Kandy, by the Scottish planter **James Taylor**, but only came into its own following the failure of the island's coffee a few years later. The introduction of tea also had a significant social byproduct. Coffee production was seasonal, meaning the migrant Tamil labourers working on the plantations returned to India for six months of the year. By contrast, tea collection continues year round, leading to the permanent settlement of Sri Lanka's so-called **"Plantation" Tamils**.

Tea remains vital to the economy – Sri Lanka is the world's second largest exporter, after India, with tea still making up around a quarter of the country's export earnings. Almost half these exports now go to Middle Eastern countries, however, which has made the industry vulnerable to the effects of warfare and sanctions in that region.

Tea production

The tea "bush" is actually an evergreen tree, *Camellia sinensis*, which grows to around ten metres in height in the wild. Cultivated tea bushes are constantly pruned, producing a repeated growth of fresh young buds and leaves throughout the year. "Ceylon" tea (as it's still known) is divided into three types, depending on the altitude at which it is grown. The best quality tea, so-called **high-grown**, only flourishes above 1200m in a warm climate and on sloping terrain – hence the suitability of the island's Central Highlands. Bushes at higher altitude grow more slowly but produce a more delicate flavour. **Low-grown tea** (cultivated below 600m) is stronger and less subtle in taste; **mid-grown tea** is somewhere between the two – in practice, blends of the various types are usually mixed to produce the required flavour and colour. The island's finest teas are grown in Uva province and around Nuwara Eliya, Dimbula and Dickoya; the flavours from these different regions are quite distinct, showing (at least to trained palates) how sensitive tea is to soil and climate. Low-grown teas are mainly produced in the Galle, Matara, and Ranapura regions of the south.

price, though he's worth a tip as well), after which you can enjoy a cup of the local unblended brew at the attractive café overlooking the plantations.

To reach the factory, either hire a **tuktuk** (Rs.300 return with waiting time; Rs.100 one way) or catch **bus** #743 to Ragala from the bus station.

Around 20km north of Nuwara Eliya lies the expansive **Labookelie Tea Estate**, the highest tea plantation in Sri Lanka, set in gorgeous rolling countryside. The tea gardens here are much more photogenic, and the countryside much more unspoilt, than at the Pedro, and the estate is well set up for visitors, with regular free factory **tours** and tastings. Labookelie is easy to reach, since all buses to Kandy pass right by the entrance. Alternatively, a taxi there and back should cost around Rs.750.

Hakgala Gardens and the Seetha Amman Temple

Hakgala Gardens (daily 8am–5.45pm; Rs.300) lie beneath the towering **Hakgala Rock** some 10km southeast of Nuwara Eliya, with majestic views across the hills of Uva Province receding in tiers into the distance. The rock is allegedly one of the various pieces of mountain scattered by Hanuman on

The entire tea production process, from plucking to packing, takes around 24 hours. The first stage – **plucking** the leaves – is still extremely labour intensive, providing work for some 300,000 estate workers across the island (mainly but not exclusively women). Tea pickers select the youngest two leaves and bud from the end of every branch – bushes are plucked every seven days in the dry season, twice as often in the wet. Following plucking, leaves are **dried** by being spread out in huge troughs while air is blown through them to remove the moisture, after which they are **crushed** for around thirty minutes, an action which releases juices and triggers fermentation – the conditions and length of time under which the leaves ferment is one of the crucial elements in determining the quality of the tea. Once sufficient fermentation has taken place, the tea is **fired** in a heated chamber, preventing further fermentation and producing the black tea which is the staple form of the drink consumed worldwide (except in China and Japan, where unfermented green teas still hold sway).

The resultant "bulk" tea is then filtered into different-sized particles and **graded**. The finest teas – often described as "leaf" teas, since they consist of relatively large pieces of unbroken leaf – are known as "pekoes", "orange pekoes" or "souchongs" (named after types of Chinese tea), sometimes with the addition of the word "flowery", "golden" or "tippy" to indicate that they use only the finest tips of the tea plant. Lower grades are indicated by the addition of the word "broken", while at the bottom of the scale come "fannings" and "dust", which form the basis of most cheap commercial tea – although scorned by the connoisseur, these tiny particles have the benefit that they produce a quick, strong brew, and so are perfect for tea bags. Sri Lankan tea-growers have also starting producing fine green (unfermented) and oolong (partially fermented) varieties.

Following production, tea is **sampled** by tea tasters – a highly specialist profession, as esteemed in Sri Lanka as wine tasters are in France – before being sent for auction. Unfortunately, although tea grows all around the Central Highlands, 94 percent of all the island's tea is exported, meaning that it's difficult to actually sample the end product in situ. Most tea is sold at auction in Colombo, though it's also possible to buy pure, unblended teas at shops around the island (see the various town listings for details) and sometimes on the estates themselves. When buying tea, look out for the Ceylon Tea Board lion logo, which guarantees that the stuff you're buying comprises only pure Ceylon tea.

his return from the Himalayas (see p.168) – its name, meaning "Jaw Rock", refers to the fact that Hanuman apparently carried the mountain in his mouth. The gardens were first established in 1861 to grow **cinchona**, a source of the anti-malarial drug quinine, and were later expanded to include a wide range of foreign species. They're also now well known, at least amongst dedicated horticulturalists, for their **roses** (in bloom from April to August).

The gardens sprawl up the steep hillside, ranging from the anodyne ornamental areas around the entrance to the far wilder and more interesting forests up the hill – the best views are from the steps and path (on the right immediately inside the entrance gate) that lead through the azalea garden up to a little pavilion. The wooded portions of the gardens include many majestic Monterey cypresses from California, plus fine old cedars, a section of enormous tree ferns, stands of Japanese camphor, and pines and eucalpyts, including a shaggy cluster of bark-shedding Australian melaleucas. The garden is also one of the best places in the island to spot endemic montane **bird** species, including the dull-blue flycatcher, Sri Lanka whistling thrush and Sri Lanka bush warbler. If you're lucky, you might also catch a glimpse of the elusive **bear monkeys** which also live here. To reach the gardens, take any **bus** heading to Welimada or Badulla (every 15min; 20min) from the private bus stand.

Head back along the main road towards Nuwara Eliya for about 1.5km to reach the **Seetha Amman Temple**, said to be built at the spot where Rawana held Sita captive, as related in the *Ramayana* (although the same claim is also made for the Rawana Cave in Ella; see p.265) – the strange circular depressions in the rock by the adjacent stream are supposed to be the footprints of Rawana's elephant. The small temple boasts the usual gaudy collection of statues, including a couple of gruesome Kali images, though there's not really much to see.

Shantipura and Uda Radella

Nuwara Eliya is the starting point for a wonderful **walk** that leads to the village of Shantipura and the unforgettable viewpoint at Uda Radella. Pioneered by Ari at the *Victoria Inn* (see p.255), who you'll need to enlist as a guide, the walk takes six to seven hours and is quite taxing, with plenty of climbing and some treacherously slippery sections in places; wear good shoes, and bring food and drink. Prices are negotiable but inexpensive – reckon on around Rs.1500 per group; maybe less if there are only two or three of you.

The walk begins by climbing up **Single Tree Mountain** (see p.253), then continues along the ridgetop above Nuwara Eliya, through tea plantations and eucalyptus forest, before dropping down on the far side past a pretty Hindu temple and into the isolated little Tamil plantation village of **Shantipura**. Despite its proximity to Nuwara Eliya, the landscape here is marvellously unspoilt, and the surrounding tea plantations are some of the most beautiful on the island, carpeting a succession of the gently rounded hills in a layer of intense green, dotted with the brightly coloured specks of sari-clad Tamil women at work. Beyond here, the walk continues through further pristine tea plantations to the astonishing viewpoint at **Uda Radella**, one of the finest panoramas in the whole of Sri Lanka, with views south to Adam's Peak – seemingly close enough to touch – and north to the hills around Kandy and beyond. You then retrace your steps through Shantipura by a different route, before dropping back down into Nuwara Eliya along Unique View Road.

Horton Plains and World's End

Perched on the very edge of the hill country midway between Nuwara Eliya and Haputale, **Horton Plains National Park** covers a wild stretch of bleak, high-altitude moorland bounded at its southern edge by the dramatically plunging cliffs that mark the edge of the hill country, including the famous **World's End**, where the escarpment falls sheer for the best part of a kilometre to the lowlands below. Set at an elevation of over two thousand metres, Horton Plains are a world apart from the rest of Sri Lanka: a misty and rainswept landscape dotted with beautiful patches of pristine cloudforest, whose characteristic umbrella-shaped keena trees, covered in a fine cobweb of old man's beard, turn from green to red to orange as the seasons progress. The cool, wet climate has fostered the growth of a distinctive range of flora, including various rhododendrons, bamboos, tree ferns and many endemic species of plant, making the Plains an area of great biological value and fragility, though the stands of cloudforest are now receding, possibly because of acid rain generated by motor traffic across the island.

The Plains' **wildlife** attractions are relatively modest. Herds of elephants formerly roamed the area, until they were all shot by colonial hunters, and though a few leopards still visit the park, you'll have to be incredibly lucky to see one. The park's most visible residents are its herds of sambar deer, which can often be seen hanging companionably around the entrance office waiting for handouts, while you might see rare bear-faced (also known as purple-faced) monkeys. The Plains are also one of the best places in the island for **birdwatching**, and an excellent place to see montane endemics such as the dull-blue flycatcher, Sri Lanka bush warbler, Sri Lanka whistling thrush and the pretty yellow-eared bulbul, as well as striking orange minivets. You'll probably also see beautiful lizards, some of them boasting outlandishly fluorescent green scales, though their numbers are declining as the result of depredations by crows, attracted to the park (as to so many other parts of the island) by litter left by loutish visitors.

Exploring the park

From the entrance, a nine-kilometre circular track leads around the Plains, walkable in a few gentle hours. For the first half-kilometre, the path leads through rolling open heathland dotted with gorse and rhododendron bushes before entering a stretch of wonderful cloudforest: a tangle of stunted, grey-barked trees covered in mosses and old man's beard. Another couple of kilometres and you reach the edge of the cliffs which bound this section of the park and the first viewpoint, **Small World's End**, after which it's a short 250m scramble up to **World's End** proper. From here, the cliffs plunge almost vertically for 884m, revealing enormous views across much of the southern island: you can see the coast on a clear day – the large lake in the near distance is at Uda Walawe (see p.283). There are also marvellous views along the craggy peaks which line the escarpment, including Sri Lanka's second and third highest, **Kirigalpota** (2395m) and **Totapolakanda** (2359m), which stand at the edge of the park. Another 200m beyond World's End, the path turns inland towards Baker's Falls. Ignore this turning for a moment and continue along the cliff edge for another 100m to another viewpoint from the overhanging rock ledge – it's said that no less than ten star-crossed couples have leapt to their deaths from here over the years.

From here, the track loops back towards the entrance, through open plains with cloudforest set back on both sides. A couple of kilometres from World's

End you pass **Baker's Falls** (named after Samuel Baker; see p.249). It's a slippery scramble down to the modest little falls themselves, after which you'll have to scramble back up again. The final couple of kilometres are relatively humdrum, crossing open moorland back to the entrance.

About 3km further along the road past the entrance to the park, a track leads off to **Poor Man's World's End**, an alternative viewpoint to World's End which acquired its name since you could enjoy the view without having to pay the hefty national park fees. The tight-fisted authorities have now closed off the track, though some guides still offer to take people to the viewpoint. Obviously, if you do this it's at your own risk, and you are, of course, technically trespassing. One other way of getting into the park without paying the fees is to do the extremely taxing walk up from **Belihul Oya** (see p.272), at the foot of the escarpment. It's eleven very steep kilometres of walking – ask for directions locally.

Practicalities

The park is open from 6am to 6pm; entry costs around US$17. You can hire a guide at the entrance for Rs.500 per group; it's fairly easy to find your own way around, although you might appreciate having someone explain the local flora. The Plains can get very cold and wet: take a thick sweater, stout shoes, something waterproof and food and drink; hot drinks are available at the tiny café attached to the entrance office. The Plains attract hoards of moronic teenagers at weekend, who come to camp out, get smashed on arrack, fool around and generally trash the place; mercifully they tend to arrive after midday, by which time you'll hopefully be on your way home.

You can reach Horton Plains from either **Nuwara Eliya** or **Haputale**. Note that the view from World's End is generally obscured by mist from around 10am onwards, especially from April to September, so you'll have to arrive early to stand a realistic chance of seeing anything. In practice this means that you'll have to **hire a vehicle**. The return trip with waiting time from either Nuwara Eliya or Haputale takes around ninety minutes and currently costs around Rs.1800 per vehicle. Most drivers will suggest you leave around 5.30am to reach the park by 7am, and World's End by 8am – it's well worth the brief pain of dragging yourself out of bed to do this. The drive from Nuwara Eliya is particularly beautiful, with trees poking their heads out of the mist in the valleys, while just before you reach the park there's a stunning dawn view of Adam's Peak (prettiest during the pilgrimage season from December to May, when the lights on the mountain are illuminated).

If you're completely strapped for cash, it's possible to reach the park by public transport, though it's a long and strenuous walk. The easiest place to start is **Haputale**; catch the 7.56am train to arrive at **Ohiya station** at 8.35am. From here it's an 11km walk (around 3hr uphill, and 2hr back down) up the road to the national park entrance, a pleasant hike with fine views (though the short-cut through the tunnel mentioned in some guidebooks is now closed). You won't reach World's End until around 1pm, however, by which time the views will probably have misted up. You should just make it back to Ohiya to catch the 4.36pm train to Haputale.

Badulla and around

Set on the eastern edge of the hill country the bustling modern town of **BADULLA**, capital of Uva Province and an important transport hub – you might pass through en route between the hill country and the east coast. If you do get stuck here overnight, there are a couple of modest attractions to while away a few hours. Thought to be one of the oldest towns on the island, Badulla developed into a major centre on the road between Polonnaruwa and the south, though the old town has vanished without trace. The town thrived under the British, developing into a vibrant social centre complete with racecourse and cricket club, though there's almost nothing left to show from those days now, save the modest church of St Mark's, a small and quaint Victorian structure which stands at the northern end of the town centre.

Easily the most interesting building in Badulla is the eighteenth-century **Kataragama Devale**, in the town centre between King Street and Lower Street (though you can only enter from the Lower Street side). It's very Kandyan in style: the main shrine consists of a long narrow wooden structure, decorated with a faded, possibly Kandyan-era painting of a perahera and terminated by a little wooden pavilion tower at the far end. Entrance to the shrine is through a colonnaded walkway and two fine carved wooden doors. Inside, the principal image of Kataragama is, as usual, hidden behind a curtain, flanked by statues of a pink Saman holding an axe and flag, and Vishnu, holding a conch shell and bell.

At the southern end of town stands the **Muthiyagana Vihara**, whose origins are believed to date back two thousand years to the reign of Sri Lanka's first Buddhist king, Devanampiya Tissa. It's a tranquil, if unremarkble, spot, though you might get a sighting of the resident elephant in the grounds.

Practicalities

The town centre is bisected by two main roads: **King Street**, the principal drag, and **Lower Street**, which runs parallel to King Street a block to the east. The **bus station** is bang in the middle of town on King Street; the **train station** is about a kilometre due south of here on the edge of town. There are branches of various **banks** in town; foreign cards are accepted in the ATMs of the Commercial Bank (Visa and MasterCard), on a small alley between King Street and Lower Street two and a half blocks south of the bus station; and Seylan Bank (Visa only), on Lower Street parallel with the bus station. The modern and well-organized **post office** is next to the bus station. For **Internet access** try Cybrain (daily 9am–7pm; Rs.4.50 per minute); follow Bank Road west from the roundabout by the entrance to the Muthiyagana Vihara for about 50m, then look for the tiny sign opposite the Bank of Ceylon. For **food**, you're limited to the guest houses and hotels listed below, plus the usual local cafés.

There are a couple of passable **places to stay**; note that Badulla is much lower and warmer than Nuwara Eliya, so you can probably get away without hot water. The pick of the bunch is the *Riverside Holiday Inn*, 27 Lower King St (☏055-222 2090; ❷). This is the smartest place in town (for what that's worth), although despite the name it's actually adjacent to an unsightly mass of Ceylon Electricity Board pylons and transformers. Rooms are pleasant, modern and very good value (though a couple are rather dark) and the rooftop restaurant is the best in town, with a big menu of inexpensive Sri Lankan and Chinese standards. Badulla's cheapest option is the good-value *Peace Haven Inn*, 18 Old Bedes Road (☏055-222 2523; ❶), set in a pleasantly quiet location on the north side of town and offering slightly basic but perfectly acceptable rooms, and decent food. The town's *Rest House*, on King Street, is rather noisy and shabby, although its restaurant dishes up cheap beer and simple but decent and good-value set meals (Rs.150–250), if you don't mind the agonizingly slow service.

Badulla is a major regional transport hub and sits at the end of the railway line from Kandy (for more details of **train** services, see timetable on p.288). The **bus station** is unusually clearly laid out, and has a helpful information office on its far side. There are regular departures to Colombo, Kandy, Monaragala, Bandarawela, Ella and Wellawaya; for Haputale either take a Colombo bus, or go to Bandarawela and change there. Heading south, there are twice-daily departures to Kataragama, and once-daily services to Matara and Galle. For full details of bus services, see p.287.

Around Badulla: Dunhina Falls and Bogoda Bridge

Around 7km north of Badulla lie the majestic, 63-metre-high **Dunhinda Falls** (entrance Rs.25), reached via a beautiful drive from town, followed by a pleasant 1.5km scramble along a rocky little path during which you cross a wobbly, Indiana Jones-style suspension bridge. The falls themselves, fed by the Badulla Oya, are the island's seventh highest, but are most notable more for their sheer volume, spewing out an impressive quantity of water which creates great clouds of spray as it crashes into the pool below. The trip from Badulla costs around Rs.200 return by **tuktuk**, including waiting time. Alternatively, **buses** running past the path to the falls leave town about every thirty minutes. Avoid weekends and public holidays, when the falls are thronged with locals. Whenever you visit, there should be a few stalls serving drinks and snacks.

Some 13km west of Badulla, the remote village of **BOGODA** is home to an extremely unusual **roofed bridge**, its tiled roof supported by elegant wooden columns. The bridge lies on a pilgrimage route which connects with Mahiyangana and the Dowa Temple near Ella, and there is thought to have been a bridge here since the twelfth century, though the present structure dates from around 1700. The nearby **Raja Maha Vihara** rock temple dates back to the eighteenth century and has a few old murals and a large reclining Buddha – though the deeply rural setting on the banks of the small Galanda Oya is at least half the attraction. You'll need your own transport to get to Bogoda; a taxi should cost around Rs.1000; a tuktuk a bit less.

Ella

Set on the southeastern edge of Uva Province, beautiful **ELLA** is one of the island's most beguiling destinations. It's the closest thing to an English country village you'll find in Sri Lanka, enjoying a pleasantly temperate climate and surrounded by idyllic green hills, covered with tea plantations and offering some good walking – and there's also the added bonus of good cheap accommodation and excellent home cooking. And, to cap it all off, the village enjoys one of the finest views in Sri Lanka, past the towering bulk of **Ella Rock** and through a cleft in the hills – the so-called **Ella Gap** – to the plains far below.

Ella is famous in Sri Lankan folklore for its *Ramayana* connections: according to one tradition, the demon king Rawana brought the captive Sita here and hid her away in a cave a couple of kilometres outside the present-day village. Rawana's name is now memorialized in the names of various guest houses, as well as in the **Rawana Ella Falls**, which plunge magnificently down a series of rock faces 6km from Ella.

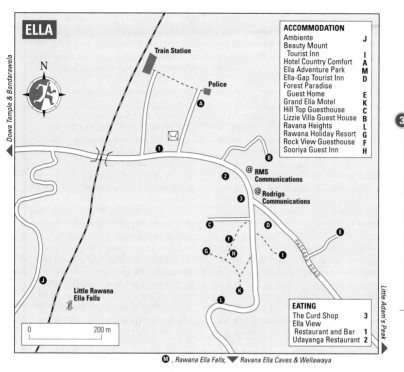

ELLA

Train Station

Police

N

ACCOMMODATION
Ambiente	J
Beauty Mount	
Tourist Inn	I
Hotel Country Comfort	A
Ella Adventure Park	M
Ella-Gap Tourist Inn	D
Forest Paradise	
Guest Home	E
Grand Ella Motel	K
Hill Top Guesthouse	C
Lizzie Villa Guest House	B
Ravana Heights	L
Rawana Holiday Resort	G
Rock View Guesthouse	F
Sooriya Guest Inn	H

@ RMS
Communications

@ Rodrigo
Communications

PASSARA ROAD

**Little Rawana
Ella Falls**

0   200 m

EATING
The Curd Shop	3
Ella View	
Restaurant and Bar	1
Udayanga Restaurant	2

M , *Rawana Ella Falls,* ▼ *Ravana Ella Caves & Wellawaya*

Arrival and accommodation

Buses drop off passengers at the road junction outside the *Curd Shop* in the centre of the village, close to all the guest houses (except the *Ambiente*). RMS Communications and Rodrigo Communications, both on the main street have **Internet** access (daily 9am–8/9pm; Rs.6 per min), IDD **phone** facilities and are open till 8–9pm. If you need a **bank**, you'll have to go to Bandarawela. **Taxis** hang out around the centre of the village. Alternatively, most of the village's guest houses can arrange taxis and tours. **Rodrigo Communication**s (☎057-223 2122, ✉tourinfo@sltnet.lk) is a good source of general info about the area, and runs a range of tours including walking trips through the hills and lowlands (Rs.600 per day guiding fee, plus transport costs), as well as conventional islandwide guest house tours, camping trips to Yala and a handy one-day tour including the Rawana Ella Falls, Buduruwagala and Diyaluma Falls (Rs.2500–Rs.3500 for 1–4 people, including lunch). Rodrigo's also have one 250cc motorbike for hire (Rs.350 per day).

Accommodation

Not the least of Ella's attractions is its good selection of characterful and good-value **guest houses**, mainly budget-oriented; there's also a couple of mid-range options, though no top-end options as yet. In general, places with a view are significantly more expensive than those without. Ella's country charm belies the state of barely suppressed warfare between the village's various guest houses, which expresses itself in some aggressive touting – a couple of places

263

have a particularly bad reputation. **Touts** sometimes get on the train at Bandarawela (the last major stop before Ella), equipped with purloined business cards and the usual tales – make your own decision and stick to it. Ella gets busiest between November to February, when prices might rise slightly. All the following have hot water, although heating isn't provided – Ella doesn't generally get too cold.

Ambiente ☎057-222 8867, ⓔkanta@telenett.net. Ella's most spectacularly located guest house, offering sublime views over Ella Gap and the Little Rawana Ella Falls. Rooms are modern and tiled (though the cheaper ones are a bit small), and there's also good, reasonably priced food – mainly rice and curry. All in all it's relatively expensive – you're paying for the view – but probably worth it. The owner's two cute dogs take guests for walks in the surrounding hills. ❸–❹

Beauty Mount Tourist Inn ☎057-222 8799. Four very cheap but perfectly OK rooms set slightly away from the road in a pleasant garden (but no views). ❶

Hotel Country Comfort ☎057-222 8532, ⓕ057-222 8501. Excellent, slightly smarter alternative to Ella's standard family guest houses. The new block has twelve sparklingly clean modern titled rooms; the old wing occupies a lovingly maintained colonial villa with eight very pleasant, good-value rooms – although a couple don't have proper windows, only skylights. No single rates, though all prices are very susceptible to bargaining. Old wing ❷, new wing ❹

Ella Adventure Park 10km south of Ella on the road to Wellawaya ☎057-228 7263, ⓦwww.jetwing.net/ella. This attractive eco-resort enjoys a tranquil forest setting and a rustic, environmentally sensitive design – including one room in a tree house. The adventure is provided by lots of gung-ho activities, including paragliding, rock-climbing, abseiling and canoeing – or just trekking and birdwatching for the less adrenalin-charged. ❻

Ella-Gap Tourist Inn ☎057-222 8528. One of the oldest guest houses in Ella, this retains a charmingly sedate air, surrounded by pleasant gardens and with a fetching restaurant on a trellised verandah stuffed with plants. The five basic rooms are simple, clean, pleasant and quite big; the two modern tiled rooms are more expensive and not so good value. Excellent food. ❷–❸

Forest Paradise Guest Home ☎057-222 8797, ⓔforestparadise@123india.com. Just three pleasant, nicely furnished but slightly small rooms set next to pine forest on the outskirts of the village, so very peaceful, though it's a bit of an uphill hike out of town. ❶

Grand Ella Motel ☎057-222 8655, ⓦceylonhotels.lk. Boasts one of the classic views of Ella Gap from its garden and most rooms – this is what you're paying for, since the rooms are nothing special. Those in the new wing are pleasant but bland; those in the old wing are shabby and overpriced. Comes a very distant second to *Ravana Heights*. Old wing ❹, new wing ❻

Hill Top Guest House ☎057-222 8780. Perched at the top of a very steep hill, though the anticipated views are partially obstructed by trees. Rooms are large and rather bare – OK, but with less character and slightly more expensive than other places. ❷

Lizzie Villa Guest House ☎057-222 8643. Modern bungalow set in a beautiful garden full of fruit trees 200m down a quiet track off the main road. The nine rooms of varying standards and prices are all fairly simple, but perfectly acceptable, and the cheaper ones are very good value. ❶–❷

Ravana Heights Opposite the 27km marker just below the village ☎057-222 8888, ⓦravanaheights.com. The nicest place in Ella, occupying a smart, modern one-storey house with just four immaculate and excellent-value rooms, three offering picture-perfect views of Ella Rock and the Gap. The charming owner leads half-day excursions (guests only) by vehicle or on foot into the hills and plains. Excellent food, too. ❺

Rawana Holiday Resort ☎057-222 8794. Perched on a hill above the village, with four simple but pleasant rooms and a lovely balcony from which to enjoy the views over a pot of home-grown tea or the good home-cooked food (see p.267). ❶

Rock View Guest House ☎057-222 8561. One of the oldest places in town and getting a bit run-down, though with lots of old-fashioned atmosphere and a marvellous view of Ella Rock from the balcony. There are just four rooms – a bit bare, but clean and perfectly OK – plus good home cooking. ❶–❷

Sooriya Guest Inn ☎057-222 8906. Friendly little place with three modern tiled rooms – spotless, albeit a bit small. Dirt cheap and good value, though precious little character. Good food, too. ❶

The village and around

There's not much to **Ella village** itself: an attractive scatter of pretty little cottages and bungalows, enclosed in neat, flower-filled gardens, it preserves a pleasingly low-key atmosphere despite the number of foreign tourists passing through. The village's single street meanders gently downhill, past assorted guest houses and a couple of cafés, before reaching the edge of the escarpment, just below the *Grand Ella Motel*, from where there's the classic view of **Ella Gap**. There's also a small Buddhist temple on the road here, where nervous motorists stop and donate a coin for good luck before negotiating the treacherously twisting highway to Wellawaya, which descends into the sheer-sided valley below.

Head down this spectacular road for 6km to reach the area's most impressive sight, massive **Rawana Ella Falls** (also known as the Bambaragama Falls), which tumble for ninety-odd metres over the valley wall. It's an impressive (if touristy) sight, and you can clamber from some way up the rocks to one side of the falls – locals will offer to show you the way for a consideration. Other hawkers here will try to flog you little coloured stones (pretty, but worthless) taken from the falls. Some also hang around with various types of foreign coins scrounged off previous visitors (or exchanged for coloured stones), which they'll ask you to change into Sri Lankan rupees. Since none of them seem to have much of an idea of current exchange rates, it's probably the only chance you'll get in Sri Lanka to rip off the locals. A taxi to the falls from Ella costs around Rs.200 return including waiting time, or catch any bus heading down to Wellawaya.

En route to the falls, a few kilometres out of Ella, lies the **Rawana Ella Cave**, in which Rama is claimed to have held Sita captive, as related in the *Ramayana* – although a similar claim is made for the Seetha Aman temple (see p.258) near Nuwara Eliya, and in any case there's remarkably little to see, given the site's alleged significance. To reach the cave, head down the road from the village into the gap for about 1.5km, from where a side road on the right makes a stiff one-kilometre uphill climb to a small and rather rustic **temple**, built underneath a rock outcrop. From here, it's a steep and slippery climb – it can become treacherous after rain – up to the uninteresting cave itself. Local kids offer themselves as guides, and will pester you mercilessly even if you've no interest in visiting the cave, but it's really not worth the effort.

Little Adam's Peak and Ella Rock

One of the best ways to spend a morning in Ella is to tackle the beautiful short walk up to the top of **Little Adam's Peak**, a pyramid-shaped rock which stands opposite the far larger Ella Rock and offers marvellous

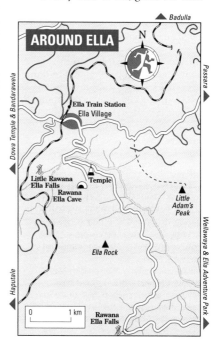

AROUND ELLA

Badulla

Passara

Ella Train Station
Ella Village

Dowa Temple & Bandarawela

Little Rawana
Ella Falls   Temple
      Rawana
      Ella Cave

Little
Adam's
Peak

Ella Rock

Haputale

Wellawaya & Ella Adventure Park

0   1 km
      Rawana
      Ella Falls

views out over the hills. The walk makes a very pleasant morning's excursion, and is fairly gentle and largely flat, apart from a small amount of climbing near the end. Count on around two hours return, and go as early as possible before the clouds set in. To begin the walk, head down the **Passara Road** for 1km, passing pine woods to your left. Just past the 1km marker the road turns sharp left by a garden centre; take the path that goes off the right-hand side of the road, straight ahead through beautiful tea plantations. Follow this path for 500m, ignoring the branch on your right which descends to a ramshackle tea pickers' village below. Keep left, following the path, with increasingly fine views to **Ella Rock** opposite and the **Newbourg Tea Factory** in the other direction. After another 500m you reach a point where two tracks go off on the right close to one another. Take the second track (past the green gate), and follow it for the final kilometre up to the top of Little Adam's Peak – the path weaves around the back of the peak and zigzags up to the summit, from where there are marvellous views of Ella Rock, Ella Gap and the very top of the Rawana Ella Falls.

If you fancy a more taxing hike, **Ella Rock** itself makes a good spot to aim for. There are various routes up, though they can become impassable during bad weather, so ask for directions and advice at your guest house before setting out. The usual route starts by following the railway line south of Ella for a couple of kilometres, passing right by the top of the **Little Rawana Ella Falls**, a small but eye-catching cascade, before striking up towards the summit. Another route starts from below Ella village, near *Ravana Heights* guest house. Take food, water and good footwear, and count on about four hours for the return trip – and take care in wet weather, when tracks can get slippery.

Dowa Temple

About 10km from Ella, and 6km from Bandarawela, the small **Dowa Temple** is set in a secluded narrow wooded valley and boasts a striking low-relief Buddha, carved into the rock face which overlooks the temple. It's similar in style to the figures at Buduruwagala, and may represent Maitreya, the future Buddha of the Mahayana pantheon who also appears at Buduruwagala. The temple itself is of some antiquity, though there's not much to show for it now apart from some fairly uninteresting paintings and a reclining Buddha. The return trip by taxi should cost around Rs.300; alternatively, take a bus from Ella to Bandarawela and ask the conductor to tell you where to get off.

Eating

Ella is perhaps the best place in the island to sample Sri Lankan **home cooking** – this effectively means rice and curry, rice and curry and more rice and curry, although the quality of the stuff served up in many places here is miles removed from the fiery slop which so often passes for the national dish. Don't come to Ella if you want **nightlife**, however: even by somnolent Sri Lankan standards, everyone seems to go to bed incredibly early – if you're planning on staying out "late" (meaning anytime past 8pm), let your guest house know, or you might find yourself locked out.

The Curd Shop Cheery little local curry house that has reinvented itself as a popular tourist caff serving rice and curry lunches, Western and Sri Lankan breakfasts and snacks, and excellent curd and honey, all at bargain-basement prices.
Ella-Gap Ella's prettiest dining room provides a pleasant setting for mouthwatering rice and curry (Rs.400) and a good range of Sri Lankan breakfasts, including pittu, kiribath, hoppers and string hoppers (Rs.200).
Ella View Restaurant and Bar Murky but sociable little café with a decent range of cheap,

It's generally more comfortable and convenient to leave Ella by **train** where possible, especially if you're heading to Haputale or Nuwara Eliya, which are rather awkward to reach by bus – and railway buffs will also enjoy the famous loop which the train tracks make just east of Ella to gain height. For timetable details, see p.288.

No **buses** originate in Ella, so you might have a problem getting a seat, although Rodrigo Communications (see p.263) can reserve places on some long-distance services for a small fee; they're also a good source of information on bus timetables. There are regular services to Bandarawela, Wellawaya and Badulla; for Haputale, change at Bandarawela. There are also occasional buses to Kandy (1 daily) and Nuwara Eliya (3 daily). Ella is a convenient jumping off point for the south coast, with around four direct buses to Matara via Tangalla and Hambantota daily. Kataragama and Tissa are served by a couple of direct buses daily; alternatively, take a Matara bus to Pamegamuwa Junction and change there, or go to Wellawaya and catch an onward connection from there. For more details, see p.288.

tourist-oriented snacks and light meals, plus several shelves full of arrack. It's about the only place in town that stays open past 9pm, so it's good for a post-prandial beer.
Ravana Heights The best food in town, with a daily changing set menu (order dinner by around 4pm; US$6) including wonderful rice and curry prepared using carefully chosen local ingredients and spices.
Rawana Holiday Resort For something a bit

different, try the special garlic curry (Rs.300) – that's a plateful of curried whole garlic cloves, rather than garlic-flavoured curry (the cloves are first fried with onions and fenugreek, then boiled with coconut milk and tamarind to remove the after-smell) – it tastes fabulous, and is good for you too. Pre-order by lunchtime. No alcohol.
Udayanga Restaurant Wholesome and ludicrously cheap rice and curry – six tasty dishes for a measly Rs.100.

Bandarawela

Midway between Ella and Haputale, but less visited than either, lies the lively little town of **BANDARAWELA**. Though it lacks either the rural charm of Ella or the dramatic setting of Haputale, Bandarawela has a couple of attractions in the shape of the area's most seductive accommodation option – the gorgeous *Bandarawela Hotel* – and the trail-blazing Woodlands Network. You could also use the town as a base for visiting Horton's Plains.

There's not much to Bandarawela itself apart from a couple of bustling but rather ramshackle streets and some views out to the surrounding green hilltops. The best thing to do here is to take advantage of the trips and other activities offered by the innovative **Woodlands Network** (☎057-223 2328, ⓦwoodlandsnetwork.org), based at the *Woodlands Hostel* (just off Esplanade Road near the bus station). The network was established in 1992 by a retired Dutch priest, Harry Haas, to provide visitor information and promote sustainable tourism. Haas died in September 2002, but the network is still going strong, offering a range of unusual local and islandwide tours featuring visits to organic tea estates, weaving cooperatives and herbariums, as well as walking tours and – for the very adventurous – homestays in plantation villages. They can also help set up **voluntary work**, doing things like working in villages or teaching English (Rs.7200 per month for accommodation and food), and organize cooking lessons and demonstrations (Rs.300 per person) – Harry Haas was a keen chef, and you can buy his books of recipes at the centre. They also arrange **ayurveda** treatments.

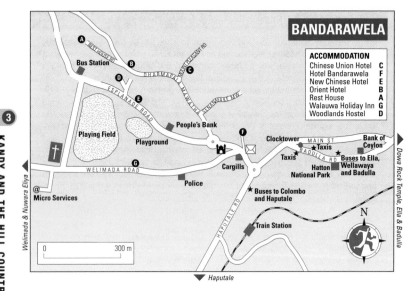

About 3km east of Bandarawela on the Badulla Road, the popular **Suwa Madhu** (☏057-222 2504) is one of the few **ayurveda** centres in the southern highlands, with a standard selection of massages, herbal and steam baths (Rs.1200 for a 45min massage, or a 90min combined massage, steam and herbal bath for Rs.2000).

Practicalities

The **bus station** is at the northwest end of town; the **train station** (and various subsidiary bus stops) are all in the town centre. To **change money**, there's a Peoples' Bank on Esplanade Road, and branches of the Bank of Ceylon and Hatton Bank close to one another on Badulla Road at the east end of town; none of the ATMs accept foreign cards. **Internet access** (Rs.9 per min) and **webcalls** (Rs.30 per min) are available at Micro Services just off the Welimada Road and at *Woodlands Hostel* (see opposite). There's a Cargills **supermarket** in the town centre for general provisions. **Food** is available at all the accommodation listed below, though apart from that you're limited to a few local cafés.

Unlike Ella and Haputale, Bandarawela is largely a local resort, and although there's plenty of **accommodation** around town, with the exception of the places listed below, it's all pretty shabby.

Accommodation

Hotel Bandarawela 14 Welimada Rd ☏057-222 2501, ⓦ www.aitkenspenceholidays.com. This gorgeous old hotel, set in a planters' clubhouse of 1893, is the biggest single reason to stay in Bandarawela. The personable, rambling wooden structure is brimful of charm, while the stylish rooms combine colonial atmosphere with modern comfort, with polished wooden floorboards, colonial fittings and quaint old metal bedsteads.

Bags of character at an extremely modest price. ⑥

Chinese Union Hotel 8 Mount Pleasant Rd ☏057-222 2502. Characterful and good-value little establishment that's been going for years. The old-fashioned rooms are very big and spotless, with crisp white sheets, and there's a pleasant little restaurant. ①

New Chinese Hotel Esplanade Rd ☏057-223 1767. One of Bandarawela's smarter and better-value budget places, with characterless but spot-

Moving on from Bandarawela

Buses leave Bandarawela from a confusing variety of places. Some depart from the main bus terminal; others from a couple of other stops elsewhere in town. Buses leave from the stop near the main roundabout just south of Cargills for **Colombo** (every 20min; 6hr) and **Haputale** (every 30min; 30min). Buses leave from the neatly labelled stands opposite Hatton Bank on the east side of town for **Ella** and **Wellawaya** (every 30min; 45min) and **Badulla** (every 10min; 1hr 30min). If you're heading for **Nuwara Eliya** or **Kandy**, it's far easier to take the train. By bus, you'll have to go first to **Welimada** (every 30min; 45min), then catch a Nuwara Eliya bus from there (and then a Kandy bus from Nuwara Eliya).

Heading to the south coast, there are regular services to **Matara** (7 daily; 7hr) and a once-daily service to **Galle**, both from the main bus stand. Heading east, there are twice-daily services from the bus station to **Monaragala**, from where you can pick up a bus to **Arugam Bay**.

For **train** timetables, see p.288.

---

less and nicely furnished modern rooms with tiled floors, and a decent range of Chinese food in the restaurant downstairs. ❷

Orient Hotel 10 Dharmapala Mw ☎057-222 2377, ℮ orient-bwela@eureka.lk. Big, functional hotel, with pleasant, good-value rooms, plus a gym, snooker table and karaoke lounge. There's a bar and restaurant with tourist-oriented Western-style dishes, and an extensive programme of tours and walking trips around the hill country and the east. Mountain bikes are available for Rs.250 per day. ❺

Rest House Rest House Rd ☎057-222 2299. Set in an attractive position above town, with good views over the hills and nine clean and pleasantly old-fashioned rooms. ❸

Walauwa Holiday Inn Welimada Rd ☎057-222 2212. Attractive, characterful colonial house – the fine old wooden doors carved with floral patterns give it the atmosphere of a Victorian vicarage. The five rooms are slightly musty but clean, well maintained and good value at the price. ❷

Woodlands Hostel 38 1/C Esplanade Rd ☎057-223 2328. Attached to the Woodlands Network (see p.267), and offering simple, clean and reasonable-value rooms. Guests have use of the kitchen, a small library, and Internet access (Rs.6 per min). Free pick-up from the bus or train station. No single rates. ❶

Haputale and around

HAPUTALE (pronounced "ha-poo-tah-lay") is one of the most spectacularly situated of all Sri Lankan towns, perched on a ridgetop at the southern edge of the hills country with bird's-eye views in both directions – south to the plains and coast, and inland across the jagged lines of hills which recede into the distance towards the high hill country. The town itself is a busy but fairly humdrum little commercial centre with a mainly Tamil population, though the mist which frequently blankets the place adds a pleasingly mysterious touch to the workaday markets and shops which fill the centre.

As with Ella, the principal pleasure of a stay in Haputale is the chance to get out and walk in the surrounding hills – most notably up to (or down from) the magnificent viewpoint at **Lipton's Seat**. Specific sights around town include the tea factory at **Dambatenne**, the evocative old country mansion of **Adisham** and the impressive **Diyalumi Falls** (see the Wellawaya account, p.274). The major drawback to Haputale is the **weather**, exacerbated by its exposed position. The marvellous views usually disappear into mist by midday, whilst the town is inundated by regular afternoon downpours for much of the year. Fortunately, Haputale boasts a few excellent places to stay and catch up on your reading, if you do get rained in.

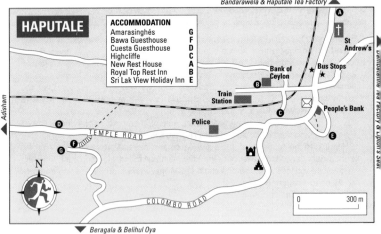

The Town and around

Views excepted, **Haputale town** has little to detain you. The most notable feature is the famously vanishing high street – a small bend in the highway as it heads west along the ridgetop out of the town creates an optical illusion, making it look as if the road simply disappears into thin air. The town itself is a small but lively mishmash of functional concrete shops and cafés. A small fruit and vegetable market straggles along the approach to the train station, offering the slightly surreal sight of crowds of loquacious Tamil locals in saris and woolly hats haggling over piles of very English-looking vegetables

Sadly little remains of Haputale's Victorian past. The principal memento is **St Andrew's**, a simple neo-Gothic barn of a building with a homely wooden interior which lies just north of the town centre along the main road to Bandarawela. The churchyard is full of the final resting places of nineteenth-century tea planters, along with the grave of Reverend Walter Stanley Senior (1876–1938), author of the once-famous but now mercifully forgotten *Ode to Lanka*, Victorian Ceylon's great contribution to world literature.

Dambatenne Tea Factory and Lipton's Seat

East of Haputale, a scenic road leads 10km along the edge of the escarpment through beautiful tea estates to the rambling **Dambatenne Tea Factory**, built in 1890 by **Sir Thomas Lipton**, the tea magnate whose name lives on in Lipton's Tea. The long white factory building is one of the most impressive in the highlands and preserves some of its original colonial-era equipment, including a pair of huge old withering trays, demonstrating the extent to which the tea-making process (and often the actual machinery as well) has remained unchanged for a hundred years or more. Disappointingly, there's no tea for sale, either to take home or drink on the premises. A rather cursory factory tour costs Rs.100 per person.

Beyond Dambatenne, a marvellous walk leads up to **Lipton's Seat**, one of the finest viewpoints in the country – the equal of World's End, but without the ridiculous entrance fee. The road offers increasingly expansive views the higher you go, leading steeply up through a perfect landscape of immaculately manicured tea plantations with scarcely a leaf out of place, connected by flights of stone steps and enclosed in fine old drystone walls. It's quite a strenuous hike to the seat – about 7km by road, though you can avoid the lengthy hairpins made by the tarmac and so reduce the overall distance by taking short-cuts up the stone steps. Lipton's Seat itself – named after Sir Thomas Lipton, who often came here to admire the view – sits perched at the edge of a cliff, with enormous panoramas over the southern part of the island all the way to the coast on a clear day. As with World's End, the viewpoint clouds over most days from about 10am, so you'll need to arrive early.

Buses for the factory leave from the south side of the bus stand in Haputale, opposite the *Muslim Hotel*. Alternatively, a **taxi** will cost around Rs.250 one-way to Dambatenne, or Rs.500 to Lipton's Seat. A good plan is to take a taxi all the way up to Lipton's Seat then walk back down, either to the tea factory or all the way back to Haputale – you should reach the viewpoint before it clouds over, after which you're walking downhill all the way.

Adisham and the walk to Idalgashina

Just east of Haputale, the grand colonial mansion of **Adisham** (Sat & Sun 9am–noon & 2–4.30pm; Rs.60) offers a misty-eyed moment of English nostalgia in the heart of the tropics. Adisham was built by **Sir Thomas Villiers**, who named it after the English village in which he was born, and modelled some of its neo-Gothic features on Leeds Castle. No expense was spared in the construction of the rather dour-looking building, with its rusticated granite walls and vaguely Tudor-style windows. The house was bought by the Benedictine monastic order in the 1960s and now functions as a monastery, though some of the chintzy original fittings remain. Adisham is about 3km east of Haputale; to get there, take the main road west from the town centre. This forks after 2km; take the left-hand (uphill) fork, marked with an easily missed sign, and follow it for a further kilometre. Alternatively, a tuktuk will cost around Rs.150 return. The road to Adisham goes through the **Tangamalai** bird sanctuary, a small patch of undisturbed highland forest. Sadly it's closed to the public, though you might see some of its avian residents from the tarmac.

Beyond Adisham, a fine walk leads west along the ridgetop towards the village of **Idalgashina**. The path starts just to the left of the Adisham gates and runs for 3km through alternating patches of dense original highland woodland, (rich in birdlife, as well as other wildlife including lots of monkeys) and airy stands of eucalyptus. The track is reasonably easy to follow at first, though it becomes indistinct in places further on (the directions below should suffice, though). After about 1km the path comes out to the edge of the ridge at the beginning of the first stands of eucalyptus. Below you can see Glenanore Tea Factory and (a little later) the railway tracks far below (they will gradually rise to meet you). From here on, the path sometimes sticks to the edge of the ridge, sometimes turns away from edge, undulating slightly but always keeping roughly to the same height. After a further 1.5km you'll see railway tracks again, now much closer. Over the next 500m the path winds down the edge of the ridge to meet the ascending railway, at which point there's a wonderful view south, with impressive sheer cliffs to the left framing views of the lines of hills descending to the south, and the flat, hot plains beyond. From here you can either continue along the railway tracks to Idalgashina (about 6km) and catch a train back, or return to Haputale along the tracks (about 4km).

Practicalities

Haputale's **train station** and **bus stops** are close to one another in the town centre. A tuktuk from here to the guest houses west of town will cost around

Rs.30. If you want to **change money** there are branches of the People's Bank and Bank of Ceylon (but no ATMs). There's an agency **post office** opposite the People's Bank. The only **Internet** access in town is at the *Amarasinghe Guest House* (Rs.7 per min). For **eating**, you're limited to the various guest houses (see the listings below); several of these do good home cooking, though you're pretty much limited to rice and curry and you'll need to order at least a couple of hours in advance, even in your own guest house.

Haputale is a good place from which to visit **Horton Plains** – both the *Cuesta* and *Amarasinghe* guest houses can arrange transport from around Rs.1800, as well as **tours** to local attractions such as the Diyaluma Falls and Buduruwagala. *Amarasinghe*'s also run camping and walking tours in the highlands, Yala, Singharaja and other locations.

Accommodation

Accommodation in Haputale is extremely good value, though not everywhere has views – the best are from the *Cuesta Guest House* and *Sri Lak View Holiday Inn*. Incidentally, if you're staying at one of the guest houses west of town, there's a useful little shortcut to the town centre, as follows: opposite where the steps come up onto the main road from the *Amarasinghe* and *Bawa* guest houses, follow the steps down to the railway line and then walk along the tracks into town (significantly quicker than following the slightly serpentine road).

Amarasinghe Guest House ☎057-226 8175. The nicest place in town, this extremely well-run family guest house has a friendly and informative manager and very good-value and comfortable (if slightly bare) rooms; those upstairs are slightly larger and nicer. Facilities include IDD phone facilities and laundry service, plus a small library – which you'll probably have recourse to, given the vagaries of the local weather. Decent food, including good rice and curry. Book ahead from December to March. Downstairs ❶, upstairs ❷
Bawa Guest House ☎057-226 8260. Five very cheap rooms in a small family guest house – nothing special, but perfectly comfortable, and good value at the price. ❶
Cuesta Guest House ☎057-226 8110, ⒺKacp@sltnet.lk. Perched right on the edge of the ridge, the rooms here are a bit basic and shabby, but have dreamy views (and small private

balconies to enjoy them from). There's also a cosy lounge and good home cooking. ❶
New Rest House ☎057-226 8099. Six pleasant and good-value rooms in a slightly old-fashioned rest house, attractively situated overlooking the hills. Standard range of cheap Sri Lankan favourites served in the big dining room. ❷
Royal Top Rest Inn ☎057-226 8178. Conveniently close to the railway station, with a mixed bag of rooms, with or without views, though three rooms share a bathroom. The two rooms with private bathroom and view are quite reasonable. ❶
Sri Lak View Holiday Inn ☎057-226 8125, Ⓦwww.srilakviewholidayinn.com. The best option in the town centre, with spotless, modern tiled-floor rooms, some with marvellous views south. The restaurant has an extensive, cheap menu of Sri Lankan and Chinese standards. ❷

West of Haputale: Belihul Oya

Around 30km west of Haputale, the pleasantly soporific little town of **BELIHUL OYA** lies in prettily wooded scenery at the foot of the hill country – a strenuous route leads from here up to World's End; ask locally for directions. The town is also the nearest jumping off point for the **Bambarakanda Falls**, whose three drops, with a total height of 241m, are the highest in Sri Lanka. The falls are 5km north of the main road between Haputale and Belihul Oya at the village Kalupahana; lots of buses pass through Kalupahana, from where you should be able to pick up a tuktuk to the falls.

There are a couple of **places to stay** in Belihul Oya. The attractive but overpriced *Rest House* (☎045-228 0156/0199; ❺) or the much more reasonable *River View* (☎045-228 0222, Ⓕ228 0223; ❹).

Heading on from Haputale to Nuwara Eliya, Kandy, Ella or Badulla it's easiest to take the **train**. For timetable details, see p.288.

   Hardly any **bus services** originate in Haputale, so it's pot luck whether or not you'll get a seat; you might prefer to go to **Bandarawela** (see p.269) and pick up a bus there in order to be sure of getting one. There are frequent buses to **Colombo** via **Belihul Oya** and **Ratnapura** (every 30min; 6–7hr); for **Badulla** and **Ella**, either pick up a through bus from Colombo or change at Bandarawela. For **Nuwara Eliya** you'll have to take a bus to Welimada and change there – it's much easier to go by train. Heading for the south coast, there are three bus services daily to **Matara** via **Tangalla** and **Hambantota**; alternatively, go to Bandarawela and pick up an onward service there (see p.269). For more details, see p.287.

Wellawaya and around

Standing in the dry-zone plains at the foot of the hills of Uva Province, the unexceptional little town of **WELLAWAYA** is, strictly speaking, not part of the hill country at all, though it's an important transport hub and provides regular connections to Ella, Haputale and beyond. The town itself is dusty and uninteresting, though there are a couple of worthwhile sights nearby – although it's also perfectly possible to visit these from Ella or Haputale. There are also a couple of excellent eco-lodges around the town of **Buttala**, about 15km east of Wellawaya – see pp.380–381 for details.

   The **bus stand** is in the middle of the extremely modest town centre, and a branch of the **Bank of Ceylon** is nearby if you need to **change money** (but no ATM). There are only a couple decent **places to stay** in town. Easily the nicest place is the *Saranga Holiday Inn*, immediately north of the market in Wellawaya's centre (☎055-227 4891; ❶, a/c ❷; not to be confused with the identically named but deeply inferior *Saranga Holiday Inn*, a kilometre further up the road). Rooms (including two with a/c) are very clean, pleasant and good value, and there's a reasonable restaurant with a long and cheap menu of Sri Lankan and Chinese staples. The *Rest House* (☎055-227 4899; standard ❶, a/c ❸), about 500m north from the bus stand, has dark and musty standard rooms and much more pleasant a/c rooms. There's also a bar and restaurant serving cheap, reasonable food. (Don't confuse this place with the filthy nearby *Rest Inn*, slightly closer to town).

   Wellawaya is the starting point for various **bus** routes, with frequent services to Ella, Haputale, Bandarawela and Monaragala. There are less frequent departures to Badulla and Nuwara Eliya. Wellawaya is also a major transit point for the south coast, with hourly services south to Pannegamuwa Junction, from where there are regular onward connections to Tissa, Kataragama, Tangalla, Matara and Colombo. There are less frequent direct services to all these places as well.

Around Wellawaya

Just south of Wellawaya lies the magical archeological site of **Buduruwagala**, located in a patch of beautifully unspoilt dry-zone forest, dotted with rocky outcrops and populated by abundant birds and butterflies. The site is home to a series of seven figures carved in low relief into the face of a large rock outcrop (whose outline is sometimes fancifully compared to that of an elephant lying down). The figures are some of the largest in the island (the biggest is sixteen metres tall), and are thought to date from the tenth century – they're unusual in displaying Mahayana Buddhist influence, which enjoyed a brief vogue in the island around this time. The large central standing **Buddha** in the *abhaya* ("have no fear") pose still bears traces of the stucco which would originally have covered his robes, as well as faint splashes of his original paint.

On the left-hand side of the rock stand a group of three figures. The central one, which retains its white paint and red halo, is generally thought to represent **Avalokitesvara**, one of the most important Mahayana divinities. To the left stands an unidentified attendant, while the female figure to his right in the "thrice-bent" pose is **Tara**, a Mahayana goddess. The three figures on the right-hand side of the rock are much more Hindu in style. No one's absolutely certain as to exactly who they are, though the general consensus is that the figure on the right is the Tibetan Bodhisattva **Vajrapani**, holding a thunderbolt symbol (a *dorje* – a rare instance of Tantric influence in Sri Lankan Buddhist art); the central figure is **Maitreya**, the future Buddha, while the third figure is Vishnu. The presence of square-cut holes in the rock above some figures – particularly the central Buddha – suggests that they would originally have been canopied.

To reach the site, head five kilometres south of Wellawaya along the main road towards Tissa, then turn right onto a side road for another 5km. Entrance costs Rs.100, and there's usually a resident guide hanging around, if you want one (he'll expect a tip). Count on around Rs.250 for the return trip from Wellawaya by tuktuk, including waiting time.

Diyalumi Falls

Around 12km west of Wellawaya and 30km from Haputale, the **Diyaluma Falls** are the second-highest in Sri Lanka, tumbling for 220m over a sheer cliff-face in a single slender cascade. The adventurous can clamber up a very steep path along the side of the falls all the way to the top, where there are a series of natural rock pools in which you can swim. There's also a gentler but more circuitous path to the top of the falls from further along the main road: walk for 500m towards Wellawaya and then take a left-hand turn up past a small rubber factory – the trail is rather indistinct, so you'll have to ask for directions as you go along. Allow an hour to reach the top.

To reach the falls, take any bus heading west from Wellawaya. If you're coming from Haputale, take one of the hourly buses to Wellawaya or catch a Colombo bus to **Beragala** (from where there are stunning views over the plains to the south) and pick up a Wellawaya bus there. Buses back from the falls to Haputale stop running at around 3–4pm, so leave early to avoid getting stuck.

Adam's Peak

Poking up from the southwestern edge of the hill country, the soaring summit of **ADAM'S PEAK (Sri Pada)** is simultaneously one of Sri Lanka's most striking natural features and one of its most celebrated places of pilgrimage – a miniature Matterhorn which stands head and shoulders above the surrounding hills, giving a wonderful impression of sheer altitude (even though, at 2243m, it's actually only Sri Lanka's fifth highest peak). The mountain has accumulated a mass of legends centred around the curious depression at its summit, the **Sri Pada** or Sacred Footprint. The original Buddhist story claims that this is the footprint of the Buddha himself, made at the request of the local god **Saman** (see box opposite); different faiths subsequently modified this to suit their own contrasting theologies. Sometime around the eighth century, Muslims began to claim the footprint as that of **Adam**, who is said to have first set foot on earth here after having been cast out of heaven, and who stood on the mountain's summit on one leg in penitence until his sins were forgiven. Hindu tradition, meanwhile, had claimed (though with no great conviction) that the footprint was created by **Shiva**. In the final and feeblest twist of the Sri Pada legend, the colonial Portuguese attempted to rescue the footprint for the Christian faith, claiming that it belonged to **St Thomas**, the founder of the religion in India, though this belief has never really taken root.

Despite all these rival claims, Adam's Peak remains an essentially Buddhist place of worship (unlike the genuinely multi-faith pilgrimage town of Kataragama). The mountain has been an object of pilgrimage for over a thousand years, at least since the Polonnaruwan period, when Parakramabahu and Vijayabahu constructed shelters on the mountain for visiting pilgrims. In the twelfth century, Nissanka Malla became the first king to climb the mountain, while later foreign travellers including Fa-Hsien, Ibn Battuta, Marco Polo and Robert Knox all described the mountain and its associated traditions with varying degrees of fanciful inaccuracy.

The climb

The ascent of Adam's Peak is traditionally made **by night**, allowing you to reach the top in time for dawn – this not only offers the best odds of seeing

---

Saman

Saman is one of the four great protective divinities of Sri Lanka, and the one who boasts the most modest and purely Sri Lankan origins. He is believed to have originally been a pious Indian trader (or possibly a king) who, thanks to the merit he had acquired, was reborn as a god residing at Sumanakuta (as Adam's Peak was then called). According to the quasi-mythological chronicle of Sri Lankan history, the *Mahavamsa*, Saman was amongst the audience of gods to whom the Buddha preached during his visit to Mahiyangana, and upon hearing the Buddha, immediately entered on the path of Enlightenment. When the Buddha returned to Sri Lanka on his final visit, Saman begged him to leave a footprint atop Sumanakuta to serve as a focus for worship; the Buddha duly obliged. Saman is still believed to reside on the mountain, and to protect pilgrims who climb it. He is regarded as an entirely benevolent and rather well-behaved god, unlike the decidedly fierce Kataragama (see p.198), whose fighting prowess and amatory naughtiness appeal to a very different sort of pilgrim. Saman is usually shown with a white elephant, an animal of both royal and Buddhist significance (the Buddha himself, in one of his previous lives, assumed this animal form); both Saman and his elephant hold a red lotus, and Adam's Peak is often shown in the background, its summit illuminated by a halo-like rising sun. He is almost only ever shown in normal human form, unlike many other gods, such as Kataragama, who are often shown with multiple arms and heads.

In characteristically Sri Lankan style, Saman has also become identified and muddled up with myriad other figures, including **Laksmana**, the brother of Rama in the *Ramayana*, or even Rama himself; some connect him with the Mahayana Bodhisattva **Samantabhadra**; while yet others believe that he is a form of **Yama**, the Hindu god of death. All these various identifications appear to be based on misinterpretations of Saman's name over the centuries, though they offer interesting examples of the way in which, in the constantly multiplying mythology of South Asia, an obscure, pre-Buddhist mountain god from a remote corner of Sri Lanka has been transformed into a figure of cosmic significance.

the extraordinary views free from cloud, but also the chance of witnessing one of Sri Lanka's strangest natural phenomena. As dawn breaks, the rising sun creates a **shadow** of the peak which seems to hang suspended in space in front of the mountain. The easiest ascent, described below, is from **Dalhousie**. An alternative, much longer route (15km; around 7hr), ascends from the **Ratnapura** side of the mountain via **Gilimale** – see p.279 for further details. An interesting walk, if you could arrange the logistics, would be to ascend from Dalhousie and then walk down to Gilimale. Another possibility is to take a tour from **Nuwara Eliya** (see p.255 for details of tour guides), climbing the peak from Dalhousie, although this makes for rather a long night.

Most visitors climb the mountain during the **pilgrimage season**, which starts on the Duruthu poya day in December or January and continues until the Vesak poya in May. During the season the weather on the mountain is at its best, and the chances of a clear dawn at the summit highest; the steps up the mountainside are also illuminated and little stalls and teashops open through the night to cater to the throngs of weary pilgrims dragging themselves up. It's perfectly possible, if less interesting, to climb the mountain **out of season**, though none of the teashops is open and the lights are turned off, so you'll need to bring a torch. Although most people climb by night, you can also go up the mountain **by day**, but the summit is often obscured by cloud and, even if it's clear, you won't see the famous shadow, or (assuming you're visiting during the pilgrimage season) be able to enjoy the spectacle of the night-time illuminations and all-night teashops on the way up.

Guides offer their services all round Dalhousie (from Rs.500), though you'll only really need one if you're a solo woman or are attempting the climb out of season at night, when the mountain can be a very cold and lonely place. A (free) alternative is to borrow a dog – all the local mutts know the track well, and will be happy to accompany you (ask for "Jimmy" at the *Green House* in Dalhousie, where they also have a three-legged dog called "Tuktuk"). You'll need a decent **torch** if you're climbing the peak out of season by night.

However fit you are, the Adam's Peak climb is **exhausting** – a taxing 7km up a mainly stepped footpath (there are some 4800 steps) which can reduce even seasoned hill walkers to quivering wrecks. The best way to go up is slowly. Allow around four hours to get up the mountain, including time for tea stops (although at particularly busy times, such as poya days, the crowds can make the ascent slower still). Taking the climb at a gentle pace also gives you the chance to mingle with the crowds of pilgrims, which is at least half the fun of the ascent. Dawn is at 6am/6.30am, so a 2am start should get you to the top in time, and there are plenty of tea houses to stop at on the way up to take shelter in if it looks like you're going to arrive at the top early (there's not much point in sitting around at the summit in the darkness for any longer than you have to). It can get bitterly cold at the summit: take warm clothing.

The track up the mountain starts at the far end of Dalhousie village, passing a copy of the Aukana Buddha and crossing a bridge. The path is easy to follow; the only possible place you might go wrong is right at the beginning, by a big but ambiguous yellow sign, where you need to go right (if you reach the *Green House* you've gone wrong). For the first thirty minutes the path winds gently through tea estates, past Buddha shrines and through the big makara torana arch which marks the boundary of the sacred area (the fact that Adam's Peak remains an essentially Buddhist place of pilgrimage, despite the claims of rival religions, is borne out by the complete absence of Christian, Hindu and Muslim shrines). Beyond here the path continues to run gently uphill to the large **Peace Pagoda**, built with Japanese aid during the 1970s. In wet weather the cliff face opposite is scored with myriad waterfalls.

Beyond the Peace Pagoda, the climb – and the steps – start in earnest; they're not too bad at first, but become increasingly short and steep. By the time you reach the leg-wrenchingly vertical section equipped with handrails you're within about 1500 steps of the summit, although by then it's a real physical struggle. One of the benefits of climbing by night is that you can't see the summit, which for most of the climb appears to tower an impossibly huge distance above. The path is very secure and enclosed, however, so unless you suffer from unusually bad vertigo, this shouldn't be a problem – and, obviously, at night you won't be able to see anything on the way up in any case. The upper slopes of the mountain are swathed in dense and largely undisturbed stands of cloudforest which are home to various species of colourful montane birdlife such as the Sri Lanka white eye and Eurasian blackbird, the sight of which might offer some welcome distraction during the slog up or down.

The **summit** is covered in a huddle of buildings. The **footprint** itself is disappointingly unimpressive: a small, irregular depression, sheltered under a tiny pavilion and painted in gold, with a concrete surround – although tradition claims that this is actually only an impression of the true footprint, which lies underground. Upon reaching the summit, pilgrims ring one of the two bells (you are meant to ring once for every successful ascent of the mountain you have made, if you want to join in). The **shadow** itself lasts for around twenty minutes, given a clear sunrise. One of the mysteries of the peak is the shadow's perfectly triangular shape, which doesn't correspond to the actual – and far more irregular – outline of the peak's summit. The Buddhist explanation is that this is not actually the shadow of the peak at all, but a miraculous physical representation of the "Triple Gem" (a kind of Buddhist equivalent to the Holy Trinity, comprising the Buddha, his teachings, and the community of Buddhist monks).

The **descent** is much quicker (count on around 2hr 30min) though no less painful, since by now your legs will have turned to jelly.

Adam's Peak practicalities: Dalhousie

The main *raison d'etre* for the extremely modest village of **DALHOUSIE** (pronounced "Del-house") is as a base for the ascent of Adam's Peak. It's usually busy with visitors during the pilgrimage season, but can seem rather desolate at other times. The village is rather beautifully situated by a river and surrounded by hills and tea plantations; various tracks head into the plantations beyond *The Green House*, in the unlikely event that you still have the urge (or ability) to walk after tackling the peak.

Dalhousie lies just over 30km southwest of the busy town of **Hatton**, which is on the main railway line through the hill country. **During the pilgrimage season** there are once-daily buses to Dalhousie from Nuwara Eliya and Colombo. Alternatively, take a bus or train to Hatton (see p.288 for train timetables), from where there are regular buses (every 30min; 90min) to Dalhousie. **Outside the pilgrimage season** there are no buses from Nuwara Eliya or Colombo and you'll have first to reach Hatton, then take a bus from Hatton to Maskeliya, and then pick up one of the battered old minibuses which ply between Maskeliya and Dalhousie (every 30min; 45min). The ride to Dalhousie is through beautiful tea country, with views of the Maskeliya reservoir. A **taxi** from Hatton to Dalhousie will cost Rs.600–700; a **tuktuk** will cost Rs.500 (or Rs.250 from Maskeliya).

Accommodation

There's not much **accommodation** in Dalhousie; you might want to ring in advance, and you should definitely reserve if staying over a poya day. In addition to the places listed below, the *Yellow House*, an old Dalhousie budget stalwart, is currently being rebuilt on a new site and should open sometime in 2004. There's also one accommodation option at the village of **Dickoya**, back down the road towards Hatton, as well as a number of tea estate bungalows in the surrounding countryside – see the box on p.247.

Dalhousie

The Green House Far end of the village, by the start of the track up Adam's Peak ☎051-222 3956. Engaging-looking place (and, yes, it *is* green), with quaint wooden gazebos in the garden. Rooms are fairly basic but adequate, with shared bathrooms and hot water on request. For Rs.450 you get food for a day, including a vegetarian dinner, breakfast and a pre-climb snack, and another Rs.100 gets you a herbal bath to ease aching muscles after the descent. Laundry and taxi service also available, and they can also arrange pick-ups from Hatton. ❶

River View Wathsala Inn On the main road by the entrance to the village ☎052-227 7427, ⓦ www.wathsalainn.com. The pleasant, spacious new upstairs rooms are the smartest in Dalhousie; the older ones downstairs are reasonable, though could be cleaner. All have beautiful views over the river to the hills. Rates are discounted by around a third out of season. Downstairs ❷, upstairs ❸

Sripalee Just past the *River View Wathsala Inn* ☎077-766 5402. Emergency standby if other places are full. Rooms are cheap, but rather shabby and depressing. ❶

Dickoya

Upper Glencairn Bungalow ☎051-222 2348. Some 7km from Hatton on the road to Dalhousie, this attractive old colonial tea planter's house is set in the middle of a working estate. Good value, though if you don't have your own transport you'll have to shell out around Rs.2000 (including waiting time) for a taxi to Adam's Peak. ❸

Kitulgala

The village of **KITULGALA** is set about halfway along the spectacular road which descends from Hatton down to the lowlands at Avissawella. The scenery is particularly dramatic hereabouts, with sheer-sided, forest-covered hills plunging down to the wild waters of the Kelani Ganga. The stretch of this river around Kitulgala provides the site for the best **whitewater rafting** in Sri Lanka, with grade three rapids some 5km upriver from the village. You can organize trips through the two hotels listed below for around Rs.2000 per person, or through other companies in advance – one of the best is Adventure Sports Lanka (see p.113), who can arrange trips to suit all abilities.

Kitulgala's other claim to fame is that it provided the location for David Lean's classic 1957 film *Bridge on the River Kwai*. If you know the film you'll probably recognize some of the locations down along the river; locals claiming to have worked as extras may descend on you en route in hope of a tip. (The "real" bridge over the River Kwai on which the film was based, incidentally, is at Kanchanaburi in Thailand, and looks totally different from the elaborate structure which was constructed here and then blown up during the making of the film.)

There are a couple of **places to stay** in Kitulgala. The *Kitulgala Rest House* (☎036-228 7528; ❺) is pleasant but rather expensive, with river-facing rooms and a dining room plastered with *Bridge on the River Kwai* memorabilia. The *Plantation Hotel* (☎036-228 7575; ❺) is similarly priced but better value, set in a restored colonial bungalow with attractively appointed rooms.

Ratnapura

Nestled amongst verdant hills at the southwestern corner of the hill country, **RATNAPURA** (literally "City of Gems") is famous for its **precious stones**, which have been mined here in extraordinary quantities since antiquity. Naturally, the town makes a big deal of this, with plenty of touts offering trips to gem mines and "museums" (read: shops), though unless you have a specialist interest in precious stones, this alone isn't really a sufficient reason to visit the place. Ratnapura does have other attractions, however. The town makes a possible base for visits to **Sinharaja** and **Uda Walawe national parks**; trips to both involve a long (3–4hr) return drive, making for a big day, but this does avoid the considerable bother of getting to Deniyaya or Embilipitiya. Most guest houses in town can arrange trips: the going rate for a jeep seating six to eight people is around Rs.3000 to Sinharaja and Rs.5500 to Uda Walawe – try *Travellers Halt* or *Kalavati* guest houses (see p.282). Ratnapura is also the starting point for an alternative ascent of **Adam's Peak**, though it's significantly longer and tougher than the route up from Dalhousie. The path starts from the

Gems of Sri Lanka

Sri Lanka is one of the world's most important sources of precious stones, and its gems have long been famous – indeed one of the island's early names was **Ratnadipa**, "Island of Gems". According to legend, it was a Sri Lankan ruby which was given by King Solomon to the Queen of Sheba, while Marco Polo described a fabulous ruby – "about a palm in length and of the thickness of a man's arm" – set in the spire of the Ruvenveliseya dagoba at Anuradhapura. The island also provided the "Blue Belle" sapphire which now adorns the crown of the British queen, while in 2003 a 478-carat Sri Lankan sapphire – larger than a hen's egg – fetched US$1.5m at auction.

Gems are actually found in many parts of Sri Lanka, but the **Ratnapura** district is the island's richest source. The origin of these gems is the geological rubble eroded from the central highlands, which is washed down from the hills along the valleys which criss-cross the area – a gravelly mixture of eroded rock, mineral deposits, precious stones and muddy alluvial deposits known as *illam*. Gem mining is still a low-tech, labour-intensive affair. Pits are dug down into riverbeds and amongst paddy fields, and piles of *illam* are fished out, which are then washed and sieved by experts who separate the precious stones from the mud. The mining and sorting is traditionally carried out by the Sinhalese, though the gem cutters and dealers tend to be Muslim. Your guest house or touts in town may be able to arrange a trip to a working mine, if you're interested in seeing the process first-hand.

Types of gem

The most valuable precious stones found in Sri Lanka are **corundums**, a mineral family which includes sapphires and rubies. **Sapphires** range in colour from blue to as clear as a diamond. Sri Lankan **rubies** are "pink rubies" (also known as pink sapphires); the better-known red rubies are not found in the island. **Garnets**, popularly known as the "poor man's ruby", and ranging in colour from red to brown, are also found. **Cat's eyes** (green to brown) and **alexandrite** (whose colour changes under different light) are the best known of the chrysoberyl group of stones. **Tourmalines** are sometimes passed off as the far more valuable cat's eye. Other common stones, found in varying colours, are **quartz**, **spinel** and **zircon**. The greyish **moonstone** (a type of feldspar) is a particular Sri Lankan speciality, though these are not mined in the Ratnapura area. Diamonds and emeralds are not found in Sri Lanka, though **aquamarine** (like emerald, a member of the beryl family) is.

279

RATNAPURA

▲ Maha Saman Devale (3 km) & Ⓐ (7 km)

▲ Ⓑ (1.5 km), Ⓒ (750 m), Ⓓ (500 m) & Katugas Falls (3 km)

National Museum

Bus station

INNER CIRCULAR ROAD

INNER CIRCULAR ROAD

GOODS SHED ROAD

CHURCH ROAD

MAIN STREET

DJ'S ROAD

People's Bank

Bank of Ceylon

Ⓖ

Cinema

Clock Tower

Public Library

Cargills

Police Station

PATTIYAWITA LANE

FRANK HETTIARACHCHI MAWATHA

Sampath Bank

Bank of Ceylon

Pizza Hut

Hatton Bank

People's Bank

Kovil

MAIN STREET

MOSQUE ROAD

WARAKATOTA ROAD

SAVIYA MAWATHA

SENANAYAKA MAWATHA

COUNCIL AVENUE

RIVERSIDE

DHARMAPALA MAWATHA

BANDARANAYAKA MAWATHA

THALAKOTUWA MAWATHA

THALGALLHARA MAWATHA

PAMBAHINNA ROAD

PULUNUGITIYA ROAD

MUWAGAMA ROAD

DHARMAPALA MAWATHA

Ⓔ

Ⓕ

Kalu Ganga

▲ Ratnapura Gem Bureau (1.5 km)

0 — 250 m

ACCOMMODATION

Darshana Inn	F
Kalavati	B
Nilani Lodge	G
Ratna Gems Halt	D
Ratnaloka Tour Inns	A
Rest House	E
Travellers Halt	C

village of **Palabaddale**, from where it's a climb of five to seven hours to the summit. Buses run to Palabaddale via Gilimale during the pilgrimage season.

Ratnapura also has the distinction of being one of the **wettest places** in Sri Lanka, with the annual rainfall sometimes exceeding four metres – and even when it's not raining, the climate is unusually humid and sticky.

The Town

A major regional commercial centre, Ratnapura is a busy and rather exhausting place, even before you've dealt with the attentions of touts trying to flog you gems or get you on visits to local mines. The heart of the town's gem trade is **Saviya Street** (also spelt Zavier, Zaviya and Zavia), just east of the clocktower, which presents an entertaining scene of locals haggling over handfuls of uncut stones; the shops of a few small dealers line the street (the town's traditional jewellers' shops are mainly located at the clocktower end of Main Street). Trading takes place on weekdays until around 3pm. You're likely to be offered stones to buy – it should go without saying that unless you're an expert, steer well clear (see p.279 for more).

If you want a more detailed look at the area's mineral riches, head out to the **Ratnapura Gem Bureau**, usually simply referred to as the "Gem Museum" (daily 9.30am–3.30pm; Rs.5), a couple of kilometres west of town on Potgul Vihara Mawatha; count on around Rs.40 by tuktuk each way. The museum is the brainchild of local gemmologist Purandara Sri Bhadra Marapana, and is intended as an altruistic and educational venture (although they might make a gentle attempt to flog you a few stones). The centrepiece is a colourful display of minerals and precious stones from around the world, including interesting Sri Lankan gems in both cut and uncut states. There are also displays of other handicrafts – stone carvings, metalwork, and so on – designed by the versatile Mr Marapana.

By contrast, there's surprisingly little coverage of the town's gem-mining heritage at the **National Museum** (Mon–Wed, Sat & Sun 9am–5pm; Rs.45), off Main Street on the northwest side of the town centre. Exhibits include the usual depressing collection of pickled and stuffed wildlife, plus chunks of rock and some unusually uninteresting bits of fossilized bone. There's also a decent if small collection of the inevitable Kandyan fabrics, jewellery, ivory carvings, pill boxes and oil lamps, plus a small selection of entertaining kolam masks and a few beautiful Buddha statues.

The most interesting sight hereabouts, however, is the **Maha Saman Devale**, 3km west of town. This is the most important temple in the island dedicated to Saman (see p.275), who is said to reside on nearby Adam's Peak. There has been a temple here since the thirteenth century. It was rebuilt by the kings of Kandy during the seventeenth century, destroyed by the Portuguese, then rebuilt again during the Dutch era (a carving to the right of the entrance steps, showing a Portuguese invader killing a Sinhalese soldier, recalls European attacks against the town and temple). The present-day structure is impressively large, and although the overall effect is not of any especial antiquity, the entire complex has a pleasantly harmonious appearance, with rising tiers of tiled roofs and white walls leading up from the entrance to the main shrine, the whole structure enclosed by a large white balustraded wall, scored with tiny triangular niches to hold oil lamps. The main shrine itself is topped by a pretty two-storey pagoda with blue pillars and yellow eaves, while inside are some fine murals of gods and a striking, splay-toothed demon. To either side stand subsidiary shrines to the Buddha and Pattini (see p.226) – the latter is very popular with local ladies, though her presence here is rather ironic: during the

Kandyan era, the rise in her cult meant that she replaced Saman as one of the island's guardian deities. There's a big **Esala perahera** here during July or August. A tuktuk from town should cost around Rs.50 each way.

Around 4km north of town, the **Katugas Falls** tumble down over boulders from a beautiful rainforested hillside – a little bit of Sinharaja on the edges of the modern town. It's possible to climb some way up the cascade into the trees. The falls are tricky to locate (ask for "Katugas Ella"); it's easiest to take a tuktuk at least one way. They're also best avoided at weekends, when they get totally overrun.

Practicalities

The **bus station** is on the north side of the town centre of Ratnapura on Inner Circular Road, within walking distance of several of the guest houses. For **money**, there are various branches, mostly on or near Main Street, of the Bank of Ceylon, People's Bank, Hatton Bank and Sampath Bank – the Sampath ATM accepts foreign cards (Visa and MasterCard). There's a Cargills **supermarket** (daily 8am–10pm) just south of the clocktower; there's a pharmacy inside. The **post office** is at the clocktower end of Main Street. There's currently no Internet access in Ratnapura, although you could check out the various computer shops around the clocktower in case something opens, as is likely.

Accommodation and eating

All the following places do **food**; the restaurant at the *Rest House* is the town's best option, though the food (mains from Rs.250) is average. Otherwise, *Pizza Hut* (nothing to do with the American chain), at the junction of Main Street and Senanayaka Mawatha on the east side of town, is a decent place for lunch, with unusually good pizzas (Rs.160–450), plus fruit juices and a few other snacks (though no booze). Don't let the manager talk you into having family-size unless you're ravenous – the pizzas are small, but thick.

Darshana Inn 68/5 Rest House Rd ☎045-222 2674. Four rather dark but perfectly clean and comfy rooms. The building doubles as a popular local bar, however, so it's not the most peaceful place. No single rates. ❶
Kalavati Polhengoda Village ☎045-222 2465, ☎223 0020. Set in a peaceful rural location about 2km from the town centre in a pleasant house full of bric-a-brac and objets d'art, although the rooms themselves are rather bare. Various ayurveda treatments are available, as well as more arcane treatments – try the "healing therapy with jewels"

or the "medicinal herb smoke". A/c supplement Rs.400. ❸
Nilani Lodge Dharmapala Mw ☎045-222 2170, ✉hashani@sltnet.lk. Functional building – it looks like an enormous air-conditioning unit – in a quiet road close to the town centre. The ten rooms (five with a/c and hot water) are clean, bright and comfy, and have nice hill views from their private balconies. The restaurant does Western, Chinese and Sri Lankan food. A/c supplement Rs.550. ❸
Ratna Gems Halt 153/5 Outer Circular Road ☎045-222 3745. The six ultra-cheap rooms here

---

Moving on from Ratnapura

The **bus station** is clearly laid out and signed; if you get stuck, the office room signed "Road Passenger Transport Authority Office" (along the left-hand side of the station) offers information. There are very frequent a/c express services for **Colombo**, plus frequent buses east to **Haputale**, **Bandarawela** and **Wellawaya**, north to **Kandy** (hourly until 1.30pm, after which you'll have to go to Kegalle and change there) and **Avissawella** (for Hatton and Nuwara Eliya) and south to **Embilipitiya** (every 10min). There are a few buses to **Matara**. For **Galle**, take a Matara bus and change at Akuressa. For more details, see p.289.

are bare and cell-like, but perfectly clean, and very good value at the price. There's also a smarter but very good-value double upstairs and a pleasant breezy eating area looking out to the hills. The only potential drawback is the owner's gem shop, which is downstairs. Expect sales talk. ❶

Ratnaloka Tour Inns Kosgala, 7km from Ratnapura ☎045-222 2455, ℮ratnaloka@eureka.lk. Comfortable if unexceptional mid-range hotel in a pleasantly rural setting,

with 53 a/c rooms with satellite TV and minibar. Popular with tour groups. ❻

Rest House Rest House Rd ☎045-222 2299 Enjoys a wonderful position on a hilltop above town with fine views. Ongoing renovations are gradually making this place better value, though it's still overpriced, and the rooms could be cleaner. ❸

Travellers Halt 30 Outer Circular Road ☎045-222 3092. Six reasonable-value rooms (three with a/c) – all are tiled and quite modern, albeit on the small side. A/c supplement Rs.500. ❷

Uda Walawe National Park and around

Uda Walawe has developed into one of Sri Lanka's most popular national parks mainly thanks to its large (and easily spotted) population of elephants – it's the best place in the island to see pachyderms in the wild, although in other respects it doesn't have the range of fauna and habitats of Yala or Bundala. The park is beautifully situated just south of the hill country, whose grand escarpment provides a memorable backdrop, while at its centre lies the **Uda Walawe Reservoir**, whose catchment area it was originally established to protect. The actual landscape of the park is rather monotonous: most of Uda Walawe lies within the dry zone, and its terrain is flat and denuded, with extensive areas of grassland and low scrub (the result of earlier slash-and-burn farming) dotted with the skeletal outlines of dead trees, killed by the resident elephants. The overall effect, however, is not without a certain austere beauty, while the lack of forest cover makes wildlife spotting easier than in any other Sri Lankan park.

The principal attraction is, of course, **elephants** – there are around five hundred, alongside hundreds of **buffaloes**; you might also see macaque and langur monkeys, spotted and sambur deer, and crocodiles. Rarely sighted residents include leopards, giant flying squirrels, jungle cats, sloth bears and porcupines. Uda Walawe is particularly good for **birds of prey** – including brahminy and black-winged kites, crested serpent, hawk and fish eagles, and the magnificent white-bellied sea eagle, one of Sri Lanka's most imposing raptors. The reservoir also attracts a wide range of **aquatic birds**, including majestic Indian darters, along with the usual egrets, cormorants, herons, kingfishers and the comical black-winged stilt, easily recognizable by its long red legs. Endemic species include the Sri Lanka spurfowl, the Sri Lanka jungle fowl, the Malabar pied hornbill and the rare red-faced malkoha. If you're lucky you might also spot the lesser adjutant, Sri Lanka's largest – and ugliest – bird, standing at well over a metre tall.

About 5km west of the park entrance on the main road is the engaging **Elephant Transit Home** – usually referred to as the "Elephant Orphanage". Founded in 1995, the orphanage is home to around 25 baby elephants rescued from the wild after the loss of their parents. Like the better-known orphanage at Pinnewala, elephants here are bottlefed milk until the age of three and a half, after which they're given a diet of grass. At the age of five, most are released into the national park (around thirty so far); a few have been donated to important temples.

The elephants are fed every three hours (at 9am, noon, 3pm, 6pm and so on), and are fun to watch, especially during the feeding sessions, but as they're kept in pens, you can't get right amongst them as you can at Pinnewala. The Transit Home is part of the national park, and entrance is free.

Park practicalities

Uda Walawe's central location makes it accessible from a number of different places, and you can arrange tours here from as far afield as Ratnapura, Hambantota, Tissa and even Unawatuna (see the relevant town accounts for more details), although all these involve long drives to reach the park. The closest starting point is **Embilipitiya**, 21km distant. It's possible to reach the park by **public transport** from Embilipitiya by catching one of the half-hourly buses to Tamanalwila, which go right past the entrance, where you can hire a jeep (seating 6–8) for around Rs.1400 for a few hours' drive – slightly but not dramatically cheaper than hiring a vehicle in Emibilipitiya.

The park **entrance** is at milepost seven along the Embilipitiya to Tamanalwila road. The usual **admission** charges apply. If you want **to stay** close to the park, there's the comfortable *Walawa Safari Village* (☎047-223 3201; ❸), just 4km from the park entrance on Right Bank Canal Road. You can arrange cheap transport to the park from here. Slightly further away, at Kithulkotte, between Thanamalwila and Kuda Oya on the main road between Tissa and Wellaway, is *Tasks Safari Camp* (☎060-247 3246, ⓦwww.taskssafari .com; ❻), Sri Lanka's best stab at an African bush camp, with nineteen smartly equipped en-suite tents. The camp is also within striking distance of both Yala and Bundala; closer to hand there's good birdwatching and local jungle walks offering a rare opportunity to track elephants on foot, rather than from the back of a jeep.

Embilipitiya

Halfway between Ratnapura and the coast, the medium-size town of **EMBILIPITIYA** is the closest base for visits to Uda Walawe, 20km distant. There's not much to the town itself. **Buses** arrive at the station about 100m south of the clocktower at the centre of town. There are several **banks** close to the clocktower; the Seylan (Visa only), Commercial (Visa and MasterCard), Sampath (Visa and MasterCard) all have **ATMs** which accept foreign cards. There's nowhere really **to eat** apart from the two hotels listed below, both of which can also arrange half-day trips to Uda Walawe for around Rs.2000.

The town has two decent **places to stay**. The mid-range *Centauria Hotel* (☎047-223 0104, ⓔcentauria@sltnet.lk; ❺), about 1.5km south of the town, is a surprisingly swish place for dusty little Embilipitiya. Rooms (all with a/c

---

Moving on from Embilipitiya

Leaving Embilipitiya, there are frequent **buses** to Ratnapura, Tangalla, Matara and Hambantota. For Tissa, change at Hambantota. If you're heading towards the south-eastern hill country, there are also buses east to Tamanalwila, from where you can pick up a bus to Wellaway, which has frequent connections with Ella, Haputale, Bandarawela and Badulla. For full details, see p.289.

If you want to combine a visit to Uda Walawe with **Sinharaja**, you'll have to make the tortuous cross-country journey to **Deniyaya**. To do this, you'll need to catch one of the early-morning buses from Embilipitiya to **Suriyakanda** (a two-hour journey), from where there's a single bus south to Deniyaya at around midday, though this often arrives full, in which case you'll have to take a tuktuk (around Rs.800). All in all it's a surprisingly time-consuming affair, though the compensation is a spectacular ride through the stunning tea plantations atop the remote and gorgeous Sabaragamuwa Mountains.

and hot water) are comfortably old-fashioned, with lots of dark wooden furniture; all have views of Chandrika Lake at the end of the grounds (some are right by the water's edge). There's also a pleasant and good-value restaurant, and the hotel cheerfully welcomes all "nature lovers and echo tourism". Alternatively, *Sarathchandra Rest* (℡047-223 0044; rooms ❷, cabanas ❸), on the main road 100m south of the bus station, has twenty very pleasant modern rooms, plus some slightly more expensive but less appealing cabanas, and one a/c room (Rs.300 extra).

Sinharaja and around

The last extensive tract of undisturbed lowland rainforest in Sri Lanka, **Sinharaja** is one of the island's outstanding natural wonders and an ecological treasure-box of international significance, as recognized by its listing as a UNESCO World Heritage Site in 1989. A staggering 830 of Sri Lanka's endemic species of flora and fauna are found here, including myriad birds, reptiles and insects, while no less than sixty percent of the reserve's trees are endemic, too.

Sinharaja stretches for almost thirty kilometres across the wet zone at the southern edges of the hill country, enveloping a series of switchback hills and valleys ranging in altitude from just 300m up to 1170m. To the north and south, the reserve is bounded by two sizeable rivers, the Kalu Ganga and the Gin Ganga, which cut picturesque, waterfall-studded courses through the trees. The oldest parts of the rainforest comprise dense stands of towering trees enmeshed in fantastic tangles of ferns and lianas; the top of the canopy reaches heights of up to 45m. Sinharaja receives as much as five metres of rain annually – you'll be struck by the sudden overwhelming humidity (approaching ninety percent) as soon as you step into the forest, as well as by the incredible noise of cicadas.

According to tradition, Sinharaja was formerly a royal reserve (as suggested by its name, meaning "Lion King"). The first attempts to conserve it were made as far back as 1840, when it became property of the British crown. Logging began in 1971, until being banned in the face of national protests in 1977, when the area was declared a national reserve. Sinharaja is now safely protected under UNESCO auspices, using a system whereby inhabitants of the twenty-odd villages which surround the reserve have the right to limited use of the forest's resources, including tapping kitul palms for jaggery and collecting rattan for building.

The reserve's most common **mammal** is the purple-faced langur monkey, while you might also encounter three species of squirrel – the dusky-striped jungle squirrel, flame-striped jungle squirrel and western giant squirrel – along with mongooses. Less common, and very rarely sighted. are leopards, rusty spotted cats, fishing cats and civets. There's also a rich **reptile** population, including 21 of Sri Lanka's 45 endemic species, amongst them rare snakes and frogs. Many of the reserve's bountiful population of **insects** remain to be classified, although you're likely to see various colourful spiders and enormous butterflies, while giant millipedes are also common.

Sinharaja has one of Sri Lanka's richest **bird** populations: 21 of the country's 26 endemic species have been recorded here (although some can only be seen in the reserve's difficult to reach eastern fringes). Unfortunately, the density of the forest and the fact that its birds largely inhabit the topmost part of the canopy means that actually seeing them is extremely difficult, and probably beyond the patience of all but committed birders – the tantalizing chirrupings of myriad invisible birds are an inevitable accompaniment to any visit to the reserve. It's much easier to spot birds around the edges of the forest, in the agricultural lands which bound the park.

Less welcome inhabitants of the park are **leeches** (see p.27), abundant after rain.

Visiting the reserve

Sinharaja is open daily from 8am to 6pm and entrance costs Rs.575, plus Rs.500 per group for an obligatory guide (unless you bring your own; see below), who will lead you on walking tours of up to three hours, depending on how taxing a hike you want. There are no driveable roads in the reserve, so you have to walk (which is, indeed, one of the pleasures of a visit, especially if you're fed up of rattling around national parks in smelly jeeps).

There are two **entrances** to the reserve. The most convenient for independent travellers is at **Mederipitiya**, about 11km east of Deniyaya (see below). The road from Deniyaya ends just short of the reserve, from where it's a pleasant 1.5km walk through tea plantations, with Sinharaja sprawling impressively across the hills ahead. The path isn't signposted and can be slightly confusing (go right at the fork by the gravestones near the beginning). A tuktuk from Deniyaya will cost around Rs.600 return with a few hours waiting time, though it's much better to go with a proper guide (see below). For information on Deniyaya, see below.

The other entrance is on the north side of the park, at **Kudawa** (see opposite); it's more difficult to reach and likely to be of interest mainly to those with their own transport approaching from the west. The forest around Kudawa is broadly similar to that around the Mederipitiya entrance, so it doesn't much matter which entrance you use in terms of what you see in the reserve.

Perhaps more than anywhere else in Sri Lanka, what you get out of a visit to Sinharaja relies on having a good **guide** – the rainforest is dense and difficult to decipher and, without skilful interpretation, can simply look to the uneducated like an awful lot of very big trees. Unfortunately the reserve's guides speak very little English, and aren't much use except to make sure you don't get lost. Two of the best are **Palitha Ratnayake**, who is based at the *Sinharaja Rest* in Deniyaya (see below), and **Martin Wijesinghe**, at Kudawa (see opposite).

The closest starting points for Sinharaja are **Deniyaya** and **Kudawa** (see below). It's also possible to arrange visits to the reserve from various guest houses in Ratnapura; from *Tropical Villas* in Beruwela (see p.130) or with a couple of tour operators in Unawatuna.

Deniyaya

The small but lively town of **DENIYAYA** is the most convenient base for visiting Sinharaja, and can be reached either from Galle or Matara on the south coast or from Ratnapura to the north. Buses arrive at the **bus station**, right in the middle of town; there are a couple of **banks** close by where you can change money, and three **places to stay**. *Sinharaja Rest*, 500m north of the bus station (T & F 041-227 3368; ❷) has six simple but adequate rooms and is owned and managed by local guide Palitha Ratnayaka, who runs six- to eight-hour trips for a very modest Rs.500 per person, entering the reserve through Mederipitiya and walking 12–14km. Shorter trips can also be arranged, as can longer excursions, such as a two-day (27km) hike across the entire reserve, or a one-day ten-hour (24km) walk to Lion Rock at Sinharaja's centre.

Alternatively, the *Rest House*, 500m south of the bus station (☎041-227 3600; ❷) has incredibly large, bare and rather dimly lit rooms – you feel you could get lost between the door and the bed, though fabulous views of hills from the verandah partly compensate. Both places are a Rs.30–40 tuktuk ride from the bus station. The third option is the *Sathmala Ella Rest* (☎041-227 3481; ❸), 4km from town on the road to Mederipitiya, which has ten pleasant rooms in an attractive rural setting. You can also arrange visits to the reserve from here.

Moving on from Deniyaya, there are a few direct buses to **Matara** and **Galle**. Otherwise change at **Akuressa** (every 30min; 1hr 30min), from where there are frequent onward connections to both these towns. Transport northwards is much more infrequent, with buses to **Pelmadulla** and **Ratnapura** every three hours (at 5.30am, 8.30am and so on).

Kudawa

The village of **KUDAWA** offers an alternative base for visiting Sinharaja, although it's rather tricky to reach and is really only worth considering if you have your own vehicle. If you're using public transport, either take a **bus** from Ratnapura to **Kalawana** (15km north of Kudawa), from where there are infrequent (around 4 daily) buses to Kudawa, or a bus from Deniyaya via Rakwana and Weddagala to Kudawa (every 1–2 hours). The best guide at Kudawa is **Martin Wijesinghe**, an extremely knowledgeable former reserve ranger. He also runs his own **guest house**, with seven simple but clean rooms (❷). It's very close to the entrance, about 3km from Kudawa village itself. Unfortunately, he doesn't have a phone; it's a good idea to leave a message for him at Kudawa Post Office (☎045-222 5528) to warn him of your arrival. He often gets booked up by tour groups, however, so the whole thing is a bit of a gamble.

There are a couple of further options at **Koswatta** village, a couple of kilometres from Kalawana and a fifteen-minute drive from Sinharaja. The first is the reasonably well set-up *Singraj Rest* (☎045-225 5201; ❸), in a modern house with pleasant rooms, plus a restaurant and bar. You can arrange transport from here to Sinharaja. The second is the luxurious new *Boulder Garden* eco-resort (☎045-225 5812, ⓦwww.bouldergarden.com; ❾), which serves up five-star style and comforts in a remote and captivating natural setting complete with the promised boulders and patches of rainforest. The resort blends seamlessly into its surroundings, with accommodation in ten beautifully rustic rooms (two of them in natural caves), and there's also fine dining in a pleasant open-air restaurant, a swimming pool, and plenty of interesting walks and tours to Sinharaja and the surrounding jungle.

Travel details

Buses

The timings given below are for the fastest express services, where they exist. Local buses are usually significantly slower, increasing journey times by anything up to fifty percent.

Badulla to: Bandarawela (every 10min; 1hr 30min); Colombo (hourly; 8hr); Ella (every 30min; 1hr); Galle (1 daily; 8hr); Haputale (change at Bandarawela; every 30min; 2hr); Kandy (hourly;

6hr); Kataragama (1 daily; 4hr); Matara (1 daily; 7hr); Monaragala (1–2 hourly; 3hr); Nuwara Eliya (every 30–45min; 3hr); Ratnapura (hourly; 5hr); Wellawaya (every 2hr; 1hr 30min).
Bandarawela to: Badulla (every 10min; 1hr 30min); Colombo (every 20min; 6hr 30min); Galle (1 daily; 7hr); Ella (every 10min; 30min); Haputale (every 30min; 30min); Matara (1 daily; 6hr); Ratnapura (every 30min; 3hr 30min); Welimada (every 30min; 45min); Wellawaya (every 30min; 45min).

Ella to: Badulla (every 30min; 1hr); Bandarawela (every 10min; 30min); Haputale (change at Bandarawela; every 10min; 1hr); Kandy (1 daily; 7–8hr); Kataragama (2 daily; 2hr 30min); Nuwara Eliya (3 daily; 4hr); Tissamaharama (2 daily; 2hr 30min); Wellawaya (every 15min; 45min).

Embilipitiya to: Hambantota (every 15min; 1hr 30min); Matara (every 20min; 2hr 30min); Ratnapura (every 15min; 2hr 30min), Tamanalwila (every 30min; 1hr); Tangalla (every 20min; 1hr 30min).

Haputale to: Badulla (change at Bandarawela; every 30min; 2hr); Bandarawela (every 30min; 30min); Colombo (every 30min; 6hr); Ella (change

at Bandarawela; every 10min; 1hr); Galle (1 daily; 6hr 30min); Matara (3 daily; 7hr); Ratnapura (every 30min; 3hr); Wellawaya (hourly; 1hr).

Kandy to: Anuradhapura (every 30min; 4hr); Badulla (hourly; 6hr); Colombo (every 10–15min; 3hr); Dambulla (every 20min; 2hr); Ella (1 daily; 7–8hr); Habarana (every 30min; 2hr 45min); Kegalle (every 15min; 1hr); Kurunegala (every 20min; 1hr 30min); Negombo (12 daily; 3hr 30min); Nuwara Eliya (every 30min; 3hr); Polonnaruwa (every 30min; 3hr 45min); Ratnapura (10 daily; 3hr 30min); Sigiriya (1 daily; 2hr 30min); Trincomalee (3–4 daily; 7hr); Vavuniya (every 30min; 4hr).

Trains in the hill country

All the following are departure times; in many cases trains arrive a few minutes earlier than the timings given below. For services from Colombo to Kandy, see p.147.

Train no.	40	30+	36	24	10+	20	6
Kandy	05.25	06.25	06.45	10.30	15.00	15.40	16.50
Colombo	08.37	09.00	10.10	13.50	17.35	18.55	19.45

+ = Intercity express

Train no.	105	126	05	15	110	159	45	47
Kandy (dep.)	–	04.00	08.55	–	–	–	23.10	–
Peradeniya Jct.	–	04.20	09.07	12.15	–	–	–	–
Gampola	–	04.47	09.23	12.33	–	–	23.40	01.25
Nawalapitiya	–	05.45	09.55	13.00	–	14.25	00.20	02.05
Hatton	–	07.35	11.30	14.15	–	16.20	01.34	03.35
Nanu Oya	–	10.00	13.00	15.40	–	19.10	02.55	05.10
Ohiya	10.30	11.55	13.56	16.36	–	20.38	03.48	06.06
Haputale	11.25	13.00	14.33	17.14	17.35	21.15	04.28	06.48
Bandarawela	12.10	14.15	15.00	17.40	18.12	–	05.00	07.28
Ella	12.41	14.50	15.30	18.09	18.50	–	05.30	07.57
Badulla	13.47	15.50	16.20	19.05	19.50	–	06.30	08.45

Train no.	524	16	505	541	6	596	506	46	48
Badulla	–	05.55	07.15	–	09.10	12.15	14.15	17.45	19.15
Ella	–	06.53	08.32	–	10.08	13.25	15.30	18.46	20.15
Bandarawela	–	07.26	09.05	–	10.42	14.20	16.03	19.21	20.50
Haputale	–	07.56	09.35	–	11.13	15.11	16.32	19.57	21.24
Ohiya	–	08.35	10.14	–	11.53	15.56	–	20.36	22.03
Nanu Oya	06.00	09.35	–	–	12.55	17.30	–	21.40	23.05
Hatton	07.29	10.55	–	10.00	14.13	19.20	–	22.52	00.24
Nawalapitiya	09.15	12.00	–	12.25	15.35	21.00	–	00.10	02.00
Gampola	10.02	12.35	–	13.02	16.07	21.38	–	00.40	02.30
Peradeniya Jct	10.46	–	–	13.23	16.24	22.05	–	00.59	–
Kandy	11.00	–	–	13.35	16.35	22.20	–	01.10	–

Trains #16, #06, #05 and #15 have first-class observation carriages; #45 and #46 night mails have 2nd and 3rd classes only; #47 and #48 have 1st class sleeping berths and 2nd and 3rd class reserved sleeperette and ordinary 2nd and 3rd class seating.

③

Nuwara Eliya to: Badulla (every 30–45min; 3hr); Colombo (every 30min; 4hr 30min); Ella (3 daily; 4hr); Galle (1–2 daily; 8hr); Hatton (every 30min; 2hr); Kandy (every 30min; 3hr); Matara (2 daily; 8hr); Welimada (every 30min; 1hr 30min); Wellawaya (3 daily; 5hr).

Ratnapura to: Avissawella (every 10min; 1hr); Badulla (hourly; 5hr); Bandarawela (every 30min; 3hr 30min); Colombo (every 15min; 3hr); Embilipitiya (every 15min; 2hr 30min); Haputale (every 30min; 3hr); Kandy (10 daily; 3hr 30min); Matara (4 daily; 5hr); Wellawaya (hourly; 4hr).

Wellawaya to: Badulla (every 2hr; 1hr 30min); Bandarawela (every 30min; 45min); Ella (every 15min; 45min); Haputale (hourly; 1hr); Monaragala (every 30min; 1hr 15min); Nuwara Eliya (3 daily; 5hr); Pannegamuwa Junction (every 30min; 1hr 45min); Ratnapura (hourly; 4hr); Tissamaharama (hourly; 2hr).

The Cultural Triangle

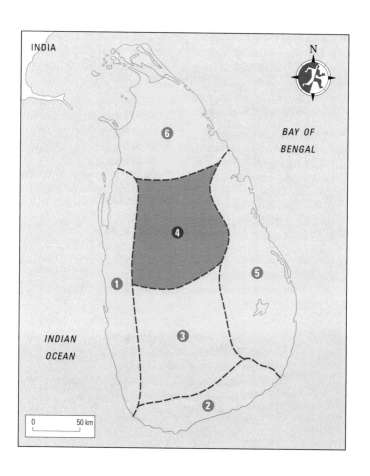

CHAPTER 4

Highlights

* **Dambulla** The atmospheric rock temples of Dambulla are a veritable Aladdin's cave of Buddhist art, packed with hundreds of statues and decorated with the finest murals in the country. **See p.305**

* **Kandalama Hotel** Cunningly buried under a layer of tropical greenery, this memorable hotel has bags of contemporary style and a stunning location by the Kandalama lake. **See p.309**

* **Sigiriya** The spectacular rock outcrop of Sigiriya was the site of Sri Lanka's most remarkable royal capital and palace, complete with water gardens, paintings of celestial nymphs, 1300-year-old graffiti and the paws of a giant lion statue. **See p.310**

* **Polonnaruwa** The ruined city of Polonnaruwa preserves an outstanding collection of ancient monuments testifying to its brief but brilliant period as the island's capital. **See p.317**

* **Minneriya National Park** Centred around the ancient Minneriya Tank, this small but scenically diverse reserve is northern Sri Lanka's premier elephant-spotting destination. **See p.332**

* **Anuradhapura** The ruins of the ancient city of Anuradhapura remain one of the island's most compelling historical sites, as well as a major place of Buddhist pilgrimage. **See p.338**

* **Mihintale** Revered as the place where Buddhism was introduced to the island, Mihintale boasts an interesting collection of religious monuments scattered across a beautiful hilltop location. **See p.357**

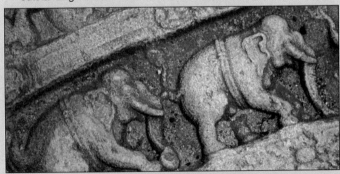

△ Moonstone, Polonnaruwa

The Cultural Triangle

N orth of Kandy, the tangled green hills of the central highlands tumble down into the plains of the **dry zone**, a hot and denuded region covered in thorny scrub and jungle and punctuated by isolated mountainous outcrops which tower dramatically over the surrounding flatlands. The region's climate is a harsh contrast of famine and plenty, with brief monsoonal deluges separated by long periods of drought during which temperatures, untempered by the sea breezes which soften the climate on the coast, can rise to parching extremes.

Despite this unpromising natural environment, these northern plains served as the cradle of Sri Lankan civilization for almost two thousand years, from the arrival of the first Sinhalese around 400 BC to the final abandonment of the city of Polonnaruwa in the thirteenth century. Much of this early civilization was centred around the great monastic city of Anuradhapura, one of the finest urban centres of its age, whose monumental **dagobas** were excelled in scale in the ancient world only by the Egyptian pyramids, and whose large-scale irrigation works succeeded in transforming the city's unpromisingly barren hinterland into an enormous rice bowl capable of supporting a burgeoning population. The innumerable man-made reservoirs (or "**tanks**") which dot the region still provide impressive physical evidence of this enormous hydraulic achievement, while the agricultural surplus produced by these irrigated farmlands supported a flourishing religious and cultural life, fostered trade with places as distant as Rome and Egypt, and even financed occasional wars overseas.

Despite its glorious achievements, however, this early Sinhalese civilization lived under the constant threat of attack from southern India. Over the centuries countless Indian adventurers turned to their wealthy island neighbour for a spot of plunder, and although the Sinhalese periodically freed themselves from the Indian yoke, ultimately the pressure of interminable warfare destroyed the civilization of northern Sri Lanka, leading to the destruction of Anuradhapura in 993 and the abandonment of Polonnaruwa three centuries later, after which the great cities of the northern plains were abandoned and reclaimed by the jungle until being rediscovered by the British in the nineteenth century. Although the modern economic and cultural life of Sri Lanka has now largely bypassed the region, its great religious monuments still serve as potent reminders of the golden age of Sinhalese culture, providing a symbol of cultural identity which goes far beyond the merely archeological.

The island's northern plains are now often referred to as the **Cultural Triangle**, the three points of this imaginary triangle being placed at the great Sinhalese capitals of Kandy (see Chapter 3), Anuradhapura and Polonnaruwa. In fact, this tourist-oriented invention presents a rather warped sense of the

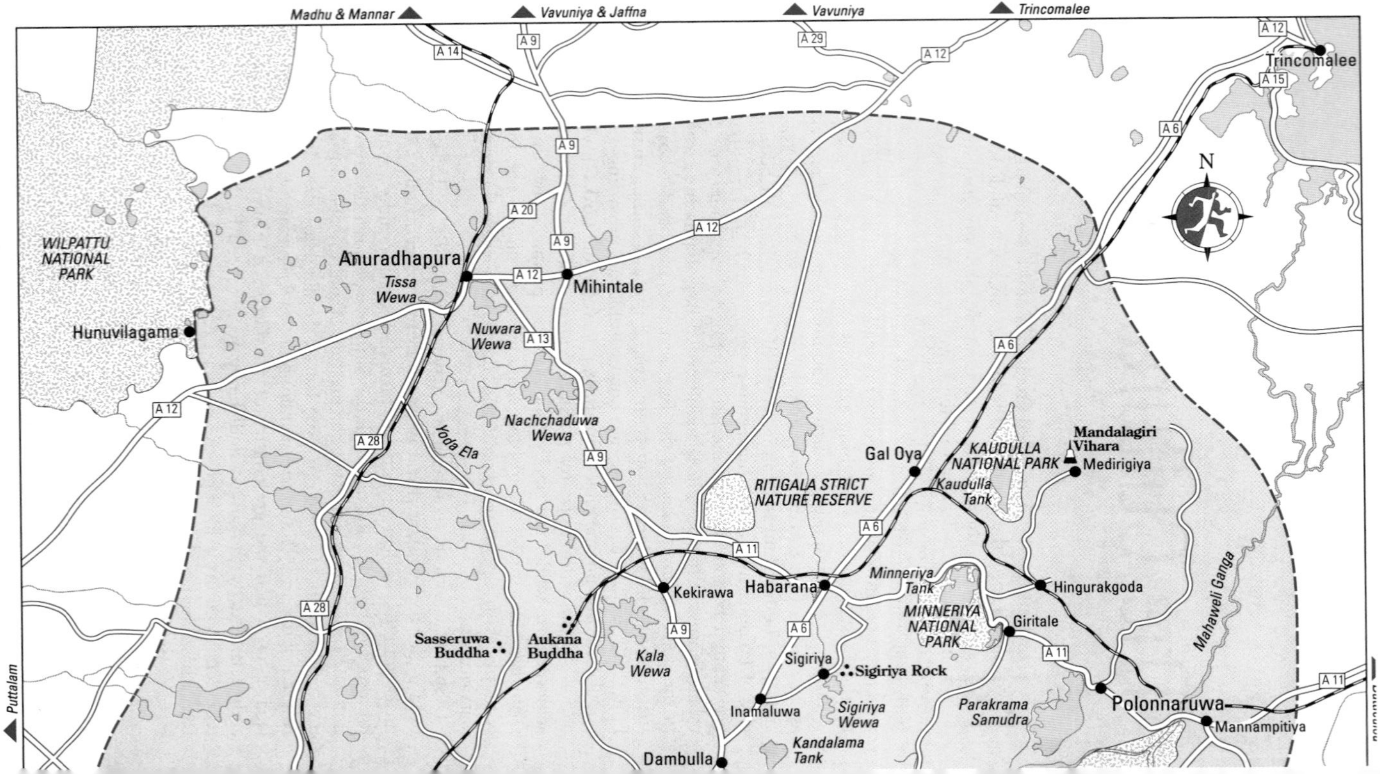
Madhu & Mannar
Vavuniya & Jaffna
Vavuniya
Trincomalee
Puttalam
A 14
A 9
A 29
A 12
A 15
A 6
A 20
A 13
A 28
A 11
N
Trincomalee
WILPATTU NATIONAL PARK
Hunuvilagama
Anuradhapura
Tissa Wewa
Mihintale
Nuwara Wewa
Nachchaduwa Wewa
Yoda Ela
Sasseruwa Buddha
Aukana Buddha
Kala Wewa
Kekirawa
RITIGALA STRICT NATURE RESERVE
Gal Oya
Habarana
Sigiriya
Sigiriya Rock
Sigiriya Wewa
Inamaluwa
Kandalama Tank
Dambulla
KAUDULLA NATIONAL PARK
Kaudulla Tank
Mandalagiri Vihara
Medirigiya
Minneriya Tank
MINNERIYA NATIONAL PARK
Giritale
Hingurakgoda
Parakrama Samudra
Polonnaruwa
Mannampitiya
Mahaweli Ganga

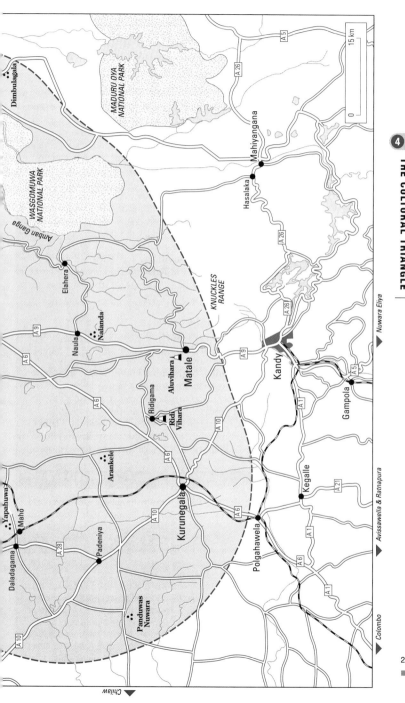

region's past, given that the history of Kandy is quite different and separate – both chronologically and geographically – from that of the earlier capitals. The real Cultural Triangle lies some distance north of Kandy, with its angles at Anuradhapura, Polonnaruwa and Dambulla, and is better described by its traditional name of the **Rajarata**, or "The King's Land".

At the spiritual heart of the triangle lie the two great ruined cities of early Sri Lanka: **Anuradhapura**, capital of the island from the third century BC to 993 AD, and its successor, **Polonnaruwa**, capital until the thirteenth century. The region's other outstanding attractions are the spectacular rock citadel of **Sigiriya**, perhaps Sri Lanka's single most extraordinary sight; the marvellous cave temples of **Dambulla**, a magical treasure-box of Buddhist sculpture and painting; and the religious centre of **Mihintale**, scene of the introduction of Buddhism to the island.

There's far more to the region than these highlights, however. The entire Cultural Triangle is peppered with intriguing ancient monuments, and one of the great pleasures of visiting the region is in getting off the beaten track and exploring these lesser sights, many of which are little visited and intensely atmospheric. Other sites worth a look include the abandoned cities of **Yapahuwa** or **Panduwas Nuwara**; the great Buddha statues of **Aukana** and **Sasseruwa**; the absorbing temples of **Aluvihara** and **Ridi Vihara**; or the haunting forest monasteries of **Arankele** and **Ritigala**. And if you begin to tire of historic monuments there are natural attractions at the national parks **Minneriya** and **Kaudulla**.

Visiting the Cultural Triangle

The major Cultural Triangle sites are all relatively close to one another, and there are all sorts of different permutations in terms of where to stay and how to plan an itinerary through the area. One possibility is to base yourself at one of the many hotels in or around **Dambulla**, **Sigiriya** or **Habarana**, at the centre of the Triangle. These hold some outstanding top-end hotels, as well as many cheaper options, and their central location makes it possible to visit all the area's major sights on day-trips if you don't mind hiring your own transport.

In terms of public transport, regular **buses** connect Kandy, Dambulla, Sigiriya, Anuradhapura and Polonnaruwa, while occasional **trains** run between Colombo, Kurunegala, Anuradhapura and Polonnaruwa. To explore the

---

Cultural Triangle tickets

Most of the principal sights in the Cultural Triangle (with the notable exception of the Dambulla rock temples) are covered by the **Cultural Triangle (CT) Ticket**. This covers six sights – Anuradhapura, Sigiriya, Polonnaruwa, Nalanda, Medirigiriya and Ritigala – plus various places in Kandy (the National and Archeological museums, Malwatta, Asigiriya and the four devales, but not the Temple of the Tooth). You can buy CT tickets at Sigiriya, Polonnaruwa, Anuradhapura, and also at the Cultural Triangle offices in Kandy and Colombo (see p.110 and p.214).

Tickets are **valid** for fourteen days from the date of first use, and you have to start using them within three months of purchase. They currently **cost** US$32.50; children aged 6–12 pay half of this (and also get half-price admission on tickets to individual sites); under 6s get in free. Buying a combined ticket offers good value compared to purchasing individual tickets at each site (individual tickets to Anuradhapura, Polonnaruwa and Sigiriya, for instance, cost US$15 each). Unfortunately, the ticket is only valid for one day's entry at each site – a particularly frustrating restriction at Anuradhapura, which needs at least a couple of days to be explored fully.

triangle's more obscure attractions, however, you really need your own transport. Although almost everywhere can be reached by public transport, doing so is often a time-consuming business, and with your own **car and driver** you'll be able to see far more.

North of Kandy: Aluvihara to Ridi Vihara

From Kandy, most visitors headed for the Cultural Triangle plough straight up the main road north to Dambulla, Sigiriya and beyond. If you have your own transport, however, there are several interesting sites en route. Two of these – the famous monastery of **Aluvihara** and the wonderful little temple at **Nalanda** – are right on the main highway, and easily visited, while the fascinating monastery of **Ridi Vihara** is a short drive westwards towards Kurunegala.

The main road between Kandy and Dambulla is also littered with innumerable **spice gardens**. The temperate climate of the region – halfway in altitude between the coastal plains and the hill country – offers ideal horticultural conditions, and if you're interested in seeing where the ingredients of Sri Lankan cuisine come from, now is your chance (and if you're travelling with a car and driver or on a tour, you'll probably be dragged into one of the gardens whether you like it or not). Entrance is generally free, but you'll be expected to buy some spices at vastly inflated prices in return for a look at the various spice-producing plants and shrubs.

Aluvihara

The monastery of **Aluvihara** (Rs.100; no photography) lies about 2km north of the busy town of Matale, right next to the main Kandy–Dambulla highway. Despite its modest size, Aluvihara is of great significance in the global history of Buddhism, since it was here that the most important set of Theravada Buddhist scriptures, the *Tripitakaya*, or "Three Baskets", were first committed to writing. During the first five centuries of the religion's existence, the vast corpus of the Buddha's teachings had simply been memorized and passed orally from generation to generation. Around 80 BC, however, fears that the *Tripitakaya* would be lost during the upheaval caused by repeated South Indian invasions prompted the industrious King Vattagamani Abhaya (who also created the Dambulla cave temples and founded the great Abhayagiri monastery in Anuradhapura) to establish Aluvihara, staffing it with five hundred monks who laboured for years to transcribe the Pali-language Buddhist scriptures onto ola-leaf manuscripts. Tragically, having survived almost two thousand years, this historic library was largely destroyed by British troops when they attacked the temple in 1848 to put down an uprising of local monks.

The heart of the complex consists of a sequence of **cave temples**, tucked away in a picturesque jumble of huge rock outcrops and linked by flights of steps and narrow paths between the boulders (many of which are carved with tiny triangular niches to hold oil lamps). The caves are relatively modern in appearance and of limited artistic merit, but the setting is atmospheric. The first temple houses a ten-metre sleeping Buddha, plus colourful standing and seated Buddhas, a kitsch makara torana entrance and a ceiling painted with lotuses and decorative patterns. From here, steps lead up to the main level, where a second cave temple conceals another large sleeping Buddha and various pictures and sculptures demonstrating the lurid punishments awaiting wrongdoers in the Buddhist hell – a subject which seems to exert a ghoulish fascination on the ostensibly peace-loving Sinhalese – including the usual images of miscreants having their skulls sawn in half or being impaled on spiky-branched trees.

Further steps lead up to a cave temple devoted to the great Indian Buddhist scholar **Buddhaghosa**, who worked at Anuradhapura during the fifth century AD (though there's no evidence that he ever visited Aluvihara). A *tableau vivant* shows the sage and his associates at work on a pile of ola-leaf manuscripts, while a golden Buddhaghosa statue from Thailand, donated to the temple in 1992, stands outside. From here, a final flight of steps leads up past a bo tree to the very top of the complex, where a dagoba and terrace offer fine views down into the temple and across to the grand hills in the distance.

Just up the hill to the left of the temple complex is a building (signed "International Buddhist Library and Museum") where a resident caretaker will pounce on you and scribble your name messily on a piece of ola leaf in return for a donation – a rather sad come-down from the monastery's days as the world's greatest repository of Buddhist learning.

Alu Vihara is easily reached by public transport: any **bus** heading north from Kandy to Dambulla goes right past the entrance; alternatively, take the train from Kandy to Matale and then a tuktuk (around Rs.200 return including waiting time). About 500m south of Alu Vihara on the main road, *Aluvihara Kitchens* (☎066-222 2404) serves up the biggest rice and curry in Sri Lanka, with no less than 25 dishes, though unfortunately you'll need to pre-order and be in a party of ten or so people to experience this gastro-fest. The *Kitchens* are located next to the home of the renowned Sri Lankan artist **Ena de Silva**, and a shop here sells outstanding tapestries, batiks, furniture and brassware.

Nalanda

Some 25km north of Matale, and a kilometre east of the main highway to Dambulla, stands the **Nalanda Gedige**, a little gem of a building and one of the most unusual monuments in the Cultural Triangle. The gedige (Buddhist image house) occupies a scenic location close to the Mahaweli Ganga, with fine views of the steep green surrounding hills – it originally stood nearby at a lower level amongst paddy fields, but was meticulously dismantled and reconstructed in its present location in 1980 when the Mahaweli Ganga hydro-electricity project led to its original location being flooded. The gedige is named after the great Buddhist university at Nalanda in northern India, though virtually nothing is known either about the gedige itself or the monastery of which it once formed part – different sources date the temple from anywhere between the seventh and twelfth centuries, when Parakramabahu I (see p.322) established a fort here during his battles against Gajabahu. According to tradition, it's claimed that Nalanda is located at the exact centre of Sri Lanka, although a quick glance at any map shows that it's actually rather closer to the west coast than the east.

The gedige is pure South Indian in style, and looks quite unlike anything else in Sri Lanka. Constructed entirely of stone, the building is laid out like a Hindu temple, with a pillared antechamber, or *mandapa* (originally roofed), leading to an inner shrine which is encircled by an ambulatory. There's no sign of Hindu gods, however, and it appears that the temple was only ever used as a Buddhist shrine – a classic example of Sri Lankan cultural miscegenation. The **main shrine** is entered through a fine square stone door flanked by beautifully carved (though eroded) columns and topped by two elephants and a line of miniature buildings; some of the chunky rectilinear decoration here looks oddly like the stone carving found on Maya buildings in Central America. The southern tympanum of the unusual horseshoe-shaped roof features a carving of Kubera, the god of wealth, seated on a lotus pedestal, and the other walls are also richly carved, with many small faces in roundels. The carvings are now much eroded, although if you look carefully you may be able to find the erotic tantric carving which adorns the southern face of the base plinth on which the entire gedige stands – the only example in Sri Lanka of a typically Indian sculptural motif. The brick base of a ruined (but much more modern) dagoba stands close by.

Entrance is included as part of the Cultural Triangle ticket (see p.296), although you can't actually buy CT tickets here. If you don't already have a CT ticket, entrance costs a ridiculous US$5. The site is open access, so if there's no one around checking tickets you can just walk in. There are no **guides** at the site, although you might be able to pick up a copy of the useful little booklet about Nalanda published by the Central Cultural Fund; it's sometimes available from the Cultural Triangle Office in Kandy (see p.214) or from bookshops around the island. Any **bus** from Kandy to Dambulla will drop you at the turn-off to the temple, from where it's a one-kilometre walk.

Ridi Vihara

Tucked away in beautiful rolling countryside 15km west of the Kandy–Dambulla highway, roughly equidistant between Matale and Kurunegala, the cave temple of **Ridi Vihara** is one of the Cultural Triangle's most absorbing smaller sights, and well worth hunting out if you have your own transport. According to legend (though it may be no more than that), Ridi Vihara, or "Silver Temple", was built by the legendary King Dutugemunu (see p.348). Dutugemunu lacked the money to complete the great Ruvanvalisaya dagoba at Anuradhapura until the discovery of a rich vein of silver ore at Ridi Vihara (along with various other miraculous treasures, as related in the island's great historical chronicle, the *Mahavamsa*) allowed the illustrious king to finished his masterpiece – he expressed his gratitude by creating a cave temple at the location of the silver lode. The vihara is hidden away behind a small monastery; one of the monks will let you in and show you around in return for a donation.

Just before the main body of the temple lies the **Varakha Valandu Vihara** ("Jackfruit Temple"), an exquisite little Hindu temple, scarcely larger than a shoe box, which was converted into a Buddhist sanctuary during the Kandyan period. The temple, which dates from around the eleventh century, is built right up against a small rock outcrop and, rather like the gedige at nearby Nalanda, is strikingly South Indian in style. The bases of the pillars are decorated with figures – a man with a spear, another with a bow and arrow – while inside the tiny shrine sits a small yellow Buddha and a few simple Kandyan-era paintings.

Beyond here, you pass through a wooden entrance pavilion (an old wooden palanquin hangs from the roof) and cross a simple courtyard painted in harmonious pastel colours to reach the main rock-cut temple, the **Pahala Vihara** (Lower Temple). To the right of the entrance is an exquisite ivory carving of five ladies, protected by an unlovely modern security grille – an altogether less aesthetic protective measure than the great plain Kandyan-era wooden locks which secure the doors of the main shrine. The temple's interior is surprisingly large; a veritable Aladdin's cave, its walls are covered in tessellated Kandyan-era pictures of hundreds of Buddhas. A huge sleeping Buddha lies to the left, in front of which is a platform inset with blue and white Dutch tiles (donated by a Dutch monk) showing pictures of Dutch village life along with a few biblical scenes – a sneaky bit of Christian proselytizing in the temple's most important Buddhist shrine. At the far end of the cave stand (from left to right) statues of the Buddha, Natha, King Dutugemunu (the last is an extremely ancient statue claimed to date from Anuradhapuran period), as well as a delicate reclining Buddha from Burma.

Behind the temple, steps lead up to the right to the Upper Temple, or **Uda Vihara**, immediately behind. This eighteenth-century structure was the work of another illustrious king, Kirti Sri Rajasinha (see p.209). The main chamber has an impressive seated Buddha set against a densely peopled background (the black figures are Vishnus), and a fine Kandyan-style moonstone plus steps flanked by elephants. Next door to the main chamber is the small "**Cobra House**". To the right of the entrance door is a painting of nine ladies – a *trompe l'oeil* which, as you walk backwards, magically transforms into the shape of an elephant. There are more Kandyan-era decorative murals of flowers and Buddhas inside the Cobra House; behind it, a dagoba sits almost completely covered under another part of the overhanging rock.

To reach the temple by public transport, take a **bus** from Kurunegala to **Ridigama** village (hourly; 45min), then either walk or take a tuktuk (around Rs.100 return) from the village for the 2km trip to the temple.

Kurunegala

Busy **KURUNEGALA** is the biggest town between Colombo and Anuradhapura, capital of the Northwest Province and an important commercial centre. The town also sits on a major junction on the roads between Colombo, Dambulla, Anuradhapura and Kandy, so you may well change buses here. There's no great incentive to visit the town in its own right, though it makes a convenient base for exploring the cluster of sights situated in the southwestern corner of the Cultural Triangle.

Kurunegala enjoyed a brief moment of eminence in Sri Lankan affairs during the late thirteenth and early fourteenth centuries, when it served as the capital of the Sinhalese kings under Bhuvanekabahu II (1293–1302) and Parakramabahu IV (1302–26), though hardly anything remains from this period. The present-day town is a tightly packed honeycomb of streets whose hustle and bustle comes as a rude awakening after the sleepy backwaters of the Cultural Triangle. Its main attractions are the breezy **Kurunegala Tank**, north of the centre, and the huge bare **rock outcrops** which surround the town, and lend the entire place a strangely lunar air. The inevitable legend professes that these are the petrified bodies of giant animals who were threatening to drink the lake dry, only to be turned to stone by a demoness who inhabited the waters. If you've an hour or so to kill, it's worth walking or taking a tuktuk up to the humdrum temple and enormous new Buddha statue atop **Etagala** (Elephant Rock), immediately above town, from where there are fine views.

Practicalities

Buses arrive at the small new station bang in the town centre; the **train** station is just over a kilometre southeast of here. If you need to **change**

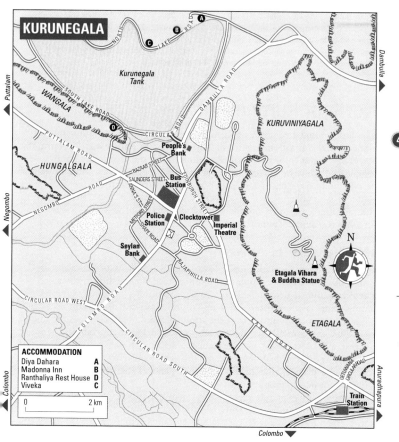

money, there are plenty of banks in town. The **ATM** at the Seylan Bank on Colombo Road accepts foreign cards (Visa only).

Kurunegala's best place **to eat** is the shady garden restaurant at the *Diya Dihara* (see below), which has a well-prepared selection of moderately priced tourist standards. The lake-facing terrace at the *Ranthaliya Rest House* is a pleasant spot for a **drink**.

Accommodation

Almost all the best places **to stay** are around the north side of the lake on North Lake Road.

Diya Dahara 7 North Lake Rd ☏037-222 3452. Big, bare a/c rooms – functional but clean, and with nice little balconies, some with lake views. It's a bit expensive for what you get, though service is good and the garden restaurant is the nicest in town. ❸

Madonna Inn 44 North Lake Rd ☏037-222 3276. The best value in town, with large,

comfortably furnished rooms in a modern house and a nice little restaurant on stilts (though the menu is very limited). ❶

Ranthaliya Rest House South Lake Rd ☏037-222 2298. The closest place to the town centre, and the most attractively located, perched on the southern side of the lake – the terrace overlooking the water is a nice place for a sundowner. The slightly shabby rooms are adequate, if nothing special, and a bit overpriced. No single rates. **②** **Viveka** 64 North Lake Rd ☏037-222 2897. Three rooms in a gracious old colonial house, with lots of period furniture on the attractive

verandah. Rooms are pleasantly old-fashioned, if a bit worn and slightly overpriced (and the a/c room is a rip-off); there's also a restaurant and a cosy little bar (though with only one table). **②**, or **④** with a/c

North of Kurunegala

The little-visited area north of Kurunegala is home to an intriguing quartet of attractions: the abandoned cities of **Yapahuwa** and **Panduwas Nuwara**; the absorbing forest monastery of **Arankele**; and the beautiful Kandyan-era temple of **Padeniya**. If you have your own transport, all four could be visited in a leisurely day's excursion, either as a round-trip from Kurunegala, or en route to Anuradhapura. (If you don't want to pay for a car all the way to Anuradhapura, ask to be dropped at Daladagama, from where it's easy to pick up a bus to Anuradhapura.)

Panduwas Nuwara

Around 12km west of the main road from Kurunegala to Puttalam lie the ruins of **Panduwas Nuwara** (24hr access; free), the first capital of **Parakramabahu I** (see p.332), the royal adventurer who would later achieve lasting fame as the greatest ruler of Polonnaruwa and the architect of that city's transformation into one of the most splendid urban centres of medieval Asia. The city which Parakramabahu created at Panduwas Nuwara is often seen as a trial run for his spectacular achievements at Polonnaruwa, and although the individual remains are relatively underwhelming, the overall scale of the place is undeniably impressive, and exudes an Ozymandias-like aura of vanished splendour.

The ruined city sprawls over an area of several kilometres. At its centre lies the **citadel**, surrounded by wide walls protected by a (now dried-up) moat and pierced by just a single, east-facing entrance – the scale of the fortifications suggests that, at this stage in his career, Parakramabahu felt far from safe. Inside the citadel, facing the entrance, the main ruin is the two-tiered **royal palace**, reminiscent in layout of Parakramabahu's royal palace at Polonnaruwa, although far less of it survives. At the top of the steps on the left stands a table inscription recording a visit by Nissankamalla (see p.327) to watch a dancing display. At the rear right-hand side of this terrace you can see the remains of an ingenious medieval latrine – a water channel leading into a well-like cesspit. The slight remains of a few further buildings around the palace have been neatly restored, but the rest of the citadel remains unexcavated, with the mounds of numerous of buildings still buried under established woodland.

South of the citadel, outside the walls, are the extensive remains of two **monasteries**. The first is some 200m south of the citadel, with a ruined brick dagoba, bo tree enclosure (*bodigara*) and the ruins of a pillared image house (only the Buddha's feet survive). Immediately south lies a second monastery, with a Tamil pillar inscription at its entrance, plus two more ruined dagobas and further monastic buildings. Further south still is a third, still-functioning monastery with an elegant Kandyan-style structure of 1977, with a walkway joined to a raised building. Driving to and from the site you'll pass the ruins of yet more dagobas and other buildings, pillars and walls.

Buses run approximately every hour from Kurunegala to Chilaw, passing through Panduwas Nuwara village, from where it's a one-kilometre walk to the site – locals will point you in the right direction.

Padeniya Raja Mahavihara

Twenty-five kilometres northwest of Kurunegala at the village of Padeniya, the **Padeniya Raja Mahavihara** is one of Sri Lanka's most attractive Kandyan-era temples, and well worth a halt en route to Anuradhapura. The unusual main shrine is set on an imposing platform and enclosed by fine walls (topped by cute lion statues) which are covered by – but not connected to – the big wooden roof. The main **image house** is topped by a fine old wooden roof supported by around thirty beautifully carved old wooden **pillars** – similar to those at the Embekke Devale near Kandy (see p.238). Panels on the pillars show various figures, including a double-headed swan, a lion, an elephant, a man smoking a pipe, a Kandyan drummer and (rather strangely for a Buddhist temple) a dancing girl. Further carved pillars support the roof of the ambulatory which, unusually for a Kandyan-style temple, completely encloses the principal shrine. The **shrine** itself is entered through an exceptionally splendid door, said to be the largest in Sri Lanka. The gloomy interior, surrounded by an ambulatory supported by old Kandyan-style wooden pillars, is home to various Buddha images and a protective Vishnu, as well as a considerable number of bats.

Next to the shrine sits a beautiful lily pond and an imposing three-tiered bo tree platform – the roots of the bo tree have worked their way down through bricks, with marvellously photogenic results.

Arankele

Hidden away on a forested hillside at the end of a rough side road some 24km north of Kurunegala lie the remains of the sixth-century forest hermitage of **Arankele**. The jungle-shrouded ruins are hugely atmospheric and seldom visited by tourists thanks to their remoteness and the difficulty of reaching them even with your own vehicle. A community of *vanavasin* monks who have devoted themselves to a reclusive, meditative life still live at the monastery by the entrance to the site.

The **entrance** is deceptive. Ignore the fine stone terrace and elaborate staircase to your left (the steps lead up through a small series of terraces to a dagoba, where the path soon peters out) and instead go straight ahead, following the covered walkway which leads to the monks' quarters – a wooden bell-chime hung at the start of the walkway is used to mark the various stages of the monastic day. Continue straight ahead through the monks' quarters, shortly beyond which the path enters a stretch of beautifully unspoilt dry tropical forest (there are plenty of other paths branching off if you want to explore further). Continue for about 500m to reach a small clearing, where an old stone monastic building nestles under a rock. Go round to the right of this to reach the beginning of the remarkable **meditation walkway**: a long, perfectly straight stone walkway, punctuated by small flights of steps, the geometrical neatness of the pathway making a strange contrast with the wild forest through which it runs. This leads after 500m past the tumbled remains of a small hypostyle chamber, like a miniature Stonehenge, and then, after another 250m, to a large **clearing** with the extensive remains of various monastic buildings and a beautiful lily-filled tank. For the casual visitor, the remains are difficult to interpret (there are no guides at – or printed guides to – the site), but the magical remoteness and unspoilt forest setting is sufficient attraction in itself.

Yapahuwa

Midway between Kurunegala and Anuradhapura lies the magnificent citadel of **Yapahuwa** (daily 8am–6pm; Rs.200), built around a huge granite rock rising almost a hundred metres above the surrounding lowlands. Yapahuwa was one of the short-lived capitals established during the collapse of Sinahalese power in the thirteenth century and served as the capital of **Bhuvanekabahu I** (ruled 1272–1284), who transferred the capital here from the less easily defensible Polonnaruwa in the face of recurrent attacks from South India, bringing the Tooth Relic (see p.219) with him. The move proved to be of little avail, however. In 1284 Yapahuwa was captured by the army of the South Indian Pandyan dynasty, who carried off the Tooth Relic to Madurai in Tamil Nadu. Following its capture, Yapahuwa was largely abandoned and taken over by monks and hermits, and the capital was moved to Kurunegala.

The site's outstanding feature is the marvellous **stone stairway**, which climbs with Maya-like steepness up to the palace. Its top flight is a positive riot of decoration. Statues of elephants, makara toranas, dwarfs, goddesses and a pair of goggle-eyed stone lions (one appears on the nation's ten-rupee note) flank the stairs, which are topped by a finely carved doorway and windows. Panels around the base and sides of each window are embellished with reliefs of dancers and musicians, one playing a Kandyan drum – the oldest pictorial record of Sri Lanka's most famous musical instrument. The quality of the craftsmanship, carving and materials (solid stone, rather than plebeian brick) is strikingly high – this doesn't look like the statement of a largely powerless king, although the decidedly Indian style pays unintentional tribute to the invaders who had driven Bhuvanekabahu here in the first place.

At the top of the stairs, the so-called **Lion Terrace** itself is deeply anticlimactic after the grandiose approach. This was the site either of the Temple of the Tooth or of Bhuvanekabahu's palace (or possibly both); there's very little to see now bar a couple of brick foundations and a few pillars – though there are fine views of the flat plains far below dotted with huge, saw-toothed mountains.

The remains of the **city** which once spread around the base of the rock are also decidedly modest. You can see the foundations of various buildings dotted round the base of the steps, bounded by a limestone wall and surrounded by a dried-up moat, though these cover a surprisingly small area.

There's a small **museum** just to the right of the site, set in one of a pair of gorgeous old Kandyan-style wooden barns separated by a quaint bell tower. Exhibits (with Sinhala labels only) include some fine stone statues, extremely Indian in style, and one of the two stone windows from the top of the stairway, intricately latticed in quasi-Arabian style (the other one is in the National Museum in Colombo). Behind the museum is a **cave temple**, its entrance projecting out from the rock outcrop and its interior containing some extremely faded Kandyan-era frescos – you can't really make anything out apart from vague colours – plus old plaster, wood and bronze Buddha images and some ugly modern statues. The temple is usually locked, though someone from the ticket office will probably offer to open it for you. A resident guide (tip) waits at the ticket office.

Yapahuwa is 4km from **Maho** Railway Station, which is served by fairly regular local **trains** from Kurunegala and by fast trains running between Colombo and Anuradhapura. Alternatively, catch any **bus** travelling between Anuradhapura and Kurunegala and get off at **Daladagama**, 5km west of the site, and pick up a tuktuk. From either Maho or Daladagama, a tuktuk should cost Rs.200–250, including waiting time.

Dambulla

Situated midway between Kandy, Anuradhapura and Polonnaruwa, the dusty little town of **DAMBULLA** is famous for its remarkable **cave temples**, one of Sri Lanka's outstanding man-made attractions – and given that they stand right next to the main road between Kandy and Sigiriya, Anuradhapura and Polonnaruwa, you're almost certain to pass right by. The temples here are little masterpieces of Sinhalese Buddhist: five magical, dimly lit grottos which seem to glow with the rich reds and golds of the innumerable statues that fill every space and the paintings that cover every surface.

Dambulla's position close to the heart of the Cultural Triangle makes it a convenient base; there are a few passable guest houses in town, and several tempting top-end hotels nearby. The **town** itself is one of the least attractive in the region, however, strung out along a single long, dusty and traffic-plagued main road. The centre is marked by the usual clocktower, north of which stretches the main run of shops, housed in a dispiriting string of ugly modern concrete buildings; to the south of the clocktower lies the town's anarchic wholesale **market** (there's usually a dangerous scrum of lorries laden with agricultural produce jockeying for position around the entrance) and most of its guest houses.

The cave temples

The **cave temples** (daily 7.30am–7pm; Rs.500) are located about 2km south of the town centre, cut out of an enormous granite outcrop which rises over 160m above surrounding countryside, offering majestic views across the plains of the dry zone as far as Sigiriya, over 20km distant. Archeological evidence suggests that these and other caves around the rock outcrop were inhabited during prehistoric times, and were later used for pre-Buddhist religious ceremonies, but their present incarnation as Buddhist shrines dates

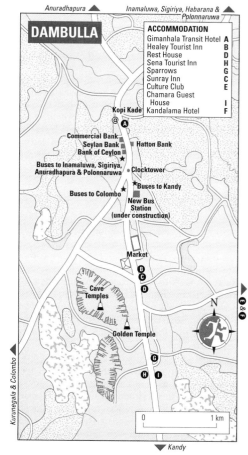

DAMBULLA

Anuradhapura ▲   Inamaluwa, Sigiriya, Habarana & ▲
                                    Polonnaruwa

ACCOMMODATION
Gimanhala Transit Hotel   A
Healey Tourist Inn   B
Rest House   D
Sena Tourist Inn   H
Sparrows   G
Sunray Inn   C
Culture Club   E
Chamara Guest
  House   I
Kandalama Hotel   F

Kopi Kade   @   A

Commercial Bank
Seylan Bank   Hatton Bank
Bank of Ceylon
Buses to Inamaluwa, Sigiriya,   Clocktower
Anuradhapura & Polonnaruwa
                          Buses to Kandy
Buses to Colombo
                 New Bus
                 Station
              (under construction)

Market
        B
        C
        D

Cave
Temples
                          E & C

Golden Temple
                  G

              H   I

N

Kurunegala & Colombo

0   1 km

Kandy

back to the days of **Vattagamani Abhaya** (also known as Valagambahu or Valagamba; reigned 103 BC and 89–77 BC). Vattagamani lost his throne to a group of Tamil invaders and was forced into hiding for fourteen years, during which exile he found refuge in these caves. Having reclaimed his throne at Anuradhapura, Vattagamani had temples constructed here in gratitude for the hiding place the rock had offered him – the individual caves which now house the temples were created by building partition walls into the space beneath what was originally a single huge rock overhang. The cave temples were further embellished by Nissankamalla (1187–96; see p.327), who gilded the interior of the caves and many of the statues, earning them the name of Ran Giri (Golden Rock). Comprehensive restorations and remodellings were carried out by the **Kandyan kings** Senerath (1604–1635) and Kirti Sri Rajasinha (1747–82), who also created the magnificent Cave 3 and commissioned many of the vast number of **murals** which now decorate the interiors – an extraordinary compendium of paintings without equal in Sri Lanka. Most of what you now see dates from the reigns of these two kings, although precise dating of individual paintings is made difficult, since these are traditionally repainted on a regular basis once their paintwork fades, and further changes and embellishments have been added right through to the twentieth century.

The entrance to the site is right on the main road at the Golden Temple (see p.308), where you buy your **ticket**. From here, it's a steep ten-minute climb up to the caves, which are concealed by a quaint white colonnaded walkway, built in 1938. Photography is now allowed in the caves, having been banned for a time after a female tourist had herself photographed sitting on the lap of a Buddha statue; the ensuing scandal also caused Dambulla to be withdrawn from the sites included in the Cultural Triangle ticket. Footwear must be removed and shoulders and knees covered. If you have them, binoculars give a better view of the frescoes, while a torch is also useful.

It's best to visit the caves in reverse order, starting at Cave 5 (at the far end from the entrance) and working backwards – this way you get to see the caves in gradually increasing degrees of magnificence, culminating in the wonderful cave 2.

Caves 4 and 5

The small and atmospheric cave 5, the **Devana Alut Viharaya** ("Second New Temple"), is the most modern of the temples, and unlike most of the site's other statues, which are fashioned from solid rock, the images here are made of brick and plaster. The main figure is a ten-metre reclining Buddha, with standing and seated Buddhas (two under enormous cobra hoods) at his head. On the wall at the Buddha's feet are paintings of a dark Vishnu flanked by Kataragama with his peacock to the right and Bandara (a local deity) to the left. To the right of the door is a mural of a noble carrying lotus flowers, perhaps the man who endowed the temple. Murals of Buddhas, flowers and chequered patterns cover the walls.

Cave 4, the **Paccima Viharaya** ("Western Temple" – although cave 5, constructed later, is actually further west), is relatively small. Multiple identical figures of seated Buddhas in the meditation posture sit around the walls, along with a few larger seated figures, one (curtained) under an elaborate makara torana arch. Figures of Vishnu and Saman stand behind the curtains. There's a small dagoba in the middle; this was broken into by thieves who believed it contained jewellery of Valagamba's wife, Queen Somawathie. Again, the walls are covered with pictures of Buddhas and floral and chequered decorative patterns, most of which were heavily repainted in the early twentieth century.

Cave 3

Cave 3, the **Maha Alut Viharaya** ("Great New Temple") was constructed by Kirti Sri Rajasinha (see p.209), and is on a far grander scale – the sloping ceiling reaches a height of up to 10m and gives the cave the appearance of an enormous tent. The cave is entered through an unpainted makara torana doorway with huge, thick wooden doors, while its edges are lined with over fifty standing and seated Buddhas. To the right of the entrance stands a statue of **Kirti Sri Rajasinha**, with four attendants painted onto the wall behind him. The meditating Buddha, seated in the middle of the cave under an exuberant makara torana, and the sleeping Buddha by the left wall, are both carved out of solid rock – an extraordinary feat in an age when every piece of stone had to be hacked off with rudimentary chisels.

The cave also has a rich collection of **murals**. Two ceiling paintings show scenes of the Buddha preaching in a Kandyan-looking pavilion. In the first (which can be seen looking up from the entrance), the Buddha preaches to a group of ascetic disciples; in the second (to the left of the entrance) he addresses a gathering of gods adorned with splendid crowns. Most of the rest of the ceiling is covered by an immense swathe of tessellated Buddhas. To the right of the door (behind a pair of seated Buddhas) is another interesting mural showing a picture of an idealized garden with square ponds, trees, elephants, cobras and Buddhas – a rather folksy, nineteenth-century addition to the original Kandyan-era murals.

Cave 2

Cave 2, the **Maharaja Vihara** ("Temple of the Great Kings"), is the biggest and most spectacular at Dambulla, an enormous, sepulchral space measuring over 50m long, almost 25m deep and reaching a height of 7m – more of a rock cathedral than a rock temple. Vattagamani Abhaya is credited with its creation, though it was altered several times subsequently and completely restored in the eighteenth century. The cave is named after the statues of two kings it contains. The first is a painted wooden image of **Vattagamani Abhaya** himself (just left of the door furthest away from the main entrance); the second is of **Nissankamalla** (see p.327), hidden away at the far right-hand end of the cave and almost completely concealed behind a large reclining Buddha – a rather obscure fate for this most vainglorious of all Sinhalese kings.

The sides of the cave are lined with an enormous collection of Buddha statues, showing a far more varied range of sizes and poses than in the other caves. The main Buddha statue, set under a makara torana in the abhaya ("Have no Fear") mudra, was formerly covered in gold leaf, traces of which can still be seen. To either side stand wooden statues of Maitreya (left) and Avalokitesvara or Natha (right), a rare touch of Mahayanist influence. Against the wall behind the main Buddha are statues of Saman and Vishnu, while images of Kataragama and Ganesh are painted onto the wall behind, an unusually varied contingent of gods within such a small space. In the right-hand corner, sitting in a wire-mesh enclosure, is a pot which is constantly fed by drips from the ceiling which are said never to run dry, even in the worst drought.

The ceiling and walls are covered in a fabulous display of **murals** – the finest in Sri Lanka. On the ceiling at the western end of the cave (to the left as you enter), Kandyan-style strip panels show pictures of dagobas at Sri Lanka's holy places and scenes from the Buddha's life (you can just make out the small white elephant which appeared in a dream to the Buddha's mother during her pregnancy, symbolizing the rare qualities of her future child). These murals pale in comparison, however, with the three adjacent ceiling panels showing the **Mara Parajaya** ("Defeat of Mara"), which depict the temptations meted out to the Buddha during his struggle for enlightenment at Bodhgaya. In the first he is shown seated under a beautifully stylized bo tree whilst crowds of hairy grey demons attack him with arrows (one technologically advanced devil even carries a musket), supervised by a magnificent Mara riding on an elephant. This attempt to break the Buddha's concentration having failed, the next panel, the **Daughters of Mara**, shows him being tempted by bevies of seductive maidens. The Buddha's triumph over these stupendous feminine wiles is celebrated in the next panel, the **Isipatana**, which shows him delivering his first sermon to a vast assembly of splendidly attired gods.

Further panels around the walls of the cave are covered in narrative paintings depicting events from the **history of Sri Lanka** – one particularly fine sequence in a recess on the south side of the cave shows the arrival of Buddhism on the island, the planting of the bo tree at Anuradhapura and the construction of Sri Lanka's first stupa.

Cave 1

Cave 1, the **Devaraja Viharaya** ("Temple of the Lord of the Gods") is named after Vishnu, who is credited with having created the caves; a Brahmi inscription outside the temple to the right commemorates the temples' foundation. Inside, the narrow space is almost completely filled by a 14-metre-long sleeping **Buddha**, carved out of solid rock, which preserves fine traces of beautiful gold gilding on his elbow. By the Buddha's head, images of Vishnu and other figures are hidden behind a brightly painted wooden screen (opened only during pujas); whilst a statue of the Buddha's most faithful disciple, Ananda, stands at his feet. The cave's unusual **murals** are quite badly eroded in places; some are said to be the oldest at the site, though constant repainting over the centuries has dulled any clear sense of their antiquity, and they lack the artistry of the murals in caves 2 and 3; the bright new frescoes behind Ananda's head (including a weird tree sporting an Italian Renaissance-style cherub) are clumsy twentieth-century additions.

Outside, next door, is a small, blue **chapel** dedicated to Kataragama; a Bo tree stands opposite.

Golden Temple

At the bottom of the steps up to the cave temples stands the bizarre **Golden Temple**, a shamelessly kitsch building topped by a huge seated **golden Buddha**, completed in 2000 and reaching a height of 30m. The sign claims it to be the largest Buddha statue in the world – which is nothing more than a barefaced lie: it's not even the largest in Sri Lanka (the genuine world's largest Buddha statue, at Leshan in China, stands over twice as tall at 71m, while plans are afoot to construct a 152-metre-tall monster Buddha at Bodhgaya in India). Exaggerated claims apart, the statue is extremely striking, and rather more artistic than the **Golden Temple Buddhist Museum** (daily 7.30am–11.30pm; Rs.100) in the building below, entered through the golden mouth of an enormous lion-like beast. The museum itself is large but rather lacking in exhibits apart from some boring copies of the cave temple paintings, a few Buddhas from around the world and a sprinkling of other artefacts, none of them labelled. Save your money.

Practicalities

Arriving in Dambulla by **bus**, you'll be deposited at the main junction in the middle of Dambulla, at one of the various stops near the clocktower (there are plans for a new bus terminal, slightly south of the clocktower, though it might be several years before this finally opens). A tuktuk from the clocktower to the hotels south of town should cost Rs.40–60. There are several **banks** in Dambulla. The ATMs at the Commercial (Visa and MasterCard) and Seylan banks (Visa only) accept foreign cards. The **post office** is on the main road just north of the *Sunray Inn*, and there's **Internet** access (Rs.120 per hour) and webcalls (Rs.25 per min) at Kopi Kade (daily 8am–8pm), at the northern end of town.

Accommodation

There's no great choice of **accommodation** in Dambulla itself, and as all the town's options are strung out along the main road, traffic noise can be a problem – always try to get a room as far from the road as possible. The area immediately **around Dambulla** is home to a couple of enticing top-end places, while there are also accommodation options 10km down the road at **Inamaluwa** (see p.317) and slightly further away at **Habarana** (see p.335). Apart from the guest houses, **eating** options are equally thin on the ground – all the places listed below do food. If you want to venture out of your guest house, the best place is the *Rest House*. The menu is limited, but there's excellent rice and curry, plus a few other inexpensive staples.

Dambulla

Chamara Guest House ☎066-228 4488. Set in a rather austere-looking custom-built modern block. Rooms are clean and comfortable, if a bit small and relatively expensive. No single rates. **②**

Gimanhala Transit Hotel ☎066-228 4864, ⓔgimanhala@sltnet.lk. The smartest place in the town, set in an attractive modern building with comfortable rooms, all with a/c and hot water. There's a decent-sized pool (residents only), free mountain bikes, an attractive pavilion restaurant and a cosy little bar with a good wine list and live music nightly. Breakfast included. **⑤**

Healey Tourist Inn ☎066-228 4940. Perhaps the best-value accommodation in Dambulla, with small, neat, clean and comfortable rooms. **②**

Rest House ☎066-222 2299. One of Sri Lanka's nicer and best-value rest houses, with large, well-maintained and characterful old rooms, plus some of the best food in town. Worth paying the few extra dollars, given the uninspiring budget alternatives. **③**

Sena Tourist Inn ☎066-228 4421. Six rooms inside a family house: small and simple, but neat, clean and perfectly comfortable. **①**

Sparrows ☎066-228 4673. Five basic but cheap and acceptable rooms, plus two smarter new rooms; all are set slightly back from the road, so quieter than many other places. Standard rooms **①**, new rooms **③**

Sunray Inn ☎066-228 4769. Slightly more expensive – but a bit smarter – than Dambulla's other budget options, with large, pleasant rooms. There's also a popular (and often noisy) in-house bar. **②**

Around Dambulla

Culture Club ☎066-223 1822, ⓦwww .connaissanceceylan.com. Set in tranquil countryside around 9km from Dambulla, this colourful hotel is a fun place to stay, although it lacks the architectural panache of the nearby *Kandalama*. The main building occupies two humungous interlocking wooden pavilions, while the rooms (all a/c twins), set in pleasant orange and white chalets, are each named after a bird and decorated with pretty floral fabrics. There's a huge pool (non-guests Rs.100), various sporting facilities, an attractive ayurveda centre, twice-daily birdwatching trips with the resident ornithologist and Kandalama Lake at the bottom of the grounds. Nothing to do with Boy George, mercifully. **⑦**

Kandalama ☎066-228 4100, ⓦwww .aitkenspenceholidays.com. Located around 10km from Dambulla on the beautiful Kandalama Lake, this is one of the country's most famous hotels, and ranks amongst the finest works of outstanding Sri Lankan architect Geoffrey Bawa (see p.132). The hotel manages to be simultaneously huge (it's the best part of a kilometre long) but almost

Moving on from Dambulla

Buses from Dambulla currently leave from three different stops (a new bus terminal is currently under construction and will presumably handle all arrivals and departures when completed, although no one seems to know when this is likely to happen). CTB buses and private minibuses to **Anuradhapura** (every 30min) and **Polonnaruwa** (every 30min) leave from the roadside just north of the clocktower. There are also buses to **Sigiriya** from this stop (every 30min); alternatively, take any northbound bus and get off at Inamaluwa Junction, from where you can catch a tuktuk to Sigiriya. Buses to **Kandy** (every 20min) leave from the stand on the Kandy Road south of the clocktower. Buses to **Colombo** (every 20min) leave from the roadside on the Colombo Road just south of the clocktower.

invisible, being built into a hillside and concealed under a carefully nurtured canopy of jungly growth, so that nature is never far away (local bats fly up and down the corridors after dark). Rooms are stylishly simple, with big picture windows and marvellous views, and the hotel has all facilities, including several excellent restaurants and one of the most spectacular swimming pools in the island. Given all this, it's surprisingly inexpensive, though it's best to come with your own transport – the in-house travel desk is shambolic, and a rip-off. **7**–**8**

Sigiriya

North of Dambulla, the spectacular citadel of **SIGIRIYA** rises sheer and impregnable out of the denuded plains of the dry zone, sitting atop a huge outcrop of gneiss rock towering 200m above the surrounding countryside. The shortest-lived but the most extraordinary of all Sri Lanka's medieval capitals, Sigiriya ("Lion Rock") was declared a World Heritage Site in 1982 and is now the country's most memorable single attraction – a remarkable archeological site made unforgettable by its dramatic setting.

Some history

Inscriptions found in the caves which honeycomb the base of the rock indicate that Sigiriya served as a place of religious retreat as far back as the third century BC, when Buddhist monks established refuges here. It wasn't until the fifth century AD, however, that Sigiriya rose briefly to pre-eminence in Sri Lankan affairs, following the power struggle which succeeded the reign of **Dhatusena** (455–473) of Anuradhapura. Dhatusena had two sons, **Mogallana**, by the most pre-eminent of his various queens, and **Kassapa**, his son by a lesser consort. Upon hearing that Mogallana had been declared heir to the throne, Kassapa rebelled, driving Mogallana into exile in India and imprisoning his father. The legend of Dhatusena's subsequent demise offers an instructive illustration of the importance given to water in early Sinhalese civilization. Threatened with death if he refused to reveal the whereabouts of the state treasure, Dhatusena agreed to show his errant son its location if he was permitted to bathe one final time in the great Kalawewa Tank, whose creation he had overseen. Standing in the tank, Dhatusena poured its water through his hands and told Kassapa that this alone was his treasure. Kassapa, none too impressed, had his father walled up in a chamber and left him to die.

Mogallana, meanwhile, vowed to return from India and reclaim his inheritance. Kassapa, preparing for the expected invasion, constructed a new residence on top of the 200-metre-high Sigiriya rock – a combination of

△ Sigiriya Rock and water gardens

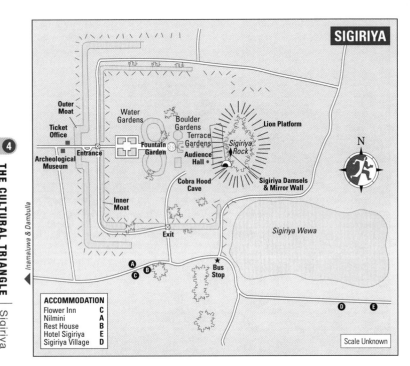

SIGIRIYA

Outer Moat
Ticket Office
Archeological Museum
Entrance
Water Gardens
Fountain Garden
Inner Moat
Boulder Gardens
Terrace Gardens
Audience Hall
Cobra Hood Cave
Lion Platform
Sigiriya Rock
Sigiriya Damsels & Mirror Wall
N
Exit
Sigiriya Wewa
Bus Stop

ACCOMMODATION
Flower Inn   C
Nilmini   A
Rest House   B
Hotel Sigiriya E
Sigiriya Village D

Scale Unknown

pleasure palace and impregnable fortress, which Kassapa intended would emulate the legendary abode of Kubera, the god of wealth, while a new city was established around its base. According to tradition, the entire extraordinary structure was built in just seven years, from 477 to 485.

The long-awaited **invasion** finally materialized in 491, Mogallana having raised an army of Tamil mercenaries to fight his cause. Despite the benefits of his impregnable fortress, Kassapa, in an act of fatalistic bravado, descended from his rocky eminence and rode boldly out on an elephant at the head of his troops to meet the attackers on the plains below. Unfortunately for Kassapa, his elephant took fright and bolted at the height of the battle. His troops, thinking he was retreating, fell back and left him cut off. Facing certain capture and defeat, Kassapa killed himself.

Following Mogallana's reconquest, Sigiriya was handed over to the Buddhist monks, after which its caves once again became home to religious ascetics seeking peace and solitude. The site was finally abandoned in 1155, after which it remained largely forgotten, excepting brief periods of military use by the Kingdom of Kandy in the sixteenth and seventeenth centuries, until being rediscovered by the British in 1828.

Sigiriya Rock

You'll need two to three hours to explore **Sigiriya Rock**; visit in the early morning or late afternoon, when the crowds are less dense and the temperature is cooler – late afternoon brings out the rock's extraordinary ochre colouration, making it look almost Australian. The site is best avoided at weekends and on public holidays, when its narrow staircases and walkways can become unbearably congested. The ascent of the rock is a stiff climb, but less gruelling than you might imagine when standing at the bottom of the towering cliff face. Sufferers of vertigo, however, might find some sections unpleasant.

The site divides into two sections: the **rock** itself, on whose summit Kassapa established his principal palace; and the area **around the base of the rock**, home to elaborate royal pleasure gardens, as well as various monastic remains pre-dating Kassapa's era. The entire site is a compelling combination of wild nature and high artifice – exemplified by the delicate paintings of the Sigiriya damsels which cling to the rock's rugged flanks. Interestingly, unlike Anuradhapura and Polonnaruwa, there's no sign here of large-scale monasteries or religious structures – Kassapa's Sigiriya appears to have been an almost entirely secular affair, perhaps a reflection of its unhallowed origins.

Tickets can be purchased at the office diagonally opposite the main entrance gate. Entrance to Sigiriya is included in the CT ticket (see p.296); otherwise it costs the rupee-equivalent of US$15. The site opens at 7am; last entrance is at 5pm (and to the Mirror Wall at 6pm), although you can stay on the rock till it gets dark. Next to the ticket office, the extremely modest **Archeological Museum** (Mon & Wed–Sun 8am–5pm; free) has a small and uninteresting collection of stone, pottery and terracotta fragments.

The Water Gardens

From the entrance, a wide and straight path arrows directly towards the rock, following the line of an imaginary east–west axis, drawn straight through the rock, around which the whole city was planned. This entire side of the city is protected by a broad moat enclosed within two-tiered walls. Crossing the moat (which once enclosed the entire west-facing side of the complex), you enter the **Water Gardens**. The appearance of this area varies greatly according to how much rain has recently fallen, and in the dry season lack of water means that the gardens can be a little underwhelming. The **first section** comprises four pools set in a square; when full, they create a small island at their centre, connected by pathways to the surrounding gardens. The remains of pavilions can been seen in the rectangular areas to the north and south of the pools.

Beyond here is the small but elaborate **Fountain Garden**. Features here include a serpentining miniature "river" and limestone-bottomed channels and ponds, two of which preserve their ancient fountain sprinklers – these work on a simple pressure and gravity principle and still spurt out modest plumes of water after heavy rain. The whole complex offers a good example of the hydraulic sophistication achieved by the ancient Sinhalese in the dry zone: after almost 1500 years of disuse, all that was needed to restore the fountains to working order was to clear the water channels which feed them.

The Boulder Gardens and Terrace Gardens

Beyond the Water Gardens the main path begins to climb up through the very different **Boulder Gardens**, constructed out of the huge boulders which lie tumbled around the foot of the rock, and offering a naturalistic wildness very different from the neat symmetries of the Water Gardens. Many of the boulders are notched with lines of holes – they look rather like rock-cut steps, but in fact they were used as footings to support the brick walls or timber frames of the numerous buildings which were built against or on top of the boulders – difficult to imagine now, although it must originally have made an extremely picturesque sight.

The gardens were also the centre of Sigiriya's monastic activity before and after Kassapa: there are around twenty rock shelters hereabouts which were used by monks, some containing inscriptions dating from between the third century BC and the first century AD. The caves would originally have been plastered and painted, and traces of this decoration can still be seen in a few places; you'll also notice the dripstone ledges which were carved around the entrances to many of the caves to prevent water from running into them. The **Deraniyagala Cave**, just to the left of the path shortly after it begins to climb up through the gardens, has a well-preserved dripstone ledge and traces of old paintings. On the opposite side of the main path up the rock, a side path leads to the **Cobra Hood Cave**, named for its uncanny resemblance to that snake's head. The cave preserves traces of lime plaster, floral decoration and an inscription in Brahmi script on the ledge dating from the second century BC.

Follow the path up the hill behind the Cobra Hood Cave to reach the so-called **Audience Hall**. The wooden walls and roof have long since disappeared, but the impressively smooth floor, created by chiselling the top off a single enormous boulder, remains, along with a five-metre-wide "throne", also cut out of the solid rock. The hall is popularly claimed to have been Kassapa's audience hall, though it's more likely to have served a purely religious function, with the empty throne representing the Buddha; a rectangular **cistern** is carved out of another part of the same boulder. The small cave to one side of the Audience Hall retains colourful splashes of paint on its ceiling and is home to another throne, while a couple more thrones can be found carved into nearby rocks.

Return back to the main path from here and you should come out at "Boulder Arch no. 1" (as the sign calls it). Continuing through here, the main pathway – now a sequence of walled-in steps – begins to climb steeply through the **Terrace Gardens**, a series rubble-retaining brick and limestone terraces that stretch to the base of the rock itself, from where you get the first of an increasingly majestic sequence of views back down below.

The Sigiriya Damsels and the Mirror Wall

Shortly after reaching the base of the rock, two incongruous metal spiral staircases lead to and from a sheltered cave in the sheer rock face that holds Sri Lanka's most famous sequence of frescoes, popularly referred to as the **Sigiriya Damsels** (no flash photography). These busty beauties were painted in the fifth century and are the only nonreligious paintings to have survived from ancient Sri Lanka; they're now one of the island's most iconic – and most relentlessly reproduced – images. Once described as the largest picture gallery in the world, it's thought that these frescoes would originally have covered an area some 140 metres long by 40 metres high, though only 21 damsels now survive out of an original total of some five hundred (a number of paintings were destroyed by a vandal in 1967, while a few of the surviving pictures are roped off out of sight). The exact significance of the paintings is unclear: they were originally thought to depict Kassapa's consorts, though according to modern art historians the most convincing theory is that they are portraits of *apsaras* (celestial nymphs), which would explain why they are shown from the waist up only, rising out of a cocoon of clouds. The portrayal of the damsels is strikingly naturalistic, showing them scattering petals and offering flowers and trays of fruit – similar in a style to the famous murals at the Ajanta Caves in India, and a world away from the much later murals at nearby Dambulla, with their stylized and minutely detailed religious tableaux. An endearingly human touch is added by the slips of the brush visible here and there: one damsel has three hands, while another sports three nipples.

Just past the damsels, the pathway runs along the face of the rock, bounded on one side by the **Mirror Wall**. This was originally coated in highly polished plaster made from lime, egg white, beeswax and wild honey; sections of the original plaster survive and still retain a marvellous polished sheen. The wall is covered in **graffiti**, the oldest dating from the seventh century, in which early visitors recorded their impressions of Sigiriya and, especially, the nearby damsels – even after the city was abandoned, Sigiriya continued to draw a steady stream of tourists curious to see the remains of Kassapa's fabulous pleasure-dome. Taken together, the graffiti form a kind of early medieval visitors' book, and the 685 which have been deciphered give important insights into the development of the Sinhalese language and script; some are also of considerable poetic merit. Sadly, the older graffiti are very small and rather hard to see under the layers of deranged scribblings left by later and less cultured hands.

Beyond the Mirror Wall, the path runs along a perilous-looking iron walkway bolted onto the sheer rock face. From here you can see a huge **boulder** below, propped up on stone slabs. The rather far-fetched popular theory is that, in the event of attack, the slabs would have been knocked away, causing the boulder to fall onto the attackers below, though it's more likely that the slabs were designed to *stop* the boulder inadvertently falling down over the cliff.

The Lion Platform

Continuing up the rock, a flight of limestone steps climbs steeply up to the **Lion Platform**, a large spur projecting from the north side of the rock, just below the summit (vendors sell fizzy drinks here at slightly inflated prices). From here, a final staircase, its base flanked by two enormous paws carved out of the rock, leads up to all that remains of a gigantic **lion statue** – the final path to the summit apparently led directly into its mouth. Visitors to Kassapa were, one imagines, suitably impressed by this gigantic conceit and by the symbolism – lions were the most important emblem of Sinhalese royalty, and the beast's size was presumably meant to reflect Kassapa's prestige and buttress his questionable legitimacy to the throne.

The wire-mesh cages on the Lion Platform were built as refuges in the (fortunately unlikely) event of bee attacks – you can see bees' nests clinging to the underside of the rock overhang above, to the left of the stairs. The whole section of rock face above is scored with countless notches and grooves which once supported steps up to the summit: in a supreme irony, it appears that Kassapa was afraid of heights, and it's thought that these original steps would have been enclosed by a high wall – though this isn't much comfort for latter-day sufferers of vertigo who have to make the final ascent to the summit up a narrow iron staircase attached to the bare rock face.

The summit

After the tortuous path up, the **summit** seems huge. This was the site of Kassapa's palace, and almost the entire area was originally covered with buildings. Only the foundations now remain, though, and it's difficult to make much sense of it all – the main attraction here is the fabulous views down to the water gardens and out over the surrounding countryside. The summit shelves quite steeply; the king's palace occupied the higher ground on the right, while the lower area to the left would have housed the living quarters of guards and servants. The two areas are divided by a wide, zigzagging paved walkway. The **Royal Palace** itself is now just a plain, square brick platform at the very highest point of the rock, next to which you can see a rectangular outline – popularly described as a "throne". The upper section is enclosed by steep terraced walls, below which is a large tank cut out of the solid rock; it's thought that water was channelled to the summit using an ingenious hydraulic system powered by windmills. Below here a series of four further terraces, perhaps originally gardens, tumble down to the lower edge of the summit above Sigiriya Wewa.

The path down takes you along a slightly different route – you should end up going right past the Cobra Hood Cave, if you missed it earlier, before exiting the site to the south.

Pidurangala Royal Cave Temple

A couple of kilometres north of Sigiriya, another large rock outcrop is home to the **Pidurangala Royal Cave Temple**. According to tradition, the monastery here dates from the arrival of Kassapa, when the monks who were then living at Sigiriya were relocated to make room for the king's city and palace; Kassapa constructed new caves and a temple here to recompense them. The main sight is a large reclining brick Buddha in the Royal Cave Temple itself, accompanied by figures of Vishnu and Saman and decorated with murals. From here you may be able to find the rough path up to the **summit** of the rock, past a few caves (one contains the remains of another reclining Buddha), and a dagoba. There's not really much specific to see, although there are fine views of Sigiriya, and the site offers an atmospheric and little-visited escape from the crowds.

Practicalities

There are **buses** to Sigiriya from Dambulla about every thirty minutes, plus one daily direct morning bus from Kandy. Approaching from Polonnaruwa, take any bus heading to Dambulla and get off at Inamaluwa Junction, 10km west of Sigiriya on the main Dambulla–Trincomalee highway, from where you can pick up a tuktuk (around Rs.200) or wait for the half-hourly bus from Dambulla. From Anuradhapura, it's probably easiest to take a bus to Dambulla, then pick up the Sigiriya bus from there (alternatively, take a bus to Habarana, then another bus to Inamaluwa Junction, then a third bus or a tuktuk as described above). Buses stop in Sigiriya village near the south side of the rock, close to all the guest houses and hotels. **Leaving Sigiriya**, it's probably worth going all the way back to Dambulla, even if you're heading up to Anuradhapura or Polonnaruwa, rather than trying to flag something down on the main road at Inamaluwa Junction. Alternatively, the site is easily visited as a day-trip from Dambulla, Habarana, or even Polonnaruwa or Anuradhapura.

Accommodation

There's only a small choice of **accommodation** in Sigiriya itself. If you don't fancy any of these places (or they're all full), there's more cheap accommodation, and one top-end establishment, about 10km down the road at Inamaluwa – most are acceptable but fairly forgettable, however, and it's better to stay in Sigiriya. It's likely that you'll **eat** where you're staying – if you do want to venture out, *Sigiriya Village* or the *Hotel Sigiriya* are the places to head for.

In addition to the places listed below, the Jetwing hotel group is constructing an ambitious new establishment, just west of Sigiriya Rock, called the *Sigiriya Wetland Lodge*; it's due to open by late 2005. This innovative project will involve the creation of an artificial wetland using a mixture of ancient Sri Lankan irrigation techniques and modern conservation know-how; the hotel itself will comprise a mix of luxury accommodation with a very strong eco-tourism focus. See ⓦ www.jetwingeco.com for latest details.

Sigiriya is also a convenient base for trips to **Minneriya** and **Kaudulla national parks** (see p.332 & 333); most of the places below can arrange tours for anywhere between Rs.1800 and Rs.3500. The *Flower Inn* in Sigiriya village is the cheapest.

Sigiriya

Flower Inn ☎078-875 3682. Cosy and very cheap little rooms set in a family house amidst a flower-filled garden – similar to, but perhaps fractionally nicer than, the *Nilmini* guest house. ❶

Nilmini ☎066-223 3313. Very cheap and cheerful little rooms in a neat little family house (although the corrugated iron roof is rather rustic). Reasonable home-cooking available. ❶

Rest House ☎066-223 1899, ⓦwww .ceylonhotels.lk. Traditional though slightly shabby rest house. The modern a/c rooms are overpriced; the older non-a/c ones are slightly better value, though still no bargain. ❹

Hotel Sigiriya ☎066-223 1940, ⓦwww.serendibleisure.com. Popular with tour groups, this large, rather forgettable resort-style establishment has comfortable a/c rooms, an ayurveda centre and a swimming pool (non-guests Rs.250). The resident naturalist leads nature walks and birdwatching trips. ❼

Sigiriya Village ☎066-223 1803, ⓦwww.sigiriyavillage.lk. Similar country-resort concept to the *Hotel Sigiriya*, though slightly smarter and more expensive. Rooms come with a/c, satellite TV and minibar, and there's a pool (non-guests Rs.100), ayurveda centre and a resident naturalist. On the down side, the chaotic service is straight out of the *Fawlty Towers* school of hotel management, while it also has the most expensive bikes in Sri Lanka (Rs.300 per hour). No single rates. ❼

Inamaluwa

Ancient Villas 1.5km from Inamaluwa Junction ☎066-228 5322, ⓔancient@sltnet.lk. The most characterful of the Inamaluwa cheapies, with cute little chalets and a couple of hexagonal cabanas with splendidly OTT wooden furniture. The whole place has a very peaceful and rather rustic feel –

elephants occasionally cross the river at the end of the garden – and ayurveda treatments are available. ❷

Eden Garden 100m from Inamaluwa Junction ☎ & ⓕ066-228 4635. Large, clean rooms with tiled floors – characterless but comfortable. There's also a nice open-air restaurant and a well-stocked bar, plus a rather shallow pool (non-guests Rs.200). A/c supplement US$5. ❺

Elephant Corridor 4km from Inamaluwa Junction, about 1.5km from the Sigiriya road ☎066-228 3333, ⓦwww.elephantcorridor.com. This new and massively hyped super-luxury boutique hotel (the proud home to Sri Lanka's first US$1000-a-night room) is set in 200 acres of scrubby dry-zone countryside with stunning views of Sigiriya. From the outside, the low cluster of ochre-coloured buildings looks understated to the point of anonymity. Inside, the 21 opulent suite-style rooms are equipped with every conceivable luxury and gimmick, including private plunge-pools and night-vision binoculars. Other facilities include a spa, gym, sauna, a fantastically expensive ayurveda centre, archery, mini-golf course, horse-riding, and (it goes without saying) a helipad. No expense has been spared, though it all looks a little bit cheap. Standard suite US$215, super-deluxe US$370, Romantic suite US$450, Presidential suite US$1500

Inamaluwa Inn 500m from Inamaluwa Junction ☎066-228 4533. Perfectly pleasant, perfectly forgettable place, fractionally nicer and pricier than the *Sigiri Holiday Inn* opposite. Upstairs rooms are slightly smarter and more expensive than downstairs. ❷

Sigiri Holiday Inn Opposite *Inamaluwa Inn*, 500m from Inamaluwa Junction ☎072-251 5210, ⓔsholidayinn@yahoo.com. The cheapest place in Inamaluwa, with acceptable if uninspiring rooms, including one family room (Rs.900). ❷

Polonnaruwa

The great ruined capital of **POLONNARUWA** is one of the undisputed highlights of the Cultural Triangle – and indeed the whole island. The heyday of the city, in the twelfth century, represented one of the high watermarks of early Sri Lankan civilization. The Chola invaders from South India had been repulsed by Vijayabahu, and the Sinhalese kingdom he established at

Polonnaruwa or Anuradhapura?

Many visitors to Sri Lanka only have the time or the archeological enthusiasm to visit one of the island's two great ruined cities, but the two are sufficiently different that it's difficult to call decisively in favour of either. The ruins at **Polonnaruwa** cover a smaller area, are better preserved and offer a more digestible and satisfying bite of ancient Sinhalese culture – and there's nowhere at Anuradhapura to match the artistry of the Quadrangle and Gal Vihara. Having said that, **Anuradhapura** has its own distinct magic. The sheer scale of the site and the number of its remains means that, although it's much harder to get to grips with, it preserves an unsanitized atmosphere and a mystery which much of Polonnaruwa has lost – and it's much easier to escape the coach parties. In addition, its status as a major pilgrimage centre also lends it a vibrancy lacking at Polonnaruwa.

Polonnaruwa enjoyed a brief century of magnificence under his successors Parakramabahu and Nissankamalla, who planned the city as a grand statement of imperial pomp, transforming it briefly into one of the great urban centres of south Asia before their own arrogance and excess virtually bankrupted the state. Within a century, their enfeebled successors had been driven south by new waves of invaders from southern India and Polonnaruwa had been abandoned to the jungle, where it remained, unreclaimed and virtually unknown, for seven centuries.

Polonnaruwa's extensive and well-preserved remains offer a fascinating snapshot of medieval Sri Lanka, including some of the island's finest monuments and compact enough to be thoroughly explored in a single (albeit busy) day. Polonnaruwa is also the most convenient base for visits to the Minneriya and Kaudulla national parks and to the vatadage at Medirigiriya (which could be combined with a visit to the evocative forest monastery of Ritigala). Most of the guest houses in town can arrange transport – count on around Rs.2500 per vehicle for any of these trips.

Some history

The **history** of Polonnaruwa stretches far back into the Anuradhapuran period. The region first came to prominence in the third century AD, when the creation of the Minneriya Tank (see p.332) boosted the district's agricultural importance, while the development of the port of Gokana (modern Trincomalee) into the island's major conduit for overseas trade later helped Polonnaruwa develop into an important local commercial centre – by 368 it was already considered sufficiently important for a royal residence to be built here. As Anuradhapura fell victim to interminable invasions from India, Polonnaruwa's strategic advantages became increasingly apparent. Its greater distance from India made it less vulnerable to attack and gave it easy access to the important southern provinces of Ruhunu, while it also controlled several crossings of the Mahaweli Ganga, one of Sri Lanka's most important rivers. Such were the town's advantages that four rather obscure kings actually chose to reign from Polonnaruwa rather than Anuradhapura, starting with Aggabodhi IV (667–83).

Throughout the anarchic later Anuradhapura era, Polonnaruwa held out against both Indian and rebel Sinhalese attacks until it was finally captured by **Rajahrajah**, king of the Tamil Cholas, in 993. Rajahrajah made it the capital of his short-lived Hindu kingdom, but in 1056, the city was recaptured by the Sinhalese king **Vijayabahu** (1055–1110), who retained it as the new

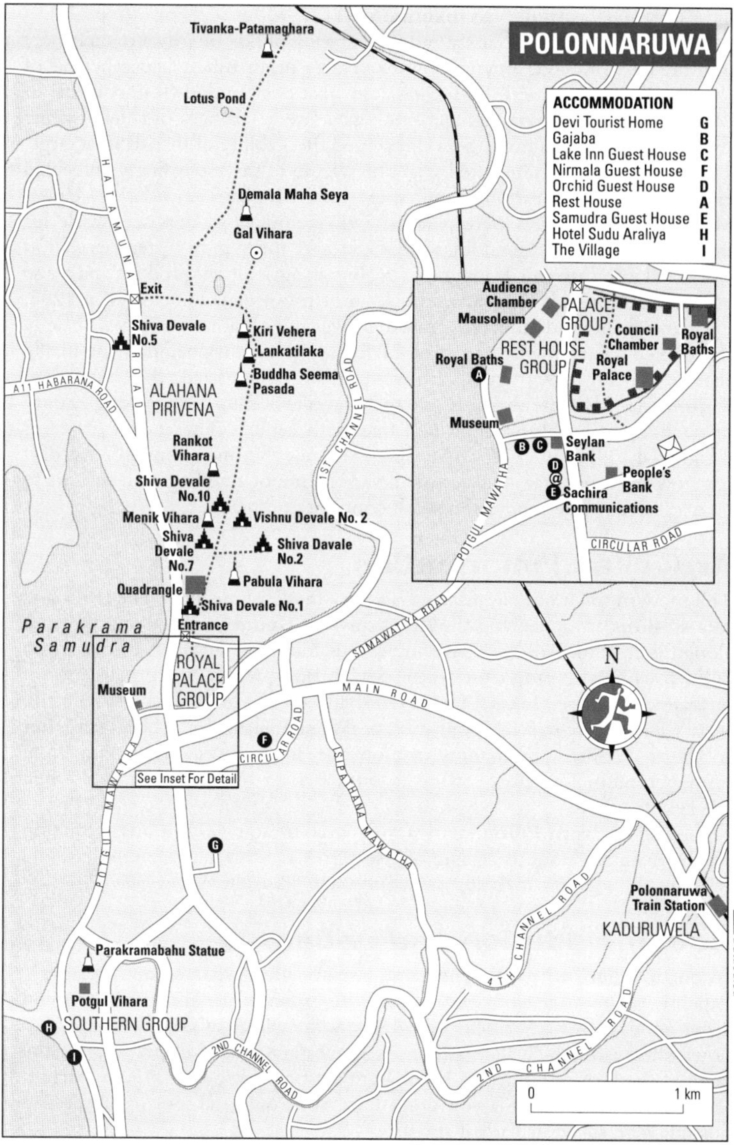

POLONNARUWA

ACCOMMODATION

Devi Tourist Home	G
Gajaba	B
Lake Inn Guest House	C
Nirmala Guest House	F
Orchid Guest House	D
Rest House	A
Samudra Guest House	E
Hotel Sudu Araliya	H
The Village	I

Sinhalese capital in preference to Anuradhapura. Vijayabahu's accession to the throne ushered in Polonnaruwa's golden age, although most of the buildings date from the reign of Vijayabahu's successor **Parakramabahu** (1153–86; see box on p.322). Parakramabahu developed the city on a lavish scale, importing architects and engineers from India, whose influence can be seen in the city's many Hindu shrines. Indian influence continued with Parakramabahu's

319

successor, the boastful **Nissankamalla** (1187–1196; see box on p.327), a Tamil from the Kalinga dynasty and the last king of Polonnaruwa to enjoy any measure of islandwide power. Nissankamalla's death ushered in a period of chaos. Opposing Tamil and Sinhalese factions battled for control of Polonnaruwa – the next eighteen years saw twelve changes of ruler – while at least four invasions from India threatened the stability of the island at large. This era of anarchy culminated with the seizure of the increasingly enfeebled kingdom by the notorious Tamil mercenary **Magha** (1215–1255). Under Magha the monasteries were pillaged and onerous taxes imposed, while his soldiers roamed the kingdom unchecked and the region's great irrigation works fell into disrepair, leading to a decline in agricultural produce and a rise in malaria. Although Magha was finally driven out of Polonnaruwa in 1255, the damage he had inflicted proved irreversible. Polonnaruwa was briefly reoccupied during the latter part of the thirteenth century before being finally abandoned in 1293, when Bhuvanekabahu II moved the capital to Kurunegala. Polonnaruwa was left to be swallowed up by the jungle, until restoration work began in the mid-twentieth century. The ancient city was designated a UNESCO World Heritage Site in 1982, and although most of it has now been painstakingly restored, various minor buildings still remain to be excavated, while renovation work continues on others.

Arrival and information

The modern town of Polonnaruwa is a very modest little affair. The **train** and **bus stations** are actually in the larger town of **Kaduruwela**, about 3km east along the road to Batticaloa. Arriving by bus, ask to be put off at Polonnaruwa "Old Town"; buses stop close to the Seylan Bank, within spitting distance of virtually all the guest houses. The Seylan Bank **ATM** accepts foreign Visa cards; there's also a branch of the People's Bank along the main road. There's **Internet** access at Sachira Communications on the main street (daily 9am–9pm; Rs.6 per min). The **post office** is on the road to Kaduruwela, just past the People's Bank.

Moving on from Polonnaruwa, you could try to pick up a **bus** at the stop on the main road, but to be sure of a seat, it's easiest to take a tuktuk (around Rs.80) to the station at Kaduruwela and catch a bus there.

Accommodation and eating

Accommodation in Polonnaruwa is no great shakes, and relatively expensive for what you get. Given the paucity of mid- and top-end accommodation, many people opt to stay at the village of **GIRITALE**, 15km down the road, which boasts three very pleasant hotels, all perched on the edge of the beautiful Giritale lake. There are frequent buses to Polonnaruwa (every 15min), so even if you don't have your own transport, Giritale is a possible base for visits to that town.

Polonnaruwa doesn't offer a great deal of choice when it comes to **eating**. As usual, all the guest houses listed below do food. If you want to eat out, the *Gajaba* has an attractive garden restaurant and a reasonable choice of inexpensive food, although quality varies. The pleasant dining room at the *Rest House* has a smaller menu but more consistent standards, with a couple of good-value set dinners from around Rs.300 and fine rice and curry. As at Anuradhapura, the rather undernourished and bony fish caught in the lake are a local staple – they're best when fried.

Polonnaruwa

Devi Tourist Home ☏ 027-222 3181, ℱ 222 3947. Set in a peaceful location 1km south of town, this is the nicest and best-run guest house in Polonnaruwa, with four comfy rooms and good home cooking. ❶

Gajaba ☏ 027-222 2394. Old Polonnaruwa stalwart and still the most popular place in town, with a varied collection of fan and a/c rooms; however some are becoming shabby, and all are relatively expensive (and those along the central corridor in the main building can be noisy). Nonetheless, the a/c rooms are quite cheerful, and there's a nice garden restaurant. ❷

Lake Inn Guest House ☏ 027-222 2321. Four basic and rather dark rooms right inside a family house. Nothing to write home about, but cheap. ❶

Nirmala Guest House Circular Rd ☏ 027-222 5163. Bright and clean rooms (including one with a/c), although very little English is spoken. ❶

Orchid Guest House ☏ 027-222 5253. Basic but very cheap rooms – a bit gloomy, but OK at the price. Bikes available (Rs.100 per day). ❶

Rest House ☏ 027-222 2299, ℮ chc@sltnet.net. In a peerless lakeside setting, this venerable old place has spacious, old-fashioned and rather lovely rooms (five with lake views) – plenty of charm, albeit no especial creature comforts. If you want to indulge a few royal fantasies, you can stay in the room occupied by Queen Elizabeth II for a night during her visit here in 1954 (❻) – a beautiful old period piece complete with photos of the old girl's visit. No single rates. A/c supplement US$7. ❺

Samudra Guest House ☏ 027-222 2817. Eight good-value rooms – fairly basic, but spacious and reasonably clean (those inside the main house are larger and cleaner, though darker, than those out the back). There's also a pretty little outdoor

restaurant and no less than forty bikes for hire (Rs.150 per day). ❶

Hotel Sudu Araliya ☏ 027-222 4849, ⓦ www.lanka.net/suduaraliya. The newest and smartest place in Polonnaruwa, with stylish public areas, pool (non-guests Rs.100) and large, comfy a/c rooms equipped with entertainingly tasteless wooden furniture, garish pink bathrooms, fridge and phone. ❻

The Village ☏ 027-222 2405, ℮ villapol@sltnet.lk. Low-slung, attractive-looking resort hotel arranged around attractive gardens. The rooms (all a/c) are a bit spartan and slightly old-fashioned, but just about OK value. There's also a reasonably sized pool (non-guests Rs.150, or free if you take a meal). No single rates. ❸

Giritale

The Deer Park ☏ 027-224 6470, ⓦ www.lanka.net/deerpark. Flash four-star establishment (although service is indifferent) with accommodation in individual cottages scattered around attractive wooded grounds – they're large and stylish, with TV, a/c and nice open-air showers, and there's also a pool. ❼

Giritale Hotel ☏ 027-224 6311, ℮ giritale @carcumb.com. The oldest and still the best value of the Giritale hotels, perched in a wonderful setting high above the lake. All rooms have a/c and hot water (most have lake views) and are cheerily decorated in bright shades of orange and yellow; the more stylish deluxe rooms come with TV and minibar, and there's also a pool, small gym and herbal massages. Standard ❹, deluxe ❺

The Royal Lotus ☏ 027-224 6316, ⓦ www.royallotus.com.lk. Comfortable and good-value two-star hotel with a pool. Rooms are bright, modern and comfy, and all have fine lake views and come with private balcony and a/c. ❺

The ancient city

The ruins of Polonnaruwa are scattered over an extensive area of dry, gently undulating woodland. The entire site is about four kilometres from north to south, and rather too large to cover by foot. The best idea is to **rent a bicycle** (available from most of the town's guest houses or from a couple of places on the main road for around Rs.150 per day); you could also hire a tuktuk, but this is far less enjoyable. The site is open daily from 7am to 6pm and is covered by the CT ticket; otherwise **tickets** cost US$15. Tickets have to be bought at the museum (see p.323) in the village; they can't be bought at the entrance itself. You can see everything at Polonnaruwa in a single long day, but you'll have to start early to do the city justice.

Polonnaruwa was originally enclosed by three concentric walls and filled with parks and gardens. At its centre lay the royal residences of successive kings, comprising the **Royal Palace Group** (containing the palace of

Parakramabahu) and the **Rest House Group** (comprising the less well-preserved remains of Nissankamalla's palace complex). South of here are the scant remains of the **Southern Group**, while just to the north of the palaces lies the city's religious heart, the so-called **Quadrangle**, which contains the densest and finest group of remains in the city, and indeed Sri Lanka. The city's largest monuments are found in the **Northern Group**, comprising the buildings of the Alahana Pirivena monastery, including the famous Buddha statues of the **Gal Vihara** and the evocative **Lankatilaka** shrine.

Although Polonnaruwa doesn't have the huge religious significance of Anuradhapura, the city's monastic remains are still held sacred by Buddhists and Hindus alike. The great statues of the Gal Vihara hold a revered place amongst the island's Buddhists, while many of the site's temples, despite their ruined appearance, are still considered living shrines. Signs outside many of the buildings ask you to remove your shoes as a token of respect – more of a challenge than you might imagine when the summer sun has heated the stone underfoot to oven-like temperatures. Wimps wear socks.

To the west of the city lies the great artificial lake, the **Parakrama Samudra** ("Sea of Parakramabahu"), encircled by rugged hills and providing a beautiful

Parakramabahu the Great

Parakramabahu I (reigned 1153–1186), or **Parakramabahu the Great**, as he is often styled, was the last in the sequence of famous Sinhalese warrior kings, stretching back to the legendary Dutugemunu (see p.348), who succeeded in uniting the entire island under the rule of a single native monarch. Like Dutugemunu, on whose example he seems consciously to have modelled himself, Parakramabahu grew up in the semi-autonomous southern kingdom of Ruhunu and harboured dreams of islandwide domination. Unlike his illustrious role model, however, Parakramabahu was not faced with an occupying foreign power, but with a series of rival Sinhalese claimants to the throne. The political and dynastic situation at this time was deeply confused, with the island having split into a number of semi-independent kingdoms, and Parakramabahu (a grandson of Vijayabahu) had no immediate prospects of kingship. He was initially farmed out by his ambitious mother to the southwestern kingdom of Dakkinadesa, which was ruled by his childless uncle, Kitsirimegha. The opportunistic Parakramabahu was soon embroiled in attempts to boot Kitsirimegha off his throne, although in the midst of his machinations, Kitsirimegha conveniently died, leaving the scheming young prince as his heir.

Becoming ruler of Dakkinadesa, Parakramabahu established a new capital at **Panduwas Nuwara** (see p.302), indulging in a flurry of building and irrigation works which appear, in retrospect, rather like a trial run for the grandiose schemes which he would later carry out at Polonnaruwa. Having established a secure base and raised at army, Parakramabahu began his campaign against the king of Polonnaruwa, his cousin **Gajabahu** (whose help he had recently solicited in his attempts to topple Kitsirimegha). Parakramabahu succeeded in capturing Polonnaruwa, but the behaviour of his troops so incensed the people that they appealed for help to another prince from Ruhunu, **Manabharana**, who arrived at Polonnaruwa under the pretence of protecting Gajabahu. It soon became clear however, that Manabharana himself harboured designs on the throne, and the hapless Gajabahu was forced to jump sides and appeal to Parakramabahu for help, buying peace by declaring Parakramabahu his official heir. Upon Gajabahu's death, the inevitable fighting resumed. Despite initial reverses, during which Manabharana drove Parakramabahu all the way back to Dakkinadesa, Parakramabahu finally triumphed and was crowned king of Polonnaruwa in 1153, although it took a brutal and protracted series of military campaigns before the entire island was finally subdued.

backdrop to the town – an evening stroll along the waterside Potgul Mawatha makes a lovely way to end a day. The lake was created by the eponymous king, Parakramabahu, though sections of the irrigation system date right back to the third century AD. Covering some ten square miles, the lake provided the medieval city with water, cooling breezes and an additional line of defence, and also irrigated over ninety square kilometres of paddy fields. After a breach in the walls in the later thirteenth century, the tank fell into disrepair, and was restored to its original size only in the 1950s.

The Polonnaruwa Museum

The modern **Polonnaruwa Museum** (daily 9am–6pm) is the best in Sri Lanka, by some distance, impressively laid out in a custom-built modern building and well worth a visit before setting off around the site (you have to buy your ticket here, in any case, if you don't have a Cultural Triangle ticket). Exhibits include a fine collection of **bronzes** and **sculptures** recovered from the site – the majority are elaborately carved images of Hindu deities, testifying to the overwhelming Indian influence in the city's culture. There are also some fascinating **scale models** showing how the city's buildings might have

Even whilst Parakramabahu was mopping up the last pockets of resistance in the south, he began to embark on the gargantuan programme of building which restored the economic fortunes of the island and transformed Polonnaruwa into one of the great cities of its age. According to the *Culavamsa*, the new king built or restored over six thousand tanks and canals, including the vast new **Parakrama Samudra** in Polonnaruwa, as well as restoring the three great dagobas at Anuradhapura and rebuilding the monastery at Mihintale. It was at his new capital, however, that Parakramabahu lavished his greatest efforts, supervising the construction of a spate of imposing new edifices, including the Royal Palace, the Alahana Pirivena's two dagobas and the Lankatilake, the Gal Vihara, the Damilathupa and the Jetvanarama complex. He also set about purifying the Buddhist clergy of disreputable elements and thoroughly overhauled the kingdom's administration.

Having secured the political and economic security of his own kingdom, the increasingly confident Paramkramabahu launched two rare Sinhalese military expeditions overseas. A fleet was sent to Burma in 1164 to punish a supposed diplomatic slight, and despite being devastated by storms in the Bay of Bengal, the expedition succeeded in capturing two towns and restoring the sense of respect in the Burmese which Parakramabahu evidently thought was his due. The second expedition was despatched in 1169 to India to assist a Pandyan ruler repel Chola advances (the countering of Chola expansionism had been a long established element of Sinhalese foreign policy). Despite initial successes, this invasion backfired massively when the infuriated Cholas launched a counter-invasion against Sri Lanka. This was repulsed, but Parakramabahu subsequently contented himself with countering Chola threats with diplomacy rather than military force.

For all his achievements, Parakramabahu seems a not entirely admirable figure. Unlike Dutugemunu's campaigns, the savage wars fought by Parakramabahu had no justification except to establish him on the throne at whatever human cost. Equally, his expansive programme of building works at home, combined with military campaigns overseas, laid a heavy burden of taxation and labour on his own subjects, and the resultant weakening of the kingdom's economy was perhaps ultimately one of the reasons for the rapid collapse in the fortunes of Polonnaruwa which followed Parakramabahu's own illustrious, but tarnished, reign.

looked in their prime, notably a fine vatadage and a rather more fanciful model of Parakramabahu's Royal Palace. Copious background descriptions (in English) of every part of ancient Polonnaruwa add interesting details and insights and help flesh out the exhibits.

Entrance to the museum is free with a ticket to the site. The only fly in the ointment is that this ticket is only valid for one day, and the longer you spend in the museum, the less time you'll have at the site itself. You can't buy a ticket just for the museum; if you want to go back the next day, you'll have to fork out another US$15.

Royal Palace Group

At the heart of the ancient city lie the buildings of the **Royal Palace Group**, created by Parakramabahu and used by subsequent kings of Polonnaruwa until the snobbish Nissankamalla (see p.327) established a new palace further to the south. The entire area is surrounded by a (heavily restored) circuit of walls. At the centre of the complex lie the remains of Parakramabahu's **Royal Palace**. According to the *Culavamsa* (see p.413), the palace originally stood seven storeys tall and boasted a thousand rooms, although this was probably an exaggeration (an interesting model in the museum shows a speculative impression of how this seven-storey palace might have looked). The remains of three brick storeys have survived (any further levels would have been built of wood and have long since disappeared), although they don't give much idea of how the building would originally have appeared – the ruin now looks more like a Norman castle than a Sinhalese royal palace. The holes in the walls were for floor beams, while the vertical grooves up to the first floor would have held stone reinforcements. The entire structure stands on a raised plinth and was originally enclosed in a rectangle of modest one-storey buildings which housed palace staff and officials; parts of these buildings' walls and foundations can still be seen, some of them rather fussily restored using modern bricks.

Just east of the Royal Palace stand the remains of Parakramabahu's **Council Chamber**, where the king would have granted audiences to his ministers and officials. The wooden roof has vanished, but the imposing base survives, banded with friezes of dwarfs, lions and galumphing elephants which seem to be chasing one another. The sumptuous steps are embellished with makara balustrades and a pair of fine moonstones, and topped with two of the rather Chinese-looking lions which came to be associated with Sinhalese royalty during the Sri Lankan middle ages; there are other fine examples at Nissankamalla's Audience Chamber (see p.331) and at the palace at Yapahuwa (see p.304) – the latter is shown on the nation's ten-rupee note. The platform supports four rows of columns, finely carved with floral decorative patterns.

Just northeast of here are the **Royal Baths** (Kumara Pokuna), designed in an unusual geometric shape (a square superimposed on a cross) and fed by two spouts carved with eroded makaras. Next to here stands the impressive two-tiered base of what was presumably some kind of royal bathhouse; each tier is decorated with lions, and there's a good moonstone on the upper level.

The Quadrangle

A couple of hundred metres north of the Royal Palace Group stands the **Quadrangle** – originally, and more properly, known as the Dalada Maluwa ("Terrace of the Tooth Relic"), since the famous relic (see p.219) was housed in various shrines here during its stay in the city. This rectangular walled enclosure, built on a raised terrace, was the religious heart of the city, conveniently close to the royal palace of Parakramabahu – the king would

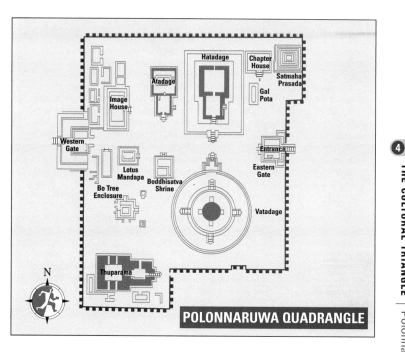

POLONNARUWA QUADRANGLE

probably have come here to listen to readings from the Buddhist scriptures – and is now home to the finest and most varied collection of ancient buildings in Sri Lanka. The buildings here exemplify the full variety and artistry of classical Polonnaruwan culture, with its range of Hindu and Buddhist influences – even if the carefully spruced-up buildings and the constant tramp of tourists mean that the Quadrangle lacks the atmosphere of more remote parts of the site.

The Vatadage

The Quadrangle is dominated by the magnificent **Vatadage** (circular relic house), arguably the most beautiful building in Sri Lanka. Built by Parakramabahu, it was later embellished by the crafty Nissankamalla (see p.327), who placed an inscription on the upper terrace claiming credit for the whole building. The entire outer structure is a fantastic riot of artistry, with almost every surface **carved** in a melee of decoration without parallel in the rest of Polonnaruwa, or indeed anywhere else on the island. The outer wall sports friezes of lions and dwarfs, and is topped by an unusually designed stone wall decorated with an abstract lotus design. Four sets of steps lead to the upper terrace, each one a little masterpiece, decorated with dwarfs, lions and makaras, as well as magnificently carved nagaraja guardstones and some of the finest moonstones in Sri Lanka – the main entrance is particularly ornate. The remains of further pillars and carved capitals which would once have supported the now vanished roof lie scattered about the upper terrace.

From the upper terrace, steps lead through four entrances, aligned to the cardinal points and each presided over by a seated Buddha, to the eroded remains of the central brick dagoba in which the **Tooth Relic** may have been

④

Polonnaruwan architecture: one city, many styles

Sri Lanka has absorbed many cultural influences over the centuries – from Portuguese names to Dutch cooking – but nowhere more strikingly than at Polonnaruwa, which for two centuries served as a melting pot of Sinhalese and Indian artistic influences, and whose buildings run through a veritable encyclopedia of styles. Some of the city's buildings, such as its dagobas and monastic foundations, are a direct continuation of the traditional Anuradhapuran Buddhist style. Others, such as the Shiva Devales 1 and 2, are pure Hindu in conception. Most interesting, however, is the syncretic style embodied by the city's three **gediges** – the Thuparama, Lankatilaka and Tivanka Pilimage. These solid, box-like structures, built entirely of stone and with exterior walls heavily decorated with pillars and niche windows, offer a characteristically Polonnaruwan example of a quintessentially Indian architectural style used in a purely Buddhist temple. Other South Indian influences also entered the Sinhalese artistic vocabulary during the Polonnaruwan period, including the finely carved, alternately square and octagonal pillars of Parakramabahu's Council Chamber, which would subsequently become one of the most characteristic features of the Kandyan era (albeit carved in wood rather than stone).

Another new departure in Polonnaruwan art was the move towards massive **Buddha images**, such as those at the Gal Vihara, or the huge standing Buddha at the Lankatilaka. The Buddha statues of Anuradhapura are on a very human scale; at Polonnaruwa, by contrast, the portrayal becomes grander, perhaps touched by Mahayanist influence in which the Buddha is seen not as an ordinary human being on a journey of personal enlightenment, but as a god-like, superhuman creature of divine abilities and proportions.

enshrined – strangely enough, this inner sanctum is virtually unadorned, in striking contrast to the remainder of the building.

The rest of the Quadrangle

The remainder of the Quadrangle is packed with a dense assortment of buildings of enormous variety and interest (though none approaches the flamboyance of the Vatadage). Opposite the Vatadage stand the rather plain remains of the **Hatadage**, originally a two-storeyed building, though the upper storey, which was perhaps made of brick, has long since crumbled away, as is the case with so many other structures at Polonnaruwa. Thought to have been built by Nissankamalla, the Hatadage is also referred to as the Temple of the Tooth, since the relic may have been placed here for a time, probably on the upper floor. It now houses three Buddha statues, the central one positioned to line up through the shrine's doorway with the Buddha directly opposite in the Vatadage. The entrance is marked by a fine moonstone and two nagarajas, whilst carvings of lions and geese run along the top and bottom of the exterior walls, which bear the very faint traces of further decorative carving. Two long Sinhala inscriptions can be found on the right of the outer and inner entrances.

Neither of these inscriptions, however, prepares one for the **Gal Pota** ("Book of Stone"), immediately east of the Hatadage, an enormous slab of granite, some nine metres long, covered in a densely inscribed panegyric praising the works of Nissankamalla, including records of his (in truth, extremely modest) conquests in India – an astonishing display of self-publicity which would put even a politician to shame. The stone itself, according to the inscription, weighs 25 tons and was brought over 90km from Mihintale, though exactly why this particular rock was considered remarkable enough to be transported from so far away remains unclear.

Next to the Gal Pota stands the strange **Satmahal Prasada** (the name means "Seven-storey temple", though only six survive). The ziggurat-like form of this temple is without parallel in Sri Lanka, its unique design perhaps the work of Khmer (Cambodian) craftsmen, although no one really knows. The heavily eroded stucco figures of a few deities in high relief decorate its walls. Behind the Satmahal Prasada are the slight remains of a seventh-century **Chapter House** – just a tiny brick outline and a few pillars, including one in the unusual "thrice-bent" style of the Lotus Mandapa (see below).

On the other side of the Hatadage, the **Atadage** is one of the oldest structures in the city, having been constructed by Vijayabahu to house the Tooth Relic; you can still see the building's brick base and the remains of finely carved pillars and door frames; a blackened Buddha statue stands in the centre. Next to the Atadage are the remains of an **image house** – the brick base inside would have supported a now vanished reclining Buddha. Continuing anti-clockwise, the next building is the small but exquisite **Lotus Mandapa** (also known as the Latha Mandapaya or Nissankalata), built by Nissankamalla

Nissankamalla the vainglorious

Along with Vijayabahu and Parakramabahu, **Nissankamalla** (1187–1196) is the third of the famous trinity of Polonnaruwan kings. A Tamil prince, Nissankamalla originally hailed from South India, but married into the Sinhalese nobility by wedding a daughter of Parakramabahu, and then succeeded in attaining the throne after a brief political skirmish following the death of his father-in-law.

Nissankamalla was notable chiefly for being the last king of Polonnaruwa to exercise real power over the whole island; he even felt secure enough to launch military expeditions against the Pandyans of South India, one of which he accompanied in person. Perhaps conscious of his foreign birth, he seems to have endeavoured to become more Sinhalese than the Sinhalese, making a great show of his religious orthodoxy, purging the sangha of disreputable monks and becoming the first king to make the pilgrimage to the summit of Adam's Peak. He is also known to have embarked on extensive tours of the island to discover the conditions under which his subjects were living, rather in the manner of a contemporary politician at election time – not that Nissankamalla would have worried much about public opinion, since he considered himself (as did many of the later Sinhalese kings) a living god.

For all his genuine achievements, however, Nissankamalla is best remembered for the long trail of **inscriptions** he left dotted around Polonnaruwa and other places in Sri Lanka, recording his valour, wisdom, religious merit and other outstanding qualities – he seems to have been the sort of monarch who wasn't able to sneeze without erecting a monument to commemorate the event. Prominent inscriptions can be found in Polonnaruwa at the Gal Pota and Vatadage in the Quadrangle, and at the Rankot and Kiri viharas, though some historians regard the claims made in them as somewhat dubious; Nissankamalla also stands accused of having stolen the credit for many of the building works carried out by Parakramabahu. Not content with leaving his scribbles all over Polonnaruwa, Nissankamalla also constructed a brand new royal palace rather than inhabit that of his predecessors, and even had the cheek to change the name of the great Parakrama Samudra tank (christened after its creator, Parakramabahu) to the Nissankamalla Samudra – subsequent generations, happily, chose to revert to the original name.

The only image of Nissankamalla stands in the Maharaja cave temple at Dambulla (see p.306) – ironically for this great self-publicist, it's tucked away in a corner, and almost completely hidden from sight.

and featuring an unusual latticed stone fence (rather like the famous Buddhist Railing at Anuradhapura; see p.352) and a small pavilion surrounded by stone pillars shaped as thrice-bent lotus buds on stalks, a beautiful and very unusual design whose sinuous organic lines look positively Art Nouveau. Inside the pavilion are the remains of a tiny dagoba which was, according to different interpretations, either used to hold relics or which served as a seat for Nissankamalla during religious ceremonies (though not, presumably, both).

Finally, in the southwest corner stands one of the oldest but also one of the most intact of the Quadrangle's structures, the **Thuparama**, an exceptionally large and well-preserved gedige (stone image house) thought to date back to the reign of Vijayabahu I. The inner shrine preserves its vaulted brick roof, the only such structure to have survived at Polonnaruwa, as well as exceptionally thick, plaster-covered brick walls whose massive dimensions keep the interior pleasantly cool – the walls are so thick that the architects were actually able to construct a staircase inside them (it's just through the door on the left), though it's usually locked. The shrine contains eight beautiful old standing and seated crystalline limestone Buddhas, which sparkle magically when illuminated. The exterior walls are decorated with the South Indian-style niches, and the heavily recessed and elaborately decorated window frames which can be found on a number of buildings across the city. The building's original name is unknown; it was confusingly christened the Thuparama ("The Stupa") by the pioneering British archeologist H.C.P. Bell, though it isn't a dagoba at all.

Shiva Devale no.1

Immediately south of the Quadrangle lies the **Shiva Devale no. 1**, one of many temples at Polonnaruwa dedicated to either Vishnu or Shiva. It dates from the Pandyan occupation of the early thirteenth century, following the collapse of Sinhalese power; the fact that the Indian invaders saw fit to construct an unabashedly Hindu shrine so close to the city's most sacred Buddhist precinct says much about their religious sympathies (or lack of), while the rounded capitals on the exterior niche windows are pure South Indian in style, and owe nothing to local traditions. The temple is made of finely cut, slate-grey stone, fitted together without the use of mortar – in fact, it may never have been finished: you can still see protruding lumps which would have helped workers when manoeuvring the blocks into place, and which would later have been carved off (in addition, the code numbers painted on almost every stone during archeological work give the whole structure the curious appearance of an enormous building set). The bottom halves of two rudely truncated guardian figures stand by the doorway, while inside there's a rather battered lingam – the extraordinary treasure-trove of **bronze images** found here are now in the National Museum in Colombo. Around the back of the shrine stand cute and tiny statuettes of a couple of venerable and heavily bearded figures which possibly represent Agni, the pre-Aryan Indian god of fire.

North of the Quadrangle

The road between the Quadrangle and the Northern Group runs through attractive light woodland and past a scatter of minor monuments. The most interesting is the finely preserved **Shiva Devale no. 2**, the oldest structure in Polonnaruwa, dating back to the original Chola occupation during the early eleventh century. This pretty little domed building is pure Indian in style, boasting the same rounded capitals and niche windows which adorn the Shiva Devale no. 1 (and also the Thuparama and Tivamka Pilimage), and four headless Nandis (Shiva's bull) standing guard at each corner.

Just to the southeast stands the **Pabula Vihara** ("Red Coral Shrine"), named by H.C.P. Bell for the red corals he discovered during excavations here. Said to have been built by a certain Rupawathi, one of Parakramabahu's wives, the vihara's main structure is a large brick dagoba, the third largest in Polonnaruwa, built in an unusual two-stepped design. The remains of various brick image houses and Buddha statues lie scattered around the base.

Continuing north along the main track to the Northern Group you pass a couple of further minor remains. The **Vishnu Devale no. 2** and **Shiva Devale no. 7** stand on the main track opposite one another. The former has a fine Vishnu image and the remains of stone (rather than brick) walls, though nothing survives of the latter apart from a lingam and a couple of columns.

Immediately north of here, the rather uninteresting remains of the **Menik Vihara** lie scattered over a large area of woodland. Little survives other than heavily restored foundations, a few armless (and sometimes also headless) Buddhas, and the lower portion of a small brick dagoba – the base of the supporting terrace has a few quaint lions carved from the brick, and you can also (unusually) see the relic chamber exposed at the top of the dagoba. North of here is a further complex of monastic buildings. Adjoining the north side of the monastery – and virtually indistinguishable from it – is the easily missed **Shiva Devale no. 10**, with a small lingam and yoni.

The Alahana Pirivena

A kilometre or so north of the Quadrangle are the remains of the **Alahana Pirivena** ("Monastery of the Cremation Grounds"), named after the royal cremation grounds which were established in this part of the city by Parakramabahu – the many minor stupas scattered about the area would have contained the relics of royalty or prominent monks. The monastery was one of the most impressive in the ancient city, and its magnificent collection of dagobas, Buddhas and other religious structures (many of which survive relatively intact) are one of Polonnaruwa's highlights.

Rankot Vihara

The Northern Group proper begins with Nissankamalla's monumental **Rankot Vihara**, an immense red-brick dagoba standing some 55m high. The fourth largest such structure in Sri Lanka, it's surpassed in size only by the three great dagobas at Anuradhapura, in imitation of which it was built, although its unusually flattened shape (it looks as though someone has sat on it) is distinctively its own. Substantial Anuradhapuran-style vahalkadas stand at the four cardinal points, decorated with the usual dwarf, elephant and lotus friezes, while an unusually large number of brick image houses, some of which still contain Buddhas, stand around the base of the dagoba. An inscription to the left of the entrance pathway describes how Nissankamalla oversaw work on the building, testifying to his religious devotion and the spiritual merit he presumably expected to gain from the building's construction – whether the forced labourers who were obliged to raise this gargantuan edifice shared the king's sense of religious idealism is not recorded.

Lankatilaka

Some 500m north of the Rankot Vihara stands one of the finest clusters of buildings and monuments in Polonnaruwa. One of the city's most emblematic structures, the **Lankatilaka** ("Ornament of Lanka") consists of a huge (though now sadly headless) standing Buddha, over 14m high, hemmed in between two narrow walls. Built by Parakramabahu, the shrine emphasizes the change in Buddhist architecture and thought from the abstract symbolic form of the dagoba to a much more personalized and devotional approach, in which attention is focused on the giant figure of the Buddha, which fills up the entire space within the shrine. The entrance is guarded by statues similar to those in the Vatadage and decorated with yet more guardstones and makara balustrades adorned with lions and dwarfs. More unusual are the intriguing **bas reliefs** on the exterior walls, showing a series of elaborate multi-storey buildings, probably intended to represent the houses (*vimanas*) of the gods.

Opposite the Lankatilaka stands the base of a fine **mandapa** (columned hall), decorated with a lion frieze around the base, while dwarf-supported steps lead up to the square terrace, dotted with quasi-Kandyan columns decorated with floral motifs. The building's original purpose remains unknown.

Kiri Vihara and Buddha Seema Pasada

Next to the Lanktilaka is the so-called **Kiri Vihara**, the best preserved of Polonnaruwa's dagobas – the name means "milk-white", referring to the white lime plaster that covers the building and which was almost perfectly preserved when the dagoba was rescued from the jungle after seven hundred years (though it's now faded to a dirty grey). Originally called the Rupavati Cetiya, it's believed to have been constructed by one of the queens of Parakramabahu. As at the Rankot Vihara, Kiri Vihara boasts four vahalkadas and an unusual number of brick shrines around its base, while to the left an inscription on a raised stone plinth records the location at which Nissankamalla worshipped.

South of the Lankatilaka, the **Buddha Seema Pasada** was the monastery's chapter house, a substantial building which might originally – judging by the thickness of its outer walls – have supported several upper storeys of brick or wood. At the centre of the building is a square pillared hall with a raised dais at its centre, surrounded by monks' cells and connected to the surrounding courtyard by four entrances, each with its own exquisite moonstone. Urns on pillars (symbolizing plenty) stand in the outer courtyard.

Gal Vihara

Just to the north, the **Gal Vihara** ("Stone Shrine"; also known as the Kalugal Vihara, or Black Stone Shrine) represents the pinnacle of Sri Lankan rock carving. The four Buddha statues here, all carved from the same massive slab of granite, originally formed part of the monastery complex – each statue would originally have been housed in its own enclosure – you still can see the sockets cut into the rock into which wooden beams would have been inserted behind the standing image (sadly, the modern answer to protecting the statues from the elements is a huge and unsightly new metal shelter).

The massive **reclining Buddha**, 14m long, is the most famous of the four statues – indeed one of the most celebrated sights in Sri Lanka – a huge but supremely graceful figure which manages to combine the serenely transcendental with the touchingly human; the face, delicately flecked with traces of natural black sediment, is especially beautiful. The seven-metre-tall **standing Buddha** next to it is the most unusual of the set: its sorrowful expression and the unusual position of its arms led some to consider it an image of Ananda, the Buddha's disciple, grieving for his departed master, though it's now thought to represent the Buddha himself. Two splendid **seated Buddhas** complete the group, though they lack the classic, iconic simplicity of the reclining figure, being posed against backdrops whose elaborate detail is rather unusual by the austere standards of Sri Lankan Buddhist art. The smaller seated Buddha is placed in a slight cave-like recess (the other three would have been housed in brick shrines), seated in the *dhyani mudra* ("meditation posture") and looking rather Oriental in style; other deities sit in the background, along with a distinctive arch modelled after the one at the great Buddhist shrine at Sanchi in India. The larger seated Buddha is also posed in *dhyani mudra* and entirely framed by another Sanchi-style arch, with tiny Buddhas looking down on him from their celestial dwellings – perhaps showing a touch of Mahayana Buddhist influence, with its belief in multiple buddhas and bodhisattvas.

North to the Tivanka-patamaghara

North of the Gal Vihara, the gargantuan **Demala Maha Seya** (or Damilathupa) is an unfinished attempt by Parakramabahu to build the world's largest dagoba, using labour supplied by Tamil (*damala*, hence the dagoba's name) prisoners of war captured during fighting against the Pandyans. The dagoba is actually constructed on top of a natural hill: a retaining wall was built around the hill, and the gap between filled with rubble, though it seemed the dagoba never reached its intended proportions. It's now largely covered in earth and looks more like a natural hill than a man-made feature.

Still further north, and just to the west of the main path, is an unusual **Lotus Pond**, almost eight metres across, and formed from five concentric rings of stone carved in the shape of stylized lotus petals. The pond may have been used as a ritual bath for those entering the **Tivanka–patamaghara** ("Tivanka Pilimage") image house at the extreme northern end of the site, an exceptionally large and fine gedige-style brick structure. Along with the lotus pond, the Tivanka-patamaghara is one of the few surviving structures of the **Jetavana monastery**. Tivanka means "thrice-bent", referring to the graceful but headless Buddha image inside which is in a position (bent at the shoulder, waist and knee) usually employed only for female images. The interior is also home to a sequence of outstanding (but rather difficult to see) **frescoes**. These depict scenes from the Buddhist jatakas, though all you can really make out (at least without the aid of a torch and binoculars) are lines of very finely painted Hindu-looking deities in sumptuous tiaras. The **exterior** shows the influence of South Indian architecture more clearly than any other Buddhist building in Sri Lanka, with the usual friezes of lions and dwarfs plus densely pillared and niched walls with celestial beings squeezed between the pillars. The overall effect is richly exuberant, and a world away from the chaste Buddhist architecture of Anuradhapura. Restoration work continues inside and out.

The southern remains

South of the main site lie two further complexes of ruins, the **Rest House Group** and **Southern Group**. Although of lesser interest, they're still worth a visit, and as entry to them is free, you don't have to try and cram seeing them and the rest of the site into a single day.

Rest House Group

The so-called **Rest House Group** comprises the modest remains of the palace of Nissankamalla, who built a brand new residence for himself here, being too vain to live in the abode of his predecessor, Parakramabahu. The most interesting structure here is the **Audience Chamber**, similar in form to that of Parakramabahu's. The roof has vanished, but the raised base survives, studded with four rows of sturdy columns, some inscribed with the titles of the dignitaries who would have sat next to them during meetings with the king. These included the heir-apparent, assorted princes, various military commanders, prominent merchants and Nissankamalla's two chief queens who, unexpectedly for the age, appear to have wielded genuine legislative power. A marvellous stone **lion** stands at the end of the plinth, probably marking the position of Nissankamalla's throne.

Just south of the Audience Chamber are the remains of a small, square brick-built **Mausoleum**, which may mark the site of Nissankamalla's cremation. The surviving walls reach heights of around five metres and retain traces of red and white paint on their exterior – surprisingly bright and well preserved in places, considering that it's over eight hundred years old. Nearby lie the remains of the sunken **Royal Baths**, currently in the throes of restoration.

Southern Group

One final group of minor ruins, the so-called **Southern Group**, lies about 1.5km south of the museum and Rest House, a scenic walk along the raised bank of the lake. The best-preserved building here is the **Potgul Vihara**, a circular image house surrounded by four small dagobas. The central room is thought to have housed a monastic library where the city's most sacred texts would have been stored, protected by massive walls which reach a thickness of around two metres at ground level. The principal attraction, however, is just to the north: an imposing 3.5-metre-high **statue** of a bearded figure, thought to date from the ninth century, which has become one of Polonnaruwa's most emblematic images. It's usually claimed that the statue is a likeness of Parakramabahu himself, holding an object which is either – depending on the state of your liver – a palm-leaf manuscript, representing the "Book of Law", or a yoke, representing the burden of royalty (the less reverent claim it's a slice of papaya). Another theory holds that the statue represents a sage named Pulasti, a hypothesis lent credence by its position near the monastic library.

Around Polonnaruwa

There are a number of attractions around Polonnaruwa, including the vatadage at **Medirigiriya** and – if you've had enough of ancient monuments – the national parks of **Minneriya** and **Kaudulla**, which offer some of the island's best elephant spotting. Polonnaruwa and Habarana are also within striking distance of **Wasgomuwa National Park**, one of the most remote, least visited and least spoilt of all Sri Lankan parks; you should be able to arrange a trip to it from either.

Minneriya National Park

Roughly halfway between Polonnaruwa and Habarana, **Minneriya National Park** offers a possibly welcome change of scenery for those saturated on ruins. Its centrepiece is the large **Minneriya Tank**, created by the famous tank-builder and monk-baiter Mahasena (see p.351), and despite its relatively small size, the park also boasts an unusually wide range of habitat types, from dry tropical forest to wetlands, grasslands and terrain previously used for slash-and-burn (*chena*) agriculture. For most visitors, the principal attraction here is **elephants**. Minneriya forms part of the elephant corridor which joins up with Kaudulla and Wasgomuwa national parks, and up to two hundred of the beasts can be found here at certain times of year during their migrations between the various parks. They are most numerous – and most visible – during the June to September dry season, when water elsewhere dries up and they come to the tank to drink and bathe. Local guides should know where the greatest concentrations of elephants are at any given time. Other **mammals** found in the park include sambur, spotted deer, sloth bears and leopards (although the last two are very rarely sighted), and there's also a good chance of seeing macaque and purple-faced langur monkeys. In addition, an enormous number of **birds** (some 160 species) have been spotted at Minneriya, including endemics such as the Sri Lankan hanging parrot and the crimson-fronted barbet.

The park's only **entrance** is on the main Polonnaruwa–Habarana road. The usual **admission fees** apply (see p.53). Most hotels and guest houses in Polonnaruwa, Habarana, Giritale, Sigiriya and Inamaluwa – all of which are close to Minneriya – can arrange a jeep to take you round the park. Some local guides also offer trips around the edges of the park, which saves you the hefty entrance fee, though the experience is likely to be less rewarding than a visit to the park itself.

Kaudulla National Park

Some 26km north of Minneriya, **Kaudulla** is Sri Lanka's newest national park; it opened in 2002, and has already become a popular fixture amongst tour operators in the Cultural Triangle. As at Minneriya, the centrepiece is a lake, the **Kaudulla Tank**, and the major attraction is **elephants** – the park was established principally to provide another link in the migratory corridor for elephants travelling between the Minneriya and Wasgomuwa national parks. The best time to elephant-spot is from around June to September, when water dries up and elephants congregate around the tank. There are up to 250 elephants in the park, depending on the season, plus sambur deer, monkeys, crocodiles and the inevitable (but very rarely seen) leopards and sloth bears, not to mention a characteristically wide array of bird life. The park's terrain consists of grasslands and scrubby forest.

The **entrance fee** is US$6.90 (half the price of most other parks), plus the other standard charges and taxes (see p.53).

Medirigiriya: the Mandalagiri Vihara

Some 30km north of Polonnaruwa, about 3km north of the town of Medirigiriya, are the remains of the **Mandalagiri Vihara**, which was built and flourished during the heyday of Polonnaruwa. It's an interesting site, but its remoteness and the difficulty (or expense, if you hire transport) of reaching it mean that unless you have an unusual interest in Sinhalese Buddhist architecture, you probably won't find it worth the effort. The main attraction here is the fine **vatadage**, dating from the eighth century, though it was probably built on top of a much earlier site dating back to the second century – it's similar in size and design to the vatadage at Polonnaruwa, though the quality of the workmanship is of a far lower level. The vatadage sits atop an unusually high terrace and is approached by a long flight of stone steps, with *punkalas* (stone urns, signifying plenty) at the top; the whole terrace is enclosed by a stone balustrade carved in a kind of fence-like pattern not unlike the Buddhist Railing at Anuradhapura. Three concentric circles of tall, delicate pillars, their capitals decorated with dwarfs, surround the inner shrine, where four large seated Buddhas at each of the cardinal points surround the remains of a small brick dagoba.

The remains of other monastic buildings lie around the vatadage. Opposite is the base of a sizeable brick dagoba, while to the left (as you face the entrance to the vatadage) are a couple of **tanks**. To the right, another high stone terrace is dotted with two **image houses** with headless Buddha fragments; next to these, a third image house contains the brick base which would have supported a now-vanished reclining Buddha. Opposite this is a stone **medicine bath** which looks unnervingly like a sarcophagus. A fourth image house stands on the far side of this terrace, with five standing and seated Buddhas still in situ. Past here, you can see the remains of the outer stone wall which girdles the entire site.

The site (unrestricted access) is covered by the Cultural Triangle ticket, though the exact situation is a muddle. At the time of writing, no tickets were sold at the site. Technically, it appears that if you don't have a CT ticket you'll have to buy a ticket from the museum in Polonnaruwa in advance, which costs a preposterous US$8 – though since there are no ticket checks at the site, you should be able to just walk in without paying.

There are **buses** roughly every hour from Giritale and Minneriya, from where you can catch a tuktuk to the site (around Rs.200, including waiting time). Alternatively, hiring a vehicle from Polonnaruwa or Giritale should cost around Rs.1500. Another possibility is to combine a trip to Medirigiya with a visit to Ritigala – count on around Rs.3000 for the trip from Polonnaruwa or Giritale.

Dimbulagala

Some 20km east of Polonnaruwa, south of the main road to Batticaloa, lies the massive rock outcrop of **Dimbulagala**, or "Gunner's Quoin", as it was rechristened by the British with characteristic militarist insensitivity. Rising over 500m above the denuded surrounding plains, the rock is scored with hundred of caves created by Buddhist monks from the third century BC onwards. A path climbs from the modern temple at its base up past a sequence of caves to a stupa at the summit – a hot climb, though the views over the dry-zone landscape from the top reward the effort. The site is rarely visited, despite being fairly close to Polonnaruwa, although it should be easy enough to hire a car or jeep (around Rs.1500) in Polonnaruwa for the trip, or even a tuktuk (around Rs.1000).

Wasgomuwa National Park

Wasgomuwa National Park was established in 1984 to protect wildlife displaced by forest clearance during the Mahaweli Development Project, in which the waters of the Mahaweli Ganga were used to irrigate large area of dry-zone land hereabouts. Wasgomuwa is one of the least visited and most unspoilt of all Sri Lanka's national parks, enjoying an isolated position and being largely enclosed – and offered a measure of protection – by two large rivers, the Amban Ganga and Mahaweli Ganga, which bound it to the east and west. The park straddles the northeastern edge of the hill country, and ranges in elevation from over 500m to just 76m along the Mahaweli Ganga; it comprises mainly dry-zone evergreen forest along the main rivers and on the hills, and open plains in the southeastern and eastern sections of the park. The park features the usual cast of Sri Lankan fauna, including up to 150 **elephants** (which migrate between here and the nearby national parks of Minneriya and Kaudulla), plus sambur and spotted deer, buffalo and rarely sighted leopards, sloth bears and fishing cats, plus 143 species of bird, including eight endemics.

Wasgomuwa is accessible either from the north via **Giritale** (see p.320); from the west from **Naula**, on the main Kandy to Dambulla road; or from the south via **Hasalaka** (see p.244), on the main Kandy to Mahiyangana road. Both the

Giritale and Naula roads lead to Elahera, from where it's a short drive to the park entrance. From Hasalaka it's 45km to the park entrance at Wasgomuwa. Sumane Bandara Illangantilake (see p.233) in Kandy is the most experienced guide to the park; alternatively, you may be able to arrange a trip in Polonnaruwa or Habarana.

Habarana

The large village of **HABARANA** is of no interest in itself, but has the geographical good fortune to sit on a major road junction almost perfectly equidistant between Polonnaruwa, Anuradhapura and Dambulla (and also conveniently close to Sigiriya, Ritigala, Minneriya and Kaudulla). You could see all of the above as day-trips from here, although it's best to bring your own vehicle with you rather than relying on finding something when you arrive, since almost all guests come with their own car and driver and the hotels aren't really set up to provide transport. If you're really bored, a few places in the village offer expensive (around US$20 per hour) **elephant rides** around the attractive lake.

Habarana boasts a couple of good **accommodation** options. *The Lodge*, 100m south of Habarana Junction (☎066-227 0011, ⓦwww.johnkeellshotels .com; ❼–❽), is one of the nicest hotels in the Cultural Triangle, comprising around fifty large white "chalets" (actually more like miniature villas) scattered around extensive tree-filled grounds running down to the lake. The chalets are extremely spacious, with stylish black and white decor; all have satellite TV and a/c, while deluxe chalets have bathtubs and minibar. There's also a large pool and an attractive open-air pavilion restaurant. Right next door is the slightly downmarket sister establishment, *The Village* (☎066-227 0046, ⓦwww .johnkeellshotels.com; ❻), with similar but less luxurious chalets dotted around sylvan grounds. There's also a pool, and live music at weekends. Those on a budget are stuck with the *Rest House*, right on Habarana Junction (☎066-227 0003, ⓔchc@sltnet.lk; ❹), an attractive-looking rest house in the usual style, though with just four rather overpriced and shabby rooms.

North from Dambulla: Ritigala to Aukana

The northern tip of the Cultural Triangle between Dambulla and Anuradhapura is home to a few relatively little-visited but interesting archeological sites, principally the two great Buddha statues at **Aukana** and **Sasseruwa** and the intriguing forest monastery at **Ritigala**. With your own transport, all three could be visited as a day-trip en route from Dambulla or Polonnaruwa to Anuradhapura.

Ritigala

Secreted away north of Habarana, on the slopes of a densely wooded mountainside protected by the Ritigala Strict Nature Reserve, lie the mysterious remains of the forest monastery of **Ritigala**. The mountainside on which the monastery sits is thought to be the *Ramayana*'s Aristha, the place from which Hanuman leapt from Lanka back to India, having discovered where Sita was being held captive. According to popular belief, Hanuman later passed by

Ritigala again, carelessly dropping one of the chunks of Himalayan mountain which he was carrying back from India for its medicinal herbs (other fragments are found at Unawatuna and Hakgala); this is held to account for the unusually wide range of plants and herbs found at Ritigala, although the mundane explanation is that the area, being higher and wetter than the surrounding plains, supports a correspondingly wider range of plant species.

The mountain's impenetrable terrain and strategic position close to Anuradhapura led to it becoming a favourite hiding place for **rebels**, from the time of Pandukabhaya in the third century BC right up to 1971, when JVP rebels hid here for several weeks before being flushed out by government troops. Ritigala's remoteness also appealed to solitude-seeking **hermits**, who began to settle here as far back as the third century BC, as testified by Brahmi inscriptions found here. In the ninth century, Ritigala became home to an order of reclusive and ascetic monks known as *pamsukulikas*, who devoted themselves to a life of extreme austerity – *pamsukulika*, meaning "rag robes", refers to the vow taken by these monks to wear only clothes made from rags either thrown away or recovered from corpses. The order (whose members also inhabited the forest monasteries at Arankele and the Western Monasteries at Anuradhapura) seems to have started as an attempt to return to traditional Buddhist values in reaction against the self-indulgent living conditions enjoyed by the island's clergy. So impressed was Sena I (831–851 AD) with the spirit of renunciation shown by the order that he built them a fine new monastery at Ritigala, endowing it with lands and servants – most of the remains you see today date from this era. Ritigala seems to have fallen into decline following the sack of Anuradhapura in 993. The last recorded reference to the monastery was at the beginning of the twelfth century until it was rediscovered by British archeologist H.C.P. Bell in 1893, who explored its remains, and oversaw the first modest efforts of restoration.

Ritigala is included in the Cultural Triangle **ticket**; otherwise, entry costs Rs.600. It's located along a dirt track 8km from the village of Galapitalgala, near the 13km marker from Habarana on the main road to Anuradhapura. There are no guides, although you might be able to pick up a copy of the useful booklet covering the site at the museum in Polonnaruwa, the Cultural Triangle office in Kandy, or other bookshops around the island.

The ruins

Ritigala is magical but enigmatic, while the setting deep in a totally undisturbed tract of thick forest (not to mention the lack of tourists) lends an additional sense of mystery. Parts of the complex have been carefully restored, while others remain buried in the forest, but despite the considerable archeological work which has been done here, the original purpose of virtually everything you now see remains largely unknown. One striking feature is the site's complete lack of residential quarters; it has been suggested that the monks themselves lived entirely in caves scattered around the forest, and that the ruined structures you now see – the tank, pavement, "roundabouts" and platform structures – had a purely ceremonial function, perhaps aimed at visitors to the monastery, rather than for the use of the monks themselves.

Past the entrance, the path runs around the edge of the tumbled limestone bricks which once enclosed the **Banda Pokuna** tank – this possibly served a ritual purpose, with visitors bathing here before entering the monastery. At the far end of the tank, steep steps lead up to the beginning of a beautifully constructed **pavement** which runs through the forest and links all the major buildings of the monastery. After around 200m the pavement reaches the first of several sunken courtyards, bounded by a retaining wall and housing three raised terraces. The one nearest is one of the **double–platform** structures which are a characteristic feature of Ritigala (and other forest monasteries such as Arankele and the Western Monasteries at Anuradhapura). These generally consist of two raised terraces linked by a stone "bridge"; one of the terraces usually bears the remains of pillars, while the other is bare; each double platform is oriented east–west. Various theories have been advanced as to the original functions of these buildings, but all are essentially glorified guesswork – one holds that the "moat" around the terraces would have been filled with water, providing a natural form of air-conditioning. These structures may have been used for meditation: communal meditation on the open terrace; and individual meditation in the cells of the building on the other terrace. A few metres to the right-hand (east) end of this enclosure is a second sunken courtyard, usually described as the **hospital**, although it may have been an alms-house or a bath house – a couple of bowls you'll see lying around here might have been used for grinding up herbs for medicine.

Beyond here, the pavement continues straight ahead to reach one of the "**roundabouts**" which punctuate its length – as with just about everything else at Ritigala, their original purpose remains unknown. About twenty metres before reaching the roundabout, a path heads off to the right, leading through enormous tree roots to the so-called "**Fort**", reached by a stone bridge high above a stream, and offering fine views over the forests below.

Continuing past the roundabout, a couple of **unexcavated platforms** can be seen off the path in the woods to the left, looking exactly as they must have appeared to H.C.P. Bell over a century ago. After another 500m you reach two further sunken courtyards. The **first courtyard** contains a large double-platform structure, one of the largest buildings in the entire monastery; one of the platforms preserves the remains of the pillars which once supported a building. A smaller raised terrace stands next to it (the elaborate urinal stone which formerly lay next to this platform had apparently vanished at the time of writing). The left-hand side of the first courtyard is bounded by two **stelae**; according to one theory, monks would have paced between these whilst practising walking meditation. A few metres beyond lies the **second courtyard** and another large double platform.

Aukana

Some 30km northwest of Dambulla, the village of **AUKANA** is home to a magnificent 12m-high standing **Buddha** (no set hours; Rs.150). The statue has become one of the defining symbols of Sri Lankan Buddhism, and full-scale copies can be found all over the country, from Dondra in the south to Trincomalee in the north. The statue stands close to the vast **Kalawewa Tank**, created by the unfortunate King Dhatusena (see p.310) in the fifth century. It was originally believed that the statue was made at the same time, until further research suggested a date of three or four centuries later, although no one's quite sure exactly when (or indeed why or by who) it was built. The later dating brings it chronologically closer to other massive stone statues in Sri Lanka, such as those at Polonnaruwa's Gal Vihara and Lankatilake, or the images at Buduruwagala and Maligawila. The brief craze for such monumental devotional statues may have been the result of Indian Mahayana influence, with its emphasis on the Buddha's superhuman, transcendental powers.

Aukana means "sun-eating", and dawn, when the low light brings out the fine detail of the east-facing statue, is the best time to visit (if you can organize a car and driver for such an early hour). The statue is in the unusual (for Sri Lanka) asisa mudra, the blessing position, with the right hand turned sideways to the viewer, as though on the point of delivering a swift karate blow. The figure is carved in the round, just connected at the back to the rock from which it's cut, though the lotus plinth it stands on is made from a separate piece of rock.

Aukana is tricky to reach by public transport. The easiest approach is to catch a **bus** between Anuradhapura and Dambulla, and get off at **Kekirawa**, from where you may be able to catch one of the infrequent local buses to Aukana or pick up a tuktuk (around Rs.500 return including waiting time). A few **trains** stop at the nearby Aukana station, though they're of little use to tourists. The only real possibility is to catch the 8am train from Polonnaruwa, arriving at Aukana 10.53, returning from Aukana 3.53pm and getting back to Polonnaruwa at 6.30pm – but this is obviously only for the incredibly committed. The best solution is to hire a car for the day and take in Aukana in conjunction with Sasseruwa and maybe Ritigala.

Sasseruwa

Some 11km west of Aukana lies the rarely visited **Sasseruwa Buddha** (no set hours; Rs.150), another standing Buddha of an almost equal height, though apparently uncompleted. Two legends connect it with the Aukana Buddha. The first, and more prosaic, says that cracks (which can be seen in the torso) started appearing during construction, and that it was therefore abandoned, with a new statue being created at Aukana. A second and more poetic legend relates that the two Buddhas were carved at the same time in competition between a master and his student. The master's Aukana Buddha was finished first and the frustrated student, realizing his own limitations, abandoned the Sasseruwa image in disappointment – although some people find that, despite lacking the Aukana's Buddha's technical excellence and high finish, the Sasseruwa image is the more endearing. The figure is in the abhaya mudra ("Have No Fear" pose) and, as at Aukana, originally stood inside an image house, as shown by the holes for beams cut into the rock around it. The statue was once part of a community of forest hermits and remains of the monastic complex can still be made out, including a few caves (one with a large reclining Buddha), inscriptions and dagobas.

Sasseruwa is difficult enough to find even with your own transport (follow the signs to Reswehera), and impossible by public transport.

Anuradhapura

For well over a thousand years, the history of Sri Lanka was essentially the history of **ANURADHAPURA**. Situated almost at the centre of the island's northern plains, the city rose to prominence very early in the development of the island, and maintained its pre-eminent position for over a millennium until being finally laid waste by Indian invaders in 993. At its height, Anuradhapura was one of the greatest cities of its age, functioning as the island's centre of both temporal and spiritual power, dotted with dozens of monasteries populated by as many as ten thousand monks – one of the greatest monastic cities the world has ever seen. The kings of Anuradhapura oversaw the golden age of Sinhalese culture, and the temples and the enormous dagobas they erected were amongst the greatest architectural feats of their time, surpassed only in scale by the great pyramids at Giza. Anuradhapura also lay at the heart of the great Sinhalese hydraulic achievements (see p.346), with vast **reservoirs** (tanks) constructed around the city to store water through the long dry seasons and irrigate the surrounding paddy fields. The city's fame spread to Greece and Rome, and judging by the number of Roman coins found here, appears to have enjoyed a lively trade with the latter.

Anuradhapura remains a magical place. The sheer scale of the ruined ancient city – and the thousand-plus years of history buried here – is overwhelming, and you could spend days or even weeks here ferreting around amongst the ruins (although sadly the manner in which the site is run by the Sri Lankan authorities – see p.344 – discourages visits of longer than a day).

Some history

Anuradhapura's origins are lost in the semi-legendary depths of early Sinhalese history. According to the *Mahavamsa*, the city was founded by the fourth king of Sri Lanka, **Pandukabhaya** (reigned 380–367 BC), a rebellious noble of the Vijaya clan who seized power around the year 380 BC and founded a new capital on the site of the palace of his great uncle, a certain **Anuradha**, after whom the new city was named. The fledgling city initially enjoyed only limited power over the surrounding region, though its status rose significantly during the reign of **Devanampiya Tissa** (c.300–260 BC), who oversaw the arrival of Buddhism in the island and established the city as a major centre of Buddhist pilgrimage and learning.

Only a few years after Devanampiya Tissa's death, however, Anuradhapura experienced the first of the recurrent attacks from southern India which were to characterize its history for a thousand years. For the better part of a century a sequence of Tamil adventurers held power, culminating in the reign of **Elara**, who reigned for 44 years before being defeated in 161 BC by the legendary **Dutugemunu** (see box on p.348). Dutugemunu succeeded in uniting Sri Lanka under Sinhalese rule for the first time, and celebrated his achievement by launching into a huge spree of building work – including the construction of two of Anuradhapura's greatest stupas: the Ruvanvalisaya and the Mirisavati – which did much to establish the city's magnificently theocratic character.

Dutugemunu's heady combination of military heroics and unimpeachable Buddhist piety proved an inspiration for all who followed him, even if none of the other 113 kings (and two queens) of Anuradhapura were able to emulate his achievements. Of the kings who followed, fifteen ruled for under a year; 22 were murdered; four committed suicide; thirteen were killed in battle; and eleven were dethroned. Soon after Dutugemunu's death, Anuradhapura was once again the target of South Indian attacks, and this constant external pressure, combined with incessant internal feuding, regularly succeeded in reducing the city to chaos. Tamil invaders seized Anuradhapura again in 103 BC, and despite being swiftly evicted by **Vattagamani Abhaya** (89–77 BC), founder of the Abhayagiri monastery and the cave temples at Dambulla, the kingdom soon descended once again into internal feuding, a period of chaos exemplified by the reign of the notorious queen **Anula** (48–44 BC), who in five years is said to have married and then murdered 32 husbands.

The great tank builders

In 67 AD, the accession to the throne of **Vasabha** (67–111), the first of the Lambakanna dynasty, inaugurated Anuradhapura's greatest era of peace and prosperity. Vasabha initiated the first of the massive irrigation works which transformed the arid plains of the northern island into fecund agricultural land capable of supporting a dense population and a highly developed civilization. Despite further struggles with invading Tamil forces – encapsulated in the legendary exploits of **Gajabahu** (114–136; see p.212) – the following four centuries of Lambakanna rule were largely peaceful. Later kings contributed further to the city's magnificent Buddhist heritage and the Rajarata's irrigation, most notably **Mahasena** (274–301), who is said to have constructed no less than sixteen major reservoirs, including the Minneriya and Kavudulu tanks, as well as the Jetavana, the last of the city's three great monasteries.

A new period of uncertainty began in 429 with yet another invasion from South India and the rule of seven Tamil generals who reigned in succession until being evicted by **Dhatusena** (455–473), who celebrated in the by now customary fashion by constructing (according to the *Mahavamsa*) no less than eighteen new temples and the enormous Kalawewa reservoir, near Aukana. Dhatusena met an unholy end at the hands of his own son, **Kassapa** (see p.310), who temporarily removed the capital to Sigiriya, before another of Dhatusena's sons, **Mogallana**, succeeded in wresting back control, albeit again with South Indian assistance. Mogallana's death, however, produced further chaos, and the following three centuries were distinguished by yet more internal feuding, punctuated, in periods of peace, by the construction of yet more grandiose irrigation works.

Decline and fall

A final interlude of peace was enjoyed during the reigns of **Aggabodhi I** (571–604) and **Aggabodhi II** (604–614), who between them restored many of the city's religious edifices and carried out further irrigation projects. The latter's death ushered in the most chaotic period in the history of the Anuradhapura kingdom, with incessant civil wars and the growing influence of South Indian mercenaries, who were recruited by disaffected Sinhalese nobles or rival claimants to the throne and frequently paid for by wealth plundered from Buddhist monasteries. By the end of the seventh century, power had effectively passed to these Tamil mercenaries, who acted as kingmakers until the last of the great Anuradhapuran kings, **Manavamma** (684–718), seized power with the help of a Pallava army. Manavamma's reign ushered in a final century of relative peace before Anuradhapura's destruction. In 853, an invading Pandyan army sacked Anuradhapura, before being bought off at great cost, and despite the best efforts of Sri Lankan diplomacy, the ever-present threat of South Indian invasion continued to hang over the kingdom, fuelled by the religious animosity which the Hindu kingdoms of South India bore towards their Buddhist neighbour. In 946–47, the Cholas sacked Anuradhapura (again), and the city's soldiers were obliged to flee to Ruhunu until the Cholas had returned home. By 992, the last king of Anuradhapura, **Mahinda V** (983–993), found he had no funds to pay the wages of his mercenaries and was forced to flee to Ruhunu. Anuradhapura and the northern areas of the island fell into chaos, with bands of soldiers pillaging at will. Attracted by the disorder, the Chola king Rajaraja despatched an army which sacked Anuradhapura for the very last time in the fateful year of **993**, reducing the once great city to ruins – the single greatest watershed in Sri Lankan history.

The Cholas established themselves a new capital at **Polonnaruwa**, which thereafter took centre stage in Sri Lankan history. Anuradhapura never recovered its previous glory, and in 1073 the city was finally abandoned, though as late as the 1260s, Parakramabahu II was restoring buildings at Anuradhapura – albeit more as a symbolic nod towards the illustrious past than as a practical attempt to restore the city to its former fortunes.

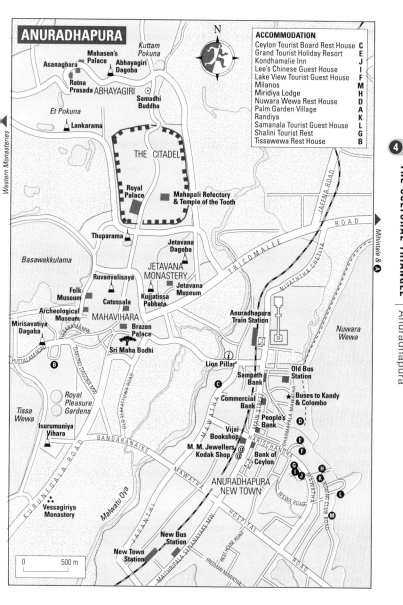

ANURADHAPURA

ACCOMMODATION

Ceylon Tourist Board Rest House	C
Grand Tourist Holiday Resort	E
Kondhamalie Inn	J
Lee's Chinese Guest House	I
Lake View Tourist Guest House	F
Milanos	M
Miridiya Lodge	H
Nuwara Wewa Rest House	D
Palm Garden Village	A
Randiya	K
Samanala Tourist Guest House	L
Shalini Tourist Rest	G
Tissawewa Rest House	B

Following the collapse of the great northern Sinhalese civilization, Anuradhapura was reclaimed by the jungle, and largely forgotten by the outside world, except by the communities of reclusive monks and guardians of the sacred bo tree who continued to live here. The British "rediscovered" the city in the nineteenth century, making it a provincial capital in 1833, after which Anuradhapura slowly began to rise from the ashes. Since the 1950s, the considerable **Anuradhapura New Town** has sprung up to the east of the Sacred Precinct, while in 1980 a huge UNESCO programme began with the goal of effecting a complete **restoration** of the ancient city. The programme continues to this day, and has assumed enormous national significance for the Buddhist Sinhalese, who see the reclamation of Anuradhapura's great dagobas and other monuments from the jungle after over a millennium as a powerful symbol of national identity and resurgence.

Arrival and information

Anuradhapura divides into two distinct areas: **Anuradhapura New Town**, which is home to almost all the town's accommodation and practical services, and the **Sacred Precinct** to the west, site of the ancient city. The entire town is hemmed in by three great artificial lakes, **Nuwara Wewa** to the east, and **Tissa Wewa** and **Basawakkulama Tank** to the west. The New Town is bisected by Main Street, where you'll find the post office, banks and other services. Most of Anuradhapura's accommodation is just east of here on or near Harischandra Mawatha.

Arriving in Anuradhapura, you'll come in at one of three places. The principal **train station**, Anuradhapura Station, is on Main Street just north of the centre of the New Town, about Rs.40–50 by tuktuk from the Harischandra Mawatha hotels and guest houses; there's a subsidiary train station, Anuradhapura New Town Station, at the southern end of Main Street, though not all services stop here.. Buses from Kandy and Colombo pull in just south of the **Old Bus Station** on Dharmapala Mawatha, east of Main Street. All other services arrive at the **New Bus Station**, at the southern end of Main Street; count on around Rs.60 for a tuktuk from here to Harischandra Mawatha.

There are various **banks** strung out along Main Street. The **ATM**s at the Commercial and Sampath banks accept Visa and Mastercard; those at the Bank of Ceylon and Seylan Bank take Visa only. There's **Internet access** at the Kodak shop and at M.M. Jewellers (both daily 9am–6pm; Rs.6 per min); they're a few doors apart on the main road diagonally opposite the **post office**; alternatively, try the *Shalini* guest house. Vijai Bookshop, opposite the Seylan Bank at the northern end of Main Street has a few English language **books**.

The ancient city is crowded with pilgrims at weekends and, especially, on poya days, and is also the focus of several **festivals**. The largest, held on Poson

---

Moving on from Anuradhapura

Private express **buses** to **Kandy** (via Dambulla) and to **Colombo** (via Kurunegala) leave every thirty minutes from the side of the road just south of the Old Bus Station. All other services leave from the New Bus Station, with regular services to **Habarana** (every 45min) and **Polonnaruwa** (every 45min until 1.30; there may be later services on demand), **Trincomalee** (3 daily), and **Vavuniya** (every 30min). For **Sigiriya**, take a Kandy bus to Dambulla and pick up the Sigiriya bus from there.

There are **trains** from Anuradhapura south to **Kurunegala** and **Colombo** at 5am, 6.40am (express nonstop to Colombo), 8.55am, 2.30pm and 11.10pm, plus five trains daily north to **Vavuniya**; most services stop at both stations in Anuradhapura, though a couple don't stop at the New Town Station. You could reach **Kandy** by train by taking a Colombo train and changing at Polgahawela, though it's much less hassle to take the bus.

poya day (June), commemorates the introduction of Buddhism to Sri Lanka with enormous processions.

Accommodation and eating

Anuradhapura has a reasonable spread of budget **accommodation**, though a relative paucity of mid- and upper-range options. Most places are located in the residential enclave east of the New Town on or near Harischandra Mawatha; those on Harischandra Mawatha itself aren't as peaceful as those closer to the lake.

As usual, most people **eat** in their guest house. If you plan to eat somewhere else it's worth dropping by in advance so that staff expect you and so you can find out what's on the menu (if anything). The restaurants at the *Milano* and *Shalini* guest houses are probably your best bet. There are a number of Chinese restaurants dotted around the guest house area, though these usually serve mainly as local drinking holes. One local speciality is **lake fish** from the local tanks – these rather undernourished creatures are fresh but decidedly bony, and are best when fried.

Budget

Ceylon Tourist Board Rest House Jayanthi Mw ☎025-222 2188. Big, modern and quite smart-looking place geared towards locals, with large a/c rooms as well as shabbier but better-value non-a/c ones. There are also very cheap but quite respectable dorms (Rs.211 per person in 2- to 8-bed dorms). A simple evening meal in the huge, breezy open-air restaurant is included in all rates. No alcohol (since you're in the Sacred Precinct), and not much English spoken. ❷

Grand Tourist Holiday Resort Off Harischandra Mw ☎025-223 5173. There's nothing grand about this small but well-run and extremely homely guest house, attractively located overlooking Nuwara Wewa with views of Mihintale in the distance. The clean, spacious modern rooms are the best value in town, and there's good food at the attractive terrace restaurant. Bikes Rs.200 per day. ❷

Kondhamalie Inn Harischandra Mw ☎025-222 2029. Varied selection of rooms: the cheaper ones in the old building are dark and depressing; the slightly more expensive rooms (including one with a/c) in the new building are much more pleasant. Not much English spoken. ❷–❸

Lee's Chinese Guest House Off Harischandra Mw ☎025-223 5476. Three large, very bare but acceptable rooms – the cheapest habitable accommodation in Anuradhapura. There's also a passable Chinese restaurant (no alcohol) attached. ❶

Lake View Tourist Guest House Off Harischandra Mw ☎025-222 1593. Modern house in a peaceful location near Nuwara Wewa with a range of rooms (including a couple with

a/c) – all OK, though nothing special. Bikes Rs.150 per day. ❷–❸

Milanos 596/40 Stage 1, J.R. Jaya Mw ☎025-222 2364. Currently the most popular place in Anuradhapura amongst foreign travellers, with large, bright and comfortable – if rather ramshackle – rooms. The inexpensive restaurant is the liveliest in town, although the food's a bit hit and miss, and the staff can be just a bit too friendly. ❷, a/c ❸

Randiya Off Harischandra Mw ☎025-222 2868, ⓦ www.hotelrandiya.com. One of Anuradhapura's better bargains, with ten cosily old-fashioned rooms (with optional a/c), all attractively and comfortably furnished. Hot water supplement Rs.200. ❸

Samanala Tourist Guest House Wasaladanththa Mw ☎025-222 4321. Four rooms in an attractive family house – they're fairly simple, but big, clean and reasonable value, and two have slight views through the trees to the lake at the bottom of the garden. Bikes Rs.200 per day. No single rates. ❷

Shalini Tourist Rest 41/388 Harischandra Mw ☎025-222 2425, ⓦ www.hotelshalini.com. Well-run guest house with sixteen varied but pleasant rooms, with or without a/c and hot water. The whimsical blue main building has an attractive restaurant under a huge wooden roof, and serves good (if slightly pricey) daily set menus for around Rs.450. Also has Internet access, bikes (Rs.200 per day) and free pick-up/drop-off from bus or train stations on arrival/departure. ❷–❹

Mid-range and expensive

Miridiya Lodge Off Harischandra Mw ☎025-222 2112, ⓦ www.galway.lk. The poshest New Town

343

option, this rather swish, recently renovated hotel has pleasant, good-value rooms (all a/c), a nice swimming pool (non-guests Rs.250) and attractive gardens running down to Nuwara Wewa. Deluxe rooms come with TV and minibar. ⑥

Nuwara Wewa Rest House Off Dharmapala Mw ℡ 025-222 1414. Tranquil place (though not a patch on the *Tissa Wewa Rest House*), nicely set back from the road, with a small swimming pool, terrace restaurant and bar (though the food is poor). The seventy rooms (all a/c) vary wildly: some are OK; some are shabby and depressing, so choose carefully. ⑤

Palm Garden Village Puttalam Rd, Pandulagama ℡ 025-222 3961, ⓔ pgvh@pan.lk. Located in a soothingly rural setting 3km from Anuradhapura,

this is the area's most upmarket option. Accommodation is in fifty a/c cottages dotted around extensive grounds, and there's an ayurveda centre, tennis courts and a fine swimming pool. Popular with tour groups. ⑦

Tissawewa Rest House Sacred Precinct, near the Mirisavatiya dagoba ℡ 025-222 2299, ⓦ www.quickshaws.com. Not Anuradhapura's plushest place, but easily its most memorable, set in a gorgeously atmospheric, rambling nineteenth-century villa (a former British governor's bungalow) in the heart of the Sacred City, with large period rooms with wooden floors, furniture and ceilings (and rather grotty bathrooms), plus optional a/c. No alcohol served, though you can bring your own. ④

The Sacred Precinct

Anuradhapura's scatter of monuments and remains is vast and potentially confusing, not helped by the paucity of signs and the sometimes obstreperous soldiers who police the site. The easiest way to get a mental handle on the **Sacred Precinct** is to think of it in terms of its three great monasteries: the Mahavihara, Jetavana and Abhayagiri – about two-thirds of the main sites belong to one of these complexes. The most logical place to start is the **Mahavihara**, at the physical and historical centre of the ancient city, beginning at the Sri Maha Bodhi, then continuing north via the Ruvanvalisaya to the Thuparama. From here you can either head east to the **Jetavana Monastery** or north to the **Abhayagiri** complex. There are further important clusters of sights at the **Citadel**, between the Mahavihara and Abhayagiri monasteries; and **south of the Mahavihara**, between the Mirisavetiya dagoba and Issurumuniya Temple. The major dagobas provide useful landmarks if you get disoriented, but beware of the confusing similarity between the Ruvanvalisaya and Mirisavetiya dagobas.

Visiting the ancient city: practicalities

The whole site is much too big to cover on foot, and it's far easier to explore by **bike**; these can be hired from virtually all the town's guest houses for around Rs.200 per day. Another possibility is to hire a **tuktuk** (around Rs.100 per hour), but this is far less pleasant. If you're determined to **walk**, you could catch a tuktuk to whichever area you're interested in and then explore on foot, though you won't be able to cover more than a limited part of the site this way. If you want a **guide**, you could try arranging something through your guest house; alternatively, you may be able to pick one up either at the Jetavana Museum (see p.352) or at the Tourist Information Office, on the main road to the precinct.

In terms of tickets and access to the Sacred Precinct, the situation is comically disorganized. Most (but not all) the sites at Anuradhapura are covered by the **Cultural Triangle ticket** (see p.296). These can be bought either at the Tourist Information Office or at the Jetavana Museum. Tickets are only valid for one day, so if you want to explore properly you'll have to shell out around US$15 on a fresh ticket each day. This is a shame, since most visitors, being reluctant to pay twice, cram it all into a day, which really isn't long enough to get the full flavour of the place.

Several notable sites – the Isurumuniya, Mirisivatiya, Sri Maha Bodhi, Folk Museum and Western Monasteries – aren't covered by the CT ticket. The logical thing to do would be to visit these on a second day. However, since all these sights (apart from the Western Monasteries) lie within the Sacred Precinct, in theory you need a CT ticket to reach them, even though they're not actually covered by the ticket. In addition, you're (theoretically) not allowed even to use the public roads which crisscross the site without a CT ticket. There's only very patchy policing of the site, however, meaning that these preposterous rules are easily broken. All sites at Anuradhapura are open-access 24hr and ticket checks are rare – some visitors don't bother buying a ticket at all; others claim that they are staying (or going for a meal or drink) at the *Tissawewa Rest House*, which lies in the middle of the Sacred Precinct.

Finding out exactly what you are or are not allowed to do, or getting any other **information** about the area, is problematic. Staff at the Tourist Information Office speak hardly any English, while the gun-toting soldiers who police the area aren't usually much help either, and can sometimes be unpleasantly officious as well. In sum, rather than encouraging tourists to spend as long as possible at Anuradhapura, the authorities are making a case for not going there at all. If all this sounds too much, rest assured that Anuradhapura is undoubtedly worth the hassle and/or expense, though until the authorities get their act together, many visitors prefer to vote with their feet and stay on the beach instead.

The tanks

Anuradhapura lies nestled between a trio of **tanks** (see box overleaf) which provided the lifeblood of the ancient city – although from the fifth century onwards their waters were supplemented by those from larger and most distant tanks such as the Kalawewa. West of the Sri Mahabodhi is the city's oldest tank, the **Basawakkulama**, created by Pandukabhaya around the fourth century BC. South of the city is the **Tissa Wewa**, built by Devanampiya Tissa, while on the east side of the city lies the largest of the city's tanks, the **Nuwara Wewa**, completed in around 20 BC and significantly expanded by later kings to reach its present imposing dimensions. The raised bunds (lakeside embankments) on the west and south sides of Nuwara Wewa are close to many of the town's guest houses and perfect for an evening stroll and some birdwatching, while there are wonderful views of the city's dagobas from the north shore of the Basawakkulama.

The Mahavihara

The centre of ancient Anuradhapura was the **Mahavihara**, the oldest of the city's monasteries and for many centuries its most important. It was founded by Devanampiya Tissa around the **Sri Maha Bodhi** (Sacred Bo Tree); Davanampiya Tissa also built Sri Lanka's first dagoba, the **Thuparama**, here, although this is now dwarfed by the great **Ruvanvalisaya** dagoba. The Mahavihara is still a living and vibrant place of pilgrimage rather than an archeological site, with pilgrims flocking to the Sri Maha Bodhi and Ruvanvalisaya – the former is still considered one of the world's most important Buddhist relics, and second in popularity only to the Tooth Relic in Kandy (see p.219).

Sri Maha Bodhi

At the spiritual and physical heart of Anuradhapura stands the **Sri Maha Bodhi**, or Sacred Bo Tree (the tree isn't included in the Cultural Triangle ticket; you may be asked for a donation). According to popular belief, this

Water world: irrigation in early Sri Lanka

The map of Sri Lanka is studded with literally thousands of man-made lakes, commonly known as **tanks** or *wewas* (pronounced, and occasionally spelt, "vavas"). The civilization of early Sri Lanka was essentially agricultural, and the need to ensure a regular supply of water for rice cultivation posed a crucial problem, given the location of the island's early capitals in the dry plains of the north. The climate in these parts – long periods of drought alternating with brief monsoonal deluges – made the use of irrigation, based on the storage of water for the regular cultivation of wet fields, a vital element in early Sinhalese civilization. The only alternative source of water was the Mahaweli Ganga, a river whose waters never ran dry, though transferring this water to places where it was needed called for considerable expertise.

The first, modest examples of hydraulic engineering date back to the earliest days of Sinhalese settlement in the third century BC, when the first farmers damned rivers and stored water in small village reservoirs. With the later increase in royal power, Sri Lanka's kings began to take an active role in the construction of irrigation schemes, leading to the creation of the three tanks which now surround Anuradhapura. The first major irrigation works were undertaken in the reign of **Vasabha** (65–110), who is said to have created twelve irrigation canals and eleven tanks, the largest with a circumference of three kilometres. Soon afterwards, Sinhalese engineers mastered the technology which allowed water in tanks to be stored until needed, then released through sluice gates and channelled through canals to distant fields.

The first giant reservoirs were constructed in the reign of **Mahasena** (274–301), who oversaw the construction of some sixteen major tanks, including the vast Minneriya tank (see p.332), and **Dhatusena** (455–473), who constructed the remarkable Jaya Ganga canal, almost 90km long and maintaining a subtle gradient of six inches to the mile, which delivered water to Anuradhapura from the huge Kalawewa (whose waters ultimately hastened that unfortunate king's demise – see p.310). Further tanks and canals were built during to the reigns of **Moggallana II** (531–551), whose Padaviya tank, in the northern Vavuniya district, was the largest ever constructed in ancient Sri Lanka, and Aggabodhi II (604–614), who was responsible for the tank at Giritale, amongst other works. Large new irrigation projects in the Anuradhapura region virtually ceased after the seventh century, and although the simple maintenance of the tanks and canals already built must have been a huge task, the entire system appears to have worked smoothly for the next three centuries until the final collapse of Anuradhapura in 993.

The construction of large-scale irrigation works became a defining feature of these Sinhalese civilizations: the maintenance of such massive hydraulic feats required skilled engineering and a highly evolved bureaucracy, and also encouraged the development of centralized control and hierarchical social structures. The captured waters allowed a second rice crop to be grown each year, as well as additional vegetables and pulses, all of which supported much higher population densities than would otherwise have been the case. The surplus agricultural produce created by large-scale irrigation and the taxes raised from the system were major sources of royal revenue, allowing expansive building works at home and military campaigns overseas – culminating in the reign of the Polonnaruwan king, **Parakramabahu I**, who famously declared that "not one drop of water must flow into the ocean without serving the purposes of man", and who oversaw the creation of the vast Parakrama Samudra at Polonnaruwa, one of the last but finest monuments of Sinhalese irrigation.

immensely venerable tree was grown from a cutting, brought to Sri Lanka by Princess Sangamitta (see p.413), which was taken from the original bo tree in Bodhgaya, India, under which the Buddha attained enlightenment. The original bo tree in India was destroyed not long afterwards, but the Sri Maha Bodhi survived, and is now officially the world's oldest tree. Cuttings from it have been grown all over the island (and indeed throughout the Buddhist countries of Southeast Asia).

The Sri Maha Bodhi sits at the centre of a large and elaborate enclosure, dotted with numerous younger bo trees and festooned with prayer flags. It grows out of the top of a series of terraces decorated with gold railings: the highest terrace is open from 2.30pm to 10pm, although you're not able to reach the tree itself, and what you can see of it is curiously unimpressive, appearing neither particularly large nor old (despite one trailing branch propped up on iron supports). Far more interesting is the general scene in the enclosure, which is usually full of rapt pilgrims (the ladies dressed neatly in white saris) contemplating the tree and praying. During poya days, huge crowds of devotees flock here to make offerings, especially during the April poya, the Snana puja, when pilgrims bathe the tree in milk.

The Brazen Palace

Just north of the Sacred Bo Tree stand the remains of the **Brazen Palace** ("Loha Pasada"), named on account of the copper roof which once covered it. The "palace" was built by Dutugemunu, though despite its name it only ever served as a monastic, rather than a royal, residence – the *Mahavamsa* describes a nine-storeyed structure with a thousand rooms (though the second part of this claim is doubtless hyperbole) at whose centre stood an empty ivory throne symbolizing the Buddha himself; the throne was inlaid with a gold moon, a silver moon and pearl stars (the sun and moon perhaps served as an inspiration for the sun and moon motif which was later adopted as the symbol of the kings of Kandy). Unfortunately, since most of the palace was made of wood, it burnt down just fifteen years after its construction and on a number of occasions thereafter, and had to be repeatedly rebuilt, most recently by Parakramabahu of Polonnaruwa (1153–86).

Little remains of the palace now apart from a dense forest of plain, closely spaced columns – some 1600 in total – each about 4m high, which would have supported the first floor, though many of these did not belong to the original structure but were salvaged from other buildings at Anuradhapura – perhaps a reflection of the dereliction which had overtaken the entire city when the palace was restored during Parakramabahu's reign. The only hint of decoration is on the fallen capitals, carved with dwarfs, which lie scattered around the ground in the southeast corner of the palace. The entire palace is currently closed to visitors, although the ugly modern wooden building at the centre is popular with grey langur monkeys.

Ruvanvalisaya dagoba

North of the Brazen Palace stands the huge white **Ruvanvalisaya** (also known as the Maha Thupa, or "Great Stupa", though it's actually only the third largest in the city). Unlike the massive stupas at the Jetavana and Abhayagiri monasteries, which are still being excavated and rebuilt, the Ruvanvalisaya dagoba is fully restored, painted a gleaming white, and busy with pilgrims throughout the day. The dagoba was the crowning achievement of **Dutugemunu** (see overleaf), built to commemorate his victory over Elara; it is popularly believed to enshrine various remains of the Buddha, and is thus the most revered in the city. Dutugemunu lavished enormous sums of money on the project, helped (according to legend) by the fortuitous discovery of a rich vein of silver at Ridi Vihara (see p.299), though sadly he died before his masterwork could be

Dutugemunu the disobedient

Of all the two hundred or so kings who have ruled Sri Lanka over the millennia, none is as revered as the semi-legendary **Dutugemunu**, the great warrior prince turned Buddhist king whose personality encapsulates a compelling mixture of religious piety and anti-Tamil nationalism which continues to provide a symbol of inspiration for many Sinhalese today. Dutugemunu grew up during the reign of the Tamil general Elara, who seized control of Anuradhapura in around 205 BC and reigned there for 44 years. Much of the island remained outside the control of Anuradhapura, however, being ruled by various minor kings and chiefs who enjoyed virtual autonomy, although they may have professed some kind of token loyalty to Elara.

The most important of these subsidiary kings was **Kavan Tissa**, husband of the legendary Queen Viharamahadevi (see p.192). From his base in the city of Mahagama (modern Tissamaharana), Kavantissa had gradually established control over the whole of the south, using a cunning mixture of marriage alliances and state-craft rather than outright military force. Despite his own growing power, the naturally cautious Kavantissa, anxious to protect his family and kingdom, demanded that his eldest son and heir, **Gemunu** (or Gamini, as it's often spelt), swear lasting allegiance to Elara. According to the *Mahavamsa*, on being asked to make this oath, the 12-year-old Gemunu threw his rice bowl from the table in a fury, saying he would prefer to starve rather than declare loyalty to a foreign overlord. Having made this declara-tion, the rebellious young prince henceforth refused to sleep with outstretched limbs, declaring that he felt unable to rest comfortably so long as he remained the subject of a foreign king, whilst demonstrating his contempt for his father by send-ing him items of women's clothing – all of which unfilial behaviour earned him the name of **Dutugemunu**, or "Gemunu the Disobedient".

On the death of his father, Dutugemunu acceded to the throne and set about raising an army; having assembled his forces, he set off to do battle mounted on his famous elephant, Kandula. He also took with him a spear with a Buddhist relic set into its shaft and a large contingent of Buddhist monks, thus casting himself not only as a political leader, but as the religious liberator of his island – the leader of a kind of Buddhist jihad. Dutugemunu's campaign was a laborious affair. For some fifteen

finished. According to the Mahavamsa, his younger brother Saddhatissa created a simulacrum of the finished stupa using bamboo frames and painted white cloth, so that the dying king could admire his masterwork in its full splendour.

The dagoba now stands 55m high, rather less than its original height. According to tradition, its original shape was inspired by the form of a bubble – a perfect hemisphere – though the effects of time and subsequent renova-tions have flattened its outline slightly. It stands on a terrace whose outer face is decorated with elephant heads (most are modern replacements). Symbolically, the elephants support the platform on which the dagoba is built, just as, in Buddhist cosmology, they hold up the earth itself (at a more prosaic level, elephants also helped in the construction of the stupa itself, being used to stamp down the dagoba's foundations).

Entering the dagoba, you pass through a security check, then up a stairway flanked by fine nagaraja guardstones. Four **vahalkadas** mark the cardinal points around the base of the dagoba – all follow the standard Anuradhapuran design, which you'll see repeated around the city and at Mihintale: tall, rectangular structures decorated with bands of elephant heads and, at the top, friezes of lions, bulls and elephants carved in low-relief – the one on the western side is the oldest and most interesting. Walking clockwise around the dagoba you reach a modern **shrine** holding five standing Buddha statues.

years he fought his way north, conquering the succession of minor kingdoms which lay between Mahagama and Anuradhapura, until he was finally able to engage Elara himself at Anuradhapura. After various preliminary skirmishes, Elara and Dutugemunu faced one another in single combat, each mounted on their elephants. As the *Mahavamsa* describes it:

King Duttahagamani proclaimed with beat of drum: "None but myself shall slay Elara." When he himself, armed, had mounted the armed elephant Kandula, he pursued Elara and came to the south gate of Anuradhapura.

Near the south gate of the city the two kings fought. Elara hurled his dart, Gamani evaded it; he made his own elephant pierce Elara's elephant with his tusks and he hurled his dart at Elara; and the latter fell there, with his elephant.

Dutugemunu buried Elara with full honours, decreeing that anyone passing the defeated general's tomb should dismount as a sign of respect – this decree was still apparently being obeyed in the early eighteenth century, some two thousand years later, though curiously enough, no one now knows where Elara's tomb is located. His conquest complete, the new king began an orgy of building works, including the Brazen Palace and Mirissavatiya dagoba. His most famous monument, however, was the mighty **Ruvanvalisaya** dagoba at Anuradhapura, which Dutugemunu himself did not live to see finished. He is supposed to have looked on the unfinished structure from his deathbed and said, "In times past . . . I engaged in battles; now, singlehanded, I commence my last conflict – with death, and it is not permitted to me to overcome my enemy."

As the leader who evicted the Tamils and united the island under Sinhalese rule for the first time, Dutugemunu is regarded as one of Sri Lanka's great heroes (at least by the Sinhalese). Despite his exploits, however, the fragile unity he left at his death quickly collapsed under subsequent, less able rulers, and within 35 years, northern Sri Lanka had once again fallen to invaders from South India.

The four identical limestone statues date back to the eighth century and are thought to represent three previous Buddhas and the historical Buddha; the fifth (modern) statue is of the future Buddha, Maitreya, wearing a tiara and holding a lotus – an unexpected Mahayanist touch in the heart of Anuradhapura's most conservative Theravada monastery. Continuing clockwise brings you to an ancient limestone **statue**, facing the dagoba's south side and popularly believed to represent Dutugemunu contemplating his masterpiece. A little further round stands a small **model** of the dagoba, reputedly an architect's model. It's meant to show the shape of the original dagoba, though the difference between the model and the real thing isn't very obvious.

A couple of hundred metres east of the Ruvanvalisaya is the **Kujjatissa Pabbata**, the remains of a small dagoba on a stone base with well-preserved guardstones. The structure dates from around the eighth century, but probably occupies the site of an earlier building – it's been suggested that this was the place, just outside what was once the south gate into the city, where Dutugemunu buried Elara and raised a memorial in his honour.

Thuparama and around
Heading north from the Ruvanvalisaya, a broad walkway leads 300m to the **Thuparama**. This was the first dagoba to be built in Sri Lanka (its name

means simply "The Stupa"), though by later Anuradhapuran standards it's a modest structure, standing less than 20m high. It was constructed by Devanampiya Tissa shortly after his conversion to Buddhism at the behest of Mahinda (see p.357), who suggested that the new Sinhalese faith be provided with a suitable focus for its worship. A monk was despatched to Ashoka, the Buddhist emperor of India, who obligingly provided Devanampiya Tissa with two of his religion's most sacred relics: the Buddha's right collarbone and alms bowl. The bowl was sent to Mihintale (and subsequently disappeared), whilst the bone was enshrined in the Thuparama, which remains a popular pilgrimage site to this day.

By the seventh century, the original structure had fallen into ruins; Aggabodhi II had it restored and converted into a **vatadage** (circular relic house), a uniquely Sri Lankan form of Buddhist architecture, with the original dagoba being enclosed in a new roof, supported by four concentric circles of pillars of diminishing height – an excellent model in the Archeological Museum shows how it would all have looked. The roof has long since disappeared and the surviving pillars now topple unsteadily in all directions, though you can still make out the very eroded carvings of geese (*hamsas*; a protective bird), which adorn their capitals. The dagoba itself is actually a reconstruction of 1862, when it was restored in a conventional bell shape – the original structure was built in the slightly ovoid "heap of paddy" form. The entrance steps are flanked with unusually fine guardstones, while no less than nine Buddha shrines surround the dagoba itself which, unusually, stands on a circular rather than a square terrace.

The area just south of the Thuparama is littered with the remains of buildings from the Mahavihara monastery, including numerous living units arranged in the quincunx pattern (like the five dots on the face of a dice) which is characteristic of so many of the city's monastic dwellings. About 100m south of the Thuparama is a colonnaded hall set on an imposing brick platform, with two fine guardstones and one of the most magnificent **moonstones** at Anuradhapura, though sadly it's protected – as are all the city's best moonstones – by an ugly metal grille.

The Archeological Museum and Folk Museum

West of the Ruvanvalisaya dagoba lie a couple of contrasting museums, although they can't be reached directly from the dagoba; you'll have to follow the road which runs north of Ruvanvalisaya east to Basawakkulama and then turn south along the lakeside road. The **Archeological Museum** (Mon & Wed–Sun 9am–5pm; entrance only with CT ticket) has attractively displayed sculptures from Anuradhapura and other places in Sri Lanka exhibited around the verandahs and in the garden of a creaking old colonial British administrative building. These include a large number of simple (but many sadly headless) standing and seated Buddhas, plus a couple of fine bronzes (including a big dancing Shiva) from Polonnaruwa. The garden is full of an entertaining troupe of dwarfs and nagarajas, as well as lots of pillar inscriptions recording grants of land and other administrative details. Other exhibits include various items of daily use – axes, ploughshares, hammers – plus the usual bits of broken pottery. There's also an interesting display explaining the various different shapes of stupas (see p.438). The sheer quantity of exhibits gives a good sense of ancient Anuradhapura's size, especially when you consider that finds from the ancient city fill another large museum at the Jetavana monastery (see p.352), as well as a considerable section of the National Museum in Colombo.

The **Folk Museum** (Mon–Wed, Sat & Sun 9am–5pm; Rs.50), a little further down the same road, explores rural life in the north central province, with forgettable displays of cooking vessels, handicrafts and the like.

Jetavana monastery

The last of the three great monasteries built in Anuradhapura, **Jetavana** was raised on the site of the Nandana Grove – or *Jotivana* – where Mahinda (see p.357) once preached, and where his body was later cremated. The monastery was founded during the reign of the great tank-building king, **Mahasena** (274-301 AD), following one of the religious controversies which periodically convulsed the ancient city. Relations between Mahasena and the Mahavihara monastery had been strained ever since the king had disciplined some of its monks. They retaliated by refusing to accept alms from the king, who responded by pulling down some of the Mahavihara's buildings and then establishing the new Jetavana monastery on land owned by the Mahavihara. The king gave the monastery to a monk called Tissa – who was then promptly expelled from the Sangha for breaking the rule that individual monks should not own any private property. Despite this, the new monastery continued under a new leader, becoming an important rival source of Theravada doctrine within the city.

The Jetavana dagoba

The centrepiece of Jetavana is its monumental red-brick **dagoba**. Descriptions of this massive edifice tend to attract a string of statistical superlatives: in its original form the dagoba stood 120m high, and was at the time of its construction the third-tallest structure in the world, surpassed only by the two great pyramids at Giza. It was also the world's biggest stupa and is still the tallest and largest structure made entirely of brick anywhere on earth: it took a quarter of a century to build and contains over ninety million bricks – enough (as the excitable Victorian archeologist Emerson Tennant calculated) to build a three-metre-high wall from London to Edinburgh. The dagoba has now lost its topmost portion, including the summit of its pinnacle, but still reaches a neckwrenching height of 70m – similar to the Abhayagiri dagoba. UNESCO-sponsored restoration began in 1981 but is still far from finished: parts of the structure are still encased in scaffolding, with rubble lying around, and sections on the north side are still awaiting excavation – at one point you can see where earth has been cut away to reveal the dagoba's base, buried deep in the soil.

The dagoba stands on an enormous but rather overgrown platform. Only two of the dagoba's four **vahalkadas** have so far been excavated; the one facing the entrance on the southern side is the finest, studded with eroded elephant heads, with naga stones to either side and two figures to the right – the top is a nagaraja, the lower one of an unidentified goddess.

The rest of the monastery

The area south of the dagoba is littered with the extensive remains of the Jetavana Monastery, all carefully excavated and landscaped – this is the most neatly presented area of ruins at Anuradhapura, though rather unatmospheric compared to other parts of the city. The monastery would once have housed some three thousand monks, and the scale of the remains is impressive, although except in a few places only the bases of the various structures survive; some preserve traces of fine stone carving. The first monastery buildings were constructed during the third century in the area north of the dagoba (which remains largely unexcavated) and gradually spread south and east as the monastery expanded over the next six centuries – most of what you see today dates from the ninth and tenth centuries. Immediately behind the Jetavana museum (see below) lies a deep and beautifully preserved **bathing pool** and the so-called **Buddhist Railing**, an unusual latticed fence pierced with four entrances oriented towards the cardinal points; the three tiers of the fence are claimed to represent Buddhism's "three jewels" (the Buddha; his teachings; and the Sangha). The building which the railing formerly enclosed was either a bo tree shrine or an image house. Slightly east of here stands the **Uposathagara** (chapterhouse), with dozens of roughly hewn and very closely spaced pillars; these probably supported upper storeys, since a room with this many pillars crowded into it would have been of little practical use.

To the west of the dagoba stands the **Patimaghara** (image house), the largest surviving building at Jetavana: a tall, slender door leads between eight-metre-high surviving sections of wall into a narrow image chamber, at the end of which is a lotus base which once supported a standing Buddha image. Below this is a latticed stone **reliquary** consisting of 25 holes in which relics or statues of other deities would have been placed. Around the image house are further extensive remains of monastic residences – many are laid out in the characteristic quincunx (five-of-dice) pattern, with a large central building, in which the more senior monks would have lived, surrounded by four smaller structures, the whole enclosed by a square brick enclosing wall.

Jetavana Museum

The interesting **Jetavana Museum** (daily 8am–5pm; entrance with CT ticket only) holds a striking collection of objects recovered during excavations at the monastery. Compared to the mass of rather plain stone carvings at the Archeological Museum, many of the luxurious items here show a level of craftsmanship and an obsession with personal display which gives an insight into the wealth – and worldliness – of ancient Anuradhapura. Most impressive in this respect is the large room devoted to coins, jewellery, ivory carvings, ear ornaments and bangles, all of extremely fine workmanship, as well as precious stones such as amethysts and garnets – hardly the objects one would associate with monastic life. There are also fine fragments of decorative friezes and carvings from the site, including Buddhas and guardstones, some of great delicacy, plus a relatively less interesting collection of pottery, though look out for the skilfully engineered three-tiered urinal pot. A pavilion outside has more stone sculptures: friezes, elephants and guardstones.

The Citadel

The area north of the Thuparama, between the Mahavihara and Abhayagiri monasteries, is occupied by **The Citadel**, or Royal Palace area. This was the secular heart of Anuradhapura, enclosed by a moat and thick walls which perhaps reached a height of five metres; little survives of this once bustling urban centre, however, and it's now one of the city's least interesting areas.

The present **Royal Palace** is one of the newest buildings at Anuradhapura, having been built by Vijayabahu I after his victory over the Cholas in 1070. By this time power had shifted to Polonnaruwa; the palace here was no more than a secondary residence, and little remains of it apart from the terrace on which it stood and a few bits of wall. The main steps up to the terrace are flanked by two fine **guardstones** featuring a pair of unusually obese dwarfs (a similar pair guard the steps on the far side). A wall on the terrace, protected by a corrugated iron shelter, bears a few splashes of paint, all that remains of the frescoes which once decorated the palace.

The kings of ancient Anuradhapura set great store by their shows of piety and beneficence – though in reality they often fell somewhat short of the ideals which they claimed to embody. The true murkiness of the Anuradhapuran royal character is famously encapsulated by the story of **King Yasalalakatissa** (reigned 52–60), who had seized the throne by murdering his brother. Yasalalakatissa had a weakness for practical jokes. Upon discovering an uncanny resemblance between himself and a palace gatekeeper called **Subha**, he swapped clothes with Subha in order to enjoy the spectacle of the island's nobles paying homage to a humble servant. So greatly did this amuse Yasalalakatissa that he had the prank repeated several times, until one day Subha, playing the role of king, ordered the execution of his "gatekeeper" for impertinence. Yasalalakatissa's claims to be the real king were met with disbelief, and he was promptly murdered. It says something about the debased standards of the Anuradhapuran monarchy that even when Subha's deception was unmasked, he was allowed to rule for a further six years before being assassinated in turn.

About 100m north of the palace, on the opposite side of the road, are the remains of the **Mahapali Refectory**. The huge stone trough here (it looks like something a horse would eat from) would have been filled with rice for the monks by the city's lay followers and could have fed as many as five thousand – any monk could find food here, even during periods of famine, and records state that a number of Anuradhapura's kings were in the habit of taking their meals here, though it's not recorded whether they mucked in at the trough with everyone else. Next to the refectory is an impressively deep stepped **well**.

Immediately east of the refectory are the remains of a building studded with a cluster of columns reaching up to 4m high; this is thought to be the very first **Temple of the Tooth**, constructed to house the Tooth Relic (see p.219) when it was originally brought to the island in 313. The columns may have supported a second storey, and it's been suggested that the Tooth Relic was kept on the upper floor, thus setting the pattern for all the shrines which subsequently housed it. The Tooth Relic was taken annually in procession from here to the Abhayagiri in a ceremony which was the ancestor of today's great Esala Perahera at Kandy.

Abhayagiri monastery

The third of Anuradhapura's great monasteries, **Abhayagiri** lies on the northern side of the city, and was found by King Vattagamani Abhaya (also known as Valagamba or Valagambahu) in 88 BC. Vattagamani had earlier lost his throne to a group of invading Tamils. Whilst escaping from the city, the deposed king was jeered by a Jain priest of the Giri Monastery, who shouted: "The great black lion is fleeing". The exiled king retorted that, "If my wish [of regaining my kingdom] is fulfilled, I will build a temple here." Fourteen years later, Vattagamani returned with an army and drove the Tamils out of Sri Lanka. Upon returning to Anuradhapura he quickly established a new Buddhist monastery in the place of the Giri Monastery, named after the second part of his own name (meaning "fearless" – as in the abhaya, or "Have No Fear" Buddhist mudra), and that of the monastery on whose ground it had been built.

Abhayagiri rapidly surpassed the older Mahavihara as the largest and most influential monastery in the country. By the fifth century it was home to five thousand monks and had become an important source of new Buddhist doctrine and a flourishing centre of artistic activity and philosophical speculation. Although it remained within the Theravada tradition, elements of Mahayana and Tantric Buddhism were taught here (much to the disgust of the ultra-conservative clergy of the Mahavihara, who labelled the monks of Abhayagiri heretics), and the monastery established wide-ranging contacts with India, China, Burma and even Java.

In many ways, Abhayagiri is the most interesting and atmospheric quarter of Anuradhapura, and one of the great pleasures here is simply in throwing away the guidebook and wandering off at random amongst the innumerable ruins which litter the area – indeed getting lost is half the fun. The sheer scale of the monastic remains is prodigious, while their setting, scattered amidst beautiful light woodland, is magical – particularly memorable early in the morning or at dusk, when with only a little imagination you could fancy yourself an intrepid Victorian explorer stumbling upon the remains of a lost city.

Abhayagiri dagoba

As at the Mahavihara and Jetavana, Abhayagiri's most striking feature is its great **dagoba**, originally built during the reign of Gajabahu I (114–136) and later restored by Parakramabahu in the twelfth century. It formerly stood around 115m tall, only slightly smaller than the Jetavana dagoba, making it the second tallest in the ancient world – the loss of its pinnacle has now reduced its height to around 70m. The dagoba is popularly believed to be built over a footprint of the Buddha, who is said to have stood with one foot here and the other one on top of Adam's Peak. It's still largely unrestored, and most of the structure remains covered in earth and vegetation – a great fuzzy mound which makes a rather mysterious sight when seen rising out of the forest from a distance, though close up looks like an enormous building site thanks to ongoing restoration work.

Flanking the main entrance stand two guardian statues of **Padmanidhi** and **Samkanidhi**, two fat and dwarfish attendants of Kubera, the god of wealth; these statues have become objects of devotion in their own right, and are enclosed in ugly little concrete sheds with grilles to which pilgrims tie prayer ribbons. At the top of the steps stand a pair of the incongruously Grecian-looking urns (*purna ghara*), symbolizing prosperity, which can be found at several points around the monastery, while just beyond there's a modern temple with a large reclining Buddha.

The dagoba's four **vahalkadas** are similar in design to those at the Ruvanvalisaya, and are in various stages of reconstruction. The eastern vahalkada is flanked by unusual low-relief carving showing Classical-looking elephants, bulls and lions, all jumping up on their hind legs, plus two winged figures looking like a pair of angels who've flown straight out of the Italian Renaissance. The western vahalkada is flanked by delicate floral patterns.

The Samadhi Buddha and Kuttam Pokuna

Around 250m east of the dagoba lies a famous early example of Sinhalese sculpture, the so-called **Samadhi Buddha**, carved from limestone in the fourth century AD and showing the Buddha in the meditation (samadhi) posture – a classic and serene example of early Buddhist art, now ignominiously enclosed in an ugly concrete shelter modelled on the Buddhist Railing at the Jetavana monastery. The image is particularly revered, which means you'll have to take your shoes off when you approach it. The Buddha was originally one of a group of four statues (the base and seated legs of another figure can be seen next to it); it's thought that all four were originally painted and had gems for eyes.

Northeast of the Buddha lie the magnificent **Kuttam Pokuna** ("Twin Baths"), constructed in the eighth century for monks' ritual ablutions, with stepped sides leading down into the baths. These survive in marvellously good condition (despite being full of fetid green water) and are one of few places where you can get an obvious sense of the ancient city's original splendour. One of the two is significantly bigger than the other. Standing at the far end of the smaller pond and looking to your right you can see three small stone pools at ground level. Water would have been fed into these and the sediment left to settle, after which the cleaned water would have been released into the smaller bath through the conduit with the eroded lion's head on one side. The superb naga (snake) stone next to this conduit was a symbol of good fortune, while the urns at the top of the stairs down into the bath symbolize plenty. Water passed from the smaller to the larger bath through small holes which connect the two.

The rest of the monastery

Immediately north of the Abhayagiri dagoba lies **Mahasen's Palace** (also known as the Queen's Pavilion), though it's not actually a royal residence at all, but an image house dating from the eighth or ninth century. It's famous principally for its delicately carved **moonstone**, arguably the finest in Sri Lanka. Behind this rise a flight of finely carved steps supported by the inevitable dwarfs, squatting like tiny Sumo wrestlers.

Continuing anticlockwise around the dagoba brings you to the **Ratna Prasada** ("Gem Palace"), formerly the main chapterhouse of the Abhayagiri monastery, which was built in the eighth century by Mahinda II. This boasts a magnificent **guardstone** dating from the eighth century and showing the usual nagaraja standing on a dwarf, shaded by a seven-headed cobra and carrying various symbols of prosperity: lotus flowers, a flowering branch and an urn. The **arch** which frames this figure shows an extraordinary chain of joined images, with four makaras swallowing two tiny human couples and two equally microscopic elephants, separated by four flying dwarfs; an unimpressed elephant stands to one side. Not surprisingly, the symbolism of this strange piece of sculpture remains obscure.

Just north of here are the remains of the **Asanaghara**, dating from the third-century BC and boasting two plain *sri pada*, a soot-blackened sandstone Buddha statue minus one arm, and a couple of pillar inscriptions, while the floor is studded with lotus-shaped pillar bases (the actual pillars are long gone). South of here is the colossal **Et Pokuna** ("Elephant Pool"). Dug out of the bedrock, this is the largest bathing pool in the ancient city and quite large enough to hold a whole herd of elephants. Spreading away east of here lie the remains of the **monastic residences**, with innumerable terraces, hypostyle rooms, stairways and baths, many set atop steep-sided plinths. There's a difficult-to-find **refectory** here with a huge, 15-metre-long rice trough.

South of here on the main road (you probably passed it on the way in) is the **Lankarama**, a first-century BC vatadage – the three rows of pillars which surround the ruins would originally have supported a roof. The present dagoba is modern, white and unusually square in shape.

The western monasteries

The countryside west of the Abhayagiri monastery, beyond the Bulankulam tank, was formerly home to Anuradhapura's **western monasteries**. These fourteen monasteries were home to the most extreme of the city's Buddhist sects – the *pamsukulika*, or "tattered-robe", monks, who decamped here during the seventh century in reaction to the relatively luxurious lifestyles enjoyed by monks in the city's great royal monasteries, devoting themselves to a life of privation and meditation. The best preserved of the monasteries lies about 2km southwest of Abhayagiri. Remains here include a double-platform structure (see p.337), similar to those found at Ritigala and Arankele, a meditation walk, the remains of monks' cells and baths, plus a sumptuously decorated urinal stone – the symbolism of monks urinating on the symbols of wealth depicted in these carvings (gems; the residence of Kubera, guardian of wealth) is obvious.

The southern city

If you have the energy for more, there's a further cluster of interesting remains west and south of the Sri Maha Bodhi along the banks of the Tissa Wewa. Around a kilometre west of the Sri Maha Bodhi lies the **Mirisavatiya Dagoba**, a huge structure which was the first thing to be built by Dutugemunu after he captured the city; it looks very similar to – and only slightly smaller than – the Ruvanvalisaya dagoba, which Dutugemunu subsequently had constructed. The obligatory legend recounts how the new king went to bathe in the nearby Tissa Wewa, leaving his famous spear (in which was enshrined a Buddhist relic) stuck in the ground by the side of the tank. Having finished bathing, he discovered that he was unable to pull his spear out of the ground – an unmistakeable sign. At the dagoba's consecration, Dutugemunu dedicated the monument to the Sangha, offering it in compensation, the great king declared, for his once having eaten a bowl of chilies without offering any to the city's monks, a small incident which says much about both the island's culinary and its religious traditions.

The dagoba was completely rebuilt by Kassapa V in the tenth century and is surrounded by various monastic ruins, although these remain largely unexcavated and are relatively unimpressive. Northeast of the dagoba you may be able to find the remains of a monks' **refectory**, furnished with the usual enormous stone rice troughs.

South of the dagoba, on the banks of the Tissa Wewa, lie the **Royal Pleasure Gardens**, also known as the "Park of the Goldfish" after the goldfish which were kept in the two **pools** here. The pools were created in the sixth century and used water channelled from the adjacent Tissa Wewa; the northern one has low-relief carvings of bathing elephants very similar to those at the nearby Isurumuniya temple, cleverly squeezed into the space between the pool and the adjacent rock outcrop – the contrast between the geometrical precision of the two pools and the untamed surroundings, littered with huge boulders and rock outcrops, is extremely picturesque.

Isurumuniya Vihara

Continuing south for 500m brings you to the **Isurumuniya Vihara** (not included in the CT ticket; Rs.100 entrance). This venerable old rock temple dates right back to the reign of Devanampiya Tissa, and though it's a bit of a hotch-potch architecturally, it's worth a visit for its interesting stone **carvings**. The entrance is embellished with the usual fine, though eroded, guardstones and moonstone, while to the right of the entrance is a pool with low-relief carvings of elephants, designed so that they appear to be bathing in the waters. Opposite the entrance, steps lead steeply up to the main shrine. To the right of the shrine door is an unusual carving showing a man with a horse looking over his shoulder. Inside, a gold Buddha sits in a niche carved directly into the rock, framed by a finely carved makara arch.

To the left of the main shrine is a modern shrine with an ugly reclining Buddha and a small **cave** full of an extraordinary number of bats. Beyond these is the temple's **museum**, now home to a number of its most famous carvings, all rather Indian in style. Perhaps the most famous is the fifth-century sculpture known as **The Lovers**, probably representing either a bodhisattva and his consort or a pair of Hindu deities, though the figures are popularly thought to represent Prince Saliya, the son of Dutugemunu, and Asokamala, the low-caste girl he fell in love with and married, thereby giving up his right to the throne. Another carving depicts a palace scene showing five figures, said to include Saliya, Asokamala and Dutugemunu.

Next to here steps lead up to the rock above the temple, passing two beautiful *sri padas* on the way up; very steep rock-cut steps go up to one of two platforms at the top. Climb the steps up to the top of the temple for a sweeping **view** over Tissa Wewa, best at sunset.

Vessagiriya Monastery

South of Isurumuniya Vihara lie the large, scattered rock outcrops which formed the core of the **Vessagiriya Monastery**, once home to five hundred monks. The monastery was first established in the third century BC by King Tissa, but it was the infamous Kassapa of Sigiriya (see p.310) who rebuilt and expanded it, constructing an extensive monastery here, though most of the stone was later carted off for use elsewhere. It's a picturesque spot, with huge boulders and rock outcrops offering views out over the Sacred Precinct from the top, though there's not much to see apart from a few rock-cut steps, the stumps of pillars and occasional fragments of carved stone. An intriguing archeological footnote is provided (if you can find them) by the extremely ancient **inscriptions** written in a proto-Brahmi script similar to that found at the Kantaka Chetiya in Mihintale (it looks rather like cuneiform) – they're on the road-facing side of a few of the rocks.

Mihintale

MIHINTALE, 12km east of Anuradhapura, is famous as the place where Buddhism was introduced to Sri Lanka. In 247 BC (the story goes) the Sinhalese king of Anuradhapura, **Devanampiya Tissa** (reigned 250–210 BC), was hunting in the hills of Mihintale. Pursuing a stag to the top of a hill, he found himself confronted by **Mahinda**, the son (or possibly brother) of the great Buddhist emperor of India, Ashoka, who had been despatched to convert the people of Sri Lanka to his chosen faith. Wishing first to test the king's intelligence to judge his fitness to receive the Buddha's teaching, Mahinda proposed his celebrated **riddle of the mangoes**:

"What name does this tree bear, O king?"
"This tree is called a mango."
"Is there yet another mango besides this?"
"There are many mango-trees."
"And are there yet other trees besides this mango and the other mangoes?"
"There are many trees, sir; but those are trees that are not mangoes."
"And are there, beside the other mangoes and those trees which are not mangoes, yet other trees?"
"There is this mango-tree, sir."

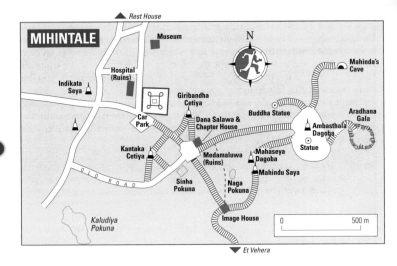

Having established the king's shrewdness by means of this laborious display of arboreal logic, Mahinda proceeded to expound the Buddha's teachings, promptly converting the king and his entire entourage of forty thousand attendants. The grateful king gave Mahinda and his followers a royal park in Anuradhapura, which became the core of the Mahavihara (see p.345), while Mihintale (the name is a contraction of *Mahinda tale*, or "Mahinda's hill") also developed into an important Buddhist centre. Although modern Mihintale is little more than a large village, it remains an important pilgrimage site, especially during **Poson Poya** (June), which commemorates the introduction of Buddhism to Sri Lanka by Mahinda, during which thousands of white-robed pilgrims descend.

The ruins and dagobas at Mihintale are relatively ordinary compared to those at Anuradhapura, but the setting – with rocky hills linked by beautiful old flights of stone steps shaded by frangipani trees – is gorgeous. Mihintale can be tiring, however: there are 1850 steps, and if you want to see all the sights you'll have to climb almost every single one of them (although you can avoid the first flight by driving up the Old Road to the Dana Salawa level). It's a good idea to visit in the early morning or late afternoon to avoid having to tackle the steps in the heat of the day.

A **tuktuk** to Mihintale from Anuradhapura costs Rs.400–500 return including waiting time. Alternatively, **buses** leave for Mihintale from Anuradhapura's New Bus Station roughly every fifteen minutes. You could also **cycle** here from Anuradhapura, but the road is quite busy and it's not a particularly relaxing ride. If you want **to stay** here, your only option is the reasonable *Hotel Mihintale* (☎025-226 6599, ✉chc@sltnet.lk; ❹), a pleasant, though rather expensive, rest house.

The site

At the bottom of the site, near the car park, lie the remains of a **hospital**, including fragments of treatment rooms and a large stone bath in which patients would have been washed in healing oils and herbs. Most of the island's larger religious complexes had similar infirmaries, where doctors used a highly developed system of ayurvedic medicines and treatments which were perhaps not so far from those used in today's hotels and clinics. On the other side of the road stand the remains of a monastic structure, its buildings arranged in a characteristically Anuradhapuran quincunx pattern.

Just north of the hospital is the site **museum** (daily except Tues; free), filled with the usual pottery fragments and figurines, as well as the remains of stone storage jars and grinding stones from the hospital. The most interesting exhibit is the model of a relic chamber from a dagoba – a rare opportunity to see what goes on inside one of these structures.

The Kantaka Chetiya

The first flight of steps heads up directly from the car park. About halfway up steps lead off on the right to the remains of the **Kantaka Chetiya** dagoba. Not much remains of the body of this dagoba, which originally stood over 30m high, but the four Anuradhapura-style vahalkadas, decorated with elephants, peacocks and nagas, are extremely well preserved. Just south of the dagoba, on a huge boulder perched precariously on its side, is an unusual inscription in a very early, proto-Brahmi script, similar to that found in inscriptions at the Vessagiriya Monastery in Anuradhapura.

The Medamaluwa monastery

Returning to the steps and continuing up brings you to a large terrace and the remains of the **Medamaluwa** monastery, the most important at Mihintale. The first building on your left is the **Bhojana Salawa** ("Alms House"), whose two big stone troughs would have been filled with food for the monks by lay followers. On the terrace immediately above are two large stone **tablets** in Sinhala, flanking the door into what was the monastery's image house. Erected by Mahinda during the tenth century, these stelae lay down the rules and responsibilities pertaining to the various monks and lay staff at the monastery – a kind of medieval Sinhalese job description. The brick bases of vanished dagobas lie all around, along with the remains of further monastic buildings, including the **Chapter House**, which preserves a few of its original 64 pillars.

Slightly lower down the same terrace, near the top of Old Road, is the small **Sinha Pokuna** ("Lion Pool"), named for the unusual, though but very eroded, sculpture of a lion rampant, through whose mouth water was fed into the pool. There are much better carvings on the small frieze above – they're small but relatively well preserved, showing lions and dancers in a rather Indian style.

The Upper Terrace

Another long flight of steps leads up to the heart of Mihintale, located (it's claimed) at the very spot at which Devanampiya Tissa met Mahinda. You have to buy a **ticket** (Rs.250) at the top of the stairs before entering the terrace, as well as removing shoes and hats. At the centre of the terrace is the **Ambasthala dagoba**, a surprisingly small and simple structure for such an important site – the name means "Mango Tree Dagoba", referring to the conundrum proposed by Mahinda to test Devanampiya Tissa's intelligence. The dagoba was subsequently roofed over, vatadage-style, as testified by the two rows of pillars around it. Immediately next to it is a single simple **sri pada** surrounded by two sets of railings covered with prayer flags; people throw coins in here for luck. Next to here is an extremely ancient **statue**, claimed to be of Devanampiya Tissa, though it might just be of a bodhisattva. Its arms have long since vanished, while its head has fallen off and now sits Yorick-like on a brick plinth in front. According to tradition, the Ambasthale dagoba covers the spot where Mahinda stood during the famous meeting, while the statue marks the position of Devanampiya Tissa, though given how far apart they are, this seems unlikely, unless their conversation – and the mango conundrum – was conducted as a kind of shouting match.

Various pathways lead from here to a number of further sights. Irregular rock-cut steps lead very steeply up the bare rock outcrop of **Aradhana Gala** ("Meditation Rock"), from which Mahinda preached his first sermon. On the other side, a shorter flight of steps lead up to a large white **seated Buddha**, dating from the 1980s and posed in an unusual composite posture: the left hand is in the meditation posture, while the right is in the "explanation" (*vitarka*) pose. A longer path leads to **Mahinda's Cave**, a bit of a hike down rough woodland path. The "cave" is actually an opening beneath a huge boulder poised precariously on the edge of the hillside at the edge of a large drop. On the floor is a simple rectangular outline cut out of rock, popularly believed to be Mahinda's bed.

Mahaseya dagoba

Once you've seen all the sights around the upper terrace, collect your shoes (but don't put them on) and head up one final set of steps to the white **Mahaseya dagoba**, claimed to enshrine some ashes and a single hair of the Buddha. The dagoba (which can be seen quite clearly all the way from Anuradhapura) is the largest and the second highest at Mihintale, in a breezy hilltop location and with wonderful 360-degree views over the surrounding countryside – you can usually just make out the great dagobas of Anuradhapura in the distance. Immediately next to it are the substantial remains of the lower portion of a large brick dagoba, the **Mahindu Saya**, which is thought to enshrine relics associated with Mahinda.

Carry on past the Mahaseya dagoba (you can put your shoes on now) down the back stairs to the ruins of an **image house** atop the usual stone base with flights of stairs and remains of pillars. From here, a tough ten-minute slog up steep steps (and lots of them) leads to **Et Vehera**, located at what is easily the highest point at Mihintale. There's nothing much to see apart from the remains of a small brick dagoba – despite the great sense of altitude, the views aren't really any better than those from the Mahaseya dagoba.

Retrace your steps to the image house, then head back downhill via the **Naga Pokuna**, or "Snake Pool", a rock-cut pool guarded by a carving of a five-headed cobra (though it's sometimes submerged by water). Romantic legends associate this with the queen of Devanampiya Tissa, though the prosaic truth is that it was simply part of the monastery's water supply system.

Outlying remains

Back on the main road by the turn-off to the site are the remains of another monastery and two dagobas – the larger is known as **Indikatu Seya**. South of here lies the hill of **Rajagiri Lena**. Brahmi inscriptions found here suggest that the caves on the hillside might have been home to Sri Lanka's first ever Buddhist monks. Some 500m south of here along the Kandy road, the tranquil **Kaludiya Pokuna** pool looks natural but is actually man-made. Beside it are the remains of a small tenth-century monastery, including a well-preserved cave-building with windows and a door – either a bathhouse or a monk's dwelling.

Travel details

Buses

The timings given below are for the fastest express services, where they exist. Local buses are usually significantly slower, increasing journey times by anything up to fifty percent.

Anuradhapura to: Colombo (every 30min; 5hr); Dambulla (every 30min; 1hr 45min); Habarana (every 45min; 2hr 15min); Kandy (every 30min; 4hr); Kurunegala (every 30min; 3hr); Polonnaruwa (every 45min; 3hr 15min); Trincomalee (3 daily; 4hr); Vavuniya (every 30min; 2hr).

Dambulla to: Anuradhapura (every 30min; 1hr 45min); Colombo (every 20min; 4hr); Habarana (every 20min; 45min); Inamaluwa Junction (every 15min; 15min); Kandy (every 20min; 2hr); Polonnaruwa (every 30min; 1hr 45min); Sigiriya (every 30min; 30min).

Giritale to: Habarana (every 20min; 30min); Polonnaruwa (every 15min; 30min).

Habarana to: Anuradhapura (every 45min; 2hr 15min); Dambulla (every 20min; 45min); Girtale (every 20min; 30min); Kandy (every 30min; 2hr 45min); Polonnaruwa (every 20min; 1hr).

Inamaluwa Junction to: Dambulla (every 15min; 15min); Sigiriya (every 30min; 15min).

Kurunegala to: Anuradhapura (every 30min; 3hr); Colombo (every 20min; 2hr); Kandy (every 20min; 1hr 30min); Negombo (every 30min; 2hr 15min).

Polonnaruwa to: Anuradhapura (every 45min; 3hr 15min); Batticaloa (8 daily; 2hr 15min); Colombo (every 30min; 6hr); Dambulla (every 30min; 1hr 45min); Giritale (every 15min; 30min); Kandy (every 30min; 3hr 45min)

Sigiriya to: Dambulla (every 30min; 30min); Inamaluwa Junction (every 30min; 15min); Kandy (1 daily; 2hr 30min)

Trains

Anuradhapura to: Colombo (5 daily; 4–5hr); Kurunegala (5 daily; 2hr 50min); Vavuniya (5 daily; 1hr–1hr 45min).

Kurunegala to: Anuradhapura (5 daily; 2hr 50min); Colombo (5 daily; 2hr 10min); Maho (10 daily; 40min–1hr).

Polonnaruwa to: Batticaloa (2 daily: 3hr); Colombo (1 daily; 8hr 30min).

5

The east

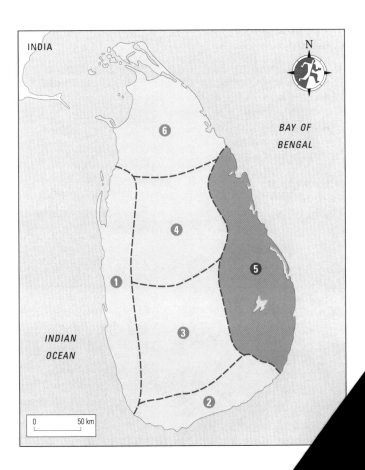

CHAPTER 5   # Highlights

✳ Trincomalee Founded around one of the world's finest deep-water harbours, the characterful town of Trincomalee has an attractive coastal setting, a fine colonial fort and an absorbing mixture of Hindu, Buddhist and Muslim traditions. **See p.367**

✳ Snorkelling at Coral Island Just offshore from the pleasant beach village of Nilaveli, Coral Island offers outstanding snorkelling in a beautiful coral garden populated by myriad colourful fish. **See p.375**

✳ Maligawila The remote village of Maligawila is home to two superb large-scale Buddha statues, hidden away in an atmospheric forest setting. **See p.380**

✳ Surfing in Arugam Bay The busy little village of Arugam Bay has an international reputation for surfing, with waves to suit all abilities. **See p.381**

✳ Lahugala This small but beautiful national park boasts the east's largest elephant population and is conveniently close to Arugam Bay. **See p.383**

△ Temple, Trincomalee

5

The east

Sri Lanka's **east coast** is a mirror image of its west. When it's monsoon season in the west, the sun is shining in the east; where the west coast in predominantly Sinhalese, the east is largely Tamil and Muslim; and where parts of the west coast are crowded with tourists and almost buried under a surfeit of hotels, the east remains largely untouched, thanks to its distance from the international airport and to the effects of the civil war, which placed most of the region off limits to visitors for two decades. Now reopened to tourism, the east remains a place of largely Edenic calm, with all the beaches but none of the crowds of the west – so far at least. How this great swathe of pristine coast is going to be protected from the sometimes crass development which has blighted parts of the west is a key problem in the wake of the peace process. For the moment, developers remain reluctant to commit their cash to major tourist projects given the region's volatile political make-up, and the continued threat of renewed fighting. The **ethnic make-up** of the east is the most complex and potentially explosive in Sri Lanka, with significant Sinhalese and, especially, Muslim communities living alongside the Tamils. Clashes between the latter two groups here have constantly disrupted the peace process, and the status of Muslims living in LTTE-controlled areas is likely to remain one of the most intractable problems in any future settlement, with Muslims facing the prospect of becoming a minority living under a Tamil hegemony.

At present, the region's most popular attractions are a trio of beaches – the adjacent resorts of **Nilaveli** and **Uppaveli**, just north of Trincomalee, and the surfing hotspot of **Arugam Bay**. All three remained (just) on the tourist trail throughout even the darkest years of the war, and are now at the centre of burgeoning plans for the development of the east coast. Arugam Bay is also the starting point for trips to the little-visited national parks of **Lahugala** and **Yala East**. Beaches aside, the main draw is the uniquely multi-ethnic town of **Trincomalee**, the shared home of Muslims, Tamils and Sinhalese, which has emerged from years at the front line of the civil war with its dignity, colonial charm and beautiful natural setting largely intact.

Getting to the east remains a bit of a slog, unless you fly from Colombo Trincomalee, and **getting around** is also less straightforward than in other parts of the country. The northeast monsoon reaches the east from Dec to March, bringing squally skies and significant rainfall. The **best time** is therefore from April to November, when it's raining in the west of

Some history

Although now something of a backwater, the east was for most outward-looking and cosmopolitan part of the island

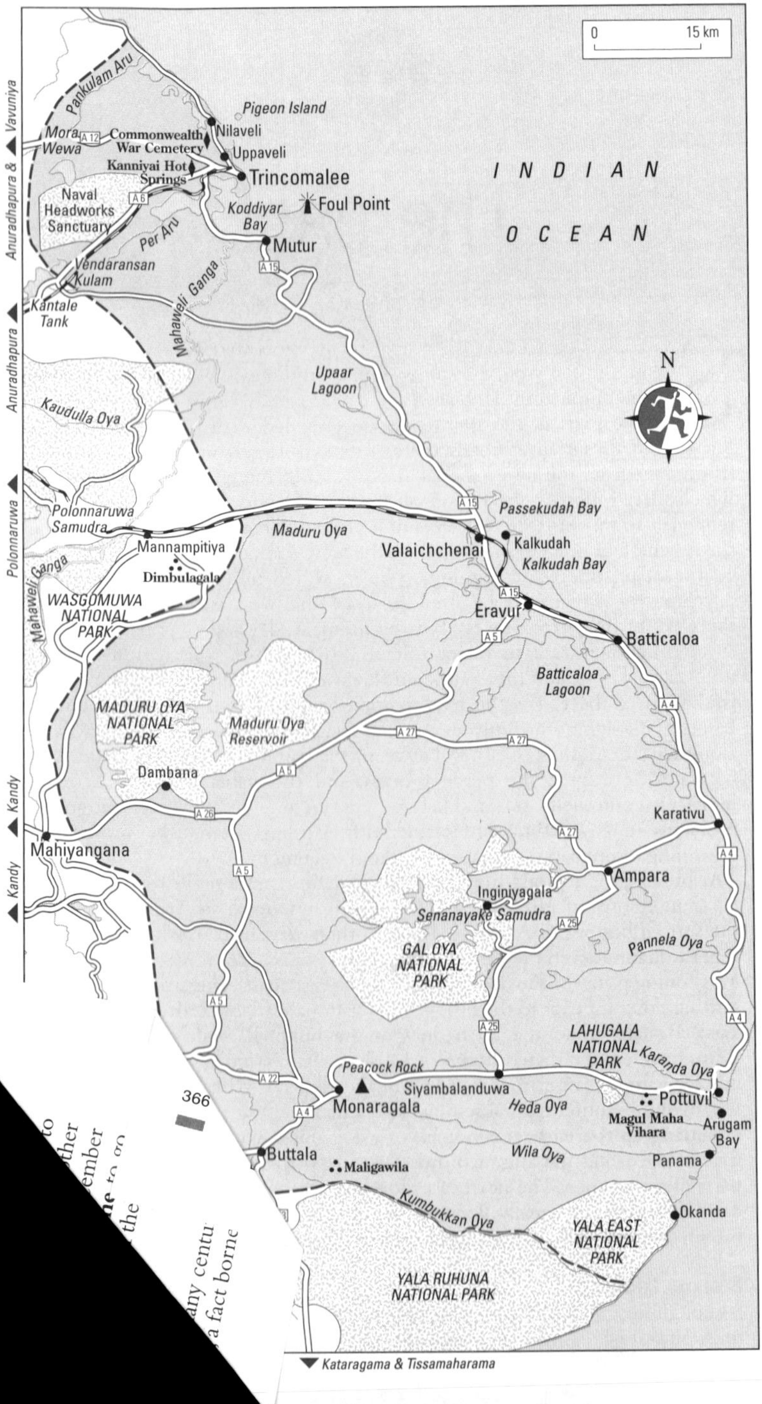
0 15 km
INDIAN OCEAN
Anuradhapura & Vavuniya
Anuradhapura
Polonnaruwa
Kandy
Kandy
Kataragama & Tissamaharama
Pankulam Aru
Pigeon Island
Nilaveli
Mora Wewa
A 12
Commonwealth War Cemetery
Uppaveli
Kanniyai Hot Springs
Trincomalee
Naval Headworks Sanctuary
A 6
Koddiyar Bay
Foul Point
Per Aru
Mutur
Vendaransan Kulam
Mahaweli Ganga
A 15
Kantale Tank
Upaar Lagoon
N
Kaudulla Oya
Polonnaruwa Samudra
A 15
Passekudah Bay
Maduru Oya
Mannampitiya
Valaichchenai
Kalkudah
Kalkudah Bay
Dimbulagala
Mahaweli Ganga
WASGOMUWA NATIONAL PARK
A 15
Eravur
A 5
Batticaloa
Batticaloa Lagoon
A 4
MADURU OYA NATIONAL PARK
Maduru Oya Reservoir
A 27
A 27
A 5
Dambana
A 26
Karativu
A 27
Mahiyangana
A 4
A 5
Ampara
Inginiyagala
Senanayake Samudra
A 25
Pannela Oya
GAL OYA NATIONAL PARK
A 5
A 25
A 4
LAHUGALA NATIONAL PARK
Karanda Oya
Peacock Rock
A 22
Siyambalanduwa
Pottuvil
Monaragala
Heda Oya
A 4
Arugam Bay
Magul Maha Vihara
Buttala
Wila Oya
Panama
Maligawila
Kumbukkan Oya
Okanda
YALA EAST NATIONAL PARK
YALA RUHUNA NATIONAL PARK

the mixture of Tamils, Muslims and Sinhalese who make the region the most ethnically diverse in Sri Lanka. Much of the area's early history revolved around **Trincomalee**, the island's principal trading port during the Anuradhapuran and Polonnaruwan eras, and the harbours of the east continued to serve as an important conduit for foreign influences in subsequent centuries. Islam spread widely along the coast thanks to visiting Arab, Malay and Indian traders, while the European powers also took a healthy interest in the region. The Dutch first established a secure presence on the island at the town of Batticaloa, while it was the lure of Trincomalee harbour more than anything else which drew the British to the island – and subsequently even attracted the attentions of the Japanese during World War II.

With the rise of Galle and later Colombo, the east gradually fell into decline, and its fortunes nosedived during the **civil war**, whose front line bisected the region and turned Tamils, Muslims and Sinhalese against one another in a frenzy of communal violence whose repercussions continue to be felt today. Trincomalee remains an important cog in the national economic machine – the LTTE have long coveted it as the commercial capital of a future Tamil Eelam (see p.392) – although its position at the front line between the island's Sinhalese and Tamil areas continues to cast a shadow over its future. Away from the coast the east remains sparsely populated and economically backward – the arid climate has always discouraged settled agriculture, and although the huge Mahaweli Development Project (see p.378) has brought some life to the area, it remains for the most part impoverished and inward-looking.

Trincomalee and around

Eastern Sri Lanka's major town, **TRINCOMALEE** (or "Trinco") has been celebrated since antiquity for its superlative deep-water **harbour**, one of the finest in Asia – the legendary Panduvasudeva (see p.414) is said to have sailed into Trincomalee (or Gokana, as it was originally known) with his followers, while the town served as the major conduit for the island's seaborne trade during the Anuradhapuran and Polonnaruwan periods. The harbour was later fought over repeatedly during the colonial period and even attracted the hostile attentions of the Japanese air force during World War II.

Trincomalee's fortunes nosedived with the onset of the **civil war** in 1983. The town became – and remains – a flashpoint for ethnic tensions, thanks to a population which is almost evenly divided between Tamil, Muslim and Sinhalese communities. In addition, although Trincomalee avoided the massive bomb damage inflicted on Jaffna, its position close to the front line made it the island's major collecting point for war-displaced **refugees**, whose presence stretched the town's resources and infrastructure to breaking point and beyond, while parts of the town were burnt to the ground during communal rioting. Following the ceasefire, thousands upon thousands of Sri Lankans fr[...] Colombo and elsewhere in the south flocked to Trincomalee – for some i[...] their first ever visit; others were seeing it for the first time in twent[...] Trincomalee's recovery has been rapid, although alleged ceasefire vio[...] the town's hinterland by the LTTE continue to cast a shadow ove[...]

Although most visitors are drawn to this part of the island by t[...] Nilaveli and Uppaveli, a day in Trincomalee makes an interesting[...] beach. Trinco has an understated but distinct charm, with a f[...] fine colonial fort and, in places, a certain old-fashioned ele[...]

of Tamil, Sinhalese and Muslim populations lends a multi-ethnic flavour whose subtle mingling of religions and traditions is unique in Sri Lanka.

Arrival

Buses arrive at the bus station, right in Trinco's centre at the bottom of Main Street, a Rs.30–40 ride from the cluster of guest houses along Post Office Road. The **train** station is at the northwest end of town, with just two services daily from Colombo. There's the usual selection of **banks** in the town centre; the Commercial Bank on Central Road has an **ATM** which accepts foreign Visa cards and MasterCard. **Internet** access is available from several places at the junction of Post Office and Power House roads, near the guest house area; try Comet.Net (daily 8.30am–midnight; Rs.80 per hour), which has a/c and several machines.

Accommodation

The main concentration of decent places to stay is along **Post Office Road** (or Kachcheri Road, as it's officially known), where you'll find several perfectly OK if fairly indistinguishable options. There are a few other places dotted around town, but avoid the string of resolutely awful places on Dyke Street, despite the ocean-front setting on one of the town's prettiest streets.

Jegas Home 108 Post Office Rd ☏026-222 7237. A handful of simple but acceptable rooms with or without bath. ❷

Kumars Guest House 102 Post Office Rd ☏026-222 7792. Fractionally nicer than its neighbours, thanks to its combination of pleasant and good-value rooms (but avoid the one right on the road) and the attractive *Kumars Cream House* downstairs, a cheery spot for snacks and drinks. ❷

Medway Hotel 250 Inner Harbour Rd ☏026-222 7655, ✉jrstrinc@slt.lk. Set in a nice location facing the Inner Harbour, this motel-style establishment is the smartest option in central Trinco, although nothing special. The huge and rather bare rooms come with a/c, phone, TV and great expanses of tiled floor. No single rates. ❺

New Silver Star 27 College St ☏026-222 2348, ☏222 1889. This medium-sized hotel close to the [ ] a bit shabby, but the rooms are

decent and inexpensive. There are also a few a/c rooms. ❷, a/c ❸

Star Inn 90 Post Office Rd ☏026-222 2740. Attached to the excellent little *Star Restaurant* (see p.372), the three cheap but pleasant and nicely furnished rooms here share two clean bathrooms. More rooms are planned. ❶

Sunflower Guest House 154 Post Office Rd ☏026-222 2963. Spacious and reasonable-value modern rooms above the *Sunflower Bake House*. No single rates. ❷

Welcombe Hotel (formerly the *7 Islands Hotel*) Orr's Hill Rd ☏026-222 237, ✉welcombehotel@sltnet.lk. Trinco's only upmarket option, a couple of kilometres west of town, with 25 rooms, stylishly furnished with sleek, colonial-style wooden furniture, and fine views over the Inner Harbour from an unusual viewing platform made from old railway sleepers. ❻

es a splendid natural setting athwart a narrow peninsula Ocean and the deep and sheltered waters of the Inner elf is a bit of a mishmash. Much of the centre is lonial **Fort Frederick**, which climbs up to the dominant feature on the coast hereabouts. West of nmercial centre comprises a surprisingly low-grid of streets, though it's worth exploring the f here, lined with pretty old colonial villas and les, mosques and, especially, dozens of colourful ism is much the most obvious of Trinco's three

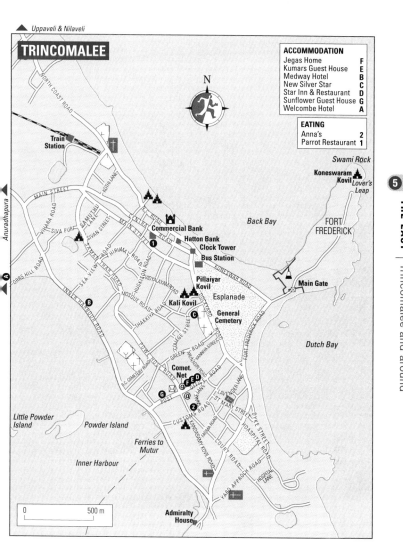

TRINCOMALEE

ACCOMMODATION

Jegas Home	**F**
Kumars Guest House	**E**
Medway Hotel	**B**
New Silver Star	**C**
Star Inn & Restaurant	**D**
Sunflower Guest House	**G**
Welcombe Hotel	**A**

EATING

Anna's	**2**
Parrot Restaurant	**1**

NORTH COAST ROAD

Train Station

MAIN STREET

VIHARA ROAD

SIVA PURE

Anuradhapura

ORRS HILL ROAD

INNER HARBOUR ROAD

SAMY LANE
CENTRAL ROAD
KOTHU LANE
SIVAN STREET
SEA VIEW HEAL ROAD
HIRUMA ROAD
VIDYALAYAM ROAD
POST OFFICE ROAD
HUSSEN ROAD
MOSQUE ROAD
THAKKIYA ROAD

Commercial Bank

Hatton Bank

Clock Tower

Bus Station

Pillaiyar Kovil

Kali Kovil

Esplanade

General Cemetery

Back Bay

Koneswaram Kovil Lover's Leap

Swami Rock

FORT FREDERICK

Main Gate

KONESWAR ROAD

FORT FREDERICK ROAD

Dutch Bay

GREEN STREET
COLLEGE STREET
R.C. CEMETERY ROAD
POST OFFICE ROAD
NARAYAN ROAD
VANNIA STREET
DYKE STREET
CUSTOMS ROAD
KANDASAMY KOVIL ROAD
COURT ROAD
HOSPITAL ROAD
YARD APPROACH ROAD
HOSPITAL LANE
ST MARY STREET
LAVENDER LANE

Comet. Net

Little Powder Island

Powder Island

Ferries to Mutur

Inner Harbour

0	500 m

Admiralty House

THE EAST | Trincomalee and around

principal religions, especially at around 4pm, when the town fills with the ringing of bells and the sound of music from myriad temples for the late-afternoon puja.

Fort Frederick

The centrepiece of Trincomalee is **Fort Frederick**, whose buildings sprawl across the narrow peninsula which pokes out into the sea from the middle of town, dividing Back Bay from Dutch Bay. The fort was originally constructed by the Portuguese in 1623 and captured in 1639 by the Dutch. The Dutch held it until 1782, after which it was captured by the British and then the French, who ceded it back to the British, who returned it briefly to the Dutch before

△ Trincomalee

getting their hands on it for good in 1795. The British rechristened it Fort Frederick in 1803 after the then Duke of York and enjoyed undisputed possession of the place until Independence, troubled only by a solitary Japanese air raid on April 9, 1942.

The fort is still in military use, but visitors are free to wander fairly much at will. The entire complex is enclosed by a solid set of stone walls; entrance is through a pretty main gate, its outer face carved with the date 1675 and a British coat of arms bearing the legend "Mon Dieu et Mon Droit". Inside, the pleasantly shady grounds are dotted with fine old trees, while a small population of deer (plus a few cows) wander around. A few colonial buildings survive, including one known variously as **Wellesley Lodge** or Wellington House. A popular legend describes the providential escape enjoyed by Arthur Wellesley, later the Duke of Wellington, who, it's claimed, stayed in here in 1800 whilst convalescing from an illness – the ship which he was to have sailed on later sank with the loss of all hands. In fact, the Iron Duke did spend some time in Trinco, but made it as far as Bombay before being struck down with a combination of fever and the "Malabar Itch". Fortunately for the future duke, a course of lard and sulphur failed to shift the infection and he was reluctantly forced to stay behind in Bombay while the doomed ship sailed off without him.

The main road through the fort leads up to **Swami Rock**, a towering clifftop vantage point offering wonderful views back to town, along the coast and down the sheer cliff face to the deep-blue waters way below. At the highest point of the rock sits a Hindu shrine, the **Koneswaram** (or Tirukoneswaram) **Kovil**, one of the five most holy Shaivate temples on the island. The original structure was destroyed by the Portuguese in the early seventeenth century – they simply shoved it over the edge of the cliff into the waters below. Divers subsequently rescued a Shiva lingam from the water, which is now enshrined in the (rather unattractive) modern temple.

Just outside the temple at the highest point of Swami Rock, a tree clings precariously to the edge of the rock, its branches adorned with prayer flags which supplicants have somehow managed to attach. This spot is popularly known as **Lover's Leap** in commemoration of a certain young Dutch lady, Francina van Rhede. The details are confused: some say that the heartbroken van Rhede, who had been abandoned by her lover, leapt but survived the fall; others claim that she didn't even jump. Whatever the truth, government archives record her subsequent marriage eight years later, after which she (presumably) lived happily ever after.

The rest of the town

West of the fort, modern Trincomalee's **commercial centre** comprises an undistinguished and low-key trio of parallel streets lined with tiny one-storey shops and dotted with the occasional small mosque (salmon pink being the preferred colour). Turn right off N.C. Road (officially Ehamparam Road) to reach a magical little stretch of **beach**, with small pastel-painted Hindu temples on one side, brightly coloured fishing boats drawn up at the water's edge on the other, and rabbit warrens of tiny shacks behind, their neat, brightly painted pastel facades giving the beachfront a spurious but undeniable prettiness.

At the southeastern end of the commercial centre lies the wide and grassy expanse of the **esplanade**. A couple of pretty Hindu temples enliven the western side of the green, the large **Kali** and the much smaller (though equally gaudy) **Pillaiyar kovils**. Both burst into life with drumming, music and lines of supplicants during the late-afternoon puja (around 4–5pm). Immediately south of these – and in stark, moribund contrast – lies the decaying and utterly neglected old **General Cemetery**, the final resting place of Trinco's Christian population, with a few picturesquely dilapidated colonial tombs dating back to the 1820s alongside more modern graves. Notable internees (if you can find them) include Jane Austen's brother, Charles, and the British railway administrator and amateur astronomer P.B. Molesworth, who discovered the Red Spot of Jupiter. The cemetery is usually locked, but it's easy enough to hop over the low wall.

A number of roads run southwest from the centre down towards the Inner Harbour – much of this quarter of town retains a pleasantly old-fashioned feel, with numerous colonial villas, some of them embellished with quirky, slightly Art Deco-looking decorative motifs. The expansive **Inner Harbour** itself is an attractively breezy spot, its choppy waters dotted with container ships and various port facilities, framed against a circle of rugged green hills which ring the bay – it's particularly lovely at night, when a thousand lights twinkle around the vast bay.

Elsewhere in town, the ocean-front Fort Frederick Road along **Dutch Bay** offers fine sea views, while the beach which edges the road is a popular spot around dusk, when half the town seems to congregate here to promenade along the seafront and loll around on the sands. Beyond here lie further low-key but charming rows of colonial villas, most particularly along **Dyke Street**, lined with quaint pastel facades.

On the far side of the enormous Koddiyar Bay lies the town of **MUTUR**, connected by ferry to Trinco (departures at 8am and 3pm; returns at 10am and 5pm; Rs.100 return). Ferries depart from the pier close to the western end of Post Office Road and provide an attractively breezy, one-hour boat ride across the bay, though there's nothing specific to do in Mutur itself.

Eating and drinking

Though there are no culinary treats in Trincomalee, you won't starve. The best selection of **places to eat** is in the guest house area around Post Office Road. The cosy little *Star Restaurant* (closed Fridays), at the *Star Inn*, has a cheap and well-prepared selection of all the usual suspects – burianis, devilled dishes, fried rice and string hoppers. *Anna's*, nearby on Court Road, is similar, though the atmosphere is rather moribund. There are also a couple of pleasant bakeries along Post Office Road selling drinks, breakfasts and snacks – try *Kumars Cream House* or the *Sunflower Bake House*. In the town centre along Main

---

Moving on from Trincomalee

Buses from Trinco are a little sketchy, with relatively infrequent services to **Colombo**, **Batticaloa**, **Kandy**, **Anuradhapura** and **Vavuniya**. As many of these leave early in the morning – around 6am – you might have to make an early start. There are services north to **Uppaveli** and **Nilaveli** about every hour – you might prefer to jump in a tuktuk.

There's a **train** from Trincomalee daily at 9.45am to Habarana and Colombo. From Gal Oya there's an onward connection to Polonnaruwa at 12.15pm. The ride is significantly slower than the bus, and no more scenic. There's also a second night-train to Colombo daily at 8pm. There are flights from Trinco to Colombo five times weekly operated by Serendib Express, 47 Kandy Rd (☎026/222-1519; US$56 return, US$30 one way); it takes about an hour to fly from Colombo, compared to eight hours on the bus.

Street, the pleasant little *Parrot Restaurant* has a reasonable selection of basic dishes, most for under Rs.100. They don't serve alcohol, but will send out for it on request. If you want to push the boat out, you'll have to make the trip out to the restaurant at the nautically themed *Welcombe Hotel*, Trinco's only upmarket eating option.

It's harder to get an alcoholic **drink** in Trinco than anywhere else in the country – almost all the town's restaurants are dry. If you get desperate, there's a liquor store on Post Office Road.

North of Trincomalee

The two main attractions north of Trincomalee are the fine beaches at **Uppaveli** and **Nilaveli**, although there are a couple of other low-key sites if you have a few hours to kill. Five kilometres north of Trinco, just past Uppaveli at the village of Sampaltivu, the **Commonwealth War Cemetery** holds the graves of the many Allied servicemen who lost their lives in Sri Lanka during Word War II, including the aircrews killed during the Japanese air raid of April 1942 and seamen who died aboard three Royal Navy vessels, including the *Hermes* aircraft carrier, which were sunk south of Trinco by the Japanese. In striking contrast to the General Cemetery in Trinco, the War Cemetery is beautifully looked after – even recent war damage has been patched up. The caretaker has a complete list of all those buried here. **Buses** to Nilaveli pass within walking distance of the cemetery; alternatively the return journey by **tuktuk** from Trinco will cost around Rs.250.

A slightly less sombre excursion can be made to the **Kanniyai Hot Springs** 6km inland from Trinco, which according to tradition were created by Vishnu himself. Count on Rs.250 for the return journey by tuktuk.

Uppaveli

Some 4km north of Trincomalee, the fine white-sand beach at the village of **UPPAVELI** continued to attract a trickle of visitors throughout the civil war years, and with the onset of peace the place looks set to boom: hotels which had shut up during the war years are now reopening, and it's possible that the whole village will change significantly in the near future – though the volatile political situation in the east continues to put a dampener on local optimism. For the present, however, it's all pretty crashed out: just a wide strip of sand, a few fishermen and good views down the coast to Trinco and Swami Rock, which affords a degree of shelter to the water here.

There are infrequent **buses** from Trinco to Uppaveli (roughly hourly), though it's much easier to catch a tuktuk (Rs.100).

Practicalities

One of Uppaveli's problems is that there's nowhere really nice to **stay**, and as prices have doubled since the ceasefire, the whole village is poor value for money, although this might change as new hotels and guest houses open and competition increases – a number of places are currently being renovated and reopened after twenty years' closure. The following are given in the order you reach them travelling north; all serve **food**, though you won't find much beyond a few tourist basics except at the *Hotel Club Oceanic*, which has a slightly wider (but still fairly average) selection of dishes.

5

Diving and snorkelling at Uppaveli and Nilaveli

Uppaveli and Nilaveli are the only two places along the east coast currently set up for **diving**. The sea here harbours a lot of live hard and soft coral – much of it close to the shore – though it lies in very shallow water (ten metres or less), so doesn't offer very exciting diving. Deeper dives are possible but not terrible interesting – at the time of writing, Trincomalee harbour – which reaches depths of over a kilometre and contains the wrecks of three scuppered Sri Lankan navy vessels – remains off limits. The diving season is from May to September.

Coral Island (see opposite), a few kilometres from Nilaveli, offers the best snorkelling in Sri Lanka, while nearby Pigeon Island (see opposite) is also worth a visit. You may also be able to arrange **snorkelling** trips from Uppaveli to Nilaveli through the companies detailed below, though it's easier and cheaper to just go to Nilaveli. Alternatively, there are boats for hire on the beach (operators hang out opposite the *Club Oceanic*): count on around Rs.2000 return to Pigeon Island for two people, including the use of snorkelling gear.

Diving the Snake *Pragash French Garden* ☎077-716 0880, ⓦwww.divingthesnake .com. The east-coast branch of the Bentota-based operation, run by an extremely clued up and informative owner.

LSR Dive School *Club Oceanic* hotel, ⓦwww.lsr-srilanka.com. Local branch of the reliable German-owned Lanka Sportsreizen chain.

New Sea Lord On the beach about 4km north of Trincomalee ☎026-222 2396. One of the nicer and better-value places in Uppaveli, catering for a mainly local crowd. Set in a sprawling low verandahed building, rooms are simple but clean and comfortable – if slightly functional-looking. No single rates. **②**

Anton French Garden Tourist Guest House (no phone) 750m north of the *New Sea Lord*. Set just back from the beach next to *Pragash French Garden*. Four clean, simple rooms – they're small and slightly dark, but OK at the price. **①**

Pragash French Garden 750m north of the *New Sea Lord* ☎026-222 4546. The longest-established cheapie in Uppaveli, though the rooms are basic, dilapidated and shamelessly overpriced. It does, however, enjoy a gorgeous beachfront location – easily the best in the village. No single rates. **②**

Nema Beach House 100m north of *Pragash French Garden*, just back from the beach ☎026-222 7613. Four rooms in a functional modern building – new, clean and rather antiseptic and expensive. **②**

Lily Motel On the main road, 100m north of *Nema Beach House* ☎026-222 7422. Seven clean, simple but quite pleasant rooms, three of which share a bathroom. The best value in the village, although the location on the main road is uninspiring. **①**

Beach Bangol On a side road to the *Hotel Club Oceanic* ☎026-222 7599. Rather austere-looking place with a faint but palpable resemblance to an army barracks. Rooms are basic and bare, but acceptable, and the friendly owner is very proud of his toilets' powerful flushes. New beach-facing rooms with a/c and hot water are planned for early 2004. No single rates. **②**

Hotel Club Oceanic 250m down a side road just north of the *Lily Motel* ☎026-222 1611, ⓦwww.johnkeellshotels.com. This rather functional-looking resort is Uppaveli's only fancy option, although if you've got the cash it's better to push on to the *Nilaveli Beach Hotel* (see opposite). Rooms all have a/c, sea-facing balconies and hot water; superior ones also have TV; chalets have TV and minibar – all are spacious and comfy, albeit fairly forgettable. Small ayurveda centre on site. **⑥–⑧**

Nilaveli

Ten kilometres north of Uppaveli, **NILAVELI** is the second of the Trincomalee area's famous pair of beaches. Like Uppaveli, it continued to attract a handful of visitors throughout the war years and now looks set to take off for good or (more likely) bad. Nilaveli has the edge over Uppaveli: better accommodation; a slightly more attractive setting further from the depressing suburbs of Trinco; and, especially, the best **snorkelling** in Sri Lanka at the nearby Coral Island.

Bus services up the coast are erratic; it's easiest to take a **tuktuk** – count on Rs.350 from Trinco to Nilaveli, or Rs.250 from Uppaveli to Nilaveli

Practicalities

As at Uppaveli, one dividend of the peace process has been the doubling of all **accommodation** prices, making the village relatively expensive, though standards here are better. The following are listed in the order you reach them heading north along the coast. All the following do **food**, although only at the *Nilaveli Beach Hotel* will you find anything more than simple tourist staples like fried noodles and fish.

❺

Coral Bay ☎026-223 2272. Ten rooms (four with a/c) in a good location close to the beach – pleasant enough, though decidedly overpriced. Breakfast included. ❹, a/c ❺

Shahira 3km north of the *Coral Bay* ☎026-223 2224. Set 100m back from the beach, rooms are large, nicely furnished and reasonable value, at least by Nilaveli standards. No single rates. Breakfast included. ❸

H & U On the access road to the Nilaveli Beach Hotel ☎026-222 6254. Nilaveli's only real budget option at present, with just three very basic rooms under corrugated-iron roofs. ❶

Nilaveli Garden 1km north of Shahira, next to the *Nilaveli Beach Hotel* ☎026-223 2228, ✉viptours@lankacom.net. One of the nicer and better-value places at Nilaveli, with pleasantly furnished rooms in a nice garden setting, and conveniently close to all the facilities of the *Nilaveli Beach Hotel*. ❸

Nilaveli Beach Hotel 1km north of Shahira ☎026-223 2295, ⓦwww.tangerinetours .com/hotels.htm. The nicest hotel along this stretch of coast, with a range of rooms. Standards are pleasant, fairly simple but comfy; deluxe ones come with a/c, fridge and big sea-facing French windows; they're also slightly bigger, with cool tiled floors. There are also a few economy rooms, with fan only, on the land side, plus a tennis court, biggish swimming pool (non-guests Rs.100) and a PADI diving and watersports centre. Economy rooms ❺, standard rooms ❻

Pigeon Island and Coral Island

About a kilometre offshore from Nilaveli, tiny, coral-fringed **Pigeon Island** was formerly one of the area's natural gems, though tragically it has been almost completely trashed by local day-trippers. The beach now lies buried under a thick layer of dead coral and the entire place is infested by crows attracted by rubbish left by visitors – a foretaste of what lies in store for the rest of the east coast without careful management. Despite the devastation, however, small patches of live coral survive on the island's ocean-facing side, and there are also lots of fish here, making for good and sheltered snorkelling.

Far more attractive, and so far undamaged, is **Coral Island**, a few kilometres north along the coast from Nilaveli. The "island" is a bit of a misnomer: it's basically just a few rocks poking up out of the water (you can't actually land on them), surrounded by an outstandingly well-preserved array of live reef, including lots of cabbage coral, which provides a home to dazzlingly colourful tropical fish – all in all, easily the best snorkelling in Sri Lanka. The only minus point is that the water here is very shallow at low tide, meaning that it's easy to knock against the coral whilst swimming, with potentially painful results for you and (more importantly) fatal consequences for the coral. Visibility is also lower at certain times of day – when the tide goes out, it flushes mud out of the lagoon which backs the shore, reducing visibility.

Boats can be hired on the beach (the majority hang out opposite the *Nilaveli Beach Hotel*); reckon on about Rs.500 per boat for the return trip to Pigeon Island and Rs.1200 to Coral Island, or Rs.1800 to both. These rates should also include the use of snorkelling equipment. You could try bargaining, though you'll need to be determined. It's also possible to arrange boats through the *Nilaveli Beach Hotel*, though this is a bit more expensive than doing it yourself. The hotel's Scuba Sri Lanka PADI centre (℡026-223 2295, ⒺIihinys @hotmail.com) rents out snorkelling equipment (Rs.300 for around three hours) and is the only place in Nilaveli to arrange **diving**; they also have kayaks and surf- and body boards.

South from Trincomalee: Batticaloa to Monaragala

The long swathe of coastline south of Trincomalee to Arugam Bay is sparsely populated and almost completely undeveloped – a small number of resort hotels established here during the 1970s were destroyed in the civil war and have yet to be rebuilt. The region remains impoverished and tensions between its Tamil and Muslim communities continue to run high, while in early 2004 there was even an outbreak of fighting near Batticaloa between rival factions of the LTTE.

The most significant town along this stretch of coast is the old Dutch colonial settlement of **Batticaloa** – a pleasant enough place, though without any compelling attractions. Inland from here lie the national parks of **Gal Oya** and **Maduru Oya**, both enormous, remote and still recovering from the effects of the civil war, whose front line ran through or close to both. Further south, the surfing village of **Arugam Bay** is the area's one genuine tourist hotspot, and a convenient base for visits to the national parks of **Yala East** and **Lahugala**, while the small inland town of **Monaragala** is the jumping-off point for the huge Buddhist statues at **Maligawila**.

Transport around the region is slow, and the infrastructure poor. The A15 highway runs the length of the coast, though it's in poor condition and is punctuated by numerous river crossings where vehicles are carried over by ferry – buses from Trincomalee to Batticaloa make the long detour inland via Habarana.

Batticaloa and around

The principal east-coast town south of Trincomalee, **BATTICALOA** (often shortened to "Batti") sits on a narrow sliver of land backed by the serpentine **Batticaloa Lagoon**. The town is surrounded by water on three sides, and the constantly shifting views of land, lagoon and ocean lend Batticaloa an interesting – if disorienting – character. It's a pleasant enough place, with a couple of decent guest houses, although there's not much reason to come here apart from sheer curiosity or, if you've got your own vehicle, to explore the attractive and totally undeveloped coastline hereabouts. At present, the only reason you might be passing through is if you're following the little-travelled (at least by tourists) route from Arugam Bay up to Polonnaruwa, though the town may begin to see more visitors when tourists start returning to the beaches at nearby **Kalkudah** and **Passekudah**.

Batticaloa was an LTTE stronghold for most of the war and survived the conflict in relatively good shape. It retains a solidly commercial feel, especially along Main Street, a neat collection of small lock-up shops with colourful signs in Tamil and huge wooden doors. It's also worth a stroll through the backstreets which meander up the hill behind Main Street, dotted with colourful churches, a few old colonial villas and the grandiose **St Michael's College**.

⑤

The singing fish of Batticaloa

Batti is famous in Sri Lankan folklore for its **singing fish**. According to tradition, between April and September a strange noise – described variously as resembling a plucked guitar or violin string, or the sound produced by rubbing a wet finger around the rim of a glass – can be heard issuing from the depths of the lagoon. The "singing" is allegedly strongest on full moon nights, though no one knows exactly what causes it – and indeed some people say the entire story is just an old wives' tale. The most popular explanation is that it's produced by some form of marine life – anything from catfish to mussels – while another theory states that it's made by water flowing between boulders on the lagoon floor. The best way to listen to the singing is apparently to dip one end of an oar in the water and hold the other end to your ear. Kallady Bridge, a couple of kilometres outside town, is traditionally held to be a good place to tune in.

Batticaloa was the first Sri Lankan stronghold of the Dutch, who constructed the town's solid-looking **Fort**, which stands some 200m behind the large public library at the west end of the town centre. The hulking and rather dour exterior walls are well preserved, whilst inside an old colonial warehouse and various modern buildings are crammed together cheek by jowl. There's a grand view of the lagoon from the far side of the fort.

Practicalities

Batticaloa's **bus station** is right in the middle of town, a couple of minutes walk from the *Subaraj* hotel. To reach either the *Riviera Resort* or *Bridge View* hotels you'll have to deal with Batti's tuktuk mafiosi, who usually charge a wildly over-inflated Rs.100 for the trip – there's a chronic shortage of tuktuks in town, and the few in business are almost totally impervious to any form of bargaining. The **ATMs** at the Commercial (Visa and MasterCard) and Seylan (Visa only) banks on Bar Road both accept foreign cards. To reach Bar Road, head straight across the river from the clocktower in the centre of town and continue straight ahead for 400m until you reach a roundabout; Bar Road is on your right.

The most convenient place **to stay** is the *Subaraj Inn* (T065-222 5983; ❶, ❸ with a/c), close to the bus station and next to the large *Lake View Inn*. This has a varied selection of good-value rooms (three sharing one bathroom) – simple but clean and comfortable. There's also an attached restaurant, though the food is only so-so. Don't even think about staying at the *Lake View Inn* next door – it looks plausible from the outside, but the rooms are disgusting fleapits. There are a couple of other options just outside town. The *Riviera Resort* (T065-222 2165; ❷) is set amidst gardens in a peaceful riverside spot 2km from town. The rooms are slightly rustic, but pleasant and good value, and simple meals are available. The nearby *Bridge View*, about 200m further along the same road (T & F065-222 3723; ❷,❸ with a/c) is more modern but less characterful, with a range of fan and a/c doubles and triples (equipped with fancy pink bathrooms). The restaurant has the biggest menu in town, with a wide range of seafood and curries (most mains under Rs.150). It's a Rs.100 ride by tuktuk to both these places, unless you bargain like crazy.

Moving on from Batticaloa, there are reasonably frequent services to Polonnaruwa (every 1–2hr), twice-daily **buses** to Colombo and Trincomalee, and services once or twice daily to Pottuvil for Arugam Bay. There are no direct services to Kandy. **Trains** leave twice daily for Polonnaruwa and Colombo.

Around Batticaloa

Around 35km north of Batticaloa lie the adjacent beaches of **Kalkudah** and **Passekudah**: two magnificent arcs of fine white sand, separated by a slender headland on which sits Kalkudah village. Until the civil war, these two villages were the most developed on the east coast, but two decades of fighting have transformed the area into a ghostly shadow of its former self. The once flourishing guest houses lie abandoned, while the bullet-riddled shells of two large resort hotels sit ominously on Passekudah Bay – a disquieting sight, though the actual beaches are still beautiful, and offer good swimming and calm, safe waters. The beaches are popular with locals, though foreign visitors are still a rarity.

The beaches are about 5km from the busy little Tamil town of **Valachchenai**, accessible by bus and train from Polonnaruwa. There are just a couple of places to **stay** hereabouts, the most reliable being the venerable *Simla Inn* (☎065-225 7184; ❶), in Kalkudah village, which somehow managed to stay open throughout the war and now offers a few simple but clean rooms.

Maduru Oya National Park

Southeast from Polonnaruwa (and northeast from Mahiyangana), the huge and remote **Maduru Oya National Park** was established in 1983 and recently reopened after a long closure during the civil war. At its heart lies the enormous **Maduru Oya Reservoir** – whose catchment area the park is intended to protect – along with four other smaller reservoirs (over fifteen percent of the park area is made up of water), all of which play an important role in the **Mahaweli Development Project** (see box below). There are plans to eventually link the park via a jungle corridor with Gal Oya National Park to the southeast. Much of Maduru Oya's predominantly low-lying terrain was previously used for slash-and-burn agriculture, and is now mostly covered by open grasslands and secondary vegetation, although there are a few rocky

---

The Mahaweli Development Project

Sri Lanka's longest river, the **Mahaweli Ganga**, flows for 335km from its starting point at Adam's Peak, meandering past Kandy and through the eastern provinces before finally reaching the sea at Trincomalee. The river was first harnessed for irrigation in the third century BC, though it wasn't until the 1960s that its full potential began to be realized with the commencement of the monumental **Mahaweli Development Project**, the largest irrigation and development scheme ever attempted in Sri Lanka. The project aimed to construct a series of **dams** across the river, most notably the enormous Victoria Dam just east of Kandy, in order to irrigate huge sections of arid and thinly populated land in the east and open them up for farming by Sinhalese colonists relocated from the island's overcrowded southern provinces.

The project really took off in the late 1970s under the government of J.R. Jayawardene – who was keenly aware of the political capital to be gained by emulating the massive hydraulic projects last attempted by the great Sinhalese Buddhist kings of Anuradhapura and Polonnaruwa. As of 2000, nearly 100,000 families had been resettled as a result of the scheme, with some 80,000 hectares of land opened up for cultivation. The scheme was not universally applauded, however. The Veddahs (see p.245) lost much of their ancestral land, while the LTTE has always regarded efforts to populate the east with Sinhalese settlers as an underhand attempt to colonize and ultimately steal land traditionally considered as belonging to the island's Tamils and Muslims – massacres of Sinhalese settlers in the east were a repeated feature of the civil war.

mountains in the southwest corner of the park reaching elevations of 685m. The usual range of fauna can be seen here: elephants, various species of monkeys and deer, abundant birdlife, rare sloth bears and even rarer leopards.

The road to the park goes via the village of **Mannampitiya**, 14km east of Polonnaruwa on the main road to Batticaloa. From here, a road leads 25km south to the park entrance. The usual national park **entrance fees** apply (see p.53). You might be able to arrange a day-trip from Polonnaruwa for around US$50, although the far more accessible parks of Kaudulla and Minneriya mean that, at least as yet, Maduru Oya sees very few visitors. If you're approaching the park from the south, you might enter via the settlement of **Dambana**, on Maduru Oya's southern border, one of the major Veddah villages in Sri Lanka.

Gal Oya National Park

The enormous **Gal Oya National Park** lies some 50km inland from the coast, in a little-visited corner of the island west of the regional capital of Ampara. Like the nearby Maduru Oya, it was recently reopened following long-term closure during the civil war, but remains poorly set up for visitors at present. The centrepiece of the park is the vast **Senanayake Samudra**, one of the largest lakes in Sri Lanka, and the tours of the park are usually made – uniquely in Sri Lanka – by boat. As usual, elephants are the main draw, with herds of up to 150 visiting the park during their annual peregrinations. Elephant-spotting is best from March to July.

The entrance is at **INGINIYAGALA**, 20km west from Ampara, where you can hire a boat for a trip around the Senanayake Samudra (around 2 hours; Rs.1000). The usual national park **entrance fees** apply (see p.53). There's a Department of Wildlife Conservation bungalow and campsite in the park itself, though these are best avoided in favour of the *Inginiyagala Safari Inn* (☎011-269 3189, ✉chilton@sltnet.lk; ❼), close to the park entrance, with around 25 newly refurbished a/c **rooms**; you can organize half-day tours into the park from here for around US$15 per person.

Monaragala and Maligawila

Just beyond the easternmost fringes of the hill country east of Badulla, the obscure little town of **MONARAGALA** (pronounced "monah*rah*gahlah") is of interest as the gateway to Arugam Bay and as a base for visiting the remote and magical Buddhist statues of Maligawila. Monaragala itself is dominated by the huge sheer sides of **Peacock Rock**, though there's nothing else to see or do except explore the town's two streets and field endless questions from curious locals – you wouldn't really choose to spend a night here unless you have a peculiar interest in experiencing Sri Lankan small-town tedium at first hand.

The **bus station** is bang in the centre of town; there's also a **taxi** (van) rank here if you need transport to Maligawila (see below). If you need to **change money**, there are branches of Hatton and Bank of Ceylon (but no ATMs) on the main road. The nicest **accommodation** in town is at the *Frashi Guest Inn* (☎055-227 6340; ❷), about 300m up a side road from the clocktower at 1/83 Pottuvil Road (take the road on the opposite side from the bus station and look out for the easy-to-miss sign); this has large and reasonably pleasant rooms, as well as reasonable food. Alternatively, the *Wellassa Inn Rest House* (☎055-227 6815; ❷) occupies a pleasant-looking building set behind gardens on the main road into town, though the rooms themselves (some with a/c) are a mite basic and grubby; good, cheap set dinners (Rs.250–300) are available. There are also two beautifully rustic eco-lodges in the surrounding countryside, the *Tree Tops Eco Lodge* and *Galapita Eco Lodge* (see below).

Moving on from Monaragala, there are currently two or three services to Arugam Bay each morning, the last leaving at 12.30pm. If you miss the last bus, you could take a bus to Ampara (about every hour until mid-afternoon) and get off at Siyambalanduwa, then catch a tuktuk to Arugam Bay, although it's a long ride – count on Rs.800–1000. Alternatively, a **taxi** from Monaragala to Arugam Bay will cost around Rs.1750. Heading west, regular buses depart for Wellawaya and Badulla, from where there are plentiful onward connections, plus less frequent services to Tissa, Kataragama and Matara.

Maligawila

Around 17km south of Monaragala, the remote village of **MALIGAWILA** is home to two giant standing Buddhist **statues**, fashioned out of crystalline limestone, which are thought to have once formed part of an extensive monastic complex. The statues, which had collapsed and fallen to pieces, were restored in 1991, when the various pieces were rescued from the jungle floor and painstakingly reassembled – though the Maitreya statue still looks rather patched up, and is missing parts of various fingers. The statues are impressive in themselves, but are made additionally mysterious by their setting, hidden away in a stretch of pristine lowland jungle. The ride to the site from Monaragala is also memorable, initially passing through rubber plantations, then winding along a tiny back road through straggling villages, avenues of majestic old hardwood trees and paddy fields, with impressive saw-tooth hills rising in the distance beyond – a perfect and unspoilt little rural corner of the island which feels a thousand miles from anywhere.

Maligawila village itself is little more than a sandy clearing surrounded by a few makeshift shacks. There's no entrance fee to the site, apart from a small parking fee. From the car park, a path leads into the woods, reaching a T-junction after about 300m. Turn left to reach the first of the two statues, an 11m-high standing **Buddha**, posed in the abhaya mudra ("Have No Fear") pose, freestanding apart from a discreet supporting brick arch at the back. Return to the T-junction and follow the other path for 200m to reach the second statue, dating from the seventh century AD and thought to represent either the Bodhisattvas **Maitreya** or **Avalokitesvara**. This is a more elaborate structure, with the remains of ornate entrance steps, a moonstone and two flanking guardstones, plus a pillar inscription in medieval Sinhala erected during the reign of Mahinda IV (956–972), recording acts performed by the king in support of the Buddhist order. The statue itself is set on a sequence of five raised plinths, like a ziggurat, and clothed in a richly ornamented dress; unfortunately, it's currently protected by an ugly concrete pavilion.

If you have your own transport, it's worth making the short detour about 6km west of Maligawila to the **Detamahal Vihara**, a mildly interesting temple with marvellous views over the paddy fields. Its origins date right back to the first or second century BC, and an ancient-looking, red-brick stupa survives, along with traces of Polonnaruwa-era stonework in the main shrine, itself built on an even older stone base. Next to here a modern brick building houses a striking, blackened twelfth-century Buddha image.

The area boasts a couple of remote, eco-oriented **accommodation** options. The first is the excellent *Tree Tops Eco Lodge* (no phone; ⓦ www.ecoclub .com/treetopsfarm; ❼ full board; book at least 3 days in advance), 9km from the town of **Buttala**, easily reachable by bus from Wellawaya or Monaragala.

The lodge is really out in the wilds – visitors are advised to arrive no earlier than 9am and no later than 3pm to avoid wandering elephants – with accommodation in rustic clay and wood huts in an unspoilt forest setting close to the edge of Yala National Park. There are no mod cons here (and no electricity) but it manages to be very comfortable even so, and there's plenty to do – safaris, walking, cycling, or just crashing out in a hammock.

Further south, roughly halfway between Buttala and Kataragama, the tiny *Galapita Eco Lodge* (℡011-250 8755, ⓦwww.galapita.com; ❼ full board) occupies a gorgeous riverside setting complete with natural pool and waterfall. The four open-sided pavilion-rooms are beautiful but very rustic. You're awfully close to nature here (there's only a mosquito net between you and the elements) – you might feel like a very style-conscious forest hermit. There's not much to do apart from kick back, enjoy the setting and explore the river and a few low-key local sights – but then, that's virtually the point of the place.

Buses from Monaragala to Maligawila leave roughly every 45 minutes and take around an hour. Alternatively a **taxi** will cost around Rs.1000, while tuktuks make the trip for Rs.700 (though it's a long journey, and you won't be able to appreciate the views).

Arugam Bay and around

Some 60km due east from Monaragala, **ARUGAM BAY** has long been popular with hardcore **surfers**, who come here to ride what are generally acknowledged to be the best waves in Sri Lanka, and the village still has an impromptu, palm-shack feel that reflects its origins as a low-key surfing hangout. Nowadays, however, Arugam Bay is beginning to draw a wider clientele, attracted by the village's remote, crashed-out ambience, as well as by

Surfing at Arugam Bay

With waves fresh from Antarctica crashing up onto the beach, Arugam Bay is sometimes claimed to be one of the top ten surf points in the world. The best surfing is between April/May and October/November. There are three main point breaks fairly close to Arugam Bay, plus several others further afield. The biggest and most popular waves are at **The Point**, a long right-hand break close to Arugam Bay, which has (on a good day) two-metre waves and a 400m ride. Thirty minutes north of Arugam Bay by tuktuk, **Pottuvil Point** breaks off a long and deserted sandy beach and is less crowded than The Point, though the waves are a bit smaller. Thirty minutes by tuktuk south of Arugam Bay, then a twenty-minute walk, **Crocodile Rock** is the smallest of the three points but, if there's sufficient swell, is an excellent spot for beginner and intermediate surfers. In Arugam Bay itself, there's a beach break in front of the *Stardust Hotel* which can be fun for body surfing or for beginners.

The best place for general **surfing** info and equipment hire is the A-Bay Surf Shop, at the south end of the main road through the village. In addition, many of the village's guest houses rent surfboards (Rs.350–450 per day) and bodyboards (Rs.250–Rs.350 per day), as well as offering **surfing safaris** to various hotspots along the idyllic coastline south of Arugam Bay (prices vary depending on the length of the trip and the amount of driving involved); various places also run combined surf and safari tours to Yala East, featuring surfing at assorted "secret" locations and the well-known surfing point at **Okanda**, at the entrance to the park – ask at the A-Bay Surf Shop or look for signs around the village advertising trips.

THE EAST | Arugam Bay and around

its proximity to **Lahugala** and **Yala East national parks**, newly accessible again after the years of civil war.

Having said that, some people find Arugam Bay a disappointment. The **beach** is fairly ordinary and not even especially clean – there are far more attractive stretches of sand in more convenient locations around the island (although, in compensation, there is a huge and magnificently untouched stretch of sand a couple of kilometres south of the village around the next headland). The village itself is uninspiring – essentially a single main road running parallel to the beach – and has none of the charm or atmosphere of, say Unawatuna or Mirissa. It also suffers from a poor and overpriced selection of accommodation, while the atmosphere in the village is far from relaxing – requests from children (and often adults too) for schoolpens, bon bons and money are probably more relentless here than anywhere else in the island, and can turn a quiet stroll along the beach into a bit of a trial.

Practicalities

There's not much to Arugam Bay: just a single main road running parallel to the ocean; most of the village's accommodation is squeezed in between the road and beach. If you need to **change money**, there's a branch of the Bank of Ceylon attached to the *Siam View Beach Hotel*; the *Siam View* also has an extremely well-equipped, a/c **Internet** cafe (Rs.250–500 per hour depending on time of day).

Moving on from Arugam Bay, there are currently around five buses daily to Monaragala (two continue to Colombo; one to Badulla). Two of these originate in Arugam Bay and leave from outside the *Siam View Beach Hotel*, where you can check latest times. There are also one or two buses daily to Batticaloa leaving from the town of Pottuvil, a couple of kilometres north of Arugam Bay.

ARUGAM BAY

Lagoon

Arugam Bay

N

A Bay
Surf Shop

Okanda & Yala East National Park

ACCOMMODATION	
Arugambay Hilton	G
Beach Hut	C
Chuttis Place	J
Galaxy Hotel	B
Hideaway	F
Royal Village Hotel	D
Siam View Beach Hotel	H
Star Dust Beach Hotel	A
Sooriya's Beach Hut	H
Tri Star Beach Hotel	E

0   500 m

Accommodation

Accommodation in Arugam Bay is a bit of a mishmash – a couple of good options, plus a lot of very indifferent places, including plenty which are seriously overpriced. Many owners have opted to put up rustic-style palm cabanas, although some are so rustic that you may as well be sleeping in someone's garden shed. These cabanas are usually built with the roofs raised slightly above the top of the walls, which keeps the rooms ventilated, although it also means insects and mosquitoes can fly in; the closer you are to the shore and sea breezes, the less of a problem this is likely to be.

Arugambay Hilton ☎063-224 8189. One of the better-value and more solid-looking places in town, with seven boxy concrete rooms with secured flat roofs set around a pleasant courtyard garden, slightly back from the beach. ❷

Beach Hut ☎063-224 8202. Friendly place with a selection of good-value concrete rooms and palm-thatch cabanas (with and without bath), some right on the beach, others set slightly back on a second point of land. ❶

Chutti's Place Seven tiny and very basic but dirt-cheap little cabanas. ❶

Galaxy Hotel ☎063-224 8415. Friendly place on the beach, with a mixture of poky little concrete rooms (with and without bath) plus some basic palm-thatch cabanas – simple but cheap, and the shared toilet is clean. ❶

Hideaway ☎063-224 8259, ✉tissara@eureka.lk. Beguiling guest house, set on the land side of the main road in a characterful two-storey house swathed in tropical greenery, with a gorgeous veran-dah upstairs. The rooms are excellent value and attractively furnished, with open latticework brick walls and slatted wooden fronts – pleasantly cool, if not especially private. There are also a few spacious and pleasant cabanas. Excellent food, too. ❷

Royal Village Hotel (no phone). Seven cheap and relatively good-value rooms (with and without bath) with concrete walls and thatched roofs. ❶–❷

Siam View Beach Hotel ☎063-224 8195, ⓦwww.arugam.com. Set in a rambling and attractive Thai-style wooden building, this is the most fun (if not the most peaceful) place in the

village, and the epicentre of pretty much every-thing that's going on at Arugam Bay, with an excellent restaurant (see below) and even the occasional full-moon party. There's a huge spread of accommodation ranging from dirt-cheap thatched cabanas, through more expensive cabanas and rooms right up to the luxurious "royal suite". Also has its own massive generator (a real bonus in powercut-prone Arugam Bay), formerly the property of Saddam Hussein's Republican Guard. ❶–❻

Sooriya's Beach Hut ☎063-224 8232. Set on the land side of the main road, with accommoda-tion in a motley but characterful collection of eccentric and ramshackle structures dotted around a long, rambling garden, including several huts on raised stilts and a genuine treehouse, plus huts, cabins and a few dingy rooms. It's all pretty basic and a bit grubby, but very cheap. ❶

Stardust Beach Hotel ☎063-224 8191, ⓦwww.arugambay.com. The swankiest place in town: attractive, but wildly overpriced. The pleasant rooms (those upstairs are nicer, brighter, and have better views) come with stylish cane furnishings and a vaguely colonial feel, though they're rather poky; there are also some attractive and relatively better-value bungalows. Rooms ❻, bungalows ❹

Tri Star Beach Hotel ☎063-224 8404, ✉tristar3@sltnet.lk. Reasonable mid-range option, on the land side of the main street, with functional standard rooms, plus smart new a/c ones with TV and minibar. Also has a swimming pool. Standard rooms ❸, a/c rooms ❺

Eating

Food is available at all the village's guest houses. If you want to eat out, try the *Siam View*, whose upstairs terraced restaurant is one of the nicest and liveliest places in town, with authentic Thai cuisine prepared by the resident Thai chef (mains from around Rs.300), plus other Sri Lankan and international dishes. A smarter but more sedate alternative is the *Stardust Beach Hotel*, which has a big, attractive restaurant under an enormous pavilion and a tempting (albeit overpriced) menu of international dishes – although you might find that very few items on the menu are actually available.

Around Arugam Bay: Lahugala and Yala East national parks

About 15km inland from Arugam Bay, the main road passes through the small but beautiful **Lahugala National Park** (pronounced "lao–gala"). The park is best known for its **elephants** – up to a hundred of them congregate around the park's tanks during July and August, when the rest of Lahugala's waters dry up. The tanks are also good for spotting a wide range of water birds. When the rains come the elephants disperse, and large sections of the park are transformed into gorgeous green floodplain and beautiful mature dry-zone woodlands.

Lahugala is technically closed at present, meaning you can get in for free, though this is likely to change soon. A number of guest houses in Arugam Bay can arrange jeeps for Rs.1000–1500 per half-day – try the *Siam View* or *Tri Star Beach Hotel* – although there's no guarantee your driver will know anything about the park's wildlife. Some locals claim that you've just as much chance of spotting elephants and other wildlife from the main road. If you want to test this theory, catch any bus heading towards Siyambalanduwa.

Just outside the eastern border of the park lies the **Magul Maha Vihara**, according to some locals the site of the marriage between Kavan Tissa and Viharamahadevi, though this is far more likely to have been at the identically named temple in Yala West National Park (see p.196). Despite this, it's an interesting and evocative site, with the remains of a dagoba, vatadage and the bases of several other ruined structures, made all the more enticing by its remote jungle location.

Yala East National Park and around

Yala East National Park is the forgotten twin of the relentlessly popular Yala West, which it adjoins (though it's impossible at present to travel directly between the two). Off limits during the civil war, the park reopened in 2003 and now offers the opportunity of enjoying some of the wildlife – including elephants, leopards and a huge variety of birdlife – of Yala West with none of the crowds; however it's still recovering from depredations suffered during the war years. Twenty kilometres from the entrance, the tank of **Kumana Wewa** and its surrounding mangroves are home to an outstanding array of aquatic birds.

The park entrance is at **OKANDA**, some 30km south of Arugam Bay; the usual national park entrance fees apply (see p.53). Okanda is a popular surfing spot, and also boasts a major **Hindu temple**, marking the spot where Kataragama is said to have landed on the island, and now an important staging point on the overland pilgrimage to Kataragama. A few kilometres inland from Okanda lies the extensive forest hermitage of **Kudimbigala**, whose hundreds of caves are thought to have been occupied by Buddhist monks as far back as the first century BC.

Some Arugam Bay guest houses – try *Siam View* or *Tri Star Beach Hotel* – can arrange transport to Yala East for Rs.3000 per jeep for a day-trip, rising to Rs.6000 for trips to Kumana. *Siam View* also run a fun day-safari (Rs.5000 per person; minimum 2 people) using quad bikes and combining a visit to Panama beach, about halfway to the park, with Okanda and Yala East.

Travel details

Buses

The timings given below are for the fastest express services, where they exist. Local buses are usually significantly slower, increasing journey times by anything up to fifty percent.

Arugam Bay/Pottuvil to: Batticaloa (1–2 daily; 5hr); Monaragala (2–3 daily; 3hr).

Batticaloa to: Arugam Bay (1–2 daily; 5hr); Colombo (2 daily; 8hr); Polonnaruwa (8 daily; 2hr 15min); Trincomalee (3 daily; 5hr).
Monaragala to: Ampara (hourly; 3hr); Arugam Bay (2–3 daily; 3hr); Badulla (1–2 hourly; 3hr); Buttala (every 30min; 45min); Kataragama (2 daily; 1hr 30min); Matara (5 daily; 4hr); Tissamaharama (5 daily; 2hr); Wellawaya (every 30min; 1hr 15min).
Trincomalee to: Anuradhapura (4 daily; 3hr 30min); Batticaloa (3 daily; 5hr); Colombo (hourly; 7hr); Kandy (4 daily; 5hr); Nilaveli (hourly; 45min); Uppaveli (hourly; 30min); Vavuniya (3 daily; 3hr 30min).

Trains

Batticaloa to: Colombo (2 daily; 10hr); Polonnaruwa (2 daily; 3hr).
Trincomalee to: Gal Oya (2 daily; 1hr 55min); Colombo (2 daily; 8hr).

Planes

Trincomalee to: Colombo (5 weekly; 1hr).

5

THE EAST | Travel details

6

Jaffna and the north

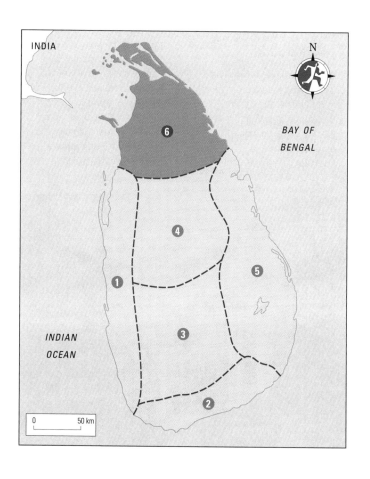

CHAPTER 6

Highlights

✳ **Jaffna** Recently reopened to visitors after two decades of isolation during the civil war, Jaffna offers a fascinating microcosm of Sri Lankan Tamil culture and a faded colonial townscape – as well as a unique insight into the ravages of the war years. See p.394

✳ **Nallur Festival, Jaffna** The largest and longest festival in Sri Lanka, attracting thousands of visitors to its 26-day extravaganza of ceremony, colour and spectacle. See p.402

✳ **Jaffna Peninsula** This densely populated peninsula is home to myriad contrasting sights, from sand dunes and hot springs to abandoned villages and war-torn temples. See p.404

✳ **The islands** Splintering off the tip of the Jaffna Peninsula, the starkly beautiful islands of Keyts, Karaitivu, Nainativu and Delft are a world away from the rest of Sri Lanka, home to little-visited colonial churches, Hindu temples and remote beaches. See p.406

△ St Martin's Seminary, Jaffna

Jaffna and the north

The **north** is a world away from the rest of Sri Lanka. Closer to southern India than to Colombo, the region was settled early on by **Tamil** migrants from southern India and has retained a unique character and culture, one which owes more to Hindu India than Buddhist Sri Lanka. The tensions and recurring conflicts between Tamils and Sinhalese lie at the very heart of Sri Lankan history. Throughout much of the island's earlier history, Tamil adventurers and mercenaries – either from the north of the island or from South India – interfered, usually with disastrous consequences, in Sinhalese affairs, creating a deep-seated suspicion which continues to cloud Sinhalese attitudes towards Tamils to this day. From 1983 to 2002, the entire region was engulfed in the **civil war** between the rebel guerrillas of the LTTE, or Tamil Tigers, and the Sri Lankan Army (SLA), and the decades of fighting have further reinforced the 2000-year history of difference that separates the Tamil north from the Sinhalese south. Much of the north remains under the control of the LTTE, and although the Tigers have renounced their original demands for complete independence, the fact remains that in many ways the north has the character of an entirely different country – a fact emphasized by the heavily policed **border** which currently separates the LTTE-controlled areas from the rest of the country.

For the traveller, the **north** is Sri Lanka's final frontier, and offers a fascinating opportunity to explore a region emerging from twenty years of isolation and civil war. Getting to and around the area is problematic due to erratic public transport, LTTE-imposed travel restrictions and the troublesome border between LTTE- and SLA-controlled areas, though for those who make the

Safety in the north

As of mid-2004, travel along the main roads to Jaffna and Mannar was still safe, although political volatility and the increasing fragility of the peace process mean that this situation may, unfortunately, change. Before heading to the region, make sure you're up to date with the latest events; if in doubt, check with your embassy in Colombo (see p.110).

The major hazard in the north is **mines** – it's been estimated that almost two million were laid here during the civil war. In the countryside, it is imperative that you stick to the main roads – do not wander off the tarmac for any reason. Even in and around towns you should avoid walking across any area which looks as though it is not in regular use – mines have been laid even in the heart of Jaffna. The same caution applies to the beaches of the Jaffna Peninsula and Mannar island.

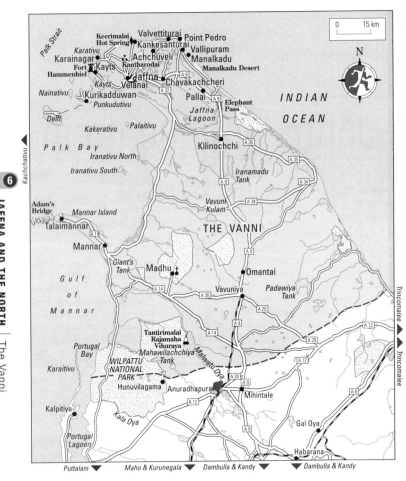

effort, there are rich rewards. Foremost of these is the fascinating town of **Jaffna**, with its strange but haunting mixture of war-torn colonial charm and vibrant Tamil culture, while the **Jaffna Peninsula** and surrounding islands offer a string of remote temples, beaches and more off-beat attractions – everything from a miniature desert to a giant boabab tree – to tempt the adventurous. In addition, the curious could head for the small town of **Killinochi**, headquarters of the LTTE, or the remote island of **Mannar** and the important Christian shrine at **Madhu** nearby, though these are destinations for the adventurous only. LTTE restrictions mean that travel to other parts of the north is currently forbidden.

The Vanni

The huge area of northern Sri Lanka between **Vavuniya** and the Jaffna Peninsula – **the Vanni** – was devastated by the civil war, and large areas now lie ruined, abandoned and heavily mined – the task of bringing life back to the region is likely to be a long and difficult one. This is the heartland of the LTTE, whose centre of operations is in the town of **Kilinochchi**, at the northern edge of the Vanni; the entire area between Omantai, north of Vavuniya, and the Jaffna Peninsula remains under LTTE control.

The spine of the region is the **A9** road to Jaffna, whose reopening to general traffic following the ceasefire was one of the most important symbolic and practical steps of the entire peace process. The road is still in poor condition, though upgrading is currently being carried out along its entire length.

Vavuniya to Kilinochchi

The town of **VAVUNIYA** (pronounced "vowvneeya") is the largest between Anuradhapura and Jaffna, sitting roughly at the borderline between Sinhalese and Tamil Sri Lanka. There's a significant Tamil population here, and if you've travelled up from Anuradhapura, you'll start to notice subtle cultural changes in language, food and attire compared with places further south. Vavuniya's only attraction is the modest **Archeological Museum** (daily except Tues 9am–5pm; free), which has a small collection of fifth- to tenth-century Buddhist statues. The town has a few basic **places to stay**, the best of which is the *Vanni Inn*, Ganana Vairavarkovil Rd, off 2nd Cross Street (☎024-222 1406; ❶); 2nd Cross Street runs off the main road near the Commercial Bank. Unless you're utterly stuck, however, it's better to press on to Anuradhapura.

Vavuniya is a major transport hub. The **train** line north (which formerly extended all the way to Jaffna) now stops here, and the town is also the starting point for **buses** west to Mannar. There are also frequent bus services to Anuradhapura, Kandy and Colombo, as well as to the border at Omantai separating LTTE- and SLA-controlled areas (see box on p.396).

North of Vavuniya, and beyond the border, the A9 runs through huge swathes of eerily deserted land, dotted with minefields, a few ruins and the odd palm-thatch hut – most of the villages marked on maps of the country along the A9 en route to Kilinochchi have virtually disappeared. About 80km north of Vavuniya, the small town of **KILINOCHCHI** is the headquarters of the LTTE. There are a couple of small and simple guest houses here (❶), including one, the *Vanni Inn*, run by the LTTE themselves. The nasty reality of war is rather more apparent some 5km west of Kilinochchi, where the **Mahavire Memorial** holds the identikit graves of almost two thousand LTTE soldiers killed in the war.

Some 15km further north along the A9 lies **Elephant Pass**, where a causeway connects the Jaffna Peninsula with the rest of the island. The pass was named for the elephants which were once driven across to the peninsula here, though it's now best known as the location of two of the civil war's most bitter battles, fought here in 1991 and 2000; it was during the latter that the LTTE finally succeeded in dislodging the Sri Lankan Army from its heavily fortified position at the entrance to the Jaffna Peninsula – a crucial moment in the progress of the war. The pass is one of the most heavily mined places in the country so do not under any circumstances leave the road – and in any case there's nothing really to see apart from the bleak, featureless stretch of land divided by a narrow strip of water.

The Liberation Tigers of Tamil Eelam

Terrorists in the eyes of some, freedom fighters to others, the **Liberation Tigers of Tamil Eelam** (LTTE), popularly known as the **Tamil Tigers**, are one of the world's most committed, effective and ruthless militant organizations. The LTTE was founded in the early 1970s, one of a string of paramilitary groups established by young Tamils in response to the decades of official discrimination meted out by the Sinhalese governments of Colombo to the Tamils of the north and east. The failure of the older Tamil politicians to secure justice for Tamils within the island's flawed parliamentary democracy drove many young Tamils to espouse violence, while the heavy-handed behaviour of the Sinhalese-dominated Sri Lankan Army and police in Tamil areas added to the discontent.

All these groups of young militants called for the establishment of an independent Tamil state in the north and east of the island, to be called **Eelam** ("Precious Land"), and a number received training from special Indian government forces who were initially sympathetic to their cause. The LTTE gradually rose to pre-eminence thanks to its ruthless suppression of all competing political groups and the assassination of rival politicians, and by the beginning of the civil war in 1983, the LTTE had become the leading player in Tamil affairs.

At the heart of the LTTE's mystique lies their founder and leader, the enigmatic **Velupillai Prabhakaran** (born 1954). Legends about this reclusive leader abound. According to some, he was a shy and bookish student with a fascination for Napoleon and Alexander the Great, who turned militant when he saw an uncle burnt alive by Sinhalese mobs, and who later trained himself to endure pain by lying in sacks of chillies. Known as *Thambi*, or "Little Brother", Prabhakaran is held in quasi-religious veneration by his recruits, and has proved a consummate political survivor who has evaded capture for two decades to emerge, in post-peace negotiations, as the self-styled "President of Tamil Eelam". He has also proved a gifted military strategist, although reports suggest that much of the LTTE's earlier engagements were based on the study of *Rambo* and Arnold Schwarzenegger videos – a classic example of life imitating (bad) art.

The LTTE began life as a classic guerrilla operation, harrying the (to begin with) far better-equipped and numerically superior forces of the Sri Lankan Army and later the Indian Peacekeeping Force (IPKF; see p.426) with hit-and-run attacks, before retreating back into the countryside and blending with local populations. These guerrilla tactics have been mixed with bloody and attention-grabbing attacks such as that at Anuradhapura in 1985, when dozens of civilians and pilgrims were gunned

North to Mannar

Some 45km from Vavuniya, north of the A14, lies the remote village of **MADHU**, the most important place of Christian pilgrimage in Sri Lanka. The large, nineteenth-century Portuguese-style **church** here is home to the allegedly miraculous statue of **Our Lady of Madhu**. The image was brought to Madhu in 1670 by Catholics fleeing Dutch persecution in the Mannar area, and subsequently became revered for its magical qualities, particularly its supposed ability to protect devotees against snakebites. In characteristic Sri Lankan fashion, the shrine has become popular even amongst non-Christians – some half a million people attended a festival here following the ceasefire in 2002. **Buses** runs from Mannar and Vavuniya to Madhu every couple of hours, taking about two hours to make the journey; the church lies within LTTE-controlled territory, so you'll have to negotiate Sri Lankan Army and LTTE checkpoints as well as baggage searches.

down by LTTE soldiers in the symbolic centre of Sinhalese culture. The LTTE also pioneered the gruesome practice of **suicide bombing** (whose technology they are believed to have exported to militant Palestinian organizations such as Hamas), with notable attacks against Colombo, the international airport and the Temple of the Tooth in Kandy, amongst many others. Suicide bombers have also been used in a string of high-profile **political assassinations** – victims have included former Indian prime minister Rajiv Gandhi in 1991, and Sri Lankan prime minister Ranasinghe Premadasa in 1993. As the war progressed and the LTTE acquired better armaments and military know-how, they gradually began to function more as a conventional army – exemplified by their seizure of Elephant Pass, at the southern end of the Jaffna Peninsula, from the heavily entrenched forces of the SLA in 2000.

The LTTE's ability to take on and defeat the huge forces of the Indian army and Sri Lankan armies reflects its legendary discipline and commitment to the cause, fostered by relentless **political indoctrination** and quasi-monastic **discipline**. Alcohol and smoking are banned, while adultery is punishable by death. In addition, hardly any LTTE fighters are ever captured alive, thanks to the phials of cyanide which all cadres wear around their necks. They also – by Asian standards at least – have impeccable **feminist** credentials. The shortage of men of fighting age has led to many women – the so-called "Freedom Birds", memorably described by English writer William Dalrymple as "paramilitary feminist death squads" – being absorbed into the LTTE military apparatus and often pitched into its toughest fighting engagements. The LTTE have also proved themselves capable **administrators**, having taken on the role of an unofficial government in areas which fell under their control during the civil war; they continue to function as the de facto local government in large parts of the Vanni.

Attitudes towards the LTTE remain divided. In the early years of the civil war they were widely regarded as heroes standing up for the rights of Tamils in a way which older politicians had failed to do. As the conflict dragged on, however, opinions changed. The LTTE's massacres of rival politicians and of anyone suspected of collaborating with the Sinhalese; their use of child soldiers and habit of extorting money under duress from Tamils at home and abroad; and their indiscriminate use of suicide bombers have earned them censure in the eyes of the world and led to them being classified, until recently, as a terrorist organization. Whether they are now fully committed to making the transition to peace remains the single most vital question in the entire peace process.

Beyond Madhu, **Mannar Island** pokes a finger westwards towards India. The island is virtually connected to the mainland, to which it's joined by a bridge; it's also the closest part of Sri Lanka to India, and was formerly the starting point for the ferry to that country, suspended since 1983. Mannar was long famous for its **pearl banks**, which were exploited from antiquity until the colonial period: as late as 1905, some five thousand divers recovered a staggering eighty million oysters here in a single season – they also provided the inspiration for Bizet's *The Pearl Fishers*, the only opera ever to be set in Sri Lanka. Arab traders also flocked to Mannar, introducing the island's donkeys (an animal virtually unknown elsewhere in Sri Lanka), and planting the baobab trees which remain another of the island's distinctive features. Mannar suffered greatly during the war, when its position close to India made it a major conduit for refugees fleeing the country. The island's large Muslim population, a legacy of its years of Arab trade, was driven out by the LTTE in 1990, though the local population still includes many Catholics – some forty percent, the highest proportion of anywhere in Sri Lanka.

The main settlement is the woebegone town of **Mannar**, at the island's eastern end. The main sight is the imposing **Portuguese fort** (later strengthened by the Dutch), near the entrance to town. A couple of kilometres south of town lies a famous **baobab tree**, said to be the largest tree in Asia, with a circumference of 20m; it's thought to have been planted in 1477. Mannar has a couple of simple but acceptable **places to stay**: the *Star Guest House*, on Moor Street in the town centre near the Bank of Ceylon (☏023-223 2177; ❶, ❷ with a/c); and the slightly smarter *Manjula Inn*, also in the town centre on 2nd Cross Street (☏023-223 2037; ❷) – it's best to book in advance at the latter.

At the far, western end of the island, the small town of **Talaimannar** was formerly the departure point for ferries to India, though it's now largely deserted in the wake of fighting during the war. West of here, a chain of islets and sandbanks known as **Adam's Bridge** stretch all the way to India, 30km distant. According to the *Ramayana*, these were the stepping stones used by the monkey god Hanuman to travel from India to Lanka, and they also served as the causeway by which the earliest human settlers reached the island some 250,000 to 300,000 years ago. These sandbanks lie less than two metres under water in many places, and may only have been submerged as recently as 1480, according to temple records from Rameswaram in India.

Jaffna

Poised close to the northernmost tip of the island, the war-torn town of **JAFFNA** lay at the heart of many of the civil war's fiercest struggles, and symbolizes more than anywhere else in Sri Lanka the terrors, absurdities and pointless destructiveness of the war years – such was the town's symbolic importance that when government forces captured it in 1995, the LTTE marched the town's entire population out into the surrounding countryside, leaving the advancing army to occupy a ghost town. Inaccessible for two decades to all but enterprising journalists and aid workers, Jaffna is now at last back in the public domain: war-torn but still unexpectedly vibrant and, in places, strangely beautiful. And although the effort of reaching the place is still considerable, anyone who makes it this far will be richly rewarded.

Jaffna is closer to India than to Colombo, and in many ways the town looks across the Palk Strait to the Indian state of Tamil Nadu rather than to Sinhalese Sri Lanka for much of its cultural and political inspiration. Arriving here can come as something of a culture shock if you've spent a while in the rest of the island, and even the most casual visitor will notice the profound **Indian influence** here, exemplified by the replacement of the Buddhist dagoba with the Hindu gopuram, and by the switch from the singsong cadences of Sinhala to the quickfire intonations of Tamil – not to mention myriad other details, like the sultry Indian pop music which blares out of shops and cafés, and the quasi-subcontinental hordes of kamikaze cyclists who rattle around the congested streets. Yet although there's a fair bit of India in Jaffna, the town has its own unique and complex identity, shaped, in true Sri Lankan fashion, by a wide cross-section of influences, including Muslim, Portuguese, Dutch, British – and even Sinhalese. Although Hinduism remains the dominant religion, Christianity is also strong, and the town presents an intriguing mixture of Tamil and European elements, with colourful temples set next to huge churches, and streets of a beguiling, faded colonial charm dotted with old Dutch and British residences. Perhaps most striking of all, however, is the sense of cultural

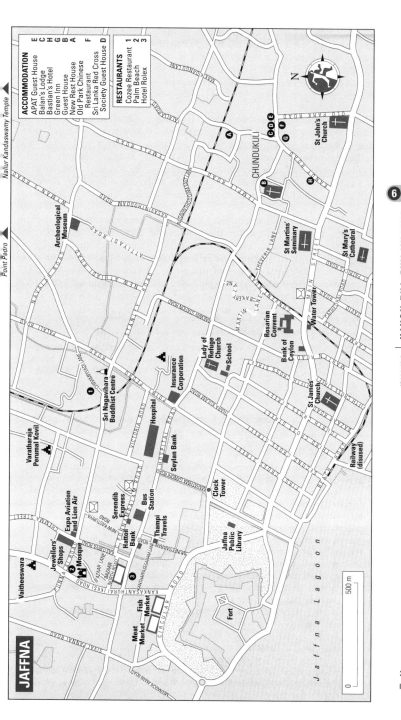

JAFFNA

Nailur Kandaswamy Temple ►

Point Pedro ►

ACCOMMODATION
APAT Guest House — E
Balan's Lodge — C
Bastian's Hotel — H
Green Inn — G
Guest House — B
New Rest House — A
Old Park Chinese Restaurant — F
Sri Lanka Red Cross Society Guest House — D

RESTAURANTS
Cozee Restaurant — 1
Palm Beach — 2
Hotel Rolex — 3

N

CHUNDUKULI

St John's Church

St Martins' Seminary

St Mary's Cathedral

Archeological Museum

ATTIYADI ROAD

Sri Nagavihara Buddhist Centre

Varatharaja Perumal Kovil

Vaitheeswara

Jewellers' Shops

Expo Aviation and Lion Air

Mosque

Serendib Express

Hatton Bank

Thampi Travels

Bus Station

Seylan Bank

Hospital

Insurance Corporation

Lady of Refuge Church

School

Rosarian Convent

Bank of Ceylon

Water Tower

St James' Church

Railway (disused)

Clock Tower

Jaffna Public Library

Fort

Meat Market

Fish Market

CIRCULAR ROAD

Jaffna Lagoon

500 m

0

sophistication here, embodied physically by the famous Jaffna library, and more intangibly by the remarkably cosmopolitan and highly educated populace who, despite battling for almost half a century against institutionalized racism and devastating civil war, retain a charm, curiosity and intelligence which is one of Jaffna's most unexpected but memorable attractions.

Some history

The Jaffna Peninsula has always been a focus for **Tamil settlement** in Sri Lanka, thanks to its proximity to the Tamil heartlands of India, not much more than 50km away across the Palk Strait. The earliest settlers arrived as far back as the second or third century BC, and this population was constantly supplemented over successive centuries by migrants, mercenaries and assorted adventurers. Interestingly, some of these early settlers may have been Buddhist rather than Hindu, as borne out by the enigmatic cluster of dagobas at Kantharodai (see p.404).

There are few records of the Jaffna region's early history, but by the thirteenth century, as the great Sinhalese civilizations of Anuradhapura and Polonnaruwa had fallen into terminal decline, Jaffna had developed into the capital of a powerful Tamil kingdom known as **Jaffnapatam**. In 1284, a Pandyan general, Arya Chakravati, seized control of the north. Over the next fifty years, his successors extended their power gradually southwards, gaining control of Mannar and its valuable pearl industry and continuing to push south. For a

---

Getting to Jaffna

Getting to Jaffna by **bus** is a long hard slog; it's infinitely easier **to fly** from Colombo. There are currently no **train** services to Jaffna, though this may change if the peace process continues successfully – as, indeed, may all the other information outlined below.

By bus

There are direct a/c **buses** to Jaffna **from Colombo** (2–3 daily; Rs.1000). A number of places along the Galle Rd in Wellawatta run services (precise details and operators change frequently); try Thampi Travels, at 296/D4 Galle Rd, Wellawatta (☎011-236 0959, ⑤554 0002).

From anywhere else, the journey is rather more problematic, and requires taking at least five different buses. The first place to aim for is **Anuradhapura**, from where there are frequent buses north to **Vavuniya** (every 30min). From Vavuniya you'll need to take a second bus for the thirty-minute trip to the **border** separating the areas controlled by the LTTE and the SLA. This is tantamount to a national border crossing, with passport and customs checks, and baggage searches (though these checks are much less stringent as you head south, out of LTTE territory). Note that you're not technically allowed to take binoculars or video cameras into LTTE territory; you might be able to argue your way around this regulation, but don't count on it. You'll first reach the **SLA checkpoint** at Omantai. Having negotiated this, you'll need to catch another bus a further 5km down the road to the **LTTE checkpoint**. Here you have to purchase and fill in a form (Rs.2) – it's in Tamil only, so you'll have to enlist the help of one of the charmless functionaries who man the checkpoint. The exact purpose of this form is unclear, though it's as well to keep it with your passport during your entire stay in the north.

Having entered LTTE territory, you'll have to catch a third bus to **Pallai**, a journey of around three hours. There are far fewer buses on the LTTE side of the border, so you face a potentially long wait – anything up to two or three hours – before you can get on a vehicle. The road itself is in poor condition (although it's being rapidly

brief period in the mid-fourteenth century they gained control of the whole of the west coast almost as far as Colombo – the greatest expansion of Tamil power in the history of Sri Lanka. In the fifteenth century, Parakramabahu VI (1411–1465), king of Kotte, turned the tables, gaining control of the whole of the north by 1450; the Tamil kingdom quickly re-established its independence, however.

Half a century later, Jaffna was faced with a new kind of invader. The **Portuguese** coveted the kingdom, since its strategic position next to the Palk Strait allowed it to control the sea route between east and west India, and also because its ruler had the revenues of the huge pearl banks at Mannar. The Portuguese were taxing the pearl industry as early as 1513, and they spent much of the sixteenth century harassing the rulers of Jaffna from their base in Mannar and converting large numbers of the local fishermen to Catholicism – though it wasn't until 1621 that they finally seized Jaffna itself. The Portuguese spent much of their time destroying Hindu temples and building churches in their place, though God appears not to have looked favourably upon their actions, since in 1658 they were evicted from Jaffna by the **Dutch**. The Dutch gave the town an imposing fort before the British took over in 1796. Jaffna became something of a backwater during the later colonial era, as the ports of Galle and, later, Colombo emerged in the south, although the railway arrived in 1905 and Jaffna Tamils continued to thrive under the British administration. Following **independence**, Jaffna found itself increasingly at the centre of the island's growing ethnic storm,

improved), which further slows your progress. At **Pallai** there's a second SLA check-point controlling access to the Jaffna Peninsula, much of which is still in SLA hands. Checks are less stringent here – you'll probably just be waved through – but once again you'll need to find another bus once you're through the checkpoint. This will take you to **Jaffna** itself (1hr 30min). Don't expect to do the journey from Anuradhapura in much under twelve hours, and try not to do it on Sundays, when buses are even more scarce in LTTE territory. You could also break your journey overnight at Kilinochchi (see p.391).

Given the hassles of the journey, you might consider **hiring your own vehicle** in Anuradhapura or Vavuniya – drivers offering rides to Jaffna hang out around the bus station in the latter place; just ask around, or try in one of the small cafés on the opposite side of the road from the station. Although it's still a long drive, you'll at least avoid the constant hanging around for buses, and you should also be fast-tracked through the various checkpoints. Count on US$50 or more for the ride from Anuradhapura, if you can find a driver willing to do the trip; you might find it easier to pick up a driver and vehicle in Vavuniya, whose Tamil population are more familiar and comfortable with the journey and its attendant bureaucracy. One final possibility is to find space in a **van or truck** heading from Vavuniya to Jaffna (Rs.800–1000) – again, this is likely to be significantly quicker than the buses. There are usually a few drivers hanging around on the main road in Vavuniya, on the opposite side of the road just south of the bus station.

By plane

Given the exhausting nature of the journey by bus, there's every incentive to fly. Jaffna is served by daily services from three companies: **Expo Aviation**, 466 Galle Rd, Kollupitiya ☎011-451 2666,; **Lionair**, 14 Trelawney Place, Bambalapitiya ☎011-451 5615, ✉lionairsales@sierra.lk; and **Serendib Express**, 500 Galle Rd, Wellawatta ☎011-250 5632, ⊛www.serendibexpress.com. The flight lasts one hour and costs around US$42 one-way, $75 return.

If you want to leave Jaffna by **local bus**, you'll have to follow the route described in the box on p.396 in reverse. Alternatively, several nonstop **a/c buses** leave for Colombo daily at around 8am – various places advertise these services around town, or ask at Thampi travel agents. The fare is Rs.1000. If you want to use one of these buses to save messing around with the local services, but you don't want to go all the way to Colombo, you'll still have to pay the full fare, and make it clear both when booking the ticket and boarding the bus where you want to get off. Some services go via Kandy, though not all go through Anuradhapura (although all pass close by).

There are between three and seven **flights** daily from Jaffna to Colombo operated by three companies: Lionair (often spelled "Llionair" on signs around Jaffna), 1T Stanley Rd ☏021-222 6026; Expo Aviation, 1E Stanley Rd, ☏&℉021-222 3891, ℮jaffna @expoavi.com; and Serendib Express, 13 Power House Rd ☏021-222 3916; Lionair is the biggest and most professional of the three, though also more expensive. Fares are around US$40/70 (single/return) on Lionair, and US$25/45 on Serendib and Expo Air.

6

JAFFNA AND THE NORTH | Jaffna

with regular clashes between young Tamil militants and Sinhalese soldiers and police culminating in the infamous destruction of the Jaffna library by government thugs in 1981. The burning of the library, however, was just a small foretaste of the destruction to come during the **civil war** itself, during which large parts of the centre were reduced to rubble by the various battles which raged in and around the town (see p.400).

Arrival and accommodation

Buses arrive right in the middle of Jaffna at the bus station on Hospital Road, the main road in the modern town centre. A tuktuk from here to the hotel area of **Chundukuli** will cost around Rs.70. (Note that, although there are usually a few tuktuks hanging around the bus station, there's an overall shortage in town, and it can be difficult to find one in Chundukuli.) **Flights** from Colombo arrive at Palali Airport, around 15km north of Jaffna; your airline should provide transport into town from here. Of the several **banks** along Hospital Road, Seylan Bank (Visa) and Commercial Bank (Visa and MasterCard) both have ATMs which accept foreign cards.

The well set-up **Thampi travels**, in the town centre at 90 Kanthappasegaram Road (☏021-222 2504, ℉222 2040), can see to most travel needs, including reservations on flights and buses to Colombo. They also have a/c cars and vans with driver for hire to explore the area around Jaffna; count on around US$30 per day.

Accommodation

Most **accommodation** in Jaffna is clustered in the suburb of **Chundukuli**. Room rates in Jaffna are about fifty percent more expensive than anywhere else in Sri Lanka (and there's a real shortage during the Nallur festival, when you should book ahead). Jaffna is also one of the few places in Sri Lanka where en suite doesn't come as standard.

APAT Guest House 43 Kandy Rd ☏077-773 8221. A cheap if rather basic option, with acceptable though gloomy rooms including doubles, triples and one very cheap single; some share a clean communal bathroom. Free morning and evening tea, but no food. ❷

Balan's Lodge (also known as *Palan's Lodge*) 71 Kandy Rd ☏021-222 3248. Emergency option, with three small and basic (but expensive) en-suite rooms, and a minuscule, bathroom-less single (Rs.400). ❷
Bastian's Hotel 37 Kandy Rd ☏021-222 2605, ℉222 3447. Pleasant-looking hotel, though the

rooms are disappointingly gloomy and expensive – those with shared bath are much better value than those with en suite. By the time you read this, a block of brand new rooms with a/c and private bathrooms should also be available. The hotel restaurant is a popular drinking hole, though the food is very average. Shared bath ❷, en suite ❹

Green Inn 60 Kandy Rd ℡ 021-222 3898, ⒻAX 222 2298. Pleasant but expensive en-suite rooms (and the noisy resident dog is a total pain). Don't expect any food, despite the large sign saying "Restaurant". ❸

Guest House US Multi Centre, 874 Hospital Rd ℡ 077-724 5810. Nameless guest house-cum-computer shop with six poky but comfortable doubles and triples, all with fridge and a/c. ❸

New Rest House Just north of Kandy Rd, opposite the Human Rights building ℡ 021-222 5928. The best-value place in town, with four simple but clean and comfortable rooms in a pleasant modern house. All meals available. ❷

Old Park Chinese Restaurant 40 Kandy Rd ℡ 021-222 3790. The best accommodation and food (see p.404) in Jaffna, with spotless and spacious a/c rooms – nothing fancy, but very comfortable. ❺

Sri Lanka Red Cross Society Guest House 73 Kandy Rd ℡ 021-222 2561. The cheapest place in town, with accommodation in two- and four-bed dorms for Rs.250 per person, plus one en-suite double. It's very basic, but bearable. No food or drink. ❷

The Town

Jaffna town is a curious mixture: in places the effects of two decades of vicious fighting are all too apparent; in others, you might think that the war never even happened. Although large areas surrounding the centre show the tragic signs of wartime damage, with huge swathes of razed ground dotted with scrub-covered ruins, the town centre itself remains surprisingly intact, vibrant and seemingly untouched by the war years, while many of the outlying districts preserve a sedate colonial air, dotted with enormous churches, venerable old religious foundations and atmospheric Dutch-era villas.

The Fort and around

Immediately south of the modern centre lies the town's immense **fort**. The largest Dutch fort in Asia, this huge structure was built on the site of the former Portuguese stronghold in the characteristic star shape favoured by the Dutch (the pointed bastions offered greater protection against cannon fire). The inner defences were completed in 1680 and the outer ring of bastions in 1792, though just three years after it was completed, the fort was surrendered to the British without a shot being fired. Sadly, having survived two hundred years without seeing action, the fort was finally pressed into military service during the civil war, when the outer defences were repeatedly bombarded by both sides and the old Dutch buildings inside, including the beautiful **Groote Kerk** ("Great Church"), destroyed. The fort is still in military use, and currently off limits. A walk around the outside gives some idea of the strength of the massive exterior walls, although war damage, tangles of barbed wire and the luxuriant spread of unchecked vegetation make it difficult to see anything very clearly.

The south side of the fort is bounded by the calm, shallow waters of the **Jaffna lagoon**, the ocean inlet which divides the Jaffna Peninsula from the rest of Sri Lanka (and from the islands of Kayts and Karaitivu). This is one of the few places in town where you can actually reach the lagoon, since most of the shoreline has been fenced off by the SLA; the low-lying bridge-cum-causeway which connects Jaffna to Kayts can be seen disappearing into the waters close to the fort.

The devastation inflicted on the area surrounding the fort is sobering. This entire quarter has been razed almost completely to the ground, with just a handful of buildings standing in incongruous isolation amidst a wilderness of

The sieges of Jaffna

As the principal town of the north and the symbolic heart of Tamil culture in Sri Lanka, Jaffna played a pivotal – and tragic – role in the **civil war**. The town was one of the flashpoints in the rising ethnic tension which preceded the war, and the thuggish behaviour of Sinhalese troops and police stationed here played a major part in fostering the rise of the many militant Tamil groups, including the LTTE, that emerged in the north in the late 1970s and early 1980s.

During the opening phase of the war, from 1983 to 1987, the LTTE gradually acquired control over much of the town and the surrounding peninsula, rendering SLA troops stationed in the area increasingly powerless. In the end, however, the first counterattack against the LTTE in Jaffna came not from the SLA but from the **Indian Peace Keeping Force** (IPKF; see p.426), who had arrived to police a cease-fire between the two sides and ensure fair treatment for the embattled Tamils – though in the event, they became embroiled in the fighting themselves and ended up attacking the people they had allegedly come to protect. In October 1987 the IPKF attacked Jaffna in an offensive called **Operation Pawan**, meaning "wind". This was expected to last just two days, though in the event the Indian advance became bogged down by the LTTE's determined resistance and a bloodbath ensued, with massive civilian casualties caused by indiscriminate IPKF shelling and bombing. IPKF forces were also widely accused of rape, looting and the random murder of civilians – most notoriously the storming of Jaffna hospital and the massacre of many of its patients. In the end it took three weeks of vicious street-by-street fighting before the IPKF could claim control of Jaffna.

The LTTE retreated into the countryside, from where they continued to harry the IPKF until the latter's **withdrawal** from Sri Lanka in March 1990, at which point the LTTE simply reoccupied Jaffna. A brief ceasefire followed, though hostilities swiftly resumed. In June 1990 the LTTE captured and massacred around eight hundred Sinhalese policemen stationed in the east of the island. In retaliation, the SLA went on the warpath once more, advancing across the Jaffna Peninsula and subjecting Jaffna to a **second siege**. This proved a far more protracted affair than the first. Once again, Jaffna was subjected to indiscriminate shelling and bombing (at one point, the Sri Lankan air force even dropped barrels of excrement on the streets), while helicopter gunships strafed the town, killing thousands of civilians. Supplies of food and medicine were cut off, while temples, schools and hospitals were all bombed – the government blamed pilot error and weather conditions, although few believed this. At the same time, the Sinhalese troops and others who had been trapped in Jaffna at the sudden resumption of hostilities took refuge in the town's fort, where they were held by LTTE forces for three months – a bizarre siege within a siege – until a raid by a force of SLA commandos succeeded in rescuing them. Although the SLA commandos attempted to gain a foothold in the town, they were soon forced to flee, leaving the LTTE to reclaim Jaffna fort – a symbolic, if ultimately useless, victory.

Jaffna finally fell to the SLA in December 1995. As they had done in 1987, LTTE forces disappeared back into the countryside and merged with the local population, whilst continuing to attack the SLA. At the time of the **ceasefire** in 2002, the SLA retained control of Jaffna town and much of the peninsula (though the LTTE's capture of Elephant Pass had rendered their position increasingly precarious) – thus explaining the anomaly whereby Jaffna, the most important Tamil town in Sri Lanka, remains to this day under the control of Sinhalese forces.

scrub and ruins – much of it still mined. The entire area exudes a sense of profound desolation, all the stranger for its close proximity to the bustling modern town centre. The most notable building hereabouts is the **Jaffna Public Library**, located in an impressive if rather functional

Indo-Saracenic-style building just east of the fort. The original library was torched by pro-government Sinhalese mobs during election riots in 1981, an act of vandalism which reduced one of South Asia's greatest public collections (including many irreplaceable works of Tamil literature) to ashes – a key event in the build-up to the civil war which erupted two years later. In a symbolic gesture, this was the first major public building to be rebuilt following the ceasefire, though ironically the new building had still not been opened at the time of writing due to infighting between rival Tamil political factions.

Pointing skywards in distinctive isolation just northeast of the library is the town's **clocktower**, an endearing architectural mongrel wantonly mixing Islamic and Gothic styles. The tower – designed by British architect J.G. Smither, who was also responsible for Colombo's Old Town Hall and National Museum – was built in 1875 to commemorate a visit by the then Prince of Wales. Fittingly enough, the four clocks which now adorn this monstrous carbuncle were presented by the current Prince of Wales, Prince Charles – a very British gift, although sadly none of the clocks can agree on the correct time, whilst one has lost its hands completely.

The new town

Just north of the clocktower, **Hospital Road** forms the spine of the modern centre, a vibrant commercial district which shows remarkably few traces of the devastation visited on the area surrounding the fort – almost the only traces of the war years are the lovingly preserved Morris Minors, Morris Oxfords, Austin Cambridges and other vintage cars, kept going through the long decades of the conflict, which still outnumber modern vehicles hereabouts.

Just northwest of the town centre, up Kankesanthurai (KKS) Road, a tall gopuram, painted an unusually plain grey-blue, announces the **Vaitheeswara Temple**, the most interesting of central Jaffna's numerous Hindu temples. Dedicated to Shiva, it was built during the Dutch era by an influential local merchant. At its centre lies a richly decorated stone shrine, painted in orange hues and surrounded by a beautiful old wooden-roofed ambulatory, rather like a Dutch verandah, complete with Doric columns, its doorways picked out in faded pastel colours. A small tank sits next to it.

A short way east of the Vaitheeswara Temple and north of the bus station is **Kasturiya Road**, the heart of Jaffna's celebrated **jewellery industry**, and the town's equivalent to the colourful Sea Street in Colombo. The street is home to a long sequence of jewellers, mainly trading in gold, each announced by a lurid Tamil sign set up on the pavement outside. Continue east along Stanley Road to reach the **Varatharaja Perumal Kovil**, a large but decidedly kitsch temple, with a huge, polychromatic gopuram and brightly coloured buildings – the whole ensemble is very Disneyland, though rather less atmospheric than the Vaitheeswara.

East of the centre

Heading east from the Varatharaja Perumal Kovil, away from the centre, Jaffna assumes a more residential and colonial character, with quiet, tree-shaded streets lined by sedate – if decaying – Dutch villas and a string of imposing churches. Heading east along Stanley Road, then a block north to Navalar Road, brings you to Jaffna's **Archeological Museum** (Mon–Sat 9am–5pm; donation), which has miraculously survived the war intact, although many of the display cabinets are broken and covered in dust. Exhibits include several small and beautiful wooden *vahanams* (chariots for gods) such as horses, elephants, nandis, and a fetching wooden model of Harischandra – the man who never told a lie – and his wives. Look out, too, for the remains of various stone Buddhas, a pair of *sri pada* found at Kantharodai, a couple of attractively carved Indian-style wooden doors and pillars and a memorably amateurish portrait of the young Queen Victoria, in which that dignified lady appears sticking her tongue out at the viewer; the tears in the canvas are apparently bullet holes.

From here you're within striking distance of the Nallur Kandaswamy Temple (see below). Alternatively, turn due south down to **Main Street**. Although Hospital Road has now taken over as the town's principal commercial thoroughfare, Main Street is still the spine of the finest surviving quarter of colonial Jaffna, notable for a sequence of remarkably large – if otherwise unexceptionable – churches, as well as two of Jaffna's most magical colonial survivors. The first is the **Rosarian Convent**, occupying a beautiful sequence of Dutch colonial buildings which are now home to the Rosarian Sisters, well known hereabouts for their home-made wine and grape juice (which you may find for sale in town – try *Bastian Hotel*). A little further east along Main Street is the equally atmospheric **St Martin's Seminary**, a gorgeous Victorian neo-Gothic period piece dating from the 1880s, with verandahed buildings and a little musty chapel in the middle.

Just south of St Martin's Seminary stands the largest of Jaffna's outsize churches, the gigantic **St Mary's Cathedral**; it's quasi-Portuguese in style, although it actually dates from the Dutch era, and built on a positively industrial scale, with a pleasingly simple interior.

Nallur Kandaswamy Temple

Jaffna's most notable sight is the large **Nallur Kandaswamy Temple**, about 2km northeast of the town centre, or 1km from Chundukuli. Dedicated to Murugam (known to the Buddhist Sinhalese as Kataragama – see p.198), this is the most impressive Hindu temple in Sri Lanka, and the only one on the island to rival the great shrines of India. The original temple is thought to date back to the mid-fifteenth century, though it was destroyed in 1620 by the Portuguese. The present structure was begun in 1807 and has now developed into an enormous religious complex, surrounded by red-and-white striped walls. There are numerous shrines inside, richly decorated corridors framed in rows of golden arches and a beautiful courtyard with a large tank. Men must remove their shirts before entering. There are no less than six **pujas** daily, with three between 4pm and 5pm, the best time to visit.

The temple is a fascinating place to visit at any time, but becomes unforgettable during the latter stages of the **Nallur Festival**, which runs for 26 days, finishing on the poya day in August. The crowds of festival-goers rival those at the far better-known Kandy Esala Perahera, and many Jaffna expatriates return for the celebrations. Men dress in fresh white sarongs, while ladies don their best saris, transforming the entire temple complex into a vast a sea of intense blues, reds and greens. Held on the 24th of the 26 days, the **Ther** festival is the biggest night, when an enormous chariot is pulled around the town by huge crowds of sarong-clad men; on the following day, particularly enthusiastic devotees mortify themselves by driving skewers through their bodies in honour of the god and making their way to the shrine accompanied by drumming and piping, stopping periodically to dance en route. Even more extraordinary are the devotees who, using skewers driven through their backs, suspend themselves from poles. These poles are then attached to the front of trucks and tractors, and the devotees are driven through town to the temple, dangling in front of their vehicle like bait on a fishing line. Suppliants who perform these self-mortifications believe that the god will protect them from

△ Nallur Kandaswamy Temple

any sense of pain. Many also carry a **kavadi**, the distinctive symbol of Murugam (or Kataragama), a semicircular yoke, placed across the shoulders, with peacock feathers at either end.

Eating

There aren't many culinary treats in Jaffna – and you'll get better South Indian **food** in Colombo. *Bastian's Hotel* (see p.398) is the liveliest place for a **drink**.

Cozee Restaurant Chirampiyadi Lane. Doesn't look like much, but popular with locals for its tasty and inexpensive Chinese and Indian (north and south) food, and even has its own tandoor oven – a rarity in Sri Lanka.

Old Park Chinese Restaurant 40 Kandy Rd, Chundukuli. The best food in town, with a big menu of cheap but mouthwatering Chinese dishes from around Rs.300 – try the fish in hot garlic sauce or the chili chicken with cadju nuts. You'll need to order at least a couple of hours in advance, however.

New Rest House Just north of Kandy Road (opposite the Human Rights building), Chundukuli. The only place in Chundukuli where you can get reliable food without pre-ordering, though there's only

a very limited choice (fried rice, noodles, and maybe burianis or rice and curry if you're lucky; other dishes are available if you order in advance). It's very cheap, however, with dishes for Rs.100–125.

Palm Beach Stanley Rd. Pleasant a/c restaurant with dirt-cheap South Indian standards including burianis, dosas, idlis – and pizza. Some items are only available after 6.30pm. No smoking and no alcohol.

Hotel Rolex Hospital Rd. Characterful and inexpensive little local café with an Indian-style curry buffet, short eats and excellent burianis (Rs.120) – rather more solid-looking than your average Sri Lankan place, complete with multicoloured lantern lights and sooty chandeliers.

The Jaffna Peninsula

The agricultural hinterland of Jaffna town – and the source of much of its former prosperity – is the **Jaffna Peninsula**, a narrow but fertile arc of land which adds a delicate flourish to the northern tip of Sri Lanka. The peninsula is virtually an island, physically and culturally almost completely detached from the rest of the country, and has always been far more densely populated than the more arid lands of the Vanni further south (although parts of the peninsula are now temporarily deserted thanks to the presence here of the controversial **high-security zones**; see box opposite).

The peninsula is host to a low-key but varied collection of sights, ranging from a string of impressive temples and a few pristine beaches to more unlikely attractions such as a miniature desert, miracle-working hot springs, and the childhood home of LTTE supremo Prabhakaran. **Buses** connect the peninsula's main towns, though there's a chronic shortage of vehicles, meaning infrequent services and horrible overcrowding. It's well worth hiring your own transport.

North of Jaffna

About 10km north of Jaffna, and 2km west of the village of Chunnakam on the main road to Kankesanturai, lies the curious archeological site of **Kantharodai**. It comprises an unusual huddle of around twenty miniature dagobas, ranging in height from 1m to 3m, crammed together in a small plot, along with the unexcavated bases of many other dagobas. The site is quite unlike anything else in Sri Lanka, and is of great antiquity, dating back at least two thousand years, though no one can quite agree on its exact purpose – a popular theory is that the dagobas enshrine the remains of Buddhist monks; others claim that they are "votive" dagobas erected in fulfilment of answered prayers.

A few kilometres north of Chunnakam at Tellipalai lies one of the peninsula's controversial **high security zones** (see box below). You'll need your own transport to go into the zone, and before entering you'll have to surrender your passport, along with any cameras, video cameras and mobile phones. A soldier will be assigned to travel with you for the length of your visit to prevent you from spying or wandering off into a minefield. From the entrance, you're allowed to drive up and down the road to the Keerimalai hot springs (see below), passing the bombed-out ruins of several deserted villages which have now been totally abandoned to – and largely swallowed up by – the encroaching jungle. The entire area offers a hauntingly strange example of the destruction wrought by the civil war, most disconcertingly in the large village immediately beyond the entrance to the zone, whose long main street achieves a positively *Marie Celeste*-like effect: its buildings still largely intact but now utterly deserted; the painted signs on its half-ruined shopfronts still visible between the branches of the trees and creepers which are slowly reclaiming it for the jungle.

A couple of large temples – the **Naguleswaram** and **Maviddapuram** – survive in proud isolation towards the northern edge of the peninsula. Both have suffered significant bomb damage but remain busy with visitors, preserving a stubborn flicker of religious life amidst the surrounding desolation. A few metres past the Naguleswaram temple on the peninsula's northern shore are the **Keerimalai** hot springs, whose therapeutic powers have been recognized since the time of the *Mahabharata*: a princess whose face had been transformed to resemble a horse and an Indian holy man who resembled a mongoose both found cures here, and a steady string of bathers now follow in their footsteps. Security is very tight, however, and unless you fancy joining the locals for a refreshing dip in the neat little concrete pool in which the springs have been captured (bring a towel), there's nothing to see or do, and you're currently unable to travel any further, or to explore the enticing beaches which stretch away from here in either direction.

High-security zones

At the time of the ceasefire in 2002, the Sri Lankan Army controlled the Jaffna Peninsula, and continues to maintain a significant military presence here, visible in the gun emplacements and barbed wire which litter the streets of Jaffna, and the checkpoints which dot the roads. Nowhere, however, is the SLA presence more obvious – or more controversial – than in their eighteen **high-security zones** (HSZs). Scattered across the peninsula and occupying over a quarter of its land area, the heavily militarized HSZs serve as the basis of SLA control of the peninsula: the local population has been evicted from them, and access to them remains tightly restricted. Not surprisingly, HSZs have become an increasing bone of contention during the peace process. Locals live with a hostile occupying army in their midst, while the thirty thousand or so Sri Lankan soldiers manning the zones work in constant fear that, should hostilities resume, they will find themselves isolated in the heart of enemy territory.

Dismantling the HSZs is a leading objective of the LTTE, who have drawn attention to the humanitarian plight of the thousands of Tamils evicted from their homes within. Meanwhile, the Sri Lankan government is reluctant to hand back these strategically vital areas to the LTTE until they are confident of lasting peace, and have made LTTE disarmament in the peninsula a precondition of the zones' return to civilian use. Even the Norwegian peace negotiators have urged the retention of the HSZs for the time being, arguing that any disturbance in the delicate balance of power in the peninsula would potentially undermine negotiations.

Northeast to Point Pedro

The road northeast from Jaffna to Point Pedro passes several points of interest. About 5km along near the main road, the village of **Kopai** is home to an enormous **LTTE cemetery**, containing the neatly ordered graves of some two thousand cadres killed in the civil war – a sobering sight. A couple of kilometres further along is the **Nilavarai well**, according to legend the work of Rama himself, who created it by sticking an arrow into the ground to assuage his thirst. Its waters (which are said to be bottomless) are a striking aquamarine colour and appear to be somehow connected directly to the sea: the water is fresh near the top, but becomes increasingly salty the deeper you go.

On the north shore of the peninsula, 30km from Jaffna, the fishing village of **VELVETTITURAI** (widely abbreviated to "VVT") is famous nowadays principally as the birthplace of the leader of the LTTE, **Velupillai Prabhakaran** (see box on p.392). Some 500km west of the town centre on the road to Kankesanturai, his childhood home now attracts a steady stream of visitors, many of whom have recorded their flattering views of the great leader in graffiti. Outside, a sign solemnly describes Prabhakaran as "The President of Tamil Eelam". Just east of Prabhakaran's house lies the large **Amman Temple**, whose newly resurrected festival in April draws enormous crowds. **Buses** to VVT run hourly from Jaffna's bus station.

Point Pedro and around

The Jaffna Peninsula's second largest town, busy little **POINT PEDRO** ("PPD"), stands at the extreme northeastern tip of the peninsula. There's not much to see here, although the curious could seek out the **Theru Moodi Madam**, a traditional travellers' rest house built across a road on the east side of town, and the chintzy little **St Thomas's Church**, dating from the 1860s, on the seafront west of the centre – one of several large churches which dot the town. Just west of here, **Point Pedro Lighthouse** marks the most northerly point in Sri Lanka. About 2km east of the lighthouse is one of the peninsula's most attractive **beaches** – safe to visit and popular with locals, although if you turn round you'll have a vista of barbed wire and military bunkers.

South of the lighthouse lies the strange **Manalkadu Desert**, an extensive range of coastal sand dunes. At the northern end of the desert, 5km from Point Pedro, is the village of **VALLIPURAM**. This was formerly one of the peninsula's principal towns, and the tiny settlement is still home to its second largest temple, which is thought to date back to the first century AD. A rather strange legend recounts that Vishnu himself appeared here in the form of a fish. About 2km south of here lie the remains of **St Anthony's Church**, built around 1900 and now picturesquely half-buried in the dunes.

There are **buses** roughly every thirty minutes from Jaffna's bus station to Point Pedro; buses on from Point Pedro to the Manalkadu Desert are infrequent; you might want to hire a tuktuk.

The islands

West of Jaffna, a string of **islands** straggle out into the waters of the Palk Bay towards India. Two of them – **Kayts** and **Karaitivu** – virtually join up with the mainland, to which they are connected by causeways, as is **Punkudutivu** further west. Punkudutivu is the starting point for ferries to **Nainativu**, home to two important religious shrines, and the remote and captivating island of **Delft**.

There are few specific sights to aim for. The point and pleasure of a trip here is in the journey, and in the subtle but memorable land- and seascapes, with the flat and largely uninhabited islands merging almost imperceptibly into the blue waters of the Jaffna lagoon and Palk Bay. There's also an undeniable pleasure in simply reaching such a remote and little-visited corner of Sri Lanka, and in discovering a relatively untroubled corner of the north – aside from the occasional checkpoint or ruined building, the war seems a long way away here.

As ever, public transport is sketchy and horribly overcrowded, with **buses** to Kayts and Punkudutivu every one to two hours

Kayts

Kayts is the largest of the islands and the closest to Jaffna – its eastern tip lies just over the lagoon from Jaffna town and is reached via a causeway through very shallow water, beyond which you'll have to negotiate the inevitable checkpoint. Like the other islands, Kayts is only lightly inhabited and largely devoid of traffic – a pancake-flat expanse studded with innumerable Palmyrah palms.

At the far (western) end of the island is **Kayts town** (actually little more than a sleepy village), just beyond which lie the scant remains of **Urundi Fort**, also known as Fort Eyrie, now no more than a couple of picturesquely decaying coral-stone walls which are being gradually swallowed up by vegetation. Urundi and Hammenhiel (see below) forts were originally built by the Portuguese to control this entrance to the Jaffna lagoon, though the Dutch neglected Urundi, concentrating their defences in Hammenhiel – of which there's a beautiful view from here, seemingly floating in the middle of the waters between Kayts and Karaitivu. Occasional **ferries** (4 daily) connect the islands of Karaitivu and Kayts, running close by Hammenhiel.

Back in Kayts town is the beautiful shell of the nineteenth-century **St James** church (the facade bears the date 1716, but the building actually dates from 1815): the facade and exterior walls survive, but the roof has gone and there's nothing inside but wooden scaffolding, giving the entire structure the appearance of an elaborate film prop.

There's a decent **beach** at **Velanai**, near the eastern end of Kayts and just a few kilometres from Jaffna.

Karaitivu and Punkudutivu

The most northerly of the islands, **Karaitivu**, is reached by road some 12km north of Jaffna. En route to the island, 10km from Jaffna, you'll pass the barn-like **Vaddukoddai Portuguese Church**, in whose churchyard lie 27 tombstones which were recently moved here for safekeeping from the Groote Kerk in Jaffna fort. Most are Dutch colonial; the oldest dates back to 1666. A kilometre further down the road is the **Punnalai Varatharaja Perumal Kovil**, dedicated to Vishnu and one of the peninsula's two oldest temples. The shrine holds an ancient stone tortoise which was apparently fished ashore here.

On the north coast of Karaitivu itself is **Casuarina Beach**, the peninsula's most popular, although it's not particularly clean. Swimming is safe (though the water is shallow), but there are no facilities beyond a few locals flogging drinks. Just off the southern tip of the island, in the waters between Karaitivu and Kayts, is the old Dutch fort of **Hammenhiel** – its name, literally "Heel of Ham", refers to the prosaic old Dutch belief that Sri Lanka resembled a leg of ham. The fort is a fine sight, seemingly floating on the waters of the lagoon, though it's still in operational use so you can't visit. There's also a good view of it from Urundi fort on Kayts (see p.407), or from one of the occasional **ferries** (4 daily) which make the short trip past Hammenhiel from Karaitivu to Kayts.

There are hourly **buses** to **Karainagar**, the main village on Karaitivu, from Jaffna's bus station. Infrequent services run direct to Casuarina Beach; alternatively take a tuktuk from Karainagar.

The island of **Punkudutivu** lies southeast of Kayts, to which it is connected by a four-kilometre causeway. There's nothing much to see here, although the journey across the causeway is unusual (you'll feel you're driving across the sea) and the village of **Kurikadduwan** ("KKD") on the island's southwest corner is the departure point for boats to Nainativu and Delft.

Nainativu

A couple of kilometres east of Punkudutivu lies the small island of **Nainativu**, just 10km from top to bottom, and a few kilometres wide. Immediately in front of the ferry jetty is the ornate **Naga Pooshani Ambal Kovil**, a Hindu temple sacred to the goddess Ambal – newborn babies are brought here to receive the goddess's blessings. The original temple was, as usual, destroyed by the Portuguese, and the large and impressive complex you see today dates from 1788; the gopuram was added in 1935. Thousands of people attend a major festival here in June/July.

A ten-minute walk south of here lies the **Nagadipa Vihara**, a rare place of Buddhist worship in the Hindu north. This marks the spot of the Buddha's second legendary visit to Sri Lanka, when he is said to have achieved the reconciliation of two warring naga kings.

There are hourly **buses** from Jaffna to Kurikadduwan on Punkudutivu, from where it's a fifteen-minute trip by **ferry** (7 daily) to Nainativu.

Delft

By the time you reach the island of **Delft**, named after the famous Dutch town, you'll begin to feel you're a long way from anywhere – although, despite its remoteness, the island was occupied by all three colonial powers. It's a place of bleak, minimalist beauty, criscrossed with coral-rock walls and boasting an unusual population of **wild ponies**, the descendants of those first introduced by the Portuguese – they're found mainly in the southern centre of the island.

Ferries from Kurikadduwan dock at the northeast corner of the island. A short distance west of the ferry dock lie the remains of the old Portuguese **fort** – better preserved than Urundi, though you'll still need a good imagination to make much sense of the remains. There's a nice **beach** just east of the fort, in the unlikely event that you have time to burn. South of the ferry dock lies a stumpy **baobab tree**, one of Central Africa's most distinctive species but almost unknown in Sri Lanka apart from this specimen and a few around Mannar. It's presumed to have been planted by Arab seamen.

Delft lies some 20km southwest of Punkudutivu island, an hour's journey by ferry from the town of Kurikadduwan, which is connected to Jaffna by hourly buses. There are only two ferries in each direction daily, so unless you can arrange accommodation locally or are prepared to camp, you'll only get about two hours on the island before you have to head back again. A single **bus** plies the island's main road. Your only other option is – unlikely as it might seem – to hire a tractor, though this won't be much quicker (and is much noisier) than walking.

A further 30km southwest of Delft lies the tiny island of **Kachchaitivu**, used as a base by passing Sri Lankan and Indian fishermen, but otherwise uninhabited, inaccessible, and boasting just a single man-made structure, the church of **St Anthony** – Sri Lanka's most isolated building and almost as close to India as to Jaffna.

Travel details

Buses

Jaffna to: Colombo (2–3 daily; 10–12hr); Karainagar (hourly; 1hr); Kayts (hourly; 1hr); Kurikadduwan (hourly; 1hr); Point Pedro (every 30min; 1hr); Velvettiturai (hourly; 1hr).
Mannar to: Colombo (4 daily; 7hr); Talaimannar (hourly; 1hr); Vavuniya (hourly; 2hr).
Vavuniya to: Anuradhapura (every 30min; 2hr); Colombo (every 30min; 5–6hr); Kandy (every 30min; 4hr); Madhu (every 2hr; 2hr); Mannar (hourly; 2hr); Omantai (every 30min; 30min); Trincomalee (3 daily; 3hr 30min).

Trains

Vavuniya to: Colombo (4 daily; 6–7hr).

Air

Jaffna to: Colombo (3–7 daily; 1hr).

Contexts

Contexts

A brief history of Sri Lanka

Sri Lanka's past is sunk in an inextricable mixture of the historical and the mythological, exemplified by the curious legend of Prince Vijaya (see box on p.414), from whom the Sinhalese people claim descent. Despite the colourful legend which surrounds the island's prehistory, however, actual archeological evidence of early settlement in Sri Lanka is relatively slight. Sri Lanka's earliest inhabitants were the Veddahs (see p.245), probably related to the aborigines of Australia, the Nicobar Islands and Malaysia, and thought to have arrived in Sri Lanka by 125,000 BC. The Veddahs initially lived by hunting and gathering, and later developed knowledge of iron and agriculture, while quartz tools have been discovered at Bandarawela and simple pottery at Balangoda. There is also evidence of early trading contacts between the island and South India.

The arrival of the Sinhalese

From around the fifth century BC, waves of Indo-Aryan immigrants began to arrive in Sri Lanka from northern India (perhaps following in the wake of Indian mariners who may already have been sailing down the coast in search of trade). Their exact origins remain obscure, though it's now thought that the first settlers came from present-day Gujarat, and were followed by subsequent waves of migrants from Orissa and Bengal. These people, the ancestors of the present-day **Sinhalese**, first arrived on the western coast of the island. At first they were limited to river valleys, these being the only areas in which they were able to cultivate rice, but as their expertise in irrigation increased, they were able to strike inland towards the island's dry northern plains – during which the indigenous Veddahs were either absorbed by the new arrivals or driven south.

The Anuradhapura period

The first major Sinhalese kingdom developed around the city of **Anuradhapura**, in the dry plains of the northern island. According to popular legend, the city was founded in 377 BC by Pandukabhaya, the third king of the Vijaya dynasty, and subsequently became the most important of the scattered, independent agricultural settlements which grew up at the same time in the north of the island. According to the *Mahavamsa*, **Mahinda**, son of the great Indian Buddhist emperor, Ashoka, arrived in Sri Lanka in 246 BC with a retinue of monks to proselytize on behalf of Buddhism, quickly converting the king of Anuradhapura, **Devanampiya Tissa** (c.300–260 BC). Mahinda was soon followed by his sister, **Sangamitta**, who arrived with a valuable collection of

---

The Mahavamsa and Culavamsa

Much of our knowledge of early Sri Lankan history is owed to the **Mahavamsa** ("Great Chronicle") and its continuation, the **Culavamsa** ("Little Chronicle"). The *Mahavamsa* was compiled by Buddhist monks during the sixth century (the *Culavamsa* dates from the thirteenth century) and was intended to commemorate and legitimize the Sinhalese royal lineage and the island's impeccable Buddhist credentials. Their narration of actual historical events is therefore at best questionably biased, and at worst totally imaginary – a fact illustrated by the *Mahavamsa*'s meticulous descriptions of the three visits which the Buddha himself is claimed to have made to the island.

Prince Vijaya

According to Sinhalese tradition, recorded in the *Mahavamsa*, the Sinhalese people trace their origins back to the union between a lion ("sinha", hence Sinhalese) and a rather disreputable North Indian princess ("Very fair she was and very amorous, and for shame the king and queen could not suffer her"). The princess is said to have been travelling in a caravan when the lion attacked. The princess's companions fled, but, as the *Mahavamsa* touchingly relates:

When the lion had taken his prey . . . he beheld her [the princess] from afar. Love laid hold on him, and he came towards her with waving tail and ears laid back. Seeing him . . . without fear she caressed him, stroking his limbs.

The lion, roused to fiercest passion by her touch, took her upon his back and bore her with all speed to his cave, and there he was united with her.

In due course the princess gave birth to twins, a boy and a girl, who subsequently married one another. The fruit of this incestuous union was sixteen sons, the eldest of whom was **Prince Vijaya**. Growing to manhood, Vijaya made such a nuisance of himself that there were calls for him and seven hundred of his male companions to be put to death. Instead, the king packed them all into a boat and sent them off into exile. Vijaya and his friends arrived on Sri Lanka sometime in the sixth century BC (although the writers of the *Mahavamsa* – ever on the lookout for an opportunity to boost Sri Lanka's Buddhist credentials – later changed this date to 483 BC, the year of the Buddha's death, claiming that the master himself had declared a blessing on Vijaya's enterprise as he lay on his deathbed, announcing that Sri Lanka would henceforth be one of the faith's principal heartlands). Landing on the island's west coast, they were confronted by a yaksa, or devil, who appeared to them in the form of a dog. Following the dog, they found another yaksa, this one in the shape of a woman hermit named **Kuveni**, who proceeded to magically ensnare all Vijaya's friends until the prince, protected by a magic thread conferred by the god Vishnu himself, seized her and threatened to cut off her head. Kuveni released the men, agreed to hand over the kingdom to Vijaya and, transforming herself into a young and desirable woman, retired with Vijaya to a splendidly appointed bed. They subsequently married and had two children, though Vijaya eventually came to feel the need for a more reputable consort, and drove Kuveni back into the forest. Their children escaped and married one another; it was their descendants who became, according to tradition, the **Veddahs**.

The lack of women on the island was finally relieved when Vijaya sent to the Pandyan court in India for wives for himself and his followers. Vijaya himself married a Pandyan princess, but failed to produce an heir, and towards the end of his reign sent for his younger brother to come and take his place as ruler. The brother, unwilling to leave his native land, instead sent his youngest son, **Panduvasudeva**. Having landed with 32 followers on the east coast at Gokanna (present-day Trincomalee), Panduvasudeva was duly enthroned and continued the Vijaya dynasty.

To what extent these mythological events reflect actual history is a matter of considerable speculation. Vijaya himself was perhaps a symbolic rather than an actual historical figure – his name means "victory", perhaps representing the victory of the North Indian immigrants over the native Veddahs. Equally, Vijaya's union with Kuveni would seem to commemorate the intermingling of the Sinhalese immigrants with the Veddahs, while his subsequent marriage to a Pandyan princess again probably has its roots in actual historic links between the early Sinhalese and the Tamils of South India – even Panduvasudeva may simply be another symbolic figure representing the second wave of settlement. The essentially symbolic nature of the tale is supported by fact that the Sinhalese themselves – and indeed the staunchly Buddhist writers of the *Mahavamsa* – feel no compunction in tracing their ancestry to a violent outcast whose immediate ancestry included both bestial and incestuous relations.

relics including the Buddha's begging bowl, collarbone and a cutting from the sacred bo tree under which the Buddha attained enlightenment in Bodhgaya – the tree subsequently grown from this cutting still flourishes today.

Buddhism found a ready audience in Sri Lanka, and within half a century the island's Sinhalese had all converted to the new faith. Buddhism gave the Sinhalese a new-found sense of national identity and inspired the development of a distinctively Sri Lankan culture, exemplified by the religious architecture of Anuradhapura, whose enormous stupas were amongst early Asia's greatest monuments. Sri Lanka's proximity to South India made it a constant target of invasions, however, while the reliance of the Sinhalese on Tamil mercenaries (given the traditional Buddhist regard for the sanctity of life, the Sinhalese have always had difficulties raising an effective army) left them at the mercy of their own fighting forces. Tamils had already begun migrating to the island from the third century BC, and shortly after Devanampiya's death, two Tamil captains in the Anuradhapura army – Sena and Guttika – staged a coup and ruled there for two decades. Following their murder, another Tamil soldier, **Elara**, seized power around 205 BC and ruled the city for a further 44 years.

Elara's reign was finally ended by **Dutugemunu** (161–37 BC; see box on p.348), who eventually defeated the old Tamil general after a protracted period of war, so bringing the whole of Sri Lanka under unified rule for first time. Dutugemunu's successors, however, were unable to preserve the unity which he had so laboriously achieved, and prolonged periods of instability followed, punctuated by a further brief period of Tamil rule from 44 to 29 BC. In AD 65, King Vasabha founded the **Lambakanna dynasty**, who ruled for about four centuries, their most noteworthy king being **Mahasena** (274–303), who constructed the first of the major irrigation systems which were to prove so important to the island's subsequent development.

In 432, a Pandyan invasion from southern India put an end to the Lambakanna dynasty and, briefly, to Sinhalese rule. In 455, **Dhatusena** (455–473) defeated the Pandyas and re-established Sinhalese rule. His son, **Kassapa** (473–491; see p.310), seized power, murdered his father and moved the capital briefly from Anuradhapura to the rock fortress of **Sigiriya**, though the capital was returned to Anuradhapura after he was deposed by his brother Mogallana, with help of Tamil mercenaries. This event signalled a renewal of Tamil influence: the island's kings again sought Tamil support in their own disputes, and South Indian mercenaries became an important and unpredictable faction in the Sinhalese state, and a powerful influence at court.

Tamil influence in Sri Lankan affairs continued to grow during the fifth century AD, following the resurgence of Hinduism in southern India and the rise of three powerful new Tamil kingdoms: the Cholas (based in Thanjavur), the Pandyas (Madurai) and the Pallavas (Kanchipuram), all of whom would at various times become entangled in Sri Lankan affairs. In 684, Manavamma was placed on the throne with the support of the Pallavas, establishing a second Lambakanna dynasty, which reigned at Anuradhapura until the ninth century, when the Sinhalese joined forces with the Pandyans in a disastrous campaign against the Cholas. The Cholas, under Rajaraja I, first defeated the Sinhalese in India and then, in the fateful year of 993, launched a punitive expedition against Sri Lanka, sacking Anuradhapura and reducing it to ruins.

The Polonnaruwa period

Having destroyed Anuradhapura, the Cholas established themselves in the city of **Polonnaruwa**, from where they ruled for the next 75 years until

Vijayabahu I ejected them from the island in 1070 AD. Although Vijayabahu had himself crowned for symbolic reasons amidst the ruins of Anuradhapura, he decided to move the capital to Polonnaruwa, which was further removed from India and situated in more easily defensible territory.

The relocation to Polonnaruwa ushered in the beginning of a final Sinhalese golden age. Vijayabahu's successor **Parakramabahu I** (1153–1186; see box on p.322), one of the most flamboyant of all Sri Lankan monarchs, reformed the island's economy, transformed Polonnaruwa into one of the great cities of south Asia and even launched raids against the Pandyas and a naval expedition against Burma. After Parakramabahu the throne passed to his Tamil brother-in-law, **Nissankamalla** (1186–96), and the influence of South India increased once again. Nissankamalla was the last effective ruler of Polonnaruwa, though his zeal for lavish new building projects came close to bankrupting the state, which had already been labouring under the expense of Parakramabahu's wars overseas. Nissankamalla's death without a designated heir resulted in the usual disorder. A series of weaker rulers followed until, in 1212, a new wave of Tamil invaders, the Pandyans, arrived in the island and seized power, only to be displaced three years later by another South Indian adventurer, the despotic **Magha** (1215–1255), who instituted a chaotic reign of terror during which the kingdom's complex irrigation systems gradually fell into disrepair, and the population began to abandon Polonnaruwa and move steadily southwards.

The Sinhalese move south

The following period of Sri Lankan history presents a complex and disordered picture, as various Sinhalese and South Indian factions jockeyed for position amidst an increasingly politically fragmented island. As Polonnaruwa fell into chaos under Magha, so the Sinhalese aristocracy began to establish rival centres of power located in inaccessible terrain away from his reach. Initially, the Sinhalese established a new capital at Dambadeniya, about seventy miles southwest of Polonnaruwa, under Vijayabahu III (1232–36). Vijayabahu III's successor, **Parakramabahu II** (1236–70), succeeded in expelling Magha with Pandyan help, though further political instability soon followed. Under Bhuvanaikabahu I (1272–84) the Sinhalese capital was moved briefly northwards to the isolated rock fortress of **Yapahuwa**. After further skirmishes, Bhuvanekabahu II (1293–1302) moved the capital south again, to **Kurunegala**, though the increasing fragmentation of power meant that none of these kings enjoyed much real power. By around 1340, the monarchy itself had split, and rival Sinhalese kings had established themselves at **Gampola** and **Dedigama**.

The southwards drift of Sinhalese power had dramatic social and economic consequences. As the island's population moved quickly from one town to another, so the complex **irrigation systems** which had supported the advanced civilization of the dry zone fell into further disrepair. The carefully oiled machinery of Sinhalese civilization wound down: the great tanks and canals of the northern plains dried up, reducing the area of cultivable land, with a consequent decline in population and revenue, whilst a losing battle was fought against the encroaching jungle, which began to reclaim the abandoned cities and villages. The Sinhalese increasingly found themselves driven into the monsoon-affected lands of the south and the central highlands. Capital cities were now selected mainly for their defensibility, and became military strongholds rather than economic centres, situated in difficult terrain and away from populous areas. As irrigation systems and large-scale agriculture broke down, so fewer taxes were paid to the state, further weakening centralized control. The southwards migration increasingly forced the population to adapt to the different climate and topography of their new surroundings, obliging them to develop new agricultural techniques. Rice cultivation remained important, but was now supplemented by other highland grains. The lack of major irrigation works meant that farming diminished to the subsistence character, with shifting cultivation practised amongst the hills, and aided by the region's copious rainfall. Coconuts, easily grown in the highlands and coastal wetlands, became an important crop.

These economic changes also had implications for the island's cherished Buddhist faith. As revenues – literally – dried up, so the funds available to the Buddhist church declined. Kings continued as patrons of Buddhism, but their own reduced circumstances meant that Buddhist institutions no longer enjoyed the wealth they once had. The great monasteries of Anuradhapura and Polonnaruwa were disbanded, and though new institutions were established around the various subsequent capitals, they lacked the scale and magnificence of their predecessors. In addition, the absence of strong royal authority affected the unity of the Buddhist Sangha (clergy), and indiscipline and theological schisms spread, so that kings were frequently obliged to purge the Sangha of disreputable elements. Along with this weakening of Buddhist cohesion came a new influence of Hinduism on Buddhist institutions. The increasing contact between the Sinhalese ruling classes and the Tamil nobility was followed by an influx of South Indian Brahmins, and Hindu gods began to assume important roles both in popular Buddhism and in elaborate festivals.

The Jaffna kingdom

The erosion of Sinhalese authority left a power vacuum in the north of the island. At the beginning of the fourteenth century a South Indian general, **Arya Chakaravarti**, seized power in the north, founding a Tamil kingdom, **Jaffnapatnam**, with its capital at Nallur in the Jaffna Peninsula. This kingdom soon expanded southwards, coming into conflict with the centres of Sinhalese power, until by the mid-fourteenth century the Tamil kingdom even attacked and defeated the rulers of Gampola, establishing its own tax collectors in the kingdom. One consequence of the Sinhalese movement southwards and the establishment of the Tamil kingdom to the north was the division of the island into two ethno-linguistic zones. Previously, Tamil settlements had been interspersed among the Sinhalese. Now, for the first time, the island's northern and eastern areas became predominantly Tamil, and fresh migrations from South India following the collapse of the Pandyan kingdom in the fourteenth century served to compound this. Jaffna became the heart of Tamil Hindu culture, with its society organized along similar lines to the Tamil regions of South India, overseen by the landowning cultivators, or Vellala. Hindu institutions were supported by the kings and were strengthened by the influx of Brahmins, while the Tamil language became entrenched in the island, developing a literary culture which was nurtured by the kings of Jaffna and enriched by contact with South India.

The rise of Kotte

The Jaffna kingdom's mid-fourteenth-century attack against Gampola marked its high-water point. In the second half of the fourteenth century a new Sinhalese dynasty, the **Alagakkonaras** (or Alakesvaras) rose to power in Gampola. Establishing a fort at **Kotte**, near Colombo, they expelled the Tamil tax collectors and re-established their independence, though internal feuding fatally weakened them. In 1405 a Ming Chinese fleet under the legendary general **Cheng Ho** arrived in Sri Lanka in a mission to gain possession of the **Tooth Relic**. The Alagakkonaras, not surprisingly, refused to hand it over. A few years later, Cheng Ho returned and carried off the last of the Alagakkonara rulers, Vira Alekesvara, to China for five years.

Vira Alekesvara was eventually returned unharmed to Sri Lanka, only to find that during his absence a minor member of the Gampola nobility had seized power and had himself crowned as **Parakramabahu VI** of Kotte (1412–67). The last of the great Sinhalese unifiers, Parakramabahu first subdued the independent kingdom of the highlands, then saw off an invasion of the Vijayanagarans, who had become the dominant power in southern India, until in 1450 he succeeded in taking possession of the Jaffna kingdom and uniting the entire island, for the final time, under Sinhalese rule. As on so many previous occasions, however, the unity achieved by one strong ruler failed to survive his death, and within a few years of Parakramabahu's demise, the kingdoms of Jaffna, Rajarata and the central highlands had once more asserted their independence, so that the subsequent rulers of Kotte, although they continued to claim sovereignty over the whole of Sri Lanka, increasingly found themselves hemmed into a small area in the island's southwestern corner.

The Portuguese

As agricultural revenues declined following the collapse of irrigation systems and the loss of territory, so **trade** became an increasingly significant Sinhalese concern. Spices were the most important exports: cinnamon, found in the southwestern forests, was first exported in the fourteenth century, and was soon followed by pepper and other spices – all of them subject to royal monopolies. Colombo, Galle and other coastal settlements in the island's southwest developed into important **ports**, becoming centres of coastal and Indian trade and attracting foreign merchants, who came both to trade and to settle permanently – the extent of this trade can be seen by the fact that King Bhuvanaikabahu I sent a mission to the Mamluk sultan of Egypt in 1283. The most important of these traders were the **Arabs**, who first began trading with Sri Lanka from around the tenth century, and who established trading settlements around the coast and brought Islam to the island, whilst exporting cinnamon and other spices, which had begun to fetch good prices in Western markets.

The island's trading possibilities soon began to attract attention from even further afield. In 1497 the **Portuguese** navigator Vasco da Gama pioneered the sea route to India around the tip of Africa, opening the Indian Ocean to European mariners. In 1505 a Portuguese fleet, prospecting for spices, was blown off course into the mouth of the Kelani Ganga, near Colombo. The Portuguese received a friendly audience from the king of Kotte, Vira Parakramabahu, who was understandably fascinated by these exotic, armour-clad foreigners, described by one of the king's scouts as "a race of men, exceeding white and beautiful. They wear boots and hats of iron, and they are always in motion. They eat white stones [bread] and they drink blood [wine]."

The Portuguese had noted the island's commercial and strategic value – in particular its vast supply of cinnamon – and soon returned, being granted trading concessions and permission to build a fort at Colombo. They found themselves rapidly overtaken by the imbroglio of Sri Lankan politics, however. In 1521 three sons of the king of Kotte, Vijayabahu, put their father to death and divided the kingdom between themselves. The oldest of the brothers,

Bhuvanaikabahu, ruled at Kotte, whilst the two others set up independent kingdoms at Sitawake and Rayigama. The ambitious king of Sitawake, **Mayadunne**, soon began the attempt to seize control of his brother's kingdom at Kotte; Bhuvanaikabahu, in turn, sought Portuguese assistance, becoming increasingly reliant on their military support.

In 1543, Bhuvanaikabahu signed an agreement whereby his son and heir, **Prince Jão Dharmapala**, was to be guaranteed Portuguese protection in return for a confirmation of Portuguese privileges and a tribute of cinnamon. Dharmapala was educated by Franciscans, and his conversion to Christianity in 1557 undermined the Kotte dynasty in the eyes of the people, transforming Mayadunne's wars against Kotte into a struggle against the Portuguese. Mayadunne succeeded in capturing a large part of the Kotte kingdom, while following his death, his son **Rajasinha** continued to prosecute the war against the Portuguese successfully on land, though he had no way of combating Portuguese sea power. Rajasinha's death in 1593, however, left the Sitawake kingdom in want of a strong ruler. The Portuguese recaptured much of the lands of Kotte and then, on the death of Dharmapala in 1597, took possession of the Kotte kingdom. Meanwhile, a series of Portuguese expeditions against Jaffna had begun, culminating in the successful annexation of the kingdom of Jaffna in 1619. The Portuguese continued to expand their control: to the lower reaches of the central highlands and to the east coast ports of Trincomalee and Batticaloa, eventually gaining control over the entire island except for the kingdom of Kandy, in the central highlands.

Portuguese rule largely retained the traditional Sinhalese systems of caste and tribute, using local officials from the Sinhalese nobility who were loyal to the Portuguese; however all tribute that had been due to the Sinhalese kings was now taken by the Portuguese, including a monopoly in elephants and cinnamon, and control of the lucrative trade in pepper and betel nuts. Even so, the burdens they placed upon the island's inhabitants led to hardship and popular hostility. In addition, Portuguese rule was also marked by intense Roman Catholic **missionary activity**. Franciscans established Sri Lankan centres from 1543, followed by Jesuits, Dominicans and Augustinians. Following the conversion of Dharmapala, many members of the Sinhalese nobility followed suit. Dharmapala endowed missionary orders lavishly, often using funds from Buddhist and Hindu temples, whilst members of the landed aristocracy embraced Christianity and took Portuguese surnames – the origins of the thousands of de Silvas and Pereiras who still fill the telephone directories of modern Sri Lanka. Many coastal communities underwent mass conversion, particularly Jaffna, Mannar, and the fishing communities north of Colombo.

Taking the Portuguese to Kotte

Following the arrival of the first Portuguese on the coast of Sri Lanka, they were invited to present themselves to the king of Kotte, who was understandably intrigued by these strange foreigners. A delegation was prepared and despatched to meet the king. However, before they could meet the king, the king's messengers, in order to disguise the smallness of their kingdom and the fact that the royal capital lay a mere thirteen kilometres inland from the coast, led the Portuguese on a convoluted three-day march around the coastal regions in a vain attempt to delude them into believing the kingdom of Kotte a much grander affair than it actually was. Sadly, the Portuguese saw straight through this attempted subterfuge, but despite the failure of the attempt, the expression "**Taking the Portuguese to Kotte**" remains to this day a Sri Lankan euphemism for all kinds of double-dealing.

The Kandyan kingdom and the arrival of the Dutch

The origins of the kingdom of **Kandy**, situated in the remote and rugged hill country at the heart of the island, date back to the early thirteenth century, during the southwards drift of the Sinhalese. By the time the Portuguese arrived, it had developed into one of the island's three main kingdoms, along with Kotte and Jaffna. The Portuguese first turned their attention to Kandy in 1591, though their attempt to place a puppet ruler on the throne was thwarted by an ambitious Sinhalese nobleman sent to accompany the Portuguese nominee, who enthroned himself instead, proclaiming independence from the Portuguese and taking the name of **Vimala Dharma Sürya**. Using guerrilla tactics, Vimala Dharma Sürya routed a Portuguese attack in 1594, as well as subsequent attacks in 1611, 1629 and 1638.

Realizing he couldn't drive the Portuguese out of Sri Lanka without sea power, Dharma Sürya saw the arrival of the **Dutch**, who had had their eyes on the island for a number of years, as an opportunity to gain naval support against his adversaries. Dutch envoys met Dharma Sürya in 1602 and determined upon a joint attack against the Portuguese. At least that was the plan. The Dutch leader, Admiral Sebald de Weert, invited the king to come back to the coast and inspect his ships. Dharma Sürya demurred, replying that he was reluctant to leave his queen, Dona Caterina, alone. De Weert, who appears to have been somewhat the worse for drink, replied that from what he had heard the queen was unlikely to be alone for long, whereupon he and his companions were, perhaps not surprisingly, hacked to death. Despite this unfortunate turn of events, Dharma Sürya's successor, **Senarat**, continued to seek Dutch support. The Dutch again promised military support, though in the event they were unable to provide it and the king turned instead to the Danes, who despatched an expedition, though by the time it arrived Senarat had concluded a peace agreement with the Portuguese (the tardy Danes instead founded a colony on the Coromandel coast of India). The truce was short-lived, however, and in 1630 the Kandyans invaded Portuguese territory, laying siege to Colombo and Galle, though again their lack of sea power prevented them from dislodging the Portuguese permanently.

In 1635 Senarat was succeeded by his son **Rajasinha II**. The new king once again sent emissaries to the Dutch, who arrived in Sri Lanka with a fleet of ships and began attacking Portuguese positions. Between 1638 and 1640 they drove the Portuguese out of a number of important coastal towns, but refused to hand over their conquests to Rajasinha, saying they had not been paid their expenses. The king of Kandy was still waiting when, in 1640, the offensive against the Portuguese was temporarily halted by a truce declared in Europe between the United Provinces of the Netherlands and Spain, which at that time ruled Portugal and its overseas possessions. Fighting didn't resume until 1652. The Kandyans launched attacks on Portuguese positions in the interior provinces, pushing them back to their coastal strongholds despite fierce Portuguese resistance. The Dutch, meanwhile, laid siege to Colombo by sea and land, and in May 1656 the Portuguese surrendered the city to the Dutch, who promptly shut the Kandyans out of its gates. Faced with this duplicity, Rajasinha torched the lands around Colombo and then withdrew back to the hills. Despite this loss of local support, the Dutch continued to drive the Portuguese from the island, attacking Portuguese strongholds in northern Sri Lanka until, with the conquest of Jaffna in 1658, they had replaced the Portuguese as masters of coastal Sri Lanka. Following their expulsion of the

Portuguese, the Dutch gradually pushed inland, until by 1665 they had reached the east coast, controlling most of the island's cinnamon-growing lands as well as its ports.

Compared with the Portuguese, the Dutch were less interested in saving souls than in making money – as an early governor, Van Goens, wrote: "It can easily be seen what a mischievous and horrible thing war is . . . All our efforts should be directed in future to reduce our expenses by a well-regulated establishment and to increase our profits by faithful economy." Even so, the early years of **Dutch rule** did see an enthusiastic effort to spread the Reformed Calvinist faith in Sri Lanka. Roman Catholicism was declared illegal, and its priests banned from the country; Catholic churches were given to the Reformed faith, and many Sinhalese and Tamil Catholics nominally embraced Protestantism. Meanwhile, the Dutch tried to promote trade with neighbouring countries, though these efforts were stifled by the strict monopolies which they maintained in the lucrative export markets of cinnamon, elephants, pearls and betel nuts. Relations with the kingdom of Kandy, meanwhile, were generally amicable, except for one outbreak of hostilities in 1776, when the Dutch sacked Kandy itself.

The arrival of the British

The French Revolution initiated a major shake-up in relations between the leading European powers. When the Netherlands fell to the French in 1794, the **British East India Company**'s forces occupied Sri Lanka, having already for some time coveted the magnificent natural harbour at Trincomalee. In theory, the British were meant to be protecting Dutch territory against the French, though the forgivably suspicious Dutch mounted a halfhearted resistance before surrendering the island in 1796 to their British "protectors". Despite the avowedly temporary nature of the British administration, the new colonists soon began to appreciate Sri Lanka's strategic and commercial value, and quickly moved to make their hold on the island permanent – in 1802, Sri Lanka was ceded to Britain under the Treaty of Amiens with France.

One of the priorities of the new colonizers was to subdue the Kandyan kingdom and finally unify the island under a single rule. The British launched a disastrous expedition against the kingdom in 1803, but it wasn't until 1815 that they finally achieved their end, when the Kandyans, enraged by the megalomaniac behavior of their king, Sri Wickrama Rajasinghe (see box on p.220), simply stood to one side and allowed British soldiers to march in and occupy the city. After two centuries of spirited resistance, the last bastion of Sri Lankan independence had finally been extinguished.

Though reluctant to upset traditional Sinhalese institutions, the British abolished slavery, relieved native officials of judicial authority, paid salaries in cash, and relaxed the system of compulsory service tenure. Agriculture was encouraged, and production of cinnamon, pepper, sugarcane, cotton, and coffee flourished. Internal communications were extended, Christian missions despatched, and restrictions on European ownership of land lifted. In 1833, a series of **reforms** laid the foundations for Sri Lanka's subsequent political and economic structures, including a unified administrative and judicial system for the whole island. English became the official language of government, and the medium of instruction in schools. In addition, the British quickly opened up the island's economy, abolishing all state monopolies. Crown land was sold off cheaply to encourage the establishment of new plantations, and capital flowed in. The most notable result of these changes was the spectacular growth in the island's **coffee** production, from around 1830 to 1870. As the area under cultivation for coffee expanded, so new roads, railways and port facilities were constructed to service the industry, while indentured labourers from southern India begin arriving in large numbers to make good the island's labour shortage – almost a million arrived between 1843 and 1859. In the 1870s, however, the island's coffee production was destroyed by a leaf disease – *hemileia vastratrix* – fondly christened "Devastating Emily". The void, however, was soon filled by the introduction of **tea**, with plantations quickly spreading around the slopes of the central highlands, while rubber and coconuts also acquired increasing importance.

The rise of nationalism

Sri Lanka's traumatic encounters with European colonial powers led to a major re-evaluation of its own traditional culture. In the nineteenth century, revivalist Buddhist and Hindu movements sprang up, with the aim both of modernizing native institutions in the face of the Western onslaught, and of defending the island's traditional culture against missionary Christianity. Gradually, this burgeoning **nationalist consciousness** acquired a political dimension. Grassroots organizations began to demand greater Sri Lankan participation in government, though the uncoordinated nature of these protests meant they were easily ignored by the government – even so, **constitutional reforms** passed in 1910 made the small concession of allowing a limited number of "educated" Sri Lankans to elect one member to the government's Legislative Council.

During World War I, the forces of nationalism gathered momentum. British arrests of prominent Sinhalese leaders after minor civil disturbances in 1915 provoked widespread opposition, leading in 1919 to the foundation of the **Ceylon National Congress**, which united both Sinhalese and Tamil organizations and drafted proposals for constitutional reforms. Gradual reforms slowly followed, and in 1931 a new constitution gave the island's leaders the chance to exercise political power and gain legislative experience with a view towards eventual self-government. In addition, the new constitution granted universal franchise, bringing all Sri Lankans into the political process for the first time (and making the country the first Asian colony to achieve universal suffrage).

During **World War II**, Sri Lankan nationalist leaders supported the British war effort whilst continuing to lobby for full independence. When Singapore, Indonesia and Burma fell to the Japanese, Sri Lanka suddenly found itself close to the frontline of the war in the east, a fact brought home by Japanese bombing raids against Colombo and Trincomalee (during which a number of British warships were sunk). By the end of 1942, Sri Lanka had become the major base of British operations in Asia. Lord Mountbatten established his South East Asia Command headquarters at Kandy, while Trincomalee hosted a wing of the Special Operations Executive, which launched saboteurs and resistance coordinators behind Japanese lines.

Independence

Sri Lanka's long-awaited **independence** finally came on February 4, 1948, with power passing from the British to the **United National Party** (**UNP**), under the leadership of **Don Stephen Senanayake**. The essentially conservative UNP was dominated by the English-educated leaders of the colonial era, though it did include people from all the country's ethno-linguistic groups. Its members were bound by the common ideals of Sri Lankan nationalism, parliamentary democracy, and gradual economic progress through free enterprise.

The first years of independence were kind to Sri Lanka: the island's exports were doing well in world markets, there was a sizeable sterling balance earned during the war, and the coalition government had a substantial majority in parliament – the island even came close to eradicating malaria. There were, however, some basic weaknesses. The ruling parties largely represented the views of the island's English-educated, westernized elite – an ideology which most of the population found incomprehensible or irrelevant. In addition, **economic difficulties** began to emerge. Falling rubber and tea prices on the world markets, rises in the cost of imported food and a rapidly increasing population ate quickly into the country's foreign exchange, while the expanded school system produced large numbers of educated persons unable to find suitable employment. Meanwhile, Tamil plantation workers found themselves suddenly disenfranchised by the UNP (conveniently so, given that they largely voted for their own, sectarian, Tamil parties). The Senanayake government insisted on classifying the **plantation Tamils** as "foreigners", even if they had been living on the island for generations, and attempted to repatriate them to India, an incident which tarnished relations between the two countries for years.

In 1952, D.S. Senanayake died after being thrown from his horse on Galle Face Green in Colombo and was briefly succeeded by his son, Dudley Senanayake, though he was forced to resign following disastrous attempts to cut rice subsidies, an act which provoked widespread strikes and rioting. In 1953 he was succeeded by his uncle, **John Kotelawala**, a bout of nepotism which earned the UNP the name of the "Uncle Nephew Party".

The Bandaranaikes

As the 1950s progressed, the UNP's westernized and elitist political leaders proved increasingly out of touch with the views and aspirations of the majority of the island's population. In the elections of 1956, the UNP lost to the socialist-nationalist **Sri Lanka Freedom Party** (**SLFP**) under the leadership of the charismatic **S.W.R.D. Bandaranaike**, ushering in an extraordinary dynastic sequence in which power alternated between various members of the Senanayake clan (through the guise of the UNP), and assorted Bandaranaikes (through various incarnations of the SLFP). The new government immediately set about changing the country's political landscape, instigating a huge programme of nationalization, making Sinhala the sole official language and instigating state support for the Buddhist faith and Sinhalese culture, largely in reaction to the Anglo-Christian culture left by the British. Bandaranaike's new policies had the unfortunate side effect of stoking the fires of ethnic and religious tension. His language policy alienated the Tamils, his educational policies outraged the small but influential Christian community, while even factions amongst the Sinhalese communities were disturbed by his cultural and religious reforms. As passions grew, Tamils were driven from Colombo and other places where they had traditionally lived alongside the Sinhalese, while Sinhalese in turn fled from Tamil areas in the north and east. In September 1959, Bandaranaike opened **talks with the Tamils** in an attempt to calm the situation, and was promptly assassinated by a militant Buddhist monk – not the first or last time the island's Buddhist clergy would play a role in stoking up religious intolerance on the island. Despite the mixed achievements of his government, Bandaranaike is still regarded (at least by the Sinhalese) as a national hero, the first genuinely populist Sinhalese leader, who returned the government of Sri Lanka to the common people after the neocolonialism of his predecessors.

Bandaranaike was succeeded by his widow, Sirimavo – or **Mrs Bandaranaike**, as she is usually known – who thus became the world's first ever female prime minister. Mrs Bandaranaike's government continued to implement the policies of Sinhalese nationalism: all private schools were nationalized in an attempt to neutralize the influence of Christian missions in the educational system, while important national industries were also taken over by the state; in addition, she had half a million plantation Tamils deported to India. Despite her symbolic importance for women worldwide, Mrs Bandaranaike was less appreciated at home, and had to survive an attempted coup before being finally trounced at the polls in 1965 by the UNP, who returned to power under **Dudley Senanayake**, with the emphasis once again put on private enterprise and economic stability.

The JVP and the road to civil war

The Sri Lankan electorate's habit of kicking out whichever party happened to be in power repeated itself in the **1970 elections**, when the UNP were defeated and the irrepressible Mrs Bandaranaike once again became prime minister at the head of a new SLFP-led coalition, the **United Front**. The interminable yo-yoing between parties and policies thus continued, with Mrs Bandaranaike reversing the policies of the UNP and resuming her old aims of restricting private enterprise and increasing nationalization of key industries, whilst introducing policies aimed at reducing social inequality via an ambitious programme of land reform. Her government also ditched a further element of the island's colonial past by changing its **name** from Ceylon to Sri Lanka (see box below).

Though these measures appeased the island's underprivileged, they did nothing to address basic economic problems such as the mounting trade deficit. The country's youth, impatient for radical change, expressed their discontent through the extreme left-wing and anti-Tamil **JVP** (Janatha Vimukthi Peramuna, or People's Liberation Front). In 1971 the JVP launched an armed rebellion with the aim of overthrowing the government, but despite brief

---

Sri Lanka or Ceylon?

The origins of the island's colonial name of Ceylon stretch back to the island's ancient Sanskrit name of **Sinhaladvipa**, as it was known to the very first Aryan settlers, who were from the Sinhala – or Lion – tribe (*dvipa* is Sanskrit for "land" or "continent"). Arab traders who began visiting the island in the early centuries of the new millennium transformed this name into **Serendib** (the root of the English word "serendipity", or the making of fortuitous discoveries by accident, which was invented in the eighteenth century by the English man of letters Horace Walpole, and inspired by a Persian fairy tale, "The Three Princes of Serendip"). Further linguistic transformations mutated Sinhaladvipa (or at least its first two syllables) into the Portuguese **Ceilão**, and thence into the Dutch **Zeylan** and the British **Ceylon**.

Not that this was the only name by which the island was known overseas. The Greeks and Romans had previously called the island **Taprobane**, derived from another ancient Sanskrit name for the island, **Tambapanni**, after the copper-coloured beach on which Prince Vijaya and his followers (see p.414) are claimed to have first landed. The island's own inhabitants, however, have always known the island by a different name entirely: in Sinhalese, **Lanka**, and in Tamil as **Ilankai**. The reversion from the British colonial Ceylon to the indigenous Sri Lanka (or, to be precise, the Democratic Socialist Republic of Sri Lanka) was finally made in 1972 – the additional Sri is Sinhalese for "auspicious" or "resplendent".

successes, the insurrection was easily and ruthlessly suppressed by the army, with thousands of the poorly organized rebels (mainly students) losing their lives. Meanwhile, Sri Lanka's **economic decline** continued, and the immense power held by the state provided the party in power with the opportunity for patronage, nepotism, and corruption. Mrs Bandaranaike continued her nationalization programme, seizing hold of tea estates and private agricultural lands, two of the few areas of the economy which were still functioning successfully. By 1977, unemployment had risen to about fifteen percent.

The LTTE and civil war

In June 1977, the United Front was defeated by a reinvigorated UNP under the leadership of **J.R. Jayawardene**, who became the first non-Senanayake to control the UNP. Jayawardene began to tamper with the democratic process, writing yet another new constitution in 1978 which gave the country's president (previously an essentially ceremonial role) new powers – with, as it would later turn out, disastrous effects. Jayawardene resigned as prime minister and was promptly elected the country's first president (and re-elected in 1982, after further tinkering with the constitution).

The Jayawardene government again tried to revitalize the private sector and attract back some of the foreign capital driven away by Mrs Bandaranaike. These policies enjoyed some success: by 1983, unemployment had been halved, while the island became self-sufficient in rice by 1985. Meanwhile tourism and expatriate Sri Lankans working in the Middle East brought in valuable foreign currency, though these gains were undercut by rampant inflation, unstable tea and rubber prices, and, most seriously, by the country's descent into **civil war**. The origins of this latest Sinhalese–Tamil conflict had first been sparked in the early 1970s via new legislation designed to cut the number of Tamil places at the country's universities, whilst the new constitution of 1972 further aggravated Tamil sensibilities by declaring Buddhism to hold the "foremost place" amongst the island's religions. These measures provoked growing unrest amongst Sri Lanka's Tamils, culminating in a **state of emergency** which was imposed on northern areas of the island for several years from 1971. Since the police and army who enforced this state of emergency included few Tamils (one result of the constitution's insistence that only Sinhala speakers be allowed to occupy official posts), and were often undisciplined and heavy-handed, they were increasingly seen by the Tamils as an occupying force.

By the mid-1970s some young Tamils had begun to resort to violence, calling for an independent Tamil state, **Eelam** ("Precious Land"). Tamil bases were established in jungle areas of northern and eastern Sri Lanka, as well as in the southern districts of the Indian state of Tamil Nadu, where Tamil groups received considerable support. The Liberation Tigers of Tamil Eelam (LTTE), usually known as the **Tamil Tigers**, were the strongest of these, but there were other competing groups which were sometimes hostile to each other.

Despite limited **reforms** – such as the promotion of Tamil to the status of a "national language" to be used in official business in Tamil areas – violence continued to escalate in the north. The point of no return arrived in 1983, following the ambush and massacre of an army patrol by a group of Tamil Tiger guerrillas in the Jaffna region. For several days afterwards, Sinhalese mobs indulged in an orgy of killing and looting against Tamils all over the country – the so-called "**Black July**" saw the slaughter of as many as two thousand people, and virtually levelled areas with a large Tamil population, such as Colombo's Pettah district.

The government, police and army showed themselves unable – or unwilling – to stop this violence. Tens of thousands of Tamils fled to the north of the island, while many others left the country altogether. Equally, Sinhalese started to move out of Jaffna and other Tamil areas. In the following years, violence continued to escalate, with several massacres, including a notorious attack at Anuradhapura in May 1985, when 150 mainly Sinhalese victims were gunned down at one of the symbolic centres of the island's Sinhalese and Buddhist culture. Both sides were accused of torture, intimidation and disappearances.

The government's offer, in the mid-1980s, of **limited Tamil self-government**, proved to be too little and too late. By the end of 1985 fighting between Sri Lankan government forces and the LTTE had spread across the north and down the east coast, while there were also conflicts between Tamils and the east coast's significant Muslim population. War had a devastating effect on the economy. Tourism slumped, military spending rose and aid donors threatened to cut money over human rights abuses. And, to add to the country's woes, tea prices collapsed.

The Indian Peace Keeping Force

In 1987, government forces pushed the LTTE back to Jaffna city, prompting a further exodus of Tamil refugees to India. The Indian government (for whom the fate of the Sri Lankan Tamils has always been a sensitive issue, given the massive number of Tamils in India itself) began supplying food by air and sea to the beleaguered Tamils, leading to clashes between the Indian and Sri Lankan navies. In the same year, President Jayawardene came to an arrangement with India whereby the government pledged that the Sri Lankan army would hand their positions over to an **Indian Peace Keeping Force**, or **IPKF**, whose aim would be to disarm the Tamil rebels and maintain peace in the north and east.

The deal attracted opposition from all quarters, including Muslims and the LTTE, and provoked riots in Colombo amongst Sinhalese, who saw the Indian presence in the north as a threat to national sovereignty and a latter-day re-enactment of previous Indian invasions. In the event, the Indian army's hopes of simply keeping the peace proved to be purest fantasy. No sooner had they arrived than they became embroiled in clashes with the LTTE, which soon escalated into full-scale war, culminating in the bloody siege and capture of Jaffna (see p.400).

Then, in 1987–88, a second **JVP rebellion** broke out in the south and centre of the island, launching a series of strikes and political assassinations which terrorized the inhabitants of the highlands and crippled the economy. At the end of 1988, President Jayawardene retired, and the new UNP leader, **Ranasinghe Premadasa**, defeated the indefatigable Mrs Bandaranaike in new presidential elections. Premadasa was a new thing in Sri Lankan politics: a low-caste boy made good, who had grown up in a shack in Colombo and who introduced a blast of fresh air into the insular world of island politics. Premadasa promised to end the fighting against both the JVP and the LTTE and succeeded at least in the first pledge. When the JVP refused to lay down their arms, Premadasa sent out paramilitary death squads, which went about the country assassinating suspected JVP activists. By the end of 1989, most JVP leaders were dead or in prison, whilst thousands of their sympathizers disappeared amidst an international human rights outcry. Some estimates put the number of those killed in the insurrection as high as 17,000.

The IPKF, meanwhile, remained in an impossible position. Despite having managed to contain the LTTE, Sinhalese nationalists were vociferous in demanding that the IPKF leave the country. The LTTE themselves, who had suffered so greatly at their hands, agreed a ceasefire in the hope of seeing the back of them, and the IPKF finally pulled out in March 1990. At their height they had numbered some eighty thousand soldiers, a thousand of whom had died in the fighting.

The 1990s

No sooner had the IPKF withdrawn than LTTE hostilities began all over again, with the introduction of a new and deadly weapon: the **suicide bomber**. By the end of 1990, the LTTE had recaptured much of the north, though the east was back under government control. This new war reached a peak in mid-1991 with a series of battles around Jaffna, while the LTTE's influence also reached into India itself, where they were implicated in the assassination of India's former prime minister, Rajiv Ghandi. In mid-1992 a major new assault against the LTTE was launched by the Sri Lankan army, coupled with a long-overdue attempt to rebuild relations with terrorized Tamil civilians. By this time, tens of thousands had died in the conflict, whilst 700,000 people had been displaced, including 200,000 Sri Lankan Tamils who had fled to Tamil Nadu in India, about half of whom were living in refugee camps.

In 1993, President Premadasa became the first Sri Lankan head of state to be **assassinated**, blown up by a 14-year-old suicide bomber – the LTTE, though suspected, never claimed responsibility. At around the same time, **Chandrika Bandaranaike Kumaratunga**, the daughter of none other than S.W.R.D. and Sirimavo Bandaranaike, gained leadership of the SLFP and became head of the **People's Alliance (PA)** coalition. Following her election victory in 1994, Kumaratunga became Sri Lanka's first female president. One of her first acts was to appoint her mother prime minister, thus continuing the clannishness which had marked Sri Lankan politics since the early days of independence.

The new PA was largely unrecognizable from the old SLFP, having abandoned Sinhalese nationalism and pseudo-socialism in favour of national reconciliation and free-market economics. The PA's principal pledge was to end the civil war, but Kumaratunga's attempts to negotiate with the LTTE in 1995 soon broke down, leading to yet another round of attacks against LTTE positions and to retaliatory LTTE **bomb attacks**, most notably the devastating strikes against the Central Bank in Colombo in 1996 and the Temple of the Tooth in Kandy in 1998. By the end of 1995 thousands of troops had been despatched to the Jaffna peninsula, and Jaffna itself was taken by the Sri Lankan Army in December 1995 – further major offensives against the LTTE followed in 1997 and 1998. In December 1999, shortly before new presidential elections, Kumaratunga survived an assassination attempt, though she was blinded in one eye. A few days later, she was re-elected president for a second term.

Despite her electoral success, Kumaratunga was unable to make any steps towards a lasting peace. In addition, her policy of trying to negotiate from a position of military strength received a huge blow in April 2000 when the LTTE captured the strategic **Elephant Pass** (see p.391) – perhaps their greatest military success of the entire conflict. In addition, in July, LTTE suicide bombers led a daring raid against the **international airport**, destroying half of SriLankan Airlines' fleet. The pictures of bombed-out planes and eyewitness accounts by hapless holidaymakers caught in the cross-fire made headline news around the globe, and had a predictably disastrous effect on the country's already fragile tourist industry.

Peace

In October 2001, Kumaratunga dissolved parliament just before a no-confidence vote which the PA looked likely to lose. In the ensuing **elections of December 2001**, the UNP won a narrow victory under the leadership of **Ranil Wickramasinghe** – although, despite her party's defeat, Kumaratunga remained president, a situation which would have disastrous political consequences. Wickramasinghe had made an end to the civil war central to his candidacy, and he quickly moved to open **negotiations with the LTTE**, mediated by diplomats from Norway – who had previously played a key role in securing the famous peace deal between Israel and the Palestinians in 1993. The timing for talks seemed propitious. Both the Tamil and Sinhalese people had become intensely war-weary, whilst the LTTE appeared to have increasingly lost the support of its own people. Wickramasinghe's conciliatory approach was also an important factor, while the events of September 11 and the subsequent US-led "War on Terror" threatened to cut off international funding for the LTTE, who were proscribed as a terrorist organization by many countries, including the US and UK.

In December 2001 the LTTE declared a temporary **ceasefire**, which was made permanent in February 2002. Events thereafter moved with unexpected swiftness: decommissioning of weapons began; the road connecting Jaffna to the rest of the island was reopened; and in September 2002 the government lifted the ban on the LTTE, opening the way for the group's official recognition by the international community. A crucial breakthrough was made at this first round of **peace talks**, held in Thailand, when the LTTE abandoned their most cherished principal – the demand for complete independence – in favour of a **federal system**, thus removing the single most intractable barrier to peace. Under this plan, the Tamil areas of the island would enjoy a large degree of autonomy, with their own parliament, prime minister and even army. Subsequent rounds of talks discussed a complex raft of issues: LTTE disarmament and the outlawing of child soldiers; aid and rehabilitation packages for war-affected areas; human rights issues; the fate of Muslim minority communities in Tamil areas; the returning home of war-displaced refugees – just some of the most important of the many deep-rooted problems produced by almost two decades of conflict.

The initial stages of the peace process proved hugely positive, but despite early successes, the inevitable **problems** began to emerge during the latter part of 2002 and 2003. President Kumaratunga became an increasingly vociferous critic of the peace process, claiming that the government was making too many concessions to the Tamils, and accusing the Norwegian mediators of bias – including one famous outburst during which she labelled them "salmon-eating busy-bodies"; the possibility that she would exercise her presidential powers to dissolve parliament and call fresh elections began increasingly to undermine the peace process. Sporadic clashes between the LTTE and Sri Lankan army, as well as serious civilian conflicts between Tamils and Muslims in the east of the country, were seen by Kumaratunga and her allies as evidence that the LTTE was simply using the peace process as a cover under which to regroup and re-arm, whilst the proposed federal system was described as a Tamil ploy from which they would once more launch a bid for full independence. In April 2003, against a background of increasing political uncertainty and arguments over the implementation of the peace process, the LTTE pulled out of talks.

Even with talks stalled, the ceasefire held, and attention increasingly turned to the growing **tension between Kumaratunga and Wickramasinghe**.

Events came to a head in November 2003, when Kumaratunga invoked her presidential powers, sacking three of Wickramasinghe's ministers and taking personal charge of the key Defence Ministry. At the same time, the LTTE (who had been watching the political standoff in Colombo with concern) themselves faced a unprecedented crisis, as their commander in the east, Colonel Karuna, broke away from the rest of the movement, taking several thousand troops with him and raising the spectre of a further battle for power amidst the protagonists in the increasingly precarious peace process.

With the peace process paralysed and the government rendered virtually powerless, fresh **elections** were called for April 2004. The hope was that a new government would be produced with a clear mandate to pursue the peace process, but in the event the results were inconclusive. Kumaratunga's new coalition, the so-called **Freedom Alliance**, won a narrow victory, but without an overall majority – the main gains were made by the Tamil **National Alliance**, who became the new parliament's third-largest party, and the **Buddhist Party**, whose monks-turned-politicians ended up holding a small but potentially crucial share of seats. Amidst frantic political horse-trading, the PA managed to create an unlikely **coalition government**, their principal partners being the newly respectable JVP (Kumaratunga thus found herself sharing power with the people who had killed her husband). The populist southern politician **Mahinda Rajapakse** was appointed prime minister, whilst reassuring noises were made about the coalition's commitment to the peace process. The LTTE leadership, meanwhile, regained control of its eastern wing after brief fighting, forcing Colonel Karuna to flee.

Thus, as of mid-2004, Sri Lanka faced an ambivalent future. The LTTE found itself confronted with a new and far more hardline government in Colombo in an atmosphere of mutual suspicion, despite both sides asserting their continued commitment to the peace process. Not that a return to war seemed imminent. After eighteen months of the ceasefire, the desire for peace – and an appreciation of its benefits – remained undimmed amongst the general population, whilst even the hardliners on both sides increasingly seemed to believe in finding a political rather than a military solution to the conflict, even if they were unable to agree on the means to reach it. Even in peace, however, Sri Lanka remained divided. Although the peace dividend was plain to see in many parts of the country, Tamils in war-affected areas had experienced little improvement in their living conditions, with many still unable to return home or to gain access to basic services. It will be on the success of meeting these people's needs and aspirations, more than anything, that the future of peace in Sri Lanka will depend.

Sri Lankan Buddhism

Sri Lanka has always been considered one of the heartlands of Buddhism, thanks to the fact that it was one of the first countries to be converted to the faith as well as its vital role in preserving the religion and its most important scriptures. Although Buddhism had more or less died out in neighbouring India by the eighth century, it has remained the dominant religion in Sri Lanka in the face of considerable adversity, including repeated invasions by Hindu Tamils, the arrival of proselytizing Muslim traders and the onslaught of colonialism and missionary Christianity. Despite these challenges, Sri Lanka has preserved the Theravada tradition (indeed it was in Sri Lanka that the principal Theravada Buddhist scriptures were first written down) and subsequently exported it to Southeast Asia, via Burma and on to Thailand – Buddhists in Southeast Asia still regard Sri Lanka as the guardian of the original Theravada tradition. But while it's true that Buddhism in Sri Lanka hasn't experienced the byzantine transformations it experienced in, say, China or Japan, the religion in Sri Lanka has acquired its own particular flavour and local characteristics.

The life of the Buddha

Siddhartha Gautama, the Buddha-to-be, was (according to tradition) born the son of the king in the small kingdom of Lumbini in what is now southern Nepal during the fourth or fifth century BC – 563 BC is often suggested as a possible date, though no one really knows. Auspicious symbols accompanied the prince's conception and birth: his mother dreamt that a white elephant had entered her womb, and according to legend Siddhartha emerged from beneath his mother's right arm and immediately talked and walked, a lotus flower blossoming beneath his foot after each of his first seven steps.

Astrologers predicted that the young prince would become either a great king or a great ascetic. His father, keen to prevent the latter, determined to cater to his son's every desire, and to protect him from all knowledge of worldly suffering. Thus as Siddhartha grew up he knew only the pampered life of a closeted prince. Not until the age of 29 did he venture out of his palace to ride through the city. Despite his father's attempts to clear all elderly, ugly and sick people from the streets, a frail elderly man wandered into the path of Siddhartha's chariot. The young prince, who had never seen an old person before, was, not surprisingly, deeply troubled by the sight, having previously been spared all knowledge of the inevitability of human mortality and physical decay.

On subsequent occasions the prince travelled from his palace three more times, seeing first a sick person, then a corpse, and finally an ascetic sitting meditating beneath a tree – an emblematic representation of the inevitability of age, sickness and death, and of the possibility of searching for a state which transcended such suffering. Determined to discover the path which led to this state, Siddhartha slipped away from the palace during the night, leaving his wife and young son asleep, exchanging his royal robes for the clothes of his servant, and set out to follow the life of an ascetic.

For six years Siddhartha wandered the countryside, studying with sages who taught him to achieve deep meditative states. Siddhartha quickly equalled the attainments of his teachers, but soon realized that these accomplishments failed to release him from the root causes of human suffering. He then met up with five other ascetics who had dedicated themselves to the most extreme austerities. Siddhartha joined them and followed their lifestyle, living on a single grain of rice and a drop of water each day until he had wasted away virtually to nothing. At this point, Siddhartha realized that practising pointless austerities was equally unhelpful in his spiritual quest. He therefore determined to follow the so-called **middle way**, a route which involved neither extreme austerities nor excessive self-indulgence.

His five companions having contemptuously abandoned him on account of his apparent lack of willpower, Siddhartha sat down beneath a bo tree and vowed to remain there until he had found an answer to the riddle of existence and suffering. Siddhartha plunged himself into profound meditation. Mara, the god of desire, seeing that the prince was attempting to free himself from craving, and therefore from Mara's control, attempted to distract him with storms of rocks, coals, mud and darkness. When this failed, he sent his three beautiful daughters to tempt Siddhartha, but this attempt to distract the prince also proved fruitless. Finally, Mara attempted to dislodge the prince from the ground he was sitting on, shaking the very earth beneath him. Siddhartha extended his right hand and touched the earth, calling it to witness his unshakeable concentration, after which Mara withdrew.

Having conquered temptation, Siddhartha continued to meditate. As the night progressed he had a vision of all his millions of previous lives and gained an understanding of the workings of karma and of the way in which good and bad actions and desires bear fruit in subsequent lives, creating a potentially infinite and inescapable sequence of rebirths. During the final phase of his great meditation, Siddhartha realized that it was possible to pass beyond this cycle of karma and to reach a spiritual state – which he called **nirvana** – where desire, suffering and causality finally end. At this point he attained **enlightenment** and ceased being Prince Siddhartha Gautama, instead becoming **the Buddha**, "the Enlightened One".

Following his enlightenment, the Buddha at first felt reluctant to talk to others of his experience, doubting that it would be understood. According to tradition, it was only at the intervention of the god Brahma himself that the Buddha agreed to attempt to communicate his unique revelation and help others towards enlightenment. He preached his **first sermon** to his former ascetic companions, whom he found in the Deer Park in Sarnath, near present-day Varanasi in north India. In this sermon he outlined the **Four Noble Truths** (see p.433). The five companions quickly understood the Buddha's message and themselves became enlightened. After this, the Buddha's teaching spread with remarkable rapidity. An order of monks, the **Sangha**, was established (a less successful order of nuns was also subsequently created) and the Buddha appears to have travelled tirelessly around northeast India preaching. He continued to travel and teach right up until his death – or, to be precise, his passing into nirvana – at the age of around eighty at the town of Kusinagara.

The history of Buddhism in Sri Lanka

Over the centuries following the Buddha's death, Buddhism rapidly established itself across much of India, becoming the state religion under the great Indian emperor **Ashoka**. Ashoka sent out various Buddhist missions to neighbouring countries, one of which, under the leadership of his son, Mahinda, arrived in Sri Lanka in 247 BC (see p.357). Mahinda's mission was spectacularly successful and Buddhism quickly became the dominant faith on the island, the religion giving the Sinhalese people a new-found sense of identity. Buddhism and Sinhalese nationalism have remained closely connected ever since, linked to a view of Sri Lanka as the chosen land of the faith – a kind of Buddhist Israel.

Buddhism gradually withered away in India over the following centuries, but continued to flourish in Sri Lanka despite repeated Tamil invasions and the attendant influx of Hindu ideas. It was the chaos caused by these invasions, and the fear that the main Buddhist teachings, which had hitherto been passed orally from generation to generation, would be lost that prompted King Vattagamani Abhaya to have them transcribed in the first century BC – the first time that the key Buddhist texts were committed to writing.

Although Buddhism in India had fallen into terminal decline by the fourth century AD, it continued to spread to new countries. From India it travelled north into Nepal, Tibet and China, developing in the process into a new type of Buddhism, **Mahayana** (see p.434). Sri Lanka, by contrast, preserved the **Theravada** tradition (see opposite), which it subsequently exported to Burma and Thailand, from where it spread to the rest of Southeast Asia. Buddhism continued to flourish throughout the Anuradhapuran and Polonnaruwan periods (see pp.413–415) – indeed for much of these epochs Sri Lanka was virtually a theocracy. Huge monasteries were established and much of the island's agricultural surplus went to supporting a vast population of monks – the resources devoted to maintaining the clergy meant that the practice of begging from alms largely disappeared in Sri Lanka from an early date, while the Buddha's traditional requirement that monks lead a wandering life in order to spread the religion was similarly ignored.

Not until the abandonment of Polonnaruwa in the face of further Tamil assaults in the thirteenth century did Sri Lankan Buddhism begin to face serious difficulties. As Sinhalese power and civilization fragmented over the following centuries, so Buddhism lost its central role in the state. Monasteries were abandoned and the population of monks declined. Hinduism became entrenched in the north, where a new Tamil kingdom had been established in the Jaffna Peninsula, while further religious competition was provided by the traders who began to arrive from Arabia from around the eighth century, and who established sizeable Muslim enclaves around parts of the coast.

Buddhism reached its lowest point in Sri Lanka during the seventeenth and eighteenth centuries, as the coast fell to Portuguese (and later Dutch) colonists. Portuguese missionaries set about winning over the natives for the Roman Catholic faith with a will, ordering the destruction of innumerable temples and converting considerable sections of the population. Meanwhile, the throne of the kingdom of Kandy, the island's last independent region, passed into Tamil hands, and Hindu influence gradually spread.

By 1753, the situation had become so bad that there were not enough monks left to ordain any further Buddhist clergy. The king of Kandy, Kirti Sri Rajasinha, sent out for monks from Thailand, who performed the required ordination services, thus re-establishing the Sangha in the island and founding the so-called **Siyam Nikaya**, or "Siam Order". The revived order flourished, although it became increasingly exclusive, so that only members of the upper-caste Goyigamas were allowed to be ordained (a very un-Buddhist practice). A second sect, the **Amarapura Nikaya**, was established, again with Thai monks providing the initial ordinations. Further disputes over points of doctrine led to the foundation of the **Ramanna Nikaya** in the late nineteenth century. These three nikayas remain the principal orders right up to the present day, with each sect preserving its own ordination tradition.

The Buddhist belief system

The Buddha's teachings, collectively known as the **Dharma**, were codified after his death and passed on orally for several centuries until finally being written down at Alu Vihara in Sri Lanka in the first century BC. The essence of Buddhist belief is encapsulated in the **Four Noble Truths**. Simply put, these are (1) life is suffering; (2) suffering is the result of craving; (3) there can be an end to suffering; (4) there is a path which leads to the end of suffering, the so-called **Noble Eightfold Path**, which consists of a set of simple rules to encourage good behaviour and morals.

All beings, Buddhism asserts, will experience a potentially infinite sequence of rebirths in various different forms: as a human, an animal, ghost or god, either on earth on in one of various heavens or hells. The engine which drives this permanent sequence of reincarnations is **karma**. Meritorious actions produce good karma, which enables creatures to be reborn higher up the spiritual food chain; bad actions have the opposite result. In this classically elegant system, good deeds really are their own reward. No amount of good karma, however, will allow one to escape the sequence of infinite rebirths – good behaviour and the acquiring of merit is simply a stage on the route to enlightenment and the achievement of nirvana. Every desire and action plants seeds of karma which create the impetus for further lives, and further actions and desires – and so on. Some schools of ancient Indian philosophy took this idea to its logical conclusion – the Jains, for example, decided that the best thing to do in life was nothing at all, and more extreme proponents of that religion were known to sit down and starve themselves to death in order to avoid involvement in worldly actions, for good or bad.

The exact route to enlightenment and nirvana is long and difficult – at least according to the older schools of Buddhism – requiring millions of lifetimes. Exactly what **nirvana** is meant to be remains famously vague. The Buddha himself was notoriously elusive on the subject. He compared a person entering nirvana to a flame being extinguished – the flame doesn't go anywhere, but the process of combustion ceases.

Theravada and Mahayana

Theravada Buddhism (the "Law of the Elders") is the dominant form of the religion in Sri Lanka, as well as in Southeast Asia. It is the older of the two main schools of Buddhism and claims to embody the Buddha's teachings in their original form. These teachings emphasize that all individuals are responsible for their own spiritual welfare, and that any person who wishes to achieve enlightenment must pursue the same path trodden by the Buddha himself, giving up worldly concerns and developing spiritual attainments through meditation and self-sacrifice. This path of renunciation is, of course, impossible for most members of the Theravada community to follow, which explains the importance of **monks** in Sri Lanka (and in other Theravada countries), since only members of the Sangha are considered fully committed to the Theravada path, and thus capable of achieving enlightenment – and even then only in rare instances. Lay worshippers do have a (limited) role in the Theravada tradition, though this is mainly to earn merit by offering material support to monks. Otherwise they can hope for little except to lead a moral life and hope to be reborn as a monk themselves at some point in the future.

The rather elitist aspect of Theravada doctrine led to it being dubbed **Hinayana Buddhism**, or "Lesser Vehicle", a slightly pejorative term which compares it unfavourably with the **Mahayana**, or "Greater Vehicle", sect. Mahayana Buddhism developed as an offshoot of Theravada Buddhism, eventually becoming the dominant form in China, Tibet and Japan, although it has had only a slight influence on Sri Lankan Buddhism. As Theravada Buddhism developed, it came to be believed that the Buddha himself was only the latest of a series of Buddhas – Sri Lankan tradition claims that there have been either 16 or 24 previous Buddhas, and holds that another Buddha, Maitreya, will appear at some point in the remote future when all the last Buddha's teachings have been forgotten. The Mahayana tradition expanded this aspect of Buddhist cosmology to create a grand array of additional deities, including various additional Buddhas and **bodhisattvas** – a Buddha-to-be who has chosen to defer entering nirvana in order to remain on earth (or in one of the various Buddhist heavens) to help others towards enlightenment. Instead of trying to emulate the Buddha, devotees simply worship one or more of the Mahayana deities and reap the spiritual rewards. Not surprisingly, this much more populist – and much less demanding – form of the religion became widely established in place of the Theravada tradition. Compared with the countless lifetimes of spiritual self-improvement which Theravada Buddhism requires its followers to endure, some schools of Mahayana claim that even a single prayer to the relevant bodhisattva can cause one to be reborn in one of the Buddhist heavens – hence its description of itself as the "Greater Vehicle", a form of the religion capable of carrying far greater numbers of devotees to enlightenment.

The Buddhist pantheon in Sri Lanka

The odd Mahayana bodhisattva occasionally crops up in temples around the island, but almost all the additional gods and goddesses associated with Buddhism in Sri Lanka are the result of its proximity to Hindu India and to the influence of successive waves of Tamil invaders. Buddhism evolved from the same roots as **Hinduism** and makes many of the same assumptions about the universe, so the inclusion of many Hindu deities within the pantheon of Sri Lankan Buddhist gods is not as inconsistent as it might initially appear. Indeed the Buddha himself never denied the existence or powers of the myriad gods of ancient Indian cosmology, simply arguing that they were subject to the same laws of karma and rebirth as any other creature – indeed according to tradition the Buddha ascended to the various heavens to preach to the gods on several occasions. Thus, although other gods may be unable to assist in helping one towards the ultimate goal of attaining nirvana, they can still have power to assist in less exulted aims – the success of a new business; the birth of a child; the abundance of a harvest – and they can therefore be worshipped alongside the Buddha.

Various Hindu gods have been appropriated by Sri Lankan Buddhism over the centuries – and have gone in and out of fashion according to the prevailing religious or political climate. There are countless shrines across the island dedicated to these subsidiary gods, either as subsidiary shrines within Buddhist temples or as separate, self-contained temples – these shrines or temples are known as **devales** to differentiate them from purely Buddhist temples (viharas) and Hindu temples (kovils). Thus, the supreme Hindu deity, **Vishnu** (often known locally as **Upulvan**), is regarded in Sri Lanka as a protector of Buddhism and is worshipped by Buddhists, as is the god **Kataragama** (see p.198), also of mixed Hindu–Buddhist origins. Other popular gods in the Buddhist pantheon are **Saman** (see p.275) and **Pattini** (see p.226), while the elephant-headed Hindu god **Ganesh** is also widely worshipped. Recent decades have also seen a dramatic increase in the popularity of the fearsome goddesses **Durga** and Kali.

Daily Buddhist ritual and belief

For all the Buddha's emphasis on the search for enlightenment and nirvana, for most Sri Lankans, daily religious life is focused on more modest goals. Theravada Buddhism traditionally states that only monks can achieve enlightenment, and even then only on very rare occasions: Sri Lanka's last arhat (enlightened monk) is supposed to have died in the first century BC. Thus, rather than trying to emulate the Buddha's own spiritual odyssey and attempt the near-impossible task of achieving enlightenment, the average Sri Lankan Buddhist will concentrate on leading a moral life and on acquiring religious merit in the hope of ensuring rebirth higher up the spiritual ladder.

To become a Buddhist, one simply announces the fact that one is "taking refuge" in the **Three Jewels**: the Buddha, the Dharma and the Sangha. There is no form of organized or congregational worship in Buddhism, as there is in Christianity or Islam – instead, devotees visit their local temple as and when they please, saying prayers at the dagoba or Buddha shrine (or that of another god), perhaps offering flowers, lighting a candle or reciting (or having monks recite) Buddhist scriptures, an act known as **pirith**. Although Theravada holds that the Buddha himself should not be worshipped, many Sinhalese effectively do so. Buddhist **relics** are also objects of devotion, and many Sinhalese still visit Kandy to pay homage to the Buddha's Tooth.

Full-moon – or **poya** – days are considered particularly important, since the Buddha himself is said to have been born, achieved enlightenment and passed into nirvana on a poya day. Buddhist devotees traditionally visit their local temple on poya days to spend time in prayer or meditation; they might also practise certain abstinences, such as fasting or refraining from alcohol and sex.

The Sangha

Sri Lanka's twenty thousand-odd **Buddhist monks** form a distinctive element of national life, instantly recognizable in their brightly coloured robes. The monastic tradition is deeply embedded in the national culture, and the importance of the Buddhist clergy can be seen in myriad ways, from the monks who sit in the nation's parliament to the seats in every bus which are reserved for their use. The Sinhala language, meanwhile, features special forms of address only used when talking to a monk, even including a different word for "yes". (There are no Buddhist nuns in Sri Lanka, incidentally, the order having died out in the eleventh century.)

Young boys are chosen to be monks if they show a particular religious inclination or if their horoscope suggests that they would be suitable candidates – material factors can also play a part for children of poor families, since entering the Sangha offers access to education and a reasonable standard of living. Boy monks are first initiated as novices around their tenth birthday (there is no minimum age at which boys can be ordained – according to tradition, a boy can become a novice when he is old enough to chase away crows). Higher ordination occurs at the age of 20. At this point the monk becomes a full member of the **Sangha**. Monks generally enter the Sangha for life – the custom, popular in Thailand and Burma, of laymen becoming monks for a short period then returning to normal life is not an accepted practice in Sri Lanka.

On entering the Sangha the new monk shaves his head and dons the characteristic robes (usually saffron, sometimes red or yellow) of a Buddhist cleric. He also takes a new name: the honorific *thero* or *thera* is often added after it, while "The Venerable" (or "Ven.") is frequently added as a prefix. Monks commit themselves to a code of conduct which entails various prohibitions. These traditionally include: not to kill; not to steal; not to have sex; not to lie about spiritual attainments; not to drink alcohol; not to handle money; not to eat after midday; and not to own more than a bare minimum of personal possessions.

The great monastic foundations of ancient Sri Lanka have largely vanished, and most monks now live in small groups attached to their local village temple, and as such are often intimately connected to the life of the village. The actual functions required of a Buddhist monk are few. The only ceremonies they preside at are funerals, although they are sometimes asked to recite Buddhist scriptures (*pirith*). Monks traditionally act as spiritual advisers; some monks also gain reputations as healers or astrologers, whilst many teach (and some attain considerable intellectual accomplishments).

A less savoury aspect of the Sri Lankan Buddhist clergy has been their involvement in **ultra-nationalistic politics** – the view which many monks hold of Sri Lanka as the "chosen land" of Buddhism has disturbing parallels with hard-line Jewish attitudes towards Israel. In 1959 the country's prime minister, S.W.R.D Bandaranaike, was shot dead by a Buddhist monk, and the clergy have constantly involved themselves in politics ever since – some of the more right-wing monks reputedly formed a clandestine ultra-nationalist group called the Circle of Sinhalese Force, whose members used Nazi salutes and spouted wild propaganda about the perceived threat to their land, race and religion – a mixture of *Mahavamsa* and *Mein Kampf*. In earlier decades monks contented themselves with influencing politicians, though in recent years they have started entering politics on their own account – a Buddhist monk was first elected to parliament in 2001, while in the elections of 2004 a total of seven were voted into office, forming a significant political grouping in a delicately balanced minority government. Leading monks have consistently denounced any attempts by the government to cede autonomy to the Tamils of the north and have campaigned vigorously for a military rather than a negotiated solution to the civil war, apparently seeing no contradiction between the Buddhism which they profess to believe and their aggressively warmongering and anti-Tamil rhetoric – all the more unfortunate, given that they continue to command widespread popular support and respect.

Sri Lankan Buddhist art and architecture

Sri Lanka's art and architecture – ranging from Dravidian temples to Portuguese Baroque churches – offers a fascinating visual legacy of the varied influences which have shaped the island's eclectic culture. Despite the number of races and religions which have contributed to the artistic melting pot, however, the influence of Buddhism remains unchallenged at the centre of the nation's cultural fabric, and it is in Buddhist art and architecture that Sri Lanka's greatest cultural achievements can be found.

Sri Lanka's early Buddhist art exhibits a restrained classicism, exemplified by the monumental simplicity of the great dagobas of **Anuradhapura**. Although the **Mahayana** doctrines (see p.434) which transformed Buddhist art in many other parts of Asia largely bypassed Sri Lanka, the island's religious art was significantly enriched from around the tenth century by the influence of **Hinduism** introduced by the numerous Tamil dynasties which periodically overran parts of the north. This influence first showed itself in the art of **Polonnaruwa** and later blended with Sinhalese traditions to create the uniquely syncretized style of **Kandyan** temple architecture, which reached its apogee during the fifteenth to eighteenth centuries.

Buddha images

Early Buddhist art was symbolic rather than figurative. The Buddha himself (according to some traditions) asked that no images be made of him after his death, and for the first few centuries he was represented symbolically by objects such as dagobas, bo trees, thrones, wheels, pillars, trees, animals, footprints.

Exactly why the first **Buddha images** were made remains unclear, though they seem to have initially appeared in India in around the first century BC. Buddha images are traditionally highly stylized: the intention of Buddhist art has always been to represent the Buddha's transcendental, superhuman nature, rather than to describe a personality (unlike, say, Western representations of Jesus). The vast majority of Buddha figures are shown in one of the canonical poses, or **mudras** (see box overleaf).

Many sculptural details of Buddha figures are enshrined in tradition and preserved in the *Sariputra*, a Sinhalese treatise in verse for the makers of Buddha images. Some of the most important features of traditional Buddha images include the **ushnisha**, the small protuberance on the top of the head, denoting superior mental powers; the **sirsapata**, or flame of wisdom (the Buddhist equivalent of the Christian halo), growing out of the *ushnisha*; the elongated **earlobes**, denoting renunciation (the holes in the lobes would have contained jewels which the Buddha gave up when he abandoned his royal position); the shape of the **eyes**, modelled after the form of lotus petals; the **eyebrows**, whose curves are meant to resemble two bows; the **mouth**, usually closed and wearing the hint of a smile; and the **feet**, which traditionally bear 32 different auspicious markings.

The one area in which Mahayana Buddhism has had a lasting impact on Sri Lankan religious art is in the **gigantic Buddha statues**, some standing up to 30m high, which can be found all over the island, dating from both ancient

Buddhist mudras and their meanings

Abhaya mudra The "Have No Fear" pose shows the Buddha standing with his right hand raised with the palm facing the viewer.

Dhyana or **samadhi mudra** Shows the Buddha in meditation, seated in the lotus or half-lotus position, with his hands placed together in his lap.

Bhumisparsha mudra The "Earth-Witness" pose shows the Buddha touching the ground with the tips of the fingers of his left hand, commemorating the moment in his enlightenment when the demon Mara, in attempting to break his concentration, caused the Earth to shake beneath him, and the Buddha stilled the ground by touching it.

Vitarka mudra ("Gesture of Explanation") and **dharmachakra mudra** ("Gesture of the Turning of the Wheel of the Law") In both positions the Buddha forms a circle with his thumb and one finger, representing the wheel of dharma. Used in both standing and sitting poses.

Reclining poses In Asian Buddhist art, the reclining pose is traditionally considered to represent the Buddha at the moment of his death and entrance into nirvana – the so-called **Parinirvana** pose. Sri Lankan art makes a subtle distinction between two types of reclining pose: the **sleeping** pose, and the true *parinirvana* pose. Sleeping and *parinirvana* Buddhas are distinguished by six marks (although the distinctions between the two are often quite subtle). In the sleeping pose: the eyes are open; the right hand is at least partially beneath the head; the stomach is a normal size; the robe is smooth beneath the left hand; the bottom of the hem of the robe is level; and the toes of the two feet are in a straight line. In the *parinirvana* pose, the hand is away from the head; the eyes are partially closed; the stomach is shrunken; the robe is bunched up under his left hand (the clenched hand and crumpled robe indicating the pain of the Buddha's final illness); the hem at the bottom of the robe is uneven; and the toes of the two feet are not in a straight line. Reclining poses are particularly common in Sri Lanka.

(Aukana, Sasseruwa, Maligawila, Polonnaruwa) and modern (Dambulla, Weherehena, Wewurukannala) epochs. Such larger-than-life depictions reflect the change from Theravada's emphasis on the historical, human Buddha to Mahayana's view of the Buddha as a cosmic being who could only be truly represented in figures of superhuman dimensions.

Dagobas (stupas)

The stupa, or **dagoba**, as they are known in Sri Lanka, is the world's most universal Buddhist architectural symbol, ranging from the classically simple hemispherical structures found in Sri Lanka and Nepal to the spire-like stupas of Thailand and Burma and the pagodas of China and Japan (indeed the Sinhalese name dagoba has been mooted as one possible source for the word pagoda). Dagobas originally developed from the Indian burial mounds which were raised to mark the graves of important personages, although popular legend traces the distinctive form of the dagoba back to the Buddha himself. Upon being asked by his followers what shape a memorial to him should take, the Buddha is said to have folded his robe into a square and placed his upturned begging bowl and umbrella on top of it, thus outlining the dagoba's basic form. As Buddhist theology developed, so the elements of the dagoba acquired more elaborate symbolic meanings. At its simplest level, the dagoba's role as an enormous burial mound serves to recall the memory of the Buddha's passing away and entering into nirvana. A more elaborate explanation describes the dagoba in cosmological terms: the main dome (*anda*), built in the shape of a hill, is said to represent Mount Meru, the sacred peak which lies at the centre of the Buddhist universe, while the spire (*chattravali*) symbolizes the axis mundi, or cosmic pillar, connecting earth and heaven and leading upwards out of the world towards nirvana.

The earliest dagobas were built to enshrine important **relics** of the Buddha himself or of other revered religious figures (the Buddha's own ashes were, according to tradition, divided into forty thousand parts, providing the impetus for a huge spate of dagoba building, while many notable monks were also interred in dagobas). These relics were traditionally placed in or just below the *harmika*, the square relic chamber at the top of the dome. As Buddhism spread, the building of dagobas became seen as an act of religious merit, resulting in the construction of innumerable smaller, or "votive", dagobas, some no larger than a few feet high.

It was in the great dagobas of Anuradhapura and Polonnaruwa, however, that early Sri Lankan architecture reached its highest point. These massive construction feats were Asia's nearest equivalent to the Egyptian pyramids. The foundations were trampled down by elephants, then the main body of the dagobas filled with rubble and vast numbers of bricks (it's been estimated that the Jetavana dagoba at Anuradhapura uses almost one hundred million), after which the entire structures were plastered and painted with a coat of limewash. Constant repairs, and the fact that new outer shells were often constructed around old stupas, means that it's often difficult to determine the exact origins or original shape of some of the island's most famous dagobas.

Sri Lankan dagobas preserve the classic older form of the stupa, following the pattern of the great stupa at Sanchi in central India, erected in the third century BC by the emperor Ashoka, who was also responsible for introducing Buddhism to the island. Despite the superficial similarities shared by all Sri Lankan dagobas, there are subtle variations, with six different basic shapes being recognized (ranging from the perfectly hemispherical "bubble-shape" to the narrower and more elongated "bell-shape"), as well as innumerable other small nuances in design. Dagobas consist of four principal sections. The entire structure usually sits on a square terrace whose four sides are oriented towards the cardinal points. Many larger stupas have four small shrines, or **vahalkadas** (a uniquely Sri Lankan architectural element), arranged around the base of the dagoba at the cardinal points. The main hemispherical body of the stupa is known as the **anda**, surmounted by a cube-like structure, the **harmika**, from which rises the **chattravali**. In the earliest Indian stupas this was originally a pillar on which a series of umbrella-like structures were threaded, though in Sri Lankan-style dagobas the umbrellas have fused into a kind of spire. Dagobas are solid structures (apart from a single hollow example at Kalutara).

Dagobas still serve as important objects of pilgrimage and religious devotion: as in other Buddhist countries, devotees typically make clockwise circumambulations of the dagoba – an act known as *pradakshina* – which is meant to focus the mind in meditation, although this practice is less widespread in Sri Lanka than in other countries such as Nepal (similarly, the prohibition against walking around dagobas in an anticlockwise direction, which is frowned upon in other countries, isn't much observed).

Buddhist temples

Sri Lankan **Buddhist temples** (viharas or viharayas come in a bewildering range of shapes and sizes, ranging from the intimate cave temples of Dambulla and Mulkirigala to the enormous monastic foundations of Anuradhapura and Polonnaruwa. Despite their variety, however, most of the island's Buddhist places of worship comprise three basic elements: an image house, a dagoba (see above), and a bo tree enclosure. The **image house** (*pilimage* or *patimaghara*) houses the temple's Buddha image, or images, along with statues and/or paintings of other gods and attendants; it may be preceded by an antechamber or surrounded by an ambulatory, although there are countless variations in the exact form these shrines take and in the particular gods found inside them. During the late Polonnaruwan and early Kandyan period, image houses developed into the **gedige**, a type of Buddha shrine strongly influenced by South Indian Hindu temple architecture, being constructed entirely out of stone on a rectangular plan, with enormously thick walls and corbelled roofs. Important examples can be found at Polonnaruwa, Nalanda and at the Natha Devale in Kandy.

The **bo tree enclosure** (*bodhighara*) is a uniquely Sri Lankan feature. The Buddha achieved enlightenment while meditating beneath a bo (or bodhi) tree, and these trees serve as symbols of, and a living link with, that moment – many of the island's specimens have been grown from cuttings taken from the great tree at Anuradhapura, which is itself believed to have been grown from a cutting taken from the very tree under which the Buddha meditated. Bo tree enclosures are often surrounded by gold railings and raised on terraces, with tables set around them on which devotees place flower offerings; the trees themselves (or the surrounding railings) are often draped in colourful strings of prayer flags. Some bo trees are also surrounded by a kind of brick plinth with ducts at each corner, into which devotees pour water to feed the tree's roots.

Larger temples often have two or even three bo tree enclosures and perhaps one or two subsidiary **shrines** or devales devoted to different deities from the Sinhalese Buddhist pantheon, such as Vishnu or Kataragama. Temples attached to monasteries also have dormitories and refectories for the monks, as well as a **poyage** ("House of the Full Moon") in which monks assemble to recite Buddhist scriptures on poya (full moon) days. Kandyan-era temples sometimes have a **digge**, or drummer's hall, usually an open-sided columned pavilion, where drummers would have performed during temple ceremonies – there's a good example at the Vishnu Devale in Kandy.

Even more unusual is the **vatadage**, or a circular image house, of which only a few examples remain. These have a small dagoba at their centre, flanked by four Buddha images at the cardinal points, and then surrounded by concentric rows of pillars which would originally have supported a wooden roof. There are notable examples at Medirigiya, at the Thuparama in Anuradhapura and in the Quadrangle at Polonnaruwa.

Buddhist temple iconography

Sri Lankan temples typically sport a wealth of symbolic decorative detail. The bases of stairways and other entrances into temples are often flanked by **guardstones** (*doratupalas*), showing low-relief carvings of protective deities who are believed to ward off malign influences. These guardian figures are sometimes the Hindu god **Vishnu**, regarded as a protector of Buddhism in Sri Lanka, and sometimes **nagarajas** (snake kings; see box on p.442). Another notable feature of Sri Lankan art found at the entrances to temples is the **moonstone** (see box opposite), carved either in the classic semicircular shape found at Anuradhapura, Polonnaruwa and elsewhere, or in the more asymmetric examples typical of Kandy.

Originally from India, the **moonstone** developed in Sri Lanka from a plain slab to the elaborate semicircular stones, carved in polished granite, which are found at Anuradhapura, Polonnaruwa and many other places across the island. Moonstones are placed at the entrances to shrines to concentrate the mind of the worshipper upon entering. Carved in concentric half-circles, they represent the spiritual journey from samsara, the endless succession of deaths and rebirth, to nirvana, the escape from endless reincarnation.

The exact design of moonstones varies; not all contain every one of the following elements, and the different animals are sometimes combined in the same ring.

Flames (often in the outermost ring), representing the flames of desire – though they also purify those who step across them.

The four **Buddhist animals**, representing the inevitability of birth, death and suffering, are the **elephant** (symbolizing birth), the **horse** (old age), the **lion** (illness) and the **bull** (death and decay) – the way in which the images in each ring chase one another around the moonstone symbolizes samsara's endless cycle of deaths and rebirths. The animals are sometimes shown in separate rings, but more usually combined into a single one.

Vines (or, according to the interpretations of some art historians, snakes), representing desire and attachment to life.

Geese, representing purity (the goose is a Hindu symbol: as Hamsa it is the vehicle of Brahma, and a sign of wisdom).

A **lotus** at the centre of the design is the symbol of the Buddha and nirvana, and of escape from the cycle of reincarnation.

The classic moonstone pattern described above experienced two important modifications during the **Polonnaruwa period**. To begin with, the bull was omitted: as an important Hindu image (the bull Nandi is the "vehicle", or chariot, of Shiva) this particular animal had become too sacred to be trodden on in the increasingly Hinduized city. In addition, the lion was also usually absent (although one can be seen in the moonstone at the Hatadage) due to its significance as a royal and national symbol of the Sinhalese.

Moonstone design continued to evolve right up until the **Kandyan period**, by which time the moonstone had evolved into the almost triangular designs found at the Dalada Maligawa and many other temples in the central highlands. During this evolution, the moonstone also lost virtually all its symbolic meaning; the floral designs found on Kandyan-era moonstones are of purely decorative import, although the lotus survives at the heart.

Many details of Buddhist iconography depict real or imaginary animals; the most common are described in the box overleaf. Another standard decorative element is the **lotus**, the sacred flower of Buddhism; the fact that these pure white flowers blossom directly out of muddy waters is considered symbolic of the potential for Buddhahood which everyone is believed to carry within them. Lotuses are found everywhere in Buddhist design, often painted decoratively on ceilings and walls; Buddha figures are usually shown seated on lotus thrones. Other common symbolic devices include the **chakra**, or Buddhist wheel, symbolizing the Buddha's teaching – the eight spokes represent the Eightfold Path (see p.433). A common detail in the doors of Kandyan temples is the **sun and moon** motif, originally a symbol of the Buddha during the Anuradhapura period, though later appropriated by the kings of Kandy as a royal symbol.

Temples are often decorated with **murals** of varying degrees of sophistication, ranging from primitive daubs to the great narrative sequences found in

C

CONTEXTS | Sri Lankan Buddhist art and architecture

A Buddhist bestiary

Animals, both real and imaginary, form an important element in Buddhist iconography. The following are some of the most common.

Makaras The *makara* is a mythical beast of Indian origin, formed from parts of various different animals: the body of a fish; the foot of a lion; the eye of a monkey; the trunk and tusk of an elephant; the tail of a peacock; the ear of a pig; and the mouth of a crocodile. One of the most ubiquitous features of Sri Lankan Buddhist architecture is the **makara torana**, or "dragon arch", made up of two *makaras* connected to a dragon's mouth, which is designed to ward off evil spirits and used to frame entrances and Buddha images in virtually every temple in the island.

Nagarajas, or snake kings, are human figures canopied by cobra hoods. They apparently derive from pre-Hindu Indian beliefs and are regarded as symbols of fertility and masters of the underground world. Despite their apparently pagan origins, they derive some Buddhist legitimacy from the fact that the *nagaraja* Muchalinda is said to have sheltered the meditating Buddha as he achieved enlightenment – as a result of which cobras are held sacred. *Nagarajas* (plus attendant dwarfs) are often pictured on the **guardstones** which flank the entrances to many buildings of ancient Sri Lanka, and were intended, like makara toranas, to prevent evil influences from entering the building.

Dwarfs *Nagarajas* are often shown with dwarfs (*gana*), who can also often be seen supporting the base of steps or temple walls – these jolly-looking pot-bellied creatures are associated with Kubera, the god of wealth, though their exact significance and origins remain obscure.

Elephants Carved in low relief, elephants commonly adorn the walls enclosing religious complexes, their massive presence symbolically supporting the temple buildings.

Lions Though they possess no definite religious significance except to suggest the Buddha's royal origins, lions are also common features of Buddhist architecture. The lion is also an emblem of the Sinhalese people, who trace their ancestry back to – and indeed owe their name to – a lion.

Geese (*hamsa*) Considered a symbol of royal spiritual knowledge, geese are often found on moonstones, and used decoratively elsewhere in temples.

the cave temples at Dambulla. Perhaps the most popular subject for murals, especially in the south of the island, is tales from the **jatakas**, the moral fables describing the Buddha's 547 previous lives, while pictures of **pilgrimage sites** around the island are another common theme.

The Kandyan style

The distinctive architectural tradition which developed during the **Kandyan era** (seventeenth to early nineteenth centuries) is quite different from the earlier styles of Anuradhapura and Polonnaruwa. As the power and prosperity of the Sinhalese waned, it was no longer possible for kings and clergy to construct new monasteries and dagobas on the scale of the great structures of the past, and Sri Lankan Buddhist architecture became much more small-scale and intimate, as exemplified by the dozens of beautiful little temples which dot the city of Kandy and the surrounding countryside.

Few of these structures were built in stone, and wood became the principal material of Kandyan craftsmanship, encouraging the development of elaborate **carving**, as displayed in the highly ornate pillars which are one of the most typical features of Kandyan architecture (though they owe much of their inspiration to South Indian styles which had already appeared in stone in Polonnaruwa; see p.326). Architects often used these pillars to create open-sided pavilions for ceremonial functions or musical performances, topped with the elegant hipped roofs which are also typical of Kandyan architecture, as in the Audience Hall at the Temple of the Tooth at Kandy (see p.224). The Kandyan era also saw a great flourishing of **mural painting**, typically executed in vivid red and arranged in strip panels. Two of the finest examples are the great *Mara Parajaya* sequences in Cave no. 2 at Dambulla (see p.307) and the Degaldoruwa temple (see p.241) just outside Kandy.

Sri Lankan wildlife

S ri Lanka boasts a variety of wildlife quite out of proportion with its modest physical dimensions, including one of the world's largest populations of both wild and captive elephants plus an array of other fauna ranging from leopards, sloth bears and giant squirrels through to huge monitor lizards and crocodiles – not to mention a fascinating collection of endemic birdlife. This richness is partly a result of Sri Lanka's complex climate and topography, ranging from the denuded savannahs of the dry zone to the lush montane forests of the hill country, and partly due to its geographical position, which makes it a favoured wintering spot for numerous birds, as well as a nesting site for five of the world's species of marine turtles.

Elephants

No animal is as intimately connected with the history and culture of the island as the **Sri Lankan elephant** – indeed such was the regard in which they were held that killing one was formerly a capital offence. Elephants are accorded an almost religious veneration on account of their size and strength, and play an important role in religious festivals across the country, nowhere more so than at the Esala Perahera in Kandy, where the Tooth Relic itself (or at least its casket) is borne through the city by the Maligawa Tusker. Ceremonial occasions aside, elephants have been put to many uses throughout the island's history. Dutugemunu (see p.348) went to war mounted on one, while later kings of Anuradhapura used them to trample down the foundations of their city's great religious monuments (bas reliefs of elephant heads still adorn the encircling walls of many of the islands' temples and dagobas). During the Kandyan era, elephants were used to trample condemned prisoners to death, while the pragmatic Dutch employed them to haul gun-carriages and tow barges along their newly constructed canals – even now, trained elephants are used to move heavy objects in places inaccessible to machinery. Elephants were also a valuable commercial commodity. The colonial authorities organized huge elephant hunts where wild elephants were rounded up, tamed and then exported – you can see a sling in Colombo's National Maritime Museum with which they were lifted aboard ships. Elephants can now be seen in virtually all the island's national parks – Yala, Uda Walawe and Minneriya are three of the best – and you can also see captive elephants in various places, most famously the Pinnewala Elephant Orphanage, outside Kandy.

The Sri Lankan elephant (*elephas maximus maximus*) is a subspecies of the Asian elephant (*elephas maximus*), which is lighter and has smaller ears than the African elephant (*loxodonta africana*), and also differs from African elephants in that only a small proportion (about one in ten) of male elephants have tusks, so-called **tuskers**. This at least had the benefit of discouraging ivory poachers, although it failed to deter British colonial hunters, who saw the elephant as the ultimate big-game target – the notorious Major Rogers is said to have despatched well over a thousand of the unfortunate creatures during a twelve-year stint in Badulla before his murderous career was terminated by a well-aimed blast of lightning. By the beginning of the twentieth century there were only around 12,000 elephants left in Sri Lanka, and this figure has now fallen to 2000–2500; although this is still a remarkably large population for such a small island, there are fears that these numbers will continue to fall. Many elephants were injured or killed in the civil war, though the principal pressure on them nowadays is **habitat loss**, as more and more of the island's undeveloped areas are cleared for agriculture. This has led to numerous conflicts between villagers and roaming elephants, with tragic consequences – it has been estimated that between 1997 and 2001, more than seven hundred elephants (and nearly three hundred people) were killed in such clashes. Elephant herds still migrate across the island for considerable distances, particularly in the southeast around Yala and Bundala national parks and in the north between Minneriya, Kaudulla and Wasgomuwa national parks, and there are frequent conflicts between farmers and wandering herds, which trample crops and raid sugar plantations (elephants have a pronounced sweet tooth). Herds are periodically rounded up and chased back to the island's national parks, though these so-called "elephant drives" have frequently become a source of conflict between locals and conservationists. In an attempt to solve this problem the government is attempting to create so-called "**elephant corridors**" along traditional migratory routes linking the various national parks.

Wild elephants usually live in close-knit family groupings of around fifteen, under the leadership of an elderly female; each herd needs a large area to survive – around five square kilometres per adult – not surprising, given that a grown elephant drinks 150 litres of water and eats up to 200kg of vegetation daily. Elephants' gestation period averages 22 months and they can live up to seventy years.

Trained elephants are still a major feature of Sri Lankan life, and can often be seen shambling along roads around the island. Captive elephants work under the guidance of skilled **mahouts**, who manipulate their charges using a system of 72 pressure points, plus various verbal commands – a measure of the animals' intelligence is given by the fact that elephants trained to recognize instructions in one language have been successfully re-educated to follow commands in a different one. The life of a trained elephant can be demanding, and it's likely that not all are treated as well as they should be – mahouts are occasionally injured or even killed by their disgruntled charges, proving the truth of the old adage about elephants never forgetting (one particular elephant who had killed two of his mahouts was even put on trial in a court of law – and subsequently acquitted after evidence was presented that he had been mistreated by his handlers). Having said that, elephants can also become objects of remarkable veneration, most famously in the case of the venerable Maligawa Tusker Raja (see p.224), whose death in 1998 prompted the government to declare a day of national mourning.

Leopards

The Sri Lankan **leopard** (*Panthera pardus*) is the island's most striking – and one of its most elusive – residents. These magnificent animals, which can grow to over two metres in length, are now highly endangered in Sri Lanka due to habitat destruction, although the island still has more of the creatures than almost anywhere else in the world. It's thought that there are around five hundred in the whole of the island, with some two hundred concentrated in **Yala National Park** (see below). Each hunts within a set territory, preying on smaller or less mobile mammals, most commonly deer; most hunting is done at dawn or dusk, which is generally the best time to spot them. Leopards have a diverse diet and will eat anything from insects to deer, although some leopards develop a taste for certain types of meat – the notorious man-eating leopard of Punanai (whose story is recounted in Christopher Ondjaate's *The Man-Eater of Punanai*; see p.451) is said to have acquired a particular fondness for human flesh. They are also expert climbers, and can sometimes be seen sitting in trees, where they often store the remains of their kills; they are also commonly spotted basking in the sun on rocky outcrops.

Leopards can be found in various parts of the island, including many national parks. Easily the best place to spot one is Yala National Park, though you'll have to be amazingly lucky to come across one anywhere else. Block 1 of Yala (the area which is open to the public) is thought to have a leopard density of as high as one animal per kilometre, probably the highest in the world. Leopards here, particularly young males, have become remarkably habituated to human visitors, and often stroll fearlessly along the tracks through the park.

Monkeys and other mammals

Three species of **monkey** are native to Sri Lanka. The most distinctive and widely encountered is the graceful **grey langur** (*Presbytis entellus*; also known as the common or Hanuman langur), a beautiful and delicate long-limbed creature with silver-grey hair, a small black face and an enormous tail. Grey langurs can be seen all over the island and are particularly numerous around the southeast, both in national parks and in areas of human habitation, ranging from Bundala National Park to the sacred precinct at Kataragama. They are naturally shy, though some troupes in places frequented by humans have become slightly less reclusive, albeit still engagingly skittish.

Also relatively common, though rather less attractive, is the **toque macaque** (*Macaca sinica*; also known as the red-faced macaque), a medium-sized, reddish-brown creature with a rather baboon-like narrow pink face topped by a distinctive circular tuft of hair. Macaques are much bolder (and noisier) than langurs, and sometimes behave aggressively towards humans when searching for food; they also frequently raid gardens with destructive results. They can be found in most rural parts of the island, usually in troupes of around twenty to thirty.

The third native species is the **purple-faced langur** (*Presbytis senex*; also known as the purple-faced leaf monkey or bear monkey), which is endemic to the island. This is similar in build to the grey langur, with long, slender limbs, but with a blackish coat and a pair of large, striking white side-whiskers.

Sri Lanka's most endearing mammal is the rare **sloth bear** (*Melursus ursinus*), an engagingly shaggy, shambling creature, about a metre in length, which is occasionally spotted in Yala and other national parks. You're far more likely to see the island's various types of **deer** – species include the spotted deer, sambur deer and muntjac or barking deer. Wild **buffalo** are also common. Sri Lanka boasts several species of **squirrel**, ranging from the beautifully delicate little palm squirrels, instantly recognizable by their striped bodies and found everywhere (even on the beach), to the rare giant squirrels which can occasionally be seen in montane forests. **Flying foxes** – large, fruit-eating bats which can reach up to a metre in length – are a common sight islandwide, while **mongooses** are also often encountered in the island's national parks, as are rabbits. Less common is the **wild boar**, similar to the wild boars of Europe, and equally ugly. Rare species include the reclusive **porcupine** (or pangolin), most commonly seen by night, and the even rarer, and also largely nocturnal, **fishing cat**, a large, greyish-brown creature which can grow up to almost a metre in length. They usually live near water, scooping prey out with their paws – hence the name.

Birds

Sri Lanka is a rewarding and well-established destination for dedicated birders: the island's range of habitats – from coastal wetlands to tropical rainforest and high-altitude cloudforest – supports a huge variety of birdlife, which is further enriched by migrants from the Indian subcontinent and further afield. The island boasts 233 **resident species**, including 26 **endemics**, while another two hundred **migratory** species have been recorded as visiting the island. Most of the latter visit the island during the northern hemisphere's winter, holidaying in Sri Lanka from around August through to April. In addition, some species of pelagic bird visit Sri Lanka during the southern hemisphere's winter.

Some species are confined to particular **habitats**, and most of the island's endemic species are found in the wet zone which covers the southwestern quarter of the country. For casual bird-spotters, any of Sri Lanka's national parks should yield a large range of species – Bundala, Yala and Uda Walawe are all excellent destinations, and a day's birdwatching in any of these could easily turn up as many as a hundred species. Dedicated birders generally head to more specialist sites, such as Sinharaja, which is home to no less than seventeen endemics (although they are difficult to see), and Horton's Plains and Hakgala in the hill country, both excellent for spotting montane species. With careful planning, dedicated birders might succeed in seeing all the island's endemics in a week or two.

Sri Lanka's 26 **endemic birds** range from the spectacular, multicoloured Sri Lanka blue magpie to relatively dowdy and elusive species such as the tiny Legge's flowerpecker, the Sri Lanka whistling thrush and the ashy-headed laughing thrush. Other attractive endemics include the dusky-blue flycatcher, yellow-eared bulbul, black-crested bulbul, yellow-fronted and crimson-fronted barbets, Layard's parakeet, Sri Lanka hanging parrot and the Sri Lanka white-eye – even for nonspecialists, catching a glimpse of one of these rare and beautiful birds is a memorable moment.

Even if you don't manage to catch any of the endemics, there are plenty of other eye-catching birds to watch out for. **Common species** include bee-eaters, scarlet minivets, orioles, parakeets, Indian rollers, Indian pittas, hoopoes, sunbirds and the various species of dazzling kingfisher – the latter is a frequent sight around water (or perched on cables) throughout the island. Other ubiquitous, albeit less colourful, species include the common myna, bulbul, spotted dove and the yellow-billed babbler, the last instantly recognizable thanks to its distinctive hopping gait. Another frequently encountered resident of the national parks is the peacock (or, more precisely, the Indian peafowl), a common but always memorable sight when perched in the trees of the dry-zone jungle. Other spectacular Sri Lankan birds include the Malabar pied hornbill, with its strange double beak, and the Asian paradise-flycatcher, with its sweeping brown tail feathers.

The rich population of resident and migrant **water birds** includes various species of grebe, cormorant, pelican, bittern, heron, egret, stork, ibis, plover, lapwing, sandpiper, tern and stilt. Look out particularly for the colourful painted stork, the magnificent Indian darter and the huge (and impressively ugly) lesser adjutant, while Bundala National Park attracts huge flocks of migrant flamingos. **Birds of prey** include the common Brahminy kite (frequently spotted even in the middle of Colombo), the majestic sea eagle and the huge black eagle and grey-headed fish eagle. The island's fine range of **owls** includes the extraordinary-looking spot-bellied eagle owl, oriental scops owl and the difficult-to-spot frogmouth.

Finally, one bird you can't avoid in Sri Lanka is the **crow** – indeed the rasping and cawing of flocks of the creatures is one of the distinctive sounds of the island. Burgeoning numbers of these avian pests can be found wherever there are heaps of rubbish, and infestations are now common not only in towns but also in formerly unspoilt areas as diverse as Pigeon Island near Nilaveli and Horton Plains National Park, where they have been responsible for eating many of the beautiful lizards which formerly lived here.

Reptiles

Sri Lanka boasts two species of **crocodile**: **mugger** (also known as marsh or swamp) crocodile (*Crocodilus palustris*) and the **saltwater** (or estuarine) crocodile (*Crocodilus porosus*); both species live in burrows and feed on fish, birds and small mammals, killing their prey by drowning. Muggers can grow up to 4m in length and tend to frequent shallow freshwater areas around rivers, lakes and marshes; the larger and more aggressive saltwater crocs can reach lengths of up to 7m and prefer the brackish waters of river estuaries and lagoons near the sea. Crocodiles are commonly seen in Bundala and Yala – despite their fearsome appearance they aren't usually considered dangerous unless provoked, although attacks are not unknown.

Sri Lankan crocodiles are occasionally confused with **water monitors**, or *kabaragoya* (*Varanus bengalensis*), though these only grow up to 2m in length and have a quite different – and much more lizard-like – appearance, with a narrower, blue-black head and body with pale yellow stomach and markings on the back. Water monitors are just one of numerous impressive monitor species found on the island, including the similar land monitor, or *talagoya* (*Varanus salvator*). The island also boasts wide and colourful range of smaller lizards, which can be seen islandwide, from coastal beaches to the high-altitude moorlands of Horton Plains National Park.

Sri Lanka is home to eighty-odd species of **snake**, including five poisonous varieties, all relatively common (especially in northern dry zones) and including the cobra and the extremely dangerous Russell's viper. The island has the dubious distinction of having the highest number of **snakebite** fatalities, per capita, of any country in the world – see pp.27–28 for more information.

Turtles

Five of the world's seven species of **marine turtle** visit Sri Lanka's beaches to nest, a rare ecological blessing which could potentially make the island one of the world's leading turtle-watching destinations; however official support for conservation efforts remains depressingly half-hearted, despite the number of privately run turtle hatcheries which have sprung up along the west coast.

Turtles are amongst the oldest reptiles on earth, and offer a living link with the dinosaur age, having first evolved around two hundred million years ago. They are also one of the world's longest-lived creatures, reaching ages of over a hundred years. Tragically, despite having survived for so long, the world's population is now on the point of being wiped out – a fact which makes the lack of official support for conservation efforts in Sri Lanka all the more frustrating. All five of the species which visit the island are now highly endangered, thanks to marine hazards such fishing nets and rubbish thrown into the sea, as well as widespread poaching of eggs, hunting for meat and shells, and the disturbance or destruction of nesting sites. The magnificent leatherback turtle is particularly threatened – recent scientific studies have concluded that the species will be extinct within thirty years if current fishing practices are not changed.

Sea turtles occupy an unusual evolutionary niche. Originally land-dwelling reptiles like tortoises, their limbs evolved into flippers, transforming them into marathon swimmers, and they now generally only leave the water during the breeding season, when females emerge onto land to lay eggs in a hole scooped out of the sand (male turtles, by contrast, rarely leave the ocean). The eggs take six to eight weeks to hatch – if they escape the attentions of human poachers or avoid being dug up by dogs or other creatures. When the newborn turtles hatch, they head instinctively towards the sea – the first journey across the beach to the water is the most dangerous, since they're at the mercy of birds, crabs and other predators. Most females go back to lay their own eggs on the very same stretch of sand on which they were born – their so-called **natal beach** – proof of an extraordinary natural homing instinct, although the disturbance or destruction of such beaches is one of the crucial factors in declining turtle populations. This homing instinct is particularly remarkable given the immense distances sea turtles sometimes travel to return from their feeding grounds to their natal beaches – green turtles can travel up to 5000km, while tagged leatherbacks have swum across the Atlantic, though exactly how they navigate over such vast distances is imperfectly understood.

The most widespread marine turtle – and the one most commonly sighted in Sri Lanka – is the **green turtle** (*Chelonia mydas*), named for its greenish fat; green turtles are actually brown in colour, albeit with a greenish tinge. The green turtle grows to up to 1m in length and 140kg in weight and is found in warm coastal waters worldwide, feeding mainly on marine grasses. Female green turtles are the most prolific egg-producers of any sea turtle, laying six or seven hundred eggs every two weeks. The largest and more remarkable sea turtle is the **leatherback** (*Dermochelys coriacea*), which commonly grows to over 2m in length (indeed unconfirmed sightings of 3m-long specimens have been reported) and weighs up to 800kg. The leatherback is one of the planet's greatest swimmers and can be found in oceans worldwide, ranging from tropical waters almost to the Arctic Circle; they can also dive to depths of up to a kilometre and hold their breath for half an hour. The leatherback's name derives from its unique carapace – the "shell" is actually made up of separate bones buried in blackish skin; another unique evolutionary adaptation is their spiny throats, designed to help them swallow their favourite food, jellyfish.

The reddish-brown **loggerhead** (*Caretta caretta*) is another immense creature, reaching lengths of up to 2m; it's similar in appearance to the green turtle, but with a relatively larger head. The **hawksbill** (*Eretmochelys imbricata*) is one of the smaller sea turtles, reaching a length of around 0.5m and a weight of 40kg – it's named for its unusually hooked jaws, which give its head a rather bird-like appearance. Both the hawksbill and loggerhead are found in warm waters worldwide and feed on both plants and animals. The **olive ridley** (*Lepidochelys olivacea*) – one of the ridley turtles, named for its greenish colour – has a wide, rounded shell and reaches sizes of up to 1m. It inhabits the warm waters of the Indo-Pacific region and feeds on both animal and vegetable material.

Books

Contemporary Sri Lanka has a rich literary tradition, and the island has produced a string of fine **novelists** in recent years, including Booker Prize-winner Michael Ondaatje. Although virtually all of them now live abroad, the island, its culture and twentieth-century history continue to loom large in their work – all the novels of Shyam Selvadurai and Romesh Gunesekera, for instance, deal with Sri Lankan themes, even though Gunesekera now lives in London and Selvadurai in Canada.

The wealth of home-grown talent contrasts with a relative paucity of other books dealing with the island. Perhaps not surprisingly, Sri Lanka hasn't (with one notable exception) featured significantly in the works of **foreign novelists**, and, in striking contrast to neighbouring India, few foreign writers have written **travelogues** about the country. There are literally thousands of works about **Buddhism** and **Buddhist art**, though very few include much material on Sri Lanka. Coverage of the island's **history** and archeological sites is similarly lacking: there are a reasonable number of locally published works on various Cultural Triangle sites and other notable locations, though most are patchy and poorly written.

Fiction

Romesh Gunesekera *Reef.* This deceptively simple but haunting story about a house boy, his master and their twin obsessions – cooking and marine science – beautifully captures the flavour of the island, as well as plumbing some surprising depths. Gunesekera's other three books, *Monkfish Moon*, *The Sandglass* and *Heaven's Edge*, are also partly or wholly set in Sri Lanka, though none is a patch on *Reef*.

Michelle de Kretser *The Hamilton Case.* Set in the years just before and after independence, this beautifully written and cunningly plotted novel – part period piece, part elegant whodunnit – chronicles the career of lawyer Sam Obeysekere, a loyal subject of empire, whose life and loyalties are blighted by his chance involvement in the mysterious murder of a British tea planter.

Carl Muller The prolific novelist and journalist Carl Muller is some- thing of a cultural institution in Sri Lanka. His most famous work, *The Jam Fruit Tree* trilogy (*The Jam Fruit Tree*, *Yakada Yaka* and *Once Upon a Tender Time*), is an intermittently entertaining account of the lives, loves and interminable misadventures of the von Bloss clan, a family of ruffianly, party-loving and perma- nently inebriated Burghers. Other books include the comic short stories of *A Funny Thing Happened on the Way to the Cemetery*; the chunky historical epics *The Children of the Lion* (based on the mythological history of early Sri Lanka) and *Colombo*; and a collection of essays, *Firing At Random*.

Michael Ondaatje *Running in the Family.* Perhaps the best book ever written about the island, this marvellous memoir of Ondaatje's Burgher family and his variously dipsomaniac and wildly eccentric relations is at once magi- cally atmospheric and wonderfully comic. Ondaatje's other Sri Lankan book, the altogether more sombre *Anil's Ghost*, offers a very lightly fictionalized account of the civil war and JVP insurrection seen through the eyes of a young forensic pathologist attempting to expose government-sponsored killings.

Shyam Selvadurai *Funny Boy* and *Cinnamon Gardens. Funny Boy* presents a moving and disquieting picture of Sri Lanka seen through the eyes of a young gay Tamil boy growing up in Colombo in the years leading up to the civil war. *Cinnamon Gardens* offers a similarly simple but eloquent account of those trapped by virtue of their sex or sexuality in the stiflingly conservative society of 1930s Colombo.

A. Sivanandan *When Memory Dies.* Weighty historical epic describing the travails of three generations of a Sri Lankan family living through the end of the colonial period and the island's descent into civil war. Look out too for Sivanandan's *Where The Dance Is*, a sequence of inventive and acutely observed short stories set in Sri Lanka, India and England.

★ **Leonard Woolf** *The Village in the Jungle.* Future luminary of the Bloombury set, Leonard Woolf served for several years as a colonial administrator in the backwaters of Hambantota. First published in 1913, this gloomy little masterpiece tells a starkly depressing tale of love and murder in an isolated Sri Lankan village, stifled by the encroaching jungle and by its own poverty and backwardness.

History and travelogues

Yasmine & Brendan Gooneratne *This Inscrutable Englishman: Sir John D'Oyly (1774–1824).* Detailed biography of the brilliant English diplomat who brokered the surrender of the Kandyan kingdom to the British in 1815 – the sheer drama of the events described makes it an interesting read, despite the authors' laboriously academic tone.

Robert Knox *An Historical Relation of Ceylon.* Knox's account of his twenty-year captivity in the Kandyan kingdom (see p.229) is still an interesting read, especially the autobiographical section of the book, dealing with Knox's own Job-like trials and tribulations and culminating in the nail-biting story of his carefully planned escape.

★ **William McGowan** *Only Man Is Vile.* Written in the late 1980s, this classic account of the civil war and JVP insurrection combines war reportage, travelogue and social commentary to produce a stark, compelling and extremely depressing insight into the darker aspects of the Sinhalese psyche.

Roy Moxham *Tea: Addiction, Exploitation and Empire.* This detailed and very readable account of the development of the tea industry in the British colonies paints a compelling portrait of Victorian enterprise and greed – and of the terrible human price paid by Indian plantation workers. Includes extensive coverage of Sri Lanka.

Christopher Ondaatje *The Man-Eater of Punanai.* Famous Sri Lankan expatriate and entrepreneur Christopher Ondaatje (brother of Michael) returns to the island of his birth to go searching for leopards in the war-torn east, and for memories of his own youth – including the spectre of his maverick father

451

(who also appears as one of the stars of *Running in the Family*; see p.450).

Riccardo Orizio *Lost White Tribes: Journeys Amongst the Forgotten.* Orizio's account of the "lost white tribes" – the descendants of European colonists, scattered around the globe – includes an interesting

chapter devoted to the Burghers of Sri Lanka.

KM de Silva *A History of Sri Lanka.* The definitive history of the island, offering a considered and intelligent overview of events from prehistory to the present day, although somewhat spoiled by gaps and some baffling inconsistencies.

Religion

Karen Armstrong *Buddha.* Readable and intelligent biography which resolutely strips away millenia of accumulated myth in order to focus on the historical person of the Buddha and the society and culture from which his teachings evolved.

Richard Gombrich *Theravada Buddhism: A Social History from Ancient Benares to Modern Colombo.* This academic but accessible guide to Theravada Buddhism gives an absorbing account of the religion from a social and cultural, rather than theological, angle, with extensive coverage of the faith's develop-

ment in Sri Lanka. The same author's difficult-to-find *Precept and Practice: Traditional Buddhism in the Rural Highlands of Ceylon* offers a revealing insight into the idiosyncrasies of local Buddhist practice.

★ **Donald S. Lopez** *Buddhism.* Outstanding general introduction to Buddhism, written with great verve and insight, and wearing its considerable learning very lightly.

R.K. Narayan *The Ramayana.* Concise and extremely readable retelling of the great Hindu epic by India's foremost storyteller.

Art, architecture and culture

Joe Cummings & Bill Wassman *Buddhist Stupas in Asia: the Shape of Perfection.* Beautiful coffee-table book with inspirational photos of some of Asia's most spectacular stupas and interesting accompanying text; includes a short section devoted to Sri Lankan stupas.

Robert E. Fisher *Buddhist Art and Architecture.* Concise, well illustrated overview of Buddhist architecture, sculpture and painting. There's little specific coverage of Sri Lanka, although the discussions of different

national styles provide illuminating context.

★ **Ronald Lewcock, Barbara Sansoni & Laki Senanayake** *The Architecture of an Island: the Living Heritage of Sri Lanka.* This gorgeous book is a work of art in itself, and offers revealing insights into the jumble of influences that have gone into creating Sri Lanka's distinctive architectural style. The text discusses 95 examples of traditional island architecture – from palm shacks and hen coops to

Kandyan temples and colonial cathedrals, all beautifully illustrated with line drawings by Barbara Sansoni. Sadly, it's only available in Sri Lanka itself.

Meher McArthur *Reading Buddhist art.* Absorbing, richly illustrated introduction to the myriad signs and symbols of Buddhist iconography, with clear explanations of everything from sacred footprints to mythical animals, as well as introductions to the main deities of Mahayana Buddhism.

George Michell *Hindu Art and Architecture.* Copiously illustrated and well-presented introduction to Hindu architecture.

★ **David Robson** *Geoffrey Bawa: The Complete Works.* Written by a long-term Bawa associate, this comprehensive volume offers the definitive overview of the work of Sri Lanka's outstanding modern architect, with copious beautiful photographs and fascinating text on Bawa's life and creations, plus many revealing insights into Sri Lankan culture and art.

Flora and fauna

John Harrison and Tim Worfolk *A Field Guide to the Birds of Sri Lanka.* The definitive guide to Sri Lanka's avifauna.

Sriyanie Miththapala and P.A. Miththapala *What Tree is That?* Well-presented basic guide to the most common tree species of Sri Lanka, with good line drawings.

Gehan de Silva Wijeyeratne, Deepal Warakagoda and T.S.U.

de Zylva *A Photographic Guide to Birds of Sri Lanka.* Invaluable pocket-sized tome, with excellent photos of all listed species and clear descriptions.

Gehan de Silva Wijeyeratne *Where to Watch Birds and other Wildlife in Sri Lanka.* Excellent guide to the key wildlife sites in Sri Lanka, with descriptions and maps.

Miscellaneous

Philippe Fabry et al. *The Essential Guide for Jaffna and its region.* Useful little guidebook to Jaffna and the peninsula, although it's only available in Sri Lanka.

Suharshini Seneviratne *Exotic Tastes of Sri Lanka.* Good introduction to Sri Lankan cuisine, with 150 recipes, plus information about spices, cooking techniques and traditional utensils.

Language

Language

Language

S ri Lanka is a trilingual nation. The main language, **Sinhala**, is spoken by around 75 percent of the population; **Tamil** is spoken by around 25 percent (including not only the Tamils themselves, but most of the east coast's Muslim population). **English** is also widely used by westernized and urban sections of the population, and is the first language of most Sri Lankan Burghers. English also serves as a link language between the island's communities – relatively few Tamils speak Sinhala, and even fewer Sinhalese speak Tamil.

Language is an emotive issue in Sri Lanka – the notorious "Sinhala Only" legislation of 1956, which downgraded Tamil from the status of an official language and effectively barred Tamils from most forms of government employment, was one of the most significant root causes behind the subsequent civil war, and although Tamil was restored to the status of an official language in 1988, the subject is still politically sensitive. All official signs, banknotes, government publications and the like are printed in all three languages, and (except in the north, where Sinhala is rarely seen or heard) many businesses and shops follow suit.

Useful Sinhala and Tamil words and expressions

Basics

	Sinhala	Tamil
hello/welcome	hello/ayubowan	vanakkam
goodbye	ayubowan	varavaanga
yes	oh-ooh	aam
no	nay	illai
please	karuna karala	thayavu seithu
thank you	es-toothee	nandri
excuse me	sama venna	enga
sorry	kana gartui	mannikkavum
do you speak English?	Oh-ya Inghirisee kata karenavada?	ningal angilam paysu virhala?
I don't understand	matah obahvah thehrum gahna baha	enakku puriyavillaiye
what is your name?	nama mokada?	ungaludaya peyr enna?
my name is . . .	mahgay nama . . .	ennudaya peyr . . .
how are you?	kohomada?	ningal eppadi irukkirigal?
well, thanks	hondeen innava	romba nallayirukkudhu
not very well	vadiya honda nay	paruvayillai
this	mayka	ithu
that	ahraka	athu
when?	kawathatha?	eppa?

457

where?	kohedah?	enge?
when does it open/close?	ehika kiyatada ahrinnay/vahhannee	eppa thirakkiruthu/ moodukiradu
I want	mata onay	enakku venam
is there any ...?	...-da?	vere ethavathu irikkirutha?
how much?	ahhekka keeyada	ahdu evvalah-vur?
can you give me a discount?	karuna karala gana adukaranna	ithil ethavathu salugai irikkirutha?
big	loku	pareya (perisu)
small	podi	sarreya
excellent	hari hondai	miga nallathu
hot (weather)	rasnai	ushnamana
open	erala	thira
closed	vahala	moodu
shop	kaday	kadi (kadai)
post office	teppa kantorua	anja lagam
bank	bankua	vangi
toilet	vesikili	kahlippadem
police	polisiya	kavalar
pharmacy	farmisiya/bayhet sapua	marunthu kadai
doctor	dostara	maruthuvar (vaidyar)
hospital	rohala	aspathri
ill	asaneepai	viyathi

Getting around

English	Sinhala	Tamil
boat	bohtua	padadur
bus	bus ekka	bas
bus station	bus stand	baas nilayem
train	kohchiya	rayil
train station	dumriya pala	rayil nilayem
car	car	car
bicycle	bicycle	saikal
road	para	pathai
left	vama	idathu
right	dakuna	valathu
straight on	kelin yanna	naerakapogavum
near	langa	arukkil
far	athah	turam
station	is-stashama	nilayem
ticket	tiket ekkah	anumati situ

Accommodation

English	Sinhala	Tamil
hotel	hotelaya	hotel

guest house	guesthouse ekka	virun-dhinnar vidhudheh
bathroom	nahnah kamarayak	kulikkum arai
clean	suda	suththam
cold	seethai	kulir
dirty	apirisidui	alukku (azhukku)
room	kamaraya	arai
do you have a room?	kamara teeyenavada	arekil kidehkkumah?
may I see the room?	kamaraya karuna karala penvanna	koncham kanpikkireengala
is there an a/c room?	a/c kamarayak teeyenavada?	kulir seithu arayai parka mudiyama?
is there hot water?	unuvatura teeyenavada?	sudu thanir irukkuma?
please give me the bill	karuna karala bila ganna	bill tharavum

Time and numbers

L

LANGUAGE | Useful Sinhala and Tamil words and expressions

	Sinhala	Tamil
1	ekka	ontru
2	dekka	erantru
3	toona	moontru
4	hatara	nangu
5	paha	ainthu
6	hiya	aru
7	hata	aelu
8	ahta	ettu
9	navighya	onpathu
10	dahhighya	pattu
20	vissai	erpathu
30	teehai	mupathu
40	hatalihai	natpathu
50	panahai	ompathu
100	seeya	nooru
200	dayseeya	irunooru
1000	daha	aiyuram
2000	daidaha	iranda iuram
100,000	lakshaya	latcham

	Sinhala	Tamil
today	ada	indru
tomorrow	heta	naalay
yesterday	eeyai	neh-truh
morning	udai	kaalai
afternoon	havasa	matiyam
day	davasa	pakal
night	reh	eravu
last/next week	giya/ilanga sahtiya	pona/adutha vaaram

Food and drink

Basics

	Sinhala	Tamil
food	kanda	unavu
restaurant	kamata	unavu aalayam
the menu, please	menu eka penvanna	thayavu seithu thinpandangal patti tharavum
I'm vegetarian	mama elavalu vitaray kannay	naan oru saivam
please give me the bill	karuna karala bila ganna	bill tharavum
bread	paan	rotti/paan
egg	bittaraya	muttai
ice	ay-is	ice
rice (cooked)	baht	arisi
water	vaturah	thannir
mineral water (bottle)	drink botalayak genna	oru pottal soda panam tharavum
tea	tay	teyneer
coffee	kopi	kapi
milk	kiri	paal
sugar	seeni	seeni
butter	bahta	butter/vennai
chilli	miris wadi	karam
jaggery	hakuru	seeni/vellam

Fruit and vegetables

	Sinhala	Tamil
fruit	palaturu	palam
banana	keselkan	valaipalam
coconut	pol	thengali
mango	amba	mangai
papaya	papol	pappa palam
pineapple	annasi	annasi
vegetables	elavelu	kai kari vagaigal
carrot	karat	carrot
cauliflower	malgova	pookos
green/red pepper	ratu/kola malu miris	pachha/sivappu kudamulakai
mushrooms	haatu	naikudai
onion	luunu	venkayam
potato	ala	uruka kilangu
tomato	thakkali	thakkali

Meat and fish

	Sinhala	Tamil
meat	harak mas	mamism

Sinhala place names

Aluthgama	අලුත්ගම
Ambalangoda	අම්බලන්ගොඩ
Anuradhapura	අනුරාධපුර
Arugam Bay	ආරුගම්බේ
Badulla	බදුල්ල
Bandarawela	බන්ඩාරවෙල
Batticaloa	මඩකලපුව
Bentota	බෙන්තොට
Beruwala	බේරුවල
Colombo	කොළඹ
Dambulla	දඹුල්ල
Ella	ඇල්ල
Galle	ගාල්ල
Giritale	ගිරිතලේ
Habarana	හබරණ
Hambantota	හම්බන්තොට
Haputale	හපුතලේ
Hikkadduwa	හික්කඩුව
Jaffna	යාපනය
Kalutara	කළුතර
Kandy	මහනුවර
Kataragama	කතරගම
Kitulgala	කිතුල්ගල
Kurunegala	කුරුණෑගල
Matara	මාතර
Mihintale	මිහින්තලේ
Mirissa	මිරිස්ස
Monaragala	මොණරාගල
Negombo	මීගමුව
Nilvaveli	නිලාවේලි
Nuwara Eliya	නුවර එළිය
Polonnaruwa	පොළොන්නරුව
Ratnapura	රත්නපුර
Sigiriya	සිගිරිය
Tangalla	තංගල්ල
Tissamaharama	තිස්සමහාරාමය
Trincomalee	ත්‍රිකුණාමලය
Unawatuna	උණවටුන
Uppaveli	උප්පුවේලි
Weligama	වැලිගම
Wellawaya	වැල්ලවාය

chicken	kukulmas	koli (kozhi)
pork	uroomas	pantri
beef	harak mas	maattu mamism
lamb	batalu mas	aattu mamism
crab	kakuluvo	nandu
prawns	isso	iraal
lobster	pokirissa	periya iraal
fish	malu	min

Glossary

abhaya mudra "Have no Fear" pose; see p.438.

anda The main, hemispherical section of a dagoba.

apsara heavenly nymph.

arhat enlightened monk.

Avalokiteshvara Mahayana boddhisattva who is worshipped as the lord of infinite compassion, able to save all beings from suffering.

ayurveda Ancient Indian system of holistic healthcare; see p.128.

-arama or **-rama** park, garden or monastic residence.

betel Popular and mildly narcotic snack, combining leaves from the betel tree with flakes of areca nut, a pinch of lime and sometimes a piece of tobacco. Produces the characteristic red spittle whose stains can be seen on pavements throughout the country.

bhikku Buddhist monk.

bo tree (*ficus religiosa*; also known as the bodhi tree), Species of tree held sacred by Buddhism since the Buddha is believed to have achieved enlightenment while meditating under one.

boddhisattva A Buddha-to-be who, rather than passing into nirvana, has chosen to stay in the world to improve the spiritual welfare of other, unenlightened beings; see p.434.

bodhigara bo tree enclosure.

bund bank of a reservoir or tank.

Burghers Sri Lankans of European (usually Dutch) descent.

chaitya/cetiya stupa; see p.293.

chattravali spire-like pinnacle at the top of a stupa

chena slash-and-burn farming.

Cholas (or **Colas**) The dominant power in South India from the tenth to the twelfth centuries, with their capital at Thanjavur in Tamil Nadu. They overran Sri Lanka in the late tenth century, sacking Anuradhapura in 993, after which they established a new capital at Polonnaruwa.

coir fibre made out of coconut husks.

Culavamsa the "Lesser Chronicle" and continuation of the *Mahavamsa*; see p.43.

dagoba stupa; see p.293.

devale Shrine or temple to a deity, either freestanding or part of a Buddhist temple. Devales are nominally Buddhist, but often show strong Hindu influence.

dhyani mudra meditation pose; see p.438.

digge Drummer's hall; often a pillared hall or pavilion in a temple where drummers and dancers rehearse.

Durga The most terrifying of female Hindu deities, the demon-slaying Durga is considered an aspect of Shiva's consort, Parvati. Worshipped by Hindus and also occasionally found in Buddhist temples.

duwa small island.

dwarfs Attendants of Kubera, the god of wealth, and thus symbols of prosperity.

-ela stream.

-gaha tree.

-gala rock.

-gama village.

Ganesh Popular elephant-headed Hindu god, the son of Shiva, remover of obstacles and bringer of success and prosperity.

ganga river.

-ge hall or house.

gedige Shrine built in South Indian style, with thick, richly decorated stone walls and vaulting.

-giri rock.

gopuram Tower of a Hindu temple, usually richly decorated with multi-coloured statues.

guardstone Carved figure placed at the entrance to a temple to protect against malign influences; often shows a figure of a nagaraja (see opposite).

Hanuman Monkey god who assisted Rama in recovering Sita from the demon Ravana, as related in the *Ramayana*.

harmika The box-shaped section of a dagoba which sits on top of the dome (*anda*) and supports the *chattravali*.

Hinayana Alternative and pejorative name for Theravada Buddhism.

hypostyle Building constructed using many columns.

image house (pilimage) building in a Buddhist temple housing a statue of the Buddha.

jataka Stories describing the 547 previous lives of the Buddha.

JVP (Janatha Vimukthi Peramuna, or People's Liberation Front). Marxist party with an extreme nationalist, anti-Tamil agenda. Originally made up largely of rural poor and students, the JVP launched armed insurrections against the government in 1971 and 1987–89, both put down with considerable loss of life. Since the second insurrection it has transformed itself into an important mainstream political party with a strong parliamentary presence.

Kataragama One of the principal Sri Lankan deities, believed to reside in the town of Kataragama.

kavadi "peacock dance" performed by devotees of the god Kataragama; see p.200.

kolam Masked dance-drama; see 139.

kovil Hindu temple.

-kulam tank, lake.

Lakshmi Hindu goddess of wealth; Vishnu's consort.

lingam Phallic symbol representing Shiva; often placed within a *yoni*, representing female sexuality.

LTTE Liberation Tigers of Tamil Eelam, popularly known as the Tamil Tigers; see p.392.

maha great.

Mahavamsa The "Great Chronicle", containing an account of Sri Lankan history from the time of the Buddha up to the fourth century AD; see p.413.

Mahayana Buddhism One of the two major schools of Buddhism, and the dominant form of the religion in China, Japan and Tibet, though it has had only superficial influence on Sri Lankan Buddhism; see p.432.

Maitreya The next Buddha. Mahayana Buddhists believe Maitreya will reintroduce Buddhism to the world when all knowledge of the religion has been lost.

makara Imaginary composite animal derived from Indian bestiary.

makara torana Arch formed from two linked makaras.

mawatha (abbreviated to "Mw") street.

moonstone Carved semi-circular stone placed in front of entrance to shrine; see p.441. Also a type of gemstone mined in the island.

moors Sri Lankans of Arab or Indian-Arab descent.

mudra Traditional pose in Buddhist iconography; see p.438.

nagaraja serpent king.

naga stone Stone decorated with the image of a hooded cobra.

nuwara town.

ola/ola leaf Parchment made from the talipot palm (see p.237) used as a writing material in Sri Lanka up to the nineteenth century. Individual leaves were often bound up into ola-leaf manuscripts and books.

oya stream, small river.

Pali The sacred language of Theravada Buddhism, this early Indo-European language, related to Sanskrit, is close to the language spoken by the Buddha himself. The scriptures of Theravada Buddhism were originally written in Pali and are still recited in this language in Buddhist ceremonies.

Pallavas South Indian Tamil dynasty (5th–9th centuries), based in Kanchipuram, who, along with the Pandyans and Cholas, periodically interfered in Sri Lankan affairs.

Pandyans Major Tamil dynasty (6th–14th centuries), based in Madurai, who vied for control of South India with the Cholas and Pallavas from the ninth to thirteenth centuries and periodically involved themselves in Sri Lankan affairs. Sacked Anuradhapura in the ninth century.

parinirvana mudra Reclining pose showing the Buddha on the point of entering into nirvana. One of the most common mudras (see above) in Sri Lankan art.

463

pasada palace.

Pattini Hindu goddess worshipped as paragon of marital fidelity; see p.226.

perahera procession.

pirith Ceremonial chanting of Buddhist scriptures.

-pitiya field or park.

poya full-moon day.

poyage Building in a monastery used for ceremonial gatherings of monks on poya days (hence the name); sometimes translated as "chapter house".

puja Hindu or Buddhist religious offering or ceremony.

-pura/-puram town.

Rama The seventh incarnation of Vishnu and hero of the *Ramayana*.

Ravana (or **Rawana**) Demon-king and arch villain of the *Ramayana*; responsible for kidnapping Rama's wife Sita and holding her captive in Sri Lanka.

samadhi (dhyani) mudra Pose showing Buddha in state of meditation, seated in the lotus or half-lotus position.

Saman The god of Adam's Peak; see p.274.

samudra large tank.

Sangha The worldwide community of Buddhist monks.

Shiva One of the two principal Hindu gods, worshipped in many forms, both creative and destructive.

Shiva Nataraj Classic subject of Hindu sculpture, showing a four-armed dancing Shiva enclosed by a circle of fire.

sinha lion.

Skanda Son of Shiva (also known as Murugam and Subramanian). His identity in Sri Lanka has merged with that of Kataragama.

SLA Sri Lankan Army.

SLFP One of the two main Sri Lankan political parties, led successively by S.W.R.D. Bandaranaike, his wife and his daughter. Policies have tended to be the opposite of the pro-Western, free-market UNP, leaning instead towards a brand of populist nationalism (often with an anti-Tamil bias) featuring extensive state control of the economy.

sri pada holy footprint.

tank Large man-made lake constructed for irrigation; almost always much larger than the English word suggests; see p.346.

-tara/-tota port.

Theravada Buddhism The older of the two main schools of Buddhism, and the dominant form of the religion in Sri Lanka; see p.432.

tuktuk motorized rickshaw; also know as a three-wheeler, trishaw or taxi.

UNP United National Party; one of Sri Lanka's two main political parties and the first ruling party of independent Sri Lanka. Policies have traditionally tended to be pro-Western and free market. Leadership dominated by Senanayake and Jayawardene families.

Upulvan Sri Lankan name for Vishnu.

vahalkada Shrines placed at the four cardinal points of a stupa.

vatadage Characteristic Sri Lankan style of building formed by adding a roof and ambulatory to a dagoba.

Veddah Sri Lanka's original aboriginal inhabitants; see p.245.

ves dancer Style of traditional costume and dancing employed by Kandyan dancers.

Vibhishana The youngest brother of Ravana. Despite his demonic nature, Vibhishana is revered in Sri Lanka, since he pleaded the captive Sita's cause with Ravana and later fought with Rama against his brother, suggesting the potential for right action in even the lowest creature.

vidaya street (in Kandy).

vihara (sometimes spelt *vehera* or *wehera*) Buddhist temple or monastery.

Vishnu One of the two principal Hindu gods, considered a protector of Buddhism in Sri Lanka.

VOC Vereenigde Oost Indische Compagnie (Dutch East Indies Company).

-watte garden.

-wewa man-made reservoir (tank).

-wila pond.

Rough
Guides

advertiser

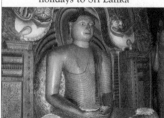

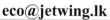

small print and Index

A Rough Guide to Rough Guides

In the summer of 1981, Mark Ellingham, a recent graduate from Bristol University, was travelling round Greece and couldn't find a guidebook that really met his needs. On the one hand there were the student guides, insistent on saving every last cent, and on the other the heavyweight cultural tomes whose authors seemed to have spent more time in a research library than lounging away the afternoon at a taverna or on the beach.

In a bid to avoid getting a job, Mark and a small group of writers set about creating their own guidebook. It was a guide to Greece that aimed to combine a journalistic approach to description with a thoroughly practical approach to travellers' needs – a guide that would incorporate culture, history and contemporary insights with a critical edge, together with up-to-date, value-for-money listings. Back in London, Mark and the team finished their Rough Guide, as they called it, and talked Routledge into publishing the book.

That first *Rough Guide to Greece*, published in 1982, was a student scheme that became a publishing phenomenon. The immediate success of the book – with numerous reprints and a Thomas Cook prize shortlisting – spawned a series that rapidly covered dozens of destinations. Rough Guides had a ready market among low-budget backpackers, but soon also acquired a much broader and older readership that relished Rough Guides' wit and inquisitiveness as much as their enthusiastic, critical approach. Everyone wants value for money, but not at any price.

Rough Guides soon began supplementing the "rougher" information about hostels and low-budget listings with the kind of detail on restaurants and quality hotels that independent-minded visitors on any budget might expect, whether on business in New York or trekking in Thailand.

These days the guides – distributed worldwide by the Penguin group – offer recommendations from shoestring to luxury and cover more than 200 destinations around the globe, including almost every country in the Americas and Europe, more than half of Africa and most of Asia and Australasia. Our ever-growing team of authors and photographers is spread all over the world, particularly in Europe, the USA and Australia.

In 1994, we published the *Rough Guide to World Music* and *Rough Guide to Classical Music*; and a year later the *Rough Guide to the Internet*. All three books have become benchmark titles in their fields – which encouraged us to expand into other areas of publishing, mainly around popular culture. Rough Guides now publish:

- Travel guides to more than 200 worldwide destinations
- Dictionary phrasebooks to 22 major languages
- History guides ranging from Ireland to Islam
- Maps printed on rip-proof and waterproof Polyart™ paper
- Music guides running the gamut from Opera to Elvis
- Restaurant guides to London, New York and San Francisco
- Reference books on topics as diverse as the Weather and Shakespeare
- Sports guides from Formula 1 to Man Utd
- Pop culture books from *Lord of the Rings* to Cult TV
- World Music CDs in association with World Music Network

Visit **www.roughguides.com** to see our latest publications.

Rough Guide Credits

Text editor: Polly Thomas
Layout: Ajay Verma
Cartography: Miles Irving, Ashutosh Bharti, Animesh Pathak and Rajesh Chhibber
Picture research: Harriet Mills
Proofreader: David Price
Production: Julia Bovis
Editorial: **London** Martin Dunford, Kate Berens, Helena Smith, Claire Saunders, Geoff Howard, Ruth Blackmore, Gavin Thomas, Polly Thomas, Richard Lim, Lucy Ratcliffe, Clifton Wilkinson, Alison Murchie, Fran Sandham, Sally Schafer, Alexander Mark Rogers, Karoline Densley, Andy Turner, Ella O'Donnell, Keith Drew, Andrew Lockett, Joe Staines, Duncan Clark, Peter Buckley, Matthew Milton; **New York** Andrew Rosenberg, Richard Koss, Hunter Slaton, Chris Barsanti, Steven Horak
Design & Pictures: London Simon Bracken, Dan May, Diana Jarvis, Mark Thomas, Jj Luck, Harriet Mills; **Delhi** Madhulita Mohapatra, Umesh Aggarwal, Ajay Verma, Jessica Subramanian

Production: Julia Bovis, John McKay, Sophie Hewat
Cartography: **London** Maxine Repath, Ed Wright, Katie Lloyd-Jones, Miles Irving; **Delhi** Manish Chandra, Rajesh Chhibber, Jai Prakash Mishra, Ashutosh Bharti, Rajesh Mishra, Animesh Pathak, Jasbir Sandhu, Karobi Gogoi
Cover art direction: Louise Boulton
Online: **New York** Jennifer Gold, Cree Lawson, Suzanne Welles, Benjamin Ross; **Delhi** Manik Chauhan, Narender Kumar, Shekhar Jha, Rakesh Kumar
Marketing & Publicity: **London** Richard Trillo, Niki Smith, David Wearn, Chloë Roberts, Demelza Dallow, Kristina Pentland; **New York** Geoff Colquitt, Megan Kennedy
Finance: Gary Singh
Manager India: Punita Singh
Series editor: Mark Ellingham
PA to Managing Director: Julie Sanderson
Managing Director: Kevin Fitzgerald

Publishing Information

This first edition published November 2004 by
Rough Guides Ltd,
80 Strand, London WC2R 0RL.
345 Hudson St, 4th Floor,
New York, NY 10014, USA.
Distributed by the Penguin Group
Penguin Books Ltd,
80 Strand, London WC2R 0RL
Penguin Putnam, Inc.
375 Hudson Street, NY 10014, USA
Penguin Books Australia Ltd,
487 Maroondah Highway, PO Box 257,
Ringwood, Victoria 3134, Australia
Penguin Books Canada Ltd,
10 Alcorn Avenue, Toronto, Ontario,
Canada M4V 1E4
Penguin Books (NZ) Ltd,
182–190 Wairau Road, Auckland 10,
New Zealand
Typeset in Bembo and Helvetica to an original design by Henry Iles.

Printed in Italy by LegoPrint S.p.A

480pp includes index
A catalogue record for this book is available from the British Library

ISBN 1–843531887

3   5   7   9   8   6   4

Help us update

We've gone to a lot of effort to ensure that the first edition of **The Rough Guide to Sri Lanka** is accurate and up-to-date. However, things change – places get "discovered", opening hours are notoriously fickle, restaurants and rooms raise prices or lower standards. If you feel we've got it wrong or left something out, we'd like to know, and if you can remember the address, the price, the time, the phone number, so much the better.

We'll credit all contributions, and send a copy of the next edition (or any other Rough Guide if you prefer) for the best letters. Everyone who writes to us and isn't already a subscriber will receive a copy of our full-colour thrice-yearly newsletter. Please mark letters: **"Rough Guide Sri Lanka Update"** and send to: Rough Guides, 80 Strand, London WC2R 0RL, or Rough Guides, 4th Floor, 345 Hudson St, New York, NY 10014. Or send an email to **mail@roughguides.com**

Have your questions answered and tell others about your trip at
www.roughguides.atinfopop.com

Acknowledgements

The editor would like to thank Gavin Thomas for being really pleasant to work with, and Claire Saunders for taking over at the crucial stages.

Gavin Thomas: In Sri Lanka, thanks to all those who provided entertainment, information and inspiration along the way, including (in no particular order): Tilak Conrad; R.K Koddikara; the Khalid family; Jith in Ella; Faiesz and Sue Samad; J.P. Jayasinghe; Gamini at Midigama; Asoka Rapwatte; Asela Pethiyagoda; S. Ravindra; Diane and Mike in Jaffna; Fred at Arugam Bay; Sumane Bandara Illangantilake; Dr Will Cave; Jezima Mohamed; and all at Jetwing for their wonderful hospitality. Thanks also to all at the Silver Sands in Negombo, the Hemadan in Aluthgama, and the Nippon Hotel in Colombo. Special thanks to Gehan de Silva Wijeyeratne for birdwatching and nightlife expeditions, and for bearing my interminable questions so patiently; and especially to Dominic Sansoni for putting me up (and putting up with me) in Colombo, for inspirational photography, and for sharing so many insights into the island.

At Rough Guides, thanks to all who helped make this book happen, including Harriet Mills, Ajay Verma, Jessica Subramanian and

Miles Irving. Thanks also to Kate Berens and Martin Dunford for unshackling me from my desk and letting me do it, and to Mark Ellingham for not doing it himself, as well as for the Burgher box and invaluable contacts in Colombo. Very special thanks to my masterly editor Polly Thomas, whose contributions were always apposite but never intrusive, and also to Claire Saunders for last-minute editorial mopping-up and long-term moral support (I look forward to reading her Sri Lankan novel one day). Also in London, thanks to Charmarie Maelge and all her staff at the Sri Lanka Tourist Board (especially Saroja – *bohomah stoothiy*), as well as Kieran Falconer and Alice Berry.

Finally and most importantly, thanks to Allison, with whom I first discovered Sri Lanka (and so many other countries), and to Laura, who I hope will one day discover it for herself. Both bore my prolonged absences patiently, and kept me sane during the endless months of writing which followed my return. This book is dedicated to the two of them, with all my love.

Index

Map entries are in colour.

INDEX

475

T

INDEX

Map symbols

maps are listed in the full index using coloured text

– – –	Chapter boundary	@	Internet access
═══	Major road	ⓘ	Tourist office
──	Minor road	⊠	Post office
⊞⊞⊞	Steps	◉	Accommodation
──▬──	Railway line	▣	Restaurant
- - - -	Path	✈	Airport
– –	Ferry route	★	Bus stop
────	River	‿	Bridge
▬▬▬	Wall	⊞	Hospital
Rocks	Rocks	⊠	Gate
Reef	Reef		Gardens
/∣\	Hill shading	Ⓐ	Stupa/Buddhist temple
⁄ \ ⁄\	Earthworks	▲	Hindu temple
▲	Peak		Mosque
◠	Cave		Church (regional maps)
	Waterfall	⊞	Church (town maps)
	Banyan tree		Building
♦	Place of interest	☐	Market
⊙	Statue		Christian cemetery
∴	Ruin		Muslim cemetery
	Lighthouse		Park
	Fortress		Beach
	Golf course		Swamp
			Jungle/forest